Vyākaraṇa Mahābhāṣya of Patañjali on Pāṇini 3.1 (Āhnikas 1 to 6)

Vyākaraṇa Mahābhāṣya of Patañjali on Pāṇini 3.1 (Āhnikas 1 to 6)

Text, Translation with Introduction and Technical Notes

STEPHEN PETER THOMPSON

MOTILAL BANARSIDASS PUBLISHERS
PRIVATE LIMITED • DELHI

First Edition : Delhi, 2010

ISBN: 978-81-208-3444-6

MOTILAL BANARSIDASS
41 U.A. Bungalow Road, Jawahar Nagar, Delhi 110 007
8 Mahalaxmi Chamber, 22 Bhulabhai Desai Road, Mumbai 400 026
203 Royapettah High Road, Mylapore, Chennai 600 004
236, 9th Main III Block, Jayanagar, Bangalore 560 011
Sanas Plaza, 1302 Baji Rao Road, Pune 411 002
8 Camac Street, Kolkata 700 017
Ashok Rajpath, Patna 800 004
Chowk, Varanasi 221 001

PRINTED IN INDIA
By Jainendra Prakash Jain at Shri Jainendra Press,
A-45 Naraina, Phase-I, New Delhi 110 028
and Published by Narendra Prakash Jain for
Motilal Banarsidass Publishers Private Limited,
Bungalow Road, Delhi 110 007

Contents

Foreword

The unique importance of the Pāṇīnan tradition of Sanskrit Grammar and its place in the grammatical literature of the world need not be articulated since it has been sufficiently highlighted. The position at the top occupied by Patañjali, the author of the *Vyākaraṇamahābhāṣya,* within the Trimuni tradition of the Pāṇinīan school also has been an accepted fact. A complete translation of this magnum opus in any Indian (except marathi) or non-Indian language has been a strongly felt desideratum. Apart from Dr. S.D. Joshi and Dr. A.A.F. Roodborgen who translated some important sections of the *Bhāṣya,* we do not come across any other attempt to undertake this Herculean task. The present book, which attempts the first translation in English of one of the largest sections of the Bhāṣya is, indeed, a praiseworthy effort.

The concept of *pratyaya* is one of the seminal concepts in Pāṇinī's metalanguage. It is, in fact, one of the two building-blocks and, as pointed out by the author of this book, lies at the heart of Pāṇini's grammar. Patañjali writes in colloquial Sanskrit and in dialectical style. A good translation of his text is, therefore a challenging task The author of this translation deserves our compliments for accepting the challenge and for having accomplished the task.

This book contains a comprehensive treatment of *pratyaya* including its etymology, pre-Pāṇinīan and post-Pāṇnīan attestations, and a thorough analysis of different categories of Pratyayas in the Aṣṭādhyāyī, The translation of the six *Āhnikas* of the *Bhāṣya* which cover the first section of the third chapter is more literal and faithful to the text. Dr. Thompson has added critical notes which are very useful to understand the text and its context. At the end there is an attempt to uplift the linguistic notion of Pratyaya to a higher spiritual level. This is in consonance with the Indian tradition of learning with a three-fold approach to reality, *ādhibhautika, ādhidaivika* and *ādhyātmika.*

The book will, I am sure, be of great help to the students of Sanskrit grammar.

Saroja Bhate
Hon. Secretary
Bhandarakar Oriental Research Institute, Pune
bori1@vsnl.net

Preface

The *Sanskṛta* language is acknowledged to have the finest and oldest grammatical system in the world today, besides possessing an incomparable literature. Hence for understanding the nature of language and of the Word itself it becomes imperative to study the greatest authorities on *Sanskṛta* Grammar, viz. *Pāṇini, Kātyāyana* and *Patañjali.*

At the heart of *Pāṇini's* great *Aṣṭādhyāyī* lies the concept of *pratyaya,* being by far the largest *adhikāra sūtra,* governing the three central *adhyāyas* of the *Aṣṭādhyāyī* and virtually half the *sūtras.* This in itself bears witness to the importance of the concept in language. Indeed it has been said that to understand the Word, one needs first to understand the relation between the stem which is known and the *pratyaya* which is unknown but joins the stem to bring forth the meaning of the whole Word.

Thus this thesis focuses on the first and most important *pāda* within the province of the *Pratyaya Adhikāra,* the *pratyayapāda,* with a view to shedding some light on the concept of *Pratyaya* and indirectly on the Word itself.

Acknowledgements

I would first like to express my gratitude to my father and mother who through their godliness enabled me to experience the unity of life, which they witnessed to as the grace of the Lord Jesus Christ, the love of God and the fellowship of the Holy Spirit without which none of this study would have been possible.

Next I would like to express my profound gratitude to Mr. Leon MacLaren for revealing afresh the teaching on the unity of the Self and introducing so many of us to the *Sanskṛta* language as a unique instrument to bring one to the *rasa,* the sweet taste of goodness, that only the connoisseurs enjoy.

I wish to thank my teachers at the School of Oriental and African Studies, Professor Wright, Mr. Grey, Dr. Geldblum and Dr. J. Smith for all the help and encouragement they gave me with my studies of *Sanskṛta.*

I would like to thank all those in Pune who have so generously helped me during the last four years. Firstly, Principal V.K. Nulkar and his family not only for putting up with me but for treating me truly as their second son. Next I would like to express my gratitude for having had the great privilege to study under the last of the great *Vyākaraṇa Paṇḍits* in Pune, whose presence really brought me here, Pandit Bhagavat Sastri. It has been an inspiration to be with him. I would also especially like to thank my first guide at C.A.S.S., Professor Laddu for not only giving the benefit of his wisdom but for kindness and consideration. Similarly Dr. S.D. Joshi, Dr. G. Palsule and Dr. S. Bahulkar have throughout my four years been generous teachers, guides and friends. Lastly but not least I would express my gratitude to my present guide Mrs. Saroja Bhate, Head of the Department of *Sanskṛt and Prākṛt* at the University of Poona, Pune, who has shown patience, wisdom and generosity at every step and will, I am sure, continue to inspire many to study this uniquely fine and truthful *Sanskṛta language.*

Further, I would like to express my gratitude to the Garware Trust for the scholarship they have generously provided during the last two years covering my living expenses.

Finally, the loving company of my wife Linda has always been a source of inspiration as she has contributed in her own way in bringing this work into manifestation.

Bibliography

Primary Sources :

Srī Bhagavat Patañjali viracitam vyākaraṇa mahābhāṣyam with Kaiyaṭa's Pradīpa and Nāgojibhaṭṭa's Uddyota.	Edited by Vedavrata, 5 Volumes, Gurukula Jhaggar (Rohtak), Haryana Sāhitya Samsthāna, Volume 3, mainly utilised.
Eighteen Principal Upaniṣads	Vaidika Samśodhana Maṇḍala, 1972
Kāśikā Vṛtti with the Nyāsa of Pañcika commentary and Padamañjarī Śudhirakāśanam	Vāranasī, 1983, Volume 1-6,
Patañjali's Vyākaraṇa Mahābhāṣya	S.D. Jodhi and J.A.F. Roodbergen, University of Poona, No.3 P.2.1.1; No.5 P.2.1.2-49 No.6 2.1.51-72, No.7 P.2.2.23; No.9 P.2.2.23-38; No.10 P.1..23-55; No.11 P.2.3.1-7; No.12 P.2.3.18-45; No.14 P.2.3.46-71; No.15 Paśpaśāhnika.
The Paribhāśenduśekhara of Nāgojibhaṭṭa	Ed. F. Kielhorn, Part I and 2, Text, Translation and Notes, Second Edition by K.V. Abhyankar.
Ṛgveda Samhitā	Vaidika Samśodhana Mandala, 1972.
Siddhāntakaumudī with the Tattvabodhinī commentary	Edited by Pt. V.L.S. Panshikar, Chaukhamba Prakashan, 1985 reprint of 1915 edition.
Upaniṣatsaṅgrahaḥ	Motilal Banarsidass, Delhi, 1980.
Vākyapadīya of Bhartṛhari	Eds. K.V. Abhyankar and V.P. Limaye, Poona, 1965.

Vyākaraṇa Mahābhāṣya of Patañjali — Edited by F. Kielhorn, Volume 1, Third Edition by K.V. Abhyankar, Pune, 1962; Pandith Nityananda Panta Parvatiya, 1946. Volume 2, Third Edition by K.V. Abhyankar, Pune, 1965; Volume 3, Bombay, 1885.

Secondary Soruces :

Abhyankar, K.V. — *A Dictionary of Sanskrit Grammar,* Baroda, 1977.

Sri Aurobindo — *The Origins of Aryan Speech,* 1971 in 'The Secret of the Veda'.

Bloomfield, L. — *Language,* Reprint, Motilal Banarsidas, Delhi, 1961.

Böhtlink and Roth — *Sanskrit Wörterbuch.*

Cardona, G. — *Pāṇini, A Survey of Research,* 1980.
Linguistic Analysis and some Indian Traditions, 1983

Chatterji, K.C. — *Technical Terms and Technique of Sanskrit Grammar.*

Deussen, P. — *Sixty Upaniṣads of the Veda,* translators Bedekar and G.B. Palsule, 1980.

Devasthali — *Anubandhas of Pāṇini,* Poona, 1967.

Heimann, Betty — *Sphoṭa and Artha,* Festschrift P.V. Kane, 1941.

Iyer, K.A.S. — *Vākyapadīya of Bhartṛhari,*
Ch. 1, Deccan College, 1965,
Ch. 2, Motilal Banarsidass, Delhi, 1977,
Ch. 3 Part 1, Deccan College, 1971,
Ch. 3, Part 2, Motilal Banarsidass, Delhi, 1974.

V.P. Some Problems, BORI, Poona, 1932

Joshi, S.D. — *Sphoṭanirṇaya,* Poona, 1967.

Kartre, S.M. — *Dictionary of Pāṇini,* Deccan College, Poona, 1968-69.

Keith, A.B. — *A History of Sanskrit Literature,* Oxford, 1928.

Keilhorn, F. — *Kleine Schriften,* Teil 1, 1969.

Laddu, S.D. *The Evolution of the Sanskrit Language, from Pāṇini to Patañjali,* Poona, 1967.

Limaye, V.P. *Critical Studies on the Mahābhāṣya,* Hoshiarpur, 1974.

Macdonell, A.A. *A Sanskrit Grammar,* Oxford, 1927.

Monier-Williams, M. *Sanskrit-English Dictionary,* Oxford, 1899.

Nāgeśa Bhaṭṭa *Parama Laghu Mañjuṣā. Pandit Nityananda Panta Parvatiya, 1946.*

Palsule, G.B. *The Sanskrit Dhātu Pāṭhas,* Poona, 1961.

Robbins, R.H. *Ancient and Medival Grammatical Theory in Europe.*

Sharman, K.M.K. *Pāṇini, Kātyāyana and Patañjali,* Delhi, 1968.

Shefts, B. *Grammatical Method in Pāṇini,* New Haven, 1961 ?.

Vasu, S.C. *The Aṣṭādhyāyī of Pāṇini,* Volume 1 and 2, Allahabad, 1891.

The Siddhānta Kaumudī of Bhaṭṭoji Dīkṣita, Allahabad, 1905-07.

Wackernagel, J. *Altindische Grammatik,* Gottingen, 1986.

Detailed Contents Index for

The Pratyayapāda of the Vyākaraṇa Mahābhāṣya 3.1.1-149

First *Āhnika*

Second *Āhnika*

Third *Āhnika*

Sūtra	Type	Meaning	*Vā/Ślo*	Page
3.1.27	*vidhi yak*	*svārthe*	*Vā* 4	285
3.1.28	*vidhi āya*	*svārthe*		
3.1.29	*vidhi īyaṅ*	*svārthe*		
3.1.30	*vidhi ṇiṅ*	*svārthe*	*Vā* 3	291
3.1.31	*vidhi āya, iyañ, ṇiṅ*	*(ārdhadhātuke)*	*Vā* 4	299
3.1.32	*sañjñā san etc.*		*Vā* 1	307
3.1.33	*vidhi sya/tāsi vikaraṇa*	*svārthe*	*Vā* 0	311
3.1.34	*vidhi sip*	*svārthe*	*Vā* 6	316
3.1.35	*vidhi ām vikaraṇa*	*svārthe*	*Vā* 1	322
3.1.36	*vidhi ām vikaraṇa*	*svārthe*	*Vā* 6	323
3.1.37	*vidhi ām vikaraṇa*	*svārthe*		
3.1.38	*vidhi ām vikaraṇa*	*svārthe*	*Vā* 1	335
3.1.39	*vidhi ām vikaraṇa*	*svārthe*	*Vā* 1	337
3.1.40	*vidhi ām vikaraṇa*	*kṛñ anuprayujyate*	*Vā* 9	338

Fourth *Āhnika*

Sūtra	Type	Meaning	*Vā/Ślo*	*Page*
3.1.41	*vidhi ām vikaraṇa*	*svārthe*		
3.1.42	*vidhi ām vikaraṇa*	*svārthe*		
3.1.43	*vidhi cli vikaraṇa*	*svārthe (luṅi)*	*Vā* 5	347
3.1.44	*vidhi sic ādeśa*	*svārthe (luṅi)*	*Vā* 7	359
3.1.45	*vidhi ksa ādeśa*	*svārthe (luṅi)*	*Vā* 5	370
3.1.46	*vidhi ksa ādeśa*	*svārthe (luṅi) (āliṅgane)*	*Vā* 4	373
3.1.47	*niyama ksa ādeśa*	*svārthe (luṅi)*		
3.1.48	*vidhi caṅ ādeśa*	*svārthe (luṅi) (kartari)*	*Vā* 3	378
3.1.49	*vidhi caṅ ādeśa*	*svārthe (luṅi) (kartari)*		
3.1.50	*vidhi caṅ ādeśa*	*svārthe (luṅi) (kartari) chandasi*		
3.1.51	*vidhi caṅ ādeśa*	*svārthe (luṅi) (kartari) chandasi*		
3.1.52	*vidhi aṅ ādeśa*	*svārthe (luṅi) (kartari) chandasi*	*Vā* 2	381
3.1.53	*vidhi aṅ ādeśa*	*svārthe (luṅi) (kartari) chandasi*		
3.1.54	*vidhi aṅ ādeśa*	*svārthe (luṅi) (kartari) chandasi*		
3.1.55	*vidhi aṅ ādeśa*	*svārthe (luṅi) (kartari) chandasi*		
3.1.56	*vidhi aṅ ādeśa*	*svārthe (luṅi) (kartari) vā*		
3.1.57	*vidhi aṅ ādeśa*	*svārthe (luṅi) (kartari) vā*		

Fourth *Āhnika* Continued

Fifth *Āhnika*

Sūtra	Type	Meaning	*Vā/Ślo*	Page
3.1.87	*atideśa*	*karmavatkarmaṇā tulyakriyā kartari*	*Vā* 18	434
3.1.88	*niyama*	*karmavatkarmaṇā tulyakriyā kartari*		
3.1.89	*niyama*	*karmavatkarmaṇā tulyakriyā kartari*	*Vā* 1	460
3.1.90	*vidhi/śyan*	*karmavatkarmaṇā tulyakriyā kartari*	*Vā* 2	462
3.1.91	*adhikāra*	*dhātoḥ*	*Vā* 11	467
3.1.92	*adhikāra/sañjña*	*upapada tatra saptamīstham*	*Vā* 6	484
3.1.93	*adhikāra/sañjña*	*kṛt atiṅ*	*Vā* 0	493
3.1.94	*adhikāra*	*vāsarūpo'striyām*	*Vā* 10	498
3.1.95	*adhikāra*	*kṛtyāḥ*	*Vā* 2	516
3.1.96	*vidhi tavya tavyat anīyar*	*bhāvakarmaṇoḥ*	*Vā* 3	517
3.1.97	*vidhi yat*	*bhāvakarmaṇoḥ*	*Vā* 3	519
3.1.98	*vidhi yat*	*bhāvakarmaṇoḥ*		
3.1.99	*vidhi yat*	*bhāvakarmaṇoḥ*		
3.1.100	*vidhi yat*	*bhāvakarmaṇoḥ anupasarge*	*Vā* 1	524
3.1.101	*vidhi yat*	*garhyapaṇitavyānirodheṣu*		
3.1.102	*vidhi yat*	*karaṇam*		
3.1.103	*vidhi yat*	*svāmivaiśyayoḥ*	*Vā* 1	525
3.1.104	*vidhi yat*	*kāyā prajane*		
3.1.105	*vidhi yat*	*saṅgatam*	*Vā* 1	525
3.1.106	*vidhi yat/kyap*	*bhāvakarmaṇoḥ supi anupasarge*	*Vā* 1	528
3.1.107	*vidhi kyap*	*bhāve*	*Vā* 0	530
3.1.108	*vidhi kyap*	*bhāve supi anupasarge*	*Vā* 1	531
3.1.109	*vidhi kyap*	*bhāve supi anupasarge*	*Vā* 2	532
3.1.110	*vidhi kyap*	*bhāve supi*		
3.1.111	*vidhi kyap*	*bhāve*	*Vā* 0	535
3.1.112	*vidhi kyap*	*bhāve asañjñayām*	*Vā* 4	536
3.1.113	*vidhi kyap*	*bhāve vibhāṣā*		
3.1.114	*vidhi kyap*	*bhāve*	*Vā* 3	542
3.1.115	*vidhi kyap*	*nade*		
3.1.116	*vidhi kyap*	*nakṣatre*		
3.1.117	*vidhi kyap*	*muñjakalkahaliṣu*		

Fifth *Āhnika* Continued

Sixth *Āhnika*

PART ONE
GENERAL INTRODUCTION

A. The Concept of Pratyaya in relation to the terms *Prakṛti, Aṅga, Dhātu, and Prātipadika*

Etymology and definitions of Pratyaya

The word *pratyaya* is derived from the root/*dhātu* *i* preceeded by *prati* and followed by the *pratyaya ac.*[1]

According to Pāṅini *3.3.56 ac* comes after a *dhātu* ending in *i* or *ī* (when mere action is denoted, or when the sense is that of a name, the word being related to the *dhātu* from which the name is derived but not as an agent).

Here the *dhātu* *i* in the sense of 'movement' is preceded by the *upasarga prati* creating a special result in the *prakṛti*/base or stem, in the sense of before, forward, in front, on, forth; so in the verbal form meaning to go forward, to meet, to resort to, to receive, to accept, to admit, to recognise, *(c.f. pratītaye R.V. 1.36.20, pratītyena R.V. 4.5.14)* to be certain of, to be convinced that, *(Gṛhya* - and *Śrauta-Sūtra, Nirukta* and *Rāmāyaṇa);* to trust and believe *(Kathāsaritsāgara).*

Attestations of the Word Pratyaya

The *dhātu* *i* followed by the *pratyaya ac* to form a noun *nāman* (by *erac 3.3.56*) which *pratyaya* is recorded in the literature in the following meanings:

---

1 Formation: प्रति+इ+अय:। निरु॰ 1.3 अभि इत्याभिमुख्यम्।
प्रति इत्येतस्य प्रातिलोम्यम् प्रति इण् (धा॰ पाठ गतौ 1045 अदादिगण परस्मै अनिट्)
अभिरभागे 1.4.31 - (अच् भावे)

लक्षण – *upasarga prati* used in the sense of *abhi/lakṣaṇa* meaning away from

(लक्षणे = sign, 'in direction of', i.e. away from) एरच् 3.3.56 (भावे, अकर्तरि, कारके)

इवर्णान्ताद् धातो भावे (3.3.18) अकर्तरि चकारके संज्ञायाम् (3.3.19) अच् प्रत्ययो भवति। घञोऽपवाद:।

By चित: 6.1.163 (अन्त: उदात्त:) the *it c* is for the final *udātta* accent.

1. Upaniṣads :

In the meanings knowledge, consciousness, faith in, belief in, firm conviction, confidence, hopefulness, certainty, ...

the earliest reference in the *Upaniṣads* is found in the *Māṇḍūkyopaniṣad C 7):*

> नान्तः प्रज्ञं न बहिष्प्रज्ञं नोभयतः प्रज्ञं न प्रज्ञानघनं न प्रज्ञं नाप्रज्ञम्।
> अदृष्टमव्यवहार्यमग्राह्यमलक्षणमचिन्त्यमव्यपदेश्यमेकात्मप्रत्ययसारं
> प्रपञ्चोपशमं शान्तं शिवमद्वैतं चतुर्थं मन्यन्ते स आत्मा स विज्ञेयः
>
> "They consider the Fourth *(turīya)* to be that which is not conscious of the internal (subjective) world, nor conscious of the external (objective) world, nor conscious of both the worlds, nor is a concrete consciousness, nor conscious, nor unconscious: which is unseen, beyond empirical dealings, beyond grasp (intangible), devoid of qualifications, beyond thinking, and beyond description; essentially of the nature of **consciousness** as the Self alone *(ekātma pratyaya-sāram)* in which all phenomena cease; which is peaceful, auspicious and non-dual. That is the Self, and that is to be known." In accordance with the Vedic text 'it is to be meditated upon as the Self' *(Bṛh. 1.4.7).*

The next reference to *pratyaya* is in the *Maitrāyaṇīya Upaniṣad (6.10):*

> पुरुषश्चेता प्रधानान्तःस्थः। स एवं भोक्ता प्राकृतमन्नं भुङ्क्त इति।
> तस्यायं भूतात्मा ह्यन्नम्। अस्य कर्ता प्रधानः। तस्मात् त्रिगुणं भोज्यम्।
> भोक्ता पुरुषोऽन्तस्थः। अत्र दृष्टं नाम प्रत्ययम्।
>
> "The conscious Person (*puruṣa*) stands in the midst of matter (*pradhāna*). He is an enjoyer—he enjoys the food of nature (*prakṛti*). Even this elemental soul (*bhūtātman*) is food for him; its maker is matter. Therefore, that which is to be enjoyed consists of the three 'qualities' (*guṇa*) and the enjoyer is the person (*puruṣa*) who stands in the midst. Here observation is clearly **consciousness** (or Knowledge)."

Other *Upaniṣads* use the concept in a similar sense.

In the following passages the word pratyaya carries the sense of comprehension, knowledge or realisation:

Mahopaniṣat 5.12.13:

> नवप्रसूतस्य परादयं चाहमिदं मम।
> इति यः प्रत्यय स्वस्थस्तज्जाग्रत्प्रागभावनात्।।12
> अयं सोऽहमिंद तन्म इति जन्मान्तरोदितः
> पीवरः प्रत्ययः प्रोक्ता महाजाग्रदिति स्फुटम्।।13

Sarasvatīrahasyopaniṣad 3:

तस्यैव स्तुवतो नित्यं समभ्यर्च्य सरस्वतीम्।
भक्तिश्रद्धाभियुक्तस्य षण्मासात्प्रत्ययो भवेत्।।

However here it is found in its technical sense 'affix':

Prāṇopaniṣat or *Praṇavopaniṣat 2.34*
६२ - *Gopatha Brāhmaṇa 1.1.24-30*

ओंकारं पृच्छामः को धातुः किं प्रातिपदिकं किं नामाख्यातं
किं लिङ्गं किं च वचनं का विभक्तिः कः प्रत्ययः ...

को धातुरित्याप्तेर्धातुरवतिमप्येके। रूपसामान्याद्यर्थसामान्यान्यन्य
नेदीयस्तस्मादापेरोंङ्कारः सर्वमाप्नोतीत्यर्थः।

कृदन्तमर्थवत्प्रातिपदिकम् अदर्शनं प्रत्ययस्य नाम संपद्यते।

"We are asking questions about the sound *'Om'*.

Which is (its) *dhātu?* Which is (its) *prātipadika?* What is (its connection with) *nāman* and *ākhyata* (verb)? What is its *liṅga* (gender)? What is its *vacana* (number)? What is its *vibhakti* (case)? What is the *pratyaya?*

Its *dhātu* is *āp* or according to others *av* (to protect etc.). According to the former, being common to all forms and meanings, it pervades all as *'Om'*.

Ending in a *kṛt pratyaya* it is meaningful and is thus *prātipadika.* The disappearance of its *pratyaya* (still) means it is valid as a *nāman* (noun)."

In the *Śrī Rāmapūrvatopaniṣat 39.4.7* the sense is 'belief':

स तु रामे शङ्कितः सन्प्रत्ययार्थं च दन्तुमेः।
विग्रहं दर्शयामास यो रामस्तम्न्चिक्षिपत।।

In the Sāmarahasyopaniṣat 227.12 the sense is 'realisation':

रसलीलायां प्रकृतिरन्यधर्मविस्मरणपूर्वका जाता।
तस्याः सेवाकथायां प्रत्ययो बभूव।।

२५०-१ तल्लीलाकथा परा काष्ठा तस्यां लीलायां प्रत्ययः परा काष्ठा।

२८८-१६ यदा महाभाग्योदयो भवति तरां तदस्य लीलायां प्रत्ययो भवेत्।

2. Nirukta

In the *Nirukta*, we find Yāska is using the word in the sense of conception, assumption, notion; or according to Abhyankar, the word *pratyaya* is used in the sense of realization, in which case the *dhātu i* in *pratyaya* means knowing (Nor conscious nor unconscious:) according to the maxim (quoted by Abhyankar from an unknown source); c.f. *sarve gatyarthā jñānārthāḥ* "All *dhātus* meaning to go have (also) the meaning to know"), and *yadi mantrārthapratyayāya nirarthaka bhavati* ("(The *Nirukta*) as means for the realisation of the meaning of the *mantras* (Vedic stanzas) it is of no use" *Nirukta 1.15*).

Incidentally, Yāska uses other terms, e.g. *nāmakaraṇa, upabandha* etc. to convey the idea of grammatical *pratyaya.*

3. Prātiśākhya

The word *pratyaya* is used in the *Prātiśākhya* works in the sense of 'following' or 'that which follows', i.e. the literal meaning.

The word *pratyaya* is used in the *Prātiśākhyas* and their commentaries in the sense of 'subsequent word or sound' *sparśe copaḥ pratyaye pūrvapadyaḥ. (R.P. 1.30) upa* forming the first member of a compound is designated *riphita* when a mute follows.

> मेधातिथौ वरूणान्तव्रतान्तौ स्पर्शान्तःस्थाप्रत्ययौ लिर्हसेते। *(R.P. 1.90.)*
>
> "In the Medhātithi hymns compounds ending in '*Varuṇa*' and 'Vrata' are shortened when a mute or semi-vowel follows."
>
> स्पर्शः स्वे प्रत्यये पूर्वान्तसस्वरो भवति। (Commentary on R.T. 25)

In the *Vājasaneyī Prātiśākhya* the word is used both in the sense of 'following' and in the sense of 'a suffix'/*pratyaya.* Thus in *pratyayasavarṇamadi Śākaṭāyana(3.9) 'Śākaṭāyana'* prescribes the change of a *Visarjanīya* into the homogeneous letter of the following sound when a sibilant follows. *Pratyayasavarṇa* is used in the sense of *parasavarṇa.*

In *hrasvavyañjanābhyāṃ vakārādau vibhaktipratyaye (5.13)* however *vibhaktipratyaye* means a "suffix which is a case ending".

In *C.A. pratyaya* is used in the sense of a suffix, c.f. *nābhikarephātpratyayakārasya (2.86) vyavadhāvapratyaye* (3.3). But in the commentary it is used in the sense of subsequent also.

> पूर्वरूपस्य मात्रार्थं समानकरणं परम्।
> प्रत्ययेन भवेत् कार्यमेतत् संयुक्तमिष्यते।। १-५०

In *Taittirīya Prātiśākhyaya pratyaya* is used in the sense of augment in *akurva iti ca pratyayāt paraḥ (5.7),* whereas in *Pāṇini* as we shall see, we find the word used in the specialised sense of a suffix, as *apṛkta* is used in reference to a *pratyaya* only.

In the Gopatha Brāhmaṇa (1.1.26):

का धातुर इत्यादिर्धातुः। रूपसामान्यादर्थसामान्यं नेदीयः। तस्मादापेरोङ्कार। सर्वमाप्नोतीत्यर्थे कृदन्तमर्थवत्प्रातिपदिकम्। अदर्शनं प्रत्ययस्य। नाम सम्पद्यते। निपातेषु चैनं वैयाकरणा उदात्तं समासनन्ति तदव्ययीभूतमन्वर्थवाची शब्दो नो व्येति कदाचनेति।

See page 5 for translation.

In the *Brāhmaṇa* as well as *Prātiśākhya* it is clear the word means not only 'that which follows' (*V.Pr.3.9*) 'augment' (*Tai Pr. akurva iti ca pratyayātparaḥ. (5.7)* and 'case ending' (*'adarśanam pratyayasya' Gopatha Brāhmaṇa 1.26*) but at one time included the sense of suffix, prefix, infix, and augment.

4. Other Grammarians

'Pratyaya' is used in this wide sense only once by Pāṇini in *aṇuditsavarṇasya cāpratyayaḥ. 1.1.69.* Hence the objector urges in the *M.Bh:*

अत्यल्पमिदमुच्यते अप्रत्यय इति अप्रत्यय आदेश टित् किन्मित इति वक्तव्यम्

"It is too narrow to say 'not a *pratyaya*/affix'. It should be stated 'not a *pratyaya,* or *an ādeśa*/substitute or having an *it 'ṭ',* or an *it 'k'* or an *it* 'm.'"

The etymological sense is thus shown in *M.Bh. 3.1.1:8 yastamarth-ampratyāyayati sa pratyayaḥ* as we shall see in more detail subsequently. *Nāmakaraṇa* and *upabandha* would appear to be the earlier names for a *'pratyaya'*. Both are found in the *Nirukta.*

While explaining *kiṃ punardvigusaṃjñā pratyayotarapadayorbhavati* under *taddhitārthottarapadasamāhāre ca 2.1.51 Kaiyaṭah* says *kāśakṛtsnasya pratyayotta-rapadayoḥ iti sūtram.*

From this it is clear that *Kāśakṛtsna* also used *pratyaya* in the sense of a *pratyaya.* All the different systems of Sanskrit grammar use *'pratyaya'* for a 'suffix' with the exception of the Jainendra and Mugdhabodha. Jainendra uses the second syllable *tya* for *pratyaya* and Mugdhabodha follows Jainendra.

Kātantra, Saṁkṣipta and *Supadima Vyākaraṇam* use *pratyaya* without defining it.

5. Classical Literature

Kālidāsa has used the two technical terms *Prakṛti*[2] and *pratyaya* in *Raghuvaṃśa 11.56.*

---

[2] That to which the प्रत्यय is added is known as प्रकृति. प्रकृति has the sense of 'original form' in the *Nirukta 2.2,*

ता नराधिपसुता नृपात्मजैस्ते च ताभिरगमन् कृतार्थताम् सोऽभवद् वरवधूसमागमः प्रत्ययप्रकृतियोगसन्निभः।।

"The princesses attained the object of their being, on being united with the princes, as did the princes by being joined with the princesses. The union of the bride and bridegroom was like the combination of the *prakṛti* /base with the *pratyaya*/ affix."

Bhāravi also uses the term in *kirātārjunīyaḥ. 13.19* -

स भवस्य भवक्षयैकहेतोः सितसप्तेश्चविधास्यतोः सहार्थम्।
रिपुराप पराभवाय मध्यं प्रकृतिप्रत्यययोरिवानुबन्धः।।

"The enemy came for his own overthrow between Śiva, the sole cause of creation, and Arjuna of the white steeds, both about to accomplish their object simultaneously, even as the indicatory letter comes for elision between the *prakṛti* and the *pratyaya* which together express the meaning."[3]

Bhaṭṭoji quotes in *Prauḍhamanoramā*

उदितवति परस्मिन् प्रत्यये शास्त्रयोनौ गतवति विलयं च प्राकृतेऽपि प्रपञ्चेसपदि पदमुदीतं केवलः प्रत्ययो यत् तदियदिति मिमीते को हृदा पण्डितोऽपि।।

अथापि प्रकृतय एवैकषु भाष्यन्ते विकृतय एकेषु (धातोराख्यातपदभावेन स यः प्रयोगः सा प्रकृतिः। नामीभूतस्य तस्यैव यः प्रयोगः सा विकृतिः दुर्गः।)

"Further, primary forms alone are used in speech among some people; secondary forms among others".

Pāṇini uses the term *aṅga* or base as his synonym of Prakṛti.

यस्मात् प्रत्ययविधिस्तदादि प्रत्ययेऽङ्गम् 1 । 4 । 13

"Whatsoever is followed by an enjoined *pratyaya* the prior part of that (combination), in its state prior to any change resulting from combination, is named *aṅga* (in relation to and) in the presence of that following *pratyaya*."

Similar to the usage in the *Prātiśākhyas* and *Pāṇini, Saṁkṣiptasāra Vyākaraṇa* uses *Prakṛti* in this sense in *prakṛtivad dvirguṇādiśca 2.566* etc.

In *2.289 mūlaprakṛti* is used. *Goyīcandra* explains it thus -

प्रकृतिपदेन यस्मात्प्रत्ययोत्पतिस्तस्यैव ग्रहणे सिद्धे व्युत्पादितस्तदग्रहणार्थं धातुरेव शब्दस्य मूलप्रकृतिः।
धातुजत्वात् सर्वशब्दः। मूलप्रकृतीति कृतम् यस्माद् धातोः शब्दः।

3 (N.B. - In Kālidāsa's simile the masculine *'Pratyaya'* and feminine *Prakṛti* are *upamānas* for the bridegroom and bride respectively. But in Bhāravi's simile the *upamāna Prakṛti* is feminine but the *upameya bhāva* is masculine and since the sense of *prakṛti* is subordinate to *pratyaya*, Śiva becomes inferior to Arjuna. Moreover generally *anubandhas* come at the end of a *pratyaya* (and not between it and the *prakṛti*).)

> "When the Supreme Knowledge (*pratyaya*) which has its source in scripture, arose and the visible world created by *Māyā* (or illusion) melted away, lo! There arose an entity which is pure knowledge. Who however learned he may be, can now measure by heart its extent? When the *pratyaya gh-a* which acts after the *prakṛti* as prescribed in grammar, added to *idam* and everything belonging to the *prakṛti* was elided, there sprang into existence a word which is solely a *pratyaya*. That word is *iyat*. Who, however learned he may be, can thoroughly explain this?"[4]

Paṇḍitrāja Jagannātha has a similar stanza in *rasagaṅgādhara*

> गुणवृद्धि परे यस्मिन् नैव स्तः प्रत्ययात्मके बुधेषुसदितिख्यातं तदु ब्रह्म समुपास्महे।।
>
> "We worship that *Brahma* in whom the Supreme Being consisting of pure thought (*pratyaya*) there is neither any attribute nor any growth or development who is known among the wise as the existent or eternal one."

Finally there is a *subhāṣita*—

> हरिहरयोरिह भेदं कलयति लोको विनाशास्त्रम्।
> अनयोः प्रकृतिरभिन्ना प्रत्ययभेदात् विभिन्नवद् भाति
>
> "People here regard *Hari* and *Hara* as different and dig their own graves (*vināśa astram*) though there is nothing in the *śāstras* to warrant this. Their nature (*prakṛti*) is the same but appears different owing to a difference in knowledge (*pratyaya*)."

Pratyayas as a rule come after the base to which they have been added. Hence *Pāṇini* has framed the *adhikāra sūtra Paraśca 3.1.2* immediately after the *sūtra pratyaya 3.1.1.* So in *Kādaṃbarī* (page 47) Bāṇabhaṭṭa uses the *parisaṃkhyā "pratyayānāṃ paratvam"* being subsequent (is characteristic) of *pratyayas*. The major exception is the *pratyaya bahuc* by *Pāṇini sūtra Vibhāṣā supo bahuc purastāt tu 5.3.68 (Candra (4.3 vṛtti)* and his followers refuse to

---

4 This *pratyaya* वत् is added to इदम् and the व of वत् changed to घ (i.e. इय्) by किमिदंभ्यां वो घः 5.2.4 so we get इदम् इय त्. Then by इदम् इश 5.3.3 ई replaces इदम् so we have इइयत्. The ई is elided by यस्येति च 6.4.148. So that the whole base is elided. Only *pratyaya* इयत् remains. Similarly
अधुना 5.3.17 *adhunā* etc.

c.f. In English 'bus' is an abbreviation of omnibus, dative plural of Latin 'omnis'. 'Bus' corresponds to Sanskrit *bhyas* (भ्यस्).

(In Gathic Avesta *tā* (*Yas. 11.7.3*) for Sanskrit पिता in *Y. Avesta turiya* (*Vis. 12.15*) for पितृव्य.)

regard *bahuc* as a *pratyaya*), c.f. 'more' and 'most' in English forming comparative and superlative suffixes, c.f. also

Mahābhāṣya 3.1.2 vā. 6

> द्वयसजादीनां च केवलानां प्रयोगो दृश्यते।
> किमस्य द्वयसम् किमस्य मात्रम् काद्य तिथीति।।
> द्वयसादयो वै वृत्तिजसदृशा अवृत्तिजा यथा बहुस्तथा।।
>
> "The usage of *'dvayasac' pratyaya* and the rest alone (i.e. without a base or *prakṛti*) is seen (as) 'What is the measure (*dvayasac*) of that? What number day is it today?'
>
> *dvayasac* and the rest are indeed like verbal activities or *prakṛtis*. As non-verbal, (not *prakṛtis*) so they are like *bahuc*".[5]

In *Madhyama Vyāyoga* of Bhāsa (?) we find

> "रूपं सत्त्वं बलं चैव पितृभिः सदृशं बहु

where *bahu* is used separately, as also

> जनयति च मनोज्वरं स्वरो यं बहुसदृशो हि धानञ्जयस्वरस्य (25)

where *'bahu'* has been compounded with *sadṛśa*.[6]

6. Platonic Dialogue on Pratyaya

Rather than specifically defining the concept, Pāṇini frames the *adhikāra sūtra pratyayaḥ. (3.1.1)* and thereby indicates that the prescribed items which fall in the third, fourth and fifth *adhyāyas*, (making it much the largest governing *sūtra* in terms of sphere of influence) and come after *aṅga* (which come into existence only after a *pratyaya* is added), are all *pratyayas*. The tradition particularly that of Kātyāyana and Patañjali has interpreted the word consistently in the sense of that which causes one to understand a meaning —

> "Or else we can resort to the meaning (for explaining the *pratyaya* rule). A *pratyaya* is that which causes the meaning to be meant or understood."
>
> "Is this (going) to be stated? 'Not at all.' How will it be understood— if unexpressed?"

---

5 बहुच् can easily have the secondary sense of 'to a large extent' (c.f. Germ. 'fast' and Fr. 'asse') and both the position of '*bahu*' and the accent along with the gender of the word show there is a compound of '*bahu*' and a following word.

6 See Wackernagel, 'Altindische Grammar', *2.1.236.*

"'*Pratyaya*' is formed as a great *saṃjñā*/technical term."

"And *saṃjña* is verily (normally) that than which nothing is shorter."

"How is this? For the purpose of the technical name is brevity."

"In that context the reason/cause of the 'great *saṃjñā*' is so that its purpose as an '*anvartha saṃjña*' (a term whose meaning is intelligible in itself and opposed to such technical terms as '*bha*', '*ghu*' coined by Pāṇini), may be known."

"A *pratyaya* leads towards, i.e. causes to recognise or acknowledge, convince (anyone of the truth of anything)"

[*Kālid*–'makes clear', proves (*Saṁ K., Sāh.*)]

"If '*pratyaya*' leads towards, i.e. causes (the listener) to recognise (the meaning) then the technical term *pratyaya* does not obtain for '*avika*' (c.f. *aveḥkaḥ* अवे: क: ५४.२) ("The *pratyaya* '*ka*' acts after '*avi*' in the sense of '*avi*'/*svārthe* itself, i.e. without change of sense") and the rest (of *svārthe pratyayas*) for they do not cause one to recognise anything."

"Well then '*pratyaya*' is that which is led towards, i.e. is caused to be recognised or acknowledged, (i.e. the *pratyaya* is recognised but not as having an independent meaning)."

"Then the term *pratyaya* does **not** obtain for the *pratyaya* 'san' (desiderative) etc. which causes to recognise a meaning."

"Well then this word is expressive of both, expressive of the agent (who causes to recognise, i.e. know the meaning) and expressive of the Object (which is caused to be recognised or is made known)."

"Even then how is it that although (both the pratyaya and the *āgama*) have in common the state of not previously being taught, in the forms *trāpuṣam* and *jātuṣam* (derived by *trapujatunoḥ ṣuk 4.3.138.*"

"The *pratyaya* '*aṇ*' with the augment/*āgama ṣuk* acts in the sense of modification *vikāra* and *jatu* (n., lac, gum) thus *trāpuṣam* made of tin, *jātuṣam* m.f.n. "made or covered with lac or gum".

"Here the letter '*a*' (of the *pratyaya* '*aṇ*') causes the meaning to be meant or understood, not (the augment/*āgama*) letter '*ṣ*'."

"Elsewhere also it is by reason of the letter '*a*' (that there is) pronunciation of that meaning. We think it is the letter '*a*' which causes the meaning to be meant or understood, not the letter '*s*'."

"Where else?"

"After *'bilva'* etc. the *pratyaya 'aṇ'* acts in the sense of its modification or part (*vikāra* or *avayava*) *bailva* m.f.(ī)n. relating to or coming from the *bilva* tree, (made of *bilva* wood, modification, part of the *bilva* tree)."

7. Nāgeśa's Discussion on Svārtha Pratyayas

Generally a meaning is assigned to a *pratyaya* when it is prescribed. When the meanings are not assigned, the *pratyaya* is said to bear the sense of the base.

One might say that the term *'pratyaya'* which implies that which is termed so, conveys a meaning, ought properly not to be applied to those (*pratyayas* which convey no meaning[7] whatever). (The author of the *Paribhāṣa*) says therefore

प्रत्ययाःस्वार्थेः
नागेश। नवत्यन्तस्वार्थिकानामर्थप्रत्यायकत्वरूपः
प्रत्ययत्वानुपपत्तिरत आह अनिर्दिष्टार्थाः
प्रत्ययाः स्वार्थे।। परि. ११३

(*Pari. 113*) "*Pratyayas* to which no meaning has been assigned (in grammar) convey the meaning of the (bases) to which they (are added)."

यस्यार्थः प्रकृत्या प्रत्याय्यते सोऽपि प्रत्यय
इत्यस्यप्यङ्गीकारात्तस्य प्रत्ययत्वमिति न दोष।

"As we hold (not only that a *pratyaya* conveys a meaning but hold) likewise[8] that, the meaning of which is conveyed by the base (to which it is added) too may be termed a *pratyaya,* it cannot be improper to apply the term *pratyaya* to the latter (i.e. to *pratyayas* which convey no meaning of their own)."

स्वार्थ इत्यस्य स्वीयप्रकृयर्थ इत्यर्थः।

Svārthe (in this *Paribhāṣā*) means that they convey the meaning of their own bases.[9]

What gives rise to the present *(Paribhāṣā)* on this:

महासंज्ञाबलादर्थाकाङ्क्षायामन्यानुपस्थितिरस्या बीजम्।

---

7 such as क् *5.4.28*

8 namely in accordance with *Bhāśya* on 3.1.1 प्रत्यय इति महती संज्ञा

9 i.e. स्व in the sense of स्वीय
सुपि स्थः (3.2.4) इत्यादि सूत्रेषु भाष्ये स्पष्टैषा।

"When (*Pāṇini*) adopts so long a technical term (as *pratyaya*) his doing so shows that (what is denoted by that term) must (in accordance with the etymological meaning of the latter necessarily convey) a meaning and as no other (meaning) can be conveyed (by the *pratyayas* spoken of in this *Paribhāṣā* they must convey the meaning of the bases to which they are added)."

(This (*Paribhāṣā*) is found in the *Bhāṣya* on *P.3.2.4* and other rules.)

Nāgeśa 83

ननु कुटीर इत्यादौ स्वार्थिकत्वात्स्वार्थिकानां
प्रकृतितो लिङ्गवचनानुवृत्तेर्न्यायप्राप्तत्वात्
पुंस्त्वानुपपत्तिरप्कल्पमित्यत्र नपुंसकत्वैकवचनयोरनुपत्तिश्चेत्यत आह

"One might say e.g. in *kuṭīra* 'a small hut' (*pratyaya ra* which has been added by *5.3.88* has been added to the feminine *kuṭī* does not add any meaning of its own) but leaves (*kuṭīra*) with the same meaning that would be denoted by the original base (*kuṭī*), *kuṭīra* ought not to be masculine because (derivative bases formed by means of) *pratyayas* 'that do not convey any particular meaning of their own, should in accordance with the practice of ordinary life receive their gender and number from the original base (from which they are derived) and that (for the same reason) *ap-kalpa* 'almost water' (*ap, āp* — in accordance with *5.3.67* is derived from the feminine plural *āp, āpaḥ,* by means of the *pratyaya kalpap*) ought not to be neuter and singular (the author of the *Paribhāṣās*) says therefore:

क्वचित्स्वार्थिकाः प्रकृतितो लिङ्गवचनान्यतिवर्तन्ते।।८३

"(Pari. 83): Sometimes (it happens that bases which are derived by means of) *pratyayas* that (do not convey any particular meaning of their own, but) leave the meaning which is conveyed by the original base (to which they are added unchanged) do not take their gender and number from these original bases (from which they are derived)."

Pratyayas taught in *5.3.1 prāg-diśo vibhakti* etc. convey no meaning of their own but merely indicate that the base to which they are added must be understood in some particular sense or other; the new bases therefore which are formed by them convey the same meaning as the original bases to which they are added and might accordingly be expected to receive their gender and number from the latter.[10]

---

[10] See *P.V. 3.7* and *55*
स्वार्थिका इति। प्रायेणेति शेषः। स्वकीयप्रकृतेऽर्थे भवा इत्यर्थः।
तसिलाद्यर्थनिर्देशाभावादतिशायन इत्यादीनां प्रकृत्यर्थविशेषणत्वादिति भावः

णच स्त्रियामञ् 5.4.14 इति सूत्रे स्त्रियामित्युक्तिरस्या ज्ञापक।

The fact that (*Pāṇini*) has stated in the *sūtra 5.4.14* (that *añ* shall be added to bases in *ṇac*) *striyām*, i.e. in the feminine, indicates (the existence of) this (*Paribhāṣā*).

अन्यथा कर्मव्यतिहारे "णच् स्त्रियां" ३.३.४३
इति स्त्रियामेव विधानात्किं तेन।

"If on the other hand (the *Paribhāṣā* did not exist) that (*striyām* in *5.4.14*) would serve no purpose, because *ṇac* by *3.3.43* can be added only in the feminine (and because new bases derived from such bases in *ṇac* by means of *añ* could likewise be nothing but feminine)."

स्पष्टा चेयं बहुज्विधायके भाष्ये।

This (*Paribhāṣā*) is found in the *Bhāṣā* on *Sūtra 5.3.68* which teaches the addition of बहुच्.

Mbh. 3.2.4.2 line 10, also on *3.3.19* and *3.4.9* etc. (the sense given in the language long before this formulation) is stated as the composite sense of the base and *pratyaya* together. Usually there is stated to be *pratyayārthasya prādhānyam,* c.f. *prakṛtipratyayau sahārthaṃ brūtaḥ na kevalaḥ pratyayaḥ.*

(Mbh. on *P.1.2.64, Vārt. 1.5 p.234.1.15*) "Pre-eminence for the meaning of the *pratyaya.* The base and the *pratyaya* are spoken of together; neither the base alone should be used for making sense nor the *pratyaya* alone." [Cf. also *1.3.1 Vārt. 4 p.254.1.26; 2.3.1 Vārt. 10 p.442.1.2; 3.1.4 Vārt. 3 p.79.1.5,6* .]

The Concept Dhātu Defined

Dhātu is from the *dhātu ḍu-dhāñ juhotyādi* Cl. 3 *dhāraṇapoṣaṇayoḥ dāne'pi ityeke.*

To hold, nourish and sustain

Some say it means to give; also derived according to *uṇādi 1.70.*

सितनिगमिमसिच्यविधाञ्कुशिभ्यस्तुन्

"Pratyaya tun comes after the *dhātus si (si) tani* (spread), *gamḷ* (go), *masi* (complete), *sic* (sprinkle), *avi* (protect), *dhāñ* (bear support), *kuś* (lament).

"Originally it meant layer, essential or constituent part, component, ingredient (esp. and in *R.V.* only i.f.c. where often = fold, e.g. *tridhātu* threefold etc. *R.V. 1.34.6* etc.). Then it meant element, primitive matter (e.g. *mahābhūtaḥ kṣiti āp tejas marutaṃ vyoman*) or the constituent elements of the body *rasādayaḥ saptaḥ dhātavaḥ to rasa, rakta, mānsa, medas-asthi majjā śukrāṇi; Caraka Saṃhitā, 15.16* etc.

The last meaning, both semen, and more generally 'seed' indicate a more 'essential' nature for the word-meaning than the analogy of 'root' used to translate the term when speaking in linguistic terms. It is also used in the sense of the five *jñānendriyas* or the *tanmātras*, namely (*'gandha, rasa, rūpa, sparśa* and *śabda'*).

Attestations of the Word Dhātu

In grammar it means 'element' or 'essential ingredient'. Thus 'seed' rather than 'root' is the more accurate translation. It is first found in the *Gopaṭha Brāhmaṇa* (in the grammatical sense (see earlier reference under *pratyaya*, page 5).

1. Upaniṣads

In the *Chāndogya Upaniṣad* we have the earliest *Upaniṣadic* reference *6.5.1 ff.*

> अन्नमशितंत्रेधा विधीयते।
> तस्य यः स्थविष्ठो धातुस्तत्पुरीषं भवति।
> यो मध्यमस्तन्मांसम्। योऽणिष्ठस्तन्मनः।
>
> 'Food when eaten becomes divided in three ways: that which is the grossest 'ingredient'/element (*dhātu*) of it turns into faeces, that which is the medium (ingredient) becomes flesh. That which is the subtlest becomes mind.'

The second earliest is the *Kaṭhopaniṣat 2.20:*

> अर्णोरणीयान्महतो महीयानात्मास्य जन्तोर्निहितो गुहायाम्।
> तमक्रतुः पश्यति वीतशोको धातुप्रसादान्महिमानमात्मनः।।
>
> "The Self is subtler than the subtle, greater than the great, is lodged in the heart (of every creature). A desireless man sees the glory of the Self, through the serenity of the organs and (thereby) becomes free from sorrow."

Commentary on *Kaṭha. 2.20:*

> शंकरभाष्ये। मन आदीनि करणानि धातवः शरीरस्य धारणात्प्रसीदन्तीत्येषां धातूनाम् प्रसादाद्।
>
> The organs such as mind etc., become composed; *dhātus* being so called because of holding the body, (so) "through serenity of the organs".

2. In Nirukta (1.20)

एतावन्तः समानकर्माणो धातवः धातुर्दधातेः।

So many *'dhātus'* have the same meaning. *'Dhātu'* is derived from *'dhā'* (to put).

3. In R.V., Prāt. 6.6

तदाख्यातं येन भावं (अभिदधाति) स धातु

That by which being/action is declared or made known. It is the original basis of words, as it is the basic component of earth when it is used in the sense of mineral.

4. Bṛhat Devatā

It is found several times in the *Bṛhat Devatā 2.101-102:*

लिङ्गं धातु विभक्ति च सन्नमेत् तत्र तत्र च। यद् यद् स्याच्छन्दसंमन्त्रे तत्तत्कुर्यात्तु लौकिकम्।।

" '*Liṅga*' (gender), *'dhātu'* and *'vibhakti'* (inflection) one should in their respective places adapt (to the sense). Whatever is Vedic in a formula one should turn into everyday speech."

5. Pāṇini

Pāṇini does not define *dhātu* but merely names two important *dhātūs* — one of the first conjugation and one of the second ... (according to one view) and says that *'dhātus'*, are of the nature of these. His rule is:

भूवादयो धातवः *1.3.1.*

"Bhū and the rest are (called) *dhātus* (beginning with one, i.e. *bhū*) and of the nature of the *dhātu* i.e. *vā*

(or, *bhū* and the rest, and *vā* and the rest are called *dhātus.*)"[11]

भा. 1.3.1. वा. 11
प्रत्येकं चाऽऽदिशब्दः परिसमाप्यते भ्वादय इति च
वादय इति च . . . क्रियावचनो
धातुरित्येष पक्षस्तदा भू इत्यत्र य आदिशब्दः स

---

11 A *śloka* explains that the '*v*' in the *sūtra* is for auspiciousness:

भूवादीनां वकारोऽयं (लक्षणार्थ) मंगलार्थः प्रयुज्यते।
भूवो वार्थ वदन्तीति भ्वर्था वा वादय स्मृताः
(found in *Kāśikā* on *1.3.1.*)

व्यवस्थायां वर्तते वा इत्यत्र य आदिशब्दः स
प्रकारे। भू इत्येवमादयो वा इत्येवंप्रकारा
इति। यदा तु भाववचनो धातुरित्येष पक्षस्—
तदा वा इत्यत्र य आदि शब्द स व्यवस्थायाम्
भू इत्यत्र य आदिशब्दः स प्रकारे। वा
इत्येवं साऽयो भू इत्येवमादयो भू प्रकारा इति।

i.e. *bhūvādi* is to be derived with one *aunādika* agent *pratyaya i*; thus *bhūvo'rthaṃ vadantīti.*

It is possible that in some ancient *Dhātu Pāṭha, 'vā'* stood at the head of the *'vādi' dhātus* and so some predecessor of *Pāṇini* framed the *sūtra bhūvādayo dhātavaḥ* which was taken over by *Pāṇini.*

Kātyāyana says *kriyā vacano dhātuḥ 1.1.1* and *kriyā bhāvo dhātuḥ 2.1.3*—a word denoting a verbal activity. It is just possible that we have nouns from the two general *dhātus* 'to go' etc. and 'to be' (in the words of *Rāma Tarkayāgīśa parispandattasādhanasāghya gamanādi aparispandanasādhana sāghya avasthānādi* and that the author intended us to understand 'that which denotes action and that which denotes existence are *dhātus'*. *Nirukta 1.1 bhāvapradhānamākhyāttam; sattvapradhānāni nāmāni* "The verb has becoming as its fundamental notion, nouns have being as their fundamental notion".

The Concept Prātipadika: Attestations of Meaning

1. Pāṇini

(i) *Prātipadika* literally available in every word, express, explicit. Ṣṛṣṭdhara, a Bengali commentator of the 17th century derived from *pratipada* 'every word' with the *pratyaya ṭhak* according to *sūtra padottarapadaṃ gṛhṇāti 4.4.39.* "The *pratyaya ṭhak* comes in the sense of who takes, after a word having *pada* as its second member, the word being in the second case in construction." So *prātipadika* means that which embraces every inflected word, i.e. words like *vṛkṣa* etc., which are inherent in all the different inflected forms, like *vṛkṣaṃ vṛkṣāṇi* etc.

It is, however, possible that *ṭha(k)* has been added to *pratipada* in the sense of *prayojanam 5.1.109.* The *pratyaya ṭhañ (ik)* comes after a word in the first case in construction in the sense of 'that whose occasion or purpose is this' and the word *prātipadika* means that which is necessary for each inflected word (*prayojana* is similar to *phala* here) since no inflected word (*subanta* or denominative) can be formed without the help of the *prātipadika.*

Monier-Williams notes that *prātipada* occurs in the *Sāṃkhyāyāna Śrauta Sūtra* in the sense of 'forming the commencement'. Thus *prātipadika* forms the beginning of words which cannot be used unless and until a *vibhakti pratyaya* is added *suptiṅantaṃ padam 1.4.14.*

(ii) *Pāṇini* defines *prātipadika* as *arthavadadhāturapratyayaḥ prātipadikam 1.2.45 kṛt-taddhitasamāsāśca 1.2.46,* i.e. that which conveys meaning and is neither a *dhātu* nor a *pratyaya* (nor a word ending in a *pratyaya*) is a *prātipadika.* 'Samāsa' (compounds) as well as words ending in primary or *kṛt pratyaya* and secondary or *taddhita pratyayas* are also called *prātipadikas* which we shall consider in relation to *pratyaya* in the appropriate section.

Pāṇini implies four kinds of *prātipadika: mūlabhūta, kṛdanta, taddhitānta,* and *samāsa.*

2. Brāhmaṇa

The term, though mentioned in the *Brāhmaṇa,* i.e. *Gopatha Brāhmaṇa* of the *Atharva Veda*

महासंज्ञाकरणं श्रुत्यनुयोधानं तथा चाथर्वणे पठ्यम्।
को धातुः किं प्रातिपदिकं कः प्रत्यय इति।

is not mentioned in the *Prātiśākhyaya* works, probably because those works were concerned with formed words which had actually been in use. *Bhā 1.2.45 vā 8*

3. Mahābhāṣya Kātyāyana

नित्यसम्बन्धावेतावर्थौ प्रकृति प्रत्यय इति प्रत्ययेन नित्यसम्बन्धात्
केवलस्यप्रयोगो न भविष्यति।

"The meaning of *prakṛti* and *pratyaya* are always connected together. One should know from the eternal connection there will (never) be use of (either) alone."

B. Uses of the Pratyaya in Pāṇini's *Aṣṭādhyāyī* in Order of Occurence (26)

1. प्रत्ययस्य लुक्श्लुलुपः (1.1.61) (अदर्शनम्)

"The disappearance of a *pratyaya,* when it is caused by the words *'luk', 'ślu'* or *'lup',* is designated by those terms respectively."

2. प्रत्ययलोपे प्रत्ययलक्षणम् (1.1.62)

"When there is a *lopa* (elision) of a *pratyaya,* the *pratyaya* still exerts an influence (and the operations dependent upon it take place as if it were present)."

3. अणुदित्सवर्णस्य चाप्रत्ययः (1.1.69) (स्वं रूपम्)

"The letters of the *pratyāhāra* अण्, i.e. vowels and semi-vowels and a term having उँ as its indicatory letter, refer to names of their own form as well as to their homogeneous letters, except when they are used as *pratyayas.*"

Here प्रत्यय is explained by Bhaṭṭoji Dīkṣita in *Siddhānta Kaumudī* in similar terms to Patañjali's explanation *pratīyate* ('it is admitted, recognised, known, understood, implied-M.W.), but then itself glossed by *vidhīyate* (it is anything enjoined, ordained by rule), indicating the word has a much wider scope here, including prefixes and augments and *ādeśas* (substitutes).

4. अपृक्त एकाल्प्रत्ययः (1.2.41)

"A *pratyaya* consisting of a single letter is called *apṛkta* (अपृक्तः) not mixed." Here the word is used in the specialised sense of a *pratyaya.*

5. प्रधानप्रत्ययार्थवचनमर्थस्यान्यप्रधानत्वात् (1.2.56) (अशिष्यम्)

"(Nor need be taught) the rule relating to the dependence of the meaning of a word on the principle (प्रधान) in a compound or on the *pratyaya* because the authority of the meaning (of a word, compound or derivative) consists in something else."

That is, inasmuch as the meaning of a word is fixed by usage and idiom, the proofs, for the meaning of a word is not only to be searched either in the *pratyayas* which go to form it nor by its principal word if it is a compound, for the proof of the meaning is the usage of a people.

6. षः प्रत्ययस्य (1.3.6) (आदिर् इति इत्)

"The initial ष of a *pratyaya* is indicatory (and thus goes *lopa* when the *pratyaya* comes into operation)."

7. यस्मात्प्रत्ययविधिस्तदादिप्रत्ययेऽङ्गम् (1.4.13)

"After whatsoever there is a *pratyaya* enjoined (whether it be a *dhātu* or a *prātipadika*) that which begins therewith in the form in which it appears when the *pratyaya* follows is called अङ्ग (an inflective base, called प्रकृति by Patañjali and the later tradition)." (N.B. Philosophically this leads some to suggest a parallel between the प्रकृति and पुरुष in *Sāṁkhya* and *Śrīmadbhagavadgītā* and अङ्ग and प्रत्यय in *Pāṇini.*)

8. षष्ठ्यतसर्थप्रत्ययेन (2.3.30)

"Sixth case *pratyaya* is used in connection with words ending with *pratyayas* having the sense of the *pratyaya* अतसुच् (दक्षिणोत्तराभ्यामतसुच् ५-३-२८ स्वार्थे)", i.e. of its base *dakṣiṇa* or *uttara* (direction, locality or time).

9. प्रत्ययः (3.1.1)

"A *pratyaya*/affix." This *sūtra* regulates the sense of others. From this place forward to the end of the fifth book all will get the name *pratyaya* or affix except the अङ्ग or प्रकृति (base), the उपपद (dependent word) or the उपाधि (the attribute or special case) that occasion changes.

10. कास्प्रत्ययादाममन्त्रे लिटि (3.1.35) (प्रत्ययः धातोः)

"आम् is the *pratyaya* of the *dhātu* कास् to cough, and of those *dhātus* that are formed by *pratyaya* (i.e. derivative verbs) when लिट् (perfect tense) follow except in the mantra (i.e. *Veda*)."

Here one special class of *pratyaya* is mentioned as conveying the function and meaning of *dhātus* to certain nominal forms.

11. अ प्रत्ययात् (3.3.102) (स्त्रियाम्)

"After *dhātus* that end in a *pratyaya* there is the *pratyaya* अ, the word being feminine." This refers to the first group of *pratyayas* सनाद्यन्ताः (3.1.32) the words ending with the *pratyaya san* etc. (conveying the sense of desire etc.) which are called धातवः (*dhātus*) in spite of this. The *kṛt* (कृत्) *pratyaya* is then added to these enabling the *strī* (or feminine) *pratyaya* to be added, which finally prepares the way for the *pada* forming *pratyaya* or *sup-vibhakti* enabling the word to fully manifest its meaning in the 'cosmos' of the sentence.

> ज्ञा+सन्+अ ⇨ जिज्ञास ⇨ जिज्ञास+टाप् ⇨ जिज्ञासा+जस् ⇨ जिज्ञासाः,
> the ladies desire to know.

12. धातुसम्बन्धे प्रत्ययाः (3.4.1)

"Words formed with *pratyayas* stand (in reference to time) in closer relation to the *dhātu* (with which they are allied)", or more literally, "*Pratyayas* are employed in denoting the relation between (the sense of) *dhātu*" which confirms the special function of the *pratyaya* in the sentence in bringing forth the meaning, i.e. making manifest what without them is not known. (Here when a relation between two *dhātus* as qualifier and qualified is intended then *pratyayas* may be employed in denoting other times than that specifically ordained for them, i.e. *pratyaya* is related directly to *dhātus* and not to whole sentences (तत्र वसन् ददर्श).

13. स्वाङ्गे तस्प्रत्यये कृभ्वोः (3.4.61) (क्त्वा णमुलौ)

"*Pratyaya ktvā* and *ṇamul* act after *dhātu kṛ* (make) and *bhū* (become) in composition with a word denoting a member of one's own body when *pratyaya tas* is enjoined thereto,"

e.g. मुखतः कृत्य गतः having placed himself at the head/front, he went.

14. नाधार्थप्रत्यये च्व्यर्थे (3.4.62)

"*Pratyaya* क्त्वा and णमुल् act after कृ and भू when a word ending in *pratyaya* ना or a *pratyaya* with the meaning of धा or having the sense of the *pratyaya* च्वि, is in composition,"

e.g. नाना कृत्य गतः having performed variously (sacrifices etc.), he went.

15. ञितश्च तत्प्रत्ययात् (4.3.155)

"*Pratyaya* अञ् acts in the sense of 'its product or part' after a word ending in a *pratyaya* having an indicatory ञ् denoting its product or part,"

e.g. दैवदारवम्, made of the tree *Devadāru*, or being part of it.

16. वान्तो यि प्रत्यये (6.1.79)

"The substitution of those ending in व् (namely अव् and आव्) for ओ and औ also takes place before a *pratyaya* beginning with य्."

गो+यम् ⇨ गव्यम्, belonging to a cow; नौ+यम् ⇨ नाव्यम्, belonging to a boat.

17. भीह्रीभृहुमदजनधनदरिद्राजागरां प्रत्ययात्पूर्वं पिति (6.1.192)

For the benefit of the *dhātus* भी, ह्री, भृ, हु, मद, जन, धन दरिद्रा and जागृ and their reduplicates the *udātta* accent is before the सार्वधातुक unaccented *pratyaya* (called तिङ् विभक्ति conveying the sense of the three पुरुष (persons) in the singular पित्), on the syllable which precedes the *pratyaya*," e.g. बिभेति, he is afraid; जागर्ति, he awakes or keeps himself awake.

18. अनिगन्तोऽञ्चतौ वप्रत्यये (6.2.52) (प्रकृतिस्वरः)

"An immediately preceding *gati* not ending in इ or उ or ऋ retains its original accent before अञ्च् when a *pratyaya* having a व् follows."

For instance प्राङ् (क्विन् प्रत्यय).

19. इच एकाचोऽप्रत्ययवच्च (6.3.68)

"A monosyllabic word, ending in an इच् (any vowel other than अ), when followed by a word formed by a खित् *pratyaya* receives the augment अम्, which is added in the same way as the *pratyaya* अम् of the Accusative/*karman* singular signifying that most desired of the agent (कर्तुरीप्सिततमं कर्म 1.4.49),"

e.g. दर्शनीयंमन्यः, thinking oneself handsome, by आत्ममाने खश्च 3.2.83 or नरंमन्यः, thinking oneself a man, by ऋतो ङिसर्वनामस्थानयोः (7.3.110)

[*Guṇa* is substituted for the final ऋ of a stem in the *adhikaraṇa* (locative) singular and in the strong cases. As a result नृ becomes नर.]

20. विष्वग्देवयोश्च टेरद्र्यञ्चतौ व प्रत्यये (6.3.92)

"In place of the last vowel with consonant that follows it, of a pronoun and of the words विष्वक् and देव is substituted अद्रि when अञ्च with प्रत्यय व् follows,"

e.g. विष्व्+अञ्च्+क्विप् ⇨ विष्वद्र्याङ् going everywhere or in all directions. *śiś* ind. °*dryāk* forth, on both or all sides *(R.V. 7.25.1)*.

21. उतश्च प्रत्ययादसंयोगपूर्वात् (6.4.106) (हिः लुक्)

"The imperative हि is *luk* elided after the उ of a *vikaraṇa pratyaya* called श्नु, and उ of the स्वादि and तनादिगणऽ respectively (i.e. class 5 and 8 for the special conjugations, namely present, imperative, optative and imperfect) provided the उ is not preceded by a संयोग (conjunct consonant),"

e.g. सुनु, do thou press out the (*soma*); तनु, thou shouldest expand.

22. प्रत्ययोत्तरपदयोश्च (7.2.98) (युष्मदस्मदोः मपर्यन्तस्य त्वमावेकवचने)

"त्व is substituted for युष्म् and म् for अस्म् when they signify a single individual, even when a *pratyaya* follows or a word is in composition."

For Example त्वदीयः thine; मदीयः mine.

23. प्रत्ययस्थात्कात्पूर्वस्यात इदाप्यसुपः (7.3.44)

"Let the vowel इ be in the place of the vowel अ coming before the letter क standing in a *pratyaya* when the feminine *pratyaya* आप् follows, provided that the feminine *pratyaya* does not come after a सुप् विभक्ति प्रत्यय/case affix."

For Example सर्वक:, सार्विका, every female.

24. वित्तो भोगप्रत्यययो: (8.2.58)

"The (irregularly formed participle) वित्त denotes 'possessions' and 'known/ recognised'." (Again tradition says प्रतीयते इति प्रत्यय: it is known or makes known. Some indication that Pāṇini was perhaps conscious of this dimension as also applicable to the concept in the broader context of शब्द.)

25. क्विन्प्रत्ययस्य कु: (8.2.62)

"A stem formed with the *pratyaya* क्विन् (under स्पृशोऽनुदके क्विन् 3.2.58) substitutes at the end of a word a guttural for the final consonant."

For Example, घृतस्पृक्, touching ghee.

26. आदेशप्रत्यययो: (8.3.59) (इण्को: 8.3.57).

"ष् is the substitute for that स् which is an आदेश substitute (of the ष् of a *dhātu* in the *dhātupāṭha* by *6.1.64* धात्वादे: ष: स:) or which is a portion of a *pratyaya* (under the above condition of being preceded by an इक् vowel or a guttural, इण्को: (8.3.57)."

For Example, रामेषु, in (all) *Rāmas.*

From these instances we conclude:

(1) That Pāṇini himself uses the concept primarily in the technical sense of 'affix' coming after a base or अङ्ग. Similarly, from an examination of all instances in the *Mahābhāṣya,* we conclude Patañjali used it in the same sense.

(2) That *8.2.58* particularly acknowledges the state of 'making known' as being central to the meaning of 'प्रत्यय'.

C. Nine Major Types of *Pratyaya* referred to in the *Aṣṭādhyāyī*

A description with illustrations from the *Īśopaniṣad* etc., namely:

Following the order of Pāṇini, we find that after first establishing the *pratyayaḥ (3.1.1)*, its position is then defined as परश्च (*3.1.2*) that is 'following' a *dhātu*[12].

Then by yet another अधिकार or *paribhāṣā sūtra* आद्युदात्तश्च *(3.1.3) (pratyayaḥ)* "That which is called a *pratyaya* has *udātta* accent on its first syllable." Except for the सुप् and तिङ् *pratyayas* which are *anudātta* अनुदात्तौ सुप्पितौ 3.1.4.

Sanādi Section—(dhātu forming pratyayas)

Then begins the first group of *pratyayas* having in common their capacity to form verbs and to technically acquire the full nature of *dhātu* or 'seed' forms सनाद्यन्ता धातवः *(3.1.32)*. "All the words ending with the *pratyaya* सन् and others (twelve in all) are called *dhātu"*, having the same functions, taking तिङ् विभक्ति etc., as the original *dhātu* defined at *1.3.1* as भूवादयो धातवः and collected in the *dhātupāṭha* (being about 2000 in number, 1943 in *S.K.*). This in itself illustrates the enormous potency of a *pratyaya* to manifest meaning. Our first illustration relates to the first of this group of *pratyaya*, namely गुप्तिज्किद्भ्यः सन् *(3.1.5*) प्रत्ययः "after the *dhātus* गुप् तिज् and कित् comes the *pratyaya* सन्."

धातोः कर्मणः समानकर्तृकादिच्छायां वा *3.1.7* "The *pratyaya* सन् optionally attached in the sense of 'wishing' after a *dhātu* expressing the object wished and having the same agent of action as the wisher thereof".

Thus we find the धातु गुप् गोपने 'to hide' when सन् is added and there is reduplication of the धातु by (*6.1.9*) सन्यङोः "of a non-reduplicate धातु ending in सन् (desiderative) or यङ् (intensive) *pratyayas,* there is reduplication" and a palatal replaces the guttural in the reduplicate syllable by कुहोश्चुः (*7.4.62*) जुगुप्स to which is added प्रथम पुरुष एकवचन आत्मनेपद तिङ विभक्ति literally, 'he', first (Western third) person singular, (the action being related to one's own self), receives ए by टित आत्मनेपदानां टेरेः (*3.4.79*) जुगुप्सते in the sense of 'he censures' or 'despises' (*"San"* in the sense of its *prakṛti* or base.)

---

12 (except in the case of बहुच् which by "विभाषा सुपो बहुच् पुरस्तात्तु" (*5.3.68*) is placed 'before' (a *dhātu* etc.), or the *pratyaya* कल्प can be used after, and in the case of *pratyayas* with the indicator '*m*' like the *vikaraṇa* श्नम् of रूधादिभ्यः श्नम् (3.1.78) they are infixed after the last of the vowels by मिदचोऽन्त्यात् परः (1.1.47))

यस्तु सर्वाणि भूतान्यात्मन्येवानुपश्यति।
सर्वभूतेषु चात्मानं ततो न विजुगुप्सते।।

"He who sees all creatures in Himself, Himself in all creatures, feels (no desire to hide or) hatred (as a result)" (*Īśā 6*).

Vikaraṇa Section

The second major group of *pratyayas* is called विकरण since they bring about a modification in the nature of a *dhātu's* expansion, which manifests finally as a पद by सुप्तिङन्तं पदम् (*1.4.14*) "That which ends in a *sup* (nominal *vibhakti pratyaya* (case ending)) or in a *tiṅ kriyā vibhakti pratyaya* (verbal/conjugational ending) is a *'pada'* or fully inflected word". Unlike the previous group, they do not appear to convey any distinctive meaning except that related to time or mood. Primarily they are said to be स्वार्थिकप्रत्ययाः. They, therefore, come to modify the verb in the very sense of their own (*dhātu*) to which they become attached.

This group begins with the 'future and conditional *pratyayas*' 'स्यतासीलृलुटोः' (*3.1.33*) when लृट् लृङ (2nd future and conditional) and लुट् (the first or periphrastic future) follow then स्य and तासि are respectively the *pratyayas* of a धातु, and ends with 'reflexive *pratyayas*' कुषिरञ्जोः प्राचां श्यन् परस्मैपदं च (*3.1.90*) कर्मकर्तरि "The *pratyaya* श्यन् comes after the *dhātu* कुष् pull and रञ्ज to colour in the reflexive voice according to the opinion of Eastern Grammarians and those *dhātus* take *parasmaipada pratyayas.*"

Within this broad section are given, first of all, subjunctive सिब् बहुलं लेटि (*3.1.34*), then the periphrastic perfect कास्प्रत्ययादाममन्त्रे लिटि (*3.1.35*), then are the forms of the aorist च्लि लुङि (*3.1.43*) च्लेः सिच् (*3.1.44*) (The Western *'S'* aorist).

शल इगुपधादनिटः क्सः	(*3.1.45*)	(*'Sa'* aorist)
णिश्रिद्रुस्रुभ्यः कर्तरि चङ्	(*3.1.48*)	(Reduplicated aorist)
अस्यतिवक्तिख्यातिभ्योऽङ्	(*3.1.52*)	(*'a'* aorist)
कृ मृ दृ रुहिभ्यश्छन्दसि	(*3.1.59*)	(*'a'* aorist)
चिण् ते पदः	(*3.1.60*)	(The aorist passive)
चिण् भावकर्मणोः	(*3.1.66*)	(The aorist passive)
सार्वधातुके यक् (भावकर्मणोः)	(*3.1.67*)	(Impersonal/passive)

(For example "पूर्णमेवावशिष्यते" ईशा शान्तिपाठः "The full, complete and perfect alone remains".) Then the first and other *gaṇas.* Let us first consider a development,

कर्तरि शप् (अ-) (3.1.68)

"The *pratyaya* शप् comes after *dhātu* भू etc. when a *sārvadhātuka pratyaya* follows signifying an agent, i.e. तिङ् शित्सार्वधातुकम् (*3.4.113*)"

"The *pratyayas* called *'tiṅ'* and those with an *'it'* ś' are called *sārvadhātuka* (*7.3.84*)"

सार्वधातुकार्धधातुकयोः "When a *sārvadhātuka* (3.4.113) or an *'ārdhadhātuka'* (*3.4.114*) *pratyaya*, (the remainder), follows there is *guṇa*[13] of the final of an (*aṅga*) ending in इक् (इ उ ऋ लृ)." Thus भू becomes भो and अव् being substituted by एचोऽयवायावः (*6.1.78*) followed by the अ of शप्[14,15] and ति of तिप्[15], we have भवति 'he becomes'. The sense of agent being indicated by तिप् आदेश of 'ल' (लस्य *3.4.77*) according to लःकर्मणि च भावे चाकर्मेभ्यः' (३.४.६९) (कर्तरि).

This is followed by श्यन् विकरण for the formation of the fourth conjugation दिवादिभ्यः श्यन् (३.१.६९).

न is for accent ञ्नित्यादिर्नित्यम् (*6.1.197*). "Whatever is derived with a *pratyaya* having an indicatory ञ् or न् has उदात्त on the first syllable." Then in the case of *'div'* to play and other *dhātus* ending in *'r'* or *'v'* the penultimate *'i'* is lengthened before a consonantal *pratyaya* by हलि च (*8.2.77*) giving the form दीव्यति 'he plays'; or *jṝ* becomes *jir* and then *jīr;* or *stṝ* becomes *stir* and then *stīr.*

Similarly the श्नु is the *vikaraṇa* of class five *dhātus* taking *guṇa* before the *'pit'* ending, i.e. एकवचनं परस्मैपदम् enabling us to form the स्वादिगण by "स्वादिभ्यः श्नुः" (३.१.७३) (सार्वधातुके, कर्तरि) सुनोति "he presses out (the soma)". (*Guṇa* by सार्व-धातुकार्धधातुकयोः (*7.3.84*)

The sixth class, like class one and four, ending in *'a'* nonetheless debars शप् thus preventing medial *guṇa* by पुगन्तलघूपधस्य च (*7.3.86*) तुदादिभ्यः शः (*3.1.77*) (सार्वधातुके कर्तरि) सार्वधातुकमपित् १.२.४ therefore 'श्' is ङित् therefore by क्ङिति च १.१.५ न गुणवृद्धी.

"*Pratyaya śa* is employed after the *dhātus* of the *tudādi gaṇa* when a *sārvadhātuka pratyaya* follows denoting the agent, and *'it' ś* makes this *sārvadhātuka.*"

So, for example, तुद् श ति ⇨ तुद् अ ति ⇨ तुदति He strikes

प्र-विश् श अन्ति-प्रविशन्ति झोऽन्तः (P.7.1.3) अतो गुणे (*P.6.1.97*) (Here the *bahuvacana* form) अन्धं तमः प्रविशन्ति। "They enter into blinding darkness (who worship *avidyā*)." (*Īśā v.9*)

The seventh class has the rare characteristic of its *pratyaya* being infixed within the *dhātu* and not after (contrary to परश्च (*3.1.2*) the general rule)

---

13 अदेङ्गुणः (1.1.2) 'अ, ए and ओ are called *guṇa*"

14 लशक्वतद्धिते (1.3.5) श् is इत्)

15 By हलन्त्यम् प् is इत्

रुधादिभ्यः श्नम् (*3.1.78*).

The *pratyaya* श्नम् (= 'न') in the *'pit'* or strong forms and न् elsewhere comes after *dhātus* of the रुधादि गण in denoting an agent when a *sārvadhātuka pratyaya* follows debarring शप् of कर्तरिशप् (*3.1.68*)).

Thus we have रुणद्धि (by अट् कुप्वाङ् नुम्व्यवायेऽपि (ण् or न्) (*8.4.2*) "He obstructs". Even when a separation is caused by the intervention of the *pratyaya 'ku'* (gutturals) and *'pu'* (five labials), *āṅ* (particle ā) and *num* (*anusvāra*), singly or combined in any way, the substitution of the cerebral for the dental *'n'* following *'r'* or *ṣ'* in the same '*pada*' shall take place and by 'झषस्तथोर्धोऽधः' (*8.2.40*) "There is ध् in place of the त् or थ् coming after a झष् (soft aspirate) but not if the *'t'* or *'th'* is part of the *dhātu* धा to hold."

[Note— We find the same *dhātu* but without the *vikaraṇa 'śnam'*, because it is an aorist form, in the *Kaṭhopaniṣad* (*1.21*) मा मा उपरोत्सीः. *Yama* says to *Naciketas,* 'do not press me (for knowledge of the Self)]'.

The eighth class has the *vikaraṇa* उ after it and in development is the same as class five स्वादिगण except for the absence of the न् of श्नु.

By तनादिकृञ्भ्य उः (*3.1.79*) it is stated that 'after the *dhātu* तन etc. and the *dhātu* कृ (to make) comes the *pratyaya* उ when a *sārvadhātuka pratyaya* follows signifying the agent.

This debars the शप् or कर्तरिशप् (*3.1.68*). Thus we have तनोति or तनुते. "He or she expands" or again with the present stem of *kṛ* by अत उत्सार्वधातुके *(6.4.110)* "In place of the short अ of कृ to make (in the *guṇated* form 'कर् by *3.1.79)*, there is short उ when a सार्वधातुक प्रत्यय (with a *it k* or *ṅ*) follows". कुरु अन्त्.

By इको यणचि (*6.1.77*) कुरु-अन्त (from शतृ present participle *parasmaipada*) becomes कुर्वन् (उ is replaced by व्).

As in कुर्वन्नेवेह कर्माणि (*Īśā. 2*) "(By) doing *karma* should indeed one wish to live here for a hundred years."

The ninth class has the *vikaraṇa 'śnā'* that is ना in the *'pit'* or strong forms and नी elsewhere before consonants and न् before vowels by the *sūtra* 'क्र्यादिभ्यः (ना) श्ना' (*3.1.81*) ई हल्यघोः (*6.4.113*) श्नाभ्यस्तयोरातः (*6.4.112*) (लोपः)

After the *dhātu* क्री to buy etc. there is श्ना when a *sārvadhātuka pratyaya* follows denoting the agent. Again there is अपवाद or debarring of शप् (*3.1.68*). Thus क्रीणाति 'He or she buys'.

The tenth class, causatives and so-called denominatives or *pratyaya-dhātus* have already been referred to in the first section सनाद्यन्ता धातवः and by the general designation of *vikaraṇa* for *dhātus* कर्तरि शप् (*3.1.68*) (सार्वधातुके).

The remaining classes two and three are dealt with prior to (*3.1.1* 'प्रत्यय') because for them an 'elision' rather than a positive *pratyaya* replaces the शप्.

Thus by अदिप्रभृतिभ्यः शप् (*2.4.72*) "There is *luk* elision of *śap* after अद् to eat etc." लुक् acts in place of शप् but there is अदर्शनं 'disappearance of that' (and is not characterised by any of the qualities of the *pratyaya* it replaces in contrast to लोप ("प्रत्ययलोपे प्रत्ययलक्षणम्" (*1.1.62*) by न लुमताङ्गस्य (*1.1.63*).

We then have अत्ति 'He eats'. (By खरि च (*8.4.55*) "When खर् (ख फ छ ठ थ च ट त क प श ष स) follows there is चर् (च ट त क प श ष स) in the place of (any consonant except a semi-vowel or a nasal) झल्." Thus *'d'* is replaced here by *'t'* because no 'positive' *vikaraṇa* intervenes.

Another example from this *gaṇa* is the *ātmanepada* form of आस बहुवचने (अन्त् of झोऽन्तः *7.1.3*). Because "it is replaced by *'at'* in the place of *'jh'* not coming after the vowel *'a'* (*vikaraṇa* of class 1, 4, 6, and 10) when terminations are *ātmanepada"*. So येऽविद्यामुपासते *Īśā*.9 "Those who worship *avidyā* (rites), enter blinding darkness"). Finally the third class is formed by substituting श्लु blank (of प्रत्ययस्य लुक् श्लुलुपः *1.1.61*) and reduplicating. Thus जुहोत्यादिभ्यः श्लुः *2.4.75*). "श्लुः is to be substituted in place of the *pratyaya* शप् (*3.1.69*) after the *dhātu* हु to sacrifice or eat etc."

When there is '*ślu*' there are two in the place of a *dhātu*, (i.e. *dhātu* is doubled). Thus जुहोति 'He sacrifices'. कुहोश्चुः (*7.4.62*). "A letter of the palatal class (here *'j'*) is the substitute of the letter of the guttural class or of an *'h'"* (as here) in a reduplicate and सार्वधातुकार्धधातुकयोः (७.३.८४)

"When a *sārvadhātuka* or *ārdhadhātuka pratyaya* follows, then *guṇa* is ādeśa/ substitute of *aṅga* ending in *ik* (*i, u, ṛ*)".

From the same *gaṇa* we have the *dhātu* धा धारणपोषणयोः to hold, sustain, nourish, occuring in *Īśā. 4* दधाति

> तिष्ठत् तस्मिन् अपो मातरिश्वा दधाति.
>
> "It (the Self) being there, *Mātariśvā* allots (or supports) all activities".

Kṛt Section

We turn now to the next major group of *pratyayas* marked by two more अधिकार सूत्रs 'धातोः' (*3.1.91*). "As far as the end of the third *Adhyāya* from this *sūtra*, the *pratyayas* are understood to come after some *dhātu*" and तत्रोपपदं सप्तमीस्थम् (*3.1.92*) "here in this third *Adhyāya* referring to *dhātu* the word implied in a term exhibited in the '*adhikaraṇa*' or seventh or locative case is called *'upapada'* or dependent word". कृदतिङ् (*3.1.93*) "(In this section in which there is a reference to a *dhātu*) any *pratyaya* except तिङ् (क्रियाविभक्तिप्रत्यय or verbal tense terminations) is called कृत्. This कृत् is a very large term strictly including within it several subordinate terms कृत्य, निष्ठा, सत्, शित्सार्वधातुक and आर्धधातुक प्रत्यय. Comprising 125 in all, as well as the 748 उणादिसूत्राणि listed separately from the *Aṣṭādhyāyī* (but nonetheless referred to). Of these यत् (*3.1.97*), ण्यत् (*3.1.124*), घञ् (*3.3.16* etc.), तृच् (*3.1.133*), क्तिन् (*3.3.94*), ल्युट् (*3.3.115* etc.), तुमुन् (*3.3.10* etc.), क्त्वा (*3.4.18*) are very general. The rest are added to particular *dhātus* under specific conditions. कृत्या (प्राङ् ण्वुलः) ३.१.९५ (A *kṛt* (कृत्) *pratyaya* usually indicates the agent (कर्तरिकृत् ३.४.६७). They come immediately after the *dhātu* (*3.1.91*) with the exception of cases such as the लुटः शतृशानचाव- प्रथमासमानाधिकरणे (*3.2.124*). A शित् प्रत्यय is separated from the *dhātu* by a *vikaraṇa*).

"From this *sūtra* as far as ण्वुल्तृचौ (*3.1.133*) all the *pratyayas* will bear the name कृत्य" like its genus (कृत्), it represents the type of verbal base formed with the *pratyaya* it stands for. य is common to all six in this group (केलिमर is added by कात्यायन on *3.1.96.* (६ in total). तव्यत्-तव्य अनीयरः (३.१.९६) (धातोः).

"The *pratyaya* तव्यत् तव्य and अनीयर् come in the sense of object or mere action" (तयोरेवकृत्यक्तखलर्थाः ३.४.७० *dhātus.*) For example, अनीयर् occurs in *Kaṭha Up. 2.13,* after *dhātu* मुद् in the sense of future passive participle. स मोदते मोदनीयं हि लब्ध्वा "That (mortal who has become the enlightened man) rejoices having obtained that which causes delight (but which is to be delighted in)". अचो यत् (*3.1.97*) (धातोः).

"The *pratyaya* यत् comes after a *dhātu* that ends in a vowel". For example स आत्मा स विज्ञेयः *Māṇḍ.* 7 "That is the Self and that is to be known". Here the letter *'t'* of the *pratyaya* shows that the *udātta* accent falls on the first vowel if it is of no more than two syllables वि being a separate पद by यतोऽनावः (*6.1.213*). Therefore the accent 'is' on ए. The ā of *dhātu* ज्ञा is changed to ई by ईद्यति (*6.4.65*). "Final आ of a stem or *aṅga* is changed into ई before the *kṛt pratyaya yat*", which in turn became गुण ए by सार्वधातुकार्धधातुकयोः (*7.3.84*).

The next major *kṛt pratyaya* is ण्यत् ऋहलोर्ण्यत् (*3.1.124*).

The *pratyaya* ण्यत् comes after a *dhātu* ending in ऋ (i.e. long or short) or in a consonant. For example अव्यवहार्यम् *ibid.* 7

After the *dhātu* हृ preceded by अ वि अव the *pratyaya 'ṇyat'* comes causing *vṛddhi* (वृद्धिर् आदैच् *1.1.1* - by उरण् रपरः *1.1.52* आ is followed by र्) thus आर्

अव्यवहार्यम् "(That Self) is beyond empirical dealings". Let us consider तृच् ण्वुल् तृचौ *3.1.133* (धातोः). "The *pratyayas* ण्वुल् (युवोरनाकौ *7.1.1* = अक्) and तृच् (तृ) are placed after all *dhātus* expressing the agent". For example, न कर्ता असि न भोक्ता असि युक्त एवासि सर्वदा (*Aṣṭāvakrasaṁhitā 1.6*) "You are neither the doer nor the enjoyer. Verily (in truth) you are ever free".

Here, when the first case ending *'su'* follows, it is in the sense of *prātipadika* by प्रातिपदिकार्थ लिङ्ग परिमाणवचनमात्रे प्रथमा २.३.४६. (not in the sense of vocative).

"The sound अनङ् is the augment of what ends in short *'ṛ'* (here kartṛ = kṛ + tṛc) and of uśanas' ("regent of the planet Venus",) *'purudaṅśas* and *anehas* (time).' (= *kart* + *an* + *s*) by ऋदुशनपुरुदंशोऽनेहसां च (*7.1.94*). Then by

अप् तृन् तृच् स्वसृनप्तृ नेष्टृ त्वष्टृ क्षतृ होतृ पोतृप्रशास्तृणाम् (६.४.११)

"When the first five *sup vibhakti* or case affixes excluding the vocative singular come after the word अप् 'water', what ends in तृन् or तृच्, स्वसृ sister, नप्तृ grandson, नेष्टृ ' a priest who officiates at a sacrifice, (त्वष्टृ' a carpenter, क्षतृ a charioteer, होतृ a priest who recites the *Ṛgveda* at a sacrifice, पोतृ a priest at a sacrifice, and प्रशस्तृ a ruler; the penultimate letter shall be lengthened."

Thus is formed कर्तान्+स्. The 's' is elided by हलङ्याब्भ्यो दीर्घात्सुतिस्युपृक्तं हल् *(6.1.68)*. " *'su'* (1st sing. case *pratyaya*) and *'ti'* and *'si'* (terminations of two of the persons of the verb) when reduced to a single consonant अपृक्त एकाल्प्रत्ययः *(1.2.41)* and when standing after what ends in a consonant or in the long vowel deduced from the feminine terminations ङी+आप्, are elided". कर्तान् and by नलोपः प्रातिपदिकान्तस्य *(8.2.7)* "there is elision of *'n'* final in a *'pada'* which is entitled to the designation of प्रातिपदिक" by अर्थवदधातुरप्रत्ययः प्रातिपदिकम् *(1.2.45)*, i.e. it is full of meaning or significant, not being a *dhātu* or a *pratyaya* (or what ends with a *pratyaya*) कृत्तद्धितसमासश्च *(1.2.45)* except the *pratyaya* be *kṛt* or *taddhita* or the whole be called *samāsa.* Thus the form of the word finally manifests as कर्ता the agent.

The *pratyayas* from *3.1.133* ण्वुल्तृचौ to *3.2.83* आत्ममाने खश्च closely resemble the *kṛtya* in being used in all three tenses whereas those from *3.2.84* भूते to *3.2.122* पुरि लुङ्चास्मे are used only in the past tense. Of the remaining *kṛt pratyayas,* some are in the future tense, some in the present. Moreover unlike *kṛtya* they are used only as noun or objective not as a verb, with the following important exceptions क्त क्तवतु क्त्वा तुमुन् शतृशानच्. Further these *pratyayas* do not permit *taddhita*/secondary *pratyayas.*

Leaving aside *uṇādi* for separate brief consideration, let us cursorily consider five more of the most general *kṛt pratyaya* तुमुन् घञ् क्तिन् ल्युट् and क्त्वा

By तुमुन्ण्वुलौ क्रियायां क्रियार्थायाम् (*3.3.10*) "The *pratyaya 'tumun'* and *'ṇvul'* are placed after a *dhātu* with the force of the future when the word in construction is another verb denoting an action performed for the sake of the (future) action". What ends in तुमुन् since it ends in *'m'* is indeclinable according to कृन्मेजन्तः (*1.1.39*).

"What ends in a *kṛt pratyaya* ending in the letter *'m'* or in *'ec'* is अव्यय or indeclinable", e.g. कृष्णं द्रष्टुं याति कृष्णं दर्शको याति He goes to see (i.e. for the sake of seeing) कृष्ण.

By the *sūtra* भावे *(3.3.18)* घञ् comes after a *dhātu* when the sense of the *dhātu* is denoted as having attained to the complete state.

Thus by पुगन्तलघूपधस्य च (*7.3.86*) 'there is *guṇa* in place of the *'ik'* (*i, u, ṛ, ḷ*) of that inflective base/*aṅga* which ends with the augment *puk* (*VII.3.86*) or which has a light vowel ह्रस्वं लघु (*1.4.10*) as its penultimate letter. Here the *'gh'* is *'it'* by लशक्वतद्धिते *(1.3.8)* and the *'ca'* of a *dhātu* is changed to a guttural when a *pratyaya* with an indicatory *'gh'* and when the *pratyaya 'ṇyat' (3.1.124)* follows by चजोः कु घिण्यतोः *(7.3.52)*.

Thus शुच् becomes शोक् and मुह् becomes मोह् manifesting in the same line.

तत्र को मोहः कः शोकः एकत्वमनुपश्यतः *(Īśā. 7)*

"(When to the man of realisation all beings become the very Self) then what delusion and what sorrow can there be for the seer of oneness?"

स्त्रियां क्तिन् *(3.3.94)* (भावे अकर्तरि कारके) "To express an action etc. by a word in the feminine, the *pratyaya* क्तिन् is added to the *dhātu,* (superceding घञ् the word relating to the action but not as agent)."

Thus after शमु अपशमे (in the sense of deep rest) by स्त्रियां क्तिन् *(3.3.94)* क्तिन् acts in the feminine to express an action etc. and by अनुनासिकस्य क्विझलोः क्ङिति *(6.4.15)* (दीर्घः)

"A long vowel shall be the *ādeśa* (substitute) for the penultimate of that which ends with a nasal in the presence of *'kvi' pratyaya* and when a *pratyaya* beginning with a झल् and distinguished by an indicatory *'k'* or *'ṅ'* follows".

Thus शाम् ति = शाम् क्तिन्

By मोऽनुस्वारः *(8.3.23)* in place of *'m'* is *anusvāra* when a consonant follows. अनुस्वारस्य ययिपरसवर्णः *(8.4.58)* in place of *anusvāra* when *'yay'* follows a letter homogeneous with the latter acts (thus *'n'*) शान्तिः शान्तिः शान्तिः 'Peace, peace, peace (physical, natural and supernatural, to avert all evils)'.

From the *sūtra* ल्युट् च (*3.3.115*) नपुंसके भावे we learn that 'the *pratyaya 'lyuṭ'* is added to the *dhātu* when the name of the action is expressed in the neuter gender. Thus आस् (to sit) gives आसनम् *'seat'* in *Bṛhad. (6.2.4)* तस्मा आसनमाहृत्योदकमाहारयांचकार "(The king) gave him a seat, had water brought for him and made him a reverential offering". (One of the four examples of this *pratyaya* being used in the principal *Upaniṣads*).

Finally समानकर्तृकयोः पूर्वकाले (*3.4.21*) (क्त्वा) "When the actions signified by two *dhātus* or verbs have the same agent, the *pratyaya* क्त्वा comes after that verb which is related to a time prior to that of the other". For example, महान्तं विभुमात्मानंमत्वा धीरो न शोचति (*Kaṭha Up. 2.1.4*. "Having realised that great and all-pervading Self, a wise man does not grieve". From धातु मन् अवबोधने ज्ञाने to realise, *'n'* is *lopa* elided by अनुदात्तोपदेशवनति तनोत्यादीनामनुनासिकलोपो झलि क्ङिति *(6.4.37)*

"When there follows a *pratyaya* beginning with a *'jhal'* (any consonant except the semivowels and nasals) and distinguished by an indicatory *'k'* or *'n'*, there is elision of the following that end in a nasal, namely those which in their original enunciation (in the *Dhātupāṭha*) are *anudātta* or gravely accented, यम् रम् नम् गम् हन् and मन्य (to respect) and वन् to ask or beg and तन् 'to stretch' etc." (included in which as a *dhātu* of the eighth class is मन् to understand). Thus our form मत्वा 'having realised' is manifest.

Tiṅ Section

The fourth major section of *pratyayas* is called तिङ् a *pratyāhāra* of all the basic verbal endings in the Sanskrit language. This *sūtra* is preceded by the (अधिकार सूत्र) (लस्य) *(3.4.77)*. In the place of ल will be substituted the *pratyaya* (to be ordained in the following *sūtras*).

The ल stands for ten *pratyayas:*

लट्	present
लिट्	perfect
लुट्	first (or periphrastic) future
लृट्	second future
लेट्	Vedic subjunctive
लोट्	Imperative
लङ्	imperfect
लिङ्	potential/optative and benedictive
लुङ्	aorist
लृङ्	conditional

By लः कर्मणि च भावे चाकर्मकेभ्यः *(3.4.69)* "The letter *'l'* is placed after transitive *dhātus* in denoting the object कर्मन् as well as the agent कर्तृ after intransitives अकर्मक in marking the condition भाव (i.e. the action itself which the *dhātu* imports) as well as the agent".

Given that ultimately there is only one activity containing the whole diversity of creation, and that from ॐ rest to ॐ the whole creation कृ is an act, क्रिया of love प्रीति or प्रेम, these *pratyayas* in the तिङ् section play a particularly crucial part in establishing the relationship between the action, क्रिया and the parts of the sentence, वाक्य, said to be a cosmos of meaning.

To illustrate this special function, let us consider three single but profound sentences from the *Upaniṣads* which may highlight the function of the तिङ् *pratyayas.* All three are in the present. So *Pāṇini* says: वर्तमाने लट् *(3.2.123) Laṭ* is placed after a *dhātu* employed in denoting present action.

तिप्तस्झि सिप् थस्थ मिप् वस् मस् तातांझ
थासाथान्ध्वमिड्वहिमहिङ् *(3-4-78)*

These eighteen are the substitutes/आदेश *'l'* and ordered in a precise way which relates to the three persons:

प्रथम पुरुष	(First; Western third)
मध्यम पुरुष	(Middle; Western second)
उत्तम पुरुष	(The highest/best; Western first)

Pāṇini defines these respectively but perhaps significantly in another order: युष्मद्युपपदे समानाधिकरणे स्थानिन्यपिमध्यमः *(1.4.105)* "When the सर्वनामन् (name of all) (Western 'pronoun') युष्मद् (thou, you two, you) understood and also when the same expressed is the attendant word in agreement with the verb and denotes the agent or object signified by the verbal termination, then the verbal termination is मध्यम (middle)".

अस्मद्युत्तमः *(1.4.107)* "When the सर्वनामन् अस्मद् (I, we two, we) is in the same circumstances (as *yuṣmad* above) then the verbal *pratyaya* of terminations are उत्तम (highest/best)".

शेषे प्रथमः *(1.4.108)* "In all other cases, the verbal *pratyaya*/terminations are called प्रथम (first)".

Each of these is naturally distinguished as is the case with *nāman* on the basis of number, namely एकवचन expressive of one, द्विवचन expressive of two, बहुवचन expressive of many.

The eighteen then manifest as परस्मैपद and आत्मनेपद

	एक.	द्वि.	बहु.	एक.	द्वि.	बहु.
प्रथम	तिप्	तस्	झि	त	आताम्	झ
मध्यम	सिप्	थस्	थ	थास्	आथाम्	ध्वम्
उत्तम	मिप्	वस्	मस्	इट्	वहि	महिङ् *(3.4.78)*

Our first illustration starts with the मध्यम पुरुष as does *Pāṇini*, perhaps because this is the most important relationship, that with one's teacher, the person facing one, the Middle person. So in *Chāndogya (6.8.7)* etc., we find the famous वाक्य

तत् त्वम् असि "Thou art that".

Here the *dhātu* अस् भुवि is in the sense of pure existence. By तासस्त्योर्लोपः *(7.4.50)* "There is elision of the *'s'* of *tās* (of first future) and *dhātu 'as'* (to be) when a *pratyaya* beginning with *'s'* follows". Here the *pratyaya* सिप् is signifying, manifest or unexpressed, the मध्यमपुरुष, thus focusing the pure existence at that point.

Our second illustration is the equally famous वाक्य from the *Bṛhadāraṇyakopaniṣad (1.4.10)* अहं ब्रह्मास्मि "I am that Brahman".

Here, with the same *dhātu (as)* expressing pure being of the person, through that focus of मिप् *pratyaya,* उत्तम पुरुष the best person, is reached. (Perhaps this is only possible after first having acknowledged तत्त्वमसि, that which faces one reflects for one the Absolute or the light of the Self!)

Finally, in the *Māṇḍukyopaniṣad (1.2)* and *Bṛhad. 4.4.5* अयमात्मा ब्रह्म "This Self is Brahman", where the verb 'to be' is understood (as is so often in *Saṁskṛta*), for the प्रथमपुरुष. Nonetheless, though unexpressed, अस्ति "pure being" expressed through the first person *pratyaya* तिप् still operates the more powerfully to bring one to the final realisation of the non-difference of आत्मन् and ब्रह्मन्. What we normally take for granted as the 'third person', (he, she, it, they, the rest), is in reality found to be nothing else than the embodied Absolute.

Sup Section

The fifth group of *pratyayas* are like तिङ्, centered on a *pratyāhāra,* that of सुप्, this time representing all the नाम or nominal विभक्तिप्रत्यय (in Western terminology, case endings). These are so called because of the Greek word originally used for such *pratyayas* meaning a 'falling away' from the vertical position of the (noun proper). The 'stoics' fixed the use of the term 'case' as we have it today. The nominative was the 'upright case' and the rest was 'oblique' They were grouped together as 'oblique' because in at least some of their uses there was prominent not only the meaning of the noun but a particular relation between it and other word(s) (usually verbs, prepositions or other nouns). Aristotle had not regarded what we call the 'nominative' case as a case at all; he distinguished nouns between the noun proper (in its nominative case and its derivatives which included in our terms its oblique case. (Cf. 1, Bekke, Aristotle, Vol. I, p. 104.) We know that (after Aristotle) the Stoics had five cases, nominative, accusative, dative, genitive, and one other.

If it was not vocative, it must be that the adverb was regarded as a case by some Stoic grammarians then the vocative would be a separate noun form by itself. The question must be left open on the evidence available. So too must be the origin of the word (meaning 'fall' literally), as a grammatical term from which by translation are taken the Latin 'casus' and our 'case'. (Cf. R.H. Robbins, Ancient and Mediaeval Grammatical theory in Europe).

In contrast is *Pāṇini's* system of which R.H. Robbins says 'of more merit than any single work on grammar in ancient or mediaeval Europe', although because of his subject 'can receive no mention'.

The *'sup' pratyayas* taken in conjunction with the कारक सूत्र would form the basis for a totally fresh view on the parts of the sentence seen as applicable to all languages. Just as the twenty-one सुप् विभक्तिप्रत्यय represent all possible endings, though not necessarily manifest at any particular time, so too the 'concepts' underlying those *pratyayas* अपादान सम्प्रदान करण अधिकरण कर्म and कर्ता may be viewed as present though not necessarily manifest in every sentence.

This group of *pratyayas* too is headed by an अधिकार सूत्र "ङ्याप्प्रातिपदिकात्" *(4.1.1)*

"After what ends with the feminine terminations ङी or आप् or after a प्रातिपदिक अर्थवदधातुरप्रत्ययः प्रातिपदिकम् *(1.2.45)*, कृत्तद्धित समासाश्च *(1.2.46)*, स्वौजसमौट्छष्टाभ्याम्भिस् ङेभ्याम्भ्यसङसिभ्याम्भ्यस् ङसोसाम् ङयोस्सुप् *(4.1.2)*.

Coming after a *prātipadika* or a feminine ending these twenty-one *pratyayas* and their substitutes serve to manifest or realise the four universals and the two particulars, as we may describe the system of the six *kārakas.* We shall attempt to illustrate each of these in a sentence showing the contrast to the Greek system. This has as its central concept the 'upright or nominative form of the noun' from which all else is said to be a falling away, whereas in the *Pāṇinian* system we see that all six concepts are 'in relation to the action' कारके *(1.4.23)*. Such action correctly perceived in any sentence is part of the one activity (क्रिया) which manifests from rest and returns to rest.

1. The first 'universal' relation to the action is:

ध्रुसवमपायेऽपादानम् *(1.4.24)*

"In moving away from the eternal unmoving there is अपादान". That fixed point which is the limit denoted by a word dependent on the verb is called the limit of ablation in relation to the action.

अपादाने पञ्चमी *(2.3.28)* When the word denotes the eternal unmoving (from which the movement comes), the fifth case is employed, (i.e. ङसि भ्याम् or भ्यस् from स्वौजस॰ *(4.1.2)* and by टा ङसि ङसाम् इनात्स्याः *(7.1.12)*. ङसि is replaced by आत् when the *prātipadika* ends in a short *'a'*. Thus पूर्णात्पूर्णमुदच्यते "The pure, perfect and complete सगुण (conditioned *Brahman*) proceeds from the Pure, Perfect and Complete (unconditioned *Brahman*) निर्गुण ब्रह्मन्"

The Greek and Latin concepts of ablation "carrying away from" lacks the reference to the unmoving source and, therefore, is not so universal.

2. The second 'universal' we may likewise consider:

कर्मणा यमभिप्रैति स संप्रदानम् *(1.4.32)*

"By means of the object (be it gift, offering or sacrifice) whom the mind intends to connect with, that very one is called the संप्रदान or recipient in relation to the action".

Again notice how the flat concept of dative connects with giving but does not bring out either the intention of the mind or the relation to the one action.

By चतुर्थी संप्रदाने *(2.3.13),* the fourth case (i.e. सुप् (प्रत्ययङे भ्याम् भ्यस्) are employed when the sense is that of संप्रदानम् (recipient) to whom the action is dedicated.

As परमात्मने नमः, a bow to the Supreme Self.

3. The third 'universal' is the instrument:

साधकतमं करणम् *(1.4.42)*

"That which is most auspicious or effective in the accomplishment of action is called the instrument".

करणे कर्तृकरणयोस्तृतीया *(2.3.18)* When the agent and instrument are not specified by the termination of the verb (i.e. when the verb is not in agreement with them), the third case, सुप् विभक्तिप्रत्ययाः टा भ्याम् भिस् . . . are employed.

Thus ईशा वास्यमिदं सर्वम् "All this is to be covered by the Lord, (the Supreme Self)".

4. The fourth 'universal' is called locative in the Greek/Latin tradition but *Pāṇini* defines it as:

आधारोऽधिकरणम् *(1.4.5)*

"The container of the action, the substratum or substance (of the Absolute in time and space) is the अधिकरण the place in time and space where the action takes place".

सप्तम्यधिकरणे च *(2.3.36)* "When the sense is that of location, the seventh case, i.e. सुप् विभक्तिप्रत्ययाः ङि ओस् सुप् are employed". For example यस्तु सर्वाणि भूतान्यात्मन्येवानुपश्यतिसर्वभूतेषु चात्मानम्... *(Īśā.6)* "Who sees all creatures **in** himself, himself **in** all creatures (feels no hatred)".

These four, though not always manifest in a sentence remain implied:

(1) from whom/which the action arises,
(2) to whom/which it is dedicated,
(3) by means of whom/which it precedes, and
(4) in what/whether in time or space it takes place.

Whereas the agent and the Object may take on a universal aspect, generally they are relative, particularly to the desire of the agent, in so far as he/she believes he/she is the doer of the action.

Thus the Accusative in Western grammar, probably so named through a mistranslation by the Latin grammarian Varro. Its Greek name means appropriately the case 'which is acted upon' (although even here we miss the depth of the *Pāṇinian* definition) or 'the Object case'. Varro seems to have taken the Greek word as derived from (to accuse) and so passed on to us the misnomer 'casus accusativus'.

Pāṇini says कर्तुरीप्सिततमं कर्म *(1.4.49)* "That which is most beloved (or desired to be obtained) of the agent is कर्म".

कर्मणि द्वितीया *(2.3.2)* "When the Object (is not denoted by the termination of the verb, i.e. when the verb does not agree with it) the second case, i.e. सुप्विभक्तिप्रत्यया: अम् औट् शस्, are attached to the words".

तद् धावतोऽन्यान् अत्येति तिष्ठत् *(Īśā.4)* "That (Self) **other runners** overtakes, while standing".

Finally let us consider the subject, agent or Nominative. The very language of subject and object speaks of a duality which finally the वाक्य or शब्द transcends, but nonetheless this appears to be the key relative function in the sentence, since the discovery of न कर्तासि "Thou art not (in reality) the doer" is the key to the realisation मुक्त एवासि सर्वदा "Verily thou art ever free".

The depth of *Pāṇini's* definition is nonetheless of universal value. For he says, स्वतन्त्र: कर्ता *(1.4.54)* "He who holds the system within himself is the agent (of the Absolute) for the purpose of the action, the independent one".

प्रातिपदिकार्थ-लिङ्ग-परिमाण-वचनमात्रे प्रथमा *(2.3.46)* "The first case, i.e. सुप्विभक्तिप्रत्यया: सु औ जस् is where the sense is only that of *prātipadika* (crude form ready to enter the condition of the *'pada'* in a sentence) or an additional sense of gender, or measure or number".

अनेजद् एकं मनसो जवीय: (Here अस्ति is understood and the कर्तृ agent is expressed by the ल substitute by ल: कर्मणि च भावे चाकर्मकेभ्य: *(3.4.69))*. "(That Self is) unmoving, one, faster than the mind".

नैनद् देवा आप्नुवन् पूर्वमर्षत् *(Īśā.4)* "The senses could not reach it. It ran ahead".

Strīpratyaya Section

The next major group of *pratyayas* are the स्त्रीप्रत्यय. These too have a special अधिकार सूत्र स्त्रियाम् *(4.1.3)*. "When feminine nature is to be indicated, the *pratyayas* which are enjoined hereafter must be employed".

Thus by अजाद्यतष्टाप् *(4.1.4)* स्त्रीयां ङ्याप् प्रातिपदिकात् "The *pratyaya* टाप् employed to indicate feminine nature after the *prātipadika*/(nominal stem) अज etc. and after the stems ending in short अ".

For example ज्ञाज्ञौ द्वावजावीशानीशावजा ह्येका भोक्तृभोगार्थयुक्ता *(Śvetā 1.9)*

"There are two unborn ones *(ajau)*, the knowing (Lord) and the unknowing (individual soul) the omnipotent and the impotent. She (i.e. Nature, *Prakṛti)* too is unborn *(ajā)* who is connected with the enjoyer and the objects of enjoyment".

In a similar manner the various स्त्री प्रत्यय are decreed as उगितश्च (स्त्रियां ङीप्) *(4.1.6)* "After what has an indicatory *uk* (i.e. उ, ऋ, ऌ) the *pratyaya* ङीप् is employed". So *jagatī* the feminine form of the present participle with the *pratyaya* शतृ therefore has taken ई in the feminine. In denoting singular location or अधिकरण by ङेराम् नद्याम्नीभ्यः *ām* is the substitute of the locative *'i'* after a stem called *nadī* (यूस्त्र्याख्यौ नदी *1.4.3)* words ending in long *ī* (as *jagatī*) or *ū* always feminine, are called *nadī*) and after the feminines in आप् and after the word नी". So, यत् किं च जगत्यां जगत् *(Īśā.1)* "(By the Lord is to be covered) whatever in the universe (or world) moves".

Taddhita Section

The last two groups of *pratyayas* are called तद्धित *pratyayas.* Numerically the largest group, comprising two hundred and eighty-one different प्रत्ययाः from तद्धिताः *(4.1.76)* to निष्प्रवाणिश्च *(5.4.160)* thus comprising nearly two whole *adhyayas* in extent. The last group of तद्धितप्रत्यया 'समासान्ताः' *(5.4.68)* to *(5.4.160)*, we consider separately, as they deal with a whole class of words, समास, which distinguishes them from the general *taddhita pratyayas.*

They are prescribed as secondary *pratyayas* and as such they follow by ङीप् आप् (ङ्यान्त आबन्त) प्रातिपदिकात् *(4.1.1.)* but do not precede them. However, in the case of the *taddhita/strī pratyaya* ति and the समासान्ताः *pratyayas* the order is reversed.

Hence in the case of युवति बहुगोमतिका etc. ति and क prevail over ङीप् and टाप् respectively. Similarly in the case of सुप् (nominal endings) and *taddhita/* secondary *pratyayas,* as a rule, the former gets priority over the latter, though nowhere is this stated categorically by *Pāṇini.* Still, it is like other important conclusions deduced from his own treatment of language in the *sūtras,* (namely ज्ञापकs, परिभाषाs, and वार्तिकs) i.e. सुबन्तात्तद्धितोत्पत्ति "The addition of secondary *pratyaya* is to a *subanta* base". This is born out by घकालतनेषु कालनाम्न *(6.3.17)* which prescribes "अलुक् (non-inclusion of *sup/* nominal ending, here seventh/ *adhikaraṇa* case), optionally after a word denoting time, ending in a consonant or अ when तरप् or तमप् or the word काल and *pratyaya* तन् follows".

In instances such as पूर्वाह्णतरे पूर्वाह्णेतमे पूर्वाह्णेतने if we do not accept the principle सुबन्तात्तद्धितोत्पत्ति then in the above instances the *taddhita pratyayas* तरप् तमप् and तन् cannot follow the *subanta* or *prātipadika* पूर्वाह्णे. Hence the question of the elision of the *adhikaraṇa*/locative endings in the above instances by सुपो धातुप्रातिपदिकयोः *(2.4.71)* would not arise at all. As such the very utility of the above *sūtra 2.4.71* becomes quite questionable. We have to conclude as the matter stands that *taddhitas* are added to *subanta* bases and then the *sūtra* in question becomes essential to rule out elision of the termination of *adhikaraṇa*—singular in the instances noted above.

However, in the case of अत्यन्तस्वार्थक तद्धित प्रत्ययs (with indication of the sense of the bases to which they are added), we find a different practice. The *pratyayas* of the above description are added to *prātipadikas* not to सुबन्त (nouns in their fully inflected state) as is the case for the rest of the *taddhitas.*

Thus *taddhitas* are divisible into:

(1) अस्वार्थिक (*pratyayas* which add to the meaning of the base), and

(2) स्वार्थिक (*pratyayas* which are simply indicative of the meaning of the base found in *Paṇini 5.3* and *5.4* only).

अस्वार्थिका: take priority because the true representatives of तद्धित (तस्मै हितास्तद्धिता:) and also of far greater number.

There is no consistency in the तद्धित प्रकरण (apart from स्वार्थिक) between *pratyayas* and their meanings. A single *pratyaya* is prescribed in a number of senses and vice versa, e.g. अण् is enjoined in more than six senses as

तस्यापत्यम्	*(4.1.92)*	तेन रक्तम्	*(4.2.1)*
नक्षत्रेण युक्त काल:	*(4.2.3)*	दृष्टं साम	*(4.2.7)*
संस्कृतं भक्षा:	*(4.2.16)*	परिवृतो रथ:	*(4.2.10)*

Similarly in the sense of तस्यापत्यम् many *pratyayas* are prescribed from *4.1.83* to *4.1.179.* Therefore the arrangement of *taddhita pratyayas* has not been made entirely on the basis of their meaning, because in that case the fallacy of अव्याप्ति (inadequate pervasion) will be inevitable.

To say that specification of the meaning of the अस्वार्थिक *pratyaya* has been made keeping in view a particular *pratyaya* as the limit of its extension does not appear warrantable.

In the majority of cases a particular meaning has been taken as a limit to the jurisdiction of a general *pratyaya.* For instance

प्राग्वहतेष्ठक् *(4.4.1)*

प्राग्घिताद्यत् *(4.4.75)*

प्राक्क्रीताच्छ: *(5.1.1)*

In between two general *pratyayas* several meanings are specified in which various *pratyayas* both उत्सर्ग and अपवाद are enjoined for various bases. The jurisdiction of one meaning ends before the commencement of the next one, e.g. तस्यापत्यम् *4.1.92* runs up to *4.1.178.*

Henceforward begins तेन रक्तम् *(4.2.1)*, which in turn continues until the next meaning takes over नक्षत्रेण युक्त कालः *(4.2.3)*.

Thus we find the jurisdiction of a particular meaning has to be ascertained while keeping in view the advent of the next meaning and not the *pratyaya.*

There is no technicality in specification of meanings etc. The change of a *pratyaya* is not essential with the change of meaning, for the same *pratyaya* is prescribed in various meanings (see above).

The option of meaning is clearly mentioned in the course of the प्रत्ययाधिकार with which it is concerned, e.g. within अण् अधिकार *(4.1.83)* all the optional meanings such as तस्यापत्यम् *(4.1.92)*, तेन रक्तम् *(4.2.1)*, दृष्टं साम *(4.2.7)* etc. are clearly mentioned, leaving no scope for confusion with regard to their fields of operation. As such there is no बाध्यबाधक भाव (relation of exclusion of one *pratyaya* by another) amongst the *pratyaya,* on account of variation in their meaning.

Still the *śloka vārttika* on तस्यापत्यम् *(4.1.92)* hints at the instance of the above phenomena in some cases of *pratyaya* based on the relative priority of meaning—

तस्येदमित्यपत्येऽपि बाधनार्थकृतं भवेत्।
उत्सर्गः शेष एवासौ वृद्धान्यस्य प्रयोजनम्।।

Similarly the *vārttika* on दित्यदित्यादित्यपत्युत्तरपदाण्यः।। *(4.1.85)* ण्यादशोऽर्थविशेषलक्षणा-दणपवादात्पूर्वविप्रति testifies to the working of the पूर्वविप्रतिषिद्धम् also in the *taddhita* section. Although, on the ground of variation in meaning there is almost no prevalance of one *pratyaya* over another, still the relation of बाध्यबाधकभाव between उत्सर्ग and अपवाद *pratyaya* cannot be ruled out.

The general *pratyaya* though penetrating through each and every *sūtra* within the limits of the jurisdiction is prevailed over by many particular *pratyayas.*

For instance the उत्सर्ग, प्रत्ययs अण् ठन् ठक् and यत् etc. within their respective jurisdictions are invariably passed over by अपवाद *sūtras.* One may also note the systematic and scientific arrangement.

(1) First अणधिकार *(4.1.83)* Jurisdiction of *aṇ* to the end of *4.3.*
(2) Second ठगधिकार *(4.4.1)* to *(4.4.74)*.
(3) Third यत् अधिकार *(4.4.75)* to *(144)* . . . etc.

Within these प्रत्ययाधिकार are enunciated several अर्थाधिकार, e.g. तस्यापत्यम् तेनरक्तम् रागात् संस्कृतम् तरति, तद्वहति रथयुगप्रसङ्गम् तत्र साधु etc.

The *apatyādhikāra* being the largest claims priority over the rest. A particular *arthādhikāra* generally being mentioned at the very outset is followed by the particular *pratyaya* prescribed therein.

This is the general plan in the whole *Taddhita prakaraṇa* with certain variations dealing with शैषिक and स्वार्थिक प्रत्ययs.

The 'primitive' or primary nouns having been formed from धातुs by adding the कृत् प्रत्ययः, other nouns may again be derived from the primary nouns to imply every possible relation to the things, actions or notions, which the primary or primitive कृदन्त expresses. The *pratyayas* forming these derivative (or secondary) nouns are called तद्धित. *Sandhi* for तद् हित because the nouns denote something relating or belong to 'that which is primitive or primary'. Or the literal sense is तस्मै हितस्तद्धिः *(5.1.5)* that which renders some 'good' to a word whether *laukika* or Vedic by occasioning some improvement in its significatory power. *Taddhita* is a sample having representative meaning, cf. तस्मै हितम् *(P.5.1.5)*.

A term of the ancient pre-*Pāṇinian* grammarians used by *Paṇini* just like सर्वनाम or अव्यय without giving any specific definition. The term occurs in the *Nirukta* of *Yāska at 11.2:*

> अथतद्धितसमासेषु एकपर्वसु वानेकपर्वसु पूर्वं
> पूर्वमपरमपरं प्रविभज्य निबूयात्। दण्ड्यः पुरुषः।
> दण्डमर्हतीति वा। दण्डेन संपद्यत इति वा।
> दण्डो ददातेर्धारयतिकर्मणः।

"Now with regard to secondary derivatives and compounds whether of one or more than one member, one should explain their component parts in their respective order having first divided (the words) into them, e.g. 'punishable', i.e. a person (liable of punishment) deserving punishment or something to be accomplished by punishment. *Daṇḍa* (punishment) is derived from *dhātu daṇḍa* meaning to hold".

And the *Vājasaneyī Prātiśākhya (1.27)* तिङ् कृत्तद्धितचतुष्टयसमासाः शब्दमयम्

Pāṇini has used the word तद्धित not for words but for the *pratyayas* which are added to form such words at all places, e.g. in तद्धितश्चासर्वविभक्तिः *(1.1.38)* "And the words ending in *taddhita* (or secondary) *pratyaya* which are not 'derived' in all the cases are also indeclinables".

प्राचां ष्फ तद्धितः *(4.1.17)* "In the opinion of the Eastern grammarians, the *pratyaya* ष्फ is employed after what ends with the *pratyaya* य and is to be regarded as a *taddhita pratyaya*".

तद्धिताः *(4.1.176)* "The *taddhita pratyayas* are treated of hereafter".

ये च तद्धिते *(6.1.61)* "There is the substitution of that stem शीर्षन् for शिरस् when a *taddhita pratyaya* with य follows." In fact, he has begun the enumeration of the *taddhita pratyayas* with the *sūtra* तद्धिताः *(4.1.76)* by putting the term तद्धित for *pratyayas* such as ति ष्यङ् अण् etc., which are mentioned thereafter.

In his rule कृत्तद्धितसमासाश्च (*1.2.46*) and in the *vārttika* समासकृत्तद्धिताव्ययाः (*1.4.1, Vārttika 41*) which are similar to *Vāj. Pr. 1.27* quoted above, the word तद्धित appears to be actually used for the words derived from nouns by secondary *pratyaya*, although commentators have explained there the terms कृत् and तद्धित for कृदन्त and तद्धितान्त.

The term तद्धित is evidently echoed in the *sūtra* तस्मै हितम् (*5.1.5*), which although not the first *sūtra* of the *taddhita* section may imply that there were possibly long lists of secondary nouns with the sense of secondary *pratyaya*, and तद्धित was perhaps the first sense given there (*Abhayankar*). The number of *taddhita pratyayas* are clearly very large (*1110 sūtras*). The main sub-divisions mentioned are preceded by the 'great option' समर्थानां प्रथमाद्वा (*4.1.82*).

If we assume the same meaning to समर्थ as in *2.1.1* समर्थपदविधिः we may accept Scharfe's translation cf. *4.1.82*. "After the first of (words) with a single meaning preferably (*taddhita*) *pratyayas*", following Kiparsky's interpretation of *vā*. For words with a same meaning there would be as a general rule/ *utsarga* compounding. In special cases however, composition may be superseded by *taddhita* formation. These are listed in rules following *4.1.16*.

1. अपत्यार्थक तस्यापत्यम् (प्राग्दीव्यतोऽण्)

वैश्वानरः by ऋष्यन्धकवृष्णिकुरुभ्यश्च (*4.1.114*) and e.g. औपगवः offspring of *Vaiśvānara* and *Upagu*.

"The *pratyaya* अण् (*4.1.83*) and those that follow it denote the descendant of someone", to
न प्राच्यभर्गादियौधेयादिभ्यः (*4.1.178*)

"The *tadrāja pratyaya* is not elided in the feminine if it forms the names of *kṣatriyas* of the east, *yaudheya* etc.", e.g. प्राचाली a *kṣatriya* woman of the east.

2. रक्ताद्यर्थक तेन रक्तं रागात् (*4.2.1*)

The *pratyaya* अण् etc. already ordained (*4.1.83*) comes after the name of a colour in the sense of 'coloured' thereby as far as नडादिनांकुक् च (*4.2.91*), e.g. काषायम् brown-red cloth or garment.'

"The augment कुक् comes after the word नड etc. when the *pratyaya* छ follows in the four senses: 'तदस्मिन् नस्तीतिदेशे' 'तन्नाम्नि' (*4.2.67*); तेन 'निर्वृत्तम्' (*4.2.68*); 'तस्य निवासः' (*4.2.69*); 'अदूरभवश्च' (*4.2.70*)", namely 'That thing, is in this (a place named)' तदस्मिन्नस्तीति देशे (*4.2.67*)

> completed by him, तेन निर्वृत्तम् (*4.2.68*)
> his dwelling place, तस्य निवासः (*4.2.69*)
> after what is near, अदूरभवश्च (*4.2.70*)

3. शैषिक, शेषे (*4.2.92*)

"The *pratyayas* taught hereafter have senses other than those mentioned above".

आथर्वणिकस्येकलोपश्च *(4.3.133)* तस्येदम् *(4.3.120)* "The *pratyaya* अण् comes in the sense of 'this is his' after the word *ātharvaṇika* and the penultimate *'ika'* is elided". आथर्वणो धर्म आम्नायो वा

4. प्राग्दीव्यतीय तस्य विकारः *(4.3.134)*

"A *pratyaya* (*4.1.83* अण् etc.) comes after a word in the sixth case in construction in the sense of 'a modification thereof'".

अश्मनो विकारः आश्मनः made of stone
बैल्वः (बिल्वादिभ्योऽण् made of *Bilva* wood *(4.3.136)*)
त्रापुषम् जातुषम् (त्रपुजतूजतुनोःषुक् *(4.3.138)*)
कंसीयपरशव्ययोर्यजजो लुक् च *(4.3.168)*

"The *pratyayas* यञ् and अञ् come respectively in the sense of its product after the word *'kāṅsīya'* and *'paraśavya'* and there is elision (of the छ and घ *pratyayas* of those words)".

5. प्राग्वहतीय प्राग्वहतेष्ठकः *(4.4.1)*

"The *pratyaya* ठक् comes as a governing *pratyaya* in the sense enumerated hereafter up to *sūtra 4.4.76*", e.g. आक्षिकः.

आवसथात् ष्ठल् *(4.4.74)* "The *pratyaya* ष्ठल् comes in the sense of who dwells there after the word *āvasathā* in the seventh case in construction".

तद्वहति रथयुगप्रासङ्गम यत् *(4.4.76)* "*Pratyaya* यत् acts in the sense of what bears it after the words रथ युग प्रसङ्ग being in the second case in construction", e.g. रथं वहतिः रथ्यः.

6. प्राग्घितीय। 'प्राग्घिताद्यत्' *(4.4.75)*

"In each *sūtra* from this one forward to *tasmai hitam (5.1.5)* the *pratyaya* यत् bears rule".

"The *pratyaya* यत् comes after the word *'sodara'* in the sense of who sleeps, the word being in the seventh case in construction", e.g. सोदर्यः *(4.4.110-114)* छन्दसि only.

7. आर्हीय। प्राक् क्रीताच्छः *(4.1.1)*

"From this *sūtra* onwards to tena *krītam (5.1.37)* (तस्मै हितम् *(5.1.5)*), e.g. वत्सेभ्यो हितो वत्सीयो गोधुक् यज्ञियो ब्राह्मणः आर्त्विजीनो ब्राह्मणः the *pratyaya 'cha'* bears rule to यज्ञर्त्विग्भ्यां घखञौ *(5.1.71)*.

"The *pratyaya* घ (इय) and ख (+ईन) come respectively after the words *yajña* and *ṛtvij* in the sense of deserving that".

8. ठनधिकारस्थ। पारायणतुरायणाचंद्रायणं वर्तयति (ठञ्) प्राग्वहतोष्ठञ् *(5.1.72)*

"The *pratyaya* ठञ् (इक्) *(5.1.18)* comes in the sense of who performs this after the words *'pārāyaṇa' 'turāyaṇa'* and *'cāndrāyaṇa'* being in the second case in construction. आकलिकडाद्यन्तवचने *(5.1.114)* पारायणिकश्छात्रः तौरायणिको यजमानः चान्द्रायणिकस्तपस्वी "The *ākalikat* is irregularly formed in the sense of 'what coincides with the beginning and the end', i.e. what lasts only an instant".

9. भावकर्मार्थक। तेनतुल्यक्रियाचेद्वतिः *(5.1.115)*, e.g. ब्राह्मणवत्

"The *pratyaya* वत् comes after a word in the third case in construction in the sense of 'like that' when the meaning is similarity of action".

ब्रह्मणस्त्वः (भावः कर्म) *(5.1.136)* "The *pratyaya* त्व comes in the sense of nature or action thereof after the word *Brahman* denoting a kind of *hotṛ* priest". (e.g.ब्रह्मत्वम्).

10. पाश्चमिक धान्यानांभवनेक्षेत्रे खञ् *(5.2.1)*

The *pratyaya khañ* खन् (+इन) comes after the name of any particular corn being in the genitive case in construction in the sense of a place of growing when the place is a field, e.g. मुद्गानां भवनं क्षेत्र ⇨ मौद्गीनाम्.

To इन्द्रियमिन्द्रलिङ्गमिन्द्रदृष्टमिन्द्रसृष्टमिन्द्रजुष्टमिन्द्रदत्तमिति वा (घञ्) *(5.2.93)* "The word *'indriyam'* (showing *udātta* on the last) is anomalous meaning an organ of sense and so called either because it is the characteristic from which the existence of *Indra* is inferred; or 'it is seen by *Indra'* or 'it is created by *Indra'* or 'wished by *Indra*' or 'given by *Indra'* ".

11. मत्वर्थीय। तदस्यास्त्यस्मिन्निति मतुप् *(5.2.94)*

"The *pratyaya matup* (मत मन्तf. ई) comes after a word in the first case in construction in the sense of 'where it is' or 'in whom it is'", e.g. गावोऽस्य सन्ति गोमान् अहं शुभयोर्युस् *(5.2.140)*.

"The *pratyaya* युस् comes in the sense of *matup* after the word *'aham'* and the indeclinable *'śubham'* (good)".

12. विभक्तिसंज्ञक। प्राग्दिशोविभक्तिः *(5.3.1)* स्वार्थे प्रकरणम्

The *pratyaya* taught from this *sūtra* forward as far as *5.3.27* (exclusive) are called *'vibhakti'*.

थाहेतौ च च्छन्दसि *(5.3.26)* *"Pratyaya* था comes in the sense of cause also (as well as 'manner') in the *chandas* after the word *kim"*. कथा

13. स्वार्थिक। दिक्शब्देभ्यः सप्तमीपञ्चमीप्रथमाभ्यो दिग्देशकालेष्वस्तातिः *(5.3.27)*

"After the words of 'direction' ending in the locative, ablative and nominative, and referring to direction, locality, or time, comes the *pratyaya* अस्ताति (=अस्तात्) without change of sense". e.g. पुरस्तात् निष्प्रवाणिश्च *(5.4.160)*

(N.B. Sometimes includes *samāsānta* from *(5.4.68))*

The word निष्प्रवाणिश्च is irregularly formed without adding the *pratyaya* कप् though the last word is a *nadī* word.

तद्धितः समर्थानां प्रथमाद्वा *(4.1.82)*

"The *taddhita pratyayas* on the alternative (of their being employed at all) come after the word that is signified by the first of the words in construction in a *sūtra* up to but excluding प्राग् दिशो विभक्तिः *(5.3.1)"*.

We shall consider a few of these by way of example.

अश्वपत्यादिभ्यश्च *(4.1.84)* And let the *pratyaya* अण् in the sense of various *pratyayas* occuring antecedently to तेन दीव्यति खनति जयति जितम् *(4.4.2)* "When the sense is 'who plays, digs, conquers or is conquered therewith' there is the *pratyaya* ठक् after these". आश्वपतिः by तद्धितेष्वचामादेः *(7.2.117)* and यस्येति च (*6.4.148*) (तद्धितेभस्य लोपः) "When a *taddhita pratyaya* follows with an indicatory *ñ* or *ṅ* there is *vṛddhi* in place of the first vowel among the vowels".

The offspring of (one of the kings styled *Aśvapati*) is आश्वपत्यम् by दित्यदित्यादित्य-पत्युत्तरपदाण्ण्यः *(4.1.85)* "The *pratyaya* ण्य in the sense of the various senses occuring antecedently to *4.4.2,* comes after the proper names दिति अदिति आदित्य 'the sun' and that which has the word पति as its final member". Thus दैत्यः descendant of दिति *Diti,* आदित्य descendant of *Aditi* or a descendant of the sun, प्राजापत्यः descendant of *Prajāpati.*

For example: पूषन्नेकर्षे यम सूर्य प्राजापत्य *(Īśā.16)*

"O *Pūṣan* (thou who art the nourisher), the solitary traveller, the controller, the acquirer, the son of *Prajāpati* (do remove the rays, gather up thy dazzle)". Again this *taddhita* may serve as a representative of one of a very large group of powerful secondary *pratyayas,* which indeed links with one of the senses of *taddhita* itself.

By असुरस्य स्वम् *(4.4.123)* the *pratyaya* यत् comes in the *chandas* after the word असुर in the sixth case in construction (i.e. in the sense of belonging).

असुर having in turn been derived from *Uṇādi 5.1.42* असेरुरन् from *dhātu* असु दि॰ प॰ से॰ 209 —क्षेपणे in the sense of throwing up. Thus when यत् is added in the sense of तस्मै हितम् *(5.1.5)* "A *pratyaya* (like *yat*) comes after a word in the fourth case in construction in the sense of good for that' " the difference in *vibhakti* being due to Vedic context.

We have the form of असुर्यः belonging to, 'good for the *Asuras*'.

So in *Īśā.3* असुर्या नाम ते लोका अन्धेन तमसाऽऽवृताः। "Those worlds of devils are covered by blinding darkness." (*Śankara* comments: As compared with their attainment of the non-dual state of the Supreme Self, even Gods are *Asuras* (devils), and the worlds belonging to them *'asuryaḥ')*.

तांस्ते प्रेत्याभिगच्छन्ति येके चात्महनो जनाः॥ "Those people who kill, i.e. deny the Self after giving up this body, go to those (worlds)".

Another extremely important *taddhita pratyaya* is decreed by तस्य भावस्त्वतलौ *(5.1.119)* which states "the *pratyayas* त्व and तल (= त or ता) come after a word in the sixth case in construction in the sense of the nature thereof.

So एक followed by त्वम् gives us एकत्वम् literally of the nature of one, as in *Īśā. 7* = oneness, unity तत्र को मोहः कः शोक एकत्वमनुपश्यतः।

"In the self, of the man of realisation (in whom all beings become the Self) what delusion and what sorrow can remain for that seer of oneness".

Our last example is the so-called comparative *pratyaya,* which in English is often represented by final '-er'. This is ordained by द्विवचनविभज्योपपदे तरबीयसुनौ *(5.3.57)* which states that "the *pratyayas* तरप् (तर) and ईयसुन् (ईयस्) come in the sense of 'surpassing' (अतिशायने) after a *prātipadika* (as comparison between) the things or when that which is added to it *(upapada)* is to be distinguished from another".

Thus from the *dhātu* जुङ् (भ्वा० आ० अ० 358 गतौ) in the sense of swift movement manifests जवीयः when followed by ईयस्, for this causes गुण of the उ of जु (सार्वधातुक-आर्धधातुकयोः) *(7.3.84)* giving जो—small +ईयम् and जवीयस् by एचोऽयवायावः *(6.1.78)* the स् becoming first रु by ससजुषो रुः *(8.2.66)* then उ by हशि च *(6.1.114)* before the following न, finally in संहिता (union of one *vākya*) by आद् गुणः *(6.1.87)* manifests as जवीयो as the example from *Īśā.4* अनेजद् एक मनसो जवीयो नैनद्देवा आप्नुवन् पूर्वमर्षत् "It (the Self) is unmoving, one, and faster than the mind *(manasas)*. The senses *(devāḥ)* could not overtake it, since it ran ahead".

Samāsāntaḥ Section

We turn to our final group of *pratyayas,* also called *taddhitas,* the समासान्ताः प्रत्ययाः forming the final section of the स्वार्थिक तद्धित section which have the characteristic of conveying or bringing forth the meaning of that to which they are attached without adding anything additional, from *5.4.68* to *5.4.160.* These are all prescribed at the end of compounds in specific cases.

Again a few examples only are possible within this general context. By the *sūtra* अव्ययीभावे शरत्प्रभृतिभ्यः *(5.4.107) Pāṇini* states "When the compound is an *avyayībhāva* or 'indeclinable compound' the *taddhita pratyaya* टच् (=ac by

चुटू *(1.3.7)* and अ by हलन्त्यम् *(1.3.3))* comes after the words शरत् etc. as final of the compound", e.g. उपशर्दम् 'near the autumn'.

Again अनश्च *(5.4.108)* "And after that *avyayībhāva* which ends in अन् let there be टच्".

नस्तद्धिते *(6.4.144)* (भस्य, टेः, लोपः) "And when a *taddhita pratyaya* follows, there is elision of the last vowel with what follows it of what ends in *'n'* and is called *bha"* (c.f. यचि भम् *(1.4.18)*. "When a *pratyaya* with an initial *'ya'* or a vowel follows, what precedes (not being *sarvanāmasthāna*) is called *bha"*.

Thus there is elision of the अन् of आत्मन् because the following *taddhita pratyaya 'tac'* when stripped of its indicatory letters really begins with *'a'*, e.g. अध्यात्मम् relating to the Self). As in *Kenopaniṣad 4.5 :* अथ अध्यात्मं यदेतद् गच्छतीव "there is (the instruction through analogy) in the context of the individual self. This (known fact that the mind) seems to go to It *(Brahman)*... ."

Again, there is the context of a बहुव्रीहि समास (in respect whereof for the most part the sense of a different word is the main one to which the sense of the compound epithet is subordinate).

We have the *sūtra* सुहृद-दुहृद मित्रामित्रयोः *(5.4.150)* "The forms of *suhṛd* and *duhṛd* occur with the sense of friend and foe (the अय of हृदय being elided in the *bahuvrīhi*)". Thus सुहृद 'whose heart is well-affected' and दुहृद् 'whose heart is ill-affected'.

For example सर्वस्य प्रभुमीशानं सर्वस्य शरणम् सुहृत् *(Śvet.3.17)* "The Lord, the ruler of all, the Friend (and) the Shelter of all".

For an example of तत्पुरुष समास प्रत्यय again we take the *pratyaya* टच् ordained by राजाहस्सखिभ्यष्टच् *(5.4.91)*. Whereby "the *taddhita pratyaya ṭac* comes after a *tatpuruṣa samāsa* (in which for the most part the sense of the last of its elements is the main one) that ends with the word राजन् (a king), अहन् (day), सखि (friend)" and by आन्महतः समानाधिकरणजातीययोः *(6.3.46)*.

"Long *'ā'* is the substitute (cf. the final of *'mahat'* (great), when a word in the same case follows and when *jātīya* (like) follows". Thus स यथा कुमारो वा महाराजो वा as in *Bṛhad. 2.1.19* महाब्राह्मणो वाऽतिघ्नीमानन्दस्य गत्वा शयीत "Verily as a youth of a great king or a great *Brahman* might rest when he has reached the utter oblivion of bliss, so this one now rests".

Finally, "the *pratyaya* टच् comes after the word *varcas* when preceded in a compound by the words *'Brahma'* or *'hasti'*".

ब्रह्महस्तिभ्यां वर्चसः *(5.4.78)* which may be read in the *Tai.1.3 :* सह नौ यशः मह नौ ब्रह्मवर्चसम् "May we both attain fame together. May spiritual eminence be vouchsafed to both of us together".

Uṇādi Section (Appendix)

The last major section of *pratyaya* still comes under the general category कृत्, referred by *Pāṇini* yet listed separately in tradition, may be considered as somewhat distinct. The उणादि *pratyayas* headed by the *pratyaya* अण् are similar to *Pāṇini's kṛt pratyayas,* giving derivation mostly of such words as are not derived by the *sūtras* of *Pāṇini.* No particular sense such as agent, object etc. is mentioned in connection with these *pratyayas,* as *Pāṇini* has stated in ताभ्यामन्यत्रोणादयः *(3.4.75).*

(They are, however, *kṛt pratyayas* under the general meaning *sūtra* कर्तरिकृत् and are placed on a level with other *pratyayas* (Comp. तितुत्रतथसिसुसरकसेषु *(7.2.9)* (अनिट्)).

"The words formed by *uṇādi pratyayas* denote other ideas than these two (i.e. सम्प्रदान recipient and अपादान ablation)". In other words any one of the senses कर्तृ agent, कर्मन् object, करण instrument, अधिकरण location is assigned to the *uṇādi pratyaya* as suits the meaning of the word.

Although some scholars believe that the *uṇādi pratyayas* were given by a grammarian later than *Pāṇini,* as there are words like ताम्बूल, तीनार and others included in the list of *uṇādi* words, and that there are many interpolated *sūtras,* still the *uṇādi* collection must be looked upon as an old one containing at least some pre-*Pāṇini*an material, which is definitely mentioned by *Pāṇini* in two different *sūtras,* namely उणादयो बहुलम् *(3.3.1).* "The *pratyayas 'uṇ'* and the rest with the force of the present (i.e. implying neither past time nor future) and with a sense simply appellative (and not descriptive) are attached diversely", and ताभ्यामन्यत्रोणादयः *(3.4.75)* (see above for translation). Some *pratyayas,* though there be no express injunction regarding them, are to be inferred as belonging to the class केचिदविहिता एव प्रयोगत उन्नीयन्ते. The maxim in regarded to the *pratyaya 'uṇ'* etc. in this.

संज्ञासु धातुरूपाणि प्रत्ययाश्च ततः परे।

कार्याद् विद्यादनुबन्धमेतच्छास्त्रमुणादिषु।। *(M. Bh. 3.3.1.2.138)*

"When in appellatives we find the forms of *dhātus* and *pratyayas* coming after them, then one may know from the result (as presented in the word) what are the indicatory letters which the *pratyaya* must have possessed in order to produce the result". This is a frank admission of the arbitrary nature of these *pratyayas,* in contrast to most of *Pāṇini's pratyayas.*

The technical terms ह्रस्व दीर्घ प्लुत उदात्त उपधा लोप संप्रसारणं अभ्यास are used in the same sense as in *Pāṇini.* The *anubandhas* are similar. However, *Kātyāyana* shows the particular *sūtras* of *Pāṇini* :

(8.3.50) कःकरत्करतिकृधिकृतेष्वनदितेः
(7.4.15) आपोऽन्यतरस्याम्
(7.2.78) ईडजनोर्ध्वे च
(8.3.59) आदेशप्रत्यययोः

do not apply to *Uṇādi (4.226)* which is an exception to गतिकारकोपपदात्कृत् *(6.2.139)*

गतिकारकोपपदयोः पूर्वपदप्रकृतिस्वरत्वं च *(Uṇ. 4.226)* "The *pratyaya* असि acts after compounds which have for their first member either a *gati* word or when the *upapada* is a *kāraka;* and the first member retains its original accent". *Patañjali* apparently ascribing the collection to *Śākaṭāyana* in *Mahābhāṣya* on उणादयो बहुलम् *(3.3.1)* states on the strength of the *Vārttika* तत्रोणादिप्रतिषेध that these *pratyayas* and the words given in the *uṇādi* collection should not be considered as genuinely derived. The derivation is not a very systematic and logically correct one and therefore, for practical purposes the words derived by the application of the *pratyayas* अण् etc. should be looked upon as underived. Cf. उणादयोऽव्युत्पन्नानि प्रातिपदिकानि *(M.Bh. on P.1.1.16, 3.4.77)*.

There is a counter statement also seen in the *Mahābhāṣya* उणादयो व्युत्पन्नानि "*Uṇādi* (should be looked upon) as derived" representing the other view prevailing at the time. *M.Bh.* on *3.1.133*; but not much importance (according to *Abhyankar*) seems to be attached to it, nor any trace of it in Kielhorn's edition!

The different systems of grammar have different collections of such words which are also known by the term *uṇādi.* Of the collections belonging to *Pāṇini's* system, three collections are available. The collections in five *pādas* given in the printed edition of *Siddhānta Kaumudī,* the collection in ten *pādas* given in the printed edition of the *Prakriyā Kaumudī* and the collection in the *Sarasvatī Kaṇṭhābharaṇa* of *Bhoja* forming *pādas* 1, 2 and 3 of the second *adhyāya* of the work. The first *sūtra* in *S.K.* is कृवापाजिमिस्वदिसाध्यशूभ्य उण् "Let the *pratyaya* उण् come after the *dhātu* कृ to make, वा to blow, पा to drink, जि to overcome, मि to scatter, स्वादि to taste, साधि to accomplish, अशु to pervade". Thus कारुः an artisan, वायुः 'Air', as in वायुरनिलममृतमथेदंभस्मान्तं शरीरम् (*Īśā.* 17) "Let (my) vital force (or wind) now attain the (all pervading) immortal Air, and now let this body be reduced to ashes". पायुः the organ of excretion, जायुः a drug (which overcomes diseases), मायुः the bile, स्वादुः sweet, साधु who accomplishes the object of another, hence virtuous, आशु quickly.

One more example of *uṇādi sūtra* will serve to illustrate their special function in providing some derivation for many words, particularly in the *Upaniṣads* which otherwise would remain underived.

अवतेष्टिलोपश्च *(Uṇ. 1.139)* The *pratyaya* सन् comes after the *dhātu* अव (600)

रक्षण रतिकान्ति प्रीतितृप्ति अवगमप्रवेश श्रवण स्वामी अर्थ याचन क्रिया इच्छा

दीप्ति अवाप्ति आलिङ्गन हिंसा आदान भाग वृद्धिषु "in the sense of protecting, movement, beauty or brilliance or desire (to return to the Absolute etc.) pleasing, satisfaction, understanḍing, penetration, hearing or listening, lordship, purpose or aim, asking, action, desire (of the Self), shining, obtaining or pervading, embracing, injuring or killing, accepting, disturbing or alloting and finally in prospering." In the twenty activities perhaps we get a glimpse of the manifest nature or the *dhātu* of all *dhātus,* the seed of all seeds at work, and there is *lopa* (elision) of the अन् (टि) portion of सन्. Thus अव + म् = उ उ + म्.

The penultimate अ and the final व् are both changed to उ by ज्वरत्वरसिव्यवि-मवामुपधायाश्च *(6.4.20)* "In ज्वर त्वा सिव् अव् and मव् before the above mentioned *pratyayas* (वि-व, a nasal or a *jhalādi* कित् or ङित्) there is the single substitution of उ for the व् and for the vowel preceding the final consonant". These two coalesce into one long ऊ, then गुण by सार्वधातुकार्धधातुकयोः *(7.3.84)* giving as in the second line in *Īśā.17* quoted above.!

ओम् क्रतो स्मर कृतं स्मर क्रतो स्मर कृतं स्मर "O my mind remember–remember all that has been done. Remember, remember all that has been done !"

PART TWO
TEXT AND TRANSLATION

A Note on the Translation

The oldest complete grammar that has been preserved is the *Aṣṭādhyāyī* of *Pāṇini.* It is one of the greatest monuments of human intelligence. It represents a fully developed system describing in minute detail, every inflection, derivation and composition as well as syntactic usage of its author's speech. No other language, to this day, has been so perfectly described. *Pāṇini* stands at the end of a long line of predecessors whose grammatical works have perished owing to the excellence of his work.

Later than *Yāska* (probably about 500 B.C.), whom *Pāṇini* mentions, and much earlier than his interpreter *Patañjali* (author of the *Mahābhāṣya* and third of the great *Munitraya), Pāṇini* probably flourished in *Śalātura* near modern Atak, where Hsuan Tsang saw a statue in his memory, c.350 B.C. If so then *Kātyāyana* (second of the great *Munitraya),* may be placed c.250-200 B.C., there being found sufficient divergence of speech due to passage of time and difference of region to justify his corrections.

The first commentatorial work on *Pāṇini's Aṣṭādhyāyī* available to us is *Kātyāyana's Vārttikas,* or critical annotations on 1245 or nearly one third of *Pāṇini's sūtras,* the object of which was to consider whether *Pāṇini's sūtras* are correct or not, and to improve on them where this may be found to be necessary. *Kātyāyana* belonged to the Deccan and belonged to a school of grammar different from that of *Pāṇini.* When *Kātyāyana's* criticisms show him to differ from *Pāṇini,* an oversight on the part of the latter is usually to be assumed, but in estimating the extent of such oversights one must take into account that he lived both later and in a part of India far removed from that of *Pāṇini.* Other grammarians made similar notes on *Pāṇini* both before and after *Kātyāyana.* Subsequent to the latter's time are the numerous grammatical *kārikās* or comments in metrical form.

All this critical work was collected by *Patañjali* in his Great Commentary, the *Mahābhāṣya,* based on the *saṃgraha* of *Vyāḍi* with many supplementary notes and discussions of his own, commenting on *Pāṇini's* rules as well as *Kātyāyana's Vārttikas.* His discussions take the form of a kind of dialogue and deal with 1713 *sūtras* of *Pāṇini. Patañjali* is regarded as an incarnation of the snake *Śeśa, Viṣṇu's* resting place during His slumber, and believed to be the author of the *Yoga Sūtra* by much later tradition, due to likeness of name. His date is still disputed. However, statements in the *Bhāṣya* refer to a sacrifice for *Puṣyamitra,* whose reign began c.185 or 178 B.C., and to a recent attack on *Sāketa* and *Madhyamika* by a *Yavana,* who is identified with the Greek Menander (c. 156-153), which give c.150-149 for the composition of the work. Slight confirmation comes from the fact that *Kātyāyna* notes the title *"devānāṃ priya", (Pāṇini* does not), famed in *Aśoka's* inscriptions, suggesting that he fell after 250 B.C. Finally *Kalhaṅa* records a revival of the study of the *Mahābhāṣya* under *Abhimanyu.* Since this statement and date is suspect the next lower limit is *Bhartṛhari's* date, namely fifth or fourth century A.D.

The *Māhabhāṣya* is in the first instance a commentary on the *Vārttikas* of *Kātyāyana.* Rarely does *Patañjali* explain *Pāṇini* for the simple purpose of explanation, as does the later *Kāśikā Vṛtti,* but like a second *vārttikākāra* on the whole he enquires whether anything has been omitted in the *sūtras* that should have been stated or whether in them there is anything superfluous, faulty to objection.

The *Mahābhāṣya* is interesting stylistically as giving us a lively picture of the mode of discussion of the day. The language is lucid and elegant, presenting arguments in a conversational style, remotely comparable to the dialogues of Plato. The *pūrvapakṣin* having raised doubts, asked questions and attacked *Pāṇini's* or *Kātyāyana's* formulations, a question is posed; an *Ācāryadeśiya* deals with it. The latter also called *Siddhāntyekadeśin,* is the person who refutes the objections and defends *Pāṇini* and *Kātyāyana* by providing partially correct answers. Thus he deals with the question posed, not altogether incompetently but not quite satisfactorily. The *Ācārya* or *Siddhāntin* solves the issues. He gives final decisions on particularly difficult issues, either

(i) by saying that *Kātyāyana's* additions to and rephrasings of *Pāṇini's sūtras* are unfounded or unnecessary, or

(ii) by defending *Kātyāyana's* rephrasing of the rules, or

(iii) by suggesting that a particular rule of *Pāṇini* is not needed even if *Kātyāyana* defends it.

The style, therefore, is lively, simple and animated and as in *Aśoka's* inscriptions not rarely do we find the question 'Wherefore?' 'How' or 'What?' put and then answered. Proverbial expressions and references to matters of everyday life are introduced and serve both to enliven the discussions and to give us valuable hints of the conditions of life and thought in the time of *Patañjali,* who is thus a source of information for religious and social history as well as for literature.

The *Mahābhāṣya* like the *Aṣṭādhyāyī* is divided into eight *adhyāyas* of four *pādas* each; each pāda being further subdivided into from one to nine *āhnikas*. (Which, in former times, may have been read in one *ahan* (day)). Within this the *pratyayapāda* comprises six *āhnikas* and in fact serves to introduce the heart of the *Pāṇinian* grammar as interpreted by *Kātyāyana* and *Patañjali,* namely the third, fourth and fifth *adhyāyas.*

The first *āhnika* provides the *sañjña* and *adhikāra sūtras 3.1.1-4* which apply throughout the subsequent three *adhyāyas,* as well as the first *pratyaya san* firstly as *svārthe* and then in the sense of *icchā.*

The second *āhnika* deals with the next seven *dhātu*-forming *pratyayas kyac, kāmyac, kyaṅ, kvas, ṇiṅ, ṇic* and *yaṅ* with various meanings including *svārthe, karaṇe* and *hetumati.*

The third *āhnika* discusses the last four of the *dhātu*-forming *pratyayas,* namely *yak, āya, īyaṅ* and *ṇiṅ,* with the *adhīkāra* for the last three and the *sañjñā dhātu* for all twelve. The first four *atyantika-svārthe vikaraṇa pratyayas,* namely *sya, tāsi, sip* and *ām* are then evaluated.

The fourth *āhnika* starts by considering the aorist *vikaraṇa cli* and then its five *ādeśas,* namely *sic, ksa, caṅ,* aṅ and *ciṇ.* Then a selection of the conjugational *vikaraṇas* are discussed, namely *śyan, śnam, u, śnā* (with *ādeśas śānac* and *śāyac*), preceded by the passive *yak,* all in the sense of *svārthe.* It ends with *vyatyayo bahulam* and the Vedic *vikaraṇa aṅ.*

The fifth *āhnika* begins with a long discussion on the *atideśa karmavat* for the reflexive passive, followed by a *niyama* and special ordaining of *śyan* to end the section dealing with verbal forms. The remainder deals with the three *adhikāras, dhātoḥ, upapada* and *kṛt,* which introduce the formation of primary noun formation with *kṛt pratyayas.*

The sixth and last *āhnika* of the *pratyayapāda* begins with the *vāsarūpo paribhāṣā* and the *adhikāra kṛtyāḥ* followed by a discussion of the six *pratyayas* in its province, namely *tavya, tavyat, anīyar, yat, kyap* and *ṇyat* in the sense largely of *bhāva* and *karman.* The last section deals with all but two of the remaining *pratyayas* of the *pāda,* in the sense of *kartṛ,* namely *ṇvul, lyu, tṛc, ṇin, ac, ka, śa, ṇa, ṇvun* and *vun.*

The Sanskrit text and the English translation of the Vyākaraṇa Mahābhāṣya by Patañjali on 3.1, the Pratyayapāda comprising six *Āhnikas* and dealing with Kātyāyana's *Vārttikas* on Pāṇini 3.1.1. - 149

प्रत्ययः ॥ 3 । 1 । 1 ॥

Pāṇini 3.1.1: Affix.

1.2 अधिकारेणेयं[1] प्रत्ययसंज्ञा क्रियते। सा प्रकृत्युपपदोपाधीनामपि। प्राप्नोति। तस्याः
प्रतिषेधो वक्तव्यः। प्रकृति[3]। गुप्तिज्किद्भ्यः सन् (3.1.5)। उपपद[4]। स्तम्बकर्णयो
रमिजपोः (3.2.13)। उपाधि[5]। हरतेर्दृतिनाथयोः पशौ (3.2.25)। एतेषां
प्रतिषेधो वक्तव्यः। किं च स्याद्यद्येतेषामपि प्रत्ययसंज्ञा स्यात्। परत्वमाद्युदात्तत्व–[6,7]
1.6 मङ्गसंज्ञेत्येते[8] विधयः प्रसज्येरन्।। अत उत्तरं पठति।

Bhāṣya: This technical term *pratyaya* is formed (with the function) of a governing *adhikārasūtra.* That (technical term) obtains also for the *prakṛti* (base), *upapada* (subordinate word in a compound) and *upādhi* (qualifying words). A prohibition of that should be stated.

Example of *prakṛti*: *'San pratyaya* acts after the *prakṛtis gup tij* and *kit' (3.1.5)*

Example of *upapada* (subordinate in compound): *'ac pratyaya* acts after *dhātus ram* (sport) and *jap* (whisper) when the *sup* (case inflected) *upapadas stamba* (clump of grass) and *karṇa* (ear) are in composition with them respectively' *(3.2.13).*

Example of *upādhi*: When the *upādhi* is 'agent' as an animal, *pratyaya in* acts after *dhātu hṛ* (to take the *karman* or object in composition as *upapada,* being) the words *dṛti* (leather bag) and *nātha* (nose string) *(3.2.25).* Prohibition should be stated of these having the name *pratyaya.* What would be (wrong) if these also had the technical name *pratyaya*? The rules of *paraś ca* ('a *pratyaya* is subsequent') *(3.1.2) ādyudāttaḥ* ('a *pratyaya* has initial *udātta* acute accent') *(3.1.3)* and the technical name *aṅga* (*yasmāt pratyavidhistadādi 1.4.13)* would be applicable. Therefore (the *Vārttikakāra*) recites the reply:

1.7 प्रत्ययाधिकारे प्रकृत्युपपदोपाधीनामप्रतिषेधः ॥ 1 ॥

Vārttika 1: (There is) no prohibition (of the technical term) for *prakṛti* (base), *upapada* (subordinate word in compound) and *upādhi* (qualifying word) when *pratyaya* is a governing rule.

1.8 अधिकारेणापि प्रत्ययसंज्ञायां सत्यां प्रकृत्युपपदोपाधिनामप्रतिषेधः। अनर्थकः
प्रतिषेधोऽप्रतिषेधः[9] ॥ प्रत्ययसंज्ञा कस्मान्न भवति।

Bhāṣya: Even when the technical term *pratyaya* exists as the governing rule, no prohibition (of the term *pratyaya*) for *prakṛti, upapada* and *upādhi* (is necessary).

The word *apratiṣedha* means a superfluous prohibition.

Why does the technical name *pratyaya* apply to them?

1.10 निमित्तस्य[10] निमित्तिकार्यार्थत्वादन्यत्रापि[11] ॥ 2॥

Vārttika 2: Because the cause is meant for that which is possessed of cause elsewhere also.

1.11 निमित्तानि हि निमित्तिकार्यार्थानि भवन्ति। किं पुनर्निमित्तं को वा निमित्ती।
प्रकृत्युपपदोपाधयो निमित्तं प्रत्ययो निमित्ती। अन्यत्रापि[12] चैष न्यायो दृष्टः।
क्वान्यत्र। लोके। तद्यथा। बहुष्वासीनेषु कश्चित्कंचित्पृच्छति कतमो देवदत्तः
कतरो यज्ञदत्त इति। स तस्मा आचष्टे। योऽश्वे यः पीठ इत्युक्ते निमित्तस्य[13]
निमित्ति-
1.15 कार्यार्थत्वादध्यवस्यत्ययं देवदत्तोऽयं यज्ञदत्त इति नेदानीमश्वस्य पीठस्य वा
देवदत्त इति संज्ञा भवति॥ किं पुनर्निमित्तं को वा निमित्ती। निर्ज्ञातोऽर्थो[14]
निमित्तमनिर्ज्ञातोऽर्थो[15] निमित्ती। इह च प्रत्ययोऽनिर्ज्ञातः प्रकृत्युपपदोपाधयो निर्ज्ञा-
1.18 ताः। क्व। धातूपदेशे[16] प्रातिपदिकोपदेशे च ते निर्ज्ञाता निमित्तत्वेनोपादीयन्ते॥

Bhāṣya : For the causes indeed are meant for the sake of the operations of those which are possessed of cause.

But what is the cause and what is that which is possessed of cause? *Prakṛti, upapada* and *upādhi* are the causes: the *pratayaya* is that which is possessed of a cause. This principle is also seen elsewhere. Where else? In the world. For example, when many are seated, someone asks someone else 'Who (among these) is *Devadatta*? Who (among these) is *Yajñadatta* ?' He says to him, 'He who is on the horse is *Devadatta,* he who is on the footstool (is *Yajñadatta*).' When this has been said, he determines 'this is *Devadatta*' and 'this is *Yajñadatta*', because of the cause being for the sake of the operation of that (main statement) caused. Now the name *Devadatta* is not that of the horse or the footstool. What again is the cause and what is that which is possessed of cause?

The object which is known is the cause, whereas that object which is unknown is that which is operated on by a cause. And here *pratyaya* is not known while *prakṛti, upapada* and *upādhi* are known. Where? In the original teaching of *dhātus* (verbal roots) and of *prātipadikas* (crude bases). Those which are known are used/employed as causes.

2.1 प्रधाने[17] कार्यसंप्रत्ययाद्वा सिद्धम् ।। 3।।

Vārttika 3 : Or else it is established, because in relation to the chief thing, there is sure knowledge of the operation.

2.2 अथवा प्रधाने कार्यसंप्रत्ययो भवति। किं च प्रधानम्। प्रत्ययः तद्यथा।
बहुषु यात्सु कश्चित्कंचित्पृच्छति को यातीति। स आह राजेति। राजेत्युक्ते प्रधाने
कार्यसंप्रत्ययाद्यः[18] पृच्छति यश्चाचष्ट उभयोः संप्रत्ययो भवति।। किंकृतं पुनः
2.5 प्राधान्यम्। अर्थकृतम्। यथा पुनर्लोकेऽर्थकृतं प्राधान्यं शब्दस्येदानीं किंकृतं
प्राधान्यम्। शब्दस्यापूर्वोपदेशः प्राधान्यम्। यस्यापूर्वोपदेशः स प्रधान्यम्। प्रकृत्युपपदोपाधि-
यश्चोपदिष्टाः।क्व। धातूपदेशे प्रातिपदिकोपदेशे च।

यद्येव निमित्तस्य निमित्तिकार्यार्थत्वादथापि प्रधाने कार्यसंप्रत्ययात्प्रकृत्यु-
पपदोपाधीनां न भवति विकारागमानां तु प्राप्नोति। हनस्त च[19]
(3.1.108) त्रपु-
2.10 जतुनोः षुक् (4.3.138) इति। एतेषां ह्यपूर्वोपदेशात्प्राधान्यं निमित्तिनश्चैवैते।

Bhāṣya: Or else there is sure knowledge of the operation in relation to the chief thing. And what is the chief thing? *Pratyaya.* As for example, when many are coming, someone asks someone else, "Who is going?" He says 'The king'. When the reply is given as 'the king', then since an operation is understood as pertaining to the principal, there exists sure knowledge for both him who asks and him who answers. But on what account is the preeminence? On account of purpose. As again, in the world, preeminence is on account of purpose. On what account is the preeminence of word? The preeminence of words consists in not being previously taught. Whatever has not previously been taught, that is predominant. *Prakṛti, upapada* and *upādhi* were previously taught. Where? In the teaching (lists) of *dhātus* and *prātipadikas.*

Whether it is "because of having for its purpose the operations of that having 'that as its cause'" (elsewhere *Vārttika*) or whether it is because an operation is understood to have reference only to that which is most important, (the name *pratyaya*) is not applicable for *prakṛti, upapada* and *upādhi,* but it does obtain for *vikāra* (substitutes etc.) and *āgamas* (augments).

(As for example) in the rule *hanas ta ca (3.1.108)* ("After the *dhātu 'han'* (kill), when in construction with a case-inflected word as *upapada* and without an *upasarga,* the *pratyaya kyap* is added, in denoting condition and *ta* is the substitute of a final") and *trapujatunoḥ ṣuk (4.3.138)* ("The *pratyaya aṇ* with the *āgama* (augment) *ṣuk* acts in the sense of its modification after the words *trapu* and *jatu*"). Since these (also) are not previously taught, there is preeminence and they are operated on by a cause.

2.12 विकारागमेषु[20, 21] च परविज्ञानात् ।। 4।।

Vārttika 4: And in relation to *vikāras* and *āgamas* also (the term *pratyaya* does not apply), because of the understanding that *pratyaya* is *para* (subsequent).

2.13 विकारागमेषु च परविज्ञानात्प्रत्ययसञ्ज्ञां [22] न भविष्यति। प्रत्ययः परो भवती-
त्युच्यते न च विकारागमाः परे संभवन्ति। किं पुनः कारणं समानेऽपूर्वोपदेशे
2.15 प्रत्ययः परो विकारागमा न परे।

Bhāṣya: And in relation to *vikāras* and *āgamas*, because of the understanding *para* (subsequent), the technical term *pratyaya* will not apply. It is said *(3.1.2)* that "a *pratyaya* is subsequent" (follows *prakṛti*), and *vikāras* and *āgamas* are not found to follow. But why is it so? The state of 'not being previously taught' being common (to all), the *pratyaya* follows while the *vikāras* and *āgamas* do not follow.

2.16 षष्ठीनिर्दिष्टस्य[23] च तद्युक्तत्वात् ।। 5।।

Vārttika 5: And because the sixth case indication is connected with those (*vikāras* and *āgamas*).

2.17 षष्ठीनिर्दिष्टं विकारागमयुक्तं पञ्चमीनिर्दिष्टाच्च प्रत्ययो विधीयते।।

Bhāṣya: That which is connected with the *vikāras* and *āgamas* is mentioned in the sixth case, and the *pratyaya* is ordained after that which is mentioned in the fifth case.

2.18 प्रत्ययविधानानुपपत्तिस्तु ।। 6 ।।

Vārttika 6: However the ordaining of *pratyaya* is not justified.

2.19 प्रत्ययविधिस्तु नोपपद्यते। क्व। यत्र विकारागमा विधीयन्ते। हनस्त च। त्रपु-
जतुनोःषुगिति। किं पुनः कारणं न सिध्यति। विकारागमयुक्तत्वादपञ्चमी-
2.21 निर्दिष्टत्वाच्च[24]।।

Bhāṣya: The statement of the *pratyaya* rule however is not justified. Where? Where *vikāras* (substitutes etc.) and *āgamas* (augments) are ordained. As in the rules *'hanas ta ca' (3.1.108)* (in which *vikāra* is shown in the *sūtra* and not the *pratyaya*), and *trapujatunoḥ ṣuk (4.3.138)* (in which the *āgama ṣuk* is shown but not the *pratyaya aṇ*). But what is the reason? (The statement of *pratyaya* for them) is not valid, because of being connected with *vikāras* and *āgamas* and not being mentioned in the fifth case.

2.22 तस्मात्तत्र पञ्चमीनिर्देशात्सिद्धिम् ।। 7।।

Vārttika 7: Therefore it is justified there by the mention in the fifth case.

2.23 तस्मात्तत्र पञ्चमीनिर्देशः कर्तव्यः।। न कर्तव्यः। इह तावद्धनस्त चेति धातोः
(3.1.91) इति वर्तते। इह त्रपुजतुनोः षुगिति प्रातिपदिकादिति वर्तते। यद्येवं
2.25 हनस्त च धातोः क्यब्भवतीति धातुमात्रात्क्यप् प्राप्नोति। नैष दोषः।
आचार्यप्रवृतिर्ज्ञापयति[25] न धातुमात्रात्क्यब्भवतीति यदयमेतिस्तुशास्वृदृजुषः[26]
क्यप् (3.1.109) इति परिगणनं करोति। अथवा हन्तिमेवात्र
धातुग्रहणेनाभिसंभन्त्स्यामः[27]। हनस्तो भवति।
3.2 भवति धातोः क्यब्भवतीति। कस्मात्। हन्तेरिति।

Bhāṣya: Therefore, there (in the *sūtra*), mention in the fifth case should be made. It should not be made. Just here in this rule *'hanas ta ca' (3.1.108)* the word *dhātoḥ (3.1.91)* ("after a *dhātu*") is present (by *anuvṛtti)*. Here in the *sūtra, "trapujatunoḥ ṣuk" (4.3.138)* exists (by *anuvṛtti)* and the word *prātipadikāt* 'after a *prātipadika*' (from *4.1.1)*. If that is the case then the *sūtra* becomes *"hanasta ca dhātoḥ kyab bhavati". 'Ta* is *'ādeśa* of the final of *han* and *kyap* acts after a *dhātu* and so, *kyap* obtains after all *dhātus"*. This is not a fault. The usage of the master (*Pāṇini* himself) makes known (by *jñāpaka)* that *kyap* is not to act after all *dhātus* because he makes a complete enumeration of this *sūtra eti stu śās vṛdṛjuṣaḥ kyap (3.1.109) "kyap* acts after *dhātus eti, stu, śās, vṛ, dṛ* and *jus"*. Or else we will here connect *dhātu han* alone with the word *dhātu,* as *'hanasto bhavati'*. "For *han* there is the *ādeśa ta"* and *'dhātoḥ kyap bhavati'*. "For the *pratyaya kyap* acts after a *dhātu"*. After which one? After *hanti.*

3.3 अर्थाश्रयत्वाद्वा[28] ।। 8 ।।

Vārttika 8: Or (the object of excluding the *ādeśas*/substitutes and *āgamas*/ augments from the application of the name *pratyaya*) is achieved because of resort to meaning.

3.4 अथवार्थाश्रयः प्रत्ययविधिः। यस्तमर्थं संप्रत्याययति[29] स प्रत्ययः।। किं
वक्तव्यमेतत्। न हि। कथमनुच्यमानं गंस्यते। प्रत्यय इति महती संज्ञा क्रियते।
संज्ञा च नाम यतो न लघीयः। कुत एतत्। लघ्वर्थं हि संज्ञाकरणम्। तत्र
महत्याः संज्ञायाः करण एतत्प्रयोजनमन्वर्थसंज्ञा यथा विज्ञायेत। प्रत्याययतीति[30]
प्रत्ययः। यदि प्रत्यायतीति प्रत्ययोऽविकादीना[31] प्रत्ययसंज्ञा न प्राप्नोति। न हि
ते किंचित्प्रत्याययन्ति। एवं तर्हि प्रत्याय्यते[32] प्रत्यय इति। एवमपि सनादीनां न

3.10 प्राप्नोति। एवं तह्युभयसाधनेऽयं कर्तृसाधनः कर्मसाधनश्च[33]।। एवमपि कुत
एतत्समानेऽपूर्वोपदेशे त्रापुषम्[34] जातुषमित्यत्राकारस्तमर्थं संप्रत्याययति न पुनः
षकार इति। अन्यत्राप्यकारेण तस्यार्थस्य वचनान्मन्यामहेऽकारस्तमर्थं संप्रत्याययति न
3.13 षकार इति। क्वान्यत्र। बिल्वादिभ्योऽण्[35] (4.3.136) बैल्वः।

Bhāṣya: Or else the rule of *pratyaya* is based on meaning. What causes the meaning to be understood, [that] is *pratyaya* . Is this to be stated? Not at all. How will it be understood without being stated? *Pratyaya* is made a great technical name. A technical name is "that than which nothing (else) is briefer". Why (do you say) this? It is for the purpose of brevity that a technical name is formed. The purpose then of the 'great technical name' is that it should be known as a significant name. A *pratyaya* is that which, (leads towards) i.e. causes one to recognise or know. If a *pratyaya* causes one to recognise (meaning etc.) the technical name *pratyaya* does not obtain for *avi-ka* and the rest.

For they (*ka* etc.) do not cause anything to be known. Well then a *pratyaya* is that which is caused to be known. Then also (the term *pratyaya*) does not obtain for *'san'* and the rest. Well, then this term is derived with both factors as the meaning of the *pratyaya,* i.e. it is expressive of both, expressive of the agent (who causes to recognise, i.e. know the meaning) and expressive of the Object (i.e. which caused to be recognised or is made known).

Even then how is it that although (both the *pratyaya* and the *āgama*) have in common the state of not previously being taught, in the forms *trāpuṣam* and *jātuṣam* the letter *'a'* (of the *pratyaya*) causes the meaning to be understood but not the *(āgama)* letter *'ṣ'* ?

Elsewhere too, also because of the expression of meaning by the letter *'a'* we know that the letter *a'* causes that meaning to be understood but not the letter *'ṣ'*. Where else? (In the *sūtra*) *bilvādibhyo 'ṇ (4.3.136)* "*aṇ pratyaya* acts after the word *bilva* and the rest (in the sense of its modification or its part)", e.g. *bailvaḥ* '*a* modification or part of the *bilva* tree, relating to or coming from the *bilva* tree, made of *bilva* wood'.

Pradīpa

Pradīpa : 1.2 अधिकारेणेति।

"Pratyaya is formed with (the function of) a governing *sūtra."*

Patañjali (introduces the first *vārttika* by illustrating) different functions *prakṛti* etc. and stating the consequences of having the name *pratyaya,* namely *paratva aṅga* technical name etc.

This technical term *pratyaya* is formed with the function of a governing/ *adhikāra sūtra.*

The technical term obtains also for the *prakṛti*/base, *upapada* and *upādhi.* A prohibition of that should be stated.

Examples of *prakṛti 'san pratyaya* acts after *prakṛtis gup tij* and *kit (3.1.5)'.*

However, if by another way the technical name is formed, by the indication etc. of the very form of that having the name, then there would be occasion for an unwarrantable stretch of the rule. (The meaning is) i.e. when however, a technical name is made with the function of a governing rule, it is to remove any possibility of needless multiplication of causes/cumbrousness etc., then there is 'an unwarrantable stretch of the rule/ *atiprasaṅga'*. However, in that context if all those elements possessing the technical name were indicated with their own form then there would be cumbrousness/ *gauravam.*

Example of *upapada* (subordinate in a compound): *Ac pratyaya* acts after the *dhātus ram* and *jap* when the *sup*/case inflected *upapadas stamba* and *karṇa* are in composition with them respectively (*3.2.13*). *stamberamaḥ karṇejapaḥ*

Now if the *sūtra* were framed as *'sap-pratyaya'*, resorting to a *pratyāhāra* beginning with the letter s of *san (3.1.5)* until the *p* of *kap (5.4.151)* the technical name *(pratyaya)* would be so ordained. Then due to the possiblity of more than one letter *p* there would be doubt. Surely, even if present in every rule, due to the possibility of a division of the (implied) sentence (namely the *sūtra*), the technical name *pratyaya* will not be applicable for *prakṛti* and the rest. For so, one sentence (may be) "After the *dhātu hṛ* when the words *dṛti* and *nātha* are objects as dependent words/ *upapadas,* when the qualification/ *upādhi* is "the agent as an animal', the *pratyaya in* acts." *(3.2.25)*

Example of *upādhi* (qualifying words):

When the *upādhi* is agent as an animal, *pratyaya in* acts after the *dhātu hṛ* (to take) the *karman* or object in composition as *upapāda* being the words *dṛti* and *nātha (3.2.25).*

[*dṛtihariḥ* carrier of skin/dog; *nāthahariḥ* that carries the master/ beast.]

A second sentence (would be) "and the words *harati, dṛti, nātha* and *paśu* have the technical name *pratyaya."* And when being one sentence/*ekavākyatā* is possible, it is not proper there be division of the sentence.

This is not so. Even for *san* and the rest the technical name is in fact to be ordained by a division of the sentence, for in the absence of those possessing technical names, ordaining of technical names does not take place. In that context by one sentence the rule is for *san* and the rest. By the other for them is in fact the technical name *(pratyaya)* rule. And hence, just as by a division of the sentence there is the technical name rule for *san* and the rest, so due to the force of close proximity to the technical name *pratyaya* to everything having a technical name, by the supplying of another case/*vibhakti* ending suitable for understanding a connection between the technical name and that possessing it, it (wrongly) obtains even for *prakṛti* (base) and the rest. In fact, in the sentence, for the arising of *san* and the rest, first is understood their dependence on another (namely *pratyaya*). However, in the second sentence teaching the connection of the technical name with 'that possessing it, when connection took place there would be 'the state of', i.e. it would have its own meaning (peculiar to the base)', just as (in *3.1.92*) by reason of dividing the sentence (into two) due to its function as a governing *sūtra,* the technical name *upapada* is applicable for that indicated in the seventh case (*3.1.92*), so (here too) the technical name *pratyaya* also obtains.

3.1.92 Here in this third book referring to *dhātus* the word implied in a term exhibited in the seventh case is called *upapada* (dependent word).

Pradīpa: 1.4 उपाधिशब्देन ।

"Example of *upādhi* (qualifying word as cause of *pratyaya*)."

And here because of equal propriety, by the word *upādhi* is expressed qualification as well (as attribute). However, in some places the practice is seen with a distinction between them both, as for example,

"There exists no attribute of an attribute nor qualification of a qualification".

Śloka Vārttika : "*Upādhi* is an attribute of the meaning, which is (in) the same case relationship with the word as that which is to be expressed by what (word) ends in that *(pratyaya)*.

A non-*upādhi* is what is other than that. A qualification which is like *ślāgha* etc. (*5.1.134*)."

[*Pratyaya vuñ* acts in the sense of action or nature thereof after a family name when one boasts thereby.

Vacaspatimiśraḥ in *Nyāyavārttikatātparyaṭīkāyām (Uddyota)*]

Uddyota: In usage, in the context of different words to be known that word to be known as in the same case relationship to be expressed by the word ending in the *pratyaya*, is the *upādhi*.

As in context of *dṛtihari* 'the carrier of skin' (with *pratyaya in*) the dog (*kartṛ*/agent etc. is animal/*paśu* (*upādhi*), prohibition should be stated of these having the name *pratyaya*.

What would be (wrong) if these also had the technical name *pratyaya*? The rules of *paraśca* (*pratyaya* is subsequent) (3.1.2) and *ādyudātta* (a *pratyaya* has initial *udātta*) (3.1.3) and the technical name *aṅga* (*1.4.13*) would be applicable.

Pradīpa: 1.5 किं च स्यात्।

"And what would be (wrong if these also had the technical name *pratyaya*)?"

For the fault is not only from the occurrence of the technical name but the occuring of the operations which are the cause of that, and for *prakṛti* and the rest it is not possible for there to be any operation which is the cause of that. Just by the mention of a particular limit, *para* (subsequent), it is in fact applicable to be obtained by *san* and the rest. And 'the nature of being subsequent' is not employed with respect to *gup* and the rest and *san* and the rest mutually because of (their functions) being opposed.

'Upapadasyāpi' Also for an *upapada* (subordinate word in compound) when there is a compound, by reason of the irregular placing of a word first in compound it would be applicable because of which there is the absence of being subsequent (*paratva*).

'Upādherapi' Also for an *upādhi* (limit or attribute). Due to absence

of restriction in popular usage of priority or posteriority, and because of reiteration by the *Śāstra* (or Grammar) of the established nature of 'being subsequent'/*paratva;* further, due to the absence of its having the nature of being ordained by the *Śutra,* but nevertheless being reiterated, because of its nature of being an attribute/*upādhi* of the meaning and because of the impossibility of *paratva* for it, there is absence of *paratva.*

Also initial *udātta* will not be applicable due to their accent being ordained each on its own account.

Further the technical name *aṅga* is not dependent on ordaining taking place but *prakṛti* and the rest are not ordained. Thus when they follow, the question is, Will that (name *aṅga*) be applicable for that and none other? (According to *yasmāt-pratyaya vidhis-tadādi pratyaye 'ṅgam 1.4.13*).

Pradīpa : 1.5 परत्वमिति।

"(The rules of) *paraśca* (a *pratyaya* is subsequent) etc. (would be applicable)."

There would be the expectation of 'being subsequent', being mutually applicable in turn for *prakṛti* and *pratyaya.* Or else for the *prakṛti* it would be applicable with respect to another word but for the *pratyaya* it would apply with regard to the *prakṛti.*

Also for the *upapada*—due to *paratva* having been barred by *'upasarjanam pūrvam'* (2.2.30) there being scope of application in the words *rāja puruṣa* etc. *paratva* would be applicable (wrongly). The order of the phrase *'bhoktum vrajati'* (He goes to eat) would be invariable and the (permitted alternative) *'vrajati bhoktum'* however would not be applicable, (if *'paraśca'* applied).

Even for expressing the *upādhi* (attribute), when a lack of restriction on usage obtains, the restriction *'paraśca'* 'and subsequent' would (wrongly) be applicable. Due to the *paribhāṣā* statement, "That which is a *pratyaya,* that is subsequent/*para*". Also having barred another accent initial *udātta* would be (wrongly) applicable.

Pradīpa: 1.6 अंगसंज्ञेति।

"And the technical name *aṅga* (would be applicable)."

'Aṅgasañjñeti' Surely the technical name *aṅga* is dependent on (a *pratyaya* being) ordained and here *prakṛti* etc. are being ordained. This is no fault:

1. Due to the ordaining of them also by the *Śāstra* and for the purpose of the explanation of established words, and

2. Due to the objection to being limited to the prior position by reason of 'being subsequent'/*paratva.*

Surely even when there is objection to the 'prior' when there is *paratva,* the *'tasmāt . . .'* rule (fifth case signifies 'after that' *1.1.67*) is not applicable so that the technical name *aṅga* will not be applicable. This needs to be (re)considered.

Pradīpa: 1.10 निमित्तस्येति।

". . . because the cause (is meant for that which is possessed of cause elsewhere)."

For the causes are indeed meant for the sake of those which are possessed of cause.

Due to the indication of *prakṛti* etc. with established/known *vibhaktis* and because of being accepted as dependent on another, by reason of their being the causes or occasions, when there is arising of *san* and the rest, there is absence of being prompting agents in relation to their own correct formation. This is the meaning. In that context even by the division of the sentence (into two) the technical name *pratyaya* being ordained, is connected with *san* etc. only, because of them alone having the nature of possessing a cause and prompting agency in relation to that (*prakṛti*), and due to the indication of the suitable *vibhakti* (namely *prathama*/first) for understanding connection with the technical name. Even when there exists expectation mutually for the two (*pratyaya* and *prakṛti*) the connection (of technical name) is not applicable so when there is expectation (of the word to complete the sense) either way, as between *'Sītā* and *Rāvaṇa*'.

It is stated that when there is expectation of a technical name to complete the sense, because of the nature of *prakṛti* and the rest as being distinguishers and not having expectation of another word to complete their sense, there is absence of connection with the technical name.

Pradīpa: 1.11 किं पुनरिति।

"But what (is the cause, and what is that which is possessed of cause)?"

Question: Due to the eternal nature of words the condition of cause and that possessing a cause is (surely) not possible?

Pradīpa: 1.12 प्रकृतीति।

"Prakṛti (*upapada* and *upādhi* are the causes . . ., *pratyaya* possessed of cause)."

Due to the establishing of teaching words by *Śāstrika* device through the indication with suitable *vibhakti*/case endings, there is (evident) the condition of cause and that possessing a cause.

This principle is seen elsewhere. Where else? In the world, for example, when many are seated, someone asks someone else 'Who among . . .?'

Pradīpa : 1.13 कतर इति।

"Who among these (is *Yājñadatta*)?"

The word *katara* is used in the specifying of one out of many due to rejecting the *upādhi*/attribute (*dvayoḥ* of two) in the two *sūtras* *'kimyattador-nirdhārane dvayor-ekasya ḍatarac' (5.3.92)* 'After the words *kim, yad,* and *tad,* in specifying one out of two acts the *pratyaya ḍatarac* (= *atara,* with elision of the final *im* and *ad*)', and *'Vā bahūnām jātiparipraśṇeḍatamac'* (*5.3.93*) 'The *pratyaya ḍatamac* (=*atama* with elision of the last syllable) acts after *kim, yat,* and *tad,* optionally, when the aim is the specifying of one out of many, the question being one of caste.'

Pradīpa : 2.1 प्रधान इति।

"(It is established because in relation to) the chief thing (there is sure knowledge of the operation)."

The technical name *pratyaya* has regard to the chief thing, for being right in its own sphere; not, however, because of its being dependent on another (with regard to) a secondary thing/non-principal.

Pradīpa : 2.4 किं कृतमिति।

"But on what account (is the pre-eminence)?"

Let there be pre-eminence for the king because of fixity of those dependent on him; but the question is how is that so here?

Pradīpa : 2.5 अर्थकृतम्।

"On account of purpose."

The meaning is made for a purpose.

Pradīpa : 2.6 यस्याऽपूर्व इति।

"(The pre-eminence of words consists in) not previously (being taught)." The meaning is due to having that purpose. For it in fact there is pre-eminence over others.

Pradīpa : 2.8 यद्वेति।

"Whether it is (because of the cause having for its purpose the operations of that having that as its cause) or whether it is because an operation is understood to have reference only to that which is most important (the name *pratyaya*) is not applicable for *prakṛti, upapada* and *upādhi* but it does obtain for *vikāras* and *āgamas*)."

Surely, those which are just *vikāras* (substitutes) and *āgamas* of the *prakṛti,* though entering into the *prakṛti* will not connect with a technical name like the *prakṛti.* However, those which are (substitutes and augments) of a *pratyaya* they are in fact denoted by that word mentioned (c.f. *Pari. 89*).

तन्मध्यपतितस्तद्ग्रहणेन गृह्यते (*Pari. 89*)

(Any term) that may be employed (in grammar) denotes (not merely what is actually denoted by it but denotes also whatever word form may result when) something (is) inserted in that (which is actually denoted by it).

Thus there is the undesired possibility that this is not so. This is not so. Even when there is the 'nature of connection with that' for *Prakṛti vikāras* and *āgamas,* because of its nature as prompting agent and being the principal or chief thing, that alone would have the technical name. Even when it is established there is 'the nature of being a part of that' for those connected with *pratyaya* there would in fact be a separate technical name *pratyaya* because of its possible usefulness.

Pradīpa : 2.12 विकारागमेष्विति।

"In relation to *vikāras* and *āgamas* (also the term *pratyaya* does not apply)."

That which is subsequent is a *pratyaya',* and '*vikāras* and *āgamas* are not subsequent, therefore they will not have the technical term *pratyaya* applicable (to them)'. It should not be explained thus. For the technical name *pratyaya* is not the cause of *paratva* but *paratva* is the cause of the technical name *pratyaya.* And so even in the absence of *paratva* the technical name *pratyaya* is applicable for *śnam bahuc* and *akac.* Therefore, thus it is explained — due to the absence of any purpose, the technical name *pratyaya* is not applicable for *vikāras* and *āgamas*. For so, the effect of the technical name *pratyaya* is the knowledge that iṭ is *para* (subsequent), and that is not possible for them, due to teaching by means of the sixth case 'connection in place of original'/*sthānasambandha* and 'connection as a part of the original'/*avayavasambandha* (respectively). There is absence of initial *udātta* because of the statement 'And there should be *anudātta* for *āgamas*'. The *vikāras* too, which have no vowels do not partake in accent. However, those having vowels, due to being *antaraṅga* (requiring fewer operations) at the time of application, are endowed with the accent of the original/*sthānin*. The technical name *aṅga* too, being a cause of that (*pratyaya*) does not obtain for another. For that is dependent on *paratva* being ordained with *pratyaya*. However, when there is the existence of a purpose, as in the case of *śnam,* even when it has the nature of *āgama* the technical name *pratyaya* applies for the purpose of the technical name being applicable to the letter ś.

Pradīpa: 2.13 परविज्ञानादिति।

". . . because of the understanding *para* (subsequent) the technical name *pratyaya* will not apply."

Fifth case here is in the sense of cause by '*vibhāṣā guṇe 'striyām* (*2.3.25*) (*hetau pañcamī*) "The fifth *vibhakti* acts optionally when the *nāman* expresses an attribute/*guṇa,* being the cause of an action, and not being in the feminine gender". The result/fruit also because of its nature of being prompter is that it is called *hetu* (cause), as similarly 'he dwells (near) because of study' (*adhyayena,* third case).

Hence this is the meaning: When there is the technical name *pratyaya* then the fruit is *paratva* and that is not possible here. Thus because of the absence of a purpose the technical name *pratyaya* will not be applicable.

Pradīpa: 2.14 किं पुनरिति।

"But why is it so?"

The sense is 'let *paratva* in fact be (inapplicable but let) the purpose (be) the technical name *pratyaya.*'

Pradīpa: 2.16 षष्ठीनिर्दिष्टस्येति।

"...because the sixth case indication (is connected with *vikāras* and *āgamas*)."

The meaning is that, because of teaching the previously spoken about connection, by means of the sixth case, due to incompatability, there is absence of *paratva.*

Pradīpa: 2.17 पञ्चमीनिर्दिष्टाच्चेति।

"(*Pratyaya* is ordained) after that which is mentioned in the fifth case."

The meaning is that there is in fact no incompatability because when there is indication in the fifth case there obtains in turn 'for the prior' and 'for the subsequent' but by the *sūtra 'paraśca'* (*3.1.2*) *paratva* is fixed upon.

Pradīpa: 2.18 प्रत्ययेति।

"(The ordaining of) *pratyaya* (is not justified)."

The sense is: When there are indicators in the sixth case.

Pradīpa: 2.19 क्वेति।

"Where?"

In the *sūtras 'gāpoṣṭak'* (*3.2.8*) "The *pratyaya ṭak* acts after the *dhātus gai* (to sing) and *pā* (to drink) when use without a preposition, and when the *karman* (object) is in composition" etc. because of understanding the sixth case in the sense 'connection as immediate succession' the *pratyaya* rule (surely) is possible? Thus is the question.

hanasta ceti (3.1.108) "After the *dhātu han* when in construction with a *sup*/case inflected word as its *upapada* and 1.1.4 when used without a preposition, acts the *pratyaya kyap* in denoting condition and the letter *t* is the *ādeśa* for its final". (Here the *vikāra* is shown in the *sūtra* and not the *pratyaya*).

The meaning is that the *pratyaya* rule is not possible, when there is understanding of a connection between the original and the substitute between the possessor of the augment and the augment, when they are actually heard, because of the usage of a sentence (requiring it) and because of the absence of another sentence.

Pradīpa: 2.23 इह तावदिति।

"Just here (in the rule *'hanasta ca' dhātoḥ* is present by *anuvṛtti*)."

The meaning is that due to the force of the *anuvṛtti* of *prakṛti* and *pratyaya,* even the *pratyaya* will be ordained, as also the *vikāras* and *āgamas.*

Pradīpa: 2.24 यद्येवमिति।

"If that is the case (then the *sūtra* becomes . . .)."

The sense is in the rule ordaining an *ādeśa* for *dhātu han,* it is because of the use of the *vibhakti* (to indicate the *ādeśa*) and because of *'dhātoḥ'* 'after a *dhātu'* not being qualified.

Pradīpa: 3.1 अथवेति।

"Or else (we will here connect *dhātu han* alone here with *dhātu*)."

The *'dhātu'* heard previously by indication (of being *adhikāra* rule) is drawn into *hanti* (*dhātu* to kill), and now by a division of the sentence into two parts, due to proximity, there is connection of *hanti* and the letter *t* possible, and *'dhātu'* distinguishes or defines (the *prakṛti*).

Pradīpa: 3.3 अर्थाश्रयत्वाद्वेति।

"Or else the rule *pratyaya* exists because of a need to resort to meaning."

The meaning is, by resorting to a technical name whose meaning is intelligible in itself, because of ordaining it as being 'meaningful/possessed of meaning', due to the *vikāras* and *āgamas* being meaningless, the technical name *pratyaya* is not applicable.

Pradīpa: 3.4 किं वक्तव्यम्।

"Is this to be stated?"

Having thought thus 'By abandoning the previously accepted meaning with its own form, the technical name words express their own nature as technical names, so *pratyaya* (means) 'the causing to know'/*pratyaya'*. So is this to be stated?

Pradīpa: 3.5 महतीति।

"(*Pratyaya* is made) a great (technical name)."

Due to greatness (of size) of the word *pratyaya* its (etymological) use is inferred. Therefore that which causes to know is *pratyaya.* 'Greatness' (of size of a term) is shown as applicable in another context (where *sarvanāman* 'name of all' is similarly) explained in the *'sarvādīni sarvanāmāni'* (*1.1.27*) *sūtra* and from that in fact is to be ascertained (as valid).

Pradīpa: 3.8 न हि त इति।

"For they (*ka* etc.) do not (cause anything to be known)."

By the methods of 'the same and the different/*anvayavyatireka,* it is ascertained that there is not expressive meaning for the *pratyaya ka* etc. because even in the absence of that (*ka*) etc. there is understanding of the meaning of that *prakṛti* on its own. The sense is there is not even, like *tarap* (comparative *pratyaya*) etc. any illuminating (indirectly or secondarily) of the meaning. Although it is stated (in *Pari. 113*) '*anirdiṣṭārthāḥ pratyayāḥ svārthe*' '*Pratyayas* to which no meaning has been assigned convey the meaning of the bases to which they are added', their meaning is in fact only in the sense of the *prakṛti,* that also is mere fancy/imagination. When there is possession of meaning, the technical name *pratyaya* should be applied. When thus it has been expressed in the absence of that (meaning) it is not possible, there be 'meaningfulness' for *ka* and the rest (simply) from the understanding that they are *svārthe* (conveying the meaning of their own *prakṛti*). (I say mere imagination) because of the difficulty of replying to what has been stated (i.e. of showing it conveys any meaning at all).

Pradīpa: 3.9 प्रत्याय्यत इति।

"(Well then *pratyaya*) is that which is caused to be known."

Due to the figurative use of the nature of that to be named, in the sense of the name, thus it was stated. This is the meaning in that context: That whose meaning is caused to be known by the *prakṛti,* due to its meaning being caused to be known, has applicable the technical name *pratyaya* which is *svārthika,* having its meaning being made known (by the *prakṛti*).

Pradīpa: 3.9 एवमपीति।

"Then also (the term *pratyaya* does not obtain for *san* etc.)"

The sense is: For *san* etc., being ordained in the sense of 'desire' etc. do not have their meaning made known by *prakṛti.* (If it is said) the *san* after *gup* etc. (*3.1.5-6*) has its meaning being made known by *prakṛti* (then we say) here it is intended, the *san* in the sense of desire (*3.1.7*).

Pradīpa: 3.10 एवं तर्हीति।

"Well then (this term is derived with both factors as the means of the *pratyaya*)."

A word which is in fact one, due to being joined to more than one power is placed at the head of a governing *sūtra,* accepted as having two reasons for use as a term. In that context in accord with possibility, by resorting to the reason (applicable), there is occurence of the technical name *pratyaya* for *san* etc. and for *ka* etc.

ण्यन्तस्य निपातनाद् अचि णिलुक्

Due to *nipātana* (being laid down irregularly) there is *luk* elision of the *ṇi* (causative) of that ending in *ṇi* when *ac* (*pratyaya*) follows.

Pradīpa: 3.10 एवमपीति।

"Even then (how is it . . . the letter *a* causes meaning to be understood (in the form *trāpuṣam* and *jātuṣam*) not the *āgama ṣ*) ?"

This statement is made to deny meaningfulness for the *āgama.*

Pradīpa: 3.12 अन्यत्रापि।

"Elsewhere also (... we know that letter *a* causes that meaning to be understood)."

There is understanding of *pratyaya* as meaningful because of its use even without the *āgama.* The meaning is: However, due to the *āgama* not being used without the *pratyaya,* by the method of 'the same and the different' (it is ascertained that the *āgama* is not meaningful).

NOTES

[1]अधिकारेण, see detailed note page 571.

[2]प्राप्नोति, 'It obtains' (but is not desired). 'It results from a rule'. Always used to indicate obtains or follows from a rule as valid but not desired.

[3]प्रकृति, see full note page 572.

[4]उपपद, see full note page 573.

[5]उपाधि, see full note page 576. Additional note on *3.2.25.*

[6]परत्वम् see 3.1.2.

[7]आद्युदात्तत्वम् see 3.1.3.

[8]अङ्गसंज्ञा, see *1.4.13, 'yasmāt pratyaya-vidhis-tadādi pratyaye 'ṅgam'.*

"After whatsoever (be it *dhātu* or *prātipadika*) *a pratyaya* is enjoined that which begins therewith in the form in which it appears in the presence of the *pratyaya* is called an *aṅga* (uninflected base)."

Thus the presence of a *pratyaya* to be enjoined is the condition for anything receiving the technical name *aṅga*.

[9]अप्रतिषेधः, useless prohibition; unnecessary prohibition.
c.f. *'anarthakaḥ pratiṣedhaḥ apratiṣedhaḥ bhāṣya 1.1.6/1.55.25* etc.

[10]निमित्तस्य। Def. 'formal cause of a grammatical operation; (in Phil.) instrumental or efficient cause (opp. to *upādāna* the operative material cause).

Veds.40 c.f. *'nimittabhāve naimittikasyābhavaḥ' Pari vyādi*

S.D. Joshi 'conditioned form' *P.3.3.139, 5.1.38, 6.1.80, 6.3.39, 7.2.36.*

[11]निमित्तिन्। Def. 'Operated on or influenced by a cause, having a cause or reason'. *T.Prat.* a *pratyaya* or *āgama* (augment) or *ādeśa* (substitute) taking place on account of certain formal causes or *nimittas.*

'conditioned form', c.f. *2.2.1 Vā. 32.* (Only other reference outside this *sūtra*).

[12]अन्यत्रापि चैष न्यायोदृष्टः "This principle is also seen elsewhere."
The only occurence of this whole phrase in the *M.Bh.* but the illustrative example is typical.

[13]निमित्तस्य निमित्तकार्यार्थत्वाद् . . . *Devadatta* is equivalent to the *pratyaya,* that having a cause, the horse and the footstool are equivalent to *prakṛti* etc., the causes which are already known, and serve to make known the yet unknown *Devadatta/pratyaya.*

[14]निर्ज्ञातोऽर्थो निमित्तम्, The thing, the object or meaning which is known as the meaning.

[15]धातूपदेशे = *Dhātu-Pāṭha,* 'original enunciation of *dhātus*'. *'Upadeśa ādyoccāraṇam'* S.K. on *'upadeśe 'janunāsika it'* (*1.3.2*), c.f. *'bhūvādayo dhātavaḥ'* (*1.3.1*)

prātipadikopadeśe = *gaṇa-pāṭha,* c.f. *arthavad-adhāturapratyayaḥ prātipadikam (1.2.45)*

[16] अनिर्ज्ञातोऽर्थो निमित्ती। That meaning or object (which is unknown is that) having a cause or operated on by a cause.

[17]प्रधाने, c.f. *'pradhānāpradhānayoḥ pradhāne kāryasampratyayaḥ' Pari. 97.*
"When of two things one is more important than the other, an operation (which is applicable to both) is understood to have reference only to that which is more important."

[18]कार्यसम्प्रत्ययाद् "Because an operation is understood" . . . or right conception of (the grammatical operation); c.f. *Bhā 1.1.15/71.18 gaunamukhyayormukhye kāryasampratyayaḥ* etc.

[19]हनस्त च (*3.1.108*) see text. त्रपुजतुनोः षुक् *(4.3.138)*
"The *pratyaya aṅ* (by *anuvṛtti* from *4.3.136*) acts with the augment *ṣuk* (augmenting the final of the *aṅga* by *'ādyantau ṭakitau' 1.1.46*) in the sense

of its modification/ *'tasya vikāraḥ' 4.3.134* to give the forms *trāpuṣam* 'made of tin' *Kad.*) *jātuṣam* 'made of or covered with lac or gum' (*Go.Br.3.8.6*).

[20]विकार see detailed note page 576;

[21]आगम see detailed note page 577.

[22]परविज्ञानात् "Because of understanding that (*pratyaya*) is subsequent."
Only occurence of this compound in *M.Bh.*

[23]षष्ठीनिर्दिष्टस्य "Because of the sixth case indication", by *'ṣaṣṭhī sthāneyogā' (1..1.49)*.

"The significance of the sixth case in the *sūtras* is that of the phrase 'in the place of' (when no other special rule qualifies the sense of the sixth case)." *Sthāne* means 'where there is occasion for'. Hence the *vikāra* or *ādeśa* act in place of the original or *sthānin* when there is occasion for such a change; similarly the *āgamas* (augments) augment that in the sixth case.

[24]पंचमीनिर्दिष्टाच्च "After that mentioned or indicated in the fifth case", by *'tasmād-ityuttarasya'* (*1.1.67*).
"When there is indication of a term in the fifth case an operation is (to be understood) in connection with that immediately following (that in the fifth case)."

[25]आचार्यप्रवृत्तिज्ञापयति। The master's (*Pāṇini's*) usage. "The spiritual preceptor or teacher makes known." A designation usually given to *Pāṇini* by *Patañjali* and with this phrase indicates *jñāpaka* (implied rule).

[26]एतिस्तुशास् (*3.1.109*) see text.

[27]अभिसंभन्त्यामः, from *abhi* + *sam* + *bandh*

"We shall (require to) connect with." (Instr. *Pat.*, or Acc.) c.f. *2.3.6* अपवर्गे तृतीया.

[28]अर्थाश्रयत्वाद् वा। "Or else because of resorting to meaning."
Only here but *bhāṣya* uses *'arthāśraya' 1.1.15/71.20* etc.

[29]सम्प्रत्याययति स प्रत्ययः। "What makes known or causes the meaning to be understood, that is *pratyaya*", from *sam* + *prati* + *ṇi* + *iṇ gatau* 'to cause to be meant or understood.'
Contrast *pratyāyyate* '(A *Pratyaya*) is that which is caused to be known'. *Bhā 2.3.9* see *Kaiyaṭa.*

[30]प्रत्याययतीति प्रत्ययः। "A *pratyaya* is that which (leads towards or) causes one to recognise or know."
Caus. (with pass. *pratyāyyate*) to lead towards, i.e. causative of *prati+i* to recognise or acknowledge, convince (anyone of the truth of anything) *Kālid..*

[31]अविकादीनाम् "(The technical name *pratyaya* does not obtain) for *avika* etc.", by *'aveḥ kaḥ'* (*5.4.28*). "The *pratyaya ka* acts after *avi* without changing the sense or in the sense of its own *prakṛti* (base)." *svīyaprakṛtyarthe* = *svārthe*,

aviḥ m.f. a sheep *R.V.9.78.1, avikaḥ* m. a sheep *Pāṇ. 5.4.28,* (*ā*) f. *R.V.1.126.7 A.V.20.129.17*

[32]प्रत्याय्यते। "A (*pratyaya*) is that which is caused to be known", passive of the causative of *prati + i.*
sanādīnām. "(The term *pratyaya* does not obtain) for *san* etc. (because they cause one to recognise or know the meaning **but** are not caused to be known)."
san = dhātoḥ karmaṇaḥ samānakartṛkād-icchāyām vā (3.1.7) "The *pratyaya san* optionally acts in the sense of desire after a *dhātu* expressing the object desired and having the same agent as the one desiring."

It is this desire which *san* causes one to recognise/understand as in *cikīrṣati* 'He desires to make'.
[33]उभयसाधनयोऽयम् कर्तृसाधन: कर्मसाधन:। "This term is effective for both, effective as a means for the agent and effective as a means of action for the *karman* (object; i.e. in the passive sense)", i.e. derived in both senses; the *pratyaya ac* acting after *prati + i* conveys both *kartṛ* and *karman: pratyāyayati* and *pratyāyyate.* In both the cases irregular *ṇi luk* is redundant — see *Kaiyaṭa.*
Kartṛsādhanaḥ, (a *pratyaya*) applied in the sense of *ṇyantasya* the agent of an activity: *kartṛsādhana,* derived in the sense of *kartṛ. Bhā 1.2.64/246.1* etc.
karmasādhanaḥ, n. implement, means, articles essential for performing of any religious act. m.f.n. (a *pratyaya*) prescribed in the sense of an object. Contrasted with *kartṛsādhana* or *bhāvasādhana.*
कर्मसाधन:, e.g. the *pratyaya ki* in the word *vidhi* by *'upasarge ghoḥ kiḥ'* (*3.3.92*) (*bhāve, kartari kārake*) explained as *vidhīyate iti vidhi* (or in the word *bhāva* by *śriṇībhuvo 'nupasarge (3.3.24) (ghañ)* explained as *bhāvyate yaḥ saḥ bhavaḥ*) *1.1.15/144.13* etc.

[34]त्रपुषम्, 1. adj. tin. *P.4.3.138* made of tin, 2. silver *Harc. 160*

जातुषम् made of lac, gum. *P.4.3.138 Go.Bh.3.8.6 M.Bh.1.151.2247.*
[35] 'बिल्वादिभ्योऽण्' (*4.3.136*) "The *pratyaya aṇ* (*a*) acts after *bilva* etc. in the sense of its modification or part/*tasya vikāraḥ,*" (*4.3.134*).
bailvaḥ = yūpaḥ Ait.Br.2.1 T.S.2.1.8.1.

परश्च ॥ 3 । 1 । 2 ॥

Pāṇini 3.1.2: And (*a pratyaya*) is subsequent.

3.15 किमर्थमिदमुच्यते। परो यथा स्यात्पूर्वो मा भूदिति। नैतदस्ति प्रयोजनम्। यमिच्छति पूर्वमाह तम्। विभाषा सुपो बहुच्पुरस्तात्तु (5.3.68)[1] इति। मध्ये तर्हि मा भूदिति। मध्येऽपि यमिच्छत्याह तम्। अव्ययसर्वनाम्नामकच्प्राक् टे:[2] (5.3.71)

इति। य इदानीमतोऽन्यः प्रत्ययः शेषः सोऽन्तरेण वचनं पर एव भविष्यतीति[3]
नार्थः परवचनेन।। एवमपि येषामेव प्रत्ययानां देशो नियम्यते त एव नियतदेशाः
3.20 स्युर्य इदानीमनियतदेशः स कदाचित्पूर्वः कदाचित्परः कदाचिन्मध्ये स्यात्।
तद्यथा। मातुर्वत्सः कदाचिदग्रतः कदाचित्पृष्ठतः कदाचित्पार्श्वतो भवति। पर एव
यथा स्यादित्येवमर्थं परवचनम्।।

Bhāṣya: Why is this said? So that (a *pratyaya*) should follow and not be prior. That is not the purpose. That which he desires to be 'prior' he states that as such *'vibhāṣā sup bahuc purastāt tu'* (*5.3.68*) "To a declined noun is optionally (rarely) added the *pratyaya 'bahuc'* (*bahu*) but it stands before (when the sense is slight incompleteness)".

Then (this rule is stated) so that it should not be in the middle. Also that which he desires (to be) in the middle that he states as such. *avyaya sarvanāmnām akac prākṭeḥ* (*5.3.71*) "The *pratyaya akac* is added to an indeclinable and to a pronomial, before the last vowel of those words; (in the sense of *Prāgivīya pratyayas 5.3.27-95*)". Now, any other *pratyaya* than that (i.e.) the remainder will be applicable only as following, without the rule (*paraśca*). (So) there is no purpose in the statement *para.*

Even if it is so for those *pratyayas* whose place is fixed (by rule) that they alone would have fixed positions that which has no fixed place, sometimes is prior, sometimes follows, sometimes would be in the middle. That is like a calf, sometimes in front of his mother, sometimes behind and sometimes at her side. In fact the reason for the *para* (subsequent) rule is so that (the *pratyaya*) should be **only** subsequent.

3.23 परवचनमनर्थकं पञ्चमीनिर्दिष्टाद्धि परस्य ।। 1 ।।

Vārttika 1: The statement of *para* (subsequent) is pointless, because the operation in connection with *para* is indicated by the fifth case.

3.24 परग्रहणमनर्थकम्। किं कारणम्। पञ्चमीनिर्दिष्टाद्धि परस्य ।। 1 ।। कार्यमुच्यते[4]।
तद्यथा। द्व्यन्तरुपसर्गेभ्योऽप ईत्[5] (6.3.97) इति। विषम उपन्यासः[6]। सतस्तत्र
परस्य कार्यमुच्यत इहेदानां कस्य सतः परस्य कार्यं भवितुमर्हति। इहापि सत
एव। कथम्। परत्वं स्वाभाकिम्[7]। अथ वाचनिके परत्वे सत्यर्थः स्यात्। परग्रगणेन।
वाचनिके[8] च नार्थः। एतद्धि तत्परस्य कार्यं यदसौ परःस्यात्।
4.5 अथवा यदस्य परस्य सतः संज्ञा स्यात्।।
4.6 यत्र तर्हि पञ्चमी नास्ति तदर्थमयं योगो वक्तव्यः। क्व च पञ्चमी नास्ति। यत्र
विकारागमाः शिष्यन्ते। क्व च विकारागमाः शिष्यन्ते। हनस्त च
4.8 (3.1.108) त्रपुजतुनोः षुक् (4.3.138) इति।

Bhāṣya: The mention of *'para'* (subsequent) is pointless. What is the reason? Because (the operation for that which follows) is indicated by the fifth case.

As (for example) in the *sūtra dvyantarupasargebhyo'pa īt (6.3.97)*. "Long *ī* is the substitute of *ap* after *dvi, antar* and an *upasarga"*. The statement is inaccurate. There (in that *sūtra*) the operation is taught (i.e. laid down) with reference to an existing (word) which follows. But here now (when enjoining all *pratyayas* as subsequent/*para*) in place of what following existing element is it possible for there to be an operation? Here too, only of one existing. How? Being subsequent is natural (for a *pratyaya*). Now when subsequent nature is expressly stated, let the meaning be applicable by means of a specific mention of the word *para* (subsequent). But there is no purpose (in reading *paraśca 3.1.2*) if the (subsequent nature of a *pratyaya*) has to be expressly stated. This (statement) 'That it should follow' is in fact the operation for that which follows. Or else that 'the technical name *pratyaya* should be (given to that) which follows' (is the operation for that which follows).

Then this rule should be stated for such cases where the fifth case does not occur, and where does not the fifth case occur? Where *vikāras* (substitutes) and *āgamas* (augments) are taught. And where are *vikāras* and *āgamas* taught? In *hanasta ca* (*3.1.108*) and *trapu jatuṇoḥ ṣuk (4.3.138)*.

4.9 विकारागमेषु चोक्तम् ॥ 2 ॥

Vārttika 2: And it was stated 'in connection with *vikāras* and *āgamas*'.

4.10 किमुक्तम्। प्रत्ययविधानानुपपत्तिस्तु’ तस्मात्तत्र पञ्चमीनिर्देशात्सिद्धमिति॥

Bhāṣya: What was stated? However the ordaining of (the technical name) *pratyaya* is not justified in connection with *vikāra* and *āgamas*. Therefore (the technical name *pratyaya*) is established as valid by mention in the fifth case *(3.1.1 Vā. 6-7)*.

4.11 अत्यन्तापरदृष्टानाम्[10] वा परभूतलोपार्थम् ॥ 3 ॥

Vārttika 3: Or (*para* rule) is for the purpose of the elision of those subsequent (*pratyayas*) which are completely unseen as 'subsequent'.

4.11 अत्यन्तापरदृष्टानाम् तर्हि परभूतलोपार्थं परग्रहणं कर्तव्यम्। य एतेऽत्यन्तापरदृष्टाः
क्विबादयो लुप्यन्ते[11] तेषां परभूतानां लोपो यथा स्यादपरभूतानां मा भूत्। किं
पुनरत्यन्तापरदृष्टानां परभूतलोपवचने प्रयोजनम्। किति णितीति कार्याणि[12]
4.15 यथा स्युरिति। एतदपि नास्ति प्रयोजनम्। आचार्यप्रवृत्तिर्ज्ञापयत्यत्यन्ता- परदृष्टापरभूता
लुप्यन्त इति यदयं तेषु कादीननुबन्धानासजति। कथं कृत्वा ज्ञापकम्[13]।
अनुबन्धासञ्जन एतत्प्रयोजनं किति णितीति कार्याणि यथा स्युरिति। यदि चात्रा-

4.18 त्यन्तापरदृष्टाः परभूता लुप्यन्ते ततोऽनुबन्धासञ्जन मर्थवद्भवति।

Bhāṣya: The mention of *para* should be made so that the elision (will be prescribed) for those *pratyayas* which become subsequent (because of the specific mention) and which are completely unseen as subsequent.

These *kvip* and the rest which are completely unseen are elided; (the mention of *para*) is so that they should be elided as subsequent and not as non-subsequent. But what is the purpose of the statement 'elision/ *lopa* for these made subsequent'? What are completely unseen as subsequent? (The purpose is) that the operations (which take place) when (*pratyayas* possessed of) *it k* and *it ṅ* follow be (applicable). This is also not a purpose. The master's usage makes it known that those which are completely unseen, which have become subsequent, are elided since to those he attaches the indicatory letters *'k'* and the rest. How is this indicated as an implied rule/ *jñāpaka?* This is the purpose when indicatory letters are attached, namely that the operations, when *it k* or *it ṅ* follows, be applicable. And if here those which are completely unseen are elided as existing subsequent, then the attaching of indicatory letters becomes meaningful.

4.19 प्रयोगनियमार्थं[14] वा ॥ 4 ॥

Vārttika 4: Or the (*para* rule) is for the purpose of a general rule restricting the use (of the term *pratyaya*).

4.20 प्रयोगनियमार्थं तर्हि परग्रहणं कर्तव्यम्। परभूतानां प्रयोगो यथा स्यादपरभूतानां मा
भूदिति। अस्ति पुनः किंचिदनिष्टं दृश्यते यदर्थो नियमः स्यात्।अस्ती-
4.22 त्याह।

Bhāṣya: Then the mention of *para* should be made for the purpose of a general rule restricting use (of the term *pratyaya*), so that the use of the *pratyayas* should be subsequent and not non-subsequent. But is there something undesired seen for which purpose there would be a restriction? There is, he states:

4.23 प्रकृतिरर्थाभिधाने प्रत्ययादर्शनात् ॥ 5 ॥

Vārttika 5: (The restriction with reference to use should be made) because (of example of) *pratyaya* not being seen when the meaning of the base (*prakṛti*) is expressed (by the *prakṛti* itself).

4.24 प्रकृतिर्थाभिधानेऽप्रत्ययिका[15] दृश्यते। क्व स देवदत्तः क्व स यज्ञदत्तो बभ्रु-[16]
र्मण्डुर्लमक[17]। बाभ्रव्यो माण्डव्यो लामकायन इति प्रयोक्तव्ये बभ्रुर्मण्डुर्लमक
4.26 इति प्रयुज्यते॥

Bhāṣya: The base is seen expressing a meaning (in the language) without a *pratyaya* (e.g.) Where is that (son of) *Devadatta?* Where that (son of) *Yajñadatta?* (Where is) *Babhrur* (*gotra* descendant of *Babhrur*)? (Where is) *Maṇḍur* (*gotra* descendant of *Maṇḍu*)? Or (where is) *Lamaka* (*gotra* descendant of *Lamaka*)? When (the forms) *Bābhravyaḥ* (*yañ*), *Māṇḍavyaḥ* (*yañ*), and *Lāmakāyanaḥ* (*phak*) should be used, *Babhrur, Maṇḍur* and *Lamakaḥ* are (in fact) used.

5.1 द्वयसजादीनां च केवलदृष्टत्वात् ॥ 6 ॥

Vārttika 6: And because *dvayasac* and the rest are seen (to be used) alone.

5.2 द्वयसजादीनां[18] च केवलानां प्रयोगो दृश्यते। किमस्य द्वयसम् किमस्य मात्रम्[19] काद्य तिथीति[20]। द्वयसादयो वै वृत्तिजसदृशा अवृत्तिजा यथा बहुस्तथा[21] ॥

Bhāṣya: And the usage is seen (to occur in the language) of *dvayasac* and the rest alone (without *prakṛti*) (e.g.) *kimasya dvayasam.* What is its *dvayasa*/ measure? *kimasya mātram.* What is its *mātra*/measure? *kādya tithi.* Which number day is it today? Verily *dvayasa* and the rest are like those produced from a compounded form (complex formation) (though they are) not produced from a compounded form as *bahu* (can optionally be).

5.4 वावचने चानुत्पत्यर्थम् ॥ 7 ॥

Vārttika 7: And when there is the expression by the word *vā* 'optionally' (it is) for the purpose of non-production (of the *san* etc.).

5.5 वावचने चानुत्पत्यर्थं[22] परग्रहणं कर्तव्यम्। वावचनेनानुत्पत्तिरपि यथा स्यात्। अथ क्रियमाणेऽपि वै परग्रहणे कथमिव वावचनेनानुत्पत्तिर्लभ्या। क्रियमाणे पर-ग्रहणे वावचनेन वा पर इत्येतदभिसंबध्यते। अक्रियमाणे पुनः परग्रहणे वावचनेन

5.8 किमन्यच्छक्यमभिसंबन्द्धुमन्यदतः संज्ञायाः। न च संज्ञाया भावाभावाविष्येते॥

Bhāṣya: Moreover the mention of *para* should be made when the expression *vā* is used for the sake of non-production (of *san* etc.) *para* should be mentioned so that by reason of the mention of *vā* the non-production will also be there.

Now, even when the mention of *para* is being made, how is it that by reason of the expression *vā* non-production (of the rule for *san* etc.) is obtained? When the mention of *para* is being made, the expression *vā para* is connected.

But when the mention of *para* is not being made what else is it possible to connect by reason of the expression *vā* other than the technical name (*pratyaya*)? And it is not desired that there be existence or non-existence of a technical name. (i.e. optionality)

5.9 वावचने चोक्तम् ॥ 8 ॥

Vārttika 8: And it was stated where there is the expression of *vā* (option).

5.10 किमुक्तम्। वावचनानर्थक्यं च तत्र नित्यत्वात्सन[23] इति॥
प्रयोगनियमार्थमेव तर्हि परग्रहणं कर्तव्यम्। अथैतस्मिन्प्रयोगनियमार्थे सति
किमयं प्रत्ययनियमः। प्रकृतिपर एवं प्रत्ययः प्रयोक्तव्योऽप्रकृतिपरो नेति।
आहोस्वित्प्रकृतिनियमः। प्रत्ययपरैव प्रकृतिः प्रयोक्तव्याऽप्रत्ययपरा नेति। कश्चात्र
5.14 विशेषः।

Bhāṣya: What was said? "And the word *vā* has no purpose there because of *san* being always applicable".

Then the mention of *para* should be made only for the purpose of restricting usage. But when this mention of *para* exists for the purpose of restricting usage is this a restriction on *pratyaya*? (Does it mean) that a *pratyaya* is to be used only following a *prakṛti* and not (to be used if) not following a *prakṛti*? Or else is it a restriction on *prakṛti* ? Does it mean that a *prakṛti* is to be employed only when a *pratyaya* is following and not without a *pratyaya* following? What is the difference here?

5.15 तत्र प्रत्ययनियमे प्रकृतिनियमाभावः ॥ 9 ॥

Vārttika 9: When there is restriction on the *pratyaya* there is absence of restriction on the *prakṛti.*

5.16 यत्र प्रत्ययनियमे सति प्रकृतेर्नियमो न प्राप्नोति। अप्रत्ययिकायाः प्रकृतेः
प्रयोगः प्राप्नोति। क्व स देवदत्तः क्व स यज्ञदत्तो बभ्रुर्मण्डुर्लमक इति॥ अस्तु
5.18 तर्हि प्रकृतिनियमः।

Bhāṣya: When there is restriction on the *pratyaya* there does not obtain a restriction of the *prakṛti.* The usage obtains of the *prakṛti* without a *pratyaya,* (e.g.) Where is that *Devadatta* ? Where is that *Yajñadatta* ? *Babhru, Maṇḍu,* and *Lamaka* ? Let there be then a restriction on the *prakṛti.*

5.19 प्रकृतिनियमे प्रत्ययानियमः ॥ 10 ॥

Vārttika 10: When there is the restriction on the *prakṛti* there is no restriction on the *pratyaya.*

5.20 प्रकृतिनियमे सति प्रत्ययस्य नियमो न प्राप्नोति। किमस्य द्वयसम् किमस्य
मात्रम् काध्य तिथीति। अप्रकृतिकस्य प्रत्ययस्य प्रयोगः प्राप्नोति॥

Bhāṣya: When there is restriction on the *prakṛti* restriction of the *pratyaya* does not obtain (e.g.) What is its height? What its measure? and What is the *tithi*/lunar day today? The usage obtains of a *pratyaya* without its *prakṛti.*

5.22 सिद्धं तूभयनियमात् ॥ 11 ॥

Vārttika 11: But it is established from both restrictions.

5.23 सिद्धमेतत्। कथम्। उभयनियमात्। उभयनियमोऽयम्। प्रकृतिपर एव प्रत्ययः प्रयोक्तव्यः प्रत्ययपरैव च प्रकृतिरिति॥ किं वक्तव्यमेतत्। न हि। कथमनुच्यमानं गंस्यते। परग्रहणसामर्थ्यात्[24]। अन्तरेणापि परग्रहणं स्यादयं परः।
6.2 पर एव यथा स्यादित्येवमर्थं परग्रहणम् ॥

Bhāṣya: But it is established from both restrictions. This is established. How? Because of the restriction of both. This is a restriction on both "a *pratyaya* is to be used only following a *prakṛti* and a *prakṛti* (is to be used) only having a *pratyaya* following".

Should this be stated? Not at all. How will this be understood without being expressed? By the force of the mention of *para.* Even without the force of specific mention of *para* this (*pratyaya*) will be subsequent. The mention of *para* is for the sake of conveying that (the *pratyaya*) will be *para,* i.e. 'subsequent' only.

Pradīpa

Pradīpa: 3.15 परश्च। किमर्थमिति।

"Why is this said?"

When there is indication in the fifth case by the act of supplying the (implied) word *para,* (simply) due to the ordaining of the fifth case, *paratva* is established as valid. The sense is: even when there is indication in the sixth case (this is so as) in the case of *sūtras* like *'gāpoṣṭak'* (3.2.8), due to an understanding of the sixth case in the sense of 'connection as immediate succession'.

Pradīpa: 3.15 पर इति।

"(So that a *pratyaya* should) follow (and not be prior)."

Even though supplying (an implied) word *'para',* though ordaining the fifth case (there the sense is *paratva*), there would still also be the (alternative) *pūrvatva* 'being prior'. The *para* rule is for the purpose of a restriction (to the subsequent only). So also due to the existence of 'immediate succession' even in relation to that 'being prior', when there is indication in the sixth case (of that), the (*para* rule) is for the purpose of restricting the (sense of sixth case to subsequent only).

Pradīpa: 3.16 यम् इच्छति।

"That which he desires (to be subsequent he states as such)."

'The *pratyaya bahuc* alone is applicable before, and no other *pratyaya*'; thus because of the restriction of prior position in relation to *bahuc,* the meaning is that a *pratyaya* will only be applicable subsequent (to the *prakṛti*).

Pradīpa : 3.16 मध्ये तर्हीति।

"Then (so that it should not be) in the middle."

The sense is that even with the supplying of the (implied) word *madhya,* there would be ordaining of sixth case.

Pradīpa: 3.17 मध्येऽपीति।

"Also (that which he desires to be) in the middle (he states as such)."

Due to the ordaining of sixth case with the supplying of (an implied) *madhya* word by the *sūtra 'avyayasarvanāmnām akac prāk-ṭeḥ'* (*5.3.71*), *akac* is in fact established as before the last vowel/ *ṭi* and this is for the purpose of a restriction, namely *'Akac* only is applicable in the middle of the *prakṛti* and no other *pratyaya'*. And by the mention of 'only in the middle' the restriction is understood. However, *akac* alone before the *ṭi* portion (is not thus specified) so (that is achieved) by the resort to the qualification 'in the middle'. Otherwise without *madhya,* there would be another *pratyaya* (possible). However, when there is the qualification *madhye* (that which is equally 'in the middle'), by resorting to that, when it is known there is a restriction, there is no fault.

Pradīpa: 3.19 एवमपीति।

"So also (those *pratyayas* whose place is fixed by rule, alone would have fixed positions)."

By reason of their fitness to be enjoined, because of pre-eminence, those two in fact are restricted with regard to a particular position—*bahuc* is only before, and *akac* only (in the middle) before the last of the vowels. This is the sense.

Pradīpa: 3.19 देशो नियम्यते।

"Whose place is fixed."

Even when there is a restriction on the *pratyaya,* when there is the possibility of place being unregulated, with the intention in fact of teaching of a particular place, it was stated 'whose place is fixed'.

Pradīpa: 3.21 मर्तुर्वत्स इति।

"(Like) a calf (sometimes in front) of its mother . . . ."

When there is perception of the operation word (*pratyaya*) as for the *prakṛti* by that it is expressed as like the nature of belonging to the mother.

Pradīpa: 3.23 परवचनम् इति।

"Statement of *para* (is pointless because the operation . . . is indicated by the fifth case)."

The sense is, because of the restriction being established by this *sūtra* in fact '*tasmād-ityuttarasya*' (*1.1.67*) 'When there is indication in the fifth case, an operation takes place for that immediately after that in the fifth case'.

Pradīpa: 4.2 सतस्तत्रेति।

"There (in that *sūtra*) the operation is said to be in place of an existing (word which follows)."

Where it is indicated by that possessing an operation has the purpose of ordaining another existent operation, there the *paribhāṣā* '*tasmād* . . .' is applicable for the purpose of a restriction.

Pradīpa: 4.2 कस्य सत इति।

"In place of what following existing element?"

The sense is 'what is not in fact *san*' is caused to exist by *san* etc.

Pradīpa: 4.2 इहापीति—

"Here too (only for one existing)."

Words are eternal, remaining in usage. The meaning is, in that context the mere correctness is produced for *san* etc. following *gup* etc. in fact quite naturally first case would have as its purpose mere indication. At a subsequent time sixth case is put in place of it. And that which is stated elsewhere—'And in a *pratyaya* rule there is not putting of another case in place of the fifth case'—whether that is established as valid in this *sūtra,* has to be looked at.

Pradīpa: 4.5 अथवेति।

"Or else (that the technical name *pratyaya* should be given to that which follows, for the operation of that which follows)."

This is the meaning: Let the arising of *san* etc. have an unrestricted place (of origin). However, afterwards, for that actually existing subsequently, that which is ordained as a *Śāstrika* operation for the technical name of the *pratyayas kṛt kṛtya* etc., is not for (any) other place (than subsequent). The meaning is that as the *Śāstrika* operation is that of 'pointing out' or 'exemplification' due to the correctness of that very place, the usage will be applicable.

Pradīpa: 4.9 विकारागमेष्विति।

"(And it was stated) in connection with *vikāras* and *āgamas.*"

The meaning is that in fact that is also to be understood here too. Thus in *sūtras* like *'gāpoṣṭak'* (*3.2.8*), it is to be explained that the *pratyaya ṭak* acts/is applicable after the *dhātu, 'dhātoḥ'* (being an *anuvṛtti*) and afterwards *'gāpoḥ'* (as the specific *dhātus* are mentioned) when the object is in composition.

Pradīpa: 4.11 अत्यन्तापरदृष्टानां वेति।

"Or *para* rule is for the purpose of the elision of those subsequent *pratyayas* which are completely unseen as subsequent."

In the sense then of the word *vā* (optionally). Nowhere seen by the principal means of valid knowledge, perception, are those which (are called) *kvip* etc. Due to the absence of existence, whether in the seeing of an invariable word or in seeing an operation for them, and due to the absence of abiding by *'tasmādityuttarasya'* (*1.1.67*), *lopa* would have an unregulated place. This rule is for the purpose of *lopa* being (only) subsequent. The understanding is arisen, 'For when this is so *kvip* etc. being subsequent are elided'. In that context the sense is that, when *agnicit* etc. (manifest as words) the augment *tuk* etc. is established as valid having resort to the *pratyayas* as being subsequent, (*k* of *tuk* showing the augment is for the first of what follows by *'ādyantau ṭakitau' 1.1.46*) but *lopa* of *kvip* etc., being prior (would) not (achieve the desired form).

Surely when there is perception of an operation, the action is for that which follows. Due to it being explained thus *kvip* etc. will be applicable as being subsequent (only). This is not so. For there is no notion of action/becoming in them, due to the coming forth of the idea of non-becoming with the ordaining of *lopa*. For becoming is the obtaining of one's own form, and they never obtain their own form due to being like the horns of a hare. Due to that very fact it was stated, 'Of those subsequent *pratyayas* which are completely unseen as subsequent'. Only the mere operation is ordained for them by the rule of *lopa*-elision of the *pratyaya* even when they are totally non-existent.

Pradīpa: 4.16 यदयमिति।

". . . since (to those he attaches *k* etc.)."

If those 'become prior', were elided the attachment of the indicatory letters would be pointless, due to all the operations connected with the indicatory letters being based on *pratyayas,* 'becoming subsequent'. Surely, even when the nature of the place is not regulated, when *lopa* has become subsequent, then due to the attached indicatory letter having scope (elsewhere), some say, 'How is it there is a sign (attached) ?' This is not proper. Then in the alternative view, it would be accepted that the attachment of the *anubandha* would be pointless. And in the *sūtras* like *'spṛśo'nudake kvin (3.2.58)* ('The *pratyaya kvin* acts after the *dhātu spṛś* (to touch) when it is in composition with a *sup*/case inflected word other than *udaka*') the fifth case is heard once. Is that applicable with the word *pūrva* (prior) supplied or with the word *para* (subsequent) supplied? Thus is doubt, when there exists the fifth case with the word *pūrva* supplied, the attachment of the *anubandha* is pointless. Thus the knowers of the *bhāṣya* say 'How when there is *lopa* of that become subsequent, could there (possibly) not be a sign for the attachment of an *anubandha* ?'

Pradīpa: 4.19 प्रयोगनियमर्थं वेति।

"Or the *para* rule is for the purpose of a general rule restricting the use of the term *pratyaya.*"

The previous purpose established, the *Vārttikakāra* recites the word *vā* for the purpose of option. However, the *Bhāṣyakāra* by implication rejecting the previous purpose (says) 'then' the meaning is explained.

Pradīpa: 4.24 क्व स देवदत्त इति।

"Where is that (son of) *Devadatta* ?"

Devadatta etc. are seen occurring in the sense of descendants and by the (following) restriction is taught their irregular nature. 'The *prakṛti* is not to be used alone and the *pratyaya* is not to be used alone. Surely due to the connection *'so'yam'* (He is that) metaphorically there is no difference because of (such) usage in indicating descendants. How is there a wrong form? This is not so. Even for *bhṛtya* (servant) etc., due to seeing the superimposition and non-difference as a cause of companionship or association etc. the meaning of descendant would not be understood by such restrictions. That was stated by *Bhartṛhari*:

सोऽयमित्यभिसम्बन्धात् तद्धितेन विना यदि। *V.I. Pratyayana*

बभ्व्रादयः प्रयुज्येरन् नाऽपत्येनियमो भवेदिति।। *3-14-84 (2) Vā. Pad.*

"If it is said that, because of the relation of identity, words like *babhru* would be considered without *'taddhita pratyaya'* then elision should be considered as meant for restriction to progeny."

(The teaching of the elision of *apatya taddhita pratyaya yañ* and *añ* by *'yañañośca' (2.4.64)* in the plural, when expressive of descendants in *gargāḥ* etc. may be so that the meaning of progeny may be understood and not some other meaning like disciples. If the meaning of the ancestor and the progeny are identified (as indicated above *'so'yam-ityabhisambandhaḥ'* then the word *gārgāḥ* even without the *pratyaya* can denote progeny, but it cannot denote disciples also. In order that it may denote progeny only, the *luk*-elision of the *pratyaya* expressive of it is taught) (c.f. K.A.S. Iyer).

Therefore, without the metaphorical use treating them as 'not different' when it is desired to express 'descendant of' the rule is for the purpose of a restriction 'Do not use *babhru* etc., ending in the singular like *gargāḥ* ending in the plural (with *taddhita pratyaya* elided by *luk*).'

Here, 'Where is that *Devadatta*?' (is read) some say simply *'kva sa iti'* (Where is that . . . ?). As when for *sup*/case endings there is *luk* or *lopa* effected, and the *prakṛti* is seen being used on its own, so *Babhru* etc. are presented in this example.

Pradīpa: 5.2 किमस्य द्वयसमिति।

"What is its *dvayasa* (measure)?"

Here this usage is seen in the sense of 'What is its measure?' In that context like *gāvya* etc., so for the rest by this is taught a wrong form.

Pradīpa: 5.3 काद्य तिथीति।

"What number day is it today?"

The meaning is 'Is today the completing of the number two etc., i.e. the second day (feminine ordinal number)?. And having obtained usage of the word *tithī* in cases like *bahutithī* ('manifold, various') in error they use it alone. However, when *ṅīs* is effected after the word *tithi* then the word *tithī* is in fact the correct form, (meaning lunar day).

Pradīpa: 5.3 द्वयसजादय इति।

"(Verily) *dvayasa* etc. are (like those produced from a compounded form)."

The meaning is, that although not produced from a compound form, in error they are seen being used alone in the world (i.e. in spoken Sanskrit).

Pradīpa: 5.3 यथा बहुरिति।

"As *bahur* (can optionally be produced from a compounded form)."

c.f. *Pramāne dvayasajdaghnañmātracaḥ' (5.2.37)*

"The *pratyayas dvayasac, daghnac* and *mātrac* act in denoting 'that whereof this is the lineal measure' after a word in the first case in construction."

'Bahupūgagaṇasaṅghasya tithuk '(5.2.52)

"When *ḍaṭ pratyaya* follows, *tithuk* is the *āgama* of the words *bahu, pūga, gaṇa* and *saṅgha."*

'Vibhāṣā supo bahuc purastāt-tu' (5.3.68)

"Optionally for a declined noun/*supaḥ* there may be added the *pratyaya bahuc* (*bahu*) but it stands before when the sense is slight incompleteness."

That *bahuc pratyaya* which acts in the sense of slight incompleteness has, like it, the word *bahu* expressing largeness of number; as it is used in the world so *dvayasac* etc. also, some explain. Others however, say that word *bahu* only, which is used in the world in the sense of slight incompleteness, is accepted as an example, when there is a wrong form accepted for *dvayasac* etc.

Pradīpa: 5.4 वावचने चेति।

"And when there is expression of the word *vā* ('optionally') (it is for non-production of *san* etc.)."

When *paratva* is established for a *pratyaya* by the *sūtra 'tasmād-ityuttarasya' (1.1.67)* in fact, by means of the word *vā* ('optionally') the rule *para* teaches in the alternative the non-arising of the *pratyaya*. In one alternative *san* has *paratva* expressed by implication as 'Optionally *san* acts after . . .'. However, in the (other) alternative the meaning is that it does not in fact arise. It is not however, the *paratva* which is optional as 'In the alternative it acts before'. Due to the invariable nature of *paratva* in usage or because of the invariable nature of *vā* due to the *sūtra 'tasmād-iti' (1.1.67)*.

Pradīpa: 5.7 अक्रियमाण इति।

"When the (mention of *para*) is not being made (how is non-production by the expression *vā*)?"

Due to the technical name *pratyaya* being present in every *sūtra,* there would be option for that alone. However, when this *para* governing rule is effected, there is established in every *sūtra 'paro vā bhavati'* applicable subsequently optionally. In one alternative *paratva* is understood, in the other alternative it is not in fact applicable. Thus the meaning turns out well.

Pradīpa: 5.10 नित्यत्वात्सन इति।

"(*Vā.* has no purpose) because *san* being *nitya* (invariably applicable)."

In the compounding alternative, *san* is invariably desired and in the non-compounding alternative as *'kartum-icchati'* ('He desires to make'), the arising of *san* does not in fact obtain. Thus when the expression *vā* has been rejected, this is a restriction of usage for us.

When *paratva* is established as valid, because of the *sūtra 'tasmād-iti'*, due to the force (of its being stated), a restriction is obtained both ways. "So that a *pratyaya* should always be subsequent, and should never not be used after."

Notes

[1]विभाषा सुपो बहुच् पुरस्तात् *(5.3.68)* This is the only exception to the general rule that a *pratyaya* acts after a word. The *pratyaya bahuc* is added before the word (by *'citaḥ' 6.1.163 c* indicates *udātta* on the first vowel), e.g. *bahupatuḥ* 'a many skilled person'.

[2]अव्ययसर्वनाम्नामकच्प्राक्टे: *(5.3.71) Akac pratyaya* (*c* for *udātta,* as above, on final) bars *ka* (from *'prāg-ivāt-kaḥ' 5.3.70) 'ceḥ.'* (before the last of the vowels) by *'aco'ntyādi ṭi' 1.1.64.*

[3]सोऽन्तरेण वचनं पर एव भविष्यति The (remainder) will be applicable only as following without the rule (*paraśca*). By the law of *'śeṣa' pratyaya* will be *para.*

The final answer given by *Patañjali* on this matter is that the *śeṣa* rule is not applicable here (i.e. *'tasmād-ityuttarasya' 1.1.67*). In the remaining cases *pratyaya* may come at the beginning, middle or end. Thus *paraśca* is **not** a *parisaṅkhyā* rather than a *niyama.*

[4]परस्य कार्यमुच्यते। c.f. *'tasmād-ityuttarasya' 1.1.67 (nirdiṣṭe).* (The general *paribhāṣā sūtra)* 'By the indication in the fifth case it is to be known that an operation takes place for that immediately following that in the fifth case'. Thus by *'dhātoḥ' (3.1.91)* and *'ṅyāpprātipadikāt'* (*4.1.1*) all *pratyayas* act after a *dhātu,* a *prātipadika* or a feminine ending in *ī* or *ā.*

[5]द्व्यन्तरुपसर्गेभ्योऽप ईत् *(6.3.97)* By *'ādeḥ parasya'* (*1.1.54*) *ī* replaces only the first letter of *ap,* namely *a.* Thus *dvīpaḥ* (an island), *antarīpaḥ* (an island), *nīpam* (situated low or deep), *vīpam* (destitute of water), *samīpam* (near). *The final pratyaya* by *'ṛk-pūrabdhūḥpathāmānakṣe' (5.4.74).*

[6]विषम उपन्यास:। Literally uneven putting down or juxtaposition, irregular, inaccurate proposition or statement; of frequent occurrence in the *M.Bh.*. Here the statement is said to be inaccurate or defective because in general a *pratyaya* does not replace that which follows that element in the fifth case. This example only in fact relates to the *ādeśa* (substitute) *ī* acting in place of the *sthānin* (original) *a.* However, *san* etc. act after a *dhātu* without replacing anything subsequent, for that does not exist.

Pra. "Yatra vidyamānam-eva kāryāntaravidhānārtham kāryatvena nirdiśyate tatra tasmāditi — paribhāṣā niyamārtham-avatiṣṭhate. Atra tu sanādayo 'pūrvā evotpadyanta iti na tasyāḥ paribhāṣāḥ pravṛttir-iti bhāvaḥ' see full translation of *Kaiyaṭa* given in the notes *(page 85 Pra. 4.2)* for further discussion.

[7]परत्वं स्वाभाविकम् "Being subsequent is **natural** (for a *pratyaya*)", "unartificial, inherent; used in the capacity of denotation which words naturally possess." c.f. *'abhidānam punaḥ svābhāvikam' 1.1.64 Vā. 36.*

[8]वाचनिके "When founded on express statement", "expressly cited by a *vacana* or statement of the *munitraya* (by *sūtra, vārttika* or *bhāṣya*) as contrasted with what naturally occurs or is inferred from their statements."

c.f. *'nedam vācanikam-āliṅgatā asaṅkhyatā (avyayānām). svābhāvikametat. 1.1. 39 Vā. 5 Bhā.*

[9]प्रत्ययविधानानुपपत्तिस्तु। [*3.1.1 Vā. 6*]. "However the ordaining of (the technical name) *pratyaya* is not justified . . .". *'Tasmāt-tatra pañcamīnirdeśāt-siddham' 3.1.1 Vā. 7.* "Therefore *pratyaya* is established as valid by mention in the fifth case."

[10]अत्यन्तापरदृष्टानाम्। "(For the sake) of those (*lopa, ślu, lup* and *luk pratyayas* like *kvip* etc.) which are completely unseen as subsequent." c.f. *'kriyā nāmeyam-atyantāparadṛṣṭa', P.1.3.1/254.15 Bhā., P.3.2.102/114.10 Bhā., P.3.2.115/ 120.9 Bhā.*

[11]क्विबादयो लुप्यन्ते। *"Kvip* etc. (completely unseen) are elided." c.f. *'sat-sū-dviṣa-druha-duha-yuja-vida-bhida-cchida-ji-nī-rājām-upa-sarge'pi kvip' 3.2.61 (supi).* "The *pratyaya kvip* acts after the following *dhātus sad* etc. when in composition with a *sup*/case *pratyaya* even though it may be an *upasarga.*"

e.g. *śuciṣad,* "Dwelling in purity or heaven", *Kaṭhopaniṣad 2.2.2.*

This *pratyaya kvip* is totally elided = zero: *k* by *laśakvataddhite 1.3.8; v* by *verapṛktasya 6.1.67; i* by *upadeśe'janunāsika it 1.3.2; p* by *halantyam 1.3.3, tasya lopaḥ 1.3.9.* Other zero *pratyayas: vic, vit, ṇvi, ṇvin, kvin, cvi.*

[12]क्ङिति ञ्णितीति कार्याणि। "(So that) the operations (which take place when *pratyayas* possessed of) indicatory *k* or *ṇ* follow (should be applicable; *'kit'* having as *it*/indicatory letter/*anubandha,* the mute letter *k*)."

Applied to *pratyayas* by *Pāṇini* for preventing *guṇa* and *vṛddhi ādeśa* for the preceding *ik* (*i u ṛ ḷ*) vowel. c.f. *'kṅiti ca'* (*1.1.5*) e.g. *i* + *k-ta* = *ita* not *eta; ṇit* 'having an indicatory letter *ṇ*, A *pratyaya* with a mute consonant *ṇ*, to signify the substitution of *vṛddhi* for the preceding vowel by *'aco ñ-ṇ-iti' 7.2.115,* e.g. *iyāya* (*ṇal*), *kāraḥ* (*ghañ*); or for the penultimate *a* by *'ata upadhyāyaḥ' 7.2.116,* e.g. *pāci* (*ṇi*); or for the first vowel of the word, if it is a *taddhita* formation by *'taddhitesvacāmādeḥ'* 7.1.117, *e.g. aupagavaḥ (aṇ).*

[13]कथं कृत्वा ज्ञापकम्। "How is this indicated as an implied rule/*jñāpaka*?"

m.f.n. causing to know, teaching, informing, suggesting, (indirect or implicit revealer).

n. an expression or rule giving particular information (as a rule of *Pāṇini* implying some other grammatical law than that resulting from the mere words of the rule itself).

The *paribhāṣās* or rules of interpretation are mostly derived by indication or implication/*jñāpakasiddhi* from a word or words in a *sūtra.* These words which are apparently *vyartha* (without purpose) and which are shown as *sārthaka* (with purpose), after the particular *jñāpaka* indication is drawn from them. The term in this special sense is first used by *Vyādi* in *Paribhāṣa-sūcana.* The *jñāpaka* is said by *Nāgeśa* to have four parts:

(1) *vaiyarthya,* 'uselessness', (2) *jñāpana,* 'making known or suggesting its purpose', or (3) *svasmiñcaritārthya,* 'successfulness in attaining one's purpose', or having its own scope of application, (4) *anyatraphala,* '(the implied rule is seen to) have effect elsewhere (as well)'.

[14]प्रयोगानियमार्थम्। "For the purpose of restricting the use of the term *pratyaya;* a general rule laid down regarding the use of words in language and literature", e.g.

(1) a word recognised as correct should always be used. c.f. *'evam-ihāpi sāmānyām-arthagatau śabdena cāpaśabdena ca dharmaniyamaḥ kriyate śabdenai-vārtho'bhidheyo nāpaśabdeneti. evam kriyamāṇam-adhyudayakārī bhavati* '*1.1.1 Pas. Pas. Ahnika.*

(2) 'Never should a base alone or a *pratyaya* alone be used but always a base should be used with the necessary *pratyaya.*'

'yāvatā samayaḥ kṛto na kevalā prakṛtiḥ prayoktavyā na kevalaḥ pratyayaḥ' Bhā. on 1.2.64 Vā. 8, 3.1.92 Vā. 3 etc.

[15]प्रत्ययिक। The alternative reading *'apratyayika'* is more suitable to the context. "Without a *pratyaya.*" *Patañjali* uses the word as a synonymn for *pratyaya,* but in *M.Bh.* (in *atmapra.*) = 'that of which everyone can convince himself'.

[16]बभ्रुर् c.f. *'madhubabhror-brāhmaṇakauśikayoḥ' (yañ) 4.1.106 (apatyam, gotre)* "The *pratyaya yañ (vṛddhi by 'taddhiteṣvacāmādeḥ' 7.1.117)* acts in the sense of *gotra* (*'apatyam pautraprabhṛti gotram' 4.1.162*) descendant after the words *madhu* and *babhru* when the words so formed mean *brāhmaṇa* and *kauśika* (patr. of *Viśvāmitra* son or grandson of *Kuśika:* without *yañ, bābhravaḥ*) respectively." Thus *mādhavaḥ* and *bābhravyaḥ.*

[17]मण्डुः। by *'gargādibhyo yañ' 4.1.105 (gotre)* (irregularly without *yañ*) "The *pratyaya yañ* acts in the sense of *Gotra* descendant after the words *garga* and the rest."

māṇḍavyaḥ grandson or still lower descendant of *Maṇḍu.* (29 in *gaṇa*); *lamakaḥ* (irregularly without *phak*) *'naḍādibhyaḥ phak' 4.1.99 (gotre);* "The *pratyaya phak* acts, in denoting a *Gotra* descendant after the *prātipadika naḍa* and the rest."

lāmakāyanaḥ grandson or still lower descendant of *Lamaka.* c.f. *Go. Bra. 1.3.1.6 lāmakāyana sagotra lamaka + phak = lamaka + ayana = lāmakāyanaḥ by 'kiti ca' 7.2.118* "*Vṛddhi* is *ādeśa* for the first vowel of the stem when a *taddhita pratyaya* with an indicatory *k* follows." *Kuśika:* without *yañ, bābhravaḥ*) and *'āyaneyīniyīyaḥ phaḍhakhacchaghām pratyayādīnām* (*7.1.2*) "In place of *ph ayan,* of *ḍh ey,* of *kh īn,* of *ch īy,* and of *gh iy* when these consonants are of *pratyayas."*

Unādi S. 2.33 'rame raśca lo vā' ujjvala- raseḥ ktun (2.32) rephasya vā latyam. ramako vilāsī. lamakastīryartha-śodhakaḥ nadāditvāt 4.1.99 lāvakāyanaḥ.

[18]द्वयसजादीनाम्। "(Because) of *dvayasac* etc. (being seen used alone). . .", c.f. *'pramāne dvayasaj-daghnañ-mātracaḥ 5.2.37 (tadasya). "The pratyayas dvayasac, daghnac,* and *mātrac* act in denoting its lineal measure after a word in the first case in construction."

[19]*uruḥ pramānam-asya = urudvayasam* reaching to the thighs (Kāś. on *4.1.5*). *urudaghnam* reaching to the thighs *Pat.* on *5.2.37*; *urumātram* reaching to the thighs *Pat.* on *5.2.37.*

[20]काद्य तिथि। "What number day is it today?" by *'bahupūgagaṇasaṅghasya tithuk' 5.2.52* "When the *pratyaya ḍaṭ* (causing elision of the *ṭi* portion by *'teḥ' 6.4.143 bhasya, ḍi lopaḥ)* follows, *tithuk* is the augment of the words *bahu, pūga, gaṇa* and *saṅgha."*

bahūnām pūraṇo bahutithaḥ manifold, various, many, much.

bahutithe'hani 'on the many-eth day during many days' (*Nal. 9.12*).

-am. ind. much, greatly

pūgatithiḥ numerous, manifold; *gaṇatithiḥ* forming troops or assemblage (*Vop.7.42*); *saṅghatithiḥ* m.f.n. numerous, abundant (*Vop. 7.42*)

Wrong usage is found where this is treated of as noun *tithi* m.f. lunar day (30th part of whole lunation of rather more than 27 lunar days).

[21]यथा बहुस्तथा। "(They are not produced from a compounded form) as *bahus* (optionally can be)." by *'vibhāṣā supo bahuc purastāt '5.3.68.* "Optionally to a *sup/* case inflected *nāman/* noun may be added to the [*i.e. omit to*] *pratyaya bahuc (bahu),* but it stands before, when the sense is slight incompleteness."

bahupaṭuḥ, rather clever; *bahumṛdu,* rather soft, delicate, mild.

[22]अनुत्पत्त्यर्थम्। "For the purpose of non-production (of a *pratyaya*)." c.f. *'tatrotpattir -vā prasaṅgo yathā taddhite' 3.1.94 Vā. 2, also 'kṛṣyādiṣu cānutpattiḥ* (*ṇicaḥ*)*' 3.1.26 Vā.3.*

[23]वावचनानर्थक्यं च तत्र नित्यत्वात्सनः *[3.1.7 Vā. 9]*

[24]परग्रहनसात्र्यात् Kiel. misprint for सामर्थ्यात्। "Through the force of circumstances, by reason of, on account of, through the force of the specific mention of *para."*

आद्युदात्तश्च ॥ 3 । 1 । 3 ॥

Pāṇini 3.1.3: And a *pratyaya* has initial *udātta* (acute accent).

6.4 किमर्थमिदमुच्यते। आद्युदात्तो यथा स्यादन्तोदातो मा भूदिति। नैतदस्ति प्रयोजनम्। यमिच्छत्यन्तोदात्तं करोति तत्र चकारमनुबन्धमाह च चितोऽन्त[1] उदात्त इति। मध्योदात्तस्तर्हि मा भूदिति। मध्योदात्तमपि यमिच्छति तत्र रेफमनुबन्धं करोत्याह चोपोत्तमं[2] रिति। (6.1.217) इति। अनुदात्तस्तर्हि मा भूदिति। अनुदात्तमपि यमिच्छति तत्र पकारमनुबन्धं करोत्याह चानुदात्तौ सुप्पितौ[3] (3.1.4) इति। स्वरितस्तर्हि मा भूदिति। स्वरितमपि यमिच्छति करोति तत्र तकारमनु-

6.10 बन्धमाह च तित्स्वरितम्[4] (6.1.185) इति। य इदानीमतोऽन्यः प्रत्ययः शेषः सोऽन्तरेणापि वचनमाद्युदात्त एव भविष्यतीति नार्थ आद्युदात्तवचनेन।। एवमपि येषामेव प्रत्ययानां स्वरो नियम्यते त एव नियतस्वराः स्युर्य इदानीमनियतस्वरः स कदाचिदाद्युदात्तः कदाचिदन्तोदात्तःकदाचिन्मध्योदात्तःकदाचिदनुदात्तःकदाचित्सवतिःस्यात्।

6.14 चित्स्वरितः स्यात्। आद्युदात्त एव यथा स्यादित्येवमर्थमिदमुच्यते।।

6.15 अथ किमर्थं च प्रत्ययसंज्ञासंनियोगेनाद्युदात्तत्वमुच्यतेऽनुदात्तत्वं च न यत्रैवान्य-स्वरस्तत्रैवायमुच्येत। ञ्नित्यादिर्नित्यम्[5] (6.1.197) प्रत्ययस्य च। अदुपदेशाल्ल-सार्वधातुकमनुदात्तम्[6] सुप्पितौ चेति। तत्रायमप्यर्थो द्विराद्युदात्तग्रहणं द्विश्चानुदात्त-

6.18 ग्रहणं न कर्तव्यं भवति। प्रकृतमनुवर्तते।। अत उत्तरं पठति।

Bhāṣya: Why is this said? (It is said) so that there should be initial *udātta* and not be final *udātta*. This is not the purpose. Whatever he desires to have final *udātta* he produces (the *pratyaya*). An indicatory *c* and says *"citaḥ" (6.1.163) (antaḥ, udāttaḥ)* "A stem formed by a *pratyaya* or *āgama* or *vikāra* having an indicatory *c* has *udātta* accent on the end syllable". Then it is so that middle *udātta* should not be applicable. Also whatever (*pratyaya*) he wants with middle *udātta* there he produces the indicatory letter *r* and says *'upottamam riti' (6.1.217)*. "What is formed by a *pratyaya* having an indicatory *r* has *udātta* on the penultimate syllable, the full word consisting of more than two syllables". Then so that there should not be *anudātta* (on the *pratyaya*). (Here) too whatever words he wants with *anudātta* there he produces the indicatory letter *p* and says *'anudāttau suppitau' (3.1.4)*. "The *sup* case *pratyayas* and the *pratyayas* having an indicatory *p* (*pit*) are *anudātta* (grave)". Then so that it be not *svarita* (circumflex). (Here) too whatever *pratyaya* he wants with a *svarita* accent there he produces the indicatory letter *t*. And he says *'titsvaritam' (6.1.185)*. "A *pratyaya* having an indicatory *t* is *svarita* (circumflex).

Now whatever other *pratyaya* remains there will be *udātta* even without this statement. So there is no pupose in the statement of *ādyudāttaḥ*.

Even then, these *pratyayas* whose accent is fixed, would have only fixed accents but those which do not have a fixed accent are sometimes initial *udātta*, sometimes final *udātta*, sometimes middle *udātta*, sometimes *anudātta* and sometimes *svarita*. This rule is stated so that there be initial *udātta* only.

Now why is initial *udātta* or (final) *anudātta* stated here in conjunction with the technical name *pratyaya*? In that place in the Sixth *Adhyaya* where in fact there is another reference to accent, this accent also should have been taught. (For instance) where indeed there is stated *ñ-n-ityādir nityam (6.1.197)* ("Whatever is derived with a *pratyaya* having an indicatory *ñ* or *n* has *udātta* accent invariably on the first syllable"). *Pratyayaśca* 'also for a *pratyaya*'. Also (*tāsy-anudāten ṅid-ad-upadeśālla-sārvadhātukam anudāttam* (*ahnviṅoḥ*) *(6.1.186)* "The personal endings and their substitutes = *la (3.2.124-126)* when (they are) *sārvadhātuka (3.4.113)* etc. are unaccented, after the (characteristic of the periphrastic future) *tāsi*, after a *dhātu* which in the *Dhātu Pāṭha* has an unaccented vowel or *ṅ* (with the exception of *hnuṅ* and *iṅ*) or *n* as indicatory letter, as well as what has a final *'a'* in the *dhātupāṭha*/original teaching/*upadeśa* and also that which has an indicatory *p* (*pit*) or a *sup* (case ending) has *anudātta*". And there also the purpose is that two mentions of *udātta* and two mentions of *anudātta* should not be made. The original (words) (namely *udātta, anudātta*) follow on from previous *sūtras*. Therefore he reads as follows:

6.19 आद्युदात्तत्वस्य प्रत्ययसंज्ञासंनियोगे प्रत्योजनं यस्य संज्ञाकरणम् तस्याद्युदात्तार्थम् ॥ 1 ॥

Vārttika 1: 'The purpose of the statement of there being initial *udātta*/acute in conjunction with the technical term *pratyaya* is so that whatever is given the technical name (*pratyaya*) also has initial *udātta*'.

6.21 आद्युदात्तत्वस्य प्रत्ययसंज्ञासंनियोगकरण एतत्प्रयोजनं यस्य संज्ञा क्रियते तस्याद्युदात्तत्वं यथा स्यात्॥

Bhāṣya: This is the purpose of the statement of initial *udātta*/acute with the technical name *pratyaya*, namely that whatever is given the technical name *pratyaya* is characterised by having an initial *udātta*.

6.23 असंनियोगे हि यस्मात्स तदादेराद्युदात्तत्वं तदन्तस्य चानुदात्तत्वम् ॥ 2 ॥

Vārttika 2: For when there is no conjunction there is the characteristic of initial *udātta* for that after which that *pratyaya* is ordained and the characteristic of *anudātta*/acute accent for final of the same.

6.24 अक्रियमाणे हि प्रत्ययसंज्ञासंनियोगेनाद्युदात्तत्वे प्रत्ययग्रहणे[7] यस्मात्स तदादेर्ग्रहणं भवतीति
तदादेरेवाद्युदात्तत्वं प्रसज्येत तदन्तस्य चानुदात्तत्वम्।। अथ

7.1 क्रियमाणेऽपि प्रत्ययसंज्ञासंनियोगेनाद्युदात्तत्वे ऽनुदात्तत्वे च कस्मादेव
तदादेराद्युदात्तत्वं न भवति तदन्तस्य चानुदात्तत्वम्। उत्पन्नः प्रत्ययः प्रत्ययाश्रयाणां
कार्याणां निमित्तं भवति नोत्पद्यमानः। तद्यथा घटः कृतो
घटाश्रयाणां कार्याणां निमित्तं

7.4 भवति न क्रियमाणः ।।

Bhāṣya: For when initial *udātta* characteristic is not being produced in conjunction with the technical term *pratyaya* (initial *udātta* characteristic would attach to the beginning of that alone which ends in the *pratyaya*) and the final *anudātta* would attach to that (word which ends with the *pratyaya*) because (of the *paribhāṣā* rule) *pratyayagrahaṇe yasmāt sa (vihitas) tadādeḥ (tadantasya) grahaṇam* "a *pratyaya* denotes whenever it is employed (in grammar, a word form) which begins with that to which the *pratyaya* has been added and ends (with the *pratyaya*)".

Now even while initial *udātta* (characteristic) and/or *anudātta* characteristic is being produced in conjunction with the technical name *pratyaya,* why does not in fact initial *udātta* (characteristic) and final *anudātta* apply to the initial of that word (which ends with a *pratyaya*) ? A *pratyaya* (which is) produced is the cause of the operations dependent on the *pratyaya* and not the (*pratyaya*) which is being produced. As for example: The pot which has been made is the cause of the operations dependent on that pot and not the (pot) which is being made.

7.5 न वा प्रकृतेराद्युदात्तवचनं ज्ञापकं तदादेरग्रहणस्य ।। 3 ।।

Vārttika 3: This difficulty does not (arise because) the rule of the initial *udātta* for the *prakṛti* (base) indicates that there is no mention of the initial of that (*pratyaya* which helps form it).

7.6 न वैष दोषः। किं कारणम्। यदयं ञ्नित्यादिर्नित्यमिति प्रकृतेराद्युदात्तत्वं शास्ति
तज्ज्ञापयत्याचार्यो न तदादेराद्युदात्तत्वं भवतीति।। तदन्तस्य तर्ह्यनुदात्तत्वं

7.8 प्राप्नोति।

Bhāṣya: Nor is this a fault? What is the reason? When he teaches *ñ nityādirnityam (6.1.197)* ('whatever is derived with a *pratyaya* having an indicatory *ñ* or *n* that has *udātta* invariably on the initial'), there is thus the characteristic of initial *udātta* for the base/*prakṛti* . The master thus makes known that there is not then the characteristic of initial *udātta* for that beginning of the word formed with (a *pratyaya*). Then the characteristic of *anudātta* obtains for that word ending with a *pratyaya.*

7.9 प्रकृतिस्वरस्य च विधानसामर्थ्यात्प्रत्ययस्वराभावः ।। 4 ।।

Vārttika 4: And because of the force of the rule for accent of the base, there is absence of accent for the *pratyaya.*

7.10 यदयं धातोरन्तः[8] प्रातिपदिकस्यान्त इति प्रकृतेरन्तोदात्तत्वं शास्ति तज्ज्ञापयत्याचार्यो न तदन्तस्यानुदात्तत्वं भवतीति। कथं कृत्वा ज्ञापकम्। यत्र ह्यनुदात्तः

7.12 प्रत्ययः प्रकृतिस्वरस्तत्र प्रयोजयति।।

Bhāṣya: When he teaches *dhātor* (*antaḥ*) 'For a *dhātu* there is *udātta* on the final syllable' and *prātipadikasya antaḥ* 'For a *prātipadika* (base) there is *udātta* on the final syllable', the master makes known (by *jñāpaka*) that the characteristic of *anudātta* is not for that (word) which ends with the *pratyaya.* How is the *jñāpaka* (implied rule) formed? Where the *pratyaya* is *anudātta* there the accent of the *prakṛti* (base) becomes applicable.

7.13 आगमानुदात्तार्थं वा ।। 5 ।।

Vārttika 5: Or (the rule is) for the purpose of *anudātta* accent for *āgamas.*

7.14 आगमानुदात्तर्थं तर्हि प्रत्ययसंज्ञासंनियोगेनाद्युदात्तत्वमुच्यते। प्रत्ययसंज्ञासं-नियोगेनाद्युदात्तत्वे कृत आगमा अनुदात्ता यथा स्युरिति।।

Bhāṣya: Then the characteristic of *udātta* is stated in conjunction with the technical name *pratyaya* for the purpose of the *anudātta* accent for *āgamas.* So that when the characteristic of *udātta* is produced by the simultaneous (conjunction) with the technical name *pratyaya,* the *āgamas* (augment) may be *anudātta* (grave).

7.16 न वागमस्यानुदात्तवचनात् ।। 6 ।।

Vārttika 6: Nor is (the rule valid) because of the rule of *anudātta* for augments.

7.17 न वैतदपि प्रयोजनमस्ति। किं कारणम्। आगमस्यानुदात्तवचनात्[9]। आगमा अनुदात्ता भवन्तीति वक्ष्यामि। के पुनरागमा अनुदात्तत्वं प्रयोजयन्ति। इट्[10]। लविता। इट् तावत्र प्रयोजयति। इदमिह संप्रधार्यम्। इट् क्रियतामाद्युदात्तत्वमिति

7.20 किमत्र कर्तव्यम्। परत्वादिडागमः[11]। नित्यमाद्युदात्तत्वम्। कृतेऽपीटि प्राप्नोत्यकृतेऽपि प्राप्नोति। इडपि नित्यः। कृतेऽप्याद्युदात्तत्वे प्राप्नोत्यकृतेऽपि प्राप्नोति। अनित्य इट्। अन्यथास्वरस्य कृत आद्युदात्तत्वे प्राप्नोत्यन्यथा स्वरस्याकृते स्वरभिन्नस्य च

प्राप्नुवन्विधिरनित्यो भवति। आद्युदात्तत्वमप्यनित्यम्। अन्यस्य कृत इटि
प्राप्नोत्यन्यस्याकृते शब्दान्तरस्य च प्राप्नुवन्विधिरनित्यो भवति। उभयोरनित्ययो:
7.25 परत्वादिडागम:। अन्तरङ्गं तह्याद्युदात्तत्वम्। कान्तरङ्गता। उत्पत्तिसंनियोगेना-
द्युदात्तत्वमुच्यत उत्पन्ने प्रत्यये प्रकृतिप्रत्ययावाश्रित्याङ्गंस्येडागम:। आद्युदात्तत्व-
8.1 मपि नान्तररङ्गं यावता प्रत्यय आश्रीयमाणे प्रकृतिरप्याश्रिता भवति।
अन्तरङ्गमेवाद्युदात्तत्वम्। कथम्। इदानीमेव ह्युक्तं न प्रत्ययस्वरविधौ तदादिविधि
र्भवतीति।सीयुट्[12] तर्हि प्रयोजयति।

Bhāṣya: Nor is this also the purpose. What is the reason? Because of the rule of *anudātta* for augments, I will say 'Augments are *anudātta*'. But which augments have the characteristic of *anudātta* applicable to them?

The augment *iṭ* has the characteristic of *anudātta,* e.g. *lavitā* "He will cut". The augment *iṭ* does not have the characteristic of *anudātta.* This is to be considered here: Let *iṭ* be formed with *udātta.* What is to be done? Because of the *iṭ* rule being *para* (subsequent) the *iṭ āgama* (is applicable). Initial *udātta* characteristic is invariable. For it is applicable even when it is produced or not produced. (The *āgama*) *iṭ* is also invariable. It obtains even when initial *udātta* is effected or it is not effected. It is variable, for it obtains in one way when the accent is made initial *udātta,* while *iṭ* obtains in another way when the initial accent is not made (*udātta*); and the rule applicable to that which contains different accents (at different times) is variable. Initial *udātta* accent is also variable. For it is effected for one when *iṭ* is not added to it and the rule obtaining for a different word becomes variable. When both are variable *iṭ āgama* rule applies because of being a subsequent or *para* rule.

Then the characteristic of initial *udātta* is *antaraṅga.* What is the state (or condition) of *antaraṅga?* The characteristic initial *udātta* is stated simultaneously in connection with the arising (of the *pratyaya*). Whereas the *āgama iṭ* obtains being dependent upon *prakṛti* and *pratyaya,* only after the *pratyaya* is produced. Also the characteristic of initial *udātta* is not *antaraṅga* inasmuch as when the *pratyaya* is being resorted to, the *prakṛti* is also resorted to. Initial *udātta* is in fact *antaraṅga.* How? Just now it was said—in a rule for *pratyaya* accent the *tad ādi* (for a word beginning with that) rule does not apply. Then *sīyuṭ* has the characteristic of *udātta.*

8.4 अवचने हि सीयुडादेराद्युदात्तत्वम् ॥ 7 ॥

Vārttika 7: For when there is not a specific rule (for *āgama* to be *anudātta*) there is the characteristic of initial *udātta* for the actual initial of *sīyuṭ.* (*āgama*).

8.5 अक्रियमाणे ह्यागमानुदात्तत्वे क्रियमाणेऽपि प्रत्ययसंज्ञासंनियोगेनाद्युदात्तत्वे
सीयुडादेर्लिङ[13] आद्युदात्तत्वं प्रसज्येत। लविषीय पविषीय।।
तत्तर्हि वक्तव्यमागमा अनुदात्ता भवन्तीति। न वक्तव्यम्। आचार्यप्रवृत्तिर्ज्ञाप-
यत्यागमा अनुदात्ता भवन्तीति यदयं यासुट्[14] परस्मैपदेषूदात्तो ङिच्च (3.4.103)
इत्याह। नैतदस्ति ज्ञापकम्। वक्ष्यत्येतत्। यासुटो ङिद्वचनं पिदर्थमुदात्तवचनं
8.10 चेति। शक्यमनेन वक्तुं यासुट् परस्मैपदेषु भवत्यपिच्च लिङ् भवतीति।
सोऽयमेवं लघीयसा[15] न्यासेन सिद्धे सति यद्गरीयांसं यत्नमारभते तज्ज्ञापयत्याचार्य[16]
8.12 आगमा अनुदात्ता भवन्तीति। शक्यमिदं लब्धुम्।।

Bhāṣya: When the characteristic of *anudātta* for an *āgama* is not (stated even when initial *udātta* characteristic is) stated, *udātta* characteristic would be wrongly attached to the *liṅ* with the initial *āgama sīyuṭ* even when initial *udātta* characteristic is stated in connection with the technical name *pratyaya*, e.g. *laviṣīyá,* May I cut; *pariṣīyá,* May I purify.

Then should that be stated as 'augments are *anudātta*' ? No, it (need) not be stated. The master's usage causes this to be known that augments have *anudātta* accents since he states this rule, *yāsuṭ parasmaipadeṣūdātto ṅic ca (3.4.103) 'yāsuṭ* is added to the *parasmaipada* ending in *liṅ*, and it is *udātta* as well as *ṅit'*. This is not an implied rule or *jñapaka.* He will say that "the stating of *it ṅ* for *yāsuṭ* is for expressing not *'pit'* (and being not *p-it*) states *udātta* (for *yāsuṭ*)" *(3.4.103 Vā. 1)*. By reason of that it is possible to say 'there is the augment *yāsuṭ* when *parasmaipada pratyayas* of *liṅ* follow and *liṅ* is without indicatory *'p'* (therefore accented *udātta*)'.

When this can be achieved thus by a briefer (written or) literal text the fact that he begins a great expression or effort suggests that the master makes known (by the implied rule) that *āgamas* have *anudātta* accent.

Then it is possible thus to obtain (this rule).

8.13 यद्येव वचनादथापि ज्ञापकादागमा अनुदात्ता भवन्त्यागमैस्तु व्यवहितत्वा-
दाद्युदात्तात्वं न प्राप्नोति। आगमा अविद्यमानवद्भवन्तीति वक्ष्यामि। यद्यागमा
अविद्यमानवद्भवन्तीत्युच्यते लविता[17] अवादेशो न प्राप्नोति। स्वरविधाविति वक्ष्यामि।
एवमपि लविता[18] उदात्तादनुदात्तस्य स्वरितः (8.4.66) इति स्वरितो न प्राप्नोति।
षाष्ठिके स्वर इति वक्ष्यामि। एवमपि शिक्षितः[19] निष्ठा च द्व्यजनात् (6.1.205)
8.20 अविद्यमानवद्भवन्तीति यदयं यासुट् परस्मैपदेषूदात्तो ङिच्चेत्याह। नैतदस्ति ज्ञाप-कम्।
वक्ष्यत्येतत्। यासुटो ङिद्वचनं पिदर्थमुदात्तवचनं चेति। शक्यमनेन वक्तुं यासुट्
परस्मैपदेषु भवत्यपिच्च लिङ् भवतीति। सोऽयमेवं लघीयसा न्यासेन सिद्धे
8.23 सति यद्गरीयांसं यत्नमारभते तज्ज्ञापयत्याचार्य आगमा अविद्यमानवद्भवन्तीति।।

Bhāṣya: Although it is from a rule, still it is from an implied rule (*jñāpaka*) that it is known that *āgamas* have *anudātta* accent, (still) because of being separated by *āgamas* the characteristic of initial *udātta* does not obtain (for the *pratyaya*). I will say "augments are as if they did not exist". If it is said "*āgamas* are as if they did not exist" then the substitute *av* for *lavitā* does not obtain. I will say "(this applies) in the context of an accent rule (only)". Even then also (in the case of *lavitā* because of the rule *udāttād anudāttasya svaritaḥ (8.4.66)*. 'The *svarita* accent is in place of an *anudātta* accent following after an *udātta* accent'. *Svarita* accent does not obtain (as required for the *i* of *lavitā*). (Then) I will say (this applies only) in relation to accent rules in the sixth *adhyāya.* Also thus (there in the example) *udātta* accent obtains for *śikṣitáḥ* (learnt, studied, taught) because of the rule *niṣṭhā ca dvyajanāt (6.1.205)* ("A two-syllable participle in *'ta'* (*niṣṭhā*), when a name, has the *udātta* on the first syllable, but not if the first syllable has an *ā*". I will say, "In the context of the (rules of) *pratyaya* accent (the *āgamas* are as if non-existent *avidyamānavat*).

Then is that to be stated, "Augments are as if they did not exist"? It (need) not be stated. The master's usage makes known that augments are 'as if they did not exist' since he states the rule *'yāsuṭ parasmaipadeṣūdātto ṅicca' (3.4.103) "Yāsuṭ* is added to the *parasmaipada* endings of *liṅ* and it is *udātta* as well as *ṅ-it*".

This is not an implied rule (*jñāpaka*). For he will say that the statement of *ṅ-it* (having an indicatory *ṅ*) for "*yāsuṭ* is for the purpose of *pit* (i.e. not *pit*) and thus for expressing *udātta* accent". *(3.4.103 Vā. 1 and 2)*

It is possible for him to say, "*yasuṭ* is the augment of *parasmaipada liṅ* and *liṅ* is not *pit* (without an indicatory *p*). Since this (teacher) begins a greater effort when it could be achieved by a briefer written text, the master's usage makes known 'augments are as if non-existent'.

8.24 आद्युदात्तस्य वा लोपार्थम् ॥ 8 ॥

Vārttika 8: Or (the rule is) for the sake of (the situation where there is) elision for that word with the initial *udātta.*

8.25 आद्युदात्तस्य तर्हि लोपार्थं प्रत्ययसंज्ञासंनियोगेनाद्युदात्तत्वमुच्यते। प्रत्ययसंज्ञा-
संनियोगेनाद्युदात्तत्वे कृत उदात्तनिवृत्तिस्वरः[20] सिद्धो भवति। स्रौघ्नी[21] माथुरीति।
8.27 अत्र हि परत्वाल्लोपः[22] प्रत्ययस्वरं बाधेत॥

Bhāṣya: Then characteristic initial *udātta* is stated in conjunction with the technical name *pratyaya* for the sake of the situation where there is elision of initial *udātta.* When that having the *udātta* accent is formed in conjunction with the technical term *pratyaya,* the accent resulting from the cessation (elision) of a (preceding) *udātta* is established (as for example) *Sraughna*— born or living in *srughna, māthurī* a female coming from or born in belonging to *Mathurā.* Because of being a *para* rule the *lopa* by *yasyeti ca (6.4.148))* would cancel the *pratyaya udātta* accent.

9.1 न वा बहिरङ्गलक्षणत्वात् ।। 9 ।।

Vārttika 9: Nor is the rule necessary because of the rule being characterised as *bahiraṅga.*

9.2 न वैतदपि प्रयोजनमस्ति। किं कारणम्। बहिरङ्गलक्षणत्वात्। बहिरङ्गलक्षणो लोपोऽन्तरङ्गलक्षणः स्वरः। असिद्धं[23] बहिरङ्गमन्तरङ्गे।। अवश्यं चैषा परिभाषा-
9.4 श्रयितव्या ।।

Bhāṣya: Nor is this the purpose. What is the reason? Because of being characterised as *bahiraṅga.* The *lopa*/elision rule is *bahiraṅga.* The accent rule is an *antaraṅga* (inner rule). 'That which is *bahiraṅga* is (regarded as) not having taken effect (or as not existing) when that which is *antaraṅga* (is to take effect)'. And it is essential to resort to this *paribhāṣā.*

9.5 अवचने हि ञ्नित्कित्स्वतिप्रसङ्गः ।। 10 ।।

Vārttika 10: For when there is not statement of *antaraṅga* rule there is an over- application of the rule in relation to *it ñ, n* and *k.*

9.6 अनाश्रीयमाणायामस्यां परिभाषायां क्रियमाणेऽपि प्रत्ययसंज्ञासंनियोगेनाद्युदात्त-त्वे ञ्नित्कित्स्वतिप्रसङ्गः स्यात्। औत्सीं[24] कंसिकी आत्रेयीति। अत्र हि परत्वाल्लोपो ञ्नित्कित्स्वरान्बाधेत।। नैष दोषः। ञ्नित्कित्स्वराः प्रत्ययस्वरापवादाः। न चापवादविषय उत्सर्गोऽभिनिविशते। पूर्वं ह्यपवादा अभिनिविशन्ते पश्चादुत्सर्गाः।
9.10 प्रकल्प्य वापवादविषयं तत उत्सर्गाऽभिनिविशते। न तावदत्र कदाचित्प्रत्यया-द्युदात्तत्वं भवत्यपवादान् ञ्नित्कित्स्वरान्प्रतीक्षते।। कंसिक्यां[25] भूयान्परिहारः। अन्य-स्यात्रोदात्तत्वमन्यस्य लोपः। आदेरुदात्तत्वमन्त्यस्य लोपः।। इदं तर्हि आत्रेयीति[26]। अत्र हि परत्वाल्लोपः कित्स्वरं बाधेत। तस्मादेषा परिभाषाश्रयित्व्या। एतस्यां च
9.14 सत्यां शक्यंप्रत्ययसंनियोगेनाद्युदात्तत्वमवक्तुम्।।

Bhāṣya: For when this *paribhāṣā* is not being resorted to there would be unwarrantable stretch of rule in relation to *it ñ, n* and *k,* even when the characteristic of initial *udātta* is being produced in conjunction with the technical name *pratyaya.*

e.g. in *autsī* (female produced or being in a well, female descendant of *Utsa*)

káṅsikī (a feminine thing made of or relating to bell-metal)

ātreyī (female descendant of *Atri*)

For here *lopa* being a following (i.e. latter/*para*) rule would cancel the accent of those having *it ñ, n* and *k.*

This fault does not obtain. The (*udātta*) accents associated with those having *it ñ, n* or *k* are exceptions to the general rule stating *pratyaya* accent. And the general *sūtra* does not enter the domain of the exceptional rule. For first, the *apavāda* rules enter, then afterwards the *utsarga*/general rules. And having (first) settled or fixed the sphere of the exceptional rule, the general/*utsarga* rule enters. Just here there is never *pratyaya* accent (because of this *apavāda sūtra*). One expects exceptional/*apavāda* rules concerning accents for those *pratyayas* having *it ñ, n* or *k.*

Another device to remove (the difficulty) in relation to *kansikī* (feminine thing, made of bell-metal) is as follows: for there is *udātta* characteristic for one and *lopa* elision for another. *Udātta* for the initial and *lopa* for the final.

Then (there is) this (example) *ātreyī (udātta on i)* (female descendant of *Atri*). Here *lopa* by *yasyeti ca (6.4.148)* being subsequent would cancel the *udātta* accent (on the final) of that conjoined with that having the *it k (6.1.165)*. There-fore, this *paribhāṣā* should be resorted to, and when this exists, it is possible not to say there is characteristic initial *udātta*. Simultaneously in conjunction with the technical name *pratyaya* (i.e. outside the domain of *vipratiṣedhe param kāryam (1.4.2)* because it is part of the technical name and not a *vidhisūtra*).

9.15 प्रत्ययाद्युदात्तत्वाद्धातोरन्तः ॥ 11 ॥

Vārttika 11: Instead of the characteristic of initial *udātta* for a *pratyaya,* final *(udātta)* for a *dhātu* (verbal seed form) is to be applied.

9.16 प्रत्ययाद्युदात्तत्वाद्धातोरन्त[27] इत्येतद्भवति विप्रतिषेधेन। प्रत्ययाद्युदात्तत्वस्याव-
काशो यत्रानुदात्ता[28] प्रकृतिः। समत्वम्। सिमतवम्। धातोरन्त इत्येतस्यावकाशो
यत्रानुदात्तः प्रत्ययः। पचति पठति। इहोभयं प्राप्नोति। गोपायत्ति[29] धूपायत्ति।

9.19 धातोरन्त इत्येतद्भवति विप्रतिषेधेन॥

Bhāṣya: Instead of the characteristic of initial *udātta* for a *pratyaya,* a final *udātta* (for a *dhātu*) is applicable by reason of a conflict (of rules of equal strength). When the base has *anudātta* there is scope for initial *udātta* characteristic for the *pratyaya*

e.g. *samatvám* (equality, equanimity); *simatvám* (entirety, wholeness).

There is scope for this rule *dhator antaḥ* where the *pratyaya* is *anudātta* e.g. *pacàti* (he cooks), *paṭhàti* (he recites). Both obtain here (in the examples) *gopāyáti* (he protects), *dhūpāyáti* (he fumigates or perfumes with incense).

Equal rules being in conflict this rule *dhātor antaḥ* (being subsequent) is applicable.

9.20 पित्स्वरात्तित्स्वरष्टापि[30] ।। 12 ।।

Vārttika 12: Instead of the (*anudātta*) accent in connection with that having an indicatory *p,* the (*svarita*) accent in connection with that having an indicatory *t* (is applicable) when feminine *pratyaya ṭāp* is added.

9.21 पित्स्वरात्तित्स्वरष्टापि भवति विप्रतिषेधेन[31]। पित्स्वरस्यावकाशः पचति
पठति। तित्स्वरस्यावकाशः। कार्यम्[32] हार्यम्। इहोभयं प्राप्नोति। कार्या[33] हार्या।
9.23 तित्स्वरो भवति विप्रतिषेधेन।।

Bhāṣya: Instead of the (*anudātta*) accent in connection with an indicatory *p,* the (*svarita*) accent in connection with an indicatory *t (6.1.185)* is applicable when the feminine *pratyaya tāp* follows, by reason of a conflict of (rules of equal strength/requiring the following rule to prevail).

The *anudātta* accent followed by *it, p* has scope (in the examples) *pácati* (he cooks), *páṭhati* (he recites).

The *svarita* accent (ordained by) *it 't'* has scope here: *kāryám* (it is to be made), *hāryám* (it is to be taken). Both obtain here in the examples *kāryā, hāryā.* The *svarita* accent in connection with that having *it t* is applicable by reason of mutual conflict between two rules of equal strength (requiring the subsequent to prevail).

9.24 चित्स्वरश्चापि पित्स्वरात् ।। 13 ।।

Vārttika 13: And instead of an (*anudātta*) accent (ordained) in connection with that having *it p, udātta* ordained in connection with that having *it c* prevails when (the feminine *pratyaya*) *cāp* follows.

9.25 चित्स्वरश्चापि पित्स्वराद्भवति विप्रतिषेधेन[34]। चित्स्वरस्यावकाशः। चलनः[35]
चोपनः। पित्स्वरस्य[36] स एव। इहोभयं प्राप्नोति। आम्बष्ठ्या[37] सौवीर्या। चित्स्वरो
10.2 भवति विप्रतिषेधेन।।

Bhāṣya: And instead of an (*anudātta*) accent (ordained in connection with *it 'p'*) an *udātta* accent (ordained in connection with *it 'c'* prevails) by reason of a conflict (of rules of equal strength requiring the following rule to prevail). There is scope for the accent (ordained because of *cit*) (for example) in *calanaḥ* (moving, shaking), *copanaḥ* (moving).

The same is in fact an example of accent in connection with that having an *it p* accent. Both obtain here, namely in *āmbaṣṭhyā* (queen of the *āmbaṣṭyā*), *sauvīryā* (princess of the *sauviryā*).

The accent due to the indicatory *'c'* is applicable by reason of conflict (of rules of equal force requiring the following to prevail).

10.3 न वाद्युदात्तस्य प्रत्ययसंज्ञासंनियोगात् ।। 14 ।।

Vārttika 14: Nor is (*vipratiṣedha* applicable) because initial *udātta* is taught in conjunction with the technical name *pratyaya.*

10.4 न वार्थो विप्रतिषेधेन। किं कारणम्। आद्युदात्तस्य प्रत्ययसंज्ञासंनियोगात्।
प्रत्ययसंज्ञासंनियोगेनाद्युदात्तत्वे कृते सतिशिष्टत्वाद्धातुस्वरो[38] भविष्यति।।
10.6 अयं चाप्ययुक्तो विप्रतिषेधः पित्स्वरस्य तित्स्वरस्य च। किं कारणम्।

Bhāṣya: No purpose is achieved by *vipratiṣedha* (by which when there is a conflict of rules of equal force the following one prevails).

What is the reason? Because the (characteristic) of initial *udātta* is taught in connection with the technical name *pratyaya.* When the (characteristic of) initial *udātta* is formed (simultaneously) by connection with the technical name *pratyaya* there will be an *udātta* accent on the *dhātu* because of its being residual (the remainder in place of the previous accent in the order of the word's formation).

Moreover this conflict (of equal rules) between the accent due to *it p* and the accent due to *it t* is not proper. What is the reason?

10.7 टापि स्वरितेनैकादेशः[39] ।। 15 ।।

Vārttika 15: When *ṭāp* follows the one substitute (for the one before and the one after will be) with *svarita* accent.

10.8 टापि स्वरितेनैकादेशो भवति। इदमिह संप्रधार्यम्[40]। स्वरितत्वं क्रियतामेका-
देश इति किमत्र कर्तव्यम्। परत्वात्स्वरितत्वम्[41,42]। नित्य[43] एकादेशः कृतेऽपि हि
10.10 स्वरितत्वे प्राप्नोत्यकृतेऽपि प्राप्नोति। स्वरितत्वमपि नित्यम्। कृतेऽप्येकादेशे
प्राप्नोत्यकृतेऽपि प्राप्नोति। अनित्यं स्वरितत्वम्। अन्यस्य कृत एकादेशे
प्राप्नोत्यन्य-स्याकृते शब्दान्तरस्य च प्राप्नुवन्विधिरनित्यो भवति। एकादेशोऽप्यनित्यः।
अन्यथास्वरस्य कृते स्वरितत्वे प्राप्नोत्यन्यथास्वरस्याकृते स्वरितत्वे स्वरभिन्नमस्य
च प्राप्नुवन्विधि-रनित्यो भवति। अन्तरङ्गस्तर्ह्येकादेशः कान्तरङ्गता। वर्णावाश्रित्यै-
10.15 कादेशः परस्य स्वरितत्वम्। स्वरितत्वमप्यन्तरङ्गम्। कथम्। वक्षयत्येतत्। पद-
ग्रहणं[44] परिमाणार्थमिति। उभयोरन्तरङ्गयोः परत्वात्स्वरितत्वम् स्वरितत्वे[45] कृत

Bhāṣya: When *ṭāp* (feminine *pratyaya*) follows the one substitute (for the one before and the one after) will be with a *svarita* accent. Here this is to be deliberated upon. Let *svarita* be effected as the single substitute. What is to be done here? The (rule of) *svarita* accent being subsequent is applicable. (The rule teaching) the one substitute is a *nitya* (invariable) rule for it obtains (even) when *svarita* is produced and also when it is not produced. *Svarita* accent is also invariable. It obtains when there is a single substitute effected and also when not effected. *Svarita* accent is variable. It obtains for one when the single substitute is effected and for another when not effected. And obtaining for a different word the rule becomes variable. A single substitute is also variable. For on the one hand it obtains when the characteristic of *svarita* is produced for an accent, while on the other (it obtains) when characteristic *svarita* is not produced for the accent.

And when a rule is applicable to a different accent it is variable/ *a-nitya.*

(When both are variable because of being a subsequent) rule, *svarita* prevails.

Then the single substitute (rule) is *antaraṅga* 'interior'. What is the nature of being *antaraṅga* ? The single substitute depends upon two letters while *svarita* accent depends upon the word. *Svarita* characteristic is also *antaraṅga.* How? He will say this.

The reference to *pada* (word) is for the purpose of transformation. When both are *antaraṅga,* because of being a subsequent rule *'svarita'* prevails.

When the characteristic *svarita* accent is produced because of near relationship of *svarita* and *anudātta* accents the one substitute for both will be *svarita,* and this conflict of that having an indicatory *'p'* (*anudātta*) accent and that having an indicatory *'c'* (final *udātta*) accent is also not proper. What is the reason?

10.19 चापि चित्करणात् ॥ 16 ॥

Vārttika 16: When *'cāp'* feminine *pratyaya* follows because of having an indicatory *'c'* there will be final *udātta.*

10.20 चापि चित्करणसामर्थ्यादन्तोदत्वं[46] भविष्यति॥

Bhāṣya: When *cāp* (feminine *pratyaya*) follows because of the force of making it an *it c* (there will be final *udātta* accent).

Pradīpa

Pradīpa: 6.3 आद्युदात्तश्च।

"Due to there not being pronunciation of vowels without an accent, and because of the fixed nature of another accent (than initial *udātta*) in relation to different *pratyayas*, consequently there will only be initial *udātta* applicable for a *pratyaya.*"

So having thought, there is the question:

Pradīpa: 6.4

किम्-अर्थम्-इति।

'Why is this said?'

Pradīpa: 6.12 येषामेति।

"Even so (only those *pratyayas* whose accent is fixed would have fixed accents)."

The meaning is: When there obtains an unfixed accent for those having an *it c,* due to the restriction thus 'that having an *it c* is only final *udātta'* there would be a fixed accent only for them. However, for the others, there is the possibility of no fixed accent.

Pradīpa: 7.2 प्रत्ययाश्रयाणामिति।

"(A *pratyaya* which is produced is the cause of the operations) dependent on the *pratyaya* (and not the *pratyaya* (still) being produced)."

The meaning is this, this is a reference to those that end (with such *pratyayas* and their operations).

When there is presence of this *sūtra 'ādyudātaśca'* in every *sūtra, tavya* etc. actually while being produced have initial *udātta* applicable, so *tip* etc. (by *3.1.4*) have *anudātta.* Thus there is no fault.

Pradīpa: 7.3 घटाश्रयाणामिति।

"(The pot which has been made, is cause of the operations) dependent on that pot, (not the pot still being made)."

The meaning is 'the carrying of water' etc.

Pradīpa: 7.6 यदयमिति।

"When he (teaches *ñ-nityādir-nityam 6.1.197* there is thus initial *udātta* for *prakṛti*)."

If initial *udātta* were established by stating 'and for a *pratyaya'* (after *6.1.197*) *ñ-nityādir-nityam* (this *sūtra ādyudāttaśca*) would not have to be undertaken, if there were thus mention (of *udātta*) for its initial.

Pradīpa: 7.10 प्रातिपदिकस्यान्त इति।

"For a crude base *udātta* on the final" by *'phiṣonta udāttaḥ' phiṭ sūtra 1.1* 'There is the characteristic of *udātta* for the final of the *prakṛti*\ (base)."

Pradīpa: 7.11 यत्र हीति।

"For where (the *pratyaya* is *anudātta prakṛti* accent becomes applicable."

In the case of *yāti* 'He goes' etc. when there is a *pratyaya* with an *it p* (here *tip*), *udātta* is applicable for (the final) of the *dhātu*. However, in the case of *yātaḥ* 'They both go' and *yānti* 'They (all) go' etc., by reason of the initial *udātta* for the *pratyaya* (*tas* and *anti*), because of the rule *'sati śiṣṭa (svarabalīyastvam) 6.1.158 Vā. 9'*, 'An accent prescribed subsequently has greater strength and prevails, by replacing the earlier accent', the *udātta* on the *dhātu* is barred. And in the case of *kṛṣṇátaraḥ* (ending in *'tara-p + su* both *anudātta*) final *udātta* is heard for the *prātipadika kṛṣṇa*. And if the final of a *pratyaya* were *anudātta,* then the meaning is 'being without a sphere (of application) there would be final *udātta* for a *dhātu* and a *prātipadika'*. In the case of *āste* 'He sits' and *śete* 'He lies' etc., if there exists *anudātta* for a *sārvadhātuka ādeśa* of *la* (here *ta* of *tiṅ*), it is not an implied rule, because of the *dhātu* accent (now) having a sphere of application. Here too, because of the possibility of the *tadanta* rule applying, in fact there is an implied rule.

Pradīpa: 7.13 आगमानुदात्तार्थम् वेति।

"Or the rule is for the purpose of *anudātta* accent on *āgamas.*"

The word *vā* is in the sense of *tarhi* 'then'. In the case of *lávitàvyam* 'it is to be cut' etc., when the initial *udātta* is effected at the time of the arising of *tavya-t* afterwards the *āgama iṭ* being effected by *'seṣānighāṭa'* the remainder of (the word) is *anudātta* (= *'anudāttam padam ekavarjam' 6.1.158* 'A word is with the exception of one syllable *anudātta*'). The meaning is that otherwise, because of being subsequent when *iṭ āgama* is effected, because of forming a part of that and due to its mention with the mention of *pratyaya,* there would in fact be applicable the effecting of initial *udātta* for *iṭ* augment.

Pradīpa: 7.18 के पुनरिति।

"But which (augments have *anudatta*)?"

Here another questioner is to be seen. However, the one by whom it was stated 'Or else not', only asks from contrariety or perverseness.

Pradīpa: 7.19 लवितेति।

"He will cut."

Here is the *luṭ* (periphrastic future of *lū* to cut) replaced by *tip* and the *vikaraṇa tāsi. Tip* is then replaced by *ḍā* (*2.4.85*). Here if *iṭ* were not *anudātta*, then because of forming a part of *tāsi iṭ* would be *udātta.* And by the remainder being *anudātta* the *ā* of *tāsi* is *anudātta,* and thus due to the absence of *lopa*-elision of an *udātta,* the (*udātta*) accent resulting from the cessation of a preceding *udātta* (*'anudāttasya ca yatrodāttalopaḥ 6.1.161* 'An *anudātta* vowel has also the *udātta* when on account of it the preceding *udātta* is elided'), would not be applicable for the letter *ā.* However, when there is *anudātta* for *iṭ āgama* the *ā* of *tāsi* is in fact *udātta,* because of which the vowel resulting from cessation of (prior) *udātta* is established as valid.

Pradīpa: 7.20 परत्वादिडागमः।

"Due to the *iṭ* rule being subsequent, *iṭ āgama* is applicable." by *'ārdhadhātukasyeḍ-valāleḥ' 7.2.35* 'An *ārdhadhātuka pratyaya (3.4.114)* etc. beginning with a *val* (any consonant except *y*) receives the *āgama iṭ'*, e.g. *lav-i-tā.*

Pradīpa: 7.22 स्वरभिन्नस्येति।

"(The rule applicable to that) which contains different accents (at different times becomes variable)."

The sense is that, although an accent possesses form, because of its nature of causing difference in hearing, it in fact makes a different word.

Pradīpa: 8.1 प्रकृतिरप्याश्रितेति।

"(When the *pratyaya* is being resorted to) the *prakṛti* also is resorted to."

The sense is by reason of the *Paribhāṣā 23:*

'pratyayagrahaṇe yasmāt-sa vihitas-tadādes-tadantasya grahaṇam.' 'A *pratyaya* denotes, when employed, the word form which begins with that to which it has been added, and ends with the *pratyaya* itself.'

Pradīpa: 8. अन्तरङ्गमेवेति।

"Initial is in fact *antaraṅga.*"

'Hence *iṭ* augment is not applicable' (as *antaraṅga*) is the meaning.

Pradīpa: 8.6 लविषीयेति।

"May I cut."

This is benedictive/*āśir-liṅ*. Here, due either to being ordained as a qualification or because of being subsequent, *sīyuṭ* is effected prior, and afterwards the *ādeśa* of *la*. In that context the initial *udātta* being effected, *sīyuṭ* in fact would be applicable. Due to the statement however, *'āgamas* are *anudātta'* when there is *anudātta* for *sīyuṭ* by the *sūtra 'iṭo't' 3.4.106* ('Short *a* is the *ādeśa* of the *i ātmanepada uttama puruṣa* (first person) singular in the Optative and the Benedictive') there is established as valid *udātta* for the short *a*. This is the meaning.

Pradīpa: 8.9 पिदर्थमिति।

"(The stating of *it ṅ* for *yāsuṭ* is for expressing *pit* and being not *pit* states *udātta* for *yāsuṭo*)." *'yasuṭo ṅid-vacanam pidartham' 3.4.103 Vā. 1. udāttavacanam ca Vā 2.*

The meaning is, due to forming part of *pit*, in examples like *cinuyāt* 'May he collect', when there is the possibility of *anudātta* for *sīyuṭ*, there is the statement (by *vārttika*) not a *jñāpaka*, of *udātta*.

Pradīpa: 8.13 आगमैरिति।

". . . (because of being separated) by *āgamas* (initial *udātta* does not obtain for a *pratyaya*)."

The meaning is, due to being separated (by *āgama*) in the case of the initial nature of *laviṣīya* etc. the initial nature does not obtain for the *pratyaya*. However, when the *sūtra* has been undertaken, when initial *udātta* has been effected in conjunction with the technical name *pratyaya*, *āgamas* are applicable (as *anudātta*), there is no fault.

Pradīpa: 8.16 लवितेति।

"The cutter, (because of उदात्तादनुदात्तस्य स्वरित: *8.4.66 svarita* does not obtain for the *i* of *lavitā*)."

Due to ending in *tṛn* this has initial *udātta 'tṛn' 3.2.135* "The *pratyaya tṛn* acts after all *dhātus* in the sense of agents having such a habit."

'ñ-nityādir-nityam' 6.1.197 "Whatever is derived with a *pratyaya* having an indicatory *ñ* or *n* has the *udātta* accent invariably on the first syllable."

Pradīpa: 8.20 यदयम्।

"Since he (states the rule *yāsuṭ parasmaipadeṣūdātto ṅicca, āgamas* are as if they did not exist."

Āgamas would prevent (accent) being initial then in the forms like *cinuyātām* 'may the two collect'. Because of *yāsuṭ* being the initial of a *pratyaya udātta* is established, but that one may not be effected. The meaning is 'However, it is done, when initial *udātta* is to be effected for a *pratyaya'*, which makes known the non-existence of *āgamas*.

Pradīpa: 8.26 स्रौघ्नीति।

"Born or living in *Sṛughna*."

On the view that, a minute account has to be made for distinguishing (the word) when *sraughna* = *a* (of *Aḥ*) + *ī* (*ṅīp*) is established, due to the *paratva* (being subsequent) of the initial *udātta*, from the proposed alternative *sūtra 'pratyayasya ca'* (following after *6.1.197*), when *lopa* of *a* is effected by *'yasyeti ca' 6.4.148* ('The final *i* and *a* (long or short) or a *bha* stem are *lopa* elided before a *taddhita pratyaya* and before the feminine *pratyaya ī'*), because of the absence of 'cessation of *udātta'* the accent resulting from cessation of *udātta* (*'anudāttasya ca yatrodāttalopaḥ' 6.1.161*) would not be in place of *ī*. However, when there is simultaneous conjunction, at the time of ordaining initial *udātta* with the technical name *pratyaya*, there is no fault.

Pradīpa: 9.1 बहिरङ्गलक्षण इति।

"(Nor is the rule necessary because of the rule) being characterized as *bahir-aṅga*."

The cause of (indicating) femininity, long *ī*, is *bahiraṅga* since there is understanding of it as in regular course (being) for the sake of the meaning of the *prakṛti* etc. and the cause of *'lopa'*-elision of that is also *bahir-aṅga*.

Pradīpa: 9.7 औत्सीति।

"A female produced or being in a well, a female descendant of *Utsa*."

Born in a well. By *'utsādibhyo'ñ' 4.1.86*.

"The *pratyaya añ* acts after the word *utsa* etc., in the various senses taught prior to *'tena dīvyati'* etc. (*4.4.2*) etc."

Feminine *pratyaya ṅīp* is then added by *ṭiḍ-ḍhānañ-dvayasaj-daghnaj-mātrac-tayap-ṭhak-thañ-kañ-kvarapaḥ 4.1.15*. If here, due to being subsequent, *lopa* were to bar the initial *udātta* characteristic of that having an *it ñ*[47], then because of the nature of initial *udātta* being for a *pratyaya*, the (*udātta*) accent resulting from the cessation of (a prior) udātta, would be in fact applicable for the letter *ī*.

Pradīpa: 9.7 कंसिकी।

"A feminine thing made of or relating to bell-metal."

Bought with bell-metal. By *'kansāṭ-ṭiṭhan'* *5.1.25*

"The *pratyaya ṭiṭhan* (*ika*) acts in the senses taught up to *5.1.63* after the word *kansa.*"

And when *ṅīp* is also effected (by *4.1.15*) there is thought to be *udātta* when the *ika ādeśa* (in place of the letter *ṭh* by *7.3.50*) has not (yet) been effected.

Pradīpa: 9.7 आत्रेयीति।

"Female descendant of *Atri.*" By *'itaścāniñaḥ'* *4.1.122.*

"The *pratyaya ḍhak* (*eya*) acts in the sense of descendant, after a two-syllable nominal stem/*prātipadika* ending in short *i*, but not however, after a word ending in the patronymic *pratyaya iñ.*"

The *ādeśa eya* occurs first for the purpose of establishing the accent, which is like that in the *upadeśa* (original teaching, i.e. *ḍhak*) according to *'āyan-ey-īn-īy-īyaḥ pha-ḍha-kha-cha-ghām-pratyaya-ādīnām'* *7.1.2,* then *ṅīp.* Here the accent from cessation of *udātta* would not be applicable. However, when *antaraṅga* is being resorted to for accent, there is no fault.

Pradīpa: 9.11 कंसिक्यामिति।

"(Another device to remove the difficulty) in relation to *kansikā* (. . . *udātta* for one and *lopa* for the other).

The meaning is due to the *it c* of *ṭhac, ika ādeśa* is first, then initial *udātta* for the *pratyaya,* thus there is not *lopa* of *udātta.*

Pradīpa: 9.13 कित्स्वरम्।

"(Here *lopa* (by *'yasyeti ca 6.4.148*) being subsequent would bar the *udātta* accent on the final of that conjoined with that) having an *it k* (*'kitaḥ' 6.1.165 antaḥ, udāttaḥ, taddhitasya*)."

The meaning is that hence the accent resulting from cessation of *udātta* would not be applicable.

Now he states the purpose, 'When there is an accent rule in simultaneous conjunction with the technical name *pratyaya*'.

Pradīpa: 9.15 प्रत्ययाद्युदात्तत्वादिति। after [Vā 11]

"Instead of initial *udātta* for a *pratyaya* (final *udātta* for a *dhātu*)."

When *'pratyayasya ca'* is (proposed as) stated immediately after *ñ-nityādir-nityam' 6.1.197,* then due to being subsequent, the *pratyayasya ca'* accent would bar the *dhātu* accent. However, when it remains as read, then the *dhātu* accent bars the *pratyaya* accent.

Pradīpa: 9.20 पित्स्वरादिति।

"Instead of *anudātta* in connection with that having *it p* (*svarita* in connection with an *it t,* when feminine *tāp* follows)."

The sense is this is established as valid here, when there is ordaining of *anudātta,* (but) nowhere else.

Pradīpa: 9.22 कार्येति।

"(*It t* has scope here) 'It is to be made!'"

It is thought before *svarita* is the single *ādeśa.* In that context, due to being like the final, in relation to the prior for the single *ādeśa, it t,* accent (*svarita*) obtains. However, due to 'being like the initial in relation to the subsequent' there is occasion for *it p* accent.

Pradīpa: 10.3 न वेति।

"Nor is (*vipratiṣedha* applicable because initial *udātta* is taught in conjunction with the name *pratyaya*)."

The sense is that, due to the *antaraṅga* nature of the accent, simultaneously conjoined with the technical name *pratyaya,* there is not 'conflict of rules/*vipratiṣedha*'.

Pradīpa: 10.9 परत्वात्स्वरितत्वम्।

"The rule for *svarita* being subsequent (is applicable)."

This was stated without having regard to the *antaraṅga* of the *svarita.* For *ṭāp pratyaya* is a cause, which has regard to femininity and is a single *ādeśa* (for two) and is *bahiraṅga.*

Pradīpa: 10.17 आन्तर्यतः।

"Because of the near relationship (of *svarita* and *anudātta* accent, the one *ādeśa* for both will be *svarita*)."

However, when there is *svarita, anudātta* also exists (included within it), thus of the *svarita* and *anudātta,* the *svarita* is the nearest (in *sthāna*).

Pradīpa: 10.19 चापीति।

"And when *cāp* follows, (because of *it c,* final *udātta*)."

The sense is, if the nature of the *it c* had been for the purpose of not preventing general mention, then *'yaṅaṣṭāp'* would have been the *sūtra* enjoined in the section dealing with the *pratyaya ṭāp,* instead of the actual *sūtra* '*yaṅaścāp*' *4.1.74* 'The feminine *pratyaya cāp* acts after a stem which is formed by the *pratyaya ñyaṅ* or *ṣyaṅ*'.

Notes

[1]चितः *6.1.163* "For words formed with *pratyayas* having an indicatory *c* the *udātta* accent falls on the final, taking *prakṛti* and *pratyaya* as an aggregate."

bahu-c + *paṭuḥ* = *bahupaṭuḥ* Note: the accent is not on *'hu'* but on the last syllable of *prakṛti* + *pratyaya.* So with *akac* by *'avyayasarvanāmnāmakac-prākṭeḥ' 5.3.71. uccakaiḥ.*

Although the *pratyaya* is added in the middle of the word the accent will fall on the end.

[2]उपोत्तमम् रिति *6.1.217* A penultimate syllable can obviously be only in a word consisting of three or more syllables.

e.g. *karanīyam* to be made fr. *anīyar 3.1.96; haranīyam* to be taken. This debars *3.1.3.*

[3]अनुदात्तौ। सुपित्तौ *3.1.4 Apavāda of 3.1.3. dṛṣad au* = *dṛṣadau,* two stones (*au* is *anudātta*) *pacati* 'He cooks' (*ti* = *tip anudātta*) but not *pacataḥ* 'They two cook' because not *pit.*

[4]तित्स्वरितम् *6.1.185 cikīrṣyam* 'to be wished to be done' with *yat 3.1.97.*

[5]ञ्नित्यादिर्नित्यम् *6.1.197 gārgyaḥ* with *yañ* (*4.1.105*) Grandson or lower descendant of *Garga. vāsudevakaḥ* with *vun* (*4.3.98* '*vāsudevārjunābhyām vun*'). *Vāsudeva,* 'the God in which all dwell'.

This is an *apavāda* of *3.1.3.*

[6]तास्यनुदात्तेन्ङिददुपदेशाल्लसार्वधाकमनुदात्तमह्न्विङोः *6.1.186* "The personal endings and their sub- stitutes (*la 3.2.124-26*) are, when they are *sārvadhātuka* (*3.4.113* etc) *anudātta* accented, after the characteristic of the periphrastic future (*tāsi*), after a *dhātu* which in the *Dhātu Pāṭha* has an accented vowel or an indicatory *ṅ* (with the exception of *hnuṅ* and *iṅ*), as well as after what has a final *a* in the *Dhātu Pāṭha,"* e.g. *tāsi kārtā kātārau kārtāraḥ.*

This is *apavāda* of *pratyaya* accent by *3.1.3.*

[7]प्रत्ययग्रहनेयस्मात्स तदादेर्ग्रहणं भवति c.f. *Bhā. 1.2.48/224.4* etc.

This very important *paribhāṣā* states the guiding rule that, 'When a *pratyaya* is given in a rule as a *nimitta* (causing something) the *pratyaya* denotes a word form which begins with that to which the *pratyaya* has been added and ends with the *pratyaya* itself."

For example the *sūtra 'yañiñośca' 4.1.101* (*phak*), which prescribes *phak* (*āyana*), has the words *yañ* and *iñ* which respectively mean *yañanta* and *iñanta*. In the word *paramagārgyāyana* from *paramagārgya, gārgya* is looked upon as *añanta* to which *phak* (*āyana*) is affixed, and hence *paramagārgyāyana* is the form and not *paramagārgya*.

[8]धातोः *6.1.162* (*antaḥ, udāttaḥ*), e.g. *pacati, paṭhati* etc.

'prātipadikasyāntaḥ' 'For that ending in a *prātipadika*' is a reference to *'phiṣo'nta udāttaḥ' Phiṭ sutra 1.1* (*prātipadikam*) 'A nominal stem/*prātipadika* is finally *udātta*', e.g. *uccaiḥ*.

[9]आगमा अनुदात्ता भवन्तीति वक्ष्यामि "I will say augments are *anudātta*." *Pat.* probably refers to *3.4.103 Vā. 3/2.186.19, 20. 'āgamānudāttārtham vā' athavaitaj-jñapayatyācārya āgamā anudāttā bhavanti* c.f. *Vyāḍiparibhāṣā pāṭha pari. 105. 'āgama anudātta bhavanti'*.

[10]इट्। लविता। *lū dhātoḥ' 6.1.162 (antaḥ udāttaḥ); lū luṭ 'anudāttampadam-ekavarjam' 6.1.158 'syatāsī lṛluṭoḥ' 3.1.33; lū tāsi 'lasya' 3.4.77; lū tāsi tip 'tipthasjhi' 3.4.78 'anudāttau suppitau' 3.1.4; lū iṭ tāsi tip 'ārdhadhātukam śeṣaḥ' 3.4.114 'ārdhadhātukasyed-valādeḥ' 7.2.35 'sthānivad-ādeśo'nal-vidhau' 1.1.65; lū iṭ tāsi ḍa 'luṭaḥ prathamasya ḍāraurasaḥ' 2.4.85; lo iṭ ā 'teḥ' 6.4.143 'anudāttasya ca yatrodāttalopaḥ' 6.1.161; lavitā 'pugantalaghūpadhyasya ca' 7.3.86 'eco'yavāyavaḥ' 6.1.78.*

[11]परत्वादिडागमः। "Because of the *iṭ* rule being subsequent the *iṭ āgama* is applicable (before *ḍā* becomes *udātta* by *'anudāttasya ca yatrodātta-lopaḥ' 6.1.161*)." *'ārdhadhātukasya+iḍ valādeḥ । ṇalvidhau 1.1.56' 7.2.35* 'An *ārdhadhātuka pratyaya* (*3.4.114* etc.) beginning with a consonant (except *y*) receives the *āgama iṭ*', e.g. *lav-itā*.

[12]सीयुट् by लिङस्सीयुट् *3.4.102 'sīyuṭ is the āgama of liṅ* (optative).'

Lopa-elision of *s* by *'liṅaḥ salopo'nantyasya' 7.2.79; y lopa* by *'lopo vyor-vali '6.1.66, e.g. edheta* 'He may increase'.

[13]लिङः सीयुट् *2.4.102*

ut is indicatory; *u* usually indicates augment/*āgama*;

ṭ indicates it is to be added to the initial of that which follows, by *'ādyantau ṭakitau' 1.1.46 laviṣīya* 'May I cut'; *paviṣīya* 'May I purify'.

By *'iṭo't 3.4.106* (*liṅaḥ*) 'Short *a* is the *ādeśa* of the *i* of the *ātmanepada uttama puruṣa* (1st. Sg.) in the Optative and the Benedictive/*liṅ*'.

lūñ (kriyā. u. se. 1483 chedane) āśirliṅ

lū iṭ 'lasya' 3.4.77 'tiptasjhi '3.4.78

lo a 'sārvadhātukārdhadhātukayoḥ' 7.3.84 (iko guṇaḥ)

lo iṭ sīya 'liṅaḥ sīyuṭ' 2.4.102 'ārdhadhātukasyeḍ-valādeḥ' 7.2.35 laviṣīya 'eco'yavāyāvaḥ' 6.1.78 'ādeśapratyayayoḥ' 8.3.59

Similarly with *pūṅ (bhvā. ā. se. 966 pavane).*

[14]यासुट् परस्मैपदेषुदात्तो ङिच्च *3.4.103*

This is *apavāda* of *sīyuṭ*. The actual augment is *yās* (*u* indicates *āgama, ṭ* for the initial of that following).

All *āgamas* being *anudātta,* this *sūtra* uses the word *udātta* to show that this augment is an exception to the general rule.

Although *liṅ* has an indicatory *ṅ* and therefore, its substitute being *sthānivad 1.1.56* would also be regarded as having an *it ṅ* the repetition of *ṅit* in the *sūtra* indicates the *paribhāṣā 'lakārāśrayaṅitvamādeśānām na bhavati'* 'The *ṅ* belonging to *la* does not influence its substitutes', i.e. *laṅ* and *lṛṅ* are not regarded as having an *it ṅ,* e.g. *kuryāt 'liṅaḥ salopo'nantyasya' 7.2.79.*

[15]यासुटो ङिद्वचनं पिदर्थम् *3.4.103 Vā.1*

By *'anudāttau suppitau' 3.1.4* 'That which has an *it p/pit* is *anudātta'.*

'udāttavacanam ca' 3.4.103 Vā. 2. The corollary thus states that a *pratyaya* without an *it p* and not *sup,* is *udātta.*

So *yāsuṭ* is stated positively therefore, as being *udātta* (because of *'sārvadhātukam-apit' 1.2.4* ((*ṅit*) it would have been *ṅit* anyway). The specific statement is therefore, the basis of the *paribhāṣā 'lakāra . . .'* quoted in the previous note.

[16]लघीयसा न्यासेन सिद्धे सति यद्गरीयासंयत्नमारभते · · · (तज्-ज्ञापयत्याचार्य · · ·)

A regular formula of *Pat.* 'When this can be achieved by a briefer literal text, the fact that he begins a great effort suggests that the master makes known a *jñapaka* . . . c.f. *Bhā 1.2.27/204.24* etc.

[17] लविता अवादेश:। *av* is in place of the *o* of *lo* (*guṇa* of *lūñ*) by *eco 'yavāyāvaḥ 6.1.78* because of the following *ac* (vowel), *i-ṭ* (augment).

[18]लविता उदात्तादनुदात्तस्य स्वरित: *8.4.66.* This is 'one who cuts, a cutter *lūñ* (*1423 chedane*) + *tṛn' 3.2.135.* "The *pratyaya tṛn* acts after all *dhātus* in the sense of the agent having such a habit etc."

The *n* of the *trn* is indicatory and regulates accent by *'ñ-n-ityādir-nityam 6.1.197* 'Whatever formed by a *pratyaya* having an *it ñ* or *n* has *udātta* invariably on the first syllable.' *lū + tṛn, 6.1.197; lo tṛn 'sārvadhātukārdhādhatukayoḥ', 7.3.84; lo iṭ tṛ 'ārdhadhātukasyeḍvalādeḥ', 7.2.35, 'āgamā anudāttā bhavanti'; lav i tṛ 'eco 'yavayāvaḥ', 6.1.78; lav i tṛ su 'ṛduśanaspurudanśo 'nehasām ca', 7.1.94; lavi tṛ an s 'aptṛntṛcsvasṛnaptṛneṣṭṛtvas-tṛkṣatṛhotṛpotṛpraśāstṝṇām', 6.4.11; lavitān s'halṅyābhyo dirghātsutisyapṛktam hal', 6.1.68; lavitā 'na lopaḥ prātipadikāntasya' 8.2.7; lavitā 'udāttād-anudāttasya svaritaḥ', 8.4.66.*

Thus the augment *i-ṭ* becomes *svarita* because following the *udātta a* of *lav.*

19शिक्षित:। learnt, taught. *'niṣṭā ca dvyajanāt', 6.1.205* "A disyllabic participle (passive *kta* or active *ktavatu, 'ktaktavatū niṣṭhā 1.1.26*), when a name, has *udātta* on the first syllable but not if that syllable is an *ā*."

This is an *apavāda* of *3.1.3.*

śikṣitáḥ—Here *udātta* 'obtains' for the first *i* of *śikṣitá* because the second *i* is the augment *i-ṭ* and is 'as if it did not exist'/*avidyamānavat* (*M.Bh. 2.8.14* etc.), and this is not desired. In fact, because this form is polysyllabic the *sūtra* will not bar *3.1.3* and *udātta* falls on the *pratyaya kta.*

20 उदात्तनिवृत्तिस्वर:। "The accent resulting from the cessation of the preceding *udātta* by *'anudāttasya ca yatrodāttalopaḥ 6.1.161"*, "In the place of the *udātta* on a vowel, there is *udātta* accent, when on account of it the preceding *udātta* is *lopa*-elided", e.g. *kumāra* + *ī* (*ṅīp*) (*anudātta by 3.1.4*), *kumār-a lopa* (by *'yasyeti ca' 6.4.148*) *ī* becomes *udātta kumārī*

21स्रौघ्नी । *srughna* m. N. of a town to the N. of *Hāstināpura Var. Br. S.*

'phiṣo'nta udāttaḥ' 1.1 phiṭ; 'ādyudāttaśca' 3.1.3 (pratyayaḥ)

srughna + aṇ 'prāgdīvyato'ṇ' 4.1.83 'tatra jātaḥ' 4.3.25 (aṇ)

sraughnaḥ 'abhiniṣkrāmati dvāram' 4.3.86 born or living in *Srughna,* coming from or leading to *Srughna* etc., a gate which leads towards *Srughna.*

sraughna + ṅīp 'ṭiḍ-ḍhā-aṇ-añ-dvayasaj-daghnañ-mātrac-tayap-ṭhak-ṭhañ-kañ-kvarapaḥ' 4.1.15; anudāttau suppitau 3.1.4; sraughna ī 'yasyeti ca' 6.4.148; sraughnī 6.1.161 a woman born or living in *Srughna.* Similarly *māthurī* a woman born or living in *Mathura.*

22परत्वाल्लोप: प्रत्ययस्वराम् बाधेत। "Because of the *lopa*-elision of *a* being by a subsequent rule, namely, *'yasyeti ca' 6.4.148,* it would bar the *udātta* accent on the *pratyaya* enjoined by *3.1.3,* because of *'vipratiṣedhe paraṃ kāryam' 1.4.2* 'When rules of equal force prohibit each other, then the last in the order (of the *Aṣṭādhyāyī*) is to take effect."

23असिद्धं बहिरङ्गमन्तरङ्गे *pari. 50*

(a) *antaraṅga* is 'a rule, the causes of the application of which, lie within or before the sum of the causes of a *bahiraṅga* rule'. Put in another way we may say 'the *antaraṅga* rule always requires fewer operations than the *bahiraṅga*'. (*antaraṅga* and *bahiraṅga* are *bahuvrīhi* compounds; they are adjectives denoting a rule or an operation, or that taught in a rule). The word *aṅga* here, neither denotes 'member of a body' nor the grammatical term defined in *P. 1.4.13*; but it is equivalent to *'upakāraka'* 'that whieh assists (an operation) or it denotes the *nimitta* i.e. the cause of the operation.)

(b) *bahiraṅga* In a like manner that rule whose causes of application lie outside or beyond the causes of the *antaraṅga* rule is *bahiraṅga*, e.g. *siv* (to sew) + *na*, by *'cchvoḥ śuḍanunāsike ca'* 6.4.19; *si u* + *na* by *'pugantalaghūpadhasya ca' 7.3.86 guṇa* for *u* before *na* (*bahiraṅga*); or by *'iko yaṇaci' 6.1.77* *y* for *i* before *u* (*antaraṅga*); therefore, *syona* m.f.n. soft, n. soft couch.

(c) *asiddham c.f. 'pūrvatrāsiddham' 8.2.1* (Regarded as) not existing, or as not having taken effect (as a rule or operation taught in grammar), unaccomplished, uneffected, imperfect. see *pari. 36* and *79 Vyāḍi.*

[24]औत्सी। *utsa* + *añ*, *'utsādibhyo ñ' 4.1.86,* a spring, fountain *'tasyāpatyam' 4.1.92,* (metaphorically applied to *'ādyudattaśca' 3.1.3,* the clouds) *R.V.A.V.* etc.

utsa + *añ* + *ṅīp, 'ṭiḍ-ḍha-an-añ . . .' 4.1.15* (*ataḥ striyām*); *auts* + *añ* + *ṅīp, 'taddhiteṣvacāmādeḥ' 7.2.117* (*ñ-ṇiti, vṛddhi*); *autsa* + *ī, 'ñ-nityādir-nityam' 6.1.197* (*udāttaḥ*), *ṅīp, 'yasyeti ca' 6.4.148* (*bhasya, taddhite, lopaḥ*) *tanmitta lopaḥ bahiraṅga; autsī, 'udāttād-anudāttasya svaritaḥ' 8.4.66,* a female produced or being in a well.

See *Pradīpa 'yadyatra paratvāllopa ādyudāttatvam ñillakṣaṇam bādheta tadā pratyayasyodāttatvādudātta-nivṛttisvara īkārasya syād-eva.'*

Translation page 111 Pra. 9.7

[25]कांसिकी। *kansa,* m.n. (*dha. kamu. bhvā. ā. se. 443 kāntau* a vessel made of metal.

vṛtṝvadihanikamikaśibhyaḥ saḥ uṇ. 3.62) drinking vessel, cup. *A.V.X. 10.5*

kansa ṭiṭhan (= ika), 'kansāt-ṭiṭhan' 5.1.25, 'tena krītam' 5.1.37 etc., 'ādyudāttaśca' 3.1.3 kansa ṭiṭhan ṅīp, 'ṭiṭhānañ' 4.1.15, 'ṭhasyekaḥ' 7.3.50

kansau ika ī, 'ñ-hityadir-nityam' 6.1.197, 'yasyeti ca' 6.4.148

kansu ika ī, 'udāttād-anudāttasya svaritaḥ' 8,4,66

kasikī, a feminine thing relating to or made of bell-metal.

see *Pradīpa 'kansāt-ṭiṭhan-iti ṭiṭhani ṅīpi ca ṭhakārasyā'kṛta ikādeśe udāttatva man-yate'.*

Translation page 112. Pra. 9.7

[26] आत्रेयी। *atri,* (*ad = trini. ad. a. pa. a. 1011 bhakṣaṇe 'adestriniśca' Uṇ. 4.68*), a devourer *R.V.2.8.5;* N. of a great *ṛṣi,* author of a number of Vedic hymns.

atri ḍhak 'itaścāniñaḥ' 4.1.122 (*dvyacaḥ*), *'tasyāpatyam' 4.1.92*

ātri ḍhak, 'kiti ca' 7.2.118 (vṛddhi , taddhite Ṣv acām ādeḥ)

ātrey ṅīp, 'ṭiḍ-ḍhāṇañ ...' 4.1.15, 'āyaneyīnīyiyaḥphaḍhakhachghām pratyayādīnām' 7.1.2 [Here the *udātta* accent on the previously *anudātta ṅīp* which is the cause of the preceding *udātta* being elided, would not have been applicable if *'yasyeti ca'* operates first. But when the *antaraṅga* rule applies, there being (first resort for the sake of accent *6.1.161*) operates, there is no fault.], *'ādyudāttaśca' 3.1.3*

ātreyaī, '*kitaḥ*' *6.1.165* (*taddhitasya, antaḥ, udāttaḥ*) *ātreyī, 'yasyeti ca' 6.4.148*

ātreyī, 'anudāttasya ca yatrodāttalopaḥ' 6.1.161, female descendant of *Atri.*

Pāṇ. 2.4.65 'atribhṛgukutsavasiṣṭhagotamāṅgirobhyaśca' (bahuṣu, tenaivāstriyām luk)

See *Pradīpa 'āyannādiṣu upadeśivadvacanamsvarasiddhyarthamiti. pūrvam-eyādeśaḥ ṅīp. atrodattanivṛttisvara na syāt. antaraṅgatve tu svarasyāśrīyamaṇe doṣo'bhavaḥ.*

Translation page 112. Pra 9.7

[27]धातोरन्तः। by *'dhātoḥ' 6.1.162* (*antaḥ, udāttaḥ*) "A *dhātu* has *udātta*/acute accent on the final syllable", e.g. *pacati* (he cooks), *paṭhati* (he recites), *ūrṇoti* (he covers).

'vipratiṣedhena', by *'vipratiṣedhe paraṃ kāryam'* 1.4.2 'When rules of equal strength prohibit each other, then the last in the order of the *Aṣṭādhyāyī* is to take effect.'

i.e. *'dhātoḥ' 6.1.162* prevails over *'ādyudattaśca' 3.1.3*

[28]यत्र अनुदात्त प्रकृतिः। "When the base has *anudātta* accent." *samatvam simatvam,* e.g. equality, entirely/all. c.f. *Ph.s. 'tvattvasamasimetyanuccāni' 4.10* 'The words *tvat, tva, sama* and *sima* are wholly *anudātta*'. Examples *'nabhantāmanyake same' R.V. 8.39.1* 'May all the others die away',

'vāsastanute simasmai' R.V. 1.115.4 'Straight over all, night spreadeth out her garment'.

[29]गोपायति धूपायति। *'gupūdhūpavicchipaṇipanibhya āyah.' 3.1.28* 'The *pratyaya āya* acts after *dhātus gupū* (to protect), *dhūp* (to heat), *vicchi* (to approach), *paṇi* (to contract or praise), and *pan* (to praise)'. *'āyādaya ārdhadhātuke vā' 3.1.31* 'The *pratyaya āya* and those that follow it (*īyaṅ* and *ṇiṅ*) optionally act when it is intended to express oneself through the an *ārdhadhātuka pratyaya'.*

[30]पित्स्वरात्। "Instead of (*anudātta*) in connection with that having an *it p.*"

c.f. use of fifth case/*apādāna*/ablative similar to *Pāṇini* in *'anunāsikāt-paro'nusvāraḥ' 8.3.4/Si.K.137 'anunāsikam vihāya'roḥ pūrvasmātparo 'nusvārā-gamaḥ syāt'*

[31]विप्रतिषेधेन। "By reason of a conflict of rules of equal strength." *'anudattau suppitau' 3.1.4* 'The *sup*/case *pratyayas* and *pratyayas* having an indicatory *p* are *anudātta.*'

'titsvaritam' 6.1.185 'A *pratyaya* having an indicatory *t* is *svarita* (circumflex).'

[32] कार्यम्। 'to be made, done, effected, etc.' *ḍu-kṛñ (ta. u. a. 1472 karaṇe)* + *ñyat, 'ṛhalor-ṇyat,' 3.1.124, 'titsvaritam' 6.1.185;* similarly *hāryam*

[33]कार्या। *kārya + tāp, 'ajādyataṣṭāp' 4.1.4; 'akaḥ savarṇe dīrghaḥ' 6.1.101, 'titsvaritam' 6.1.185;* similarly *hāryā*

[34]चित्स्वरो विप्रतिषेधेन। *'citaḥ' 6.1.163,* 'A stem (formed by a *pratyaya* or *āgama* or *ādeśa*) having and indicatory *c* has *udātta* on the final syllable.' *'yaṅaścāp' 4.1.74,* 'The feminine *pratyaya cāp* acts after a stem which is formed by the *pratyaya ñyaṅ* or *ṣyaṅ*.'

[35]चलनः। moving, movable, tremulous, shaking. *cala (bhvā pa. se. 832 kampane)* + *yuc. 'calanaśabdārthād-akarmakād-yuc' 3.2.148 (tacchīlādiṣu). 'yuvor-anākau' 7.1.1.* Similarly *copanaḥ* 'moving'. *cupa (bhvā. pa. se. 403 mandāyām gatau) + yuc.*

[36]पित्स्वरस्य स एव। "The same is in fact an example of that having an *it p* because each with the *sup vibhakti su = s = ru = ḥ" by 'svaujas ...' 4.1.2, 'sasajuṣo ru' 8.2.66, 'kharavasā ...'* 8.3.15, *'anudāttau suppitau' 3.1.4.*

[37]आम्बष्ठ-, queen, princess of the *Ambaṣṭhas* or wife of the king of the *Ambaṣṭha*'s country, and people, or simply a woman of the *Ambaṣṭha* race *M.Bh. 7.3399* seqq.

ambaṣṭha, 'vaiśya ca dvijanma ca. tayoḥ sūtaḥ. ambe tisthati.'

sthā. (bhvā. pa. a. 928 gatinivṛttau) + ka

ambaṣṭha 'supi sthaḥ' 3.2.4, 'tasyāpatyam' 4.1.92 (aṇ)

ambaṣṭha + ñyaṅ = āmbaṣṭhya 'King of the *Ambaṣṭhas.' Ai. Br. 8.21.6*

'vṛddhet-kosalājādāññyaṅ' 4.1.171 (janapadaśabdāt, kṣatriyāt)

āmbaṣṭhya + cāp, 'yaṅaścāp' 4.1.74, 'anudāttau suppitau' 3.1.4, 'citaḥ' 6.1.163 Similarly *sauvīrya*

[38] सतिशिष्टत्वाद्धातुस्वरो भविष्यति। "There will be *udātta* for the *dhātu* because of its being residual'", *satiśiṣṭa* prescribed subsequently, occurring after the preceding has taken place. (c.f. *'sati śiṣṭe'pi vikaraṇasvaraḥ sārvadhātuk-asvaram na bādheta').* 'Even though prescribed subsequently, the *vikaraṇa* accent would not bar the accent on *sārvadhātuka pratyaya.*' Although the words *sati* and *śiṣṭa* are separate, they are generally taken as combined in an adjectival sense, qualifying the word *svara* accent, as in the dictum *'satiśiṣṭasvarabalīyastvam' Vā. 9* on *'anudattam padamekavarjam' 6.1.158.* 'There is comparatively superior strength for a subsequent accent which prevails by replacing all the ones obtaining before in the formation of the word.'

. . .*'anyatra vikaraṇebhya iti vaktavyam'* 'except when it is a *vikaraṇa* accent.' *S.K. 3650* c.f. *1.1.56* on *'sthānivadādeśo'nalvidhau' Vā. 33 bhā 'tatrārdhadhātu-kasāmānye'vadibhāve kṛte sati śiṣṭatvāt-pratyayasvaro bhaviṣyati' 3.2.83/2.110.13 'satiśiṣṭatvāc- svaraḥ prāpnoti'.*

[39]स्वरितेनैकदेश। "One substitute with *svarita* accent."

'akaḥ savarṇe dīrghaḥ' 6.1.101 (ekaḥ pūrvaparayoḥ) 'After an *ak* vowel (*a i u*

ṛ ḷ), in the presence of a *savarṇa* vowel (homogeneous/of the same family) the corresponding long vowel is the one for the one before and the one after (= *ekādeśa*)', but by this *vārttika* the accent on that long vowel will not overrule the *svarita*. e.g. *kārya* + *ṭāp* the one substitute here will be long *ā* with the *svarita* accent because this will be a later rule *6.1.185* than the *anudātta* by *3.1.4*.

[40]सम्प्रधार्यम्। "To be considered, deliberated upon." Frequently used by *Pat.* to indicate the view presented is now to be questioned.

[41]परत्वात्स्वरितत्वं नित्य एकादेशः etc.

See *pari*. *'paranityāntaraṅgāpavādānām-uttarottaram balīyaḥ' S.K. 46* on *'svaritenādhikāraḥ' 1.3.12*. 'Of the four kinds of rules, namely a subsequent *para*, an invariable *nitya*, an *antaraṅga* (inner, fewer operations), and an *apavāda* (special, exceptional) rule, each of the ones following possess greater force than any one of the rules mentioned before it.' (An expansion of *'vipratiṣedhe paraṃ kāryam' 1.4.2*.)

[42] परत्वात्। ··· नित्य ··· कृतेऽपि हिं ··· प्राप्नोत्यकृतेऽपि प्राप्नोति etc.

One of *Patañjali's* typical 'pattern arguments' found repeated almost word for word in many other places. c.f. *3.1.3 vā. 6/2.7.25, 3.1.36 vā. 4/2.45.23* etc.

[43]नित्य invariable, eternal.

(1) Eternal, as applied to *śabda* Word in contrast to *dhvani* sound which is *kārya* (evanescent). The sound with meaning or without meaning, made by men and animals is impermanent; but the sense of the idea awakened in the mind by the evanescent audible words, on reaching the mind is of permanent or eternal nature.

c.f. *'sphoṭaḥ śabdo dhvanis-tasya vyāyāmadupajāyate'*; c.f. *also vyāptimatvāt-tu śabdasya, Niru. 1.1*

(2) Constant, not liable to be set aside by another. c.f. *upabandhastu deśaya nityam na rundhe nityam nityaśabdaḥ prāptyantaraniṣedhārthaḥ Tai. Pra. 1.45.4.18*

(3) Unchangeable, permanent, imperishable.

c.f. *bhā on 8.1.4 'ayam nityaśabdo'styeva kūṭasthesvavicāliṣu bhāveṣu vartate'*.

(4) Always or invariably applying, as opposed to optional; in connection with rules that do not optionally apply. c.f. *'upapadasamāso nityasamāsaḥ ṣaṣṭhīsamāsaḥ punarvibhāṣā' bhā. on 2.2.19*

(5) Constant as applied to a rule which applies, if another simultaneously applying rule were to have taken effect, as well as when that rule does not take effect, c.f. *'kvacitkṛtākṛtaprasaṅgamātreṇāpnityatā' Pari. 46*. "Occasionally it happens that an operation is *nitya* solely because it would apply if (another

operation that applies simultaneously) were to have taken effect and applies when (that operation) does not take effect."

The operations which are *nitya* according to this *paribhāṣā* take effect in preference to others which are not *nitya* although they may be *para.* c.f. *'parānnityam balavat' Pari. 42* "A *nitya* rule possesses (greater) force than a subsequent rule, (which is not *nitya*) because it would apply if the subsequent rule were to have taken effect and applies when the latter does not take effect."

[44]पदग्रहणं परिसमानार्थम्। "The mention of *pada* (word) is made for the purpose of measure, so that there should be a unit fixed to a *pada* and not to a sentence as '*anudāttam padamekavarjam' 6.1.158.*" 'A *pada* is with exception of one syllable unaccented/*anudātta*', see *Uddyota on 4.3.1.40 Vā. 4 'padatvam yāvad-bhavati yāvataśca bhavati tāvat-tāvatī ca sannihitam ekavarjam sarvam-anudāttam bhavatītyathaḥ'*

[45] स्वरितत्वे कृत आन्तर्यतः स्वरितानुदात्तयोरेकादेशः स्वरितो भविष्यति।

"The *anudātta* accent exists within the *svarita,* as part of it, therefore, it is nearer in *sthāna* than *anudātta* in considering the *ekādeśa* for an *udātta*" of (*kārya*) and an *anudātta ā* (*tāp*).

Pra. 'svarita tvanudātto'pi vidyata iti svarita'nudāttayoḥ svarito'ntaratamaḥ'

c.f. *'samāhāraḥ svaritaḥ' 1.2.31, 'tasyāditaḥ udāttam-ardhahrasvam' 1.2.32*

[46]चित्करणासामर्थ्याद्। "Because of the force of mentioning *c.*"

Otherwise the *c* would be *vyartham* (useless) whereas *p* is standing for *anudātta* (otherwise it) would be for *sāmānyagrahanārtham* 'for the sake of general mention'.

[47] '"*ñ-nityādir-nityam*' *6.1.197* 'Whatever is derived with a *pratyaya* having an *it ñ* or *n* has *udātta* invariably on the first syllable'.

गुप्तिज्किद्भ्यः सन् ॥ 3 ॥ 1 । 5 ॥

Pāṇini 3.1.5: *San pratyaya* acts after the *dhātus gup, tij* and *kit.*

10.22 गुपादिष्वनुबन्धकरणं किमर्थम्।

Bhāṣya: What is the purpose of the indicatory letters in *gup-a* etc.?

10.23 गुपादिष्वनुबन्धकरणमात्मनेपदार्थम् ॥ 1 ॥

Vārttika 1: The producing of an indicatory letter in *gup-a* and the rest is for the purpose of *ātmanepada* (*vibhakti pratyayas*).

10.24 गुपादिष्वनुबन्धनाः क्रियन्ते आत्मनेपदं यथा स्यात्।। क्रियमाणेष्वप्यनुबन्धे- ष्वात्मनेपदं नैव प्राप्नोति। किं कारणम्। सना व्यवहितत्वात्। पूर्ववत्सनः (1.3.62) इत्येवं भविष्यति। पूर्ववत्सन इत्युच्यते न चैतेभ्यः प्राक्सन आत्मनेपदं नापि परस्मैपदं पश्यामः। एवं तर्ह्यनुबन्धकरणसामर्थ्याद्भविष्यति।। अथवावयवे कृतं लिङ्गं समुदायस्य विशेषकं भविष्यति। तद्यथा। गोः सक्थनि

11.5 कर्णे वा कृतं लिङ्गं गोर्विशेषकं भवति। यद्यवयवे कृतं लिङ्गं समुदायस्य विशेषकं भवति जुगुप्सयति मीमांसयतीत्यत्रापि प्राप्नोति। अवयवे कृतं लिङ्गं कस्य समुदायस्य विशेषकं भवति। यं समुदायं योऽवयवो न व्यभिचरति। सनं च न व्यभिचरति णिचं पुनर्व्यभिचरति। तद्यथा। गोः सक्थनि कर्णे वा कृतं लिङ्गं

11.9 गोरेव विशेषकं भवति न गोमण्डलस्य।।

Bhāṣya: The indicatory letters in *gup-a* and the rest are produced so that there be *ātmanepada* (*pratyayas*) applicable.

(Now) even when the indicatory letters are being produced this *ātmanepada* does not in fact obtain. What is the reason? Because of being separated by (*pratyaya*) *san*.

(The rule) *pūrvavat sanaḥ (1.3.62)* "A *dhātu* which is *ātmanepada* in its original form before taking *san*, will also be *ātmanepada* when it ends in the *pratyaya san*", thus will be applicable.

It is said that (*ātmanepada* endings are added) to a *dhātu* ending in *san* and after these not before *san* is added to we neither see *ātmanepada* nor *parasmaipada*. Then by (reason of) creating indicatory letters (*ātmanepada* endings) will be added.

Or else a sign made in a part will be distinctive of the whole. As for example, a mark on the thigh or ear of a cow is a distinguishing characteristic of the cow. If a sign made on a part becomes the distinction of the whole then (*ātmanepada* would be) wrongly applicable also to *jugupsayati* (He causes someone to seek to defend themself or be on their guard), *mīmānsayati* (he causes someone to investigate). Of which whole does the mark made on a part become the characteristic? Of that from which a part does not deviate. It does not deviate from *san*, but from *ṇic* it does deviate (i.e. *san* is *nitya*, *ṇic anitya*). For instance the mark made on a cow's thigh or ear is a characteristic of a cow and not a group of cows.

Pradīpa

Pradīpa: 10.21 गुबिति।

There the recitation of *kit* was simply for showing succession (of *dhātus* in the text), but not to indicate (having an *it k* and therefore) as being *'anudāttet'* 'having an indicatory *anudātta* vowel' (and therefore, *ātmanepada 1.3.12*).

अनुदात्तङित्त आत्मनेपदम्

'After a *dhātu* with an *anudātta* vowel or an indicatory *ṅ* the *vibhakti pratyayas* are *ātmanepada.*'

Pradīpa: 10.22 गुपादिष्विति।

'What is the purpose of the *it* letter in *gup* etc.? The question is : Is it due to the invariable nature of the *san's* sphere of application, because of the non-production of *laṭ* etc. after (*dhātus*) without any other (*vikaraṇa*) (*pratyaya*) ?

Pradīpa: 10.23 आत्मनेपदर्थम् इति। [Vā]

'(The *it* letter in *gup-a* etc.) is for the purpose of *ātmanepadam*'.

The sense is after those ending in *san.*

c.f. *'svaritaṅitaḥ kartrabhiprāye kriyāphale' 1.3.72*

'After a *dhātu* marked with a *svarita* accent or which has an indicatory *it ṅ,* the terminations of the *ātmanepada* are employed when the fruit of the action accrues to the agent.'

Pradīpa: 11.1 पूर्ववद्-इति।

'A *dhātu ātmanepada* in its original form before *san,* will be *ātmanepada* when it ends in *san.*' The sense is, due to the extended application of the sign (of *ātmanepada*).

पूर्ववत्सनः 1.3.62

'After a desiderative *dhātu ātmanepada* is employed if it would have been used after the original *dhātu.*'

The general rule: 'If the primary *dhātu* is *parasmaipada* its desiderative will also be *parasmaipada;* if the primary *dhātu* is *ātmanepada* its desiderative will be *ātmanepada*'.

Pradīpa: 11.2 न चैतेभ्य इति।

"And after these (*dhātus* without *upasarga* before *san,* we see neither *ātmanepada* nor *parasmaipada*).'

That is an extended application of an operation. The sense is that when there is extended application of a sign (of *pada*), however, there is the possibility of *ātmanepada* also in examples like '*anucikīrṣati*' 'He desires to imitate'.

Pradīpa: 11.3 एवंतर्हीति।

"Then, indeed (by force of the producing *it* letters *ātmanepada* will be applicable)."

The sense is, even when separated by *san.*

Pradīpa: 11.4 अथवेति।

"Or else (a sign made in a part will be distinctive of the whole)."

The sense is that, where there is no purpose for the attachment of a sign on a part, that is in fact for the purpose of the whole. The *bhāṣya* is taught (as words of the wise). Here in (discussion on) '*pūrvavatsanaḥ*' the explanation is diffusely given, hence it has to in fact be determined (if it is *bhāṣyakāra's* or another's view!)

Pradīpa: 11.5 लिङ्गम् गोर्विशेषकं भवति।

"(A mark on the thigh or ear of a cow) is the distinguishing characteristic of the cow."

See *lakṣaṇa* for *liṅga* in *P. 6.3.115 'karne lakṣaṇasya ...'*

'Before *karṇa* there is the substitution of a long vowel for the final of the preceding word, when it denotes a proprietorship mark on the ears of cattle ...

e.g. *dātrākarṇaḥ*

Kāś. 'yat paśūnām svāmiviśeṣasambandha jñāpanārtham dātrākarādi kriyate tad-iha lakṣaṇam gṛhyate.'

'The word *lakṣaṇa* here means a peculiar mark put or made on the ears of animals in the form of a sickle etc. showing the propriertorship.'

Pradīpa: 11.6 जुगुप्सयति।

'He causes someone to seek to be on their guard.'

'*mimānsayati*' 'He causes someone to investigate'.

Neither are found in the literature.

If the sign on a part were to become the distinction of the whole, the rule '*pūvavatsanaḥ*' *1.3.62* would become applicable to the causative of the desiderative as well. Whereas in fact the addition of *ṇi* has the effect of forming a new *dhātu* independent of this *sūtra's* influence.

मान्बधदान्शान्भ्यो दीर्घश्चाभ्यासस्य ॥ 3 । 1 । 6 ॥

Pāṇini 3.1.6: The *Pratyaya san* acts after the *dhātus mān, badha, dān* and *śān* and there is a long vowel for the reduplicative syllable.

11.15 अभ्यासदीर्घत्वेऽवर्णस्य दीर्घप्रसङ्गः ॥ 1 ॥

Vārttika 1: When a long (is ordained) for the reduplicative syllable there is occasion for lengthening of the letter *a*.

11.12 अभ्यासस्य दीर्घत्वेऽवर्णस्य दीर्घत्वं प्राप्नोति। मीमांसते।। ननु चेत्त्वे कृते दीर्घत्वं भविष्यति।। कथं पुनरुत्पत्तिसंनियोगेन दीर्घत्वमुच्यमानमित्वं प्रतीक्षते। अथ
11.14 कथमभ्यासं प्रतीक्षते। वचनादभ्यासं प्रतीक्षत इत्त्वं पुनर्न प्रतीक्षते।

Bhāṣya: When lengthening (is ordained) for the reduplicative syllable, lengthening of the letter *a* wrongly applies, e.g. *mīmānsate* 'He reflects upon, considers or investigates'. Now surely when *i* (augment) is produced, there will be lengthening. But how (when) lengthening is being stated in conjunction with the arising (of the *pratyaya*), does one expect the letter *i*? Now how does one expect a reduplicative syllable? One expects a reduplicative syllable because of the rule (*sanyaṅoḥ 6.1.9*), (because lengthening is ordained for the reduplicative syllable), but one does not expect augment *i*.

11.15 न वाभ्यासविकारेष्वपवादस्योत्सर्गाबाधकत्वात्[1] ॥ 2 ॥

Vārttika 2: Or there is no (difficulty) because of the *apavāda* (*sūtra*) not annulling the *utsarga* (*sūtra*) in case of modification in the reduplicative syllable.

11.16 न वैष दोषः। किं कारणम्। अभ्यासविकारेष्वपवादस्योत्सर्गाबाधकत्वात्। अभ्यासविकारेष्वपवादा उत्सर्गान्न बाधन्त इत्येवं दीर्घत्वमुच्यमानमित्वं न बाधिष्यते।। अथवा मान्बधदान्शान्भ्य ई चाभ्यासस्येति वक्ष्यामि। एवमपि हलादिशेषा-

पवाद ईकारः प्राप्नोति। ई चाच इति वक्ष्यामि।। अथवा मान्बधदान्शान्भ्यो दीर्घश्चेतोऽभ्यासस्येति वक्ष्यामि। सिध्यति। सूत्रं तर्हि भिद्यते।। यथान्यासमेवास्तु। ननु चोक्तमभ्यासदीर्घत्वेऽवर्णस्य दीर्घप्रसङ्ग इति। परिहृतमेतन्न वाभ्यास-विकारेष्वपवादस्योत्सर्गाबाधकत्वादिति।। अथवा नैवं विज्ञायते दीर्घश्च अभ्यासस्येति। कथं तर्हि। दीर्घश्च आभ्यासस्येति। किमिदमाभ्यासस्येति। अभ्यासविकार[2] आभ्यासः तस्येति।।

Bhāṣya: Nor is this a fault? What is the reason? Because in relation to change in the reduplicative syllable the *apavāda* do not annul the *utsarga* (*sūtras*).

When there are changes in the reduplicative syllable, the *apavāda* (*sūtras*) do not annul the *utsarga* (*sūtras*). Thus lengthening being stated, the letter *i* will not annul it.

Or else I will (rephrase the *sūtra* and) say, "after *mān, badha, dān* and *śān,* (*san pratyaya*) and long *ī* acts in place of the reduplicative syllable". So also long *ī* obtains as *apavāda* (of the rule) *halādiḥ śeṣāḥ (7.4.60)* "Of the consonants of the reduplicative syllable only the first is retained, the remainder are elided".

I will (modify the *sūtra*) and say " . . . and long *ī* is in place of the vowel (of the reduplicative syllable)".

Or else I will (modify the *sūtra* and) say " . . . *san pratyaya* acts after *mān, badha, dān* and *śān* and there is lengthening of the short *i* of the reduplicative syllable". It is (now) established. But then the *sūtra* is split (into two).

Let it be according to the text of the *sūtra* as laid down.

Now, was it not indeed surely said, "When there is lengthening of the reduplicative syllable there is occasion for lengthening of *a*" (*Vārttika 1*) ? This was avoided by *Vārttika 2.* Nor when there are changes in the reduplicative syllable do *apavādas* debar *utsarga sūtras.*

Or else (the *sūtra*) is not understood thus (as reading) *dīrghaśca abhyāsasya* "and lengthening of the reduplicative syllable". How then? *dīrghaścābhyāsasya* "and lengthening of the changed/modified reduplicative syllable". What is the meaning of *ābhyāsasya* ? *Ābhyāsa* is change of (or prescribed in connection with) the reduplicative syllable. "Of that (let there be lengthening)".

Pradīpa

Pradīpa: 11.11 अभ्यास दीर्घ इति।

"When long is ordained for the reduplicative syllable . . ."

He says this because the special rule (would) bar the general *sūtra.*

Pradīpa: 11.13 अथ कथमिति।

"Now how (when lengthening is being stated in conjunction with the arising of the *pratyaya,* does one expect the letter *i*) ?

The sense is that just as because of the statement in the rule 'for the reduplicative syllable' lengthening is expected of the vowel of the *abhyāsa,* so due to another statement of rule 'ordained *i*' also (is expected).

Pradīpa: 11.15 अभ्यासविकारेष्विति। [Vā]

"(*Apavāda* does not bar *utsarga*) in the case of modification of the reduplicative syllable."

And this (the *sūtrakāra*) will make known by the mention of *akit* in the *sūtra.* Here *'dirgho' kitaḥ'* 7.4.83 'A long vowel is *ādeśa* for the *a* of the reduplicate in the Intensive (with expressed or elided *yaṅ*) when the reduplicate receives no augment having an indicatory *k* (like *nīk* and *nuk*)'. This gives the first condition for the *jñāpaka,* 'because when the augment *n* is added the reduplicate will end in a consonant, and not ending in a vowel there will be no occasion for lengthening, hence the use of *akitaḥ*' is gone.

Pradīpa: 11.20 ई चाच इति।

"(I will say) and long *ī* (is in place of the vowel of the reduplicative syllable)."

The meaning is, 'in place of the final of that ending in a vowel'. And when *'halādiśeṣaḥ' 7.4.60* 'Of the consonants of the reduplicate, only the first is retained, the remainder *lopa*-elided', is not effected, there is no vowel ending final.

Pradīpa: 11.24 अभ्यास विकार इति।

"The *Abhyāsa* is changed (and) prescribed in connection with the reduplicative syllable."

And that is in fact 'having *i*'. For so it is not possible just for the *ādeśa* of *lopa* to be ordained, due to not having (the nature of) a form. And if there were lengthening of a short vowel, then the indication of the *taddhita* form (*ābhyāsa*) would be pointless. Due to the proximity of 'the vowel *paribhāṣā*' with the hearing of *dīrgha* (lengthening) because of ordaining lengthening for what has a final vowel; when there is ordaining of long, it is either for a short or a long vowel, because of the absence of distinction. Therefore, the nature of *i* alone is made known by the *taddhita* formation. Otherwise, having rendered that null when *san* follows, that modification/*vikāra* which is ordained by *'sanyataḥ' 7.4.79* ('*i* is the *ādeśa* for a final short *a* of *a* reduplicate in the Desiderative',) is understood to be mentioned for that alone. And short is applicble for *bādh-i* also as for *mān* etc. by the application of the maxim *parjanyavat* (like the rain, *sūtras* fall on all respectively).

Notes

[1]न वाभ्यासविकारेष्वपवादस्योत्सर्गबाधकत्वात्।

c.f. Pari. 66, 'abhyāsavikāreṣu bādhyabādhakabhyāsa nāsti' 'So far as changes of the reduplicative syllable are concerned, rules (which teach those changes) do not supercede one another.' So the substitution of short *i* (by *7.4.79*) would be superceded by the substitution of a long vowel (*3.1.6*) for the vowel of the reduplicate syllable because this latter rule is *antaraṅga* in regard to the former.

[2]अभ्यासविकार: आभ्यास:। c.f. *tasya vikāraḥ' 4.3.134*, 'The *pratyaya aṇ* (and the rest *4.1.83* etc.) act after a word in the sixth case in construction in the sense of 'a modification thereof'.'

धातोः कर्मणः समानकर्तृकादिच्छायां वा ॥ 3 ॥ 1 ॥ 7 ॥

Pāṇini 3.1.7: Optionally the *pratyaya san* acts in the sense of desire after a *dhātu* expressing the object (wished for) and having the same agent of action (as the wisher).

12.2 धातोरिति किमर्थम्। प्रकर्तुमैच्छत् प्राचिकीर्षत्[1]। सोपसर्गादुत्पत्तिर्मा भूत्[2]।

Bhāṣya: What is the purpose of saying "after a *dhātu*"? *Prakartum aicchat* or *prācikīrṣat* "He wanted to make". So that there should not be arising (of *san*) after (*dhātu*) in conjunction with/along with an *upasarga.*

12.3 कर्मग्रहणात्सन्विधौ धातुग्रहणानर्थक्यम्।। 1 ।।

Vārttika 1: Because of the mention of *karman* in the *san* rule the mention of *dhātu* is pointless.

12.4 कर्मग्रहणात्सन्विधौ धातुग्रहणमनर्थकम्। कर्मणः समानकर्तृकदिच्छायां वा सन्भवतीत्येव धातोरुत्पत्तिर्भविष्यति। सोपसर्गं वै कर्म तत उत्पत्तिः प्राप्नोति।।

Bhāṣya: Because of the mention of *karman* in the rule (ordaining) *san*, the mention of *dhātu* is pointless. Since (it was) just (stated), "Optionally (*san* acts) in the sense of desire after that expressing the object (wished for) and having the same agent of the action (as the wisher)", "there will be arising (of *san*) after the *dhātu*". A *dhātu* along with an *upasarga* (would in fact be having) an object/*karman*, hence *san* wrongly obtains after that.

12.6 सोपसर्गं कर्मेति चेत्कर्मविशेषकत्वादुपसर्गस्यानुपसर्गं कर्म ।। 2 ।।

Vārttika 2: If (you say) the *karman* is the *dhātu* together with an *upasarga*, because of an *upasarga* being a qualification of *karman* (in reality) *karman* is (a *dhātu*) without an *upasarga*.

12.7 सोपसर्गं कर्मेति चेत्कर्मविशेषक उपसर्गः। अनुपसर्गमेव हि कर्म।। अवश्यं चैतदेवं विज्ञेयमनुपसर्गं कर्मेति।

Bhāṣya: If (we say) *karman* is (a *dhātu*) together with an *upasarga* (we imply that) an *upasarga* specifies or distinguishes *karman*. Surely in reality *karman* is without an *upasarga*. And it is essential that this should be thus known that *karman* is without an *upasarga*.

12.9 सोपसर्गस्य हि कर्मत्वे धात्वधिकारेऽपि सनोऽविधानमकर्मत्वात् ।। 3 ।।

Vārttika 3: For when the *karman* is together with an *upasarga*, even in the context of the governing *sūtra*, *dhātoḥ*, there is no rule for *san* because of the *dhātu* not being the *karman*/object.

12.10 यो हि मन्यते सोपसर्गं कर्मेति क्रियमाणेऽपि तस्य धातुग्रहणे सनोऽविधिः स्यात्। किं कारणम्। अकर्मत्वात् ।।

12.12 इदं तर्हि प्रयोजनं सुबन्तादुत्पत्तिर्मा भूत्।।

Bhāṣya: For him who thinks *karman* is together with an *upasarga* even when specific mention of the word *dhātu* is being made for it, the *san* rule would not be (applicable) to *san*. What is the reason? Because of (*dhātu*) not being a *karman*.

This then is the purpose, so that (*san*) should not act after a word ending in a *sup*/case ending.

12.13 सुबन्ताच्चाप्रसङ्गः क्यजादीनामपवादत्वात् ।। 4 ।।

Vārttika 4: And there is not occasion (for *san* acting after) a word ending in *sup*/case ending because of *kyac* and the rest having the nature of *apavāda* rules (annulling the effects of the *utsarga* rules).

12.14 सुबन्ताच्चा सनोऽप्रसङ्गः। किं कारणम्। क्यजादीनामपवादत्वात्।
सुबन्तात्क्यजादयो विधीयन्ते तेऽपवादत्वादबाधका भविष्यन्ति ।।

Bhāṣya: And there is no occasion for *san* acting after a *sup*/case ending. What is the reason? Because of *kyac* and the rest having the nature of *apavāda* (*sūtras* annulling the effects of *utsarga sūtras*). *Kyac* and the rest ordained after word *sup*/case ending. Being *apavāda sūtras* they will annul (the *utsarga san sūtra*).

12.16 अनभिधानाद्वा ।। 5 ।।

Vārttika 5: Or because of not expressing (the meaning desired).

12.17 अथवानभिधानात्सुबन्तादुत्पत्तिर्न भविष्यति। न हि सुबन्तादुत्पद्यमानेन
सनेच्छाया अभिधानं स्यात्। अनभिदानात्तत उत्पत्तिर्न भविष्यति।।
इयं तावदगतिका गतिर्यदुच्यतेऽनभिधानादिति।। यदप्युच्यते सुबन्ताच्चाप्रसङ्गः
12.20 क्यजादीनामपवादत्वादिति भवेत्कस्माच्चिदप्रसङ्गः स्यादात्मेच्छायाम्। परेच्छायां तु
प्राप्नोति। राज्ञः पुत्रमिच्छतीति। एवं तर्हीदमिह व्यपदेश्यं सदाचार्यो न व्यपदिशति।
किम्। समानकर्तृकादित्युच्यते न च सुबन्तस्य समानः कर्तास्ति। एवमपि
भवेत्कस्माच्चिद्प्रसङ्गः स्याद्यस्य कर्ता नास्ति। इह तु प्राप्नोति आसितुमिच्छति
शयितुमिच्छतीति। इच्छायामर्थे सन्विधीयत इच्छार्थेषु च तुमुन्। तत्र तुमुनोक्त-
13.1 त्वात्तस्यार्थस्य सन्न भविष्यति। एवमपीह प्राप्नोति आसनमिच्छति शयनमिच्छतीति।
इह यो विशेष उपाधिर्वोपादीयते द्योत्ये तस्मिंस्तेन भवितव्यम्। यश्चेहार्थो गम्यते
आसितुमिच्छति शयितुमिच्छतीति स्वयं तां क्रियां कर्तुमिच्छतीति नासाविह गम्यते
आसनमिच्छति शयनमिच्छतीति। अन्यस्याप्यासन-
13.5 मिच्छतीत्येषोऽप्यर्थो गम्यते। अवश्यं चैतदेवं विज्ञेयम्। यो हि मन्यतेऽद्योत्ये
त-स्मिंस्तेन भवितव्यमिति क्रियमाणेऽपि तस्य धातुग्रहण इह प्रसज्येत
संगतमिच्छति
13.7 देवदत्तो यज्ञदत्तेनेति।।

Bhāṣya: Or else because of not expressing (the meaning desired in the proper way) there will not be the arising of *san* after a word ending in a *sup*/case *pratyaya.* For by (conjunction) with *san* being produced after a *sup pratyaya* there would not be expression of the meaning 'desire'.

Hence because of not expressing (the meaning of desire) there will not be production (of a word form).

This is the resort of one who has no (other) resort (i.e. last resort, c.f. *Yajñ. 1.4.345*) namely when it is said 'because of not expressing (the meaning desired)'. Moreover it is said, there is not occasion (for *san*) after a *sup*/case ending word, because of *kyac* and the rest having the character of *apavāda* (special rules setting aside general ones). That may be so. There may be no occasion after some *sub-anta* words when the sense is 'desire for oneself'. But when the desire is for the sake of another (*san*) obtains, e.g. "He desires a son for the king". Well, then this is here sometimes (something) to be indicated which the Master does not indicate. What? "After a (*dhātu*) having the same agent (as the wisher)" is stated, but the same agent is not found in connection with a word ending in a *sup pratyaya.* It may even happen that there is non-applicability (of *san*) after something (or other) which does have the same agent; but here it does obtain, "He desires to sit down", "He desires to lie down".

San is ordained in the sense of desire, and *tumun* (is ordained) in the sense of desire. There, because of being expressed by *tumun, san* will not be applicable for that meaning.

But then here it obtains "He wants a place to sit"(on), "He wants a place to lie" (on). That (*san*) should be ordained when it is understood/taken as a specific feature or quality is to be indicated. Here what is taken as a special quality or qualification, when it is expressed, should be by means of that (*pratyaya*). And here the meaning, that is understood from "He wants to sit" and "He wants to lie down", namely that he himself wants to do that action, is not understood from the expressions "He desires a seat" or "He desires a bed".

Also "He desires a seat for another" is also understood as the meaning. It is essential too that this should be realised. For he who thinks "when it is not expressed (*san*) should be there even while being formed" (would make) the specific mention of *dhātu* for that (context) wrongly be applicable. As "*Devadatta* desires friendship with *Yajñadatta*".

13.8 कर्मसमानकर्तृकग्रहणानर्थक्यं चेच्छाभिधाने प्रत्ययविधानात् ॥ 6 ॥

Vārttika 6: And the mention of the object having the same agent is pointless because of the ordaining of the *pratyaya* when 'desire is being expressed'.

13.9 कर्मसमानकर्तृकग्रहणं चानर्थकम्। किं कारणम्। इच्छाभिधाने प्रत्ययविधानात्। इच्छायामभिधेयायां सन्विधीयते।।

Bhāṣya: The mention of the agent (being) the same (for the *dhātu*) as for the *karman* /object is pointless. What is the reason? Because of the ordaining of the *pratyaya* (*san*) when desire is to be expressed. When desire is being expressed *san* is ordained.

13.11 अकर्मणो ह्यसमानकर्तृकाद्वानभिधानम् ।। 7 ।।

Vārttika 7: (*San*) is not known (to occur) after that which is not *karman*/ object and which has not the same agent (as that of the wisher of the *karman*).

13.12 इच्छायामभिधेयायां सन्विधीयते न चाकर्मणोऽसमानकर्तृकाद्वोत्पद्यमानेन सनेच्छाया अभिधानं स्यात्। अनभिधानात्तत उत्पत्तिर्न भविष्यति ।।

Bhāṣya: When desire is being expressed *san* is ordained but not after that which is not *karman* or not having the same agent (as that of the *karman*) and by the *san* being produced there may be expression of desire. Hence due to not expressing it there will not be arising (of the form).

13.14 अङ्गपरिमाणार्थं[3] तु ।। 8 ।।

Vārttika 8: However for the purpose of determining the *aṅga.*

13.15 अङ्गपरिमाणर्थं तर्ह्यन्यतरत्कर्तव्यं कर्मग्रहणं धातुग्रहणं वा। अङ्गपरिमाणं ज्ञास्यामीति।। किं पुनरत्र ज्याय:। धातुग्रहणमेव ज्याय:। अङ्गपरिमाणं चैव विज्ञातं भवत्यपि च धातोर्विहित: प्रत्यय: शेष अर्थधातुकसंज्ञ[4] भवतीति सन आर्धधातुकसंज्ञा सिद्धा भवति।।

यच्चाप्येतदुक्तं कर्मग्रहणात्सन्विधौ धातुग्रहणानर्थक्यं सोपसर्गं कर्मेति चेत्कर्मवि-
13.20 शेषकत्वादुपसर्गस्यानुपसर्गं कर्म सोपसर्गस्य हि कर्मत्वे धात्वधिकारेऽपि मनोऽवि-
धानमकर्मत्वादिति स्वपक्षोऽनेन वर्णित:। युक्तमिह द्रष्टव्यं किं न्याय्यं कर्मेति। एतच्चात्र युक्तं यत्सोपसर्गं कर्मात्। कर्म स्यात्। ननु चोक्तं सोपसर्गस्य हि कर्मत्वे धात्वधिकारेऽपि सनोऽविधानमकर्मत्वादिति। नैष दोष:। कर्मण इति नैषा ध
ातु-समानाधिकरणा पञ्चमी[5]। कर्मणो धातोरिति। किं तर्हि। अवयवयोगैषा षष्ठी[6]।
13.25 कर्मणो यो धातुरवयव इति। यद्यवयवयोगैषा षष्ठी केवलादुत्पत्तिर्न प्राप्नोति। चिकीर्षति[7] जिहीर्षतीति। एषोऽपि व्यपदेशिवद्भावेन[8] कर्मणो धातुरवयवो भवति। कामं तर्ह्यनेनैव हेतुना क्यजपि कर्तव्य:[9]। महान्तं पुत्रमिच्छतीति। कर्मणो य-त्सुबन्तमवयव इति। न कर्तव्य:। असामर्थ्यान्न भविष्यति। कथमसामर्थ्यम्।
14.2 सापेक्षमसमर्थं[10] भवतीति।।

Bhāṣya: Then for the purpose of determining the *aṅga* the reference should be made to either *karman* or *dhātu* (so that) "I will know the measure of *aṅga*".

But which one is preferable? The (specific) mention of *dhātu* is preferable (to *karman*). And in fact the measure of the *aṅga* is known, as also the technical name *ārdhadhātuka* is established for *san* (by the statement) "the rest (of the *pratyayas* ordained after a *dhātu* have the technical name) *ārdhadhātuka*" (*3.4.114*).

And as for that which was said "because of the specific mention of the word *karman* in the *san* rule, the specific mention of the word *dhātu* is pointless" (Vā 1) "If (it is argued) *karman* with an *upasarga*, because of the *upasarga's* nature of qualifying *karman*, the *karman* is (in fact) without or distinct from the *upasarga*" (*Vā 2*) "for even when there is the characteristic of *karman* for an *upasarga* conjoined (with a *dhātu*) when in the sphere of the *dhātu* governing rule (*3.1.91*), because of the absence of characteristic *karman* there is no ordaining of *san*" (*Vā 3*). By this (statement) was described (the *purva pakṣa's*) own view.

It is proper to see which is a proper *karman*. And this is proper here that (a *dhātu*) conjoined with an *upasarga* should be *karman*. But surely it was said, "for even when there is the characteristic of *karman* for an *upasarga* in conjunction (with a *dhātu*) in the sphere of the *dhātu* governing rule, because of the absence of the chacteristic *karman* there is no affixing of *san*" (*Vā 3*).

This is not a fault. (The word) *karmaṇaḥ* (in the *sūtra*) is not fifth case in the same case relationship, i.e. in apposition with the word *dhātu*, as *karmaṇo dhātor* (which would mean 'after a *dhātu* which is *karman*'). What then (is it) ? This is sixth case 'signifying part' as 'that *dhātu* which is part of a *karman*'. If this is sixth case signifying (syntactical dependence on) a part, the arising (of *san*) after (a *dhātu*) alone does not obtain e.g. *cikīrṣati* (he desires to make) *jihīrṣati* (he desires to take).

This also is a *dhātu* by reason of its nature of representing (a secondary thing as the principal one) which is part of *karman*.

Then granted, by the reason of this very cause *kyac* also is to be applied, here obtains "He desires a great son" and thus (seems to apply) 'that *sup*/ case ending word which is a part of *karman*'. It is not to be applied. Because of their being no syntactical connection (*san*) will not be applicable. How is there not syntactical connection or adequacy? The 'inadequacy' is 'That which has expectancy is not in syntactical connection (with another word)'.

14.3 वावचनानर्थक्यं च तत्र नित्यत्वात्सनः ॥ 9 ॥

Vārttika 9: And the word *vā* (optionally) is pointless because of the invariable nature of *san* in that context.

14.4 वावचनं चानर्थकम्। किं कारणम्। तत्र नित्यत्वात्सनः। इह द्वौ पक्षौ
वृत्तिपक्षश्चावृत्तिपक्षश्च[11]। स्वभावश्चैतद्भवति वाक्यं च प्रत्ययश्च। तत्र
स्वाभाविके वृत्तिविषये नित्ये प्रत्यये प्राप्ते वावचनेन
किमन्यच्छक्यमभिसंबद्धुमन्यदतः संज्ञा-
14.7 याः। न च संज्ञाया भावाभावाविष्येते। तस्मान्नार्थो वावचनेन॥

Bhāṣya: And the expression *vā* (optionally) is pointless. What is the reason? Because of the invariable nature of *san* in that context. Here are two points of view, the compounded view or of integration and the uncompounded view or of non-integration. And this is natural that there be (both) the sentence formed by simple words and the compound word formed by a *pratyaya.* There, in the sphere of natural compounding the *pratyaya* (*san*) invariably obtaining, what else is it possible to connect by the expression *vā* (optionally) other than the technical name (*pratyaya*) ? And (the possibility of) presence or absence of a technical name is not desired. Therefore the expression *'vā'* has no meaning (here).

14.8 तुमुनन्ताद्वा[12] तस्य च लुग्वचनम् ॥ 10 ॥

Vārttika 10: Optionally (*san* should be ordained) after that ending in the (*pratyaya*) *tumun* and for that (*tumun*) the (operation of) *luk* (elision) (should be stated).

14.9 तुमुनन्ताद्वा सन्वक्तव्यस्तस्य च तुमुनो लुग्वक्तव्यः। कर्तुमिच्छति चिकीर्षति।

Bhāṣya: It should be stated that (*pratyaya*) *san* acts optionally after that which ends in (*pratyaya*) *tumun*, and that there is *luk* elision of that *tumun*, e.g. *kartum icchati* (becomes) *cikīrṣati* (He desires to make).

14.10 लिङुत्तमाद्वा[13] ॥ 11 ॥

Vārttika 11: Optionally (*san* acts) after the first person of *liṅ* (optative).

14.11 लिङुत्तमाद्वा सन्वक्तव्यस्तस्य च लिङो लुग्वक्तव्यः। कुर्यामितीच्छति चिकीर्षति ॥

Bhāṣya: Optionally after *liṅ* (optative) in the Best/first person *san* acts and it should be stated that there is *luk* elision of *liṅ*, e.g. *kuryām icchati* becomes *cikīrṣati* (His desire is that he might make something).

14.13 आशङ्कायामचेतनेषूपसंख्यानम् ॥ 12 ॥

Vārttika 12: Additional enumeration (of *san*) in relation to non-sentient beings in the sense of fear or apprehension (of the speaker).

14.14 आशङ्कायामचेतनेषूपसंख्यानं कर्तव्यम्। अश्मा लुलुठिषते[14] कूलं पिपतिषतीति।
किं पुनः कारणं न सिध्यति। एवं मन्यते चेतनावत एतद्भवतीच्छेति कूलं चाचेतनम्[15]।।
14.16 अचेतनग्रहणेन नार्थः। आशङ्काया मित्येव।इदमपि सिद्धं भवति श्वा मुमूर्षति[16]।।

Bhāṣya: Additional enumeration should be made (of *san* acting) in relation to non-sentient beings in the sense of fear or apprehension).

Aśma luluṭhiṣate (I fear the stone is on the point of falling) (lit. wishes to roll).

kūlaṃ pipatiṣati (I fear the bank is about to fall).

But what is the reason (the fear) is not justified? (Thus) one thinks that desire is possible only for a sentient being but the bank is insentient.

The specific mention of 'non-sentient' is pointless. Only (the mention of) 'in the sense of fear or apprehension' (is enough). Then this (usage) also *śvā mumūrṣati* (The dog is about to die or fears he will die) is also established.

14.17 न वा तुल्यकारणत्वादिच्छाया हि प्रवृत्तित उपलब्धिः ।। 13 ।।

Vārttika 13: Or else (the distinction) is not applicable because of the same nature of the cause. For the understanding arises from the use of *icchā* (desire).

14.18 न वा कर्तव्यम्। किं कारणम्। तुल्यकारणत्वात् तुल्यं हि कारणं चेतना-
वति देवदत्ते कूले चाचेतने। किं कारणम्। इच्छाया हि प्रवृत्तित उपलब्धिः।

14.20 इच्छाया हि प्रवृत्तित उपलब्धिर्भवति। योऽप्यसौ कटं चिकीर्षुर्भवति नासावाघोष-
यति कटं करिष्यामीति। किं तर्हि। संनद्धं रज्जुकीलकपूलपाणिं दृष्ट्वा तत इच्छा
गम्यते। कूलस्यापि पिपतिषतो लोष्ठाः शीर्यन्ते भिदा जायते देशाद्देशान्तरमुप-
14.23 संक्रामति। श्वानः खल्वपि मुमूर्षव एकान्तशीलाः शूनाक्षाश्च भवन्ति[17]।।

Bhāṣya: Or else this should not be stated. What is the reason? Because of the same nature of the cause. For the cause is the same in relation to *Devadatta*, a sentient being, and the bank which is insentient. What is the reason? For the understanding of *icchā* arises from the activity. For the understanding of *icchāyā* is possible only through the behaviour. One who is desirous of making a mat, does not proclaim aloud "I will make a mat". What then? Having seen him with a bundle of rope-pins then the desire is understood. Also the clods of earth of a bank about to fall are crushed, splitting occurs and from one place it goes to another place. Dogs indeed also, who are about to die are habitually alone (and) their eyes become swollen.

14.24 उपमानाद्वा सिद्धम्[18] ।। 14 ।।

Vārttika 14: (This usage) is established because of simile.

14.25 उपमानाद्वा सिद्धमेतत्। कथम्। लुलुठिषत इव लुलुठिषते। पिपतिषतीव
पिपतिषति।। न तिङन्तेनोपमानमस्ति[19]। एवं तर्हीच्छेवेच्छा ।।

Bhāṣya: Or else this (usage) is establed because of simile. How?

luluṭhiṣate iva luluṭhiṣate

"He wishes to roll as it were or therefore he is on the point of rolling".

pipatiṣati iva pipatiṣati

"He wishes to fall as it were or therefore he is on the point of falling".

Truly simile with *tiṅ* (verbal ending) word is not possible because they are *sādhya* (to be established) not *siddha* (already established). Then the 'desire' is 'desire as it were'.

15.1 सर्वस्य वा चेतनावत्त्वात्[20] ।। 15 ।।

Vārttika 15: Or else (the usages are established) because of everything having consciousness (or being sentient).

15.2 अथवा सर्वं चेतनावत्। एवं ह्याह कंसकाःसर्पन्ति। शिरीषोऽधः स्वपिति।
सुवर्चला आदित्यमनु पर्येति[21]। आस्कन्द कपिलकेत्युक्ते तृणमास्कन्दति। अयस्कान्त-
15.4 मयः संक्रामति। ऋषुः पठति शृणोतिग्रावाणः।।

Bhāṣya: Otherwise all have consciousness. For then he says "The metal goblets creep or move gently". "The *śirīṣa* tree (acacia) sleeps (below) on the ground".

"*Suvarcala* (the wife of the sun) follows the sun in going round". When this has been said "Leap, O Reddish One (*Kapilaka*) he leaps on the grass". The magnet (made of lode-stone) comes near or approaches iron. The seer (*ṛṣi = veda*) recites. "Harken O *ye soma* pressing stones".

15.5 इम[22] इषयो बहवः पठ्यन्ते। तत्र[23] न ज्ञायते कस्यायमर्थे सन्विधीयत इति।
इषेश्छत्वभाविनः। यद्येवं कर्तुमन्विच्छति कर्तुमन्वेषणा अत्रापि प्राप्नोति। एवं
15.7 तर्हि यस्य स्त्रियामिच्छेत्येतद्रूपं निपात्यते। कस्य चैतन्निपात्यते। कान्तिकर्मणः।।

Bhāṣya: Many *iṣ* (*dhātus*) are read (in the *Dhātu Pāṭha*). In that context is it not known in the sense of which *dhātu iṣ san* is ordained? Because of the condition of *cha* (irregularly coming after) *iṣ* (with *śa pratyaya* but without *yak pratyaya* to form the *nipātana* form *icchā*). (*San* is ordained in the sense of that *iṣ* which takes the *ādeśa ch*).

If so then (*san*) wrongly applies also here in the (forms) *kartum anvicchati* (he seeks to make). *Kartumanveṣaṇā* (she is seeking to make) (*dhātu iṣ tudādi*/class 6 but not in the sense of desire). Well the (*san*) is ordained in the sense of that *iṣ* for which this form *icchā* (*3.3.101*) is laid down irregularly in the feminine. And for whom is this an irregular formation laid down? For that which is the object of desire?

15.8 अथेह ग्रामं गन्तुमिच्छतीति कस्य किं कर्म। इषेरुभे कर्मणी। यद्येवं ग्रामं गन्तुमिच्छति
ग्रामाय गन्तुमिच्छतीति गत्यर्थकर्मणि द्वितीयाचतुर्थ्यौ न प्राप्नुतः। एवं तर्हि गमेर्ग्रामः
कर्मेषेर्गमिः कर्म। एवमपि इष्यते ग्रामो गन्तुमिति परसाधन[24] उत्पद्य-
15.11 मानेन लेन ग्रामस्याभिधानं न प्राप्नोति। एवं तर्हि गमेर्ग्रामः कर्मेषेरुभे कर्मणी।।

Bhāṣya: Now here (is this example) *grāmaṃ gantum icchati* (He desires to go to the village) what is the *karman*/object of what? Both are objects of (*dhātu iṣ* to desire). If so, then the *karman*/accusative and the *sampradāna*/dative in the two forms *grāmam* and *grāmāya* (ordained by the rule *gatyārtha* etc.) do not obtain in denoting the object of (*dhātus*) with the sense of motion.

Well the *grāmam* (village) is the *karman* (of the *dhātu*) *gam* (to go), *gam* (the *karman* of the *dhātu iṣ* to desire). Thus also in the sentence *iṣyate grāmo gantum* (where the *karman*/object *iṣ* to desire is expressed by the *la*) *grāmo* is *prathamā*/nominative and *gantum* is *bhāva*/abstract notion of the verb. The *kāraka*/relation to the action is of a different *iṣ*/to go and wrongly does not obtain as expression (or the designation) of the village (as object) by means of the *la*/verbal ending being produced.

Well then *grāmaḥ* is the *karman* of *dhātu gam* and both (*grāma and gam*) are the *karman* of *dhātu iṣ.*

15.12 अथ सनन्तात्सना भवितव्यम्। चिकीर्षितुमिच्छति जिहीर्षितुमिच्छतीति। न भवितव्यम्।
किं कारणम्। अर्थगत्यर्थः शब्दप्रयोगः। अर्थं संप्रत्याययिष्यामीति शब्दः प्रयुज्यते[25]।
तत्रैकेनोक्तत्वात्तस्यार्थस्यापरस्य प्रयोगेण न भवितव्यम्। किं

15.15 कारणम्। उक्तार्थानामप्रयोग[26] इति। न तर्हीदानीमिदं भवति एषितुमिच्छति एषिषिषतीति।
अस्त्यत्र विशेषः। एकस्यात्रेषेरिषिः साधनं वर्तमानकालश्च प्रत्ययः। अपरस्य बाह्यं
साधनं सर्वकालश्च प्रत्ययः॥ इहापि तर्ह्येकस्येषेः करोतिविशिष्ट इषिःसाधनं
वर्तमानकालश्च प्रत्ययः। अपरस्य बाह्यं साधनं सर्वकालश्च प्रत्ययः। येनैव खल्वपि
हेतुनैतद्वाक्यं भवति। चिकीर्षितुमिच्छति जिहीर्षितुमिच्छतीति तेनैव हेतुना वृत्तिरपि
प्राप्नोति। तस्मात्सनन्तात्सनः प्रतिषेधो वक्तव्यः। तं चापि ब्रुवते-
15.21 षिसन इति वक्तव्यम्। भवति हि जुगुप्सिषते[27] मीमांसिषत इति॥

Bhāṣya: Now would *san* be (applicable) after that which ends in *san* ? (e.g.) *cikīrṣitum icchati* (He desires to make), *jihīrṣitum icchati* (He desires to desire to take) ? It is not to be applicable. What is the reason? The use of words is for the comprehension of meaning. A word is used thus (with the intention).

"I will cause the meaning to be known/understood". There, because of that meaning having been spoken by one (*san*), the employment of another does not take place. What is the reason? There is no employment (of linguistic units to express) meaning which have already been expressed.

Then (this) expression— *eṣitumicchati /eṣiṣiṣati* (He desires to go) does not obtain. Here is a distinction. Here (*dhātu*) *iṣ* is the instrument of the action of one (other) (*dhātu*) *iṣ* and the (*tiṅ*/verbal) pratyaya (conveys the sense of the) present time (whereas) the external instrument of the action of the other (*dhātu*) (has) a *pratyaya* conveying all. Here also then *iṣ* (*dhātu*) is distinguished by having (the infinitive of *dhātu*) *kṛ* for one of (the forms) of (*dhātu*) *iṣ* and is the instrument of the action/ *sādhana* (while the *tiṅ*/ verbal) *pratyaya* conveys the sense of the present time.

The instrument of action for the other (form) is external and the *pratyaya* (*tumun*) conveys all or any time. Indeed also by whatever cause the sentences '*cikīrṣitum icchati* ' (He desires to desire to make) and '*jihīrṣitum icchati iti*' (He desires to desire to take) are (valid), by reason of that very cause integration also obtains. Therefore after that ending in *san*, prohibition of *san* should be stated. And that too he should say as, 'it should be stated of *san* in the sense (of the *dhātu*) *iṣ* (to desire). For it is thus (applicable in the case of the *svarthe san*) (*3.1.5 & 6*) e.g. *jugupsiṣate* (He desires to abhor), *mīmānsiṣate* (He desires to investigate).

15.22 शैषिकान्मतुबर्थीयाच्छैषिको[28] मतुबर्थिकः।
सरूपः प्रत्ययो नेष्टः सनन्तान्न सनिष्यते॥

Śloka Vārttika: *Śaiṣika* (*pratyayas*) after *Śaiṣika* (*pratyayas*), *matup arthīya* (*pratyayas*) after *matup arthīya* (*pratyayas*) (are not desired; *pratyayas* of the same form are not desired (to follow after one another) neither is *san* after *san* desired.

15.24 इति श्रीभगवत्पतञ्जलीविरचिते व्याकरणमहाभाष्ये तृतीयस्याध्यायस्य
प्रथमे पादे प्रथममाह्निकम्॥

Bhāṣya: Now here ends the first *Āhnika* in the first *pāda* of the third *adhyaya* in the *Vyākaraṇa Mahābhāṣya* composed by the Blessed Master *Patañjali*.

Pradīpa

Pradīpa : 12.2 धातोः कर्मणः।

"(Optionally *san* in the sense of desire) 'acts' after a *dhātu* expressing the object."

After a *dhātu* when occasioned by the meaning it has (the function of) expressing the object and has the same agent (as the desirer). And those two, even though having the nature of the meaning of the *pratyaya* (i.e.) of desire, due to juxtaposition are understood only with regard to that. And so the meaning of the *pratyaya* is applicable as having as its subordinate word in construction/*upasarjana* the meaning of the *prakṛti.* Otherwise there would be no connection between the *prakṛti* and the *pratyaya.*

Pradīpa : 12.2 धातोरिति किमर्थमिति।

"What is the purpose of saying 'after a *dhātu*' ? " For the purpose of introducing (descending into) the *Vārttika* he asks the question. This is the sense: the *dhātu* alone expresses the verbal activity. However, the *upasarga* is a qualifier (of that activity). And hence, having the nature of expressing the object and the same agent as the desirer, as occasions of the meaning, it is only in fact possible they occur after a *dhātu.*

Pradīpa : 12.2 सोपसर्गादिति।

"(So that there be not arising of *san* after a *dhātu*) along with an *upasarga.*"

Due to (it being said) the verbal activity is distinguished by a combination (of *dhātu* and *upasarga*) alone, there is occasion for the arising of *san.* And hence the sense is, there is occasion for dual *vibhakti* etc. in fact after the combination.

Pradīpa : 12.3 कर्मग्रहनादिति।

"Due to the mention of *karman* (in the san rule, mention of *dhātu* is pointless)."

This is an implication or synecdoche (part for the whole) whereby it should also be known 'due to the mention of having the same agent (as the desirer)'.

Pradīpa : 12.5 सोपसर्गमिति

"A *dhātu* along with an *upasarga* (would in fact be 'having an object' hence *san* (wrongly)obtains after that)."

Pradīpa : 12.6 कर्मविशेषक इति।

"(We imply that) an *upasarga* specifies or distinguishes *karman.*" Hence due to this very expression, there is prohibition of sixth case (*tatpuruṣa*) *samāsa* (compound) as variable/transient/*anitya.* This is the meaning: the *dhātu* alone expresses the action because the nature of the object is of the *dhātu* alone not also (object) of the meaning of the *upasarga.* As has been stated 'The mat only is *karman*/object there because of syntactic agreement/same case relationship there will be applicable second case after *bhīṣma* etc. So how is there a separable nature of the object of the qualifier. As spoken previously *kaṭa* mat is object and so are *bhīṣma*/huge etc., nonetheless because of the non-*karma* nature of the combination of *karma* after a combination there will not be applicable arising (of a *pratyaya san*).
[*Bh. on 2.3.1 Vā. 4*]

Pradīpa : 12.7 सोपसर्गम्।

A *dhātu* that has one of the twenty-two *upasargas pra* and the rest prefixed.
अकर्मका अपि वै सोपसर्गा, सकर्मका भवन्ति

Pradīpa : 12.9 सोपसर्गस्य हि कर्मत्वे।

कै॰ – यदि संघातस्य अर्थद्वारकं कर्मत्वं स्यात्।
तदा अवयवस्य अकर्मत्वात् ततः सन्प्रत्ययो न स्यात्।

If the nature of being object were occasioned or caused by the meaning of the combination (of *dhātu* and *upasarga*), then because of the part having the nature of being not object, the *pratyaya san* would not be applicable.

कर्मण 3.1.7 इत्येषा पञ्चमी

This *karmaṇaḥ* in the *sūtra* is fifth case (agreeing with *dhātoḥ* 'after a *dhātu*').

षष्ठयां तु सत्यां कर्मनोऽवयवात् धातोः सन् इत्याश्रीयमाणोऽनुपसर्गान्न स्यात्।

But when sixth case is resorted to, the sense is '*san* (acts) after a *dhātu* which is a part of the *karman*/object'. It would not be applicable after (a *dhātu*) without an *upasarga.* Therefore, (this verse from the *Vākyapadīya*):

अडादीनां व्यवस्थायै (v.l. व्यवस्यार्थ)

पृथक्त्वेन प्रकल्पनात् (v.l विकल्पनम्)

धातूपसर्गयोर्धातुः (v.l शास्त्रे)

क्रियावाचीति निर्णयः (धातुरेव तु तादृशः)॥ वा॰ प॰ 2.180

'In expressing verbal activity, or in the science (of grammar) *dhātus* and *upasargas* are assumed to be different for the sake of establishing the augment *aṭ* and the rest, but their combination is (really) the *dhātu.*'

'It is for such purposes as fixing the position of the augment *aṭ* that *dhātus* and *upasargas* are regarded separately in the discipline. In reality the *dhātu* is like that, (i.e. joined to an *upasarga*).

Pradīpa : 12.12 सुबन्तादिति।

'(This then is the purpose so that *san* should not act) after a word ending in a *sup*/case ending.'

Because its nature is optional, in the case of *san* being (desired) the sense is *kyac* etc. have scope (instead). However, it was not stated 'after a crude base/*prātipadika* because of the expression 'for an object/*karman* and when the nature of object exists because of its very existence there is necessity for that ending in a *sup*/case *pratyaya.*

Pradīpa : 12.14 क्यजादीनामिति।

(No occasion for *san* acting after a *sup* . . . because of *kyac* etc. having the nature of *apavāda* (*sutras*).

The rule ordaining *san* is only after the *karma*/object. The sense is that *kyac* etc. act after that ending in a case *pratyaya* qualified by the object.

And where the *utsarga*/general rule and the *apavāda*/particular/exception are optional here by the particular there is no separate/free *upasarga* (from a *dhātu*) moreover it is in fact a sentence/compound.

Pradīpa : 12.16 अनभिधानाद्वा।

'Because of not expressing (the meaning desired).'

This expression occurs frequently in the *M.Bh.* referring to such words or phrases as could be formed by rules of grammar or used according to some rules but are not found in current use recognised by learned persons or scholars.

c.f. तच्चानभिधानं यत्राप्तैरुक्तं तत्रैवः
अन्यत्र तु यथालक्षणं भवत्येव। पद ज 3.2.1
अनभिधानाद् व्यधिकरणनां बहुव्रीहिर्न भविष्यति।
यत्र त्वमिधानमस्ति तत्र वैयधिकरण्येपि भवत्येव समासः।

Pradīpa : 12.19 इयं तावद् अगतिका गतिर्।

Without resort to resources. (This is the resort (of one who has no other) resort) *Kathā.S.*

Occurs in compound with *gati* in *yājñ. smṛti* 1.345 meaning the resort of one who has no resort, a last resort.

Occurs at only one other place in *M.Bh. 81.68.380, 7/8*

अगतिकस्यापि यथास्यात्।
. . . सिद्धं पूर्वणागतिकस्यापि। . . .

कै॰– लक्षणाश्रया लक्ष्यस्य व्यवस्था न्याय्या

लक्ष्याश्रयेण तु लक्षणव्यवस्थापनं गत्यन्तरा भावादिति।

The conventional rule is that the condition of that to be indicated is the resort to that indication/sign. However, by resorting to that to be indicated indirectly, there (must be) fixing of the indication (sign definition) because of the absence of any other way.

Pradīpa : 12.21 व्यपदेश्यं सदिति।

"(Well then) this is here sometimes (something) to be indicated (which the master does not indicate)," i.e. that existing good, worthy to be indicated, he does not indicate.

Pradīpa : 12.22 न च सुबन्तस्य समानः कर्तास्ति।

"And the same agent is not found in connection with a word ending in a *sup*/nominal *pratyaya*."

कै॰ –'न च सुबन्तस्येति'।

And not for that ending in a *sup*

पुत्रादेः सत्वभूतार्थामिधायित्वा।

The sense is 'Having caused the meaning of the substantive (i.e. noun) 'son' and the rest to be set forth'.

साध्यस्यैव साधनसम्बन्धयोग्यत्वादिति भावः।

Because of the appropriateness of the connection of that to be accomplished with the means of accomplishing it (i.e. noun etc.)."

कठं करोति इत्यादावपि सुबन्तेन

"He makes the mat." Also in such examples by a *sup*/noun ending word.

सिद्धरूपोऽभिधीयते। शब्दान्तरसन्निधनात्तु

The established form is designated; however, it is through proximity to another word.

Pradīpa : 12.23 आसितुमिच्छति।

"He desires to sit down."

The sense is through the nature of that ending in *tumun* as expressing the form/nature of that to be accomplished, there is a link with the agent. Here there is prohibition of *kyac* ('in presence of *kyac* prohibition of an indeclinable ending in *m*').

Pradīpa : 12.24 तुमुन्

समानकर्तृकेषु तुमुन् 3.3.158 (इच्छार्थेषु)

The *pratyaya tumun* acts after a *dhātu* when another *dhātu* meaning 'to wish' is in construction provided that the agent of both *dhātus* is the same.

इच्छति, वष्टि, or वांछति भोक्तुम 'He desires to eat'

Pradīpa : 12.24 तुमुनोक्तत्वादिति।

"(There) because of being expressed by *tumun* (*san* will not be applicable for that meaning)."

The meaning is he desires with *tumun* (signifying) as the efficient cause. And it is not proper to say having barred the usage of that 'he desires' + *tumun*/*san* is applicable. Due to there being occasion for absence when there is absence of that *tumun* due to its nature as efficient cause of the *upapada*/dependent subordinate word. साध्यता प्रतीयते। यथोक्तं हरिणा

The nature of that to be accomplished is known. As was stated by *Bhatṛhari*.

निर्वत्यो वा विकार्यो वा प्राप्यो वा साधनाश्रयः।
क्रियाणामेव साध्यत्वात् सिद्धरूपोऽभिधीयते॥ वा० प० 3.7.79

"Whether the object be something to be made, or something to be modified or something to be reached it is the substratum of power and is presented as an accomplished thing (*siddharūpa*), because it is only actions which are to be accomplished (*sādhya*)."

Pradīpa : 13.1 आसनमिच्छति शयनमिच्छति।

'He wants a place to sit, he wants a place to lie'.

It is ordained in the sense merely of a *lyuṭ* (*bhāva*) but **not** when the *upapadas* are in the sense of desire and there is the same agency with regard to the action to be expressed by the *dhātu*.

ल्युट् च 3.3.115 (नपुंसके, भावे)

"The *pratyaya lyuṭ* (*ana*) acts after *dhātus* when the name of an action is expressed in the neuter gender."

हसन छात्रस्य, 'the laughter of the student'.

Pradīpa : 13.2 इह यो विशेष इति।

"(That *san* should be ordained when what is understood as a specific feature or quality (is to be indicated)."

The sense is the meaning to be expressed by the ending that ending in *san*/ *tumun* is the same word but that a qualification/*upādhi* is distinct. Sometimes however, the (worldly) usage is without (this) difference (of meaning).

Pradīpa : 14.8 तुमुनन्तादिति।

लध्वेवं लक्षणं भवतीति भावः। वचनसामर्थ्याच्चोपपदश्रवणं बाधित्वा पक्षे तदीयेऽर्थे सन्प्रत्ययो भवति।

By force of the rule stated having barred the meaning of a subordinate word in compound, in the alternative meaning *san* is applicable.

उद्द्योत। वचनसामर्थ्यादिति। अत एव चोपपदा भावेऽपि तुमुन् वृत्तिविषये इति बोध्यम्

From the force of actual expression of the rule. Hence even in the absence of a subordinate word in construction *tumun* should be known as applicable in sphere of integration/compounding.

Notes

[1] प्रकर्तुमैच्छत् प्राचिकीर्षत्। Why the specific mention of *dhātu*? So that (the operations caused by *san* should not be related to the *dhātu* in conjunction with the *upasarga* (but to the *dhātu* alone).

[2] का सोपसर्गादुत्पत्तिर्माभूत्। Here the augment *aṭ* for the imperfect लङ् precedes the *dhātu cikīrṣa* not the *upasarga pra*, by लुङ् लङ् लृङ्क्ष्वडुदात्तः 6.4.71

[3] add to counterfootnote 'शेषा आर्धधातुकसंज्ञा'। आर्धधातुकं शेषः 3.4.114 (तिङ् शित् धातोः)।

"The remainder (i.e. the *pratyayas* other than *tiṅ*, i.e. verbal *vibhakti pratyayas* which replace *la* tense *pratyayas*) and those with an indicatory ś (*śap vikaraṇa* etc.) acting after a *dhātu* are called *ārdhadhātuka*."

Therefore the augment *iṭ* becomes applicable (because it begins with a '*val*' for the initial *san* by आर्धधातुस्येड्वलादेः 7.2.35 and it will cause *guṇa* in place of the *ik* vowel of a preceding *dhātu* by सार्वधातुकार्धधातुकयोः 7.3.84 (इको गुणः)

[4] धातुसमानाधिकरणा पञ्चमी। "fifth case in the same case relationship with the word *dhātu*."

समानाधिकरण॥ "a grammatical agreement in case with (comp.)

c.f. लटः शतृशानचावप्रथमासमानाधिकरणे 3.2.124 "The *pratyayas śatṛ* and *śānac* and *ādeśa* of *laṭ* when agreeing with what does not end with the first case", "common or same government . . . for case relation". Words which have the same individual object (*dravya*) referred to by means of their own sense and which are in the same case, co-ordinate words.

c.f. also तत्पुरुषः समानाधिकरणः कर्मधारयः 1.2.42

का अधिकरणशब्दः अभिधेयवाची। समानधिकरणः समानाभिधेयः।

[5] अवयवयोगैषा षष्ठी। "this is sixth case signifying a part", c.f. भा° on एकाचोद्वे प्रथमस्य 6.1.1 वा 2 "In place of the first portion containing a single vowel there are two"

अवयवयोगैषा षष्ठी। धातोर्य एकाजवयव इति। "That part of a *dhātu* containing a single vowel", and on दादेर्धातोर्घः 8.2.32

"Of a *dhātu* beginning with a *d* , *gh* is *ādesa* for *h* before *jhal* or when final in a *pada*."

धातोर्यो दादिरवयव इति "That *dhātu* having *d* as its initial part."

[6] चिकीर्षति॥ अ० 12.14.19 ठय° ब्र° 1.9.2, 23 "to wish, to make or do, intend to do, intend, begin, strive after . . .''

जिहीर्षति॥ अ 2.25.3, 5.29.15 "to wish to take to oneself, or appropriate, covet, desire, long for."

[7] व्यपदेशिवद्भावेन। 'By its nature of 'having a name' or representing (a secondary thing as a principal one). For example, a person or thing, without any second (or third etc.) is looked upon as the first or the last.'

c.f. "व्यपदेशिवदेकस्मिन्" परि 30 "(An operation which affects) something, on account of a special designation which attaches to the latter, affects that which likewise stands alone (and to which therefore, just because the reason for it does not exist, that special designation does not attach)."

आद्यन्तवदेकस्मिन् 1.1.21 "An operation should be performed on a single letter as upon an initial or upon a final." (Of frequent occurence in *M.Bh.*). for example, प० प० वा० 18 सूत्रे व्याकरणे षष्ठयर्थोऽनुपपन्न इति। If the term '*vyākaraṇa*' means *sūtra* (the rules), then the meaning of the genitive ending cannot be justified. S.D. Joshi 139/40 नैष दोषः ··· व्यपदेशिवद्भावेन भविष्यति।

No difficulty here by means of treating (an item which cannot have a designation in the primary sense of the term) like the item which has that designation (in the primary sense of the term).

[8] क्यजपि कर्तव्यः। "*Kyac* is also to be applied."

सुप आत्मनः क्यच् 3.1.8 The *pratyaya kyac* optionally acts in the sense of wishing, after a word ending in a *sup*/case *pratyaya* expressing the object wished as connected with the wisher himself/herself.

पुत्रीयति, 'He desires a son of his own'.

[9] असामर्थ्यात्र। "Because of there being no syntactical connection/absence of syntactical connection."

c.f. दध्ना पटुः। धृतेन पटुः। असामर्थ्यादत्र। Clever by means of curds/clever by means of ghee. Here (compounding) will not take place. (समासो) न भविष्यति। कथमसामर्थ्यम्। Because there is no semantic connection. How is there no semantic connection? सापेक्षससमर्थं भवति। न दध्नः पटुना सामर्थ्यम्। That which requires an outside word is treated as semantically unconnected. (No semantic connection of *dadhi* with *paṭa*.)

केन तर्हि। भुजिना। दध्ना भुङ्क्ते पटुरिति। भाष्य 2.1.30 There is no semantic connection of *dadhi* with *paṭuḥ*. Then with what (is *dadhi* connected) with (the supplied verb) *bhuj* (to eat) as 'a clever man eats the curds'.

सापेक्षम् 2.1.1 भा॰ असमर्थं भवित। *S.D.J.* on *SA 26* 'That which requires (an outside word, i.e. a word outside the compound as its qualifier) is (treated) as semantically unconnected/expectancy in sense'.

If a word outside is connected with a word inside a compound especially a second or further member the sense becomes ambiguous, and expectancy in such cases is looked upon as a fault.

[10] वृत्तिपक्षश्चावृत्तिपक्षश्च॥ वृत्तिपक्ष। The alternative method of compounding words as contrasted with simple words connected as a phrase or sentence. वृत्ति *vṛtti* lit. rolling, course वृ (vṛ) वर्तने

Of action use or occurrence of a word (in grammar) a complex formation which requires explanation or separation into its parts (as distinguished from a simple or uncompounded form), e.g. any word formed with a *kṛt* or *taddhita pratyayas*, any compound and even duals and plurals which are regarded as *dvandva* compounds, of which only one number is left, and all derivative verbs. Both methods are found in use:

c.f. इह द्वौ पक्षौ वृत्तिपक्षश्चावृत्तिपक्षश्च।

स्वभावतश्चैतद् भवति वाक्यं च समासश्च। भाष्य 2.1.1.394 वा 2

lines 3-6 identical except for *samāsa/pratyaya*

Two alternative views are here: the view of *vṛtti* , integration, and view of *avṛtti,* non-integration, and this is naturally there; compound and sentence/ non-compound expression.

[11] तुमुन् प्रत्यय। A *kṛt pratyaya tum* forming the infinitive: '*tu*' is उच्चारणर्थ 'u' is for purposes of pronunciation; न् for initial *udātta* accent. by ञ्नित्यादिर्नित्यम् 6.1.197 समानकर्तृकेषु तुमुन् 3.3.158 (इच्छार्थेषु) इच्छति भोक्तुम्, He desires to eat.

[12] Not discussed by *Kaiyaṭa* or *Nāgeśa.* No examples known of the usage.

डु कृञ् (करणे त० उ० अ० 1472) लिङ्। मिप्

कृ उ तनादिकृञ्भ्य: उ: 3.1.79-कर: सार्वधातुकार्धधातुकयो: 7.3.84–कुर अत उत् सार्वधातुके 6.4.110

कुर् न भकुर्छुराम् 8.2.79 (दीर्घ:, र्वो:)-कुर् यास् यासुट्परस्मैपदेषुदात्तौ ङिच्च 3.4.103

कुर्या लिङ:सलोपोऽनन्त्यस्य 7.2.79- कुर् ये च 6.4.109 (उत:, लोप:)

कुर्याम् तस्थस्थमिपां तान्तत्ताम: 3.4.101

[13] लुलुठिषते Only recorded here and *3.1.7 vārttika* 14

लुट् (भ्वा आ से उपघाते 749) सुन्; लुट् पदि प संश्लेषणे 1381; 12 लुट् दि प विलोडने 1222 पिपतिषति, to be about to fly or fall; पत्लृ (भ्वा प से गतौ 845) सन्; (c.f. zd pat Gk petomai, pipto Lat. pete) *A.V. Mantr.S. Ś.Br.*

[14] चेतनावत् एतद् कूलं चाचेतनम्। Only for that 'having consciousness'/'sentient' , but the bank lacks consciousness. *Pat.* uses this contrast seven times: 1.1.50, 11, 123, 79, 125, 15/16 etc.

[15] श्वा सुभूर्षति The dog wishes or is about to die/face death

मृङ् (तु आ अ प्राणत्यागे) सन् 1404 – इको झल् (कित्)1.2.9 – क्ङिति च 1.1.5 (न गुण) मृ अज्झनगमां सनि 6.4.16 (दीर्घ:) - मुर उदोष्ठ्यपूर्वस्य 7.1.102 (उ) - उरण् रपर: 1.1.51 (र्)- मुभूर्षति हलि च 8.2.77 (दीर्घ:)

2.18.196 कै-शुनश्चैन्येऽपि जीवितस्य प्रियत्वात् व्याध्याद्यभिभवेऽपितिर्यक्त्वात् मर्तुमिच्छा नास्ति।

Even though a dog has consciousness, because of the nature of the love for life, when attacked by disease etc. (even for an animal there is no desire to die).

[16] श्वान: खल्वपि मुमूर्षव एकान्तशीला: शूनाक्षाश्च भवन्ति। Also dogs indeed who are about to die are habitually alone and their organs of sense/eyes become swollen. ना शूनाक्षा इति प्रसृताक्षा इत्यर्थ:। शून्याक्षा इति विषयाग्राहिचक्षुष इत्यर्थ:।

Nāgeśa observes *śūnākṣa* means protuding eyes (another) reading *śūnyākṣa* ('vacant eyes')means the eyes do not perceive the object.

[17] उपमानाद्वा सिद्धम्।

उपमान॥ n. comparison, resemblance, analogy, simile: the object with which anything is compared *Pāṇ.*, standard of comparison, a particle of comparison; (in log.) recognition of likeness, comparison (the third of the four *pramāṇas* or means of correct knowledge).

c.f. उपमानानि सामान्यवचनैः 2.1.55 "The case inflected words denoting 'objects of comparison' are compounded with words denoting what is likened to them, by reason of the latter possessing qualities in common with the former and the compound is a *tatpuruṣa*", e.g. घन श्यान cloud back (*kṛṣṇa*)

उपमान उपमेय - सामान्य

[18] न तिङन्तेनोपमानमस्ति। A simile/comparison is not possible with a finite verb/*tiṅ* ending, (because they are *sādhya*, to be accomplished, not *siddha*, already accomplished).

कै० – तिङन्तार्थेनेति भावः। The sense 'with that having the meaning of a finite verb/*tiṅ* ending'.

इव शब्दप्रयोगे तु However, there is 'superimposition' in the case of the word *iva.* अध्यारोपो विद्यते रोदितीव गायति नृत्यतीव As if dancing, he sings as though weeping.

परिपूर्णन न न्यूनस्योपमानं भवति And the comparison is that of less (than perfect) with that accomplished (perfect, whole or comlete).

क्रिया च सर्वा स्वाश्रये समाप्तेति न्यूनत्वासम्भवस्तस्याम्। तदुक्तम And all verbal activity (finds) completion/perfection in its own substratum. It was stated that is not possible.

14.16 येनैव हेतुना हंसः पततीत्यमिधीयते। The reason why one uses the expression 'it flies' in regard to a swan is found completely in an *iṣṭi* . आतौ तस्य समाप्तत्वादुपमार्थो न विद्यते। वा० प० 3.9.57 (Sparrow) also. Therefore there is no scope for comparison.

भिन्न जातीयानां च क्रियाणां सादृश्यं नास्ति And there is no similarity for different types of verbal activity as भुङ्क्त इव गच्छतीति॥ 'He goes as if he eats' (is not possible).

[19] कै० – आत्मा द्वैतदर्शनेनेति भावः। The sense is 'through the perception or realisation of the non-dual self'.

[20] सुवर्चला आदित्यमनु पर्येति। '*Suvarcalā* (wife of the Sun) follows the sun in going round'.

= धन्वन्तरि Moving in a curve, N. of a deity to whom oblations were offered in the North East quarter *Kauś* 74 of the Sun *M.Bh. 3.155* Physician of the Gods *M.Bh. (Nighaṇtu)*

सुवर्चला ओषधिविशेष। A particular kind of medicinal herb or plant, linseed Polarisia Icosandra.

सुवर्चलाऽदिव्यकान्ता सूर्यभक्ता सुखोद्भवा। Beloved wife of *Āditya,* devotee of the sun, arisen from pleasure. Found in *sauvarcalam* — belonging to or coming from *suvarcala* N. of a country, n. (or in) sochal salt (prepared by boiling down soda with emblic myrobalan *Kaus.S. 36.12*. सौवर्चलं ओषधिवत् शुक्लप्रसनम्। like medicine with white blossom. *Dānlabhāṣya* explains — सुवर्चला प्रसिद्धा। त्रिसन्ध्यासदृशी

Three divisions of the day (dawn, noon, sunset) like Hibiscus Rosa Sininsis flower.

कै० – वेद: सर्वभावानां चैतन्यं प्रतिपादयतीत्यर्थ:।

The meaning is that the *Veda* teaches the consciousness of all beings/states/objects.

शृणोत ग्रावाणु॥ 'Hearken, O ye Soma pressing stones'. तै सं 1.3.13.1; मै सं. 1.3.1; का॰ सं॰ 3.9.

[21] इम इति। Many *iṣ dhātus* are read in the *Dhātu Pāṭha.*

कै॰–शश्नाश्यन्विकरणास्त्रय इत्यर्थ:। The meaning is three *vikaraṇas.*

Cl. 6 श् (इषु तु॰ प॰ स॰ 1351 इच्छायाम्)

Cl. 9 श्ना (इष क्र्या तु॰ प॰ से॰ 1525 आभीक्ष्ण्ये)

Cl. 4 श्यन् (इष दि॰ तु॰ प॰ से॰ 1127 गतौ)

[22] तत्रेति In that context.

इच्छेति निपातनं त्रयाणामपि संभवति इति मन्यते। He thinks that because there is the irregular form laid down *icchā 3.13.101* there is also possible a formation from all three of them छत्वभाविन इति॥ because of the *pratyaya śa* acting after *iṣ dhātu.* इच्छा 3.3.101 The form *icchā* is laid down as an irregular form / *nipātana* कै॰ – इच्छेति शप्रत्ययो यगभावश्च निपात्यते। The *pratyaya śa* (acts after *iṣ* and because of the indicatory *ś*) by इषुगमियमां छ:, 7.3.77 (शिति) - (छ is *ādeśa* of ष of इष्) and irregularly there is absence of *yak* ordained by सार्वधातुके यक् 3.1.67

कान्तिकर्मण:॥ for that which conveys/produces desire.

कै॰ –कान्ति: कामन। desire.

अभिलाषस्तत्क्रियस्येत्यर्थ: The meaning is of that which forms the desire.

अन्विच्छति इत्यस्य गवेषयतीत्यर्थो न तु

The meaning of this *anvicchati* is to seek after, search but not to desire, so *san* is not applicable.

कामयत इति सन्न भवति। इषेरुभेकर्मणी Both are objects of (*dhātu*) *iṣ* (to desire)

कै॰– यो हि ग्रामगमनमिच्छति तस्येषिक्रिययोभयमीप्सितं न केवलो ग्रामो नाऽपि केवलं गमनमित्यर्थ:।

For he who desires to go to the village both are desired to be attained by the action of *iṣ* (to desire) not only the village nor even only the going.

गत्यर्थकर्मणि द्वितीया चतुर्थ्यौ चेष्टायामनध्वनि 2.3.12

"In the use of *dhātus* implying motion, the place to which motion is directed takes the *pratyayas* of the second (*karman*) and fourth (*sampradāna*) *vibhaktis* in denoting the object when physical motion is meant and the *karman* is not a word expressing a road."

ग्रामं/ग्रामाय गच्छति। He goes to the village. मनसा हरिं व्रजति He goes mentally to *Hari*

[23] परसाधन इति। a different operator/*kāraka*

कै० – परस्येषे: साधनं यत्कर्म तत्र लकार उत्पद्यते। तच्च गमनमेव न तु ग्राम इत्यर्थ:।

For that *karman* which is the instrument of accomplishing of different *iṣ* to go, the *la* (tense *pratyaya*) arises and that *iṣ* is (desire for) going only, but not the (desire for) the village.

This is the meaning.

अजा नीयते ग्राममिति। 1.4.51, 335 परसाधन उत्पद्यमानेन लेनाजाया अभिमान न प्राप्नोति।

The goat is brought to the village.

Here the *pratyayas* called *l* being generated to express the different *sādhana* (operator - *kāraka*) would incorrectly not express (the object *ajā* = goat).
3.1.19 121 13, 27 see text forward

[24] अर्थगत्यर्थ: शब्दप्रयोग:। अर्थ संप्रत्याययिष्यामीति शब्द: प्रयुज्यते।

The use of words is for comprehension of meaning. A word is used thus (with the intention)

'I will cause the meaning to be understood.'

Maxim repeated word for word 1.1.44 2, 105, 2.1.1 17, 370, 5.2.94 20, 392

[25] उक्तातार्थानामप्रयोग:। There is no (re-)employment (of linguistic units to express) meanings which have already been expressed. Frequently used in *M.Bh.* see *Pari. 51* of *Paribhāṣāpāṭhas* of *Vyāḍi.* See *Par* 28, 46 *Kātantra,* 47 *Kalāpa*

[26] जुगुप्सिषते॥ गुप्तिज्किदम्य: सन् 3.1.5 He desires to abhor.

मीमांसिषते मान्बधदान्शान्भ्योदीर्घश्चाभ्यासस्य 3.1.6

3.1.7 श्लोक वार्त्तिक

[27] शैषिकान्। Remaining or remnant, used with reference to a *taddhita pratyaya* prescribed in senses other than those mentioned before the *sūtra.*

शेषे 4.2.92 'The *pratyayas* taught hereafter have senses other than those mentioned before this.'

'Let a meaning other than those of which progeny (*तस्यापत्यम् 4.1.92*) was first mentioned, and the fourfold meaning the last be called *śeṣa* शेष and in that remainder of senses let there be the *pratyayas aṇ* etc.', e.g. श्रावण: audible, namely sound from श्रवण:

औपनिषद: treated of in the *Upaniṣads,* i.e. the Self.

15.22 मतुबर्थीयान्। *Pratyayas* having the sense of *matup* मतुप्, i.e. in the sense of possession.

मत् *mat-up taddhita pratyaya* changed in some cases to वत्

मादुपधायाश्च मतोर्वो यवादिभ्य: 8.2.9 "For the *ma* of the *pratyaya mat* is substituted *va* if the stem ends in *sa* or *a* (and *ā*) or if these are in the penultimate position but not after *yava* and the rest applied after any noun or substitute/ substantive in the sense of who possesses that, which contains that or in the popular sense of possession."

(मत मन्त ई) तदस्यास्त्यास्मिन्निति मतुप् 5.2.94 "The *pratyaya matup* acts after a word with the first case in construction in the sense of whose it is or in whom it is" गावोऽस्य सन्ति गोमत् गोमान् देवदत्तः *Devadatta* having (or rich in) cows.

वृक्षा अस्मिन् सन्ति वृक्षवत् वृक्षवान् पर्वतः A mountain having trees on it.

There are other *taddhita pratyayas* prescribed in the same senses as *matup.* लच् (5.2.96–98) इलच् (99 100 105 117) श न (100) ण (101) विनि (102, 121, 122) इनि (102, 115, 116, 128, 129-137) अण् (103, 104) उरच (106) र (107) म (108) व (109, 110) ईरन् ईरच् (111) वलच् (112, 113) ठन् (115, 116) ठञ् (118, 119) यप् (120) युस् (123, 138, 140) मिनि (124) आलच् आटच् (125) अच् (127) ब भ सु ति तु त्र यस and मतुप् after रस etc.

मतुबधिकार is 5.2.92–140

सुप आत्मनः क्यच् ॥ 3 । 1 । 8 ॥

Pāṇini 3.1.8 : The *Pratyaya Kyac* acts optionally in the sense of wishing for oneself after a word ending in a *sup*/ case *pratyaya* expressing the *karman*/object (wished) connected with the wisher's self.

16.2 किमर्थश्चकारः। स्वरार्थः। चितोऽन्त उदात्तो भवतीत्यन्तोदात्तत्वं यथा स्यात्।
नैतदस्ति प्रयोजनम्। एकाजयं तत्र नार्थः स्वरार्थेन चकारेणानुबन्धेन।
प्रत्यय स्वरेणैव सिद्धम्। विशेषणार्थस्तर्हि। क्व विशेषणार्थेनार्थः। अस्य च्वौ क्यचि
16.5 च (7.4.32–33) इति। क्ये चेति ह्युच्यमाने अपि काकः श्येनायते अत्रापि प्रसज्येत्।
नैतदस्ति। तदनुबन्धकग्रहणेऽतदनुबन्धकस्य[1] ग्रहणं नेत्येवमेतस्य न भविष्यति॥ सामान्यग्र-
हणाविघार्थस्तर्हि[2]। क्व च सामान्यग्रहणाविघातार्थस्तर्हि।
16.8 नः क्ये [4] (1.4.15) इति॥

Bhāṣya: What is the purpose of the letter *c*? For the purpose of accent. So that by (the rule) *'citaḥ'* (*antaḥ udāttaḥ*) (*6.1.163*) "There should be final *udāttaḥ* for that having an *it*/indicatory *c*". There should be final *udātta.* This is not the purpose. This (*pratyaya*) has only one vowel. Therefore there is no point in (attaching) an *it* letter *c* for the purpose of accent. By the (standard) *pratyaya* accent (by *ādyudāttaśca 3.1.3*) the proper accent is established.

Then it is for the purpose of distinguishing. Where is the purpose of that which is meant for distinguishing? (In the *sūtra*) *asya cvau* (*7.4.32*) ("A long *ī* is substituted for the final *a* or *ā* of a nominal stem before the (adverbial *pratyaya*) *cvi* (*5.4.50*) *abhūta tadbhāve kṛbhvastiyoge sampadyakartari cvi*)" and *kyaci ca* (*7.4.33*) ("A long vowel *ī* is substituted for the final *a* or *ā* of an *aṅga*/nominal stem before the denominative *pratyaya kyac*").

For if *'kye ca'* is going to be uttered (instead of *kyaci ca*) here also it will wrongly apply in the form *śyenāyate* (from *kyaṅ*) in the sentence— *api kākaḥ śyenāyate* (Does the crow in fact behave like a hawk?) not 'Does the crow desire a hawk for itself'? This is not so. (The *paribhāṣa 82 tadanubandha-kagrahaṇe tadanubandhakasya grahaṇam na.* "When a term with one or more *anubandha*/indicatory letters, is employed (in grammar it does) not (denote) that which in addition to those (one or more *anubandhas*) has another *anubandha* attached to it", will not be applicable in this (form).

Then it is for the purpose of an unobstructed general mention and not a hindrance for the application of the term to others. And where is the meaning (found) of 'that which is meant for the purpose of unobstructed mention'?

(In the *sūtra*) *naḥ kye* (*1.4.15*) "The word form ending in *n* is called *pada* when *kya* follows. (i.e. the *pratyayas kyac kyaṅ* and *kyaṣ*".

16.9 अथात्मग्रहणं किमर्थम्। आत्मेच्छायां यथा स्यात्परेच्छायां मा भूदिति। राज्ञः
पुत्रमिच्छतीति॥ क्रियमाणेऽपि वा आत्मग्रहणे परेच्छायां प्राप्नोति। किं कारणम्।
आत्मन इतीयं कर्तरि षष्ठी[5]। इच्छेत्यकारो भावे[6]। स यद्येवात्मन आत्मन इच्छत्यथापि
परस्यात्मेच्छैवासौ भवति।। नात्मग्रहणेनेच्छाभिसंबध्यते किं तर्हि। सुबन्तमभि-
संबध्यते। आत्मनो यत्सुबन्तमिति।। यद्यात्मग्रहणं क्रियते छन्दसि परेच्छायां न
16.14 प्राप्नोति। मा त्वा वृकाअघायवो विदन्[7]। तस्मान्नार्थ आत्मग्रहणेन।

Bhāṣya: Now what is the purpose of the word *ātman* (being mentioned)? So that (the *pratyaya*) acts in the sense of one's own desire and should not be applicable in the sense of another's desire, e.g. *rājñaḥ putram icchati* 'He wants a son for the king'. Certainly, even when there is specific mention of the word *ātman* (for oneself), (the *pratyaya kyac*) obtains in the sense of another's desire. What is the reason? This word *ātmanaḥ* is sixth case in the sense of agent (c.f. *kartṛkarmaṇoḥ kṛti 2.3.65*). The word *'icchā'* is (derived with the) letter *a* (of the *pratyaya śa* by *3.3.101*) in the sense of state (of the *dhātu iṣ* to desire). Even if he in fact himself desires that (now) there is still his own desire for another.

(This is no fault) *icchā* 'desire' is not connected with mention of the word *ātman* (oneself). With what then? (It) is connected to that which ends in a *sup*/case *pratyaya*. Thus (it is connected with that) ending in a *sup*/case ending word (expressing his desire) for himself. If the mention of *ātman* (for oneself) is made in the *Chandas*/*Veda* (*kyac*) does not obtain in the sense of desire for another (yet, we have the example in *Yaj. 4.34*). *mā tvā vṛkā āghāyavo vidan* "Let not the wolves desirous of evil know of (thy coming)". Therefore the mention of *ātmanaḥ* (for oneself) has no purpose.

Why is it not applicable here: *rājñaḥ putram icchati* 'He desires a son for the king'? Because of the absence of syntactical connection. How is there lack of syntactical connection? That which has expectancy (for another word) cannot be syntactically connected.

Then also in the *Chandas* this (rule) does not obtain (as above *kyac* does not act in the sense of 'for another') *mā tvā vṛkā aghāyavo vidan* 'Let not the malicious wolves know of (thy coming)'.

There is a distinction here. Here, even without the use of the third word, desire for another is understood. How, even without the use of the third word, is desire for another here understood? For those wolves are indeed naturally cruel or malicious. And who can desire evil/bad for himself?

16.14 .... इह कस्मान्न
भवति राज्ञः पुत्रमिच्छतीति असामर्थ्यात्। कथमसामर्थ्यम्। सापेक्षमसमर्थं भवतीति[8]।
छन्दस्यपि तर्हि न प्राप्नोति। मा त्वा वृका अघायवो विदन्। अस्त्यत्र विशेषः।
अन्तरेणाप्यत्र तृतीयस्य पदस्य प्रयोगं परेच्छा गम्यते। कथं पुनरन्तरेणाप्यत्र तृतीयस्य
पदस्य प्रयोगं परेच्छा गम्यते। ते चैव हि वृका एवमात्मका हिंस्राः[9]
कश्चात्मनोऽघमेषितुमर्हति। अतोऽन्तरेणाप्यत्र तृतीयस्य पदस्य प्रयोगं
16.20 परेच्छा गम्यते। यथैव तर्हि च्छन्दस्यघशब्दात्परेच्छायां क्यज्भवत्येवं भाषायामपि
प्राप्नोति। अघमिच्छतीति। तस्मादात्मग्रहणं कर्तव्यम्। छन्दसि कथम्। आचार्यप्रवृत्ति-
र्ज्ञापयति भवति च्छन्दस्यघशब्दात्परेच्छायां क्यजिति यदयमश्वाघस्यात्
16.23 (7.4.37) इति क्यचि प्रकृत ईत्वबाधनार्थमाकारं[10] शास्ति।।

Bhāṣya: Therefore even without the use of a third word, desire for another is understood. Just as indeed in the *Chandas* after the word *agha* (bad, dangerous) *kyac* is applicable in the sense of desire for another, so also in the (classical) speech it obtains as *agham icchati* "He desires evil". Therefore the specific mention of the word *ātman* has to be made.

How (to explain the usage) in the *Chandas*? The usage of the master makes known that '*kyac* (is applicable) after the word *agha* in the *Chandas* in the sense of desire for another, since he states *ā* which cancels *i* when *kyac* follows by the rule *aśvāghasyāt* (*7.4.37*) "In the *Veda* long *ā* is substituted for the final of *aśva* and *agha* before the denominative *pratyaya kyac*". Thus he teaches the letter *ā* for the purpose of the annulling of the letter *ī* according to the original *sūtra kyaci ca* (*7.4.33*) (which ordained long *ī* in the place of the final *a* or *ā* of an *aṅga* before the denominative *pratyaya kyac*).

16.24 अथ सुब्ग्रहणं किमर्थम्। सुबन्तादुत्पत्तिर्यथा स्यात्प्रातिपदिकान्मा भूदिति। नैतदस्ति प्रयोजनम्। नास्त्यत्र विशेषः सुबन्ताद्वोत्पत्तौ सत्यां प्रातिपदिकाद्वा[11]।

17.1 अयमस्ति विशेषः। सुबन्तादुत्पत्तौ सत्यां पदसंज्ञा सिद्धा[12] भवति प्रातिपदिकात्पुनरुत्पत्तौ सत्यां पदसंज्ञा न प्राप्नोति। ननु च प्रातिपदिकादप्युत्पत्तौ सत्यां पदसंज्ञा सिद्धा। कथम्। आरभ्यते नः क्ये[13] (1.4.15) इति। तच्चावश्यं कर्तव्यं सुबन्तादुत्पत्तौ

17.4 सत्यां नियमार्थम्। तदेव प्रातिपदिकादुत्पत्तौ सत्यां विध्यर्थं भविष्यति।।

Bhāṣya: Now what is the purpose of mentioning *sup*? So that there should be production of a *pratyaya* after a *sup*/case ending word and not after a *prātipadika*/crude base. This is not the purpose. There is not here a distinction between the production (of a *pratyaya*) after a *sup*/case ending word and after a *prātipadika*.

This is the distinction: when there occurs production (of a form) after a *sup*/case ending word, the technical name *pada* is established. When there is production (of a form) after *prātipadika*, the technical name *pada* does not obtain. But surely when there occurs production (of *pratyaya*) after a *prātipadika* the technical name *pada* is establihsed. How? (The *sūtra*) *naḥ kye* (*1.4.16*) "The word form ending in *n* is called *pada* when *kya* follows (i.e. *kyac kyaṅ* and *kyaṣ*)", is formed. And that necessarily should be formed for the purpose of a restriction to when there is production (of a form) after a *sup*/case ending word. That alone will be purpose of the rule that it will be applicable when there is production (of a *pratyaya*) after a *prātipadika*.

17.4 ....इदं तर्हि प्रयोजनं सुबन्तादुत्पत्तिर्यथा स्याद्धातोर्मा भूदिति। एतदपि नास्ति प्रयोजनम्। धातोः सन्विधीयते स बाधको भविष्यति। अनवकाशा[14] हि विधयो बाधका भवन्ति सावकाशश्च सन्। कोऽवकाशः। परेच्छा। न परेच्छायां सना भवितव्यम्। किं कारणम्। समानकर्तृकादित्युच्यते। यावच्चेहात्मग्रहणं तावत्तत्र समानकर्तृक-

17.9 ग्रहणम्। इदं तर्हि प्रयोजनं सुबन्तादुत्पत्तिर्यथा स्याद्वाक्यान्मा भूदिति

Bhāṣya: This then is the purpose, so that there should be production (of *pratyaya*) after a *sup*/case ending word and should not be after a *dhātu*. This is also not the purpose. *San* is ordained after a *dhātu* (already) and so that will cancel (the alternative). For rules without scope are (capable of) annulling (those with scope) and '*san*' has scope.

What scope? Desire for another. *San* should not be (applicable) in the sense of desire for another.

What is the reason? It is stated after that which has 'the same agent'. For inasmauch as there is specific mention of the word *ātman* so there is mention of *samānakartṛ*/the same agent.

Then this is the purpose: so that production (of a form) should be after a *sup*/case ending word and should not be after a phrase (or sentence).

17.9 .... महान्तं
पुत्रमिच्छतीति। न वा भवति महापुत्रीयतीति। भवति यदैतद्वाक्यं भवति महान्
पुत्रो महापुत्रः महापुत्रमिच्छति[15] महापुत्रीयतीति। यदा त्वेतद्वाक्यं भवति महान्तं
पुत्रमिच्छतीति तदा न भवितव्यं तदा च प्राप्नोति। तदा मा भूदिति।। अथ क्रिय-
माणेऽपि सुब्ग्रहणे कस्मादेवात्र न भवति। सुबन्तं ह्येतद्वाक्यम्। नैतत्सुबन्तम्।
कथम्। प्रत्ययग्रहणे यस्मात्स तदादेर्ग्रहणं भवतीति।। अथ यदत्र सुबन्तं
17.15 तस्मादुत्पत्तिः कस्मान्न भवति।

Bhāṣya: (For example as) *mahāntaṃ putram icchati* — 'He desires a great son'. Or else is not *mahāputrīyati* possible? It is when this is a sentence (or a phrase) *mahān putraḥ* 'great son' (which becomes the *karmadhārya*) *mahāputraḥ; mahāputram icchati* (then becomes compounded as) *mahāputrīyati* "He desires a great son". But when this sentence occurs as *mahāntaṃ putram icchati* "He desires a great son", then the (*pratyaya kyac*) is not to be applicable; then it (wrongly) obtains and then it must not be (applicable).

Now, even while specific mention is being made of a *sup*/case ending word, for what reason does it not occur here, as this phrase ends in a *sup*? This is not ending in a *sup*/case ending. How?

Paribhāṣā 23: *pratyaya grahaṇe yasmātsa (vihitas) tadāder grahaṇam bhavati*

"A *pratyaya* denotes whenever it is employed (in grammar, a word form) which begins with that to which that (*pratyaya*) has been added and ends with (the *pratyaya*) itself".

Now why does not *kyac* occur after that *subantam*/word ending in a case/ *pratyaya*?

17.16 समानाधिकरणानां सर्वत्रावृत्तिरयोगादेकेन।

Vārttika: For words in the same syntactical case relation there is not everywhere integration (compounding) due to not joining with one (word only).

17.17 समानाधिकरणानां सर्वत्रैव वृत्तिर्न भवति। क्व सर्वत्र। समासविधौ प्रत्ययविधौ च।
समासविधौ तावत्। ऋद्धस्य राज्ञः पुरुषः[16]। महत् कष्टं श्रित[17] इति।
17.19 प्रत्ययविधौ। ऋद्धस्योपगोरपत्यम्[18]। महान्तं पुत्रमिच्छतीति।।

Bhāṣya: Everywhere in fact there is not integration of (words) having the same syntactical relation. Where is 'everywhere'? In *samāsa*/compound rules and *pratyaya* rules. Now just (for example) in relation to *samāsa* rules: *ṛddhasya rājñaḥ puruṣaḥ* "The servant of the prosperous/rich king". *mahatkaṣṭam śritaḥ* "who has resorted to great evil".

In relation to *pratyaya* rules: *ṛddhasyopagorapatyam* the son of the prosperous *Upagu*. *mahāntaṃ putram icchati* "he desires a great son".

17.19 .... किं पुनः कारणं
समानाधिकरणानां सर्वत्र वृत्तिर्न भवति। अयोगादेकेन। न ह्यत्रैकेन पदेन
योगो भवति। इह तावदृद्धस्य राज्ञः पुरुष इति षष्ठ्यन्तस्य सुबन्तेन सामर्थ्ये
सति समासो विधीयते। यच्चात्र षष्ठ्यन्तम् न तस्य सुबन्तेन सामर्थ्यं यस्य च
17.23 सामर्थ्यं न तत्षष्ठ्यन्तं, वाक्यं तत्।

Bhāṣya: But what is the reason for everywhere there not being compounding of words in the same syntactical case relation? Because there is no joining with one (word only).

For here joining with one (word only) is not possible.

Just here in the example: *ṛddhasya rājñaḥ putraḥ* 'the servant of the prosperous king'. A *samāsa*/compound is ordained when there exists syntactical relation with a *sup*/case ending word having the sixth case. But that which here has the sixth case does not have syntactical relation with a *sup*/case ending word. And that which has syntactical relation does not have the sixth case ending. That is a sentence (or a phrase).

17.23 ....ऋद्धस्योपगोरपत्यमिति च षष्ठीसमर्थादपत्येन
योगे प्रत्ययो विधीयते। यच्चात्र षष्ठीसमर्थं न तस्यापत्येन योगो यस्य चापत्येन
17.25 योगो न तत्षष्ठ्यन्तं, वाक्यं तत्।। समानाधिकरणानामित्युच्यतेऽथ व्यधिकरणानां
कथम्[19]। राज्ञः पुत्रमिच्छतीति। एवं तर्हीदं पठितव्यम् सविशेषणानां
17.27 सर्वत्रावृत्तिरयोगादेकेनेति।।

Bhāṣya: And (in the example) *ṛddhasyopagorapatyam* 'the son of prosperous *Upagu*', that *pratyaya* which has the syntactical connection with the sixth case is ordained in connection with 'offspring' (i.e. a patronymic *pratyaya*). But that which here is in syntactical relation with the sixth case has no connection with 'offspring'. And that which has connection with 'offspring' does not have a sixth case ending. This is a sentence or phrase.

It is said, "of words having the same syntactical case relation". Now how is it said "of those having different syntactical/case relations" (e.g.) *rājñaḥ putram icchati* "He desires a son for the king". Then this has to be recited "Everywhere for those words having qualifying words there is no integration because of not connecting with one (word only)".

18.1 द्वितीयानुपपत्तिस्तु।

Vārttika : However there is no justification for a second case (*vibhakti*).

18.2 द्वितीया तु नोपपद्यते महान्तं पुत्रमिच्छतीति। किं कारणम्। न पुत्र इषि
कर्म। यदि पुत्रो नेषिकर्म न चावश्यं द्वितीयैव। किं तर्हि। सर्वा द्वितीयादयो
विभक्तयः। महता पुत्रेण कृतम्। महते पुत्राय देहि। महतः पुत्रादानय।
महता पुत्रेण स्वम्। महति पुत्रे निधेहि। तस्मान्नैव शक्यं वक्तुं न पुत्र इषि-
18.6 कर्मेति। पुत्र एवेषिकर्म तत्सामानाधिकरण्यान्महतो द्वितीयादयो भविष्यन्ति।।

Bhāṣya: However (use of) second case *vibhakti* cannot be justified: *mahāntaṃ putram icchati* "He desires a great son".

What is the reason? The son is not the *karman*/object of (*dhātu*) *iṣ* (to desire) and the second case is not essential . . . What then? All the *vibhaktis*/case endings beginning with the second (would not be applicable). "Made by a great son"; "give to a great son"; "bring from the great son"; "the wealth of a great son"; "present it to the great son".

Therefore it is not possible to say *putra*/son is not the object of *dhātu iṣ* (to desire). *'Putra'* alone is (in fact) the *karman* (object) of *iṣ* (to desire). Because of the same syntactical/case relation also second-case and the rest will be applicable for *mahat*.

18.6 ....वृत्ति-स्तर्हि कस्मान्न भवति।
सविशेषणानां वृत्तिर्न वृत्तस्य वा विशेषणं न प्रयुज्यत इति वक्तव्यम्। यदि
सविशेषणानां वृत्तिर्न वृत्तस्य वा विशेषणं न प्रयुज्यत इत्युच्यते मुण्डयति[20]
माणवकमित्यत्र वृत्तिर्न प्राप्नोति। अमुण्डादीनामिति वक्तव्यम्।।
18.10 तत्तर्हि वक्तव्यं सविशेषणानां वृत्तिर्न वृत्तस्य वा विशेषणं न प्रयुज्यतेऽमुण्डादीना-मिति।
न वक्तव्यम्। वृत्तिः कस्मान्न भवति महान्तं पुत्रमिच्छतीति। अगमक-त्वात्। इह
समानार्थेन वाक्येन भवितव्यं प्रत्ययान्तेन च। यश्चेहार्थो वाक्येन
18.13 गम्यते महान्तं पुत्रमिच्छतीति नासौ जातुचित्प्रत्ययान्तेन गम्यते महान्तं पुत्रीयतीति।

Bhāṣya: Then why is there no integration? It should be stated, "There is no integration of (words) which have (other words) qualifying them, nor is a qualifying word used in conjunction with a compound (word)".

If then, it is said "there is no compounding of (words) which have (other words) qualifying them, nor is the qualifying (word) used in connection with a compounded word, then here *muṇḍayati māṇavakam* "He shaves the youth", in this case integration does not obtain. Therefore it should not be stated in the case of *muṇḍa* and the rest (*3.1.21*).

That then should be stated as "There is not integration (of words) which have (other words) qualifying them, nor is the qualifying of a compound word regular except for *muṇḍa* and the rest". No, it should not be stated. Then why is integration not possible (in the case of) *mahāntaṃ putram icchati* "He desires a great son"? Because of the inability to communicate the meaning adequately/*agamakatvāt.*

Here the same meaning by means of a sentence and by means of a *pratyaya* should be possible.

And here that meaning which is understood by means of a sentence as *mahāntaṃ putram icchati* "He desires a great son" is by no means ever understood by a *pratyaya,* as *mahāntaṃ putrīyati* (never occurs).

18.14 एतस्माद्धेतोर्ब्रूमोऽगमकत्वादिति न ब्रूमोऽपशब्दः स्यादिति। यत्र च गमकत्वं भवति भवति तत्र वृत्तिः। तद्यथा। मुण्डयति माणवकमिति।।

18.16 अथास्य क्यजन्तस्य कानि साधनानि भवन्ति। भावः कर्ता च। अथ कर्म। नास्ति कर्म। ननु चायमिषिः सकर्मको यस्यायमर्थे क्यज्विधीयते। अभिहितं तत्कर्मान्तर्भूतं धात्वर्थः संपन्नो न चेदानीमन्यत्कर्मास्ति येन सकर्मकः स्यात् कथं

18.19 तर्ह्ययं सकर्मको भवति अपुत्रं पुत्रमिवाचरति पुत्रीयति माणवकमिति।

Bhāṣya: For this reason we say "there is no integration because of the non-intelligibility/inability to communicate the intended meaning". We do not say that it would be an incorrect word or language. And where there is the ability to communicate the intended meaning there is compounding. As *muṇḍayati māṇavakam* "He shaves the youth".

Now then, how many instruments of the action are there for that which ends in *kyac*? The *bhāva*/abstract state of the verb and *kartṛ*/agent. Then (what about) *karman*/object? There is no *karman*. But surely this *dhātu iṣ* has a *karman* in the sense of which (this *pratyaya*) *kyac pratyaya* is ordained. That *karman* is expressed and has become part of the meaning of *dhātu.* Also there is now no other *karman* by which it could be transitive/*sakarmaka.* How then does this become transitive *aputram putram ivācarati putrīyati* "He who is not his son he treats like a son". *putrīyati māṇavakam* "He treats the youth like a son".

18.19 .... अस्त्यत्र विशेषः।

द्वे अत्र कर्मणी उपमानकर्मोपमेयकर्म[21] च। उपमानकर्मान्तर्भूतमुपमेयेन कर्मणा सकर्मको भवति। तद्यथा। अपि[22] काकः श्येनायत इत्यत्र द्वौ कर्तारावुप-मानकर्ता चोपमेयकर्ता च। उपमानकर्त्रान्तर्भूत उपमेयकर्त्रा सकर्तृको भवति।। अयं तर्हि कथं सकर्मको भवति मुण्डयति माणवकमिति। अत्रापि द्वे कर्मणी सामान्यकर्म विशेषकर्म च। सामान्यकर्मान्तर्भूतं विशेषकर्मणा सकर्मको भवति।

18.25 ननु च वृत्यैवात्र न भवितव्यम्। किं कारणम्।

Bhāṣya: Here there is a distinction. For there are two objects/*karman*, the object of comparison and the object to be compared. The object of comparison is inherent and (the verb) is transitive by virtue of the object to be compared.

As for example: *api kākaḥ śyenāyate* 'Does the crow behave like a hawk?' Thus here are two agents: the agent of comparison and the agent to be compared. The agent of comparison is inherent and the (verb is) together with the agent (by means of the agent) to be compared.

Then how does this have an object/*karman* ? *muṇḍayati māṇavakam* "He shaves the youth. Here also there are two objects/ *karman*, the general object and the particular object. The general/common *karman* is inherent and (the verb is) transitive with a specific object. Now surely there should be no integration? What is the reason?

18.25 .... असामर्थ्यात्। कथमसामर्थ्यम्। सापेक्षमसमर्थं भवतीति। नैष दोषः। नात्रोभौ करोतियुक्तौ मुण्डो मानवकश्च। न हि माणवकत्वं क्रियते। यदा चौभौ करोतियुक्तौ भवतो न भवति तदा वृत्तिः। तद्यथा। बलीवर्दं करोति मुण्डं चैनं करोतीति।। कामं तह्यनेनैव हेतुना क्यजपि कर्तव्यः। माणवकं मुण्डमिच्छतीति नोभाविषियुक्ताविति। न कर्तव्यः। उभावत्रेषियुक्तौ

19.2 मुण्डो मानवकश्च। कथम्।

Bhāṣya: Because of the absence of syntactical/case relationship. How is there this lack of syntactical relation? That which has expectancy cannot have syntactical connection. The expectancy or requiring (of another word to complete the sense) is *asamartham* (not having the ability to convey the intended meaning). This is not a fault. Here neither *muṇḍa* (shaving) nor *māṇavaka* (youth) are connected with *karoti/kṛ* (to make). For the quality of youth is not made. And when both are connected with *karoti* (in the sense of making) then there is no integration. As for example *balivardaṃ karoti, muṇḍam cainam karoti.* "He produces a bull and shaves him".

Granted, then, by the same reason this *kyac* also is to be employed here in *mānavakaṃ muṇḍam icchati* "He desires the youth (to be) shaved", neither is connected with the *dhātu iṣ* (to desire). It is not to be employed. Both *muṇḍa* (shaved) and *māṇavakam* (youth) are connected with the (*dhātu*) *iṣ*. How?

19.2 .... न ह्यसौ मौण्ड्यमात्रेण[23] संतोषं करोति माणवकस्थमसौ मौण्ड्यमिच्छति। इहापि तर्हि न प्राप्नोति मुण्डयति माणवकमिति। अत्रापि ह्युभौ करोतियुक्तौ मुण्डो माणवकश्च। न ह्यसौ मौण्ड्यमात्रेण संतोषम् करोति माणवकस्थमसौ मौण्ड्यं निर्वर्तयति।। एवं तर्हि मुण्डादयो गुणवचनाः। गुणवचनाश्च[24]

19.6 सापेक्षाः। वचनात्सापेक्षाणां वृत्तिर्भविष्यति।।

Bhāṣya: For (this person) does not create satisfaction by merely shaving. This one desires shaving in relation to the youth.

Here also it does not obtain. *muṇḍayati māṇavakam* "He shaves the youth". Here both *muṇḍa* (shaving) and *māṇavaka* (youth) are connected with *karoti* (make). For that (person) does not create satisfaction by merely shaving. That (person) performs the act of shaving for the youth. Well then the words *muṇḍa* and the rest are expressive of qualities. And words expressive of qualities 'expect' (other words to complete the sense). There, because of the express rule, there will be the integration of (some specific) words which expect (other words to complete the sense).

19.6 .... अथवा धातव एव मुण्डादयः। न चैव ह्यर्था आदिश्यन्ते क्रियावचनता च गम्यते।। अथवा नेदमुभयं युगपद्भवति वाक्यं च प्रत्ययश्च। यदा वाक्यं न तदा प्रत्ययः। यदा प्रत्ययः सामान्येन तदा वृत्तिः। तत्रावश्यं विशेषार्थिना विशेषोऽनुप्रयोक्तव्यः। मुण्डयति। कम्। माणवक-मिति। मुण्डाविशिष्टेन वा करोतिना तमाप्तुमिच्छति।। अथवोक्तमेतन्नात्र[25] व्यापारो-
19.11 ऽनुगन्तव्य इति। गमकत्वादिह वृत्तिर्भविष्यति मुण्डयति माणवकमिति।।

Bhāṣya: Otherwise *muṇḍa* and the rest are in fact *dhātus*. And in fact the meanings are not indicated and the expression of verbal activity is understood.

Otherwise the two (a sentence/phrase and denominative *pratyaya*) do not exist at the same time. When there is a sentence, then the *pratyaya kyac* does not apply. When the *pratyaya* applies generally, then there is integration. In that context it is essential that a qualifying (word) should be used with that which wants qualifying, e.g. *muṇḍayati* "He shaves". Whom? The youth. Or he wants to connect with him by the particular act of shaving.

Otherwise this was stated "Here the activity/(of adding *kyac*) is not to be understood". Because of causing the meaning to be understood there is integration as *muṇḍayati māṇavakam* "He shaves the youth".

19.12 अथेह क्यचा भवितव्यम् इष्टः पुत्र इष्यते पुत्र इति। केचित्तावदाहुर्न भवितव्य-मिति। किं कारणम् स्वशब्देनोक्तत्वादिति। अपर आहुर्भवितव्यमिति। किं कारणम्। धात्वर्थेऽयं क्यज्विधीयते स च धात्वर्थः केनचिदेव शब्देन
19.15 निर्देष्टव्य इति। इह भवन्तस्त्वाहुर्न भवितव्यमिति। किं कारणम्। इह समानार्थेन वाक्येन भवितव्यं प्रत्ययान्तेन च। यश्चेहार्थो वाक्येन गम्यत इष्टः पुत्रः इष्यते पुत्र
19.17 इति नासौ जातुचित्प्रत्ययान्तेन गम्यते।।

Bhāṣya: Now here *iṣṭaḥ putraḥ* "a desired son" and *iṣyate putraḥ* "A son is desired", should *kyac* be applicable? Some just say "it should not be". What is the reason? Because of the desire having been (already) expressed by its own (fully inflected) word form. Others say, "it should be applicable". What is the reason? This *kyac* is ordained in the sense of the *dhātu*. And that *dhātu* meaning should be indicated by some word. The revered one (Your Honour) says "it should not be applicable". What is the reason? Here the same meaning should be expressed by a sentence and by that which ends in a *pratyaya.* But the meaning which is here understood *iṣṭaḥ putraḥ* "a desired son" and *iṣyate putraḥ* "A son is desired" that is never at all understood by means of the word ending in a *pratyaya* (i.e. a denominative so ending).

19.18 क्यचि मान्ताव्ययप्रतिषेधः।। 1 ।।

Vārttika 1: In respect of *kyac* "a prohibition" should be made of integrating (compounding words) ending in *m* or indeclinables when the *kyac pratyaya* follows.

19.19 क्यचि मान्ताव्ययानां प्रतिषेधो वक्तव्यः। इह मा भूत्। इदमिच्छति। किमिच्छति। उच्चैरिच्छति। नीचैरिच्छति।।

Bhāṣya: In respect of *kyac* a prohibition should be stated of (integrating words) ending in *m* or indeclinables when *kyac* (*pratyaya*) follows.

(So that) here it should not be applicable *idam icchati* "He desires this". *kim icchati* "What does he want?" *uccair icchati* "He desires intensely" *nīcair icchati* "He desires humbly/modestly".

19.21 गोसमानाक्षरनान्तादित्येके।। 2 ।।

Vārttika 2: Some (say) (*kyac* is applicable) after the word *go* (cow), words with simple vowels (other than *a*) and those ending in *n*.

19.22 गामिच्छति। गव्यति[26]।। समानाक्षरात्। दधीयति मधूयति कर्त्रीयति हर्त्रीयति।। नान्तात्। राजीयति तक्षीयति।।

Bhāṣya:

(1) *gām icchati* or *gavyati* He desires a cow. (*kyac* after *go*).

(2) After words with simple vowels other than a (*kyac* acts):
dadhīyati He likes/desires *dadhī*/curds;
madhūyati He likes/desires honey;
kartrīyati He is an agent/ likes to be an agent;
hartrīyati He is or desires to be a bearer/bringer.

(3) After words ending in *n* (*kyac* acts).
rājīyati He is or desires to be a king;
takṣīyati He is or desires to be a woodcutter/carpenter.

Pradīpa

Pradīpa: 16.9 आत्मेच्छायमिति।।

आत्मन इच्छेति शेषषष्ठ्या समासो न तु कर्तृषष्ठ्या। सुबन्तद्वारकश्चात्मन इच्छया संबन्धो न तु साक्षात्। तेनाऽयमर्थः -आत्मनः सुबन्तार्थः यदेच्छति तदा यथा स्यादिति। एवं परेच्छायामिति व्याख्येयम्।

'Desire for oneself' is a *ṣeṣa ṣaṣṭhī* — compound not agent sixth case, and the reconnection is with the desire of the self occasioned or caused by a *sup* ending word but not evidently (visible/directly). Therefore, this is the meaning, when he desires a *sup* ending object for himself then let (the *pratyaya kyac*) be applicable so when desire is for the sake of another this is to be explained.

16.11 आत्मन इतीयमिति।। क्रियाकारकसंबन्धस्यान्तरङ्गत्वादिति भावः।

The sense is that this is due to the *antaraṅga* nature of the relation between verb and *kāraka* (instrument for accomplishing the action). *Udyota comments:*

अनेनैव संबन्धेनेच्छायां तदन्वयात्। परम्परासंबन्धस्तु न षष्ठ्यर्थस्तदाह क्रियाकारकसंबंधस्येति

By this there is in fact connection, due to the syntactical connection with that in the sense of desire. But traditional connection/genitive has not the sixth case meaning. That he states is as for the connection of the *kāraka*/case relation and the verb.

Pradīpa: 16.13 आत्मनो यत्सुबन्तम्।

कै० — आत्मग्रहणोपादानसामर्थ्यात्।

By force of including the specific mention of the word *ātman* (it must be connected with the *sup* ending word).

ह्येषितारमन्तरेणेच्छा भवतीति व्यभिचाराऽभावदिच्छाया विशेषणस्य निष्फलत्वात्।

For this is due to the fruitless nature of the qualification of the word *icchā* in the absence of deviation from the rule 'there is no desire without a desirer/agent of desire'.

Pradīpa: 17.10 महान्तं पुत्रमिति।

He (desires) a great son

कै० — यद्यत्र सुबन्तसमुदायात्परः क्यच् प्रत्ययः स्यात्तदा प्रत्ययार्थाभिधाने पदद्वयस्य प्रवर्तनात्परस्परस्य समासाऽभावादुत्तरपदनिबन्धनमात्वं न स्यात्

If here the *pratyaya kyac* would be applicable after a collection (combination of *sup*/case ending words) then in expressing the meaning of the *pratyaya,* due to the absence of a compound for two words occurring one after the other with each other, the connection being with the subsequent word, there would not be the *ādeśa ā* for *mahat.*

Pradīpa: 2.1716 समानाधिकरणानामिति।

कै० — समानाधिकरणानां पदानां मध्ये एकेन पदेना योगात् समुदायेनैव योगाद्वृत्तिनं भवतीत्यर्थः।

The meaning is that because of not saying 'joining with one word among the words having the same syntactical relation', there will not be indeed applicable integration/compounding through joining with a combination.

सगुणस्य हि पुत्रस्येषिणा संबन्धो न केवलस्येति भावः।

The sense is 'for the connection is with the desirer of a son with a particular quality (greatness) not alone' (i.e. a son unqualified by any other word).

Pradīpa : 18.1 द्वितीयानुपपत्तिस्त्विति।

कै० — यदि केवलस्य प्रातिपदिकार्थस्येषिसंबन्धो नेष्यते तदा कर्मत्वाऽभावात्
केवलात्प्रातिपदिकाद्वितीया न प्राप्नोति। नाऽपि समुदायात्।
तस्या प्रातिपदिकाद्द्वितीया गुणे च संख्याया विवक्षितत्वात्

If connection of the desirer with a sole (single) word and conveying simply the sense of the *prātipadika* is not desired, then the second case does not obtain after a single *prātipadika* word because of the absence of the characteristic of *karman*/object, nor even after a combination of words, because of not having the nature of being a *prātipadika* and because, in relating to the secondary objects, numbers are being intended to be expressed.

Pradīpa: 18.6 पुत्र एवेति।

कै० — तस्यै वेप्सिततमत्वाद्गुणानां चेप्साप्रकर्षाऽभावात्।
स्वयमकर्मत्वेऽपि तत्सामानाधिकरण्यनिबन्धना विभक्तिरित्यर्थः।

(The object of *iṣ* is applicable) for him (*putra*) alone because of being that most desired to be obtained by the agent.

c.f. (कर्तुरीप्सिततमं कर्म 1.4.49) and because of the absence of the preeminence of desire to be obtained for the secondary objects. Even when he himself does not have the nature of object, the meaning is that the *vibhakti* conveys the connection with the condition of relating to the same object/grammatical agreement.

Pradīpa: 18.7 सविशेषणानां वृत्तिर्न भवति।

कै० — एकस्यैकदा व्यपेक्षैकार्थीभावविरोधादितिः।

The sense is that this is because of the conflict of the condition of becoming one (integrated word) with at the same time there existing expectancy of one (other word to complete the meaning).

Pradīpa: 18.11 अगमकत्वात्।

Because of not having the nature of making the meaning intelligible. (Only in *M.Bh.*) non-communicativeness, inability to communicate adequately the intended meaning.

मा० 2.18.11 वृत्ति कस्मान्न भवति अगमकत्वात्

How then is there no integration? Because of inability to make the meaning intelligible.

कै० — लौकिके प्रयोगेऽनुमानादपि गाव्यादिभ्यो गवाद्यर्थप्रतिपत्तिवन्महान्तं
पुत्रमिच्छतीत्यादिवाक्यर्थस्य महान्तं पुत्रीयतीत्यादेः
प्रतीतिर्नास्तीत्यर्थः। सिद्धानां च शब्दानां
सङ्करनिरासायाऽन्वाख्यानं क्रियते
न त्वप्रयुक्ताऽपूर्वशब्दव्युत्पादनाय।

The meaning is: Also from the inference (made) in relation to popular usage (of words), having ascertained/knowledge of the meaning of '*go*' etc. from the words *gāvya* etc., there is not knowledge of the meaning of the sentence *mahāntaṃ putram icchati* (He desires a great son) from the (theoretical irregular form) *mahāntaṃ putrīyati.*

For the purpose of rejecting the mixing together/confusion of established words (with valid forms), the minute explanation is made, but not for deriving unused or unprecedented words.

Pradīpa: 18.14 न ब्रूम इति।

We do not say (it would be incorrect word/*apaśabda*).

कै० — अपशब्दो हि लोके प्रयुज्यते साधुशब्दसमानार्थश्च
अयं त्वप्रयुक्तत्वादपशब्दव्य पदेशस्याऽपि न भाजनमित्यर्थः।

For in the world an incorrect word is used and has the same meaning as the correct word, but this (form) because of not being used, does not even partake of the designation of incorrect word.

c.f. Paś p. म्लेच्छो ह वा एष मदपशब्दः।

Pradīpa: 18.16 कानि साधनानि भवन्ति। भावः कर्ता चेति।

"How many instruments for accomplishing the action are there (for that which ends in *kyac*)? The *bhāva* and *kartṛ.*"

Leading straight to the goal (gram), the sense of the instrumental or agent (as expressed by the case of the noun supplementary to the action itself).

Synonymous with साधक and कारक

c.f. साधनं च क्रियायाः। क्रियाभावात्साधनाभावः।

And the *sādhana* is the instrument of activity. From absence of activity, there is absense of any instrument for that activity.

कै कर्मा भावप्रतिपादनपरमेतत्। अधिकरणादौ हि ल्युडादयो यथायोगं भवन्त्येव। भावस्य च लकाराद्युत्पत्तिनिमित्ततया साधनव्यपदेशः

The chief object of this, is teaching the absence of *karman* (as a *sādhana*) for *lyuṭ*. (करणाधिकरणायोश्च 3.3.117)

and the rest (of the *pratyayas*) are in fact applicable in the sense of *adhikaraṇa* and the rest (of the *kārakas*).

And the designation of *sādhana* for *bhāva* (abstract action/state of *dhātu*) is by reason of its nature of being a cause for the arising of *la* (verbal) *pratyayas* and the rest.

Pradīpa: 18.17 अभिहितमिति।

"(That *karman*) is expressed".

कै० — ततश्च जीवतीत्यादिवदिच्छाक्यजन्तस्याऽकर्मकत्वात्कर्मणि लाद्यभावः।

And then because of the *akarmatva* (intransitive) nature of that (verbal form) ending in *kyac* (expressing) desire like 'he (desires to) live' and the rest, there is an absense of *la* (verbal *pratyayas*) and the rest in the sense of *karman*/object.

Pradīpa: 18.18 न चेदानीमिति।

"And there is now no (other *karman*)".

कै० — नियतविषयाया इच्छायाः क्यजन्तेन प्रतिपादनात्तस्याश्च वस्त्वन्तरविषयीकरणा भावादिति भावः।

The sense is, because of teaching, 'with that ending in *kyac* (meaning) desire for a fixed (specified) object and because there is (absence of) making an internal object become an object'.

Pradīpa: 18.18 कथं तर्हीति।

"How then (does this become transitive) ?"

सकर्मको भवति।।

कै० — अत्राऽपि पुत्रादिकर्मणोऽस्त्यन्तर्भाव इति प्रश्नः।

The question is 'does not here too the object *putra* and the rest become part of the (meaning of the *dhātu*)?'

This device and explanation of *Pat.* is used by *Sāyana* in his commentary on *A.V. 3.1.3:* अमित्रसेनां मघवन्नस्मान्छत्रूयतीमभि, O Indra, be an enemy for us against this hostile army.

Pradīpa: 18.18 पुत्रीयति माणवकम्।

"He treats the youth like a son."

उपमानादाचारे 3.1.10

"The *pratyaya kyac* optionally acts in the sense of conduct/treatment after a word ending in a *sup*/case *pratyaya* denoting the object of comparison."

ननु शत्रूयतीमिति शत्रुलक्षणस्य कर्मणः
क्यज वयान्तधात्वेर्थऽन्तर्मावात जीवति रोदति
इत्यादिवत् अकर्मकेण भवितव्यम्। सत्यम्।
उपमानकर्मणोऽन्तर्भावेऽपि उपमेयकर्मणोऽनमिधातात् तदपेक्षया
सकर्मकत्वात् अस्मान् इति कर्मणि द्वितीया।
तदुक्तं भवगता पतञ्जलिना सुप आत्मनः क्यच् (3.1.8) इत्यत्र।
पुत्रीयति माणवकम् इति प्रस्तुत्य
द्वे हयत्र कर्मणि ··· सकर्मको भवति इति।

'Surely the form *Śatrūyati* (he wants/behaves as an enemy for himself) should be intransitive because of being implied in the sense of a *dhātu* ending in *kyac*, has as its object *śatru*. True even when there is an implied object of comparison, because of the object to be compared not being expressed and because of the transitive nature with regard to that, the word *asmān* is second case in the sense of *karman*/object.'

Pradīpa: 18.23 मुण्डयतीति।

(How does this have an object) 'He shaves (the youth)'?

कै॰ — मुण्डगुणविशिष्टद्रव्यकर्मणो धात्वर्थेऽन्तर्भाव इति भावः।

The sense is that inherent in the meaning of the *dhātu* is that. For if there is an object to be compared, characterised by the quality (of being that object of the action) of shaving.

Pradīpa: 18.24 'अत्रापि'।

"Here too (there are two objects)"

कै॰ — ण्यन्तो धातुर्द्रव्यमात्रमन्तर्भावयितुं शक्नोति
न तु विशेषणं माणवकादिकमिति भावः।

The sense is that a *ṇi* ending *dhātu* can only make implied/inherent a mere thing or object, but not a specific qualification like 'youth' etc.

Pradīpa: 18.25 ननु चेति।

"Now surely there should be compounding?"

कै० — यद्यप्येतच्चोदितं च परिहृतं च तथापि गमकत्वाऽगमकत्वविषयविभागप्रदर्शनाय पुनरुपन्यासः।

Although this question has been urged and refuted, still for knowing the division of sphere between that which is capable of making intelligible the meaning and that which does not, again there is this juxtaposition.

Pradīpa: 18.28 तद्यथा। बलीवर्दं करोति मुण्डं चैनं करोति।

"As for example 'he produces a bull and shaves it'."

कै० — बलीवर्दमेवात्मसंबन्धित्वेन करोति तं च मुण्डं करोतीति युगपदुभयोः करोतिकर्मत्वे विवक्षिते मुण्डयति बलीवर्दमिति प्रयोगो न भवतीत्यर्थः।

The sense is, by reason of the nature of the connection with the self, he makes or produces the bull and that he shaves. But when it is intended to express the nature of the object of *dhātu kṛ* simultaneously, in both cases the usage is not applicable (in the form) *muṇḍayati balivardam.*

Pradīpa: 19.6 धातव इति।

"(*Muṇḍa* and the rest) are in fact *dhātus.*"

कै० — सौत्रा धातवो मुण्डादयस्तेभ्यश्चुरादिवत्स्वार्थिको णिजित्यर्थः।

The meaning is that *muṇḍa and* the rest are *sūtra* (formed) *dhātus* and after these act the *pratyaya ṇic* in the sense of the base/*svārthe* as it does after the *dhātus* beginning with *cur* (Cl. 10) by *sūtra 3.1.21.*

Pradīpa: 19.6 नचैवेति।

"In fact (the meanings) are not (indicated)."

यद्यपि क्रिया विशेषाभिधायित्वं मुण्डादीनां नैवोपात्तं यथापि स्वाभाविकत्वादर्थाभिधानस्य प्रयोगादेव तदवसीयत इत्यर्थः। यथा कण्ड्वादयो द्विविधास्तथा मुण्डादय इति भावः।

Although the expressing of a particular verbal activity is not accepted for *muṇḍa* and the rest, still quite naturally from usage alone of expressing their meanings, that is known.

The sense is just as *kaṇḍū* and the rest (*3.1.27*) are two-fold (both *prātipadikas* and *dhātus*) so likewise are *muṇḍa* and the rest.

Pradīpa: 19.10 मुण्डविशिष्टेनेति।

"(He wants to connect with him) by the particular act of shaving."

कै॰ — पूर्वस्मिन्परिहारे कर्मविशेषाऽनपेक्षायां प्रत्ययोत्पत्तिरित्युक्तम्।

In the previous refutation it was stated that the arising of the *pratyaya* occurred when there was no regard to the *karman* as qualification.

अस्मिंस्तु यथा गां दोग्धि पय इति शुद्धस्य दुहेर्गवा पूर्वं संबन्ध,
पश्चात्तु गोदुहिना पयसः, एवं शुद्धः करोतिमौण्ड्येन संबध्यते,
मौण्ड्यविशिष्टस्तु माणवकेनेत्युच्यते। अनेनैव न्यायेन
माणवकं मुण्डमिच्छतीति क्यच्प्राप्नोतीत्याशङ्कयाह · · ·

However, in this answer, just as it is said 'He milks the cow' ('*duh*' governing two *karmans* by *Kārika* on 1.4.51 अकथितंच), first there is connection of pure milking with the cow, but afterwards of the milk with the milker of the cow, so likewise is the pure (action) connected with the causing of shaving. However, it is stated that the (action) distinguished as shaving, is (connected there) with the youth. By this reasoning alone (though undesired) *kyac* obtains to express 'the desire to shave the youth' with this in doubt he says:

Pradīpa: 19.12 अथेहेति।

Now here *kyac* should be applicable.

कै॰ इच्छाक्यजन्तात्कर्मणि प्रत्ययोत्पत्तिः प्रकारान्तरेणाशंक्यते।

The arising of the *pratyaya* in the sense of *karman* after that ending in *kyac* in the sense of desire is conjectured (as possible) by another way.

तथाहि यद्यत्र क्यज्भवति तदेच्छामात्रस्य क्यचाऽभिधानादवश्यं
कर्मणेऽभिधानाय तद्वाचिना प्रत्ययेनोत्पत्तव्यम्।
यथा पुत्रीयतीति कर्मणोऽभिधानाय तिपा।

For so, if here *kyac* is applicable because of the expressing by *kyac* of mere desire, it is essential for the expressing of *karman*/object that it be produced by a *pratyaya* expressing that. As for example in the form *putrīyati, tip* (= *ti* is to be produced) for expressing the agent (He desires a son for himself).

Pradīpa: 19.13 स्वशब्देनेति।

"Desire already expressed by its own (fully inflected) form."

कै० — इष्टशब्दसामानाधिकरण्यात्पुत्र इत्यनेन निर्भुक्तेषिक्रियापेक्षकर्मभावस्याऽर्थस्य प्रतिपादनादित्यर्थः। अयमर्थः यदा क्रियाफलस्य कर्मणः प्राधान्यं प्रतिपिपादयिषितं तदा वाक्यमेव प्रयुज्यते पुत्र इष्ट इत्यादि न तु क्यजन्तः तस्या कर्मकत्वात् कर्मणि प्रत्ययानुत्पादात्।

The meaning is 'By reason of the statement expressing the *putra* (as *karman*), because in the sense of the same case relation with the desired word (i.e. because of *putra* the *sup* ending word failing to express the object, *kyac* does not follow) due to the understanding of the meaning of the condition of *karman* with regard to the action of *iṣ* (to desire) being distorted or (as object distorted =) abandoned. This is the meaning, when there is the pre-eminence of the *karman*, as fruit of the action desired to be taught, then a sentence alone is used 'the desired son' etc., but not a *kyac* ending word because of its intransitive nature. There is not production of a *pratyaya* in the sense of the *karman*.

Pradīpa: 19.21 गोसमानाक्षरेति।

"*Kyac* acts after the word '*go*', words with simple vowels and those ending in *n*."

कै० — अकारादयो दश समानाः। तत्र लृवर्णान्तस्य प्रातिपदिकस्याऽसंभवादृकारान्तस्य च सप्तानांग्रहणम् अस्मिंतु न्यासेऽव्याप्तिः, वाच्यतीत्याद्यसिद्धिप्रसङ्गात्। भाष्यकारेण तु मतभेदप्रदर्शनायोपन्यासः कृतः

'The ten beginning with *a* are the same. Amongst them, because of the impossiblity of a *prātipadika* in *ḷ* and *ṛ* the reference is for seven (four short and three long). In this written text there is inadequate pervasion or extent of definition (of the scope of the rule), because of the possibility of the forms *vācyati* etc. being valid forms. However, for showing a difference of opinion by the *Bhāṣyakāra/Patañjali,* this statement is made.'

NOTES

[1] 'तदनुबन्धकग्रहणे तदनुबन्धकस्य ग्रहण न'

Only in *M.Bh.* See परि० 54 तदनुबन्धकग्रहणे नातदनुबन्धकस्य

"When a term with one or more indicatory letters is employed (in grammar it does) not (denote) that which in addition to those (one or more *anubandhas*) has another *anubandha* attached to it."

Therefore, *kyac* does not denote *kyaṅ* (*Vyādiparibhāṣā pāṭha* from *PS* p.40). This is *paribhāṣā 49* of *Śākaṭāyana paribhāṣāsūtra* p.45 ibid) and is *paribhāṣā 38 of Puruṣottamadeva's Laghuparibhāṣāvṛtti* (pp.128-129 ibid.)

[2] 'सामान्यग्रहणाविघातार्थस्तर्हि'। 'Then it is for the purpose of an unobstructed general mention' and not a hindrance for the application of the term to others.

[3] सामान्यग्रहण अविघात। 'Then preservation of inclusive reference (for two or more terms) by a wording common to those terms, e.g. ङी for ङीप्, ङीष् and ङीन्: आप् for टाप्, डाप् and चाप्.

c.f. अथवा अवश्यमत्र सामान्यग्रहणाविघातार्थः ककारेणानुबन्धः कर्तव्य मा० on 3.1.83 वा० 7

[4] 'नःक्ये' *1.4.15* "A word ending in *n* is called *pada* when these denominative *pratyayas kyac, kyaṅ* and *kyaṣ* follow", e.g. राजन् + क्य = राजीयति He desires a king for himself, न लोपः प्रातिपदिकान्तस्य 8.2.7 i.e. kingship for himself. क्यचि च 7.4.33 (ई)

[5] आत्मन इतीयं कर्तरि षष्ठी। This word *ātmanaḥ* is sixth case in the sense of agent by the *sūtra* कर्तृकर्मणोः कृति 2.3.65 (षष्ठी) 'The sixth case acts after a word, in denoting the agent and the *karman*/object, when used along with a word ending with a *kṛt pratyaya.*' (कृदतिङ् 3.1.93)

[6] इच्छेत्यकारो भावे। The word *icchā* is (derived with) the letter *a* (of the *pratyaya śa* by *3.3.101*) in the sense of the action/state of the *dhātu iṣ* (to desire).

भावे follows on by *anuvṛtti* from स्थागापापचो भावे 3.3.95

श follows on by *anuvṛtti* from कृञः श च 3.3.100

इच्छा 3.3.101 The form *icchā* is *nipātana*/irregular.

इषु (तु० प० से० 1351 इच्छायाम्) श (अ)

इषुगमियमां छः 7.3.77 (शिति); ह्रस्वस्य पिति कृति तुक् 6.1.71; इच्छा टाप् अजाद्यतष्टाप् 4.1.4

इच्छा irregularly does not apply सार्वधातुके युक् 3.1.67 (भावकर्मणोः)

Thus '*ātmanaḥ icchā*' the desire of oneself. If the correct analysis is sixth case in the sense of agent, that would include desire of oneself for another.

नात्मग्रहणेन · · · ॥ *icchā* is not connected with mention of the word *ātman.*

[7] मा त्वा वृका अघायवो विदन्। यजुर्वेद 4.34. "Let not the malicious wolves know of thy coming" (and *T.S. 1.2.9.1* without *vidan*)

वा० 1 त्वा from अघायु॥ m.f.n. intending to injure, malicious, wicked, spiteful (*padap.* अघयु) from अघय्

'अश्वाघस्यात् 7.4.37 "In the *Veda* long आ acts in place of the final of अश्व and अघ before the denominative *pratyaya* क्यच्"

उ by क्याच्छन्दसि 3.2.170 "The *pratyaya u* acts in the *chandas* after *dhātus* that have received the *pratyaya kya* in the sense of 'the agent having such a habit'."

पातं नो वृकादघायोः ऋ 1.120.7, 1.27.3, etc. "Keep us safely from wicked wolf."

अघ।। अघि (भ्वा० आ० से० 109 गत्याक्षेपे) गतौ गत्यारम्भे च) अच्
नन्दिग्रहि पचादिभ्यो . . . अच: 3.1.134 (आगमशास्त्रस्यानित्यत्वान्न नुम्)

[8] सापेक्षससमर्थं भवतीति। "That which has expectancy (of another word to complete the sense) cannot be syntactically connected."

This is *paribhāṣā 27 cādraparibhāṣāsūtra (P.S.* p.47) and *paribhāṣā 85* in *Hemahainsagaṇisamgṛhīta nyayasamgraha* (p.110 ibid) frequently used by *Patañjali.*

[9] हिंस्राः। (Naturally) cruel or malicious, injurious, mischievous, hurtful, destructive.

R.V. 1087 3.5.1 only etc. a synonym for *aghāyu.* Here only in *M.Bh.*

[10] ईत्वबाधनार्थम्। "For the purpose of barring the long *ī* "

Which follows on from ई घ्राध्मो: 7.4.31 and would have been the *ādeśa* for the final *a* or *ā* of a *prātipadika* before the denominative *pratyaya kyac* क्यचि च 7. 4.33 but that is barred by the *apavāda sūtra* ordaining *ā* for the final of: अश्व (giving) अश्वायन्तो मघ्रन् ऋ 7.32.23) and of अघ (giving अघायवो etc. as in the text) by अश्वाघस्यात् 7.4.37

[11] प्रातिपदिकात् [See introduction for more detail] "After a nominal/crude base."

c.f. अर्थवदधातुरप्रत्ययः प्रातिपदिकम् 1.2.45 "Whatever is full of meaning, not a *dhātu* or a *pratyaya* is a *prātipadika.*"

कृत्तद्धितसमासश्च 1.2.46 "And what ends in a *kṛt* or *taddhita pratyaya* or has the name *samāsa*/compound has also the name *prātipadika.*"

[12] सुबन्तादुत्पत्तौ सत्यं पदसंज्ञा सिद्धा।। "When there occurs production (of a form) after a *sup*/case ending word the technical name *pada* is established (as valid)."

सुप्तिङन्तं पदम् 1.4.14 "Whatever ends in a *sup* (noun *pratyaya pratyāhāra*) (सु औ जस्, अम् औट्, शस्, टा भ्याम् भिस्, ङे भ्याम् भ्यस्, ङसि भ्याम् भ्यस्, ङस् ओस् आम्, ङि ओस् सुप्) (4. 1.2) or a *tiṅ* (verbal *vibhakti pratyaya pratyāhāra*) (तिप् तस् झि, सिप् थस् थ, मिप् वस् मस्, त आताम् झ, थाम् आथाम् ध्वम्, इट् वहि महिङ्) has the name *pada.*"

[13] नः क्ये 1.4.15 e.g. चर्मन् + क्यष् = चर्मायते ति It becomes leather.

अकृत्सार्वधातुकयोर्दीर्घः 7.4.25

Being called a *pada* the *n* is elided by न लोपः प्रातिपदकान्तस्य 8.2.7

धातोः सन्विधीयते।। *San* is ordained after *dhātu*

धातोः कर्मणः समानकर्तृकादिच्छायां वा० 3.1.7 (गुप्तिज्किद्भ्यः) सन् 3.1.5.

[14] अनवकाशा हि विद्ययो बाधका भवन्ति सावकाश्च सन्। For rules without scope (of application elsewhere) are annulling (those with scope) and *san* has scope, i.e. rules which have no opportunity of taking effect (without setting aside other rules) supersede those rules. *2.2.24*

अनवकाश। Having no occasion or scope of application. Used in connection with a rule the whole of whose province of application is covered by a general rule, and hence which becomes technically useless, unless it is allowed to set aside the general rule. See *5.4.154, 443* and on *Pari. 64.*

See *Paribhāṣā 95* (सावकाशनवकाशयोरनवकाशो विधिबलवात्) of *śākatāyana paribhāṣāsūtra* (p.s.p. 46)

paribhāṣā 76 of kātantra paribhāṣāsūtra (p. 77 ibid); *paribhāṣā 103* of *Kalāpoparibhāṣā* (p. 80 ibid)

15 महापुत्रम्। great son.

सन्महत्परमोत्तमोत्कृष्टाः पूज्यमानैः 2.1.61 But when there is no 'expectancy' by 2.1.61 "the words *sat* (good), *mahat* (great), *parama* (highest), *uttama* (best), and *utkṛṣṭa* (excellent), are compounded with words denoting the person deserving respect and the compound is a *tatpuruṣa.*"

आन्महतः समानाधिकरणजातीययोः 6.3.46 "Long *ā* is *ādeśa* in place (of the final) of *mahat* (great), when a word in the same case follows and when *jātiyar* (*5.3.69*) follows."

महाराजः a great king; महापुत्रः a great son

16 ऋद्धस्य राज्ञः पुरुषः। servant/man of the prosperous king

But when joining with one only, राज्ञः पुरुषो राजपुरुषः, king's man, by षष्ठी 2.2.8 "A word ending in the sixth case *pratyaya* is compounded with that which is in construction and the compound is a *tatpuruṣa.*"

17 महत्कष्टं श्रितः, who has resorted to great evil, but कष्टं श्रितः - कष्टश्रितः, 'who has had recourse (when joining with one only) to evil.' by द्वितीया श्रितातीतपतितगतात्यस्तप्राप्तापन्नैः 2.1.24 "A word ending with the second *sup*/case *pratyaya* is compounded with the words *śrita* (who has resorted to), *patita* (who has fallen upon), *gata* (who has gone to), *atyasta* (who has passed), *prāpta* (who has obtained), and *āpanna* (who has reached) and the resulting compound is called *tatpuruṣa.*"

18 ऋद्धस्योपगोरपत्यम्, 'The son of prosperous *Upagu*'; but without qualification compounding is possible.

उपगोरपत्यम् औपगवः the offering of *Upagu,* by प्राग्दीव्यतोऽण् 4.1.83, तस्यापत्यम् 4.1.92 The *pratyaya aṇ* mentioned in *4.1.83* and those which follow it denote the descendant of someone.

19 व्यधिकरणानां कथम्। How of those being in a different case relation?

Characterised by or possessed of different *sup*/case *pratyayas* (only on three occasions in *M.Bh.*),. c.f. कः प्रसङ्गो यद् व्यधिकरणानां समासः स्यात्

What is the occasion there might be a compound of words having different case relations?

भा॰ 2.1.67, भा॰ 2.2.24 वा॰ 10 बहुव्रीहीः समानाधिकरणानाम्।।

A *bahuvrīhi* (is formed) of words in the same case relation.

व्यधिकरणानां मा भूदिति। (this is stated) so that it should not be formed of different case relations.

[20] मुण्डयति माणवकम्, 'He shaves the youth'.

मुण्डमिश्रश्लक्ष्णलवणव्रतवस्त्रहलकलकृततूस्तेभ्यो णिच् 3.1.21 (करणे)

'The *pratyaya* णिच् in the sense of making acts after these words as the object/ *karman* of the action.'

मुण्ड, shaved, bald *Mn. Mbh.*, मुडि (भ्वा० पा० से० 326 खण्डने) घन्
अकर्तरि च कारके संज्ञायाम् 3.3.29 - मुड ए (णिच्) तिप् 7.3.84 - मुण्डयति *Hariv. 780 7.1.78*
मुण्डं करोति, He makes (him) shaved.

Here, with a compound of words having other words qualifying we have the exception to the general rule.

[21] उपमेय। "(The object) is to be compared." That which is compared, subject of comparison; *Kāś.* uses it as a synonymn of उपमितम् found in

उपमितं व्याघ्रादिभिः सामान्याप्रयोगे 2.1.56 "A case inflected word denoting the subject of comparison is compounded with the words *vyāghra* (tiger) etc. the latter being the standard of comparison and in construction with the former, and the compound is a *tatpuruṣa* provided that any word expressing the *sāmānya* (common characteristic) is not employed", e.g. पुरुषोऽयं व्याघ्र इव पुरुषव्याघ्रः, 'a man tiger' (in strength)

[22] अपि काकः श्येनायते। "Does the crow behave like a hawk?"

कर्तुः क्यङ् सलोपश्च 3.1.11 "The *pratyaya kyaṅ* optionally acts in the sense of conduct after a word ending in a *sup*/case *pratyaya* denoting the object of comparison of the agent and there is *lopa* elision of the final *s*."

श्येन क्यङ् श्यैङ् (भ्वा० आ० 963 गतौ) इनच् (उण० 2.46)
श्येना-य-श्येनायते (अकृत्सार्वधातुकयोर्दीर्घः 7.4.25)

[23] मौण्ड्यम् "(This one desires) shaving of the head", tonsure, boldness, baldness.
मौण्डयं प्राणान्तिको दण्डो ब्राह्मणस्य विधीयते। मनु० 8.379
मुण्ड ष्यन् गुणवचनब्रह्मणादिभ्यः कर्मणि च 5.1.124 (तस्य भावः) ष्यन्

"The *pratyaya ṣyan* acts after a word expressive of quality (*guṇavacana*), and after *Brāhmaṇa* or the occupation of something or someone as well as the nature thereof."

e.g. जास्य भावः कर्म वा जाड्यम् मुण्ड् ··· मौण्ड्यम् chilliness, stiffness, dullness.

[24] गुणवचनाश्च सापेक्षाः। "And words expressive of qualities expect (other words to complete the sense)." See above *5.1.124.*

[25] अथवेति।

व्यापारोऽनारम्भणीयः प्रयत्नमन्तरेणापीष्टस्य सिद्धत्वादित्यर्थः। क्यच्त्वगमकत्वान्न भवति। The activity (of adding *kyac*) is not to be undertaken because of the desired (form) being accomplished without (that) effort. And *kyac* is not applicable because of not being able to make the meaning intelligible.

तदुक्तं हरिणा [This is not found in this form in the present text of *Vākya Padīya* but *Nāgeśa* explaining *Kaiyaṭa* says:] सदपीच्छाक्यच: कर्म तदाचारक्यचा हृतम्। वाक्यवाच्यमतो व्यक्तेर्यथाऽभ्यास: क्रमादिषु।।

नगे० - अन्यत्रोक्त हरिणा सदपीच्छाक्यच: कर्म वाक्य एवं प्रयुज्यते। प्रसिद्धेन हृत: शब्दो भावगर्हाऽभिधायिना।। अभ्यासे तुल्यरूपोऽपि न यङन्त: प्रवर्तते। इति

This is with some variants *V.P. 3.14, 72-73.* 1. वृत्त: 2. रूपत्वान्न 3. प्रसुज्यते

72.B "Therefore, even though the *pratyaya kyac* expressive of desire has an object, it is used only in a sentence." पुत्रमिच्छति माणवकमिति *Helārāja:* Thus only he desires a youth as his son.

73. "The word formed with the *pratyaya yaṅ* (*P.3.1.23*) being reserved for the well-known idea of disapproval of the action; such a word is not used to express repetition because the form would be the same (and so there might be misunderstanding)."

The expressions लोलुप्यते चङक्रम्यते जङ्गम्यते formed with यद् express the idea of disapproval.

(लुपसदचरजपजभदहदंशगृभ्यो भावगर्हायाम् 3.1.24) (नित्यं कौटिल्ये गतौ 3.1.23)

Or crookedness of the gait.

That is why even though the same *pratyaya* is taught in the sense of repetition of the action it is not used in that sense, because there is a possibility of misunderstanding. To express the idea of repetition the sentence is used, not the complex formation.

पुन: पुन: क्रामति वृत्ति चङक्रम्यते (धातोरेकाचो हलादे: क्रियासमभिहारे यङ् 3.1.22)

[26] गव्यति 'He desires a cow for himself.'

वान्तो यि प्रत्यये 6.1.79 "Those ending in *v* (namely *av* and *āv*) act in place of *o* and *au* before a *pratyaya* beginning with *ya*." 'गो क्यच् तिप्'

काम्यच्च ॥ 3 । 1 । 9 ॥

Pāṇini 3.1.9: And the *pratyaya kāmyac* also (acts in the sense of desire for onself after a word ending in a *sup*/ case *pratyaya* expressing the *karman*/ object wished).

19.25 किमर्थश्चकार:। स्वरार्थ:। चितोऽन्त[1] उदात्तो भवतीत्यन्तोदात्तत्वं यथा स्यात्। नैतदस्ति प्रयोजनम्। धातुस्वरेणाप्येतत्सिद्धम्।। ककारस्य तर्हीत्संज्ञापरित्राणार्थ:

20.2 आदितश्चकार: कर्तव्य:।। अत उत्तरं पठति।

Bhāṣya: What is the purpose of the letter *c*? For the purpose of accent (so that there should be final *udātta*) by the *sūtra* (*citaḥ antaḥ udāttaḥ*) (*6.1.163*) This is not the purpose. This is also established by the *dhātu* accent. Then the initial *c* should be made for protecting the letter *k* from being an *it*/indicatory letter.

Therefore (the *vārttikakāra*) reads what follows.

20.3 काम्यचश्चित्करणानर्थक्यं कस्येदथाभावात् ॥ 1 ॥

Vārttika 1: It is pointless to form an *it* c for *kāmyac* because there exists no purpose in the letter *k* being called *it*/indicatory.

20.4 काम्यचश्चित्करणमनर्थकम्। ककारस्य तर्हीत्संज्ञा कस्मान्न भवति। इदर्थाभावात्।
इत्कार्याभावदत्रेत्संज्ञा न भविष्यति। ननु च लोप एवेत्कार्यम्। अकार्यं लोपः। इह
हि शब्दस्य कार्यार्थो वा भवत्युपदेशः श्रवणार्थो वा। कार्यं
20.7 चेह नास्ति। कार्येऽसति यदि श्रवणमपि न स्यादुपदेशोऽनर्थकः स्यात्॥

Bhāṣya: Forming an *it* c for *kāmyac* is pointless. Then why is not the technical name *it* applicable to the letter *k* (of *kāmyac*)? Because of the absence of purpose for an *it* letter. In the absence of a grammatical operation for an *it* letter the technical name *it* will not be (applicable). But surely *lopa*/elision alone is the (grammatical operation of *it*). *Lopa* is not a grammatical operation. For here the 'original teaching/*upadeśa*' is for the purpose of the grammatical operation or for the purpose of hearing.

And here there is no (grammatical operation). If, when there does not exist a grammatical operation hearing also is not there, then the original teaching *upadeśa* would be useless.

20.7 .... इदं तर्हीत्कार्यम्।
अग्निचित्काम्यति। कितीति गुणप्रषिषेधो यथा स्यात्। नैतदस्ति प्रयोजनम्।
सार्वधातुकार्धधातुकयोरङ्गस्य गुण उच्यते धातोश्च विहितः प्रत्ययः
20.10 शेष आर्धधातुकसंज्ञा लभते न चायं धातोर्विधीयते॥ इदं तर्हि। उपयट्काम्यति।
कितीति संप्रसारणं यथा स्यात्। एतदपि नास्ति प्रयोजनम्। यजादिभिरत्र कितं
20.12 विशेषयिष्यामः।

Bhāṣya: This then is the grammatical operation of the *it* letter *k*, namely (in the expression) *agnicitkāmyati* "He desires to kindle the *agnicit*/sacrificial fire for himself"; so that when *it k* follows there should be prohibition of *guṇa*. This is not the purpose. When a *sārvadhātuka* or an *ārdhadhātuka pratyaya* follows, *guṇa* is stated for an *aṅga*, and the *pratyaya* which is remaining (i.e. other than *tiṅ* or *śit*) ordained after a *dhātu* obtains the technical name *ārdhadhātuka* and this (*pratyaya*) is not ordained after a *dhātu.*

Then this is the purpose, *upayaṭkāmyati* "He desires the *upayaṭ* (two additional formulas at an animal sacrifice) for himself. So that when *it k* follows there should be *samprasāraṇam*/vocalisation of the semivowel (of the *y* of *yaj*).

This also is not the purpose. We will specify (that elsewhere) by the word *k-it* (having an indicatory *k*) in connection with *yaj* (*dhātu*) and the rest.

20.12 ....यजादीनां यः किदिति। यश्च यजादीनं कित्। यजादिभ्यो यो विहित इति।। अथापि कथंचिदित्कार्यं स्यात्। एवमपि न दोषः। क्रियते न्यास एव द्विचकारको निर्देशः। सुप आत्मनः क्यच्च्काम्यच्चेति।। अथवा छान्दसमेतत्।
20.15 दृष्टानुविधिश्छन्दसि भवति न चात्र संप्रसारणं दृश्यते।

Bhāṣya: (Saying) "And among the *dhātus yaj* and the rest whatever has an indicatory *k* . . ."

And which of the *pratyaya*s for (*dhātus*) *yaj* and the rest have an *it k* ? That which is ordained after *yaj* and the rest.

Still now, even if, somehow there should be a grammatical operation (for the *it* letter) so also there is no fault. The written/literal text is formed indicating two *c* letters as *supa ātmanaḥ kyacckāmyacca* (*c* goes by *samyogāntasya lopaḥ 8.2.23*).

Otherwise this is a usage peculiar to the *Veda.* It is seen (as an operation) according to rule/order in conformity with what is found in the *Chandas* and here *samprasāraṇam* is not seen.

Notes

[1] काम्यच्च। का० — सुबन्तात्कर्मण आत्मेच्छायां काम्यच् प्रत्ययो भवति। "The *pratyaya kāmya-c* acts/is (applicable) in the sense of desire for oneself after a (word) ending in a *sup*/case *pratyaya* (expressing) the object/*karman* desired."

[2]आत्मनः पुत्रमिच्छति पुत्रकाम्यति। 'He desires a son of his own.'

[3]चित्तोऽन्त उदात्तो। चित: 6.1.163 "A stem formed by a *pratyaya, āgama* or *ādeśa* having an indicatory *c* has *udātta* on the end syllable."

Final *udātta* follows on by *anuvṛtti.* कर्षात्वतो घञोऽन्त उदात्तः 6.1.159 धातुस्वरेण।। धातोः 6. 1.162 "For a *dhātu* final *udātta* accent." e.g. पचति गोपायति

आदितश्चकारः ।। "An initial *c* (should be formed)."

By चुटू 1.3.7 an initial चुँ (च् छ् ज् झ् ञ् तालु), "An initial टुँ (ट् ठ् ड् ढ् ण् मूर्धा) of a *pratyaya* have the technical name *it* (indicatory letter *anubandha*)" the *c* (proposed) would be *it* but without a *k* initial of *kāmyac* would be called *it* by लशक्वतद्धिते 1.3.8 "The initial *la ś* and *ku* ल श। कुँ (क् ख् ग् घ् ङ् कण्ठ) of all *pratyayas* except *taddhitas,* are called *it",* and therefore *k* would be elided by तस्य लोपः 1.3.9 इतः

उपमानादाचारे ॥ 3 । 1 । 10 ॥

Pāṇini 3.1.10: The *pratyaya kyac* optionally acts in the sense of conduct after a word ending in a *sup*/ case *pratyaya* denoting the object of comparison.

10.17 अधिकरणाच्च ॥ 1 ॥

Vārttika 1: And (after a word denoting) location or place (of comparison, *kyac pratyaya* acts).

20.18 अधिकरणाच्चेति वक्तव्यं प्रासादीयति कुट्याम् कुटीयति प्रासाद
इत्यत्रापि यथा स्यात्॥

Bhāṣya: And (*kyac*) should be stated (as coming after a word denoting) the location of comparison. So that here too *kyac* should be applicable. *Prāsādīyati kuṭyām* "In a hut, he behaves as if he were in a palace"; *kuṭīyati prasāde* "He dwells in a palace as if it were a hut, or imagining himself to be in a hut".

कर्तुः क्यङ्सलोपश्च ॥ 3 । 1 । 11 ॥

Pāṇini 3.1.11: The *pratyaya kyaṅ* optionally acts in the sense of conduct after a word ending in a *sup* case *pratyaya* denoting the *karman*/ object of comparison for the agent; and there is *lopa*/ elision of the final *s.*

20.21 सलोपसंनियोगेनायं क्यङ् विधीयते तेन यत्रैव सलोपस्तत्रैव स्यात्। पयायते[1]।
इह न स्यात्। अपि काकः श्येनायते॥ नैष दोषः। प्रधानशिष्टः क्यङ्[2]। अन्वाचयषिष्टः
सलोपो[3] यत्र च सकारं पश्यसीति। तद्यथा। कश्चिदुक्तो ग्रामे भिक्षां
20.24 चर देवदत्तं चानयेति स ग्रामे भिक्षां चरति यदि देवदत्तं पश्यति तमप्यानयति॥

Bhāṣya: The *pratyaya kyaṅ* is ordained in conjunction with *lopa*/elision of *s*. Therefore wherever there is *lopa*/elision of *s*, there should the *pratyaya* (*kyaṅ*) be applicable. *Payāyate* "It is fluid" (i.e. it behaves like *payas*/water or milk). Here in *api kākaḥ śyenāyate* "Does the crow behave like a hawk?" (*kyaṅ*) would not be (applicable). This is not the case. *Kyaṅ* is taught as of primary importance, (whereas) elision of *s* is propounded as a rule of secondary importance, being applicable where you see the letter *s* is (actually present). As for example, someone said "Go about begging for alms in the village and bring *Devadatta* ". He goes about begging for alms in the village and if he sees *Devadatta* he brings him also.

21.1 सलोपो वा ॥ 1 ॥

Vārttika 1: Optionally *lopa*/elision of *s*.

21.2 सलोपो वेति वक्तव्यम्। पयायते पयस्यते॥

Bhāṣya: It should be stated that there is optionally *lopa*/elision of *s* (e.g.) *payāyate* or *payasyate* "It is fluid".

21.3 ओजोऽप्सरसोर्नित्यम् ॥ 2 ॥

Vārttika 2: There is invariable (elision of *s*) of *ojas* and *apsaras*.

21.4 ओजोऽप्सरसोर्नित्यं सलोपो वक्तव्यः। ओजायमानं यो अहिं जघानेति[4]। अप्सरायते[5]॥

Bhāṣya: It should be stated that there is invariably elision of the *s* of *ojas* and *apsaras*.

Ojāyamānam yo ahim jaghāna (Ṛgveda 2.22.11) "Who has slain the serpent as he showed his strength". *apsarāyate* "She behaves like an *apsara*/nymph".

21.6 अपर आह। सलोपोऽप्सरस एव। पयस्यत इत्येव भवितव्यमिति॥
कथमोजायमानं यो अहिं जघानेति। छान्दसः प्रयोगश्छन्दसि च दृष्टमनुविधीयते॥

Another says, (there is) elision of the *s* of *apsaras* only. (Therefore) *payasyate* "It is fluid", alone should be its from.

How (do we get the form) *ojāyamānaṃ yo ahiṃ jaghāna* "Who has slain the serpent as he showed his strength". (This is) a usage peculiar to the *Veda*. And in the *Chandas* the operation is ordained in conformity with what is found.

21.8 आचारे गल्भक्लीबहोडेभ्यः क्विव्बा ॥ 3 ॥

Vārttika 3: In the sense of conduct *kvip* optionally acts after (*ava*) *galbha*, *klība* and *hoḍa*.

21.9 आचारे गल्भक्लीबहोडेभ्यः[6] क्विब्वा[7] वक्तव्यः। अवगल्भते अवगल्भायते। क्लीब।
विक्लीबते विक्लीबायते। क्लीब[8]। होड[9]। विहोडते[10] विहोडायते।। किं प्रयोजनम्।
क्रियावचनता यथा स्यात्। नैतदस्ति प्रयोजनम्। धातव एव गल्भादयः। न
21.12 चैव ह्यर्था आदिश्यन्ते क्रियावचनता च गम्यते।।

Bhāṣya: It should be stated that *kvip* optionally acts 'in the sense of conduct' after *avagalbha, klība* and *hoḍa.* (It should be stated) *avagalbhate* or *avagalbhāyate* "He is brave/valiant". (Thus) *galbha* (bold). So *klība* (impotent, eunuch). *viklībate* or *viklībāyate* "He behaves like a eunuch". So *klība* (Now) *hoḍa* raft? disrespect? *vihoḍate* or *viklībāyate* "He disregards or disrespects".

So what is the purpose of the *vārttika*? So that the expressing of a (verbal noun) or a verbal activity should be understood. This is not the purpose. *Avagalbha* and the rest are in fact *dhātus*. Also the meanings are not in fact indicated and expressing of the verbal activity is understood.

21.12 .... इदं तर्हि प्रयोजनम्। अव-
गल्भा[11] विल्कीबा विहोडा। अ प्रत्ययात्[12] (3.3.102) इत्यकारो यथा स्यात्।
मा भूदेवम्। गुरोश्च हलः[13] (103) इत्येवं भविष्यति।। इदं तर्हि। अवगल्भांचक्रे[14]
21.15 विक्लीबांचक्रे विहोडांचक्रे। कास्प्रत्ययादाममन्त्रे (3.1.35) इत्याम् यथा स्यात्।

This then is the purpose (to form words) *avagalbhā* (boldness, valour?) *viklībā* (impotence?) and *vihoḍā* (disregard, disrespect). So that there should be the *pratyaya a* (by the *sūtra*) *"apratyayāt 3.3.102"*. "After a *dhātu* that ends in a *pratyaya* there is the *pratyaya a,* the word being feminine". Thus it should not be applicable. It will be formed by *guruśca halaḥ 3.3.103.* "The *pratyaya a* acts after a *dhātu* having a *guru* (prosodially heavy vowel), and ending in a consonant in the feminine". Thus it will be (stated).

This then is the purpose: *avagalbhāṃcakre* "He has been bold". *viklībāṃcakre* "He has behaved like a eunuch". *vihoḍāṃcakre* "He has disregarded or shown disrespect" (i.e. to form the periphrastic perfect) so that the *pratyaya ām* should be (applicable) because of the *sūtra kāspratyayādamantre liṭi 3.1.35.* "*Ām* is the *pratyaya* of the *dhātu kās* (to cough) and of those *dhātus* that are formed by *pratyayas* (i.e. derivative verbs), when *liṭ* (*pratyaya* conveying the sense of the perfect tense) follows, except in the *mantra/Veda.*

21.16 अपर आह। सर्वप्रातिपदिकेभ्य आचारे क्विब्वक्तव्योऽश्वति[15] गर्दभतीत्येवमर्थम्[16]।।
न तर्हीदानीं गल्भाद्यनुक्रमणं कर्तव्यम्। कर्तव्यं च। किं प्रयोजनम्। आत्मने-
21.18 पदार्थाननुबन्धानासङ्क्ष्यामीति[17]। गल्भ् क्लीब् होड्।।

Another says *"kvip* should be stated as acting in the sense of conduct after all *dhātus,* for the sake of the forms *aśvati* "He behaves like a horse". *gardabhati* "He represents or behaves like an ass/donkey".

Then, there should not now be brought about a methodical enumeration of *galbha* etc.? It should be done. What is the purpose? Thus I will attach indicatory letters for the purpose of (indicating) *ātmanepadam+galbha, klība, hoḍa.*

Notes

[1] पयायते। "It is or becomes fluid." It behaves like 'पयस्'

पय (भ्वा॰ आ॰ से॰ 476 गतौ) असुन्

or पीङ् (दि॰ आ॰ अ॰ 1141 पाने)
सर्वधातुभ्योऽसुन् उण॰ 4 183
पय सलोप क्यङ् "अकृत्सार्वधातुक्योः" 7.4.25 (दीर्घः)

[2] प्रधानशिष्टः क्यङ्

"*Kyaṅ* is taught or laid down as of primary importance"

[3] अन्वाचयशिंष्टः सलोपो

sa lapa is propounded as a rule or matter of secondary importance.

"प्रधानान्वाचयशिष्टयोः प्रधाने संप्रत्यय" व्याडि परि 67

also c.f. *Vardhamāna* in his *svapajña-tika* on *GRM (4)*

च इति अन्वचय हेतुषु भिक्षाभट गां चानय

The two occur together again in *M.Bh.* only at 7.3.118 वा॰ 4

प्रधानशिष्टभौत्वसन्वाचयशिष्टमत्वं यथा क्यङि् सलोपः

[4]ओजायमानं यो अहिं जंघान
ओजस् उब्ज (तु॰ प॰ से॰ 1303 आर्जवे) असुन् उणा॰ 4.183
उब्जेबहे बलोपश्च उणा॰ 4.192
ओजाय अकृत्सार्वधातुकयोर्दीर्घः 7.4.25)
ओजाय मुक् शानच् "लटः शतृशानचावप्रथमसमानाधिकरणे" 3.2.124
आने मुक् 7.2.82
ओजायमान

Other examples of *ojāya* are:

ओजायमानस्तन्वश्च शुम्भते (ऋ 1.140.6)

"(*Agni*) proving his might, he decks the glory of his form"

ओजायमानं तुविजात तव्यान् (ऋ 3.32.11)

"(O *Indra*) thou puisssant God, more mighty (slewest *Pahi*) showing his strength." The *vārttika 1* and *2* are found in a semi-*śloka vārttika in Kāś.*

ओजसोऽप्सरसो नित्यं पयसस्तु विभाषया
(सकारस्येष्यते लोपः शब्दशास्त्रविचक्षणैः (जै॰ सू॰ 2.1.91))

[5] 21.5 अप्सरायते। "She behaves like a nymph."

The word अप्सरा in found in the *A.V.* in the form अप्सरापति अ॰ 4.37.7 which would give the form here without *s lopa* if अप्सरा were the *prātipadika* form, but it seems to be derived from अप्सरस्

अद्भ्यः सरन्ति सरतेसुरन अण्॰ 4.237

अप् सृ (भ्वा॰ प॰ अ॰ 135) गतौ असुन्

[6] गल्भ m.f.n. bold *Vop. 21.7*

गल्भय ते to be bold

अवगल्भते to अवगल्भायते to be brave, valiant, *Pat.*

गल्भ (म॰ आ॰ से॰ 392 धाष्टर्ये) अच् 3.1.34 the boldness

[7] क्विप Denominative *pratyaya* zero acting after any substantive in the sense of behaviour/conduct. (Elsewhere a *kṛt pratyaya 3.2.61, 76, 77, 87-92, 177-179*)

क् लशक्वद्धिते	1.3.8
इत् उपदेशेऽजनुनासिक इत्	1.3.2
व् वेरपृक्तस्य	6.1.67
प् हलन्त्यम्	1.3.3
तस्य लोपः	1.3.9

3.2.11 वा॰ 2.21.1

[8] क्लीब m.f.(ā)n. impotent, emasculated, a eunuch

A.V. 6.138.3/12 8.6.11

क्लीबते क्लीब् (म॰ आ॰ से॰ 381 अघाष्टर्य) क इगुपधज्ञाप्रीकिरः

'in lack of boldness' कः 3.1.125

क्लीबा य ते to behave like a eunuch *Vop. 21.7*

[9] होड m. a raft, float, boat *Trik. 1.2.13* a title of a particular class of *kāyasthas* and of *Śrotriya Brāhmanas* in Bengal (*SK.D.* Suppl.)

होड् (भ्वा॰ आ॰ से॰ 305 अनादरे) अच् 3.1.134
भ्वा॰ प॰ से॰ 354 गतौ)

to disregard, disrespect, to go, move (*Vop.*)

पृथ्वादिम्य इमानिज्वा 5.1.122 (18 होड)

[10] विहोडते and विहोडायते Not even recorded in Lex.

'He disregards or goes.'

[11] अवगल्भा। f. boldness, not recorded

विल्कीबा impotence

विहोडा disregard

[12] 'अ प्रत्ययात्' 3.3.102

Dhātus that end in *a pratyaya* are derivative *dhātus* (e.g. desiderative, causative, intensives and denominatives), all enjoined in this first section of *3.1.5-32.* Though taking *pratyayas* they are called *dhātus* by सनाद्यन्ता धातवः 3.1.32

It is after these that the *pratyaya a* is used in forming a feminine noun.

[13] गुरोश्च हलः 3.3.103 (स्त्रियाम्, अ)

'गुरु' (having) a prosodially heavy vowel is defined संयोगे गुरु 1.4.11 (ह्रस्वम्) "When a conjunct consonant follows a short vowel it is termed heavy (*guru*)."

दीर्घं च 1.4.12 (गुरु) "And a long vowel is also termed *guru.*"

Therefore all three are *guru* (*o* being a *dīrgha* vowel)

[14] अवगल्भांचुक्रे।

अवगल्भ आम् लिट् कास्प्रत्ययादाममन्त्रे लिटि 3.1.35 आमः 2.4.81(लेःलुक्)

"There is *luk* elision in place of that *pratyaya liṭ* (sign of the perfect) coming after *ām.*

कृञ्चानुप्रयुज्यते लिटि 3.1.40

"After a *dhātu* ending with *ām* the *dhātu kṛ* is annexed (as auxiliary verb) when *liṭ* follows."

[15] अश्वति का अश्व इवाचरति अश्वायते।

Kās. Some say *kvip pratyaya* (optionally acts) after all *prātipadikas*/crude bases (and *kyaṅ* in the alternative) 'to behave like a horse'

अश्वायते formed with क्यच् means 'to wish for horses'.

अश्वाघस्यात् 7.4.37 "In the *Vedas* long आ acts in place of the final of अश्व and अघ before the denominative *pratyaya* क्यच् (3.2.8)

अश्वायन्तो मघवन् ऋ० 7.32.23 "Desiring horse, O *Indra,* (we call on thee)."

अश्व अश्नुते अशू (स्वा० आ० से० 1264 व्याप्तौ) क्वन् सङःतेच

अशूप्रुषिलटि उण 1.151

[16] गर्दभवति To represent an ass *Sāh 10.21*

गर्दभ गर्दति गर्द (स्वा० प० से० 58 शब्दे) अभच्

कृशृशलिकलिगर्दिम्योऽभच्। 3। 122 ।। अभच् ।

[17] आत्मनेपदार्थाननुबन्धानासङ्गायामीति

अनुदात्तङित आत्मनेपदम् 1.3.12

"After a *dhātu* having an indicatory *anudātta* vowel (here *a*) or an indicatory *ṅ* the *pratyayas* of the *ātmanepada* are to be applied."

e.g. गल्भायते

भृशादिभ्यो भुव्यच्वेर्लोपश्च हलः ॥ 3 । 1 । 12 ॥

Pāṇini 3.1.12: The *pratyaya kyaṅ* in the sense of becoming (what the thing previously was not), acts after the *prātipadikas bhṛśa* and the rest, which do not end with the *pratyaya cvi* (*5.4.50*) (*a-bhūta tadbhāve kṛbhvastiyoge sampadyakartari cvi*) and there is *lopa*/elison of the (final) consonant.

21.20 हलो लोपसन्नियोगेनायं क्यङ्विधीयते तेन यत्रैव हलो लोपस्तत्रैव प्रसज्येत। नैष दोषः। प्रधानशिष्टः[1] क्यङ्। अन्वाचयशिष्टः हलो लोपो यत्र च हलं

21.22 पश्यसीति।।

Bhāṣya: *Kyaṅ* is ordained in conjunction/simultaneously with the elision of a (final) consonant, therefore wherever there is elision of a (final) consonant there only *kyaṅ* obtains. There is no fault—*kyaṅ* is taught as of primary importance. The elision of a (final) consonant is propounded as a rule or matter of secondary importance, i.e. (only) when you see a (final) consonant (elide it).

12.23 भृशादिष्वभूततद्भावग्रहणम् ॥ 1 ॥

Vārttika 1: In relation of the words *bhṛśa* and the rest there should be specific mention of becoming what a thing previously was not before.

21.24 भृशादिष्वभूततद्भावग्रहणं कर्तव्यम्। इह मा भूत्। क्व दिवा भृशा भवन्तीति[2]।।

Bhāṣya: A mention should be made of (the meaning) "becoming what a thing was not before" in relation to the words *bhṛśa* etc., (so that) here it should not be applicable). *kva divā bhṛśā bhavanti*— "Where do they become strong by day?"

22.1 च्विप्रतिषेधानर्थक्यं च भवत्यर्थे क्यङ्वचनात् ॥ 2 ॥

Vārttika 2: And the prohibition of *cvi* is meaningless because of the statement of (ordaining) *kyaṅ* in the sense of becoming (what the thing was not before).

22.2 च्विप्रतिषेधश्चानर्थकः। किं कारणम्। भवत्यर्थे क्यङ्वचनात्। भवत्यर्थे हि क्यङ्विधीयते।।

Bhāṣya: And the prohibition of *cvi* is meaningless. What is the reason? Because of *kyaṅ* being ordained in the sense of becoming (what it was not before). For *kyaṅ* is ordained in the sense of becoming (what it was not before).

22.4 भवतियोगे च्विविधानम् ।। 3 ।।

Vārttika 3: (There is) ordaining of *cvi* (in the sense of becoming what was not before) with the *dhātu bhū*.

22.5 भवतिना योगे च्विर्विधीयते[3]। यत्र च्विनोक्तत्वात्तस्यार्थस्य क्यङ् न भविष्यति।।
डाजन्तादपि[4] तर्हि न प्राप्नोति। पटपटायते[5]। डाजपि हि भवतिना योगे विधीयते

22.7 भवत्यर्थे क्यष्।

Bhāṣya: *Cvi* is ordained in conjunction with the *dhātu bhū*. Because of its meaning being expressed together with *cvi, kyaṅ* will not be (applicable) there. Then also after that ending in *ḍāc,* it (*kyaṅ*) does not obtain e.g. *paṭapaṭāyate* "He makes a sound (like) *paṭa paṭa* (who did not make it before)".

For *ḍāc* (also) is ordained in conjunction with the *dhātu bhū* (and) *kyaṣ* in the sense of becoming (what it was not before)

22.8 डाचि वचनप्रामाण्यात्[6] ।। 4 ।।

Vārttika 4: From the authority of (another) rule, when *ḍāc* follows (there is *kyaṣ*).

22.9 डाचि वचनप्रामाण्याद्भविष्यति। किं वचनप्रामान्यम्। लोहितादिडाज्भ्यः
क्यष् (3.1.13) इति।।

Bhāṣya: There will be (applicability of *kyaṣ*) because of the authority of (another rule).

What rule's authority? *lohitādiḍājbhyaḥ kyaṣ* (*3.1.13*) "*Kyaṣ* acts after the words *lohiṭa* (red) etc. and after those that end with the *pratyaya ḍāc* (when) they do not take the *pratyaya cvi*".

22.11 इह किंचिदक्रियमाणं चोद्यते किंचिच्च क्रियमाणां प्रत्याख्यायते। स सूत्रभेदः
कृतो भवति।। यथान्यासमेवास्तु। ननु चोक्तमिह कस्मान्न भवति क्व दिवा भृशा
भवन्तीति। नञिवयुक्तमन्यसदृशाधिकरणे तथा ह्यर्थगतिः[7]। नञ्युक्तमिवयुक्तं वा
यत्किंचिदिह दृश्यते तत्रान्यस्मिंस्तत्सदृशे कार्यं विज्ञायते तथा ह्यर्थो गम्यते।

22.15 अब्राह्मणमानयेत्युक्ते ब्राह्मणसदृश आनीयते नासौ लोष्टमानीय कृती भवति[9]।
एवमिहाप्यच्वेरिति च्विप्रतिषेधादन्यस्मिन्नच्व्यन्ते च्विसदृशे कार्यं विज्ञास्यते।
किं चातो-

22.17 ऽन्यदच्व्यन्तं च्विसदृशम्। अभूततद्भावः।।

Here something not being produced is spoken of and something being produced is to be rejected. That makes this division of the *sūtra.*

Let it be according to the text of the *sūtra,* as it is written down. And surely it was said, "Why is not (*kyaṅ*) applicable here? *kva divā bhṛśā bhavanti* "Where do they become many day by day" (By the *paribhāṣā 74*) *nañivayuktaman-yasadṛśādhikaraṇe tathā hyarthagatiḥ* "(An expression) formed by the addition of the (negative) *nañ* or (the particle of comparision) *iva,* to (some word or other) denotes something which is different from and (yet) similar to (what is denoted by the latter) because it is so that (such expressions) are generally understood in that way".

(To explain), whatever is seen here having the (negative) *nañ* or (the particle of comparison) *iva* (implies that) in respect of that an operation is effected on another similar to that because the meaning is understood (in that way). When it is said "Bring a non-*Brāhman*" one in fact brings (someone) like a *Brāhman,* but he does not accomplish the act after having brought clods of earth.

Thus here also, because of the prohibition 'not after that (ending in) *cvi*', the operation will be known in (the context of) some other non-*cvi* ending word (but in fact) like *cvi* (in meaning). And what other than this is not ending in *cvi* but is like *cvi*? That which is becoming what it was not before.

22.18 इह काश्चित्प्रकृतयः सोपसर्गाः पठ्यन्ते। अभिमनस्' सुमनस् उन्मनस् दुर्मनस्।
तत्र विचार्यते। भृशादिषूपसर्गः प्रत्ययार्थविशेषणं वा स्यात्। अभिभवतौ सुभ-
20.20 वतौ उद्भवतौ दुर्भवताविति। प्रकृत्यर्थविशेषणं वा। अभिमनस्शब्दात् सुमनस्-शब्दात्
उन्मनस्शब्दात् दुर्मनस्शब्दादिति। युक्तं पुनरिदं विचारयितुम। ननु तेनसंदिग्धेन प्रकृत्यर्थवि-
शेषणेन भवतव्यं यावता प्राक्प्रकृतेः पठ्यन्ते। यदि हि प्रत्यया-
22.23 र्थविशेषणं स्यात्प्राग्भवतेःपठ्येरन्।। नेमे शक्याः प्राग्भवतेःपठितुम्।

Here some bases are recited with *upasargas abhi manas* (m.f.n. having the mind directed towards, desirous of, longing for), *su-manas* (m.f.n. good minded, will disposed, benevolent, gracious, favourable, pleasant, agreeable), *unmanas* (m.f.n. excited or disturbed in mind, perplexed, longing or wishing for). *dur-manas* (n. bad disposition, perversity of mind, cf. Greek *dus-menes,* in bad or low spirits, sad, melancholy).

There, in that context it is doubted whether in the words *bhṛśa* and the rest the *upasarga* should be optionally qualifying the meaning of the *pratyaya* (thus *abhi*) in the sense of overcoming, conquering or approaching; (*su*) in the sense of being excellent by nature; (*ut*) in the sense of coming up to, reaching, arising or coming forth; (*dur*) in the sense of being bad.

Or else inasmuch as (the *upasargas*) serve to qualify the meaning of the base. Thus, (acting) after the word *abhimanas* (mind directed to, desirous), after the word *sumanas* (good minded), after the word *unmanas* (excited in mind), or after the word *durmanas* (bad disposition).

It is proper to ponder on this further, surely the (*upasargas*) should be undoubted qualifications of the meaning of the base, inasmuch as (the *upasargas*) are recited before the base. For if they were qualifications of the meaning of the *pratyaya* they would be recited before *bhū*. It is not possible for these to be recited before *bhū*.

22.23 .... एवं विशिष्टे हि प्रत्ययार्थे भृशादिमात्रादुत्पत्तिः
प्रसज्येत। तस्मान्नैवं शक्यं वक्तुम्।
22.25 न चेदेवं जायते विचारणा।। कश्चात्र विशेषः।

For thus when the meaning of the *pratyaya* is specified, the arising of (the *pratyaya*) after the whole of (the group) *bhṛśa* and the rest would be applicable. Therefore it is not (in fact) possible to speak thus. And if not thus the matter has to be discussed.

And what is the distinction here?

23.1 भृशादिषूपसर्गः प्रत्ययार्थविशेषणमिति चेत्स्वरे दोषः ।। 5 ।।

Vārttika 5: If (we accept the statement) "in the words *bhṛśa* and the rest . . an *upasarga* qualifies the meaning of the *pratyaya*" (there is) a fault in relation to the accent.

23.2 भृशादिषूपसर्गः प्रत्ययार्थविशेषणमिति चेत्स्वरे भवति। अभिमनायते। तिङ्ङतिङः
(8.1.28) इति निघातः प्रसज्यते।। अस्तु तर्हि प्रकृत्यर्थविशेषणम्।

Bhāṣya: If (we say) "in the words *bhṛśa* and the rest an *upasarga* qualifies the meaning of the *pratyaya*" then there is a fault in relation to accent e.g. *abhi-manāyate* "He longs for or desires". Here (by the rule) *tiṅṅatiṅaḥ* (*8.1.28*) "A finite verb is unaccented when a word precedes it which is not a finite verb" absence of accent would be wrongly applicable.

Then let it be (that) it qualifies the meaning of the base.

23.4 सोपसर्गादिति चेदटि दोषः ।। 6 ।।

Vārttika 6: If (we accept the statement after the word) together with an *upasarga* (there is) a fault when augment) *aṭ* follows.

23.5 सोपसर्गादिति चेदटि दोषो[10] भवति। स्वमनायतेति[11] ।। अत्यल्पमिदमुच्यतेऽटि
दोषो भवतीति। अड्ल्यब्द्विर्वचनेष्विति वक्तव्यम्। अट्युदाहृतम्। ल्यपि[12]। सु-मनाय्य।
द्विर्वचने। अभिमिमनायिषते[13] ।। नैष दोषः। अवश्यं संग्रामयतेः[14] सोपसर्गा-
दुत्पत्तिर्वक्तव्या असंग्रामयत शूर इत्येवमर्थम्। तन्नियमार्थं भविष्यति। संग्रामयते-
23.9 रेव सोपसर्गान्नान्यस्मात्सोपसर्गादिति।।

Bhāṣya: If (we say) after the words together with an *upasarga* there is a fault when (augment) *aṭ* follows, e.g *sv-amanāyata* "He became cheerful or happy".

This which is stated, namely "There is a fault when *aṭ* (augment) follows" is too small (a scope).

It should be stated "when there is *aṭ (*augment*), lyap* (*pratyaya*) and reduplication (there is a fault)". (The fault) "when *aṭ follows"* is already illustrated. The fault when *lyap* follows is e.g *su-manāya* "Having become cheerful or happy." When there is reduplication, *abhi-mi-manāyiṣyate* "He desires or longs for..."

This is not a fault. It is essential that the production of *pratyayas* should be stated after *samgrāmayati* in conjunction with or having its *upasarga* attached for (explaining the form) *a-sam-grāmayata śūraḥ* "The hero made war/fought".

It will be for the purpose of the restriction only after *sam-grāmayati* with its *upasarga,* not after any other verb with its *upasarga.*

23.9 .... यदि नियमः क्रियते स्वरो न सिध्यति। एवं
तर्हि भृशादिषूपसर्गस्य पराङ्गवद्भावं वक्ष्यामि[15]।। यदि पराङ्गवद्भावं उच्यते-
ऽड्ल्यब्द्विर्वनानि न सिध्यन्ति। स्वरविधाविति वक्ष्यामि। एवं च कृत्वास्तु प्रत्यया-
र्थविशेषणमपि। ननु चोक्तं भृशादिषूपसर्गः प्रत्ययार्थविशेषणमिति चेत्स्वरे दोष
23.13 इति। स्वरे पराङ्गवद्भावेन परिहृतम्।

If the restriction is made, then the accent is not valid.

Well then, I will say that in relation to *bhṛśa* and the rest there is the condition of being like a part of that which follows.

If it is said there is condition of being like a part of that which follows, the (the accent of) those words having *aṭ, lyap* or reduplication are not valid.

I will say, "in relation to an accent rule" and having done so let it be also the qualification of the meaning of the *pratyaya.*

But surely it was stated, "if it be a qualification of the *pratyaya* then there will be a fault in relation to accent". In relation to accent it is avoided by (stating) the condition of being like that which follows.

23.14 अयं तर्हि प्रत्ययार्थविशेषणे सति दोषः क्यङोक्तत्वात्तस्यार्थस्योपसर्गस्य प्रयोगो
न प्राप्नोति। किं कारणम्। उक्तार्थानामप्रयोग इति[16]। तद्यथा। अपि काकः
श्येनायत इति क्यङोक्तत्वादाचारार्थस्याङः[17] प्रयोगो न भवति। अस्त्यत्र विशेषः।
एकेनात्र विशिष्टे प्रत्ययर्थे प्रत्यय उत्पद्यत इह पुनरनेकेन। तत्र मनायत इत्युक्ते

संदेहः स्यादमिभवतौ सुभवतावुद्भवतौ दुर्भवताविति। तत्रासंदेहार्थमुपसर्गः प्र-युज्यते।।
यत्र तद्ध्येकेन। उत्पुच्छयते[18]। अत्राप्यनेकेन। पुच्छादुदसने पुच्छाव्द्यसने
23.20 पुच्छात्पर्यसन इति।।

This then is a fault, when qualifying the meaning of the *pratyaya*, because *kyaṅ* has already expressed the meaning, the use of an *upasarga* does not obtain.

What is the reason? "There is not usage (of a *pratyaya* or other word element) for (the expressing of) those meanings which have already been stated.

As for example *api kākaḥ śyenāyate* "Does the crow behave like a hawk?" So here because by *kyaṅ* has been expressed 'in the sense of conduct' there is not applicability of the *upasarga āṅ* (in the sense of conduct). There is a distinction. Here when the meaning of the *pratyaya* is specified or distinguished by one *upsarga* the *pratyaya* arises, but here (it is distinguished) by more than one. Then, when it is stated *manāyate* "He is zealous, devoted, thinks or considers" there would be doubt as to whether *kyaṅ* is added in the sense of *abhi-bhavati* (one who surpasses or overcomes), (*su*) in the sense of *su-bhavati* (being of excellent nature), (*ud*) in the sense of *ud-bhavati* (one who comes up to, reaches, arises or exists), and (*dur*) in the sense of *dur-bhavati* (existing on ill luck).

Therefore for the purpose of avoiding doubt the *upasarga* is to be attached.

Then, where (joined) with only one (*upasarga*) the *pratyaya* acts, (e.g.) *utpucchayate* "It raises its tail".

Here also (it acts) with more than one. Thus:

pucchād-ud-asane "after *puccha* (tail) in the sense of raising".

pucchād-vy-asane "after *puccha* (tail) in the sense of wagging about".

pucchāt-pary-asane "after *puccha* (tail) in the sense of throwing about *ṇiṅ* acts".

Pradīpa

Pradīpa: का॰ — भृश इत्येवमादिभ्यः प्रातिपदिकेभ्योऽच्व्यन्तेम्यो भुवि भवत्यर्थे क्यङ् प्रत्ययो भवति, हलन्तानां च लोपः अच्वे इति प्रत्येकममिंसम्बध्यते

"The *Pratyaya kyaṅ acts in the* sense of becoming (what it was not before) after the crude bases/*prātipadika bhṛśa* and the rest not ending in the *pratyaya cvi* and there is *lopa* elision (of the final) of those (words) ending in a consonant (*hal*)."

The restriction, not (ending in the) *pratyaya cvi,* is to be connected with each (word in the *bhṛśa gaṇa*).

Notes

[1] प्रधानशिष्ट ··· अन्वाचयशिष्टः see 3.1.91

[2] "क्व दिवा भृशा भवन्ति"

Where do they become strong by day?

c.f. नक्तं दद्दृश्रे कुह चिद्दिवा ईयुः ऋग्वेद 1.24.10

"Whither by day depart (the constellations) that shine at night (set high in heaven above us)?"

कै॰ — अत्राऽभूततद्भावाभावः

Here there is absence of becoming what the thing was not before.

[3] भवतिना योगे च्विर्विधीयते

"*cvi* is ordained in conjunction with the *dhātu bhū.*"

कृभ्वस्तियोगे संपद्यकर्तरि च्वि 5.1.40

see note on P.

च्विनोक्तत्वादिति

because of (its meaning) being expressed together with *cvi.*

कै॰ — च्विसहचरितेन भवतिनेत्यर्थः

The meaning is with *bhū* going with *cvi.*

[4] डाजन्तादपि After the ending in *ḍāc* also *kyaṅ* does not obtain.

अव्यक्तानुकरणात् द्व्यज् अवरार्द्धात् डाच् 5.4.57

"The *pratyaya ḍāc* acts after the half of the word denoting an imitation of an articulate sound, when that half consists of at least two syllables, and when it is not followed by the (quotation mark) *iti.*"

पटपटत् करोति पटपटा करोति

He makes a sound like *paṭat paṭat.*

In fact *kyaṣ* will be applicable by लोहितादिडाज्भ्यः क्यष् 3.1.13 (भुवि)

"The *pratyaya k-ya-ṣ* acts after the words *lohita* and the rest and after these that end with the *pratyaya ḍāc* (*5-4-57*) when those words do not receive the *pratyaya cvi* (*5.4.50*) in the sense of becoming what the thing previously was not."

[5]पटपटायते He makes a sound like *paṭ pat* (which he had not made before).

पटत् onomatopaeic (i.e. from imitation of sounds)

पटत् डाच् 5.4.57 see अव्यक्तानुकरणात्

पटत् पटत् डाच् डाचि द्वे वा॰ 8 8.1.12

प्रकारे गुणवचनस्य

पटत् पट आ डाचि कृते टि लोप टे: 6.1.143)

(त्-प्-प) (नाम्रेडितस्यान्तस्य तु वा 6.1.99)

पटपटा क्यष् ते नित्यमाम्रेडिते डाचि 1 (पररूपम्)

"For such a double sound imitation word in the presence of *ḍāc* (= *ā*) in place of the final *ṭ* of the first member and the initial consonant of the second member, the form of the subsequent is the one *ādeśa* for both."

[6] वचनप्रामाण्यात्

'Due to the authoritative statement of a rule', an expression frequently uased by the *vārttika* to refer to the pre-eminence of a statement made by the *sūtra-kāra Pāṇini.*

[7] नञिवयुक्तमन्यसदृशाधिकरणे यथा ह्यर्थगतिः
नागे परि 74 ननु भृशादिभ्यो भुव्यच्वेः 3.1.12 इत्यादौ
विधीयमान क्यङ् क्व दिक्षा भृशा भवन्तीत्यत्रापि स्यादत आह

One might say that the *pratyaya kyaṅ* which by *3.1.12* may be added to *bhṛśa* etc., when they do not end with the *pratyaya cvi* to denote the meaning expressed by the *dhātu bhū* may be added to *bhṛśa* also in the phrase क्व दिवा भृशा भवन्ति 'Where are the (stars that were) visible (by night) in daytime?' (i.e. क्व दिवा भृशायन्ते) because *bhṛśa* in this phrase does not end in *cvi* and is in construction with *bhavanti.* (The *vārttikakāra* or a previous *paribhāṣā* formulator) says therefore... (tr. in text) An expression formed ...

The *bhāṣya* then explains:

नञ्युक्तभिवयुक्तं यत्किंचिदिह दृश्यते तत्रान्यस्मिंस्तत्सदृशे कार्यं विज्ञायते तथा ह्यर्थो गम्यते

नागेश glosses on *Pari. 74*

"Whenever we see (in a rule) any term which is formed either by the addition of (the negative नञ् or by that of इव to (some other word) we know that the operation (which is taught in the rule must take effect), in something which differs from (and is at the same time similar to that which is denoted by that other word) because it is in this way, that (such terms) are generally understood (in ordinary life)."

[8] अब्राह्मणमानयेत्युक्ते ब्राह्मणसदृश् आनीयते नासौ लोष्टमानीय कृती भवति (अब्राह्मणाम् आनय)

"For when (somebody has been told) 'fetch a non-*Brāhmaṇa*' and has thereupon brought a lump of earth, he is not considered to have done what he ought to have done."

In ordinary life अब्राह्मण denotes the one who though he is not a *Brāhmaṇa* is yet similar to a *Brāhmaṇa,* e.g. a *kṣatriya,* but it cannot denote, for example, a lump of earth.

Accordingly *kyaṅ* can be added by *3.1.12* to *bhṛśa* etc. only when it does not end with *cvi* and yet is similar to words that end in *cvi.*

c.f. also the earliest (?) explanation of *na* = *iva.*

हिरण्यदन्तो रपसो नसूनुः न हि एष सूनुः

who has golden teeth is not the inciter of bodily defect for this one is not one who urges the sun

सुनुरूपो हि एष सन् न सूतुः

For (though) being of the form of the inciter he is not the one who urges (sun).

(जैमिनीय उपनिषद् ब्राह्माण 3.3.15)

i.e. when the sense to be expressed is that 'that which formerly was not *bhṛśa* becomes or is *bhṛśa.* In the other cases however, क्व् दिवा etc. it follows that *3.1.12* cannot be applied. c.f.

श्लोक वार्तिक	नाम धात्वर्थयोगी च
अपोहवाद 33	नैन नञ् प्रतिषेधकः
कुमारिल	वदतो ब्राह्मणाधर्मो
(अभूततद्भाव)	अन्यमात्राविरोधिनौ

'*nañ* having (connection with the increasing of the *dhātu* and a noun is not negative in fact, as non-*brāhmin* and non-righteousness of one speaking are not contradicting the possibility of having different mothers. (7)'

[7] अभिमनस् (मन (दि० आ० अ० 1176 ज्ञाने) असुन् (उ० 4.189) (करणे)

अभिमनाय -आ (opt. *manāyate*) to long for desire *Bhaṭṭ 5.73*

सुमनस्— सुमनाय nom. आ to become cheerful or happy

उन्मनस्— उन्मनायते to become perplexed or excited *Daś 63.7*

दुर्मनस्— दुर्मनायते to become troubled or sad, *Kāś.*

All in the *bhṛśādi gaṇa.*

तिङतिङ् 8.1.28

"A *tiṅ* ending word (i.e. a finite verb) is *anudātta* accented (when after a word not ending in a *tiṅ* (verbal *pratyaya*)."

e.g. देवदत्तः पचति

निघात इति (caus. of *ni-han*) a blow, stroke, suppression or absence of accent *A.V. Prāt* toning down, *anudātta* or grave accent.

कै० — मनः शब्दात् क्यङिकृते मनायते इत्यस्य तिङन्तस्य पदस्याऽतिङन्तात् स्वादेः पदादुत्तरत्वात् प्रकृत्यर्थविशेषणत्वे तु सुमनायत इत्यादि तिङन्तं संपद्यत इति तद्व्यतिरिक्तपदान्तरा भावानिघातऽभावः उपसर्गस्य तु धात्वन्तर्भावात्ततः

पूर्वमडाटौ प्राप्नुतः क्यङन्ते च तस्याऽनु प्रवेशात्तद्व्यतिरिक्तपदाऽभावात्सभासा भावात्लोपा प्रसङ्गः क्यङन्ताच्च सनि कृते सोपसर्गस्य द्विर्वचनप्रसङ्गः

"There is (*anudātta* accent) when *kyaṅ* is effected after the word *manas* for (the form) *manāyate,* ending in *tiṅ* because of following the word *su* and the rest, not ending in *tiṅ*. However, when (the *upasarga*) qualified the base, (the forms) *sumanāyate* etc. become *tiṅ* ending and because of the absence of another word different from it there is absence of suppressed accent/*anudātta.* However because of the *upasarga* being included in the *dhātu* these (wrongly) obtain the augment *aṭ* and *āṭ* before it (instead of directly preceding the *dhātu* itself.)

And because of its entering into a *kyaṅ* ending (*dhātu*), because of the absence of a *pada*/word separate from it, and because of the absence of a *samāsa* (technical name), there is no possibility/occasion for *lopa* (of *sup* endings). And when *san* (desiderative) is effected after a *kyaṅ* ending *dhātu,* there is the possibility (undesired) of reduplication of the *upasarga.*"

[10] सोपसर्गादिति चेदटि दोष

If we accept the statement 'after the word together with an *upasarga* there is a fault in relation to *aṭ āgama,* by लुङ्लङ्लृङ्क्ष्वड्उदात्तः 6.4.71 (अङ्गस्य)

"*Aṭ* with *udātta* accent acts as the augment of the initial of a verbal *aṅga*/ stem, in the presence of the aorist, imperfect and conditional (tense *pratyayas*)."

So here the augment would have to be for the initial of the *upasarga* preceding the *dhātu* not of the *dhātu* itself (which is required) by आद्यन्तौ टकितौ 1.1.46

[11] स्वमनायत "He was or became cheerful."

सु अद् मनाय (यङन्त) (त) लङ् (imperfect)

If the statement is accepted *aṭ* would here have to augment the initial of *su.*

[12] ल्यप् *kṛt pratyaya* य *ādeśa* in place of क्त्वा (indeclinable participle/gerund) when the *dhātu* it follows is preceded by an *upasarga* with which it is compounded, by समासेऽनञ्पूर्वे क्त्वो ल्यप् 7.1.37

"In a compound the first member of which is an indeclinable but not *nañ,* *lyap* is *ādeśa* for *ktvā.*"

ल् *by* लिति 6.1.193

'*udātta* on the syllable immediately preceding the *pratyaya* having *it l.*'

प् by ह्रस्वस्य पिति कृति तुक् 6.1.71 augment त्

सुमनाय्य सुमनाय ल्यप् अतो लोपः 6.4.48 (आर्धधातुके)

[13] अभि मि मनाय् इट् षते

'सन्यङोः' 6.1.9

"For a non-reduplicate *dhātu* ending in *san* or *yaṅ* (intensive) *pratyayas* there is reduplication."

iṭ augment by आर्धधातुकस्येड्वलादेः 7.2.35

The reduplicate syllable is *mi* because the *dhātu* is to be reduplicated not the *dhātu* and an *upasarga* together; otherwise *abhi* would have had to be reduplicated.

सन्यतः 7.4.73

"Short *i* is *ādeśa* for *a* of the reduplicate in the desiderative"

सन्यङोः 6.1.9

"(For a non-reduplicate) *dhātu* ending in *san* (desiderative) or *yaṅ* (intensive) *pratyayas* there is reduplication."

अतो लोपः 6.4.48

"The *a* at the end of a stem is elided before an *ārdhadhātuka pratyaya.*"

[14] अवश्यं संग्रामयतेः "It is essential that the form *samgrāmayati* be taken as together with its *upasarga.*"

सङ्ग्राम (चु० उ० अ० 1123 युद्धे) णि

So that this exceptional case be allowed for, where the *upasarga sam* is intended as part of the *dhātu.*

अ संग्रामयत शूरः Imperfect लङ् with *āgama* अट्

"The hero made war or fought."

[15] पराङ्गवद्भावं वक्ष्यामि

"The condition of being like a part of that which follows" I will say. . . 'treatment of a word as part of another'

c.f. सुबामन्त्रिते पराङ्गवत्स्वरे 2.1.2

"A word ending in a *sup*/case *pratyaya,* when followed by a word in the vocative/*āmantrita* (*2.3.48*) is regarded as if it was a part/*aṅga* of such a vocative word when a rule relating to accent is to be applied," i.e. a *sup* ending word enters as it were the body of the vocative word, by आमन्त्रितस्य च 6.1.198

"The first syllable of a vocative has *udātta* accent."

e.g. शुभस् पती शुभस्पती 'of prosperity' the Lords.

The *udātta* on *patī* now falls on *su* because the two words are considered as a single word.

[16] उक्तार्थानामप्रयोगः c.f. previous note.

[17] क्यङोक्तत्वादाचारार्थस्याङः

'because by *kyaṅ* has been expressed the sense of conduct (there is not applicability) of *āṅ* (in that sense).'

c.f. उपमानादाचारे 3.1.10

"*Kyac* (optionally) acts in the sense of conduct (towards someone) after a word ending in a *sup*/case *pratyaya* denoting the object of comparison."

कर्तुः क्यङ्सलोपश्च 3.1.11

"*Kyaṅ* optionally acts in the sense of conduct . . . and there is elision of final *s*."

[18] उत्पुच्छयते It raises its tail. *Vop. 21,17*

पुच्छभाण्डचीवराण्णिङ् 3.1.20 (करणे)

"The *pratyaya ṇiṅ* in the sense of making, acts after पुच्छ (tail) भाण्ड (pot) and चीरव (rags) as the *karman*/object of the action."

c.f. also विभाषोत्पुच्छे 6.2.196

In the *tatpuruṣa* fr. b. the word उत्पुच्छ may optionally have *udātta* on the final.

लोहितादिडाज्भ्यः क्यष् ॥ 3 । 1 । 13 ॥

Pāṇini 3.1.13: The *pratyaya kyaṣ* in the sense of becoming (what the thing previously was not), comes after the words *lohiṭa* etc. and after those that end with the *pratyaya ḍāc (5.4.57)*

23.22 किमर्थः ककारः। गुणवृद्धिप्रतिषेधार्थः। ङ्किकतीति गुणवृद्धिप्रतिषेधो[1] यथा स्यात्। नैतदस्ति प्रयोजनम्। सार्वधातुकार्धधातुकयोरङ्गस्य गुण उच्यते[2] धातो श्चविहितः प्रत्ययः[3] शेष आर्धधातुकसंज्ञां लभते न चायं धातोर्विधीयते। लोहितादीनि

24.1 प्रातिपदिकानि

Bhāṣya: What is the purpose of the letter *k* (of *kyaṣ*)? For the purpose of prohibiting *guṇa* and *vṛddhi*. So that there should be prohibition of *guṇa* and *vṛddi* when that having an indicatory *k, g* or *ṅ* follows.

This is not the purpose. It is stated that when a *sārvadhātuka* or an *ārdhadhātuka pratyaya* follows *guṇa* acts for the final *ik* (namely) *i u ṛ ḷ* vowel) of an *aṅga*/base. And the remaining *pratyayas* ordained after a *dhātu* receives the technical name *ārdhadhātuka* and this (*pratyaya kyaṣ*) is not ordained after a *dhātu*. The words *lohiṭa* and the rest are *prātipadikas*/crude base (not *dhātus*).

24.1 .... सामान्यग्रहणार्थस्तर्हि। क्व सामान्यग्रहणार्थेनार्थः न क्ये (1.4.15) इति। नायं नान्ताद्विधीयते[4]।। इह तर्हि। यस्य हलः क्यस्य विभाषा (6.4.49,50) इति। नायं हलन्ताद्विधीयते।। इह तर्हि। आपत्यस्य च तद्धितेऽनाति

क्यच्व्योश्च (6.4.151, 152) इति। नायमापत्याद्विधीयते।। इह तर्हि। क्याच्छन्दसि
(3.2.170) इति याच्छन्दसीत्येतावद्वक्तव्यं चुरण्युः तुरण्युः भुरण्युः भुरण्युः
24.6 भुरण्युरित्येवमर्थम्।।

Then it is for the purpose of general mention. Where is there (exhibited some) purpose in a general mention? (In the rule) *naḥ kye* (*1.4.15*) "The word form ending in *n* is called *pada* when *kya* follows" (i.e. *pratyayas kyac, kyaṅ* and *kyaṣ*). (This *pratyaya kyaṣ*) is not ordained after (a word) ending in *n*. (Therefore general mention is not the purpose).

Here applies the sutra *'yasya* the *'yasya halaḥ'* (*6.4.49*) "When a consonant precedes the final *y* in a verbal stem, this *y* is *lopa*/elided, before an *ārdhadhātuka pratyaya*" (and the *sūtra*) *kyasya vibhāṣā* (*6.4.50*) "The elision/*lopa* of *y* of the denominative stem *pratyaya kya* is optional when preceded by a consonant and followed by an *ārdhadhātuka pratyaya*". This (*kyaṣ*) has not been ordained after that ending in a consonant. (Therefore this is not the purpose).

Here then, *āpatyasya ca taddhite'nāti* (*6.4.151*) "The *y* belonging to a patronymic *pratyaya*, preceded by a consonant is *lopa*/elided before a *taddhita pratyaya* when it does not begin with *ā*" and *kyacvyośca* (*6.4.152*) (*halaḥ, lopaḥ*) "The *y* belonging to a patronymic *pratyaya* preceded by a consonant is elided before the denominative" *pratyaya kya* and the adverbial *pratyaya cvi*". This (*pratyaya kyaṣ*) is not ordained after a patronymic *pratyaya.* (Therefore this is not the purpose)

Here then, (3.2.170)" After *kya* (denominative *pratyayas kyac kyan* and *kyas*) the *pratyaya u* acts." in the *Veda,* in the sense of agens having such a habit or nature or having skill in some action. It should in fact be only stated as *yācchandasi.* (Hence the forms) *curaṇyuḥ* 'a thief, whose habit is to steal.' *turaṇyuḥ'* swift, zealous' *bhuraṇyuḥ* 'quivering, stirring, quick'. (from the *Kaṇḍvādigaṇa* 3.1.27 *yak+u* by *3.2.168*). This is the meaning.

24.6 .... इदं तर्हि प्रयोजनम्। यत्तदकृद्यकार इति दीर्घत्वं तत्र
ङिक्दग्रहणमनुवर्तते तदिहापि यथा स्यात्। लोहितायते। किं पुनः कारणं तत्र
ङिक्दग्रहणमनुवर्तते। इह मा भूत्। उरुया[5] घृष्णुयेति। यदि ङिक्दग्रहणमनुवर्तते।
पित्र्यमिति पितू रीङ्भावो न प्राप्नोति[6]।। रीङ्भावे ङिक्दग्रहणं निवर्तिष्यते।। यदि
24.10 निवर्तते कथमसूया। वसूया चं यजामहे[7]।

This then is the purpose of that letter *y* which is not a *kṛt pratyaya,* it causes lengthening. The mention of *kṅit* is continued in the statement of *dīrgha* by the rule when a non-*kṛt* letter *y* follows and should be continued in this rule also. (Thus lengthening takes place in) *lohitāyate.*

But what is the reason why the word *kṅiti* is specifically mentioned as following on (from the previous *sūtra*)? So that lengthening should not be applicable here *uruyā* (instr. of feminine ind. far, to a distance, *Maitr. S.*) *dhṛṣṇuvā* (ind.) boldly, strongly, firmly (*R.V.*).

If the specific word *kṅiti* follows on from the previous *sūtra*, then the (form) *pitryam* with the *ādeśa*/substitute *rīṅ* does not obtain. When there occurs the *ādeśa*/substitute *rīṅ* the specific mention of *it k* and *ṅ* will cease (to be applicable).

If it ceases how do we get the form *asūya vasūya ca yajāmahe* (*Ṛgveda 1.97.2*) "(For a fine field, for pleasant paths), for wealth, we sacrifice to you"?

24.10 असूयतेरसूया[8] वसूयतेर्वसूया[9]। अथवा छान्दसमेतद् दृष्टानुविधिश्च च्छन्दसि भवतीति।
यदि च्छान्दसत्वं हेतुनार्थः ङि्कद्ग्रहणेना- नुवर्तमानेन। कस्मान्न भवति उरुया
घृष्णुयेति। छान्दसत्वात्।। अथवास्त्वत्र दीर्घत्वं छान्दसं ह्रस्वत्वं भविष्यति। तद्यथा।
उपगायन्तु मां पत्नयो गर्भिणयो युवतय[10]

24.14 इति।।

From *asūyati* (discontented with) (is derived the form) *asūya* (displeasure, indignation (esp. at the merit or happiness of another), envy and jealousy) (and) from *vasūyati* ("He desires wealth") is derived *vasūyā* (ind. through desire of wealth).

Otherwise this is peculiar to the *Veda*. And the operation or application of the rule is in accordance with the words seen in use in the *Veda*.

If being peculiar to the *Veda* is the cause, then no purpose is (served) by the mention of *kṅit* (from the previous *sūtra*). Why is (*kyaṣ*) not applicable in the case of the forms *uruyā* (far) *dhṛṣṇuyā* (boldly)? Because (they are forms) peculiar to the *Veda*.

Otherwise (in classical literature) let there be lengthening of the vowel here. The shortening will be peculiar to the *Veda*. As for example *upagāyantu māṃ garbhiṇayo yuvatayaḥ* "Let the young pregnant wives sing to me".

24.15 अथ किमर्थः षकारः। विशेषणार्थः। क्व विशेषणार्थेनार्थः। वा क्यषः[11] (1.3.90)
इति। वा यादिति ह्युच्यमाने पाश्या[12] अतोऽपि प्रसज्येत। नैतदस्ति प्रयोजनम्।
परस्मैपदमित्युच्यते न चातः परस्मैपदं नाप्यात्मनेपदं पश्यामः। सामान्यग्रहणा-
विघातार्थस्तर्हि भविष्यति। क्व सामान्यग्रहणाविघातार्थेनार्थः। क्या-

24.19 च्छन्दसीति। याच्छन्दसीत्येव[13] वक्तव्यं चुरण्युः तुरण्युः भुरण्युरित्येवमर्थम्।

Now what is the purpose of the letter *ṣ*? For distinguishing (it from other *pratyayas*).

Where is the purpose for the sake of distinguishing served? (In the *sūtra*) *vā kyaṣaḥ* (*1.3.90*) "The *pratyayas* called *parasmaipada* act optionally after the denominative verbs ending in the *pratyaya kyaṣ*". For if it were simply stating "*vā yāt*" "optionally after *ya*" it would be applicable even after a short *a* of *pāśyā* "A multitude or nooses or ropes, a net"

This is not purpose that *parasmaipada* be stated, because here we do not see *parasmaipada* nor even *ātmanepada pratyayas.*

Then it will be for the purpose of common mention or inclusion without hindrance to application (of a particular term to others where it should apply). Where is shown the purpose for the common mention without hindrance to application (of a particular term to others)? (In the rule) *kyācchandas* (*3.2.170*) "The *pratyaya u* acts in the *chandas/Veda* after *dhātus* that have taken the denominative *pratyaya kyaṣ* in the sense of the agent having such a habit etc." In fact it should be stated, namely *yācchandasi* "after *ya* in the *Veda* (omitting *k*)". So the purpose is (for the forms) *curaṇyuḥ* (thief), *turaṇyuḥ* (swift), *bhuraṇyuḥ* (quivering).

24.20 लोहितडाज्भ्यः क्यष्वचनम् ॥ 1 ॥

Vārttika 1: The rule (should be) after *lohita* and after those words ending in the *pratyaya ḍāc, the pratayaya kyaṣ acts.*

24.21 लोहितडाज्भ्यः क्यष् वक्तव्यः। लोहितायति लोहितायते। पटपटायति पटपटायते॥ अथान्यानि लोहितादीनि।

Bhāṣya: It should be stated after *lohita* and those words ending in *ḍāc, kyaṣ pratyaya* acts.

lohitāyati, lohitāyate "He becomes red",
paṭapaṭāyati, paṭapaṭāyate "He makes the sound *paṭpaṭ*",
damadamāyati, damadamāyate "He makes the sound *damadama*".

Now (what about) the others in the group) *lohita* and the rest (what of them)?

24.23 भृशादिष्वितराणि ॥ 2 ॥

Vārttika 2: The others are to be read in the (*gaṇa*) *bhṛśa* and the rest.

24.24 भृशादिष्वितराणि पठितव्यानि। किं प्रयोजनम्। ङित इत्यात्मनेपदं यथा स्यादिति॥

Bhāṣya: The rest are to be read/recited in the (*gaṇa*) *bhṛśa* and the rest. What is the purpose? So that the rule (*anūdatta*) *ṅita ātmanepadam* (*1.3.12*) "That having an *it*/indicatory *ṅ* (as well as a gravely accented *dhātu* in the *Dhātu Pāṭha* takes) *ātmanepada* (*vibhaktipratyaya* when the fruit accrues to the agent)", should be applicable.

Pradīpa

Pradīpa: लोहितडाज्भ्य इति

'The *pratyaya kyaṣ* acts after the words *lohita* and words ending in *ḍāc.*"

आदिशब्दप्रत्याख्यानमेतत् अपठितसङ्ग्रहार्थोप्यादिशब्दो न भवति, तस्य वार्त्तिककारेण दूषितत्वात्

This is rejection of the word *ādi/lohita* and the rest. The word *ādi* is not applicable also in the sense of an unread complete enumeration or collection, because of its nature being refuted by the *Vārttika-kāra.*

का० - भृशादिष्वितराणि यानि लोहितादिषु पठ्यन्ते तेभ्यःक्यङेव अपरिपठितेभ्यस्तु क्यषेव भवति

The rest of *lohita-ādi* will be found in the *bhṛśādi gaṇa.*

The words quoted in the (group) *lohita* and the rest have *kyaṅ* only after them, (others) not quoted (it being an *ākṛti gaṇa*) have *kyaṣ* only after them.

e.g. वर्मायति वर्मायते to become clad with armour.

Notes

[1] का० लोहितादिभ्यो डाजन्तेभ्यश्च क्यष् प्रत्ययो भवति

"The *pratyaya kyaṣ* acts after the words *lohita* and words ending in the *pratyaya ḍāc.*"

[2] क्ङिति गुणवृद्धिप्रतिषेधो

"And that word element, which otherwise would have caused *guṇa* or *vṛddhi* does not do so, when that has an indicatory *k, g,* or *ṅ.*"

Thus the *k* of *kyaṣ* would seem to have this function.

[3] सार्वधातुकार्धधातुक्यो: (7.3.84) अङ्गस्य गुण (उच्यते)

"*Guṇa* from 7.3.82 मिदेर्गुण: acts in the place of the final *ik* vowel by 1.1.3 इको गुणवृद्धी an *aṅga*/stem (6.4.1 अङ्गस्य) before the *sārvadhātuka 3.4.113* and *ārdhadhātuka 3.4.114-17 pratyayas.*"

[4] धातोश्च विहित प्रत्यय:

c.f. *3.1.91* "As far as the end of the third *adhyaya* from *3.1.91* the *pratyayas* are understood to be enjoined after a *dhātu.*"

c.f. शेष आर्धधातुकसंज्ञा लभते

आर्धधातुकं शेषः 3.4.114 (तिङ् शित् प्रत्ययः धातोः, वर्जयित्वा)

"The remainder, (i.e. the *pratyayas* other than *tiṅ* (verbal *pratyayas*) and those with an indicatory *ś* attached) acting after a *dhātu* are called *ārdhadhātuka.*"

4A P.6.4.50 क्यस्य भाषा का० समिध्यिता समिधिता

He will wish for fuel or behave like fuel *lopa* elision of *kya* in these circumstances.

समिधमात्मन इच्छति (क्यच्) समिधम् इव आत्मनाय आचरति (क्यङ्)

4B आपत्यस्य च तद्धिते नास्ति 6.4.151 (लोपःहलः) तद्धितस्य)

"There is *lopa* elision in place of the *ya* of a patronymic *pratyaya* preceded by a consonant in the presence of a *taddhita pratyaya* beginning with a long *ā.*"

e.g. गार्य (4.1.105)'; यञ् वुञ् (4.2.39, तस्य समूहः 4.2.37) अक् (7.1.1.)

गर्गाणां समूहः = गार्गकम्

The repetition of *taddhita* is said to indicate that the elision occurs sometimes of the non-patronymic *ya,* as सौमी इष्टिः

Hence the *pūrvapakṣa* has some grounds for his statement.

4C क्यच्व्योश्च 6.4.152 (हलः लोपः यः आपत्यस्य)

"There is *lopa* elision in place of the य of a patronymic *pratyaya* preceded by a consonant in the presence of the denominative *pratyaya kyac* and the adverbial *taddhita pratyaya cvi* (all of which is elided)"

वात्सीयति वात्सीयते वात्स क्यच् (3.1.10)

He treats someone like a *vātsa* or he behaves like a *vātsa.*

गार्गीभूतः गार्य (च्वि भूतः (5.4.50))

one who has become a *gārgya*

5 नायं नान्ताद्विधीयते "This is not ordained after a word ending in *n.*"

का० — न हि पठितानां मध्ये नकारान्तः शब्दोऽस्ति

Kāś For there is no word among those read (in the *lohita gaṇa*) which ends in the letter *n.*

यस्य हलः 6.4.49

"In place of the syllable *ya* final of an *aṅga* (verbal stem) preceded by a consonant, *lopa* elision acts, in the presence of an *ārdhadhātuka pratyaya*"

(Otherwise by the previous *sutra* अतो लोप: 6-4-48 only the final *a* of *ya* would have been *lopa* by अलोऽन्त्यस्य 1.1.52

e.g. बेभिद्य तुमुन् बेभिदितुम्

क्यस्य विभाषा 6.4.50

"The *lopa* elision of *kya* in those circumstance is optional."

i.e. precedence by a consonant and followed by an *ārdhadhātuka pratyaya kya* denotes *kyac* and *kyaṅ* not *kyaṣ.*

[5A] क्याच्छन्दसि 3.2.170 (तच्छीलतद्धर्मतत्साधुकारिषु)

"After *kya* (denominative *pratyayas kyac kyan* and *kyas*) the *pratyaya u* acts in the *Veda,* in the sense of agents having such a habit or nature or having skill in some action."

याच्छन्दसीत्येतावद् वक्तव्यम्:

"It should in fact be only stated as *yācchandasi* because the *k* serves no purpose of preventing *guṇa* since this is not ordained after a *dhātu,* but in fact after *prātipadikas* (see *3.1.13.23.21* line 1) and that enables *yak* to be included."

24.5 चुरण्यु: a thief, whose habit is to steal, Not found in the recorded literature.

चुरण (कण्ड्वादिभ्यो यक् 3.1.27 & उ 3.2.170) क प से चैर्य

Instead c.f. चरण्यु: m.f.n. movable *R.V. 10.95.6 A.V. 20.48.1* With reference to उर्वशी चरण क प से गतौ

24.5 तुरण्यु: swift, zealous R.V. 1-134-5, 7-52-3, 8-51-10

तुरण (कण्ड्वादिभ्यो यक् 3.1.27 & उ 3.2.170) क प से त्वरायाम्

भुरण्यु: quivering, stirring, quick, eager, restless, active R.V. 1-68-1, 1-129-6, 6-62-7), 10-46-7, 10-123-6.

भुरण क प से धारणपोषणयो:

So in fact all four examples are formed by *yak* and found in the कण्ड्वादिगण 3-1-27,

[6]उरुया *Maitr. S. 3.7.8* for ऊर्णुञ् ind. for, far, off; *uruyā* (Instr. of the fem) to a distance from उरु ऊर्णञ् (अ० उ० से० 1039 आच्छादने) (उणोर्तनुलोपश्च)

म हृ ति ह्रस्वश्च उ० 1.31

घृष्णुया Ind. boldly, strongly, firmly, for घृष्णुप्स्स

V.S. Prāt. 520; R.V. 4.21.4 etc.

सुपा सुलुक् पूर्वसवर्णा आ आत् व्ये या डा ड्या याच् आल: 7.1.39

"The following irregular endings act in place of various *sup*/case endings in the *Veda*.

1. *sa* of nom. sg. for *as* of pl.,
2. *luk* elision of *sup* endings,
3. single substitution of homogeneous long vowel,
4. आ,
5. आत्,
6. ए for nom. pl. ending,
7. या,
8. आ (डा) with elision of last vowel and consonant,
9. या (ड्या) with similar elision (याच्)] and
10. आ (ल् accent.)

Thus (या) gives उरुया धृष्णुया for उरुणा and धृषुया the regular instrumental (or neuter) forms by इकोऽचि विभक्तौ 7-1-73

"*Num* ('*n*') is the *āgama* for a *napuṃsaka*/neuter ending when a *vibhakti*/ case *pratyaya* follows beginning with a vowel. "

[7] यदि क्ङिद्ग्रहणमनुवर्तते पित्र्यमिति पितू रीङ्भावो न प्राप्नोति

If mention of *kit* follows on then the form *pitryam* by पितुर्यच्च 4-3-79 (ठन्) तत आगत: 4-3-74

"The *pratyaya yat* as well as *ṭhan* act in the sense of come thence after the word."

पितृ for पा (अ० प० अ० 1056 रक्षणे) तृन् (उ० 2.95)

पितुरागतं पैतृकं = पित्र्यम्

derived from or relating to a father, paternal, patrimonial, ancestral, with the *ādeśa rī*

रीङ ऋत: 7.4.27 (यि च्वौ, अकृत्सार्वधातुकयो:)

"*Ri* is *ādeśa* for the final short ऋ of a stem, before a *pratyaya* beginning with य् when it is not a *kṛt* nor a *sārvadhātuka pratyaya* and before the adverbial *pratyaya cvi*."

ī of this being elided by यस्येति च 6-4-148 (भस्य तद्धिते लोप:)

"The final इ and अ (long and short) of a weak/*bha* stem, are *lopa* elided before a *taddhita pratyaya* and before the feminine *pratyaya* ई."

[8] 24.10 असूया वसूया च यजामहे

"How do we get the form *asūya* and *vasūya* needing *yak* and *kyac* and therefore an indicatory *k* to *prevent guṇa.*"

सुक्षेत्रिया सुगातुया वसुया च यजामहे ऋ 9.197.2

"With the desire for a fine field, with the desire for fine paths, and with the desire for wealth we sacrifice (to you, O *Agni*)."

सुप आत्मनः क्यच् 3.1.8

"The *pratyaya kyaṣ* acts (optionally) in the sense of desire after a word ending in a *sup pratyaya* expressing the object desired as connected with the desirer himself."

न छन्दस्यपुत्रस्य 7.4.35

"In the *Veda* the rules causing lengthening (*7.4.24*) or substitution of long *ī* for final vowel of a stem (*7.4.32*) do not apply except in the case of *putra.*"

अ प्रत्ययात् 3.3.102 (मात्रे)

सुपां लुक् 7.1.39 तृतीया लुक्

असूया displeasure, indignation (especially at the happiness of another), envy, jealousy.

असूञ् कण्ड्वादिभ्यो यक् 3.1.27

असूत्र क॰ उ॰ से॰ असूया

अ प्रत्ययात् 3.3.102

अजाद्यतष्टाप् 4.1.4

जसूया "through desire of wealth" *R.V.1.1972*

वसु क्य्च (अकृत्सार्वधातुकयोर्दीर्घः 7.4.25)

वस (भ्वा॰ प॰ अ॰ 1005 निवासे) उ (उ॰ 1.10)

[9] असूयतेरसूया (the form) *asūya* (displeasure) (is derived from the denominative *asū va ti* to be discontented with), or from

असवे स्वाहा वसवे स्वाहा - तै॰ ब्रा॰ 3.10.7

"Hail to or (may a blessing rest on) life, hail to wealth" (for असु and for वसु) by घेर्ङिति 7.3.111

[10] वसूयतेर्वसूया (the form) *vasūya* (through desire of wealth) is derived from *vāsūyati* (denom. to desire for wealth)

सुक्षेत्रिया सुगातुया वसूया च यजामहे - ऋ॰ 1.97.2

See note on P. वसूया long *ū* by *7.4.25* in spite of न छन्दस्यपुत्रस्य 7.4.35

कै० - यदि रीङ्भाव एव निवर्तते न तु दीर्घविधावपि तदा असुवसुशब्दाभ्यां

पुर्ववद्यादेशो कृते दीर्घाभावादसूयावसूयेति न सिध्यति असूयतेः

कण्ड्वादियगन्तस्याऽसूयेति वसयतेरिच्छाक्यजन्तस्य वसय्यतेत्युत्तरम्

If only the *ādeśa* is not even in the lengthening rule, then when this substitute *ya* is effected as after *asu* and *vasu,* because of the absence of a long vowel the forms *asūya* and *vasūya* are not established. *Asūya* is formed from *asūyati* from *kaṇḍvādi gaṇa.*

[11] उपगायन्तु मां पत्नयो गर्भिणयो युवतय

"Let the young pregnant wives sing to me."

सोमस्य वे राज्ञोऽर्धमासस्य

रात्रयः पत्नय आसन पै स 2.5.6.4

"The nights were wives of king *soma* of (one) fortnight..." and here *patni* is short by reason of Vedic usage.

गर्भिणयो भवन्ति वै स 2.1.2.6 'They become pregnant.'

From गर्भिणी pregnant worman, short *i* by Vedic licence.

c.f. युनस्ति 4.1.77

The feminine *pratyaya ti* acts after the *prātipadika* and this receives the name *taddhita pratyaya* thus debars ङीप् 4.1.5 or ङीष् 4.1.65

यु (अ० प० से० 1034 मिश्रणे) कन्नि

कनिन्युवृषि उ० 1.156 न लोप 8.2.7

युवति जस् by जसि च 7.3.109

युवतयः

छान्दसं ह्रस्वत्वम्

Shortening peculiar to the *Veda*

न छन्दस्य पुत्रस्य 7.4.35

by *Patañjali* on अम्बार्थनद्योर्ह्रस्वः 7.3.107

'अवश्यं छन्दसि ह्रस्वत्वं वक्तव्यम् उपगायन्तु मां पत्नयो गर्भिणयो युवतयः'

c.f. गर्भणिका स्थूलमध्या ··· कै अर्थ 2.11.42 'bulging in the middle' Vol. 3 p. 187.

c.f. प्रवालकं आलकन्दकं वैषर्णिकं च रक्तं coral, outcaste, coloured red.

पद्यराग च करणगर्भिणिकावर्जमिति

lotus, and (free from) making an embryo or product, ruby

कै० — वर्णव्यत्ययेन दीर्घः क्रियत इत्यर्थः

'The meaning is the lengthening (in the forms *asūya* and *vasūya*) is effected by interchange of letters (short for long).

by व्यत्ययो बहुलम् 3.1.85 (छन्दसि)

"In the *chandas* there is diversely interchange of various *vikaraṇas* and the rest previously ordained."

[12] वा क्यषः 1.2.90

After the *pratyaya kyaṣ, parasmaipada* act optionally.

So by this *sūtra 3.1.13 kyaṣ* is ordained and we therefore have लोहितायति or लोहितायते etc. and पटपटायति or पटपटायते etc.

He makes a sound like *paṭ paṭ*.

[13] पाश्या "If *vā yāt* (optionally after *ya*) were stated it would be applicable even after the short *a* of *pāśya*."

in fact derived by पाशादिभ्यो यः 4.2.49 (तस्यसमूहः 4.2.37)

"The *pratyaya ya* acts in the sense of collection thereof after the words *pāśa* etc."

Dh. P. पाश (चु० आ० से० 1720 बन्धने) घञ् (3.3.19)

पाश् य टाप् (4.1.4) पाशया

कै० — नैतदस्तीति सामान्यविहितानामात्मनेपदपरस्मैपदानां नियमार्थं प्रकरणमित्यदोषः

There is no fault because the matter/production (of *ṣ*) is for the purpose of a restriction to the generally ordained *ātmanepada* and *parasmaipada pratyayas.*

[14] याच्छन्दसीत्येवं

"After *ya* in the *Veda* (should be stated)" because these four words are derived from *yak* without an initial *it ka* by *3.1.27* कण्ड्वादिभ्यो यक्

कष्टाय क्रमणे ॥ 3 । 1 । 14 ॥

Pāṇini 3.1.14: The affix *kyaṅ* in the sense of exerting in dishonesty, is employed after the word *kaṣṭa* (mischief), when the latter is in the fourth case in construction.

25.2 कष्टायेति किं निपात्यते[1]। कष्टशब्दाच्चतुर्थीसमर्थात्क्रमणेऽनार्जवे। क्यङ्निपात्यते।
कष्टाय कर्मणे क्रामति कष्टायते[2]।। अत्यल्पमिदमुच्यते[3] कष्टायेति।

Why is the word *kaṣṭa* put down or mentioned as an irregular form? *Kyaṅ* is 'put down' or mentioned irregularly in the sense of undertaking moral crookedness acts after the word *kaṣṭa* (trouble or evil) which is syntactically connected through the dative *sampradāna*/fourth case. *kaṣṭāya karmaṇe krāmati kaṣṭāyate* "(He undertakes to do evil" (He has wicked intentions). The word *kaṣṭāya* speaks very little (about the usage).

25.4 सत्त्रकक्षकष्टगहनेभ्यः कण्वचिकीर्षायाम् ।। 1 ।।

After *sattra kakṣa kaṣṭa kṛcchra* and *gahana* (*kyaṅ* acts) in the sense of desiring to do evil.

25.5 सत्त्रकक्षकष्टगहनेभ्यः कण्वचिकीर्षायामिति[4] वक्तव्यम्। सत्त्रायते। सत्त्र[5]।।
कक्ष[6]। कक्षायते।। कक्ष।। कष्ट। कष्टायते। कष्ट।। गहन[7] गहनायते।।

Bhāṣya: It should be stated that (*kyaṅ* acts) after *sattra kakṣa kaṣṭa kṛcchra* and *gahana* in the sense of desiring to do evil. *Sattra* (n. session, great *soma* sacrific).

Sattrāyate "He desires to do evil"

**kakṣa (m.* lurking*) kakṣāyate* "He waits for someone in a hidden place, lies in ambush and intends something wicked."

**kaṣṭa* (evil) *kaṣṭāyate* "He has wicked intentions".

**kṛcchra* (m.n. causing trouble or pain, evil, bad) *kṛcchrāyate* "He feels pain or has wicked designs" (*Bhatt. 17.76*).

**gahana* (n. abyss, depth, inaccessible place). *gahanāyate* "He lies in wait for someone in a secret place; he has treacherous intentions towards another". *Each is repeated at the end of the sentence.

25.7 अपर आह। सत्त्रादिभ्यश्चतुर्थ्यन्तेभ्यः क्रमणेऽनार्जवे क्यङ्वक्तव्यः। एतान्येवो-
दाहरणानि।। सत्त्रादिभ्य इति किमर्थम्। कुटिलाय क्रामत्यनुवाकाय। चतुर्थ्यन्तेभ्य
इति किमर्थम्। अजः कष्टं क्रामति।।
तत्तर्हि वक्तव्यम्। न वक्तव्यम्। नैतत्प्रत्ययान्तनिपातनम्। किं तर्हि।। तादर्थ्ये
25.11 एषा चतुर्थी[8]। कष्टाय यत्प्रातिपदिकम्। कष्टार्थे यत्प्रातिपदिकमिति।।

Another says 'It should be stated that *kyaṅ* acts in the sense of undertaking moral crookedness/dishonesty after the words *sattra* etc. ending in the fourth case (in construction)'. Those in fact (just stated) are the examples.

Why (what is the purpose of) "after *sattra*" etc.? (Otherwise it would apply here) *kuṭilāya krāmatyanuvākāya (kuṭilāyanuvākāya krāmati v.l. 5.1)* "He proceeds to uneven recitation of a chapter of the *Veda*, (*vedic* text)".

What is the purpose of (saying) "after (those words) ending in the fourth *sup*/case"? (So that it be not applicable to any other case relation, like the following) *ajaḥ kaṣṭam krāmati* "The goat steps with difficulty".

Then that surely should be stated? No, it is not necssary to state it. This is not a *nipātana*/irregular form ending in a *pratyaya*. What then? This fourth case is employed in the sense of 'for the purpose thereof or being intended for that'. *Kaṣṭāya* in the rule means whatever *prātipadika* (stands) for *kaṣṭa* (in other words) whatever *prātipadika* is in the sense of *kaṣṭa* (evil).

Pradīpa

Pradīpa: 25.9 कुटिलायेति

कै॰ — दुरध्येयत्वादनुवाकस्याऽनार्जवमस्तीति भावः

The sense is that there is crookedness/unevenness of the recitation of the Vedic text because of its nature of being difficult to be studied and learnt

Pradīpa: अजः इति

कै॰ — अनार्जवयुक्तं पन्थानं गच्छतीत्यर्थः

"The meaning is that (the goat) goes on a path having unevenness."

Pradīpa: 25.11 कष्टाय यदिति

कै॰ —कष्टलक्षणार्थप्रतिपादनाय यत्प्रातिपदिकं प्रयुज्यते तस्मात् क्रमणेऽर्थे क्यङ् भवतीत्यर्थः क्रमणविशेषश्चाऽनार्जवमभिव्यवस्थितभाषाविज्ञानाच्च पापादिभ्योऽतिप्रसंगाऽभावः॥

The sense is 'That *prātipadika* which is used for teaching the sense indicated by *kaṣṭa* (bad, crookdness) has *kyaṅ* applicable after it in the sense of undertaking.'

And because of the understanding of this as a fixed limited option, there is absence of possibility of (*kyaṅ*) being applicable after the words *pāpa* (sin) and the rest.

Notes

[1]का॰ — क्यङनुवर्तते न क्यष् कष्टशब्दाच्चतुर्थीसमर्थात्
क्रमणेऽर्थेनार्जवे क्यङ् प्रत्ययो भवति

"*Kyaṅ* follows on by *anuvṛtti* (from *3.1.11*) not *kyaṣ*. The *pratyaya kyaṅ* acts in the sense of moral crookedness when meaning 'undertaking (that moral crookedness)', after the word *kaṣṭa* having the same grammatical construction as the fourth case."

Namely कर्मणा यमभिप्रैति स संप्रदानम् 1.4.32

"Whom one intends to connect with the mind by means of the *karman* (be it gift, offering, or sacrifice) that is *sampradāna*/dative/fourth case."

[2]कष्टायेति किं निपात्यत

"Why is the irregular form *kaṣṭāya* laid down?" i.e. fourth case when it should be fifth case.

कै० — विधावनार्जवमेव क्रमणमिति विशेषो न लभ्यत इति
क्रमणविशेषलाभाय निपातनाश्रयणम्

There is resort to *nipātana* form to otain the qualification undertaking/ *kramaṇa* because the sense *kramaṇa* is not obtained in the rule (without it), only (the sense of) moral crookedness.

[3]कष्टायतेकष्ट क्यङ् अकृत्सार्वधातुकयोर्दीर्घः 7.4.24

'to have wicked intentions' *Vat. 16.10*

[4]अत्यल्पमिदमुच्यते

common phrase of *Patañjali*. This (expression) *kaṣṭāya* states too little, i.e. the scope of the rule should be wider.

[5]कण्व N. of a renowned *ṛṣi R.V. 1.35.10* etc., a peculiar class of evil spirits *A.V. 25.3, 4,5;* n. sin, evil, comm. on *Uṇ 1.158*

कण (चु० उ० से० 1716 निमीलने) क्वन्

अशूप्रूषिलटिकणिस्वटिविशिभ्यः क्वन् उ० 1.152

[6]सत्र

Session, a great *soma* sacrifice (from thirteen to one hundred days) a house, an assumed form or disguise, liberality, *R.V. 7.33.13*

अमर 3.181 सत्रमाच्छादने यज्ञे सदादाने वनेऽपि च
सीदन्त्यत्र अनेन वा

Dh.P. षदल् (क्र्या० पु० अु० 854 विशरणगत्यवसादनेषु)

in dissolution, going and causing to sink, disheartening

सद् ष्ट्रन (उ० 4.159)

सत्रायते सत्र क्यङ to desire to do *evil.*

[7]कक्ष m. lurking place, hiding place *R.V. 10.28.4;* large wood (?) *R.V. 6.45.31;* dry grass, plant armpit

कषति कष्यते वा Dh.P. कष भ्वा० प० से० 685 हिंसार्थः

वृत्तवदिडनिकषिभ्यः सः उ० 3.63

कक्ष ष्यङ् — कक्षायते to wait for anyone in a hidden place, lie in ambush, intend anything wicked.

कष्ट see above.

कृच्छ्र m.f.n. causing trouble or pain, painful, *Mbh. 3.1366* etc. *R. 3.74.28* etc.

अमर 1.9.4 स्यात्कष्टं कृच्छ्रमाभीलम् कृन्तति कृती तु० प० से० 1435 छेदने

कृतेश्घः क्रू च उ० 2.21 इति रूक छश्च

कृच्छ क्यङ् कृच्छ्रायते to feel pain *Āp. Sr. p.3.1.18.*

to have wicked designs *P.3.1.14, Bhaṭṭ 17.96*

[9]गहन m. f. (*ā*) n. deep, dense, thick, inexplicable *M.Bh. 3.16.235, 4.5.12;* n an abyss, depth (water *Naigh. 1.12 Nir. 14.11) R.V. 10.129* an inaccessible place, impenetrable darkness *R.V. 1.132.6 S. Br. 15.7.2.17.*

अमर 2.4.1 अटव्यरण्यं विपिनं गहनं कानं वनम्
गाहयति गाहू भ्वा० आ० से० 649 विलोडने
बहुलमन्यत्रापि उ० 2.78 इति युच्
कृच्छ्र गहनयोः 7.2.22 इति निर्देशाद्धस्वः
गहन क्यङ् गहनायते

to lie in wait for someone in a secret place, to have treacherous intentions towards another

[9]तादर्थ्य एष चतुर्थी

"This fourth case has the sense of 'being understood intended for that' or the nature of being for the purpose of another."

चतुर्थी संप्रदाने 2.3.13

The fourth case ending acts to express the sense of *sampradāna* (recipient) if not already expressed otherwise.

कर्मणा यमभिप्रैति स संप्रदानम् 1.4.32

"Whom one intends to connect with in the mind by means of the *karman* (be it gift, offering, or sacrifice) that is the *sampradāna*/recipient."

25.10 चतुर्थीविधाने तादर्थ्ये उपसंख्यानम् 1 Vārttika

"To the rule *caturthī* (*sampradāne*) the word *tadārthye,* in the sense of being intended/for the sake of that, should be added. . ."

Bhāṣya example यूपाय दारू कुण्डलाय हिरण्यम्

Wood for the sacrificial post. Gold for the earring.

कर्मणो रोमन्थतपोभ्यां वर्तिचरोः ॥ 3 । 1 । 15 ॥

Pāṇini 3.1.15: The *pratyaya kyaṅ* acts after the word *romantha* (ruminating) and *tapas* (austerity) when they are the *karman/* objects of the action of repeating and performing repectively.

25.13 रोमन्थ इत्युच्यते को रोमन्थो नाम। उद्गीर्णस्य वावगीर्णस्य वा मन्थो
रोमन्थ इति। यद्येवं हनुचलन इति वक्तव्यम्। इति मा भूत्। कीटो रोमन्थं
वर्तयतीति।। तत्तर्हि वक्तव्यम्। न वक्तव्यम्। कस्मान्न भवति कीटो रोमन्थं
25.16 वर्तयति। अनभिधानात्।।

Bhāṣya: What is this *romantha* which is spoken of as *romantha* (in the *sūtra*)? The stirring or churning around of something vomited forth or ejected, or it is the swallowing down and emission that is called *romantha* (chewing the cud).

It should be stated "Only if there is movement of the jaws". Here it is not applicable (therefore) "The insect or worm keeps churning inside".

Should that then be stated? No, it is not to be stated. Why is it not applicable here? "The insect remains churning around inside itself". Because (*kyaṅ*) would not express (the meaning desired, though formed by the rules of grammar, as not in current use recognised by learned men).

25.17 तपसः परस्मैपदं च ॥ 1 ॥

Vārttika 1: And after (the word) *tapas* there is *parasmaipada* (*vibhakti pratyaya*).

25.18 तपसः[1] परस्मैपदं चेति वक्तव्यम्। तपश्चरति तपस्यति[2]। कथं तपस्यते
लोकजिगीषुरग्नेः।
24.20 छान्दसत्वाद्भविष्यति।।

Bhāṣya: And it should be stated that the *parasmaipada pratyaya* (act) after the word *tapas. tapaścarati tapasyati* He performs penance or austerity.

How (is there the form) *tapasyate lokajigīsuragneḥ* "He perform austerities wishing to obtain the world of *agni*/fire".

This will pertain to the *Veda* only.

Pradīpa

Pradīpa: 25.13 उद्गीर्णस्येति।

कै० — मुखप्रदेश आकृष्टस्येत्यर्थः vomited forth.

The meaning is (the chewing) of something

अवगीर्णस्येति drawn into the region of the mouth; swallowed down.

कै० — अपानप्रदेशान्निसृतस्येत्यर्थः The meaning is (the chewing) of something gone away from the region of the anus or from that vital air going downwards and out at the anus.

Pradīpa: 24.14 हनुचलन इति हनुचलनसहचरितं चर्विपस्य

सुखप्रदेश आकृष्य यच्चर्वण तत्र यथा अपाप्रदेशान्निसृतस्येत्यर्थः।

The meaning is (the chewing) of that chewed, going with movement of the jaws, having drawn into the region of the of the mouth, so that that chewed there should be applicable (as the meaning).

Pradīpa: 25.14 कीट इति

कै० — अपाप्रदेशान्निसृतस्येत्यर्थः इत्यर्थः

The meaning is that 'the insect eats that which has gone forth from the region of the anus'.

Pradīpa: 25.16 अनभिधानात्

कै० — रोमन्थायत इति क्यङन्तेन लौकिके
प्रयोगे चर्वितचर्वणस्ये वाऽभिधानं न त्वार्थान्तरस्येत्यर्थः

The meaning is that 'the verb *romānthāyate* ending with *kyaṅ* in popular use only has the sense of chewing what has been chewed, not of any other sense.'

Notes

[1]तपस् warmth, heat *R.V. 7.1.7* etc.; pain, suffering *R.V. 7.82.7;* religious austerity, penance, serve meditation, special observance (e.g. sacred learning for *Brāhmaṇas*) *Ma.11.236, R.V. 10.113.2;* personified *R.V. 10.82.2, R.V. 10.101.1*

तप (भ्वा० प० अ० 185 सन्तापे) असुन् (उ० 4.189)
तपस् क्यङ् तपस्यति (वा०)

to undergo religious austerities *Ś.Br. 1.6, 8,10, Mbh. 1.914, Bh.G. 9.27*

वर्ति न्यास वर्तनं वर्ति the act of turning or rolling (on)

(हेतुमति च 3.1.26) ण्यन्तात् स्त्रियां क्विन् 3.3.94

वृतु भ्वा० आ० से० 758 वर्तने
ननु च क्तिना न भवितव्यम्
ण्यासश्रन्थो युच् इति युचा बाधित्वात्
अस्मदेव क्तिन्भविष्यतीत्यदोष
अस्मादेव क्तिन् भविष्यतीत्यदोष
or by अच इ उणा० 4.139

[1]तपस्यति see श० ब्रा० 14.6.8.10

यो वा एतदक्षरमविदित्वा गार्गि अस्मिल्लोके जुहोति ददाति
तपस्यति अपि बहूनि वर्षसहस्राणि अन्तवानेवास्य स लोको भवति
यो वा एतदक्षरमविदित्वा गार्गि अस्माल्लोकात् प्रैति स कृपणः
अथ य एतदक्षरं गार्गि विदित्वाऽस्माल्लोकात प्रैति स ब्राह्मणः
भगवद्गीता —
यत्करोषि यदश्नासि यज्जुहोषि ददासि यत्
यत्तपस्यति कौन्तेय तत्कुरुष्व मदर्पणम् 9.27

"Whatever thou doest, whatever thou eatest, whatever thou sacrificest, whatever thou givest, in whatever austerity thou engagest, do it as an offering to Me."

तै० आ० 2.9.1
अजान् ह वै पृश्नीस्तपस्यमाशब्रह्मस्वयंभू
अभ्यानर्षत, ते ऋ षयोऽभवन् पदृषीणामृषित्वम्
quoted by यास्क on निरू० 2.11

"It is known; because the Self born of *Brahmā* manifested Himself to them while practicing austerities, they became seers, that is the characteristic of the seers."

बाष्पोष्मभ्यामुद्वमने ॥ 3 । 1 । 16 ॥

Pāṇini 3.1.16: The *pratyaya kyaṅ* in the sense of making an emition, acts after the following words *bāṣpa* (vapour) and *uṣṇa* (heat) as *karman/* object of the action.

24.22 फेनाच्चेति[1] वक्तव्यम्। फेनायते।।

Bhāṣya: And it should be stated that (*kyaṅ*) also acts after *phena* (foam, forth): *phenāyate* "It foams or froths".

Notes

[1]फेन m. (one n.) foam, forths, scum *R.V.1.104.3* (c.f. Eng. foam)

'स्फायते' स्फायी (भ्वा॰ आ॰ से॰ 487 वृद्धौ) नक् (थे)

फेनमीनौ उ॰ 3.3

फेनायते It foams or froths *M.Bh. 6.101 H.Car*

शब्दवैरकलहाभ्रकण्वमेघेभ्यः करणे ॥ 3 । 1 । 17 ॥

Pāṇini 3.1.17: The *pratyaya kyaṅ* acts in the sense of making (i.e. of *kṛ* to make) acts after those words as *karman/* object of the action, namely *śabda* (sound) *vaira* (hostility), *kalaha* (strife), *abhra* (cloud), *kaṇva* (sin) and *megha* (cloud).

26.2 अटाट्टाशीकाकोटापोटासोटाप्रुष्टाप्लुष्टाग्रहणं[1] कर्तव्यम्। अटा। अटायते।। अट्टा।
अट्टायते।। शीका। शीकायते।। कोटा। कोटायते।। पोटा। पोटायते।। सोटा।
26.4 सोटायते।। प्रुष्टा। प्रुष्टायते।। प्लुष्टा। प्लुष्टायते।।

Bhāṣya: Specific mention should be made of (the following as having the pratyaya *kyaṅ* in the sense of making) *aṭ aṭṭa śīkā koṭā poṭā soṭā pruṣṭā pluṣṭā.*

aṭāyate He enters upon a roaming life.
aṭṭāyate He is overbearing,
śīkāyate It rains in fine drops,
koṭāyate He makes a bend or fortress (?),

poṭāyate She becomes a hermaphrodite,
soṭāyate?
pruṣṭāyate It sprinkles,
pluṣṭāyate It burns.

26.5 सुदिनदुर्दिनाभ्यां[2] च ।। 1 ।।

Vārttika 1: And (*kyaṅ*) acts after the words *sudina* and *durdina*.

26.6 सुदिनदुर्दिनाभ्यां चेति वक्तव्यम्। सुदिनायते दुर्दिनायते।।

Bhāṣya: And it should be stated that (*kyaṅ* acts) after (the words) *sudina* and *durdina*.

Sudināyate It becomes a fine day/A fine day is brought about. It makes a good day. *durdināyate* It becomes an overcast day, covered with clouds/It makes a rainy day/An overcast/rainy day is brought about/made.

26.7 नीहाराच्च ।। 2 ।।

Vārttika 2: And (*kyaṅ*) acts after the word *nīhāra*.

26.8 नीहाराच्चेति[3] वक्तव्यम्। नीहारायते ।।

Bhāṣya: And it should be stated that (*kyaṅ* acts) after the words *nīhāra*. *nīhārāyate* "It becomes misty. It causes or makes mist.".

Notes

[1]अटा the act or habit of roaming or wandering about (especially as a religious mendicant) *Ratnak* + *Nila-k* in *S.K. Dr.*

अट (भ्वा॰ प॰ से॰ 295 गतौ) अच (3.1.134) टाप् (4.1.4)

अटायते to become a religious mendicant.

अट्टा overbearing conduct (?)

अट्ट (भ्वा॰ आ॰ से॰ 273 अतिक्रमणहिंसनयोः) घञ्

कर्मणि 3.3.14 अच् (3.1.14) टाप्

अट्टायते to be overbearing (?)

शीका only recorded in this *vārttika* as a feminine noun except in *T.P.-3.2*

शीकृ से 75 सेचने

शीकायते to rain in fine drops, drizzle, sprinkle.

शीकायिष्यन्तु *T.S.7.5.11.2*

शीकायन्त *V.S. 22.26*

मेघायिष्यते स्वाहा मेघायते स्वाहा

शीकायिष्यते स्वाहा शीकायते स्वाहा तै॰ 7.5.11

तै॰ प्रा॰ 3.5 प्रस्येन्द्रिया ··· पुष्यामेघा प्रा स्वा

3.2 देवा शीका ··· शुद्धा

कोटा with a bend (?), fortress (?), stronghold (?)

कुट (तु॰ प॰ से॰ 1365 कौटिल्ये) अच् 3.1.134 टाप् (4.1.4)

कुटायते to make a bond, or a stronghold.

पोटा f. a. hermaphrodite or a woman with a beard, a female servant or slave *H.534 H.Car. 18.*

अमर 2.6.15 पोटा स्त्रीपुंसलक्षणा पुट॰ प॰ से॰ 1397 संश्लेषणे

पोतायते पोतयति यु उ भाषार्था 3.1.134 to make some a hermaphrodite.

सोटा unknown, only occurs here *3.1.17 Vā.1.*

सोटा क्यङ् सोटायते

प्रुष्टा burnt or sprinkled.

अमर 2.1.99 प्रुष्टप्लुष्टोषिता दग्धे

प्रुषु प्लुषु (भ्वा॰ प॰ से॰ 702, 703 दाहे) क्व टाप् 4.1.4

क्तः (निष्ठ 3.2.102 भूते)

यस्य विभाषा 7.2.15 (न इट्)

प्रुष्टायते to make burn, or to make become wet, pour out, fill.

प्लुष्टा प्रुष क्र्या॰ प॰ से॰ 1527 श्स्नेहनसेचनपूरणेषु

प्लुष क्र्या॰ प॰ से॰ 1529 श्स्नेहनसेचनपूरणेषु

प्लुष्टायते to burn out, fill.

quoted in *Uṇ. 1.152* formation of प्लुष्टाः rainy season, drop of water.

ेसुदिन m.f (*ā*) n. clear, bright (as the/a day or morning) *R.V.7.11.2*

n. a clear or fine or auspicious day *R.V. 7.18.21*

happy time, happiness (*sukha*) *Naigh.3.6*

अमर 1.4.2 घस्रो दिनाहनी वा तु ल्कीबे दिवसवासरौ

दीयते क्षीणां भवति दीङ (दि॰ आ॰ अ॰ 1135 क्षये) नक्

इणसिनजिदीङ (उ॰ 3.2)

बाहुलकाद्ह्रस्वः

सुदिनयते to become a fine day, clear up.

दुर्दिन n. a rainy or cloudy day, bad weather *Kaus.*

m.f.n. cloudy, rainy, dark *M.Bh.7.477*

दुर्दिनायते to become covered with clouds.

³नीहार m. (once n.) mist, fog, near frost, heavy dew, *R.V. 10.82.7*

अमर 1.2.18 अवश्यायस्तु नीहारस्तुषारस्तुहिनं हिमम्

निहियते हृञ (भ्वा० उ० अ० 799 हरणे) घञ् (3.3.19)

उपसर्गस्य घन्यमनुष्ये बहुलम् 6.3.122 (दीर्घः)

नीहारायते to become or make mist.

सुखादिभ्यः कर्तृवेदनायाम् ॥ 3 । 1 । 18 ॥

Pāṇini 3.1.18: The *pratyaya kyaṅ* acts after the words *sukha* (pleasure) and the rest in the sense of the experience/ feeling of the agent.

26.10 कर्तृवेदनायामिति किमर्थम्। इह मा भूत्। सुखं वेदयते प्रसाधको देव-दत्तस्य।। कर्तृवेदनायामित्युच्यमानेऽप्यत्र प्राप्नोति। किं कारणम्। कर्तुरितीयं कर्तरि षष्ठी[1]। वेदनायामिति चानो भावे। स यद्येवात्मनो वेदयतेऽथापि परस्य कर्तृवेदनैवासौ भवति।। न कर्तृग्रहणेन वेदनाभिसंबध्यते। किं तर्हि। सुखादीन्यभि-

26.14 संबध्यन्ते। कर्तुर्यानि सुखादीनि।।

Bhāṣya: Why (is it said) "When the feeling belongs to the agent"? So that it should be applicable here: "The valet de chambre (the attendant who dresses his master) makes known/*vedayate Devadatta's* happiness". Even when it is being stated "when the feeling is that of the agent", here also (*kyaṅ*) obtains.

What is the reason? "(The *kartṛ* in the *sūtra* is for) *kartur* (of the agent), so this is *kartari ṣaṣṭhī* sixth case (used) in denoting the agent, and the *pratyaya ana,* in the word *vedanāyām,* (*yuc* (c.f. *Vart.* on *3.3.107*) acts) in the sense of state of action (abstract action of the *dhātu*) after *vid* (to know) to form *vedana,* in the sense of feeling perception or knowledge. If he experiences feeling for himself, then too that is applicable as the feeling of the agent for another.

It is not with the specific mention of the agent that the feeling is connected. What is it then? *Sukha* (pleasure) and the rest are connected. Those pleasures etc. which pertain to the agent.

Notes

[1]कर्तुरितीयं कर्तरि षष्ठी

The *kartṛ* in the *sūtra* is for *kartur* 'of the agent' so this is sixth case used in denoting the agent.

कर्तृकर्मणोः कृति 2.3.65 (षष्ठी)

"The sixth case is applicable after a word in denoting the agent and the object when used in conjunction with a word ending in a *kṛt pratyaya.*"

कृदतिङ् 3.1.93

भवतः शायिका your turn of lying down.

So this is the feeling or experience of the agent.

किं तर्हीति कै वेदनायाः कर्तारमनतरेण भावात्

कर्तृग्रहणसामर्थ्यात् सुखादीनि विशेष्यते कर्तृग्रहणं च सुपां सुलुगिति

षष्ठीलुका निर्दिष्टम् ततश्च वेदयिता यदात्मसंबन्धीनि सुखादीनि

वेदयते तदा प्रत्ययो नान्यदीयसुखादिवेदने

What is it then? Because of feeling (never) exisiting without an agent, from the force of the specific mention of *kartṛ* (agent) the words *sukha* etc. are qualified (by it). And the mention of sixth case is made by the sixth case *luk*-elision according to *supām suluk* etc. *7.1.39* (in the *Veda*), and thence the experience of feeling. When he experiences the feeling of pleasure etc. connected with himself then the *pratyaya* (*kyaṅ*) applies, not when it is a feeling belonging to anyone else.

नमोवरिवश्चित्रङः क्यच् ॥ 3 । 1 । 19 ॥

Pāṇini 3.1.19: The *pratyaya kyac* in the sense of making, optionally acts after these words, as the *karman*/object of the action, namely *namas* (bow, adoration) *varivas* (room, ease, bliss, honour) and *citra* (wonderful)".

26.16 नमसः क्यचि द्वितीयानुपपत्तिः ॥ 1 ॥

Vārttika 1: There is inapplicability of the second *sup*/case after *namas* when *kyac pratyaya* follows.

26.17 नमसः क्यचि द्वितीया नोपपद्यते। नमस्यति देवान्। किं कारणम्। नमः-
शब्देन योगे चतुर्थी विधीयते सा प्राप्नोति।।

Bhāṣya: The second case is not applicable after *namas* when *kyac* follows. Thus *namasyati devān* "He adores or pays homage to the Gods". What is the reason? In connection with the word *namas* the fourth case is ordained (*2.3.16 namas svasti svāha* etc.) and that rule obtains.

26.19 प्रकृत्यन्तरत्वात्सिद्धम् ॥ 2 ॥

Vārttika 2: Because of being a different base/*prakṛti* (the second case is) established.

26.20 नमः शब्देन योगे चतुर्थी विधीयते[1] नमस्यतिशब्द श्चायम्। ननु च नमस्यति-
शब्दे नमः शब्दोऽस्ति तेन योगे प्राप्नोति। नैष दोषः। अर्थवतो नमः शब्दस्य ग्रहणं
न च नमस्यतिशब्दे नमः शब्दोऽर्थवान्॥ अथवोपपदविभक्तेः कारकविभक्तिर्बली-
26.23 यसीति[2] द्वितीया भविष्यति।

Bhāṣya: The fourth case is ordained in connection with the word *namas,* but this is the word *namasyati.* But surely in the word *namasyati* the word *namaḥ* exists. The specific mention of the word *namaḥ* is for its having meaning in connection with that (second case). There is no fault. The word *namas* having meaning is mentioned (in the rule) but the word *namaḥ* in *namasyati* does not have any separate meaning.

Otherwise according to *Paribhāṣā 94* because of a *kāraka vibhakti pratyaya/* case ending being stronger than an *upapada* (subordinate word in construction), the second case *vibhakti pratyaya* will be applicable (not the fourth).

27.1 क्यजादिषु प्रत्ययार्थनिर्देशः ॥ 3 ॥

Vārttika 3: There (should be) indication of the meaning of the *pratyaya* in relation to *kyac* and the rest.

27.2 क्यजादिषु प्रत्ययार्थनिर्देशः कर्तव्यः। नमसः पूजायाम्[3]। वरिवसः परिचर्यायाम्[4]
चित्रङ आश्चर्ये। भाण्डात्समाचयने[5]। चीवरादर्जने परिधाने वा[6]। पुच्छादुदसने व्यसने
पर्यसने[7] चेति। किं प्रयोजनम्। क्रियावचनता यथा स्यात्। नैतदस्ति प्रयोजनम्।
27.5 आचार्यप्रवृत्तिर्ज्ञापयति क्रियावचनाः क्यजादय इति यदयं 'सनाद्यन्ता धातवः'
(3.1.32) इति धातुसंज्ञां शास्ति। कथं कृत्वा ज्ञापकम्। धातुसंज्ञावचन
27.8 एतत्प्रयोजनम् धातोः (3.1.91) इति तव्यदादीनामुत्पत्तिर्यथा स्यात्।

Bhāṣya: Indication should be made of the meaning of the *pratyaya* in relation to *kyac* and the rest.

kyac acts after *namas* in the sense of homage/worship,

kyac acts after *varivas* in the sense of waiting upon,
kyac acts after *citraṅ* in the sense of wonder/surprise,
kyac acts after *bhāṇḍa* (vessel) in the sense of putting/heaping together,
kyac acts after *cīvara* (dress/rags of a religious) in the sense of procuring/acquiring or putting on (clothes),
kyac acts after *puccha* (tail) meaning throwing up or about, wagging and moving to and fro (of the tail).

What is the purpose? So that there should be express mention of activity.

This is not the purpose. The Master's usage makes known that the *pratyayas kyac* and the rest are expressive of verbal activity, as he stated in the rule *"sanādyantā dhātavaḥ (3.1.32).* " Words ending with the (*pratyaya*) *san* and the rest are (called *dhātus*)". Thus he teaches the technical name *dhātu* (for them).

27.8 .... यदि चात्र क्रियावचनता न स्याद्धातुसंज्ञावचनमनर्थकं स्यात्। सत्यामपि धातुसंज्ञायां तव्य-दादयो न स्युः किं कारणम्। साधने तव्यदादयो विधीयन्ते साधनं च क्रियायाः। क्रियाभावात्साधनाभावः। साधनाभवात्सत्यामपि धातुसंज्ञायां तव्यदादयो न स्युः। पश्यति त्वाचार्यः क्रियावचनाः क्यजादय इति ततः सनाद्यन्ता धातव
27.13 इति धातुसंज्ञां शास्ति।।

And if here there were not to be express mention of the activity, the expression of the technical name *dhātu* would be pointless.

Even when the technical name *dhātu* does exist, *tavyat pratyaya* and the rest would not be (applicable). What is the reason? *Tavyat* and the rest are ordained in the sense of instrument *sādhana* (the means of effecting or accomplishing) and it is *sādhana* (a means) of (accomplishing) the activity. Through the absence of a verb there is (necessarily) absence of means for accomplising/*sādhana.* Even when the technical name *dhātu* is present, due to the absence of *sādhana*/means for accomplishing, *tavyat* and the rest would not be (applicable).

However the Master sees that *kyac* and the rest express activity, hence he teaches by the *sūtra: sanādyantā dhātavah (3.1.32)* "Words ending with the *pratyaya san* and the rest are called *dhātus*", the technical term *dhātu.*

27.12 .... ननु चेदं स्यात्परसाधन उत्पत्तिं वक्ष्यामीति। न परसाधन उत्पत्या भवितव्यम्। किं कारणम्। साधनमिति संबन्धिशब्धोऽयम्। संबन्धिशब्दाश्च पुनरेवमात्मका यदुत संबन्धिनमाक्षिपन्ति। तद्यथा। मातरि वर्ति-

27.15 तव्यं पितरि श्रुश्रूषितव्यमिति। न चोच्यते स्वस्यां मातरि स्वस्मिन्वा पितरीति।
संबन्धाच्चैतद् गम्यते या यस्य माता यश्च यस्य पितेति। एवमिहापि संबन्धादेतद्
27.17 गन्तव्यं यस्य धातोर्यत्साधनमिति।।

But surely this would be the purpose (of the *sūtrakāra*) 'I will state the arising of (the *pratyayas*) *tavyat* and the rest in the sense of means or instruments for accomplishing another (activity).

No, there should not be arising (of a *pratyaya*) in the sense of instrumental for another. What is the reason? The word *sādhana* (means or instrument for accomplishing) is a word expressing relationship. And the words expressing relationship again themselves imply the relationship which (exists). As for example *mātari vartitavyam* "A mother ought to be obeyed", *pitari śuśrūṣitavyam* "A father should be obeyed".

And it is not (expressly) said "(attend to or obey) your own mother" or "(obey) your own father" because that is understood from the relationship that (one should obey) 'whomsoever is one's mother' and 'whomsover is one's father'. So here also this is understood from the relationship itself, *tavyat* (etc.) which convey *sādhana* of that *dhātu*, is the *sādhana*/means or instrument for accomplishing the activity (of the *dhātu*).

27.17 .... अथवा धातव एव क्यजादयः। न चैव ह्यर्था
आदिश्यन्ते क्रियावचनता च गम्यते। कः खल्वपि पचादीनां क्रियावचनत्वे
यत्नं करोति। येनैव खल्वपि हेतुना पचादयः क्रियावचनास्तेनैव क्यजादयोऽपि।
27.20 एवमर्थं खल्वाचार्यश्चित्रयति। क्वचिदर्थानादिशति क्वचिन्न।। एवमप्यार्थादेशनं
कर्तव्यं कथमिमे बुधाऽबुध्येरन्निति।। अथवा शक्यमर्थादेशनमकर्तुम्। कथम्।
27.22 करण इति वर्तते करणं च करोतेः करोतिश्च क्रियासामान्ये वर्तते।।

Or otherwise *kyac* and the rest are *dhātus* in fact, but the meanings are not indeed indicated and the expressing of verbal activity is understood.

Indeed who does make (any) effort in expressing the verbal activity (for that matter) of the (*dhātus*) *pac* (to cook) and the rest ? By whatever cause or means *pac* and the rest express verbal activity, so indeed by the very same (cause) do *kyac* and the rest.

Thus indeed the Master surprises (us). In some places he shows meanings, some places not. Even then indication of the meaning should be made. How otherwise could the ignorant know the meanings?

Otherwise it is possible not to have to make an (express) indication of the meaning. How? The word *karaṇe* "in the sense of making" follows on (from the *sūtra 'śabda vaira'* etc. *3.1.17*) and is derived from *karoti*/the *dhātu kṛ* (to make).

And *karoti dhātu kṛ* (to make) is used in the sense of the activity in general.

Pradīpa

Pradīpa: 26.19 कै० — प्रकृत्यन्तरत्वादिति।

नमस्येति धातु व्युत्पादयितुं निपातनमः
शब्दसदृशशब्दान्तरावयवकल्पना क्रियते परमर्थतस्तु
अविद्यमानावयवाऽर्थो नमस्यशब्द पूजावाची प्रकृत्यन्तरमित्यर्थः

The meaning is the that an imaginary irregular part is made within the word, like the word *namas,* to derive the *dhātu namasya.* But in reality 'being within the base' the word *namasya* expressing worship is the meaning of a non-existent part (i.e. not existing indepedently) of the *ya* of *namasya.*

Pradīpa: 26.20 ननु चेति।

कै० — स एवायमिति प्रत्यभिज्ञानान्निपात एवऽयमिति भावः

The sense is due to the recognition of *ayam* as meaning 'this alone', it means this irregular form only (i.e. the *nipātana*)/indeclinable *namas*).

Pradīpa: 26.21 अर्थवत इति।

कै० — नमस्यशब्दस्य समुदायस्यैवाऽर्थवत्वादिति भावः

The sense is that this is because of the meaninfgul nature being only for the word *namasya* as a whole (i.e. *namas* combined with *k-ya-c*).

Pradīpa: 26.22 अथवेति। कै० · · ·

By admitting *namasya* as meaningful, choosing the meaning of 'worship by means of making a bow', there is refuting of the other (alternative). However there is scope of application for the fourth case in an example like 'let there be a bow to the Gods.'

Here too in the example 'I make a bow to *Nārāyaṇa'* (the base *namaskaromi* governs accusative by *2.3.2*) and in fact is applicable as being *kāraka vibhakti* (and therefore *pradhāna* and not *upapada*/subordinate, when it would have governed the fourth case by *2.3.16*).

Pradīpa: 27.2 क्यजादिष्विति

कै॰ — करणग्रहणस्य वेदनाग्रहणेन व्यवधानादनधिकारे स्वार्थे प्रत्ययप्रसङ्ग इति वचनम्

There is expression (of the *vārttika 3*) because there is the possiblity of the *pratyayas* (*kyac*) being *svārthe* (in the sense of its own base) when there is no governing word due to the word *karaṇa* (making) being separated by the word *Vedanā* (in *3.1.18*)

Pradīpa: 27.2 वरिवस इति

कै॰ — सपर्या सेवा परिचर्यायामिति पाठान्तरम्

Saparyā means service, worship, homage (a different reading). Another reading is in the sense of waiting upon or serving/*paricaryā*.

Pradīpa: 27.12 परसाधन इति

कै॰ — शब्दान्तरवाच्यायां क्रियायां यत्कर्मादिकारकं तत्र तव्यादीनां
वृक्षं पश्येत्यादौ द्वितीयादीनामिव स्वार्थिकत्वाद्
द्रव्यवाचित्वेऽपि क्यजाद्यन्तानामुत्पत्तिः स्यादेवेति भावः

The sense is that when the verbal activity is being expressed by another word, which is *kāraka karman* (object and the rest) there would be in fact, arising there of (forms) ending in *kyac* and the rest even when expressing substance (as distinct from a verb) a thing, because of *tavya* and the rest ending in second case, as it were being *svarthe* (expressing the meaning simply of their own base) in the example:

vṛkṣam paśya 'see the tree', and the rest.

Pradīpa: 27.13 न परसाधन इति

कै॰ — द्वितीयादीनां प्रातिपदिकाद्विधानात्तस्य च द्रव्यवचनत्वाद्
वचनप्रामाण्यात् परसाधन उत्पत्तिर्भविष्यति

There will be arising of (the *pratyaya kyac* in the sense of) instrumental for another because of second case etc. being ordained after a *prātipadika* and because of its expressing a substance, (this being derived) from the authority of the rule (itself).

तव्यादयस्तु धात्वन्तरेषु क्रियावाचिषु स्वसाधने
सावकाशाः परसाधने नोत्पद्यन्त इत्यर्थः

The meaning is that *tavya* and the rest do not arise in the sense of instrumental for another, having scope in the sense of their own *kāraka* (meaning) when other *dhātus* express the verbal activity.

Pradīpa: 27.17 अथवेति

कै॰ — अमिधानशक्तिस्वाभाव्यादन्तरेणाप्यर्थादेशनं
विशिष्ट क्रियावचनत्वस्य
सिद्धत्वादित्यर्थः

The meaning is: 'Even without showing the meaning, because of the natural power of expression (and) because the nature of expressing a particular verbal activity, it is being established as valid.'

Pradīpa: 27.20 चित्रयतीति

कै॰ — चित्र वैचित्र्यकरणे इति चौरादिकस्य रूपम्।
अनेकं मार्गमाश्रयतीत्यर्थः

The form is a derivation of the tenth class *dhātu citra* in the sense of making variety, manifoldness, diversity.

The meaning is he resorts to many paths, diversity, or more than one way.

Pradīpa: 27.22 क्रियासामान्य इति

कै॰ — सामान्येन च विशेषणामाक्षेपात्कश्चित् प्रत्ययः क्वचिदविशेषे भवतीत्यर्थः
न च वेदनाग्रहणेन करणस्य विच्छेद तयोर्विरोधाभावात्

The sense is that of a general meaning because of giving up the qualifications (of meaning) some *pratyaya* is applicable somewhere in a particular/special (sense). And by the mention of *vedanā* (in *3.1.18*) there is not a termination or *anuvṛtti* of *karaṇa* because of the absence of conflict/contradiction between them.

Notes

[1]नमः शब्देन योगे चतुर्थी विधीयते

In connection with the word *namas* the fourth case in ordained.

नमः स्वस्तिस्वाहास्वधालंवषड् योगाच्च 2.3.16 (चतुर्थी)

"The fourth *vibhakti pratyaya* acts in conjunction with the words *namaḥ* (salutations), *svasti* (well-being, may it be well), *svāhā* (hail (to the Gods)), *svadhā* (self power (to the *ātman*)), *alam* (enough, sufficient), and *vaṣat* (exclamation) (of holy priest)).

e.g. नमो देवेभ्यः homage, salutation, adoration to the Gods.

[2]अथवा उपपदविभक्तेः कारकविभक्तिर्बलीयसी

"Or else because of *kāraka vibhakti pratyaya* (case ending) directly instrumental in bringing about the action being stronger than an *upapada* (subordinate word in composition) *vibhakti pratyaya* (the second case will be applicable)."

Nāgeśa on Pari. *94*

ननु नमस्करोति देवान्नमस्यति देवानित्यादौ
नमः स्वस्ति (2.3.16) इति चतुर्थी दुर्वारीत्यत आह ···

Surely it is difficult to avoid the fourth case by *namaḥ svasti* etc. *2.5.16* (after the word *deva* when one wishes to say he adores the Gods) in cases like *namas karoti* or *namasyati devān* (*Patañjali*) therefore says...

Accordingly देव has received, in the phrase 'नमस्यति देवान्' the second *vibhakti pratyaya/ karman* (accusative) by कर्मणि द्वितीया 2.3.2 (अनभिहिते).

When the *karman* (object) is not denoted (by the verbal) *vibhakti* termination, the second case *vibhakti pratyaya* is applicable to the word). Because the *karman* shows that the Gods are the object of the action denoted by *namasyati* and therefore the *kāraka* directly instrumental for the action, it has not received the *sampradāna*/dative *vibhakti pratyaya* which case according to *2.3.16* is governed by the (*upapada*) word *namaḥ* (which is a subordinate accompanying word).

4.96.349 उपपदविभक्ते प्रथमा भविष्यति

भा० 2.3.445

2.3.9.448

वा० 2.3.19.453

भा० 1.4.96

वा० 2.2.3.22.454

Similarly in गाः स्वामी व्रजति गो has for the same reason, namely being *kāraka*, (the owner goes to the cows) received the second case termination and not the termination of the sixth or seventh (genitive or locative) which cases according to *P.2.3.39* are governed by the word *svāmin* as *upapada*/ subordinate accompanying word.

[3] नमसः पूजायाम्
(*kyac* acts) after *namas* in the sense of homage/worship.

यं नमस्यन्ति कृष्टयः ऋ० 2.36.19

"Thou *Agni* whom people adore/worship."

पत्नीवन्तो नमस्य नमस्यन ऋ० 1.72.5

पदपाठ पत्नी वन्तः नमस्यम् नमस्यन्निति नमस्यन्

"(One minded, they approached near him) with their spouses (kneeling) to him as adorable, they paid worship." the (augmentless) imperfect *namasyan* is doubled to show its distinction in accent from the preceeding *namasyam.*

[4] वरिवसः परिचर्यायाम्

Kyac acts after *varivas* in the sense of waiting upon, attendance, service, devotion, worship.

तन्नो विश्वे परिवस्यन्तु देवाः ऋ॰ 1.122.3

"May all the Gods attend upon us, vouchsafe to us this favour, or serve us." c.f. use in later literature.

स प्रातरुत्थाय कृतसन्ध्यावरिवस्यः सारस्वतः सूक्तमधीयति

"Having risen early and performed his *sandhya* devotions, he studies the *sarasvat* hymn." *Kavyamimansa* (p.52)

[5] भाण्डात् समाचने

kyac acts after *bhaṇḍa* (vessel) in the sense of putting or heaping together from *3.1.20* omitted from *M.Bh.* and may have been in a different order.

भाण्डचीवपुच्छ

पुच्छभाण्डचीवराण्णिङ् 3.1.20 (करणे)

"The *pratyaya ṇiṅ* in the sense of making acts after the words पुच्छ (tail), भाण्ड (pot), and चीवर (rags), as the *karman*/object of the action"

भाण्ड

भणति भण (भ्वा॰ प॰ से॰ 447 शब्दे) ड

चमन्ताड्ड उ॰ 1.114

प्रज्ञाद्यण 4.4.38

Only with *upasarga sam Kās.*

सम्भाण्डयति/ते to collect vessels or utensils *Bhaṭṭ 5.62;* to gather provisions.

[6] चीवरादर्जने परिधाने वा

चीवर चीयते चित्र (स्वा॰ उ॰ अं॰ चयने) चर 1251

rags of an ascetic

छित्वछत्वर उ॰ 3.1

संचीवरयति ते to assume the coarse dress or rags of an ascetic *Anarchar Vop. 21.17*

[7] पुच्छादुदसने व्यसने पर्यसने

पुच्छ पुच्छति पुच्छ प्रमादे अच् (3.1.134)

उत्पुच्छयते to raise or cock the tail *Kās.*

परिपुच्छयते to wag the tail.

मुण्डमिश्रश्लक्ष्णलवणव्रतवस्त्रहलकलकृततूस्तेभ्यो णिच् ॥ 3 । 1 । 21 ॥

Pāṇini 3.1.21: The *pratyaya ṇic* acts in the sense of making or effecting after these words, namely *muṇḍa* (shaved) *miśra* (mixed), *slakṣṇa* (smooth, soft), *lavaṇa* (salt), *vrata* (will, vow), *vastra* (cloth), *hala* (plough), *kala* (losing, die), *kṛta* (service, lucky die) and *tūsta* (dust, hair).

27.25 इमौ हलिकली स्त इकारान्तौ[8]। अस्ति हलशब्द: कलशब्द श्चाकारान्त:। कयोरिदं ग्रहणम् याविकारान्तौ तयोरत्वं निपात्यते। किं प्रयोजनम्।

Bhāṣya: These two, *hali* and *kali* (properly) end with the letter *i*, *haliḥ* (plough), *kaliḥ* (losing die). There exist (also) the words *hala* and the word *kala* ending in the letter *a*. Irregular change of the *i* into *a* is mentioned (in the rule) in respect of those two which end in *i*.

What is the purpose?

28.1 हलिकल्योरत्वनिपातनं सन्वद्भावप्रतिषेधार्थम् ॥ 1 ॥

Vārttika 1: The putting down as an irregularity, *a* for (the final of) *hali* and *kali* is for the purpose of prohibiting *san-vad-bhāva*.

28.2 हलिकल्योरत्वनिपातनं क्रियते सन्वद्भावो मा भूदिति। अजहलत् अचकलत्।। नैतदस्ति प्रयोजनम्। इकारलोपे[9] कृतेऽग्लोपिनां नेति प्रतिषेधो भविष्यति। वृद्धौ कृतायां लोपस्तत्राग्लोप्यङ्गं भवति।। इदमिह संप्रधार्यम्। वृद्धि: क्रियतामग्लोप इति किमत्र कर्तव्यम्। परत्वाद्वृद्धि:। नित्यो लोप:। कृतायामपि वृद्धौ
28.6 प्राप्नोत्यकृतायामपि प्राप्नोति।

Bhāṣya: The putting down as an irregularity the (final) *a* for *hali* and *kali* is so that there should not be *sanvad-bhāva* (having operations like that of a word ending in san/the desiderative)

a-ja-hala-t "He ploughed or took hold of the plough",

a-ca-kala-t "He took hold of the die called *kali*".

This is not the purpose. When there is effected the *lopa*/elision of *i*, then will apply the prohibition, "not for those *aṅgas* having *ak* (= *a, i, u, ṛ, ḷ*) vowels *lopa*/elided". When *vṛddhi* is effected (by *aco ñ ṇiti 7.2.115*) there is *lopa*/elison (by *ṇāviṣṭhavatprātipadikasya 6.4.155 Vā. i* (*ṭi lopa*) of causative *ṇi* (becomes *ai* by *7.2.115*) and then the *aṅga* does not become one with *ak-lopa*/elided.

Here this should be reflected on, 'Let *vṛddhi* be effected or *lopa*/elision of *ak* (be effected)'. Which here is to be applied? Because of being subsequent (*7.2.115* to the *lopa* rule *6.4.51*, by *vipratiṣedhe param kāryam 1.4.2*) *vṛddhi* rule (prevails).

28.6 .... अनित्यो लोपः। अन्यस्य कृतायां वृद्धौ प्राप्नोत्य-
न्यस्याकृतायां शब्दान्तरस्य च प्राप्नुवन्विधिरनित्यो भवति। वृद्धिरप्यनित्या। अन्यस्य
कृते लोपे प्राप्नोत्यन्यस्याकृते शब्दान्तरस्य च प्राप्नुवन्विधिरनित्यो भवति। उभयोरनित्ययोः
परत्वाद्वृद्धिः। वृद्धौ कृतायां लोपस्तन्नाग्लोप्यङ्गं भवति। अत्वे पुनः सति वृद्धिः
क्रियतां लोप इति यद्यपि परत्वाद्वृद्धिर्वृद्धौ कृतायामगप्यगेव लुप्यते।
28.11 तस्मात्सुष्ठूच्यते हलिकल्योरत्वनिपातनं सन्वद्भावप्रतिषेधार्थमिति।।

(No), *lopa* is an invariable (*nitya*) (grammatical operation). When *vṛddhi* is effected for one (situation) it obtains, when it is not effected (*lopa* obtains) for another (situation) and obtaining for another word (the operation) is variable/*anitya* when *lopa* is effected for one (word).

(Paribhāṣā 43:) śabdāntarasya prāpnuvan vidhir anityo bhavati,

A rule for which a difference of word (form) obtains (when another rule) obtains is *anitya.*

vṛddhi is also not *nitya i.e.* variable. Even when *lopa* is effected, it obtains for one (rule), and when *lopa* is not effected, it also obtains for another (rule).

śabdāntarasya prāpnuvan vidhir anityo bhavati,

A rule for which a difference of word (form) obtains (due to another rule obtaining at the same time) is *anitya.*

Neither is *nitya,* (and) because of being subsequent (to the *lopa* rule), the *vṛddhi* (rule prevails)

When *vṛddhi* is effected *lopa* (applies and) that *aṅga* (base) becomes a non-*ak lopa aṅga* (because *ai* will have been elided not *ak i.e.* (= *a, i, u, ṛ ḷ*).

But when there is the substitution of the letter *a,* the question arises whether to let *vṛddhi* be effected (then) *lopa.*

Although because of being subsequent (to the *lopa* rule) *vṛddhi* (is effected), even when *vṛddhi* is effected (giving *lopa ā* in place of short *a* and therefore still included in the *pratyādhāra ak*), *ak* is in fact elided.

Therefore it is well said "The laying down of a irregularly for *hali* and *kali* is for the purpose of prohibiting *san-vad-bhāva* (having operations like that of a word ending in *san,* namely the *i* in the reduplicative syllable which then would become lengthened)"

Pradīpa

Pradīpa: 27.23 मुण्डमिश्र क्योरिदं ग्रहणमिति

कै० — किमिकारान्तयोः कृतात्वयोर्ग्रहणमुताऽकारान्तयोरेवेति प्रश्नः

The question is whether (there should be) mention in the *sūtra* of (*hali* and *kali*) ending in *i* effected or ending in *a*?

किं प्रयोजनमिति What is the purpose?

हलिकली इत्येव कस्मान्न क्रियत इत्यर्थः

The meaning is 'Why are not (the forms) effected as *hali* and *kali*?'

शब्दान्तरस्य चेति "For which a difference of word (form obtains)"

यद्यपि वृद्धौ कृतायामपि लोपस्य प्रवृत्तिस्तथापि वाचनिकं तस्या नित्यत्वम्
अथवा अन्यस्य प्रवृत्तावप्यन्यस्य स्थानिनो प्रवृत्या लोपस्या नित्यत्वम्

Even though when *vṛddhi* is effected there is application of *lopa,* still the *anitya* nature of that is expressly mentioned. Or else even when there is application, there is the *anitya* nature of the *lopa* of another original which has not taken place.

Pradīpa: अन्यस्य कृते लोप

अन्यस्य कृते लोपे ननु लोपस्य स्थानिवद्भावात्कथमकारकस्य प्राप्नोति नैष दोषः
प्राप्तौ सत्यां स्थानिवद्भावेन प्रतिबन्धः क्रियते
पूर्वस्य विधौ स्थानिवद्भावविधानात् अप्राप्तौ तु पूर्वविध्यभावात्स्थानिवद्भाव
एव न स्यात् यद्यपि भिन्नलक्षणा भिन्नस्वभावा च वृद्धिस्तथापि
वृद्धिशब्दवाच्यत्वाद्भेदमराश्रित्य शब्दान्तरप्राप्त्यावृद्धेर्नित्यत्वं कथितम्
तत्वतस्तु लोपे कृते वृद्धेरप्राप्त्याऽनित्यत्वं वक्तव्यम्
न्यायव्युत्पादनाय त्वन्यथाऽभिहितम् सूत्रं - प्रातिपदिकाद्धात्वर्थे इति
णिचि सिद्धे प्रपञ्चार्थमित्याहुः न चु तत्करोती त्यादिना तत्र
धात्वर्थनियमः क्रियते राजानमतिक्रान्तवानत्यरराजदित्यादावपि
णिचो दर्शनात् मुण्डं करोति माणवकमित्यादौ सापेक्षेभ्योऽपि णिजर्थं वा।।

Surely because of being *lopa* like the original (*sthānivat*), how (can) (*vṛddhi*) of *a* obtain? This is no fault. When it obtains, by reason of being *sthānivat* obstruction is effected i.e. the rule is prevented. Because of the enjoining of *sthānivadbhāva* when a rule would otherwise operate on the prior letter (1.1.57). However, when it does not obtain, because of the absence of a rule operating on the prior letter, *sthānivat bhāva* in fact would not be applicable, although *vṛddhi* has a different effect and a different nature. Still, because of the nature of that to be expressed by the word *vṛddhi,* having resorted to non-difference by reason of a difference of word (form) obtaining, the *nitya* nature of *vṛddhi* is declared. However, in reality 'when *lopa* is effected' should be stated there is the nature of *anitya* for *vṛddhi* by reason of not obtaining? [Rather] however, for the derivation of the rule it is expressed otherwise. They say when the *sūtra* (*curādibhyo ṇic 3.1.25*) by which *ṇic* applies after a *prātipadika* with the sense of *dhātu* is established, it is for application (repetition in a clearer form), and not with (the sense of) 'he makes or does that etc.' There, a restriction is being made on the meaning of the *dhātu* from seeing (the example of) *ṇic* even in such cases as *atyarājat* meaning 'he overcame the king'. Or else the meaning of *ṇic* is also (seen) after those words expecting another (word to complete the sense) as in the example 'he shaves the youth' etc.

Notes

[1] मुण्ड व्रत ··· तूस्तेभ्यो णिच्

The *Bhāṣya* makes no comment on *vrata* but *Kāś.* explains

व्रताद भोजने तन्निवृत्तौ च पयो व्रतयति वृषलान्नं व्रतयति

In the sense 'due to a vow there is eating and abstaining therefrom'.

He drinks hot *payas*/milk after a fast.

He avoids *śūdra* food.

Nyāsa पयो भुङ्क्ते इत्यर्थ वृषलान्नं न भुङ्क्ते इत्यर्थः

वा॰ 1 सन्वद्भाव

सन्वल्लघुनि चङ् परेऽनग्लोपे 7.4.93

"In the reduplicative aorist of the causative stem the reduplicate is like that of the desiderative when the vowel of the *dhātu* is light (i.e. having a short vowel) and followed by only one consonant, and the *dhātu* has not lost its final vowel before the causative *pratyaya ṇi* (as it would by *6.4.51*).

[2] 27.25 ... *Kaś* on इमौ हलिकली स्त इकारन्तौ

कलिं गृह्णाति कलयति

He takes hold of the die called *kala* (the losing die).

कृतं गृह्णाति कृतयति

He seizes the die called *kṛta* (lucky, marked with four dots).

by .... अतो लोप (आर्धधातुके) 6.4.48

e.g. कम णिङ् कमेर्णिङ् 3.1.30

अत उपधाया 7.2.116

अकाम इ अत् णिश्रिदृसृभ्यः कर्तरि चङ् 3.1.48

अकाम अत् णेरनिटि (लोपः आर्धधातुके) 6.4.51

अचकम अत् चङि 6.1.11

अचीकमत् सन्यतः 7.4.79 (इत्) दीर्घे लघोः 7.4.94)

Therefore if ....

कल or *hala* were considered the base, the undesired forms would be अचीकलत् and अजीहलत् instead of the proper forms अचकलत् and अजहलत् derived so because *hala* and *kala* are ending in *a* and because of *'ato lopa'*, will not have *sanvadbhāva.*

9.1 का० समिध्यिता समिधिता He will wish for fuel or behave like fuel

lopa elision of *kya* in these circumstances.

समिधमात्मन इच्छति (क्यच्) समिधम् इव आत्मानय आचरति (क्यङ्)

3. आपत्यस्य च तद्धिते नास्ति 6.4.151 (लोपः हलः तद्धितस्य यः)

"There is *lopa* elision in place of the *ya* of a patronymic *pratyaya* preceded by a consonant in the presence of a *taddhita pratyaya* beginning with a long *ā*."

e.g. गार्ग्यः (4.1.105) यञ् वुञ् (4.2.39, तस्य समूहः 4.2.37) अक् (7.1.1)

गर्गाणां समूहः = गार्गकम्

The repetition of *taddhita* is said to indicate that the elision occurs sometimes of the non-patronymic *ya*, as सौमी इष्टिः

Hence the *pūrvapakṣa* has some grounds for his statement.

4. क्यच्व्योश्च 6.4.152 (हलः लोपः यः आपत्यस्य)

"There is *lopa* elision in place of the य of a patronymic *pratyaya* preceded by a consonant in the presence of the denominative *pratyaya kyac* and the adverbial *taddhita pratyaya cvi* (all of which is elided)."

वात्सीयति वात्सीयते वात्स — क्यच् (3.1.10)

He treats someone like a *vātsa* or he behaves like a *vātsa.*

गार्गीभूतः गार्ग्य (च्वि भूत (5.4.50)

one who has become a *gārgya*

5. क्याच्छन्दसि 3.2.170 (तच्छील तद्धर्मतत्साधुकारिषु)

"After *kya* (denominative *pratyayas kyac kyan* and *kyas*) the *pratyaya u* acts in the *Veda,* in the sense of agents having such a habit or nature or having skill in some action.

याच्छन्दसीत्येतावद् वक्तव्यम्

It should in fact be only stated as *yācchandasi* because the *k* serves no purpose of preventing *guṇa* since this is not ordained after a *dhātu,* but in fact after *prātipadikas* (see *3-1-13.23.21* line 1) and that enables *yak* to be included.

चुरण्युः a thief, whose habit is to steal. Not found in the recorded literature.

चुरण (कण्ड्वादिभ्यो) यक् 3.1.27 - उ॰ (3.2.170)

क॰ प॰ से॰ चैर्ये

Instead c.f. चरण्युः m.f.n. movable *R.V. 10.95.6 A.V. 20.48.1*

With reference to उर्वशी - चरण क॰ प॰ से॰ गतौ

27.5. तुरण्युः swift, zealous ऋ॰ 1.134.5, 7.52.3, 8.51.10

तुरण कण्ड्वादिभ्यो यक् 3.1.27

क॰ प॰ से॰ त्वरायाम्

भुरण्युः quivering, stirring, quick, eager, restless, active ऋ॰ 1.68.1 1.129.6 6.62.7, 10.46.7, 10.123.6

भुरण क॰ प॰ से॰ धारणपोषणयोः

So in fact all four examples are formed by *yak* and found in the कण्ड्वादि गण 3.1.27

[3] इकारलोपे कृते

"When *lopa* elision of *i* is effected (then will apply prohibition)", by (टेः 6.4. 155)

वार्त्तिक णाविष्ठवत्प्रातिपादिकस्य कार्यं भवतीति वक्तव्यम्

It should be taught i.e. stated that in the presence of *ṇi* the operations for a *prātipadika* are as if it had been *pratyaya iṣtha* following, namely

1) पुंवद्भाव 2) रभाव 3) टिलोपः 4) यणादिरूम्

so by 'टेः' (टिलोप) *ṭi* (final vowel and consonant) is elided.

by 'णेरनिटि' (6.4.51 आर्धधातुके लोपः)

"There is *lopa* of the *i* of of *ṇi* final of an *aṅga* in the presence of an *ārdhadhātuka pratyaya* without *āgama iṭ* (which would have become ऐ by अतो ञ्णिति 7.2.115 because in fact *ai* has been elided then the *aṅga* is not one with *ak lopa,* it being outside the scope of *ak,* therefore *sanvadbhāva* would be applicable and the undesired consequences long *i* in the reduplicative.

[4] अकृद्यकार इति दीर्घत्वम्

Ya when not a *kṛt pratyaya* causes lengthening.

अकृत्सार्वधातुकयोर्दीर्घः 7.4.25 (यि, ङ्किति)

"A long (vowel) acts in place of the final vowel of an *aṅga* (stem) before a *pratyaya* beginning with *y* having an indicatory *k* or *ṅ* when it is neither a *kṛt* nor *sārvadhātuka pratyaya.*"

e.g. सुखायते (3.1.18 क्यङ्) He feels pleasure

similarly लोहितायते He is or becomes red, he reddens *M.Bh.1.1173* etc. *Haṅv. 5825*

ङ्किद्ग्रहणमनुवर्तते The specific mention of indicatory *k* and *ṅ* follows on from

अयङ् यि ङ्किति 7.4.22 (शीङ्)

"Before a *pratyaya* beginning with a *y* and having an indicatory *k* or *ṅ ay* acts in place of the *i* of *śī.*"

शय्यते with यक् "It is slept."

अन्यस्य कृते लोप इति "When *lopa* is effected for one (word)."

अत उपधाया इत्यनेनाकारस्येत्यर्थः

The meaning is by the *sūtra ata upadhāyāḥ 7.2.116* there is *vṛddhi* in place of the penultimate *a* . . .

धातोरेकाचो हलादेः क्रियासमभिहारे यङ् ॥ 3 । 1 । 22 ॥

Pāṇini 3.1.22: The *pratyaya yaṅ* acts after the *dhātu* which has one vowel and begins with a consonant, in the sense of repetition of any act (or intensity of action as represented by the intensive).

28.13 समभिहार इति कोऽयं शब्द। समभिपूर्वाद्धरतेर्भावसाधनो घञ्। समभिहरणं समभिहारः। तद्यथा। पुष्पाभिहारः फलाभिहार इति। विषम उपन्यासः।

28.15 बह्व्यो हि ताः सुमनसस्तत्र युक्तः समभिहारः। इह पुनरेका क्रिया॥

Bhāṣya: What is this word *samabhihāre?*

Ghañ pratyaya acts (after the *dhātu hṛ*) as the *sādhana*/instrument or means of accomplishing/manifesting the action of the *dhātu hṛ* preceded by (the *upasargas*) *sam* and *abhi.*

Samabhihāra (n. the act of seizing upon, taking etc, repetition) is the equivalent to *samabhiharaṇa.*

As for example *puṣpābhihāra* "seizing of flowers" and *phalābhihāra* "the taking of fruits".

This is an unsuitable statement of illustration. For these flowers are many and there in that context the word *samabhihāra* is appropriate.

But here the action is one.

28.15 . . . . यद्यप्येका
सामान्यक्रियावयवक्रियास्तु बह्व्यः। अधिश्रयणोदकासेचनतण्डुलावपनैधो- पकर्षणक्रियाः।
ताः कश्चित्कात्स्न्र्येन करोति कश्चिदकात्स्र्येन। यःकात्स्न्र्येन करोति स उच्यते।
28.18 पापच्यत इति। पुनः पुनर्वा पचति पापच्यत इति।।
अथ धातुग्रहणं किमर्थम्। इह मा भूत्। प्राटति भृशमिति।। अत उत्तरं
28.20 पठति।

Although the general activity (of the verb) is one (in meaning) still the verbal activities of its parts are many. (The one action of cooking involves the many) activities :

adhiśrayaṇa—"the act of putting on the fire",

vdakasecana—"the pouring out of the water",

taṇḍulāvapana—"sowing or placing of the rice", and

edhopakarṣanaṇa—"the act of drawing of dragging near the fuel".

Those (activities) someone (may) perform in their entirety, someone (else) partially. About him who performs the activity in full it is said, *pāpacyate* "He cooks (it) very much". Or (it means) "he/it cooks again and again/ *pāpacyate*".

Now what is the reason for the specific mention of the word *dhātu*? So that the rule should not be (applicable) here. *pra aṭati bhṛśam* "He roams about very much", (with the *upasarga pra,* therefore not (just) after the *dhātu*).

Then he gives a reply

28.21 यङ्विधौ धातुग्रहण उक्तम् ।। 1 ।।

Vārttika 1: When there is specific mention of *dhātu* in this *yaṅ* rule it has (in fact already) been expressed (on 3.1.7 as pointless).

28.22 किमुक्तम्। तत्र तावदुक्तं कर्मग्रहणात्सन्विधौ धातुग्रहणानर्थक्यं सोपसर्गं कर्मेति
चेत्कर्मविशेषकत्वादुपसर्गस्यानुपसर्गं कर्म सोपसर्गस्य हि कर्मत्वे धात्वधि-कारेऽपि
सनोऽविधामकर्मत्वादिति। एवमिहापि क्रियासमभिहा-रग्रहणाद्यङ्विधौ धातुग्रहणानर्थक्यं

क्रियासमभिहार इति चेत्क्रियास-मभिहारविशेषकत्वा-दुपसर्गस्यानुपसर्गः क्रियास-
मभिहारः सोपसर्गस्य हि क्रियासमभिहारत्वे धात्वधि-
29.2 कारेऽपि यङोऽविधानमक्रियासमभिहारत्वादिति।।

Bhāṣya: In respect of the mention of the word *dhātu* in this rule it has already been stated. What has been expressed/spoken? Just there (*3.1.7*) *Vārttika 1-3* it was stated:

(1) Because of the mention of *karman* in the *san* rule, the mention of *dhātu* is pointless.

(2) If (we say) the *karman* is 'together with an *upasarga*' (that is not true) because *upasarga* is a qualification of *karman* (therefore) *karman* is without an *upasarga.*

(3) For if the *karman* is together with an *upasarga,* then there would be no rule for *san* in the context of the governing *sūtra dhātoḥ* because of it not being the *karman*/object.

So here also, because of the specific mention of *kriyāsamabhihāre*/'repetition of the action', the specific mention of the word *dhātu* is pointless.

If (we say) *kriyā samabhihāre* 'repetition of the action' is together with *upasarga* (this is not correct), because the *upasargas* are qualifying *kriyā samabhihāre* 'repetition of the action', then (in reality) *kriyā samabhihāre* 'repetition of the action' is without an *upasarga.* For if the 'repetition of the action' (*kriyā samabhihāra*) is together with an *upasarga,* there is no ordaining of *yaṅ pratyaya* in the context even of the *dhātu* governing rule/ *adhikāra,* because of the *dhātu* not having the character of *kriyā samabhihāra*/ repetition of the act.

29.3 अथैकाज्झलादिग्रहणं किमर्थम्। इह मा भूत्। जागर्ति भृशम्। ईक्षते भृशम्।

Now what is the purpose of the mention of *ekāc* and *halādi* (which has one vowel and begins with a consonant)? So that the rule should not be applicable here: *jāgar-ti bhṛśam* "He wakes fully or becomes intensely awake". (*jāgṛ* has two vowels). *īkṣate bhṛśam* "He looks intensely".

29.4 एकाज्झलादिग्रहणे च ।। 2 ।।

Vārttika 2: And in relation to specific mention made (in the *sūtra*) of '(after that *dhātu* which has) one vowel and begins with a consonant', (it has already been stated).

29.5 एकाज्झलादिग्रहणे चोक्तम्। किमुक्तम्। तत्र तावदुक्तं कर्मसमानकर्तृक-ग्रहणानर्थक्यं
चेच्छाभिधाने प्रत्ययविधानादकर्मणो ह्यसमानकर्तृकाद्वानभिधानमिति ।

Bhāṣya: And in relation to the specific mention made (in the *sūtra*) of '(after that *dhātu* which has) one vowel and begins with a consonat', it has (already) been stated. What was stated? There (*3.1.7 Vārttika* 6 & 7) it was just stated: 'And mention of the object/*karman* having the same agent is pointless, because of the ordaining of the *pratyaya* when desire is being expressed or (*san*) is not known to occur after that which is not *karman*/object and which has not the same agent (as that of the wisher of the *karman*)'. Here also (it can be argued in the same way) the mention of *ekāc* and *halādi* is pointless because *yaṅ* is stated in the sense of *kriyā samabhihāra* and that which is not *ekāc* and not *halādi* does not express (*kriyāsamabhihāra*).

29.7 इहाप्येकाज्झलादिग्रहणानर्थक्यं क्रियासमभिहारे यङ्वचनादनेकाचोऽहलादेर्ह्यनभि-
धानमिति।। तच्चावश्यमनभिधानमाश्रयितव्यम्। क्रियमाणेऽपि ह्येकाज्झलादिग्रहणे यत्रैकाचो।
हलादेश्चोत्पद्यमानेन यङर्थस्याभिधानं न भवति न भवति तत्रोत्पत्तिः।
29.10 तद्यथा। भृशं शोभते। भृशं रोचते। यत्र चानेकाचोऽहलादेर्वोत्पद्यमानेन यङा-
र्थस्याभिधानं भवति भवति तत्रोत्पत्तिः। तद्यथा। अटाट्यते अरार्यते अशाश्यते
29.12 सोसूच्यते सोसूत्र्यते मोमूत्र्यते।।

And it is essential that the non-ordaining be resorted to. For even when mention is made of having a single vowel and ending in a consonant, where there is no expression of the meaning of *yaṅ* (intensive) by producing the *pratyaya* after *dhātus* having one vowel and beginning with a consonant, there is no arising (of the *yaṅ* form), as for example:

bhṛśam śobhate - "He shines intensely",

bhṛśam rocate - "It is intensely resplendent or likes very much"

(both *dhātus śubh* and *ruc* having a single vowel and beginning with a consonant).

And where there is ordaining of the meaning of *yaṅ* together with the producing of the (statement) "having more than one vowel and not beginning with a consonant" (there is arising of *yaṅ*)

aṭāṭyate "He wanders very much" (*dhātu aṭ*),
arāryate "He wanders about, hastes towards" (*dhātu ṛ*),
aśāśyate "He reaches or pervades intensely" (*dhātu aś*),
sosūcyate "He intensely points out" (*dhātu suc*),
sosūtryate "He intensely strings together or puts in the form of a *sūtra*" (*dhātu sūtra*),
momūtryate "He urinates intensely" (*dhātu mūtra*).

29.14 ऊर्णोतेश्चोपसंख्यानम् ।। 3 ।।

Vārttika 3: There (should be) additionál enumeration of (the *dhātu*) *ūrṇoti/ ūrṇu* (as having the *prorṇonūyate*)

29.14 ऊर्णोतेश्चोपसंख्यानं कर्तव्यम्। प्रोर्णोनूयते। अत्यल्पमिदमुच्यते ऊर्णातेरिति।

Bhāṣya: Additional enumeration should be made of (the *dhātu*) *ūrṇoti/ ūrṇu* (as having the *pratyaya yaṅ*) as *prorṇonuyate* "He covers completely". The additional statement of *ūrṇu* is too limited as (only an additional enumeration of the *dhātu*) *ūrṇoti/ūrṇu.*

29.15 सूचिसूत्रिमूत्र्यटत्यर्त्यश्यूर्णुग्रहणं यङ्विधौ। अनेकाजहलाद्यर्थम्।

Vārttika : Specific mention (should be made) of (the *dhātus*) *sūc-i, sūtr-i, mūtr-i, aṭ-i, art-i, aś-ū* and *ūrṅo-ti* (as being) in the scope of the *yaṅ* rule for the reason that they are of more than one vowel or do not begin with a consonant.

29.17 सूचिसूत्रिमूत्र्यट्यर्त्यशूर्णोतीनां ग्रहणं कर्तव्यम्। किं प्रयोजनम्। यङ्विधाव-
नेकजहलाद्यर्थम्। सोसूच्यते सोसूत्र्यते मोमूत्र्यते अटाट्यते अरार्यते अशाश्यते
29.19 प्रोर्णोनूयते।। ऊर्णोतेर्न वक्तव्यम्।

Bhāṣya: Specific mention should be made of (the *dhātu*) *sūc-i, sūtr-i, mūtr-i, aṭ-i, art-i, aś-ū* and *ūrṇo-ti* What is the purpose? For the reason that (although) they are either of more than one vowel or do not begin with a consonant, they are in the scope of the *yaṅ* rule.

sosūcyate "He poins out intensely",
sosūtryate "He intensely strings together in the form of a *sūtra*",
momūtryate "He urinates intensely",
aṭāṭyate "He wanders about very much",
arāyate "He wanders about or hastes towards",
aśāśyate "He pervades intensely",
prorṇonūyate "He covers completely",
Yaṇ should not be stated (as acting after *ūrṇoti* without the *upasarga pra*).

29.20 वाच्य ऊर्णोर्णुवद्भावो यङ्प्रसिद्धिः प्रयोजनम्।
आमश्च प्रतिषेधार्थमेकाचश्चेड्डुपग्रहात्।।

Śloka Vārttika : It should be stated that *ūrṇu* (*dhātu* to cover) be (treated) like (*dhātu*) *ṇu* (to praise), so that *yaṇ* (the intensitive *pratyaya*) is established (as applicable after it), aslo so that *ām* (periphrastic perfect *pratyaya*) be prohibited (and) having one vowel there is prohibition of *iṭ* (augment).

29.22 क्रियासमभिहारे यङो विप्रतिषेधेन लोड्विधानम् ।। 4 ।।

Vārttika 4 : When repetition of the action (is to be expressed) by reason of a conflict of rules of equal strength, *loṭ* (being the later) rule prevails in place of *yaṇ*.

29.23 क्रियासमभिहारे लोड् भवति यङो विप्रतिषेधेन। क्रियासमभिहारे यङ् भव-
तीत्यावकाशः। धातुर्य एकाज्झलादिः क्रियासमभिहारे वर्ततेऽधातुसंबन्धः।
लोलूयते। लोटोऽवकाशः। धातुर्योऽनेकाजहलादिः क्रियासमभिहारे वर्तते धातु-
29.26 संबन्धः स भवाञ्जागृहि जागृहीत्येवायं जागर्ति। स भवानीहस्वेहस्वेत्येवायमीहते।

Bhāṣya: When repetition of the action (is to be expressed) by reason of a conflict of rules of equal force (the subsequent one) *loṭ* (imperative) applies in place of *yaṅ* because preceding it (in the *Aṣṭādhyāyī*)

The rule of *yaṅ* in the sense of repetition of the action has scope when there is a *dhātu* which has one vowel and begins with a consonant and is connected with (another *dhātu*) (e.g.) *lolūyate* "He cuts intensely or repeatedly".

There is scope for (the operation) of *loṭ* when there is a *dhātu* which has more than one vowel or does not begin with a consonant, which conveys repetition of the action (when) connected with (another) *dhātu*.

sa bhavāṅ jāgṛhi jāgṛhi ityeva ayam jāgarti

"Wake up properly, wake up! Thus the (man) awakes".

sa bhavān īhasva īhasvetyevām īhate

"Strive, strive! Thus does he strive".

30.1 धातुर्य एकाज्झलादिः क्रियासमभिहारे वर्तते धातुसंबन्धश्च तस्मादुभयं प्राप्नोति।
स भवाँल्लुनीहि लुनीहीत्येवार्यं लुनाति। लोड् भवति विप्रतिषेधेन। न तर्हीदानी-
30.3 मिदं भवति स भवाँल्लोलूयस्व लोलूयस्वेत्येवायं लोलूयत इति। भवति च।

That *dhātu* which has one vowel and begins with a consonant, in expressing repetition of the action and which is connected with (another) *dhātu* obtains both (*yaṅ* and *loṭ pratyayas* acting) after it.

(As) *bhavān lunīhi lunīḥi ityevāyaṃ lunāti*

Cut repeatedly, cut! Thus he cuts.

Loṭ (being a rule subsequent) by reason of there being a confict of rules of equal force (prevails over the *yaṅ* rule preceding it).

Then now is the following construction available:

sa bhāvān lolūyasva lolūyasva ityevāyaṃ lolūyate

Cut repeatedly Sir, cut repeatedly!

Thus (instructed) he cuts repeatedly.

(Yes it is) also applicable (with *yaṅ*).

30.4 न वा नानार्थत्वात्कर्तृकर्मणोर्हि लविधानं क्रियाविशेषे स्वार्थे यङ् ।। 5 ।।

Vārttika 5: Or else (there is) not (a conflict of rules) because of difference in meaning. For the ordaining of *la* (tense/mood *pratyaya*) occurs in the sense of *kartṛ*/agent and *karman*/object (whereas) *yaṅ* (occurs) when a qualification in the verbal activity in the sense of the meaning of its own (*dhātu*/*prakṛti*/base).

30.5 न वार्थो विप्रतिषेधेन। किं कारणम्। नानार्थत्वात्। का नानार्थता। कर्तृ-कर्मणोर्हि
लविधानम्। कर्तृकर्मणोर्हि लोड् विधीयते क्रियाविशेषे स्वार्थे यङ् तत्रान्तरङ्गत्वाद्यङा
भवितव्यम्।। न तर्हीदानीमिदं भवति। स भवाँल्लुनीहि लुनी-
30.8 हीत्येवायं लुनाति। भवति च। विभाषा यङ् यदा न यङ् तदा लोट्।।

Bhāṣya: Or else there is no purpose in (accepting) a conflict of rules of equal force (requiring the subsequent to overrule the prior). What is the reason? Because of a difference in meaning. What is the nature of the difference in meaning? For the ordaining of *la* (tense/mood *pratyaya*) is in the sense of *kartṛ*/agent and *karman*/object. For (that reason) *loṭ* (imperative) is ordained in the sense of *kartṛ* and *karman* (whereas) *yaṅ* (intensive) is ordained as qualifying the verbal activity in the sense of the meaning of its own (*dhātu*/*prakṛti*) or base i.e. *svārthe.* In that context because of being *antaraṅga* (more inner/a rule whose causes of operation occur earlier in the process of the word's formation), *yaṅ* should be applicable.

Then this, (following usage), is not possible.

sa bhavān lunīhi lunīhityevāyaṃ lunāti Cut, cut! Thus he cuts.

Thus (instructed) he cuts repeatedly.

Optionally *yan* is applicable, when *yaṅ* is not (applied) then *loṭ* acts.

30.9 उत्तरयोर्विग्रहेण विशेषसंप्रत्ययान्नित्यग्रहणानर्थक्यम् ।। 6 ।।

Vārttika 6: The specific mention of the word *nitya* (invariable) in the rule is pointless in the absence of the specific sense of repetition of the action (conveyed by *yaṅ*) in the case of the subsequent two rules and the absence of agreement of understanding on the specific meaning by constituent analysis (namely *kauṭilye* "crookedness" and *arhāyām* "contempt").

30.10 उत्तरयोर्योगयोर्विग्रहेण विशेषासंप्रत्ययान्नित्यग्रहणमनर्थकम्। न हि कुटिलं क्रामतीति चङ्क्रम्यत इति। गम्यते। अथैतेभ्य: क्रियासमभिहारे यङा भवितव्यम्।

Bhāṣya: In the two subsequent rules, because of absence of agreement or understanding on the specific meaning by constitutent analysis, the specific mention of *nitya*/invariable is pointless.

For *kuṭilaṃ krāmati* "He goes crookedly" is not understood or known in usage to occur, (only) *caṅkramyate.* Now when then should *yaṅ* not be applicable after these in the sense of repetition of the action?

30.12 क्रियासमभिहारे च नैतेभ्य: ।। 7 ।।

30.13 क्रियासमभिहारे च नैतेभ्यो यङा भवितव्यम्। भृशं जपति ब्राह्मण:। भृशं समिधो दहतीत्येव।।

Vārttika 7: *Yaṅ* does not obtain after these *dhātus* in the sense of repetition or intensity of the action.

bhṛśam japati brāhmaṇaḥ "The *Brāhmaṇa* repeatedly mutters sacred *mantras*".

bhṛśam samidho dahati "He repeatedly burns fuel".

(i.e. in such case the 'original *yaṅ*' sense of intensity or repetition can only be expressed by a *vākya*/sentence or phrase not by the *pratyaya yaṅ*).

Pradīpa

Pradīpa: 28.12 धातोरेकाचो।

इह समभिहारे नाम मूर्तस्याऽनेकस्यैककालस्य भवति।
धातुवाच्या तु क्रियैकैव, युगपदेकेन धातुनाऽनेकस्या अनभिधानात्।
सा च निवृत्तभेदा साध्यैकस्वभावत्वाद्धातुना प्रत्याय्यते।
अधिश्रयणादीनां चक्रमजन्यत्वाद्युगपदवस्थानाऽभावाच्च क्रियासमभिहारो
न संभवतीति। मन्यमान: पृच्छति समभिहार इति कोऽयमिति।

Here in the context of repetition or intensity of action, in fact (*yaṅ*) is applicable for several forms (but) one time. However, one action alone is to be expressed by the (one) *dhātu,* because of the inability to express the meaning of more than one (action simultaneously by one *dhātu*). And that has ceased from distinctions (of action) because of the naturalness of that one to be accomplished, which is made known through/by the *dhātu.* And thinking 'repetition of intensity of the action is not possible', because the act of putting on the fire and the rest have the nature of being produced sequentially, and because of the condition of simultaneous (different actions forming one *dhātu*)."

He asks: "What is this (word) *samabhihāra*?"

इतस्तद्बुद्धिपरीक्षार्थं शब्दव्युत्पत्तिमाह समभिपूर्वादिति।

The other wishing to test that idea, states the derivation of the word (*ghañ* after *dhātu hṛ* preceded by *upasarga sam* and *abhi*).

यद्यप्येकेति।

मुख्यस्य समभिहारस्येहा संभवाद् गौण आश्रीयते।

बुद्धिगोचराऽनेकसकलावयवक्रियासंगतः पौन पुन्येनाऽनुष्ठीयमानप्रधा-
नक्रियाविषयो वेत्यर्थः

The meaning is, the secondary action is resorted to here because of the impossibility of repetition of the chief/principal action. These many actions with all their parts united in the range of the (one) mind or the sphere of the principal action is being repeated again and again.

Pradīpa: 28.16 सामान्यक्रियेति।

साधारणी समूहरूपा क्रियाधातुवाच्येत्यर्थः। यथोक्तं

The meaning is that the action to be expressed by the *dhātu* is general/common, having the nature of a collection (of activities)

हरिणा

As has been stated by *Bhartṛhari*

गुणभूतैरवयवैः समूहः क्रमजन्मनाम्।
बुद्धया प्रकल्पिताऽभेदः क्रियेति व्यपदिश्यते।। 3.8.4

"What is called action, is a collection of parts produced in sequence and mentally conceived as (one and) identical with the parts which are subordinate to it."

समूहश्च तथाभूतः प्रतिभेदं समूहिषु।
समाप्यते ततो भेदे कालभेदस्य संभवः ।। 3.8.5

"Such a whole is attributed to each one of the parts. Thus when differentiation takes place, difference to tense/time become possible."

कै॰ — अथवा अधिश्रयणादीनां तादर्थ्येन प्रवर्तनाद्गुणत्वादवयवत्वं
तस्याश्च साधारणत्वमुच्यते। तदुक्तम्

Otherwise because of the actions of putting on the (fire) etc. preceding, by reason of having that as (main) purpose, and their character of being parts arising from the secondary nature (of the actions), their common nature is stated.

As was said (by *Bhartṛhari*)

अनन्तरफलं यस्याः कल्पते तां क्रियां विदुः।
प्रधानभूतां तादर्थ्यादन्यासां तु तदाख्यता।। 3.8.15

"That moment immediately after which the result is produced, has been known to be primary action. The other are also so called because they are intended to produce that very result (*tādarthyāt*)."

Pradīpa: 28.17 कार्त्स्न्येनेति।

(About the one who performs activity) in full (it is said...)

e.g. *pac* is said to have a main meaning *vicaṭana* 'separation of grain' or *vikhaṇḍita* 'softening of the grains' and the preceding subordinate moments the secondary meaning.

प्र० — विजातीयाऽव्यवहितास्साकल्येनेत्यर्थः।

The meaning is, uninterrupted by dissimilar or heterogeneous (actions).

Pradīpa: 28.19 अथेति।

धातुरेव समभिहारविशिष्टक्रियावाची
द्योतकस्तूपसर्गो न तु वाचक इत्यर्थः।

The meaning is that the *dhātu* alone expresses the action distinguished by repetition. Moreover the *upasarga* is *dyotaka* (illuminating or making clear [the meaning]) not expressing the meaning directly/ *kāraka*.

Pradīpa: 28.19 प्राटतीति।

धातूपसर्गसमुदायस्य क्रियाविशेषावगतिहेतुत्वात् ततो यदि प्रत्ययः
स्यात्ततः सोपसर्गस्य द्विर्वचनं प्रसज्येत। प्राटाट्यते इति चेष्येते।
सन्मूत्रोक्त वस्त्विहाप्यतिदिशति-यङ् विधाविति।

If because of the nature of cause (with *ṇi lopa*), there being a conception of the qualification of the action as being for the combination of *dhātu* and *upasarga*, then the *pratyaya yaṅ* would be (applicable) and the reduplication of *dhātu* together with the *upasarga* would be applicable, (and this is not desired). And what is in fact desired is the form *prāṭāṭyate* (where) just *aṭ* is redulicated not *pra.*

That matter which was stated in the *san sūtra* (*3.1.7*) is also extended here (in *Vā. 1*) *yaṅ vidhi* (referring to *Vā.1-3*).

Pradīpa: 29.1 धात्वधिकारेऽपीति।

"For if the repetition of the action is together with an *upasarga* there is no ordaining of *yaṅ* in the context given, even of the *dhātu* governing rule."

प्रपापच्यत इत्यादौ।

He cooks repeatedly (where *pac* is reduplicated not *pra*).

i.e. the *sūtra* is applicable in the relation to the *dhātu* alone (separate from the *upasarga*), *Nāgeśa.*

Pradīpa: 29.13 उर्णोतेश्चेति।

"And (additional enumeration of the *dhātu*) *ūrṇu* (as receiving the *pratyaya yaṅ*)."

यथान्यासे सिद्ध्यभावाद्वचनम्। कार्यान्तरसिद्धयेऽश्यमूर्णोर्नुवद्भावो वाच्यस्तेनैव यङोऽपि सिद्धिमाह 'वाच्य' इति।

The expression (of this *vārttika*) is because of an absence of valid (form for *ūrṇu*) when (the *sūtra* is taken) as written. For establishing other operations (than *yaṅ*) as valid, it is essential that the state of being 'like *dhātu nu*' should be expressed for *dhātu ūrṇu.*

By that means in fact the establishment of *yaṅ* as valid is also achieved. Thus is thus stated (by the *śloka vārttika*)

यत्र यङि भावाऽतिदेश आमिटोस्त्वभावातिदेशस्तयोर्नौतेरभावात्।

There, when the condition (of being like *ṇu*) is extended in the context of *yaṅ* there is extension (to *urṇu* of the absence of the *pratyaya ām* and *āgama*) *iṭ* because of the absence of those two occuring for the *dhātu ṇu.*

Pradīpa: 29.21 प्र०— इडुपग्रहादिति।

इडुपग्रहः इट्प्रतिषेधः। विभाषा गुणे इति पञ्चमी। फलस्य चाऽत्र हेतुत्वं यथाध्ययनेन वसतीति। उदाहरणानि प्रोर्णोनूयते प्रोर्णुनाव प्रोर्णुतः प्रोर्णुतवानिति। यङैव च क्रियासमभिहारस्य द्योतितत्वान्नित्यवीप्सयोरिति क्रियासमभिहारे द्वे भवत इति वा द्विवचनं न भवति। यदा तु भृशार्थेऽपि पौनः पुन्य विवक्ष्यते तदा 'पापच्यते पापच्यते' इति द्विर्वचनं भवत्येव।

"*Iḍupagraha* (means) prohibition of *iṭ* (augment)." Fifth case by *vibhāsā guṇe 2.3.25* ('optionally the fifth case acts when the noun expresses an attribute/quality which is the cause of an action and is not feminine') and here the nature of cause is for the fruit/effect as 'He stays by reason of his study'. (Because of prohibition of *iṭ* augment *ūrṇu* is to be treated like *ṇu.*)

Examples:
prorṇonūyate 'He covers completely (*yaṅ* intensive),
prorṇunāva 'He covered' (perfect not formed with *ām*),
prorṇutaḥ 'He was covered' (*kta* past participle passive without augment *iṭ*),
prorṇutavān 'He covered' (*ktavatu* p.p. active without augment *iṭ*).

And doubling of the word is optionally not applicable by the *sūtras* '*nitya vīpsayoḥ*' *8.1.4* ('The whole word is repeated when the sense is always and each') and *3.4.2 kriyāsamabhihāre loṭ loṭo hiṣvau vā ca tadhvamoḥ* ('When the repetition of the action (or frequency) is indicated, the *pratyaya loṭ* acts after a *dhātu* and the *dhātu* is repeated optionally, and the *pratyayas hi* and *sva* or *ta* and *dhvam* are substitutes of *loṭ*'). (The *vārttika* referred to says) of middle/second person singular because of repetition of the action being made clear (*dyotika*) it is (not directly expressed) by *yaṅ* alone. But when it is desired to express repetition in the sense of intensity also, then only doubling of the verb is applicable. (He cooks intensely/again and again) *pāpacyate pāpacyate.*

Pradīpa: 29.26 स भवानिति

सामान्यविशेषभवेन क्रियाभेदाश्रयो धातुसंबन्धः।

The resort to a distinction in verbal activity is by means of the condition of the general activity and the particular activity, so (there is) connection of the *dhātu* (the *loṭ* ending is the general; and the auxiliary because of embracing agent etc., is the particular activity. *Nāgeśa*).

Pradīpa: स इति

भृशार्थपौनः पुन्ययोः प्रतिपिपादयिषितत्वादेकतरस्मिन् यङ्प्रत्ययः।
अपरस्मिंस्तु लोट्। लोटश्च केवलस्य समभिहारमभिव्यङक्तुमसामर्थ्यात्तदन्तस्य
द्विर्वचनं प्रवर्तते।

The *pratyaya yaṅ* (is applicable) in one of the other (alternatives), because of the nature of seeking to (explain) or treat of intensity or repetition. In the other alternative, however, there is *loṭ*. And doubling proceeds for what ends with that, because of the inability to manifest/ reveal repetition for a solitary *loṭ* ending verb.

Pradīpa: 30.7 तत्रेति।

"There (*yaṅ* is applicable because of being *antaraṅga*)"

लोड्बहिरङ्ग कर्त्राद्यपेक्षणाद्धातुसंबन्धापेक्षणाच्च।

Loṭ is *bahiraṅga* because of (dependence on) expectation of agent etc. and because of expecting connection with/ of form of *dhātus* (when there is doubling).

विभाषा यङिति। धातोः कर्मण इत्यतो वेत्यनुवर्तनात्।

Optionally *yaṅ* because of *vā* following on from *3.1.7.*

dhātoḥ karmaṇa etc.

Pradīpa: प्र० — (नित्यं कौटिल्ये) न हीति।

Yaṅ invariably in the sense of crookedness. For *kuṭilam krāmati* is not (known to occur).

चङ्क्रम्यत इत्यस्माद्योऽर्थः प्रतीयते नासौ कुटिलं क्रामतीति वाक्येन शक्यः प्रत्याययितुमिति तदर्थाऽनभिधानादेव वाक्यं न भविष्यति। अर्थान्तरे च कौटिल्यमात्रप्रतिपादने वाक्यं निवारयितुमशक्यमिति नित्यग्रहणमनर्थकमित्यर्थः।

[*Uddyota*: From the particular essential nature of the word in the two subsequent (rules), it is understood that the two *sūtras* are in fact these *vārttikas*. Therefore the writing of the two *sūtras* beginning with '*nityam*' prior to this is an error of the scribe.

(उत्तरयोरिति पदस्वरात् धातोरेकाच् इति सूत्रे एवं इदं)

वार्त्तिकमितिलभ्यते। तेनेतः पूर्वं नित्यमिन्यादिसूत्रवद्वयलेखो लेखप्रमादात् ...)] *Pradīpa:* That meaning which is known from the form *caṅkramyate* is not able to be made known by the sentence *kuṭilam krāmati*. Thus because of not in fact expressing that meaning the sentence will not be applicable.

And the meaning is that 'because when another meaning is being conveyed as just crookedness (e.g. the path, *Nāgeśa*), it is not possible to avoid a sentence', so that the mention of *nitya* is pointless.

Pradīpa: 30.12 क्रियासमभिहार इति।

"(*Yaṅ* does not obtain after these) in the sense of repetition of the action."

तक्रकौण्डिन्यन्यायेन कौटिल्यभावगर्हाभ्यां यङः क्रियासमभिहारादाच्छिद्य स्वीकृतत्वादिति भावः।

The sense is, by the principle or maxim of buttermilk for *Kauṇḍinya* (*M.Bh.* on *1.1.47* 'a special exception to a general rule', 'though a *Brāhmaṇa Kauṇḍinya* is made a special case ('ब्राह्मणेभ्यो दधि दीयतांतक्रंकौण्डिन्याय')) ; due to having *yaṅ* 'repetition of the action' because of its being chosen with the sense of crookedness and contempt.

सत्यापपाशरूपवीणातूलश्लोकसेनालोमत्वचवर्मवर्ण-चूर्णचुरादिभ्योणिच् ॥ 3 । 1 । 25 ॥

Pāṇini 3.1.25: The *pratyaya ṇic* acts after the words *satya* (true, in the form *satyāpa*), *pāśa* (snare), *rūpa* (form), *vīṇā* (lute), *tūla* (cotton), *śloka* (fame, stanza), *senā* (army), *loma* (body hair), *tvaca* (skin), *varma* (coat of mail), *varṇa* (colour, sound), *cūrṇa* (dust, powder) and the *dhātus* beginning with *cur* (to steal)".

30.17 सत्यापेति किं निपात्यते। What is laid down as (an irregular form) like satya/truth (etc.)?

30.18 सत्यस्य कृञ्यापुक्च ॥ 1 ॥

Vārttika 1: There is irregular derivation by adding *ṇic* and *āpuk* (as the *āgama*/augment) of the word *satya* in the sense of the *dhātu kṛñ* (to make).

30.19 सत्यस्य कृञ्यापुक्व निपात्यते णिच्च। सत्यं करोति सत्यापयति।। अत्यल्पमिदमुच्यते।

Bhāṣya: *Āpuk* is the *āgama* of (the final) of the word *satya* in the sense of *kṛñ* (to make) and *ṇic* (is the *pratyaya*).

satyam karoti satyāpayati, "He speaks the truth".

Too small a scope is stated.

30.21 णिविधावर्थवेदसत्यानामपुक्च ॥ 2 ॥

Vārttika 2: In the statement of *ṇi* it should be said that *ṇi* and *āpuk* (the *āgama*/augment) are for the final of the words *artha* (aim, wealth), *veda* (knowledge) and *satya* (truth).

30.22 णिविधावर्थवेदसत्यानामापुक्चेति वक्तव्यम्। अर्थापयति देवापयति सत्यापयति।।
यद्यापुक् क्रियते टिलोपः प्राप्नोति। एवन्तर्हीति पुक्करिष्यते। एवमपि टिलोपः
प्राप्नोति। एवं तर्ह्यक्करिष्यते। एवमपि टिलोपः प्राप्नोति एवं तर्ह्यक्करिष्यते।
एवमप्य-

31.1 नाकारान्तत्वात्पुग् न प्राप्नोति। एवम् तर्ह्यापुट्करिष्यते।।

Bhāṣya: It should be stated that *ṇic* and *āpuk* (the *āgama*) act for *artha, veda* and *satya.*

arthāpayati "He treats of (or makes). . . money",
vedāpayati "He imparts knoweldge/causes to know",
satyāpayati "He speaks the truth".

If *āpuk* is effected (as *āgama* here) *lopa* of the *ṭi* (the part beginning with the *i*, last vowel) obtains (by *teḥ 6.4.155, Vā. 1*) (i.e. the whole of *āpuk*)

Then in that case *puk* will be ordained as the *āgama.* Then also *ṭi lopa* obtains. Well then he will make the augment *āk.* Then also *ṭi lopa* obtains. Well then *ak* augment is effected/will be made. Then also, because of not ending in long *ā puk* does not obtain.

31.1 .... अथवा पुनरस्त्वापुगेव । ननु
चोक्तं टिलोपः प्राप्नोतीति। आपुग्वचनसामर्थ्यान्न भविष्यति। अथवा पुनरस्तु
पुगेव। ननु चोक्तमेवमपि टिलोपः प्राप्नोतीति। पुग्वचनसामर्थ्यान्न भविष्यति।।
अथवा पुनरस्त्वागेव। ननु चोक्तमेवमपि टिलोपः प्राप्नोतीति। आग्वचनान्न

31.5 भविष्यति।।

Otherwise again let it be the augment *āpuk* alone. But surely it was said *lopa* of *ṭi* (last vowel and any consonant that follows) obtains. Because of the force of the *āpuk* rule itself (otherwise the rule will be *vyartham*/pointless) (*lopa* of *ṭi*) will not be applicable.

Otherwise, again let there be *puk* augment only. But surely it was stated (before), so also *lopa* elision of *ṭi* obtains. Because of the force of the *puk* rule itself, *lopa* will not be applicable.

Otherwise, again let there just be *ak* augment. But surely that was spoken of before. 'So also *lopa* of *ṭi* obtains'. Because of the force of the rule ordaining augment *āk* itself, (the *lopa* of *ṭi*) will not be applicable.

Pradīpa

Pradīpa: 30.23 सत्याप। एवन्तर्हीति।

"Then in that case (*tuk* will be ordained)."

आचार्यमतभेदप्रदर्शनाऽर्थोऽनेकपक्षोपन्यासः।

The mention of more than one point of view, is for the purpose of showing a difference of opinion among the masters (*trayamuni*).

Nāgeśa: Kaiyaṭa says this because by force of the rule alone. In fact everywhere there is prevention of *ṭi* elision, so the mention of various opinions (alone) is pointless.

Pradīpa: टिलोप इति।

ṭi elision (obtains)

णाविष्ठवदित्यतिदेशादिति भावः।

The sense is (there is *ṭi lopa* obtaining) because of the extension (of the scope of *P. 6.4.155*) *'teḥ'* by *vārttika* "When *ṇi* follows (a *prātipadika* undergoes the changes) as if '*pratyaya iṣṭha*' (followed), one of which is *ṭi lopa*".

अवकरिष्यत् इति। तत्र पररूपे कृतेऽचो ञ्णिति

Well then he will make the augment *ak*.

वृद्धौ कृतायां पुगागम इति भावः।

(c.f. *ato guṇe 6.1.97*) when the form of the following (is the one substitute).

The sense is that in the context when the *vṛddhi* is effected (for the *a* of *satya*) *aco ñiṇiti 7.2.115* (*ṇi* following a vowel having an *it ṇ* becoming *ai*) *p* is the augment of the final (of the base) *satya* etc. (not giving the desired form *satyāpa)*

satya + ak + puk + ṇi + śap + tip = satyā + e + śap + tip = satyāpayati

हेतुमति च ॥ 3 । 1 । 26 ॥

Pāṇini 3.1.26: The *pratyaya ṇic* acts after a *dhātu* when the sense of *hetumat* (having or proceeding from a cause) is to be expressed, (i.e. the cause which is the prompter/instigator of the agent/independent one with the system within himself).

31.7 कथमिदं विज्ञायते। हेतुमत्यभिधेये णिज्भवतीति। आहोस्विद्धेतुमति यो धातु-
र्वर्त्तत इति।। युक्तं पुनरिदं विचारयितुम्। नन्वनेनासंदिग्धेन प्रत्ययार्थविशेषणेन
भवितव्यं यावता हेतुमतीत्युच्यते। यदि हि प्रकृत्यर्थविशेषणं स्याद्धेतुमत इत्येवं
ब्रूयात्।। नैतदस्ति। भवंतीह हि विषयसप्तम्योऽपि। तद्यथा प्रमाणे यत्
31.11 प्रातिपदिकं वर्तते स्त्रियां यत्प्रातिपदिकं वर्तत इति।

Bhāṣya: How is this (rule) to be understood? Whether it means "When the sense of having a cause is to be expressed *ṇic* (*pratyaya*) is applicable" or else "to a *dhātu* which conveys the sense of that having a cause (*ṇic* is added)". It is proper to consider this further. Insofar as it is said "when that having a cause follows" surely with this without doubt it should be qualifying the sense of the *pratyaya*. For if it were a qualification of the meaning of the *prakṛti*/base, the form would in fact be *hetumataḥ* (fifth/*apādāna*/ablative agreeing with *dhātoḥ*).

This is not so. For here (in the grammar) there are examples of *saptamī*/seventh/locative in the sense of 'with regard to' or 'in the sphere of'. As for example, that *prātipadika*/crude base which occurs with regard to lineal measure (has acting after it the *pratyayas dvayasac, daghnac* and *mātrac* (*5.2.37*) or that *prātipadika* occurs with regard to feminine nature (has the following *pratyayas* acting after it *strīyām 4.1.3*).

31.11 .... एवमिहापि हेतुमत्यभिधेये णिज्
भवति हेतुमति यो धातुर्वर्तत इति जायते विचारणा।। अत उत्तरं पठति।

So here also, question is raised whether "when the sense of 'having cause' is to be expressed *ṇic* (*pratyaya*) is applicable" or (*ṇic* is applicable to) that *dhātu* which occurs with regard to having a cause.

Hence (the *Vārttika-kāra*) expresses his reply:

31.13 हेतुमतीति कारकोपादानं प्रत्ययार्थपरिग्रहार्थं यथा
तनूकरणे तक्षः[1] ॥ 1 ॥

Vārttika 1: (In the form) *hetumati,* the *kāraka* (instrumental in bringing about the action) is understood for the purpose of understanding the meaning of the *pratyaya;* as for example (in the *sūtra*) *tanūkaraṇe takṣaḥ 3.1.76* ("The *pratyaya śnu* optionally acts after the *dhātu takṣ* 'in the sense of' making thin or paring when a *sārvadhātuka pratyaya* follows denoting the agent").

31.14 हेतुमतीति कारकमुपादीयते। किं प्रयोजनम्। प्रत्ययार्थपरिग्रहार्थम्। एवं सति
प्रत्ययार्थः सुपरिगृहीतो भवति। यथा तनूकरणे तक्षः (3.1.76) इति तनूकरण-
31.16 मुपादीयते।।

Bhāṣya: In the form *hetumati* a *kāraka* is understood. What is the purpose? For understanding the meaning of the *pratyay ṇic.* When it is thus present, the meaning of the *pratyaya* is easily understood. As for example (in the *sūtra*) *tanūkaraṇe takṣaḥ 3.1.76,* the word *tanūkaraṇa* (making thin or paring) is employed (to make known the meaning of the *pratyaya śnu* after the *dhātu takṣ*).

31.16 .... यदि तर्हि तद्वत्प्रकृत्यर्थविशेषणं भवति। प्रकृत्यर्थविशेषणं हि
तत्तत्र विज्ञायते। तनूकरणक्रियायां तक्ष इति।। अस्तु प्रकृत्यर्थविशेषणम्। को
दोषः। इह ह्युक्तः करोति प्रेषितः करोतीति णिच्प्राप्नोति। प्रत्ययार्थविशेषणे
पुनः सति नैष दोषः। स्वशब्देनोक्तत्वान्न[2] भविष्यति।। प्रकृत्यर्थविशेषणेऽपि
सति नैष दोषः। यत्र नान्तरेण शब्दमर्थस्य गतिर्भवति तत्र शब्दः प्रयुज्यते। यत्र
31.21 ह्यन्तरेणापि शब्दमर्थस्य गतिर्भवति न तत्र शब्दः प्रयुज्यते।।

If then like that, (*hetumati*) is taken as a qualification of the *prakṛit*/base, this (method) is applicable. For that is understood as a qualification of the meaning of the *prakṛti* prescribed there, '(*śnu* acts) after *dhātu takṣ* having the sense of the action of paring'.

Let it be a qualification of the meaning of the *prakṛti.* What fault is there? Here *ṇic* obtains

uktaḥ karoti "(He who) was told does",

preṣitaḥ karoti "The one who was urged does".

But when the qualification of the meaning of the *pratyaya* is present this is not a fault. Because of having already been expressed by the word itself the *pratyaya. ṇic* will not be applicable.

Even when the qualification is of the meaning of the *prakṛti* there is no fault. When there is no understanding of the meaning without the word, there the word is used. Where even without a word, understanding of meaning exists, there a word is not used.

31.21 .... इह तर्हि पाचयत्योदनं देवदत्तो
यज्ञदत्तेनेत्युभयो: कर्त्रोर्लेनाभिधान[3] प्राप्नोति। प्रत्ययार्थविशेषणे पुन:
सति न दोष:। प्रधानकर्तरि लादयो भवन्तीति प्रधानकर्ता लेनाभिधीयते
31.24 यश्चात्राप्रधानं सिद्धा तत्र कर्तरीत्येव तृतीया[4]।

Then here (in the example) - *pācayaty-odanam Devadatto Yajñadattena*- "*Devadatta* causes *Yajñadatta* to cook the rice" expression of both the agents by the *la* (tense *pratyaya*) becomes wrongly applicable.

When the qualification is of the meaning of the *pratyaya*, again there is no fault. The principal agent is expressed by the *la* (tense *pratyaya*) as (is stated).

(The ten tenses or moods which all) begin with the letter *l* are applicable in the sense of or in expressing the principal agent.

And (to denote him) who is here non-principal/subordinate agent, in the context it is established that the third case alone is employed in the sense of Agent.

31.24 .... इह च गमितो ग्रामं देवदत्तो
यज्ञदत्तेनेत्यव्यतिरिक्तो गत्यर्थ[5] इति कृत्वा गत्यर्थानां क्त: कर्तरीति कर्तरि क्त:
प्राप्नोति[6]। इह च व्यतिच्छेदयन्त इत्यव्यतिरिक्तो हिंसार्थ इति
32.1 कृत्वा न गतिहिंसार्थेभ्य: (1.3.15) इति प्रतिषेध: प्राप्नोति।। अस्तु तर्हि
प्रत्यया-र्थविशेषणम्। यदि प्रत्ययार्थविशेषणं पाचयत्योदनं देवदत्तो यज्ञदत्तेनेति
प्रयोज्ये कर्तरि कर्मसंज्ञा प्राप्नोति। भवति हि तस्य तस्मिन्नीप्सा[7]। इह च ग्रामं
गमयति ग्रामाय गमयतीति व्यतिरिक्तो गत्यर्थ इति कृत्वा गत्यर्थकर्मणि
द्वितीयाचतुर्थ्यौ न प्राप्नुत:[8]।

Morever having formed (the following sentence with a sense of going not different from the causative meaning 'made to go' etc.) referred to in the *sūtra gatyartha akarmaka* etc. (*3.4.72*) *gamito grāmaṃ Devadatto Yajñadattena*- "*Devadatta* caused *Yajñadatta* to go to the village", *kta*/past participal passive obtains in the sense of Agent because of (the statement) "*Kta* acts after *dhātus* having the sense of going or movement in denoting the Agent".

And here in the verbs *vyatibhedayante* "They are bursting (crushing or destroying) forth together on each other simultaneously". *vyaticchedayante* "They cause each other to be cut", with meaning of injuring not separated from the causative meaning or that referred to in the *sūtra—1.3.15 gati hiṃsārthebhyaḥ* "After *dhātus* having the sense of 'motion' or 'injury' (when expressing interchange of action) the *ātmanepada vibhakti pratyayas* are not used" because of which, prohibition of the *ātmanepada* obtains.

Then let (the sense be) the qualification of the meaning of the *pratyaya.* If there is qualification of the meaning of the *pratyaya* then the technical name *karman*/object wrongly applies i.e. obtains in denoting the agent to be employed/caused to act, as *pācayati odanaṃ Devadatto Yajñadattena "Devadatta* causes *Yajñadatta* to cook rice". For he (*Devadatta*) has a desire in relation to him *(Yajñadatta).*

And here (in) the sentence *grāmaṃ gamayati* (and) *grāmāya gamayati* "He causes him to go to the village" with the meaning of motion/going separated from that sense expressed in the *sūtra gatyartha karmaṇi dvitīyā caturthyau ceṣṭāyām anadhvani 2.3.12* "In the case of *dhātus* implying motion, the place to which the motion is directed takes the second *vibhakti pratyaya* (accusative) or the fourth (*sampradhāna*/dative) case (in denoting *karman*/object, when physical motion is meant, and the object is not a word expressing road)", the second and fourth cases do not obtain (as alternatives).

32.5 .... इह च एवोदकस्योपस्कारयतीति व्यतिरिक्त: करोत्यर्थ इति कृत्वा कृञ: प्रतियत्ने (2.3.53) इति षष्ठी न प्राप्नोति'। इह च भेदिका देवदत्तस्य यज्ञदत्तस्य काष्ठानामिति प्रयोज्ये कर्तरि षष्ठी न प्राप्नोति। इह च अभिषावयति परिषावयतीति व्यतिरिक्त: सुनोत्यर्थ इति कृत्वोपसर्गात्सु-नोत्यादीनामिति षत्वं न प्राप्नोति।। नैष दोष: यत्तावदुच्यते पाचयत्योदनं देवदत्तो यज्ञदत्तेनेति प्रयोज्ये कर्तरि कर्मसंज्ञा प्राप्नोतीति गतिबुद्धिप्रत्यवसानार्थशब्द-कर्माकर्मकाणामणी-

32.11 त्येतन्नियमार्थं भविष्यति।

And here (in the sentence) *edhokasyopaskārayati* "The water makes the wood impart a new quality to the water with a meaning of *karoti/ dhātu kṛ* (to make) separated (from that causative sense mentioned in the *sūtra*), (by the *sūtra*) *kṛñaḥ pratiyatne 2.3.53* "The *karman*/object of the *dhātu kṛ* takes the sixth *vibhakti*/case *pratyaya,* when it means to impart a new quality or virtue" The sixth case does not obtain in the sentence *bhedikā Devadattasya Yajñadattasya kāṣṭhānām.* "The act of causing *Yajñadatta* to cut the wood is caused by *Devadatta*". The sixth *vibhakti*/case *pratyaya* does not obtain in the sense of the Agent to be prompted or caused/impelled.

And here (in the verbs) *abhi-ṣāvayati* "He causes (him) to press out the *soma*", *pariṣāvayati* "He causes (him) to press the *soma* from all sides" with the meaning of *sunoti/ dhātu su* (to press out *soma*) different (from that expressed by the *sūtra*) *upasargāt sunoti savati* etc. 8.3.65 ("ष् is substituted for स् after an इ or उ of an upasarga in the following dhātus षु षू etc.")

This is not a fault with reference to that which is stated (in the sentence). "*Devadatta* causes *Yajñadatta* to cook the rice"/*pācayaty-odanam Devadatto Yajñadattena,* the technical name *karman*/object obtains in the sense of the Agent to be employed (i.e. subordinate agent). I say, for the purpose of restricting the scope of *karman saṃjña* there will be the *sūtra gati-buddhi-pratyavasāna-artha-śabdakarmākarmakāṇām aṇi kartā sa ṇau 1.4.52:* "For *dhātus* having the sense of motion, knowledge or information and eating, and for *dhātus* that have sound or some literary work for their *karman*/object and for intransitive *dhātus* that which was the agent of the *dhātus* in its primitive (non-*ṇi*/non causal state) is called the *karman* in its causal state (when the *dhātu* takes the *pratyaya ṇic*)".

32.11 .... एतेषामेवाण्यन्तानां यः कर्ता स णौ कर्मसंज्ञो भवति नान्येषामिति।। यदप्युच्यत इह च ग्रामं गमयति ग्रामाय गमयतीति व्यतिरिक्तो गत्यर्थ इति कृत्वा गत्यर्थकर्मणि द्वितीयाच्चतुर्थ्यौ न प्राप्नुत इति नासावेवं प्रेष्यते गच्छ ग्राममिति। कथं तर्हि। साधनविशिष्टामसौ क्रियां प्रेष्यते ग्रामं गच्छ ग्रामाय

32.15 गच्छेति।।

For these (*dhātus*) alone not ending in *ṇi* that which is the Agent (in the non-causal state) has the technical name *karman* applicable to it in the causal state when *ni* follows, but this is not so for any other (*dhātus*). With reference to what was also said (above) *iha ca grāmam gamayati grāmāya gamayati* etc. And here having formed the sentence "He causes him to go to the village" with a meaning of motion not different from that expressed in the *sūtra-gatyartha karmaṇi dvitīyā caturthyau ceṣṭāyām anadhvani (2.3.12)* the second and fourth *vibhakti pratyaya*/cases do not obtain. (I say) that (person) is not impelled (by saying) "Go to the village". How then? One is impelled to do an action which is distinguished by a *kāraka* (a case-relation instrumental in bringing about the action of the verb) '*grāmam gaccha*' (or) *grāmaya gaccha* "go to the village".

32.15 .... यदप्युच्यत इह च एधोदकस्योपस्कारयतीति व्यतिरिक्तः करोत्यर्थ इति कृत्वा कृञः प्रतियत्न इति षष्ठी न प्राप्नोतीति नासावेवं प्रेष्यत उपस्कुरुष्वैधोदकस्येति कथं तर्हि। साधनविशिष्टामसौ क्रिया प्रेष्यत एधोदकस्योपस्कुरुष्वेति।।

With reference to what is also said (as above) and here having formed (the sentence) *edhodakasyopaskārayati* "He caused the preparing of the wood and water for the sacrifice" with the meaning of *karoti/dhātu kṛ* (to make) different from that expressed in the *sūtra "kṛñaḥ praṭiyatne (2.3.35)"*, the sixth case does not obtain. That (action) is not impelled (as) *apaskuruṣv-aidhodakasya* "Prepare the wood and water for the sacrifice". How then?

The action is urged on or caused, distinguished by its instruments (or agents) of the action/*sādhana* (*kāraka*). *edhodakasyopakariṣva* "Prepare the wood and water", (with sixth case because, *edhodaka* is the object of *kṛ dhātu* (to make) and not of *kāri* (causative formed with *ṇic*.)

32.17 .... यद-
प्युच्यत इह च भेदिका देवदत्तस्य यज्ञदत्तस्य काष्ठानामिति प्रयोज्ये कर्तरि षष्ठी न प्राप्नोतीत्युक्तं तत्र कृद्ग्रहणस्य प्रयोजनं कर्तृभूतपूर्वमात्रेऽपि षष्ठी यथा स्यादिति।। यदप्युच्यत इह च अभिषावयति परिषावयतीति व्यतिरिक्तः सुनोत्यर्थ इति कृत्वोपसर्गात्सुनोत्यादीनामिति षत्वं न प्राप्नोतीति नासावेवं प्रेष्यते सुन्वभीति। कथं
32.22 तर्हि। उपसर्गविशिष्टामसौ क्रिया प्रेष्यतेऽभिषुण्विति।।

With reference to this also it is said (as earlier *2.32.6*) *iha ca bhedikā* etc. "And here when the subordinate agent (is to be expressed, as for example) *Devadatta* (is) causing *Yajñadatta* to split the logs" the sixth *vibhakti*/case *pratyaya* does not obtain. (I say), it was stated there that the purpose of mentioning *kṛt* (is) so that the sixth case should be applicable even when an agent only in a former time is to be denoted.

What also is said is (as earlier *2.32.7*) *iha cābhiṣāvayati* etc. And here having formed the verbs *abhiṣāvayati* 'He causes him to press out the *soma*' *pariṣāvayati* 'He causes him to press round the *soma*', with the meaning of *sunoti*/*dhātu su* (to press out *soma*) different to that expressed in the *sūtra upasargāt sunoti* etc. (*8.3.65*). The change of *ṣ* for *s* does not obtain (for) that is not (here) urged on/caused (at this stage) when *upasarga abhi* (is to join with the simple *dhātu*) *su(sunoti)*.

How then? that act is urged on qualified by *upasarga* (i.e. change of *s* to *ṣ*/*ṣatva* and has already taken place in the non causal state, (as) *abhi-ṣuṇu* "Do thou press out the *soma*".

32.23 युक्तं पुनरिदं विचारयितुम्। नन्वनेनासंदिग्धेन प्रत्ययार्थविशेषणेन भवितव्यं यावता व्यक्तमर्थान्तरं गम्यते पचति पाचयतीति च। बाढं युक्तम्। इह पचेः कः प्रधानार्थः यासौ तण्डुलानां विक्लित्तिः। अथेदानीं तदभिसंधिपूर्वकं प्रेषणमध्ये-
32.26 षणं वा युक्तं यत्सर्वः पच्यर्थः स्यात्।

It is proper to again consider this matter. Surely the qualifier of the meaning of the *pratyaya* must be without doubt in so far as it is understood that there is obviously a different meaning (when *ṇic* is employed), (as) *pacati* "He cooks" and *pācayati* "He causes (someone) to cook". Yes indeed it is proper to consider here what is the principal meaning of *paci* (i.e. *dhātu pac*). That (activity) which softens the grains of rice. Now then that which has been intended or aimed at (whether it be) the act of urging/impelling or soliciting/asking, it is proper that all that be (part) of the meaning of *pac-i (pac dhātu+ṇic pratyaya)*.

32.27 अथ हेतुमतीति को मत्वर्थः। हेतुः कर्तास्य हेतुमान् हेतुमतीति।।

Now what is the meaning of (the *pratyaya*) *matup* in *hemati*? He whose agent is the cause is *hetuman* (having a reason or cause), as in the *sūtra hetumat-i*.

33.1 हेतुनिर्देशश्च निमित्तमात्रं भिक्षादिषु दर्शनात् ।। 2 ।।

Vārttika 2: And the mention of *hetu* is in the sense of 'mere efficient cause or instrument' (which is known) because of seeing its usage in connection with the words *bhīkṣā* (alms) and the rest mentioned in the *sūtra bhikṣādibhyo'ṅ 4.2.38.*

33.2 हेतुनिर्देशश्च निमित्तमात्रं द्रष्टव्यम्। यावद्ब्रूयान्निमित्तं कारणमिति तावद्धेतुरिति। किं प्रयोजनम्। भिक्षादिषु दर्शनात्। भिक्षादिषु हि णिज्दृश्यते।

Bhāṣya: And the mention of *hetu* should be seen (or understood) in the sense of 'mere efficient cause or instrument'. To the extent one would say it is the efficient cause or instrument, so too (one may speak of) *hetu* as cause. What is the purpose? Because of seeing (usage) in connection with *bhikṣā* (alms) and the rest? For in (connection with the words) *bhikṣā* and the rest *ṇic* is seen (after a *dhātu*).

33.3 .... भिक्षा वासयन्ति।
कारीषोऽग्निरध्यापयतीति।। किं पुनः कारणं परिभाषिके हेतौ न सिध्यति। एवं
मन्यते चेतनावत एतद्भवति प्रेषणमध्येषणं चेति भिक्षाश्चाचेतनाः। नैष दोषः।
नावश्यं स एव वासं प्रयोजयति य आहोष्यतामिति तूष्णीमप्यासीनो यस्तत्समर्थान्या-
चरति सोऽपि वासं प्रयोजयति। भिक्षाश्चापि प्रचुरा व्यञ्जनवत्यो लभ्यमाना वासं
33.8 प्रयोजयन्ति। तथा कारीषोऽग्निर्निवात एकान्ते सुप्रज्वलितोऽध्ययनं प्रयोजयति।।

As *bhikṣā vāsayanti* "Desire for alms causes them to dwell (in the town etc.)". *kāriṣo' gnir adhyāpayati* "The cow-dung fire makes (the students) learn (by enabling them to sit in the warm)".

But is not cause admissable in the sense of the conventional technical (sense of) cause (expressed by the *sūtrakāra*)? So (the *sūtrakāra*) thought "this impelling and requesting is possible for one having consciousness", but *bhikṣā* (alms) are without consciousness. This is not a fault. It is not necessarily the very one who causes someone to dwell by saying 'you may stay' (in this place). What then? Even one who is sitting silently (and) performs (deeds or actions) which are capable of making someone stay, even he causes dwelling or abiding to take place. And so also alms, foods abundant and full of seasoning (condiments) being obtained, cause (the mendicant recipients) to dwell (nearby).

So too the cow-dung burning beautifully in a solitary place, free from wind, causes study (to take place). "

33.9 इह कश्चित्कंचिदाह पृच्छतु मा भवान् अनुयुंक्तां मा भवानिति। अ-
णिच्कस्मान्न भवति। अकर्तृत्वात्। न ह्यसौ संप्रति पृच्छति। तूष्णीमास्ते किं
च भो वर्तमानकालाया एव क्रियायाः कर्त्रा भवितव्यं न भूतभविष्यत्कालायाः।
33.12 भूतभविष्यत्कालाया अपि भवितव्यम्।

Here someone says to someone else, "Ask me a question sir, do. Do engage me sir". Here, why is there not *ṇic* applicable? Because of the one commanding not being the agent (of the action he commands). For that one does not now ask. He remains silent. And Sir, should he only be Agent of an action of the present time, (and) not of past and future time? He should also be (Agent of an action) of the past and future time.

33.12 .... अभिसंबन्धस्तत्र क्रियत इमां क्रियामकार्षीत् इमां
क्रियां करिष्यतीति। इह पुनर्न कश्चिदभिसंबन्धः क्रियते न चासौ संप्रति पृच्छति
तूष्णीमास्ते। यदि तर्हि कर्ता नास्ति कथं तर्हि कर्तृप्रत्ययेन लोटाभिधीयते। अथ
कथमस्मिन्नपृच्छत्ययं प्रच्छिर्वर्तते।अभिसंबन्धस्तत्र क्रियत इमां
33.16 कुर्विति।कर्त्रापि तर्ह्यभिसंबन्धःक्रियते।कथम्।कर्ता चास्याःक्रियाया भवति।एवं
न च कर्ता कर्तृप्रत्ययेन च
लोटाभिधीयते।।

A connection is made there "He did this action. He will do this action". But here no one is made connected, and nor does he ask (nor will he ask), he remains silent. If then, there is no agent, how then is he expressed by the agent *pratyaya loṭ* (imperative)? Now then how, when this one is not asking a question does the verb *pracch* operate? A connection is made there "Do this action". Also then connection is made with the Agent. "Be the Agent of this action". And thus the Agent is not expressed by the Agent *pratyaya loṭ* (imperatve).

33.17 .... अथापि कथंचित्कर्ता स्यात्। एवमपि न दोषः।लोटोक्तत्वात्प्रे-
षणस्य णिज्न भविष्यति। विधीयन्ते ह्येतेष्वर्थेषु प्रैषादिषु लोडादयः। यत्र च
द्वितीयः प्रयोज्योऽर्थो भवति भवति
33.20 तत्र णिच्। तद्यथा। आसय शाययेति।।

Now even if somehow there would be an agent, so then too (there is) no fault. Because of ordering/*praiṣa* being expressed already by *loṭ* (imperative), there will not be applicable to the *pratyaya ṇic*. For *loṭ* and the rest are ordained in the sense of these (sending/ordering) impelling etc.

And where a second impelled agent exists, there is *ṇic prayaya.* As for example "Do thou cause (him) to sit. Do thou cause (him) to lie down or sleep".

33.21 कृष्यादिषु चानुत्पत्तिः।

Vārttika: And there is non-arising (of *ṇic pratyaya*) in the formation of *kṛṣ-i* and the rest.

33.21 कृष्यादिषु चानुत्पत्तिर्वक्तव्या। एकान्ते तूष्णीमासीन उच्यते पञ्चभिर्हलैः कृषतीति। तत्र भवितव्यं पञ्चभिर्हलैः कर्षयतीति।।

Bhāṣya: And it should be stated that there is non-arising of *ṇic pratyaya* in (the formation) of *kṛṣ-i* and the rest. By one sitting silently in a lonely/deserted place it is said "He ploughs with five polughs". There it should be *pañcabhir halaiḥ karṣayati* "He causes ploughs with five ploughs"

33.23 कृष्यादिषु चानुत्पत्तिर्नानाक्रियाणां कृष्यर्थत्वात् ।। 3 ।।

Vārttika 3: And the case of the (*dhātus*) *kṛṣ-i* and the rest, the non-arising (of nic) is because of the meaning of *kṛṣ-i* (and the rest) having a variety of verbal activities (connected with them).

33.24 कृष्यादिषु चानुत्पत्तिः सिद्धा। कुतः। नानाक्रियाणां कृष्यर्थत्वात्। नानाक्रियाः कृषेरर्थाः। नावश्यं कृषिर्विलेखन एव वर्तते। किं तर्हि। प्रतिविधानेऽपि वर्तते। यदसौ भक्तबीजबलीवर्दैः प्रतिविधानं स कृष्यर्थः। आतश्च प्रतिविधाने
33.27 वर्तते यदहरेवासौ न प्रतिविधत्ते तदहरेव तत्कर्म न प्रवर्तते।

Bhāṣya: And in relation to (the *dhātus*) *kṛṣ-i* (and the rest) the non-arising of *ṇic* is settled. From what cause? "Because of the meaning of *kṛṣ-i* (and the rest) having a variety of verbal activities (connected with them). (For) various are the verbal activities which (comprise) the meanings of *kṛṣ-i. Kṛṣ-i* does not necessarily occur only in the sense of ploughing. What then? It also occurs in the sense of disposing and arranging i.e. managing (the activity). When he makes arrangements for eatable grain, seeds and oxen that is (all involved in) the sense of ploughing. And this indeed is for the following reason: even when arrangements exist, the day when no arrangements (of the activities are actually made is) that very day the work does not proceed."

34.1 यज्यादिषु चाविपर्यासः।

Vārttika: And in the case of the *dhātus yaj* and the rest there is no interchange or transposition (regarding *pada*).

34.1 यज्यादिषु चाविपर्यासो यज्यादिषु चाविपर्यासो वक्तव्यः। पुष्यमित्रो यजते याजका याजयन्तीति। तत्र भवितव्यं पुष्यमित्रो याजयते याजका यजन्तीति।।

Bhāṣya: And it should be stated that there is no interchange of *pada* in the case of *yaj dhātu* etc. *puṣyamitro yajate* "Prince *Puṣyamitra* sacrifices for himself" (*ātmanepada vibhakti pratyaya te*) *yājakā yājayanti* "The sacrificers perform sacrifices (for others)" (therefore *parasmaipada vibhakti pratyaya anti*). There should be *puṣamitro yājayate yājakā yajanti* "*Puṣyamitra* causes a sacrifice (to take place for his benefit, for himself) (*ātmanepada*), the offerers of sacrifices (i.e. the professional priests) perform sacrifices for others (*parasmaipada*)".

34.3 यज्यादिषु चाविपर्यासो नानाक्रियाणां यज्यर्थत्वात् ।। 4 ।।

Vārttika 4: And in the case of the *dhātus yaj* and the rest there is no interchange (of *pada*) because of the meaning of *yaj-i* (and the rest) having a variety of verbal activities (connected with them).

34.4 यज्यादिषु चाविपर्यासः सिद्धः। कुतः। नानाक्रियाणां यज्यर्थत्वात्। नाना-
क्रिया यजेरर्थाः। नावश्यं यजिर्हविष्प्रक्षेपणे एवं वर्तते। किं तर्हि। त्यागेऽपि
वर्तते। अहो यजत इत्युच्यते यः सुष्ठु त्यागं करोति। तं च पुष्यमित्रः करोति
34.7 याजकाः प्रयोजयन्ति।।

Bhāṣya: And it is established that there is no interchange (of *pada*). For what reason? Because of the meaning of *yaj-i* (and the rest) having a variety of verbal activities (connected with them). (For) various verbal activities (comprise) the meaning of *yaj-i* (and the rest). It is not essential that *yaj-i* (= *dhātu yaj*) occurs only in the sense of offering an oblation. What then? It also occurs in the sense of abandoning/giving up or away. As for example *aho yajate* "Ah! He is making (some self) sacrifice." Thus it is said (of someone) who performs excellently the act of (renunciation or) abandoning. And that, *Puṣyamitra* does (while) the offerers of the oblations/the priests prompt (him to do so).

34.8 तत्करोतीत्युपसंख्यानं सूत्रयत्याद्यर्थम् ।। 5 ।।

Vārttika 5: Additional enumeration (of *ṇic*) in the sense of 'He makes/does that' for the sake of (the forms) *sūtrayati* "He makes or composes a *sūtra*" and the rest.

34.9 तत्करोतीत्युपसंख्यानं कर्तव्यम्। किं प्रयोजनम्। सूत्रयत्याद्यर्थम्। सूत्रं करोति सूत्रयति। इह व्याकरणस्य सूत्रं करोति व्याकरणं सूत्रयतीति वाक्ये षष्ठ्युत्पन्ने च प्रत्यये द्वितीया। केनैतदेवं भवति। यो सौ सूत्रव्याकरणयोरभिसंबंधः स उत्पन्ने प्रत्यये निवर्ततेऽस्ति च करोतेर्व्याकरणेन सामर्थ्यमिति कृत्वा द्वितीया
34.13 भविष्यति।

Bhāṣya: Additional enumeration (of *ṇic*) should be made in the sense of 'he does or makes that'. What is the purpose? For the sake of (the forms) *sūtrayati* "He composes *sūtras* and the rest", *sūtraṃ karoti sūtrayati* (The sentence) 'he makes a *sūtra*' (is expressed by the denominative) *sūtrayati* 'He composes a *sūtra*'.

Here in the sentence *vyākaraṇasya sūtram karoti* 'He compose a *sūtra* of grammar', we have the sixth case for the word *vyākaraṇa* but here *vyākaraṇaṃ sūtrayati* "He compose a grammatical *sūtra*", when the *pratyaya* *ṇic* has arisen (to form *sūtrayati*) the word *vyākaraṇa*/grammar (receives) the second case/*sup*. By virtue of what does that thus become applicable? That connection of (the words) *sūtra* and *vyākaraṇa* (in the sentence by means of the sixth case) disappears when the *pratyaya* (*ṇic*) arises (to form the denominative *sūtrayati*); and having made the (statement) 'there exists mutual connection of meanings/*sāmarthyam* of the *dhātu kṛ* (to make) with the word *vyākaraṇa*', the second case (is applicable).

34.14 आख्यानात्कृतस्तदाचष्ट इति कृलुक्प्रकृतिप्रत्यापत्तिः प्रकृतिवच्च कारकम् ।। 6 ।।

Vārttika 6: "(*Ṇic*) *pratyaya* is to act after (a word expressing the name of) a story tale or legend, (ending) in a *kṛt* (*pratyaya*) when *nic* has the sense of 'He relates that', the *kṛt pratyaya* being *luk* elided and (the word) restored to its original form, as also the *kāraka*/case relationship (should be in its original form i. e. not elided)".

34.16 आख्यानात्कृदन्ताण्णिज्वक्तव्यस्तदाचष्ट इत्येतस्मिन्नर्थे। कृल्लुक्प्रकृतिप्रत्यापत्तिः प्रकृतिवच्च कारकं भवतीति वक्तव्यम्। कंसवधमाचष्टे कंसं घातयति। बलिबन्धमाचष्टे बलिं बन्धयति।।
34.18 बलिबन्धमाचष्टेयति।।

Bhāṣya: *Ṇic* should be stated after (the name of) a tale/story ending in a *kṛt pratyaya* in the sense of "He tells that". It should be stated that the *kṛt* is *luk* elided, (the base) restored to its original form and *kāraka*/case ending (relating to verbal activity becomes as it was in its original, with *vibhakti* ending manifest). *Kansa vadham ācaṣṭe* = *Kansam ghātayati* "He tells the story/drama of the killing of *kansa*" (by *Śeṣa Kṛṣṇa*) (optionally using *ṇic*).

Bali bandhanam ācaṣṭe = *balim bandhayati* "He tells the story of the binding or killing of *Bali*" (by *Viṣṇu*).

34.19 आख्यानाच्च प्रतिषेधः ॥ 7 ॥

Vārttika 7: "Prohibition (of *ṇic* in the sense of 'He tells that') after (the word) *ākhyāna* (tale)".

34.20 आख्यानशब्दाच्च प्रतिषेधः वक्तव्यः। आख्यानमाचष्ट इति॥ किं पुनर्यान्येतानि
संज्ञाभूतान्याख्यानानि तत उत्पत्त्या भवितव्यमाहोस्वित् क्रियान्वाख्यानमात्रात्। किं
चातः। यदि संज्ञाभूतेभ्य इह न प्राप्नोति राजागमनमाचष्टे राजानमागमयतीति।
अथ क्रियान्वाख्यानमात्रान्न दोषो भवति। यथा न

34.25 दोषस्तथास्तु॥

Bhāṣya: And it should be stated that there is prohibition (of *ṇic*) after the word *ākhyāna* (tale). (Therefore only the sentence form without *ṇic*).

ākhyānam ācaṣṭe "He tells a tale"

But should there be the arising (of *ṇic*) (only) after these words which have become the names of tales, or after any kind of narration of actions? And what (follows) from that? If (only) after words which have become names of tales, (then) here (*ṇic*) does not obtain.

rājāgamanam ācaṣṭe = *rājānam āgamayati*

"He tells the story of the coming of the King" (optionally in fact formed with *ṇic*). Now (then in fact) there is no fault if *nic* (acts) after all narrations of action. Let it be such that there is no fault.

34.25 दृश्यर्थायां च प्रवृत्तौ ॥ 8 ॥

Vārttika 8: When the function of the activity of telling (the story etc.) is for the purpose of seeing/visualising (something, *ṇic* acts).

34.26 दृश्यर्थायां च प्रवृत्तौ कृदन्ताण्णिज्वक्तव्यस्तदाचष्ट इत्येतस्मिन्नर्थे। कृल्लुक्
प्रकृतिप्रत्यापत्तिः प्रकृतिवच्च कारकं भवतीति। मृगरमणमाचष्टे मृगान्रमयतीति।
दृश्यर्थायामिति किमर्थम्। यदा हि ग्रामे मृगरमणमाचष्टे मृगरमणमाचष्ट इत्येव
तदा

35.3 भवतीति॥

Bhāṣya: And when the function of the activity of telling (the story) is for the purpose of seeing/realising (something), it should be stated that *ṇic* acts in the sense of 'He tells that' after a word ending in a *kṛt pratyaya.* (It should be stated that) the *kṛt* being *luk* elided, the base refers to the original form, and the *kāraka*/case relationship to the verbal activity expressed becomes like the original *mṛgaramaṇaṃ ācaṣṭe* = *mṛgān ramayati* "He tells of the deer playing (so that they can visualise it)". Why (say) "for the purpose of seeing"? For (only) when in the village he sees the playing of the deer, then only *ṇic* should not be applicable.

Only the expression *mṛgaramaṇaṃ ācaṣṭe* should (then be used).

35.4 आङ्लोपश्च कालात्यन्तसंयोगे मर्यादायाम् ॥ 9 ॥

Vārttika 9: And when expressing a continous period of time up to a specific limit, (*ṇic pratyaya* acts) and there is *lopa* elision of (the *upasarga*) *āṅ.*

35.5 कालात्यन्तसंयोगे मर्यादायां कृदन्ताण्णिज्वक्तव्यस्तदाचष्ट इत्येतस्मिन्नर्थ आङ्-
लोपश्च। कृल्लुक्प्रकृतिप्रत्यापत्तिः प्रकृतिवच्च कारकं भवतीति। आरात्रिवि-
वासमाचष्टे
35.7 रात्रिं विवासयतीति॥

Bhāṣya: It should be stated that *ṇic* acts after a *kṛt pratyaya* ending (word) when expressing a continous/uninterupted period of time up to a specific limit, in the sense of "He tells that" and there is *lopa* elision of (the *upasarga*) *āṅ* (as for as etc.). (It should be stated that) the *kṛt pratyaya* being *luk* elided the base reverts to its original form and the *kāraka*/relationship expressed becomes like the original.

āratri-vivāsam ācaṣṭe = *ratriṃ vivāsayati* "He tells a tale until daybreak/banishing of night".

35.8 चित्रीकरणे प्राति[10] ॥ 10 ॥

Vārttika 10: When there is surprise at reaching (somewhere, *ṇic* is applicable).

35.9 चित्रीकरणे प्राप्यर्थे कृदन्ताण्णिज्वक्तव्यः कृल्लुक्प्रत्यापपत्तिः प्रकृतिवच्च
कारकं भवतीति। उज्जयिन्याः प्रस्थितो माहिष्मत्यां सूर्यादगमनं संभावयते सूर्य-
35.11 मुद्गमयतीति॥

Bhāṣya: It should be stated that *ṇic* acts in the sense of surprise at reaching (a place). (It should be stated that) the *kṛt pratyaya* being *luk* elided the base reverts to its original form and the *kāraka*/case relationship becomes like that of the original form.

ujjayinyā prasthito māhiṣmatyāmsūryodgamanaṃ sambhāvayate = *sūryam udgamayati* "He who has set off from *Ujjayanī* (at sunrise) reaches/arrives at *Mahiṣmatī* (to his amazement that same morning), thus he thinks it is possible" (optionally *ṇic* is applicable).

35.12 नक्षत्रयोगे ज्ञि ।। 11 ।।

Vārttika 11: *Ṇic* acts in the sense of knowledge of the conjunction of an asterism/*nakṣatra.*

35.13 नक्षत्रयोगे जानात्यर्थे कृदन्ताण्णिज्वक्तव्यः। कृल्लुक्प्रकृतिप्रत्यापत्तिः प्रकृतिवच्च कारकं भवतीति। पुष्ययोगं जानाति पुष्येण योजयति। मघाभिर्योजयतीति।।

35.15 तत्तर्हीदं बहु वक्तव्यम्।

Bhāṣya: It should be stated that *ṇic* acts after a word ending in a *kṛt pratyaya* in the sense of knowing of the conjunction of an asterism. (It should be stated that) the *kṛt pratyaya* being *luk* elided, the base reverts to its original form and the *kāraka*/case becomes like that of the original expression.

puṣyo yogam jānati = puṣyeṇa yojayati "He knows the (time of) the conjuction (of the moon) with the asterism *puṣya* (optionally with *ṇic* lit. 'He causes conjunction with the asterism *puṣya*').

maghābhir yojayati "He knows the (time of) the conjunction (of the moon) with the asterism *maghā*".

Then much has to be stated.

35.16 न वा सामान्यकृतत्वाद्धेतुतो ह्यविशिष्टम् ।। 12 ।।

Vārttika 12: Or else (this need not be stated) because (the *pratyaya ṇic*) is taught in (the sense of cause) in general. Indeed (whatever is enumerated) is not different from cause.

35.17 न वा वक्तव्यम्। किं कारणम्। सामान्यकृतत्वात्। सामान्येनैवात्र णिज्भविष्यति हेतुमतीति। किं कारणम्। हेतुतो ह्यविशिष्टम्। हेतुतो ह्यविशिष्टमेतद्भवति। तुल्या हि हेतुता देवदत्ते चादित्ये च। न सिध्यति। स्वतंत्रप्रयोजको

35.20 हेतुसंज्ञो भवतीत्युच्यते न चासावादित्यं प्रयोजयति।

Bhāṣya: Or else it should not be stated. What is the reason? "Because (the *pratyaya ṇic*) is taught in (the sense of cause) in general. Here *ṇic* will be applicable only in the general sense 'of that having a cause'. What is the reason? Because that which is mentioned is not distinguished from cause. For this is not different from cause, (thus this *ṇic*) is applicable. For the nature of cause in *Devadatta* and the sun is the same.

That is not valid. For it is said that the technical name *hetu* (refers to) the prompter of the independent one. And that (one yonder) does not prompt or direct the Sun.

35.21 स्वतन्त्रप्रयोजकत्वादप्रयोजक इति चेन्मुक्तसंशयेन तुल्यम् ॥ 13 ॥

Vārttika 13: If (it is said that) is not the prompter because he is prompter of an independent one, (this statement is equivalent to that made) by one who is free from doubt.

35.22 यं भवान्स्वतन्त्रप्रयोजकं मुक्तसंशयं न्याय्यं मन्यते पाचयत्योदनं देवदत्तो यज्ञदत्तेनेति तेनैतत्तुल्यम्। कथम्

Bhāṣya: This is just like that (*Devadatta*) whom you properly think without doubt (to be) the prompter of the independent one in the sentence *pācayatyodanam Devadatta Yajñadattena "Devadatta* causes *Yajñadatta* to cook the rice". This is like that (one who causes the Sun to rise). How?

35.24 प्रवृत्तिर्ह्युभयत्रानपेक्ष्य ॥ 14 ॥

Vārttika 14: For the inclination (to do something) in both cases is irrespective (of anything).

35.25 प्रवृत्तिर्ह्युभयत्रानपेक्ष्य किंचिद्भवति देवदत्ते चादित्ये च। नेह कश्चित्परोऽनु-
36.1 ग्रहीतव्य इति प्रवर्तते। सर्व इमे स्वभूत्यर्थं प्रवर्तन्ते।

Bhāṣya: This inclination (to do something) occurs in both cases in *Devadatta* and in the Sun irrespective of anything. There is nobody who is inclined to do something for another. All these act or proceed for the sake of their own welfare.

36.1 .... ये तावदेत्ते गुरुशुश्रूषवो नामा तेऽपि स्वभूत्यर्थमेव प्रवर्तन्ते पारलौकिकं च नो भविष्यतीह च नः प्रीतो गुरुरध्यापयिष्यतीति। ष्यतीति। यथा यदेतद्दासकर्मकरं नामैतेऽपि स्वभूत्यर्थमेव प्रवर्तन्ते भक्तिं चेलं च लप्स्यामहे परिभाषाश्च न नो भविष्यन्तीति। तथा य एते शिल्पिनो नाम तऽपि स्वभूत्यर्थमेव प्रवर्तन्ते वेतनं च लप्स्यामहे मित्राणि च नो भविष्यन्तीति। एवमेतेषु
36.6 सर्वेषु स्वभूत्यर्थं प्रवर्तमानेषु

Those who obey/serve their teacher indeed even they (in truth) act for the sake of their own welfare (under the belief) 'and for us there will be (attainment of) the world beyond and the teacher pleased with us will teach us'. Similarly indeed whosever is a servant doing his (master's) work, they too act for the sake of their own welfare (with the idea) "and we shall obtain food and clothing and their will not be any reproofs for us". Similarly indeed those called artisans, they also act for the sake of their own welfare, (with the idea) "we shall receive wages and for us there will be (many) friends".

So thus, in all these (examples) when they are acting for the sake of their owe welfare, (then applies the next *vārttika*)

36.7 कुर्वतः प्रयोजक इति चेत्तुल्यम् ।। 15 ।।

Vārttika 15: (This) is equivalent (to saying) that (*hetu*) is the prompter of one who does something.

36.8 यदि कश्चित्कुर्वतः प्रयोजको नाम भवति तेनैतत्तुल्यम् ।। यदि तर्हि सर्व इमे स्वभूत्यर्थं प्रवर्तन्ते कः प्रयोज्यार्थः। यदभिप्रायेषु सज्जन्ते। ईदृशौ वध्रौ कुरु
36.10 ईदृशौ पुटकौ कुरु। आदित्यश्चास्याभिप्राये सज्जते।

Bhāṣya: If someone is the prompter of the one who is already doing, really that is equivalent to (saying that he is) the *hetu*. If then all these acts are for the sake of their own welfare what is the sense of *prayojya* "to be prompted"? Since they are intent on (fulfilling his) intentions e.g. "Make two leather bands like this", "Make two water-cups (from leaves) like this", (they become *prayojya*). The sun is also intent on fulfilling its purpose.

36.10 .... एष तस्याभिप्राय उज्जयिन्याः प्रस्थितो माहिष्मत्यां सूर्योद्गमनं संभावयेयेति तं चास्याभिप्रायमादित्यो निर्वर्तयति।। भवेदिह वर्तमानकालता युक्ता स्यात् उज्जयिन्याः प्रस्थितो माहिष्मत्यां सूर्योद्गमनं संभावयते सूर्यमुद्गमयतीति तत्रस्थस्य हि तस्यादित्य उदेति। इह तु कथं
36.14 वर्तमानकालता कंसं घातयति बलिं बन्धयतीति चिरहते कंसे चिरबद्धे च बलौ।

This is his intention, that one having set off from *Ujjayanī* (at night) be possible amazingly to be at *Māhiṣmatī* at sunrise. *suryodgamanam sambhāvayate* (or with *ṇic*) *sūryam udgamayati* (c.f. *Vārttika 10*).

Here it may be that the present time would be appropriate in this case: Having set off from *Ujjayanī* he contemplated on the sunrise at *Māhiṣmatī* (optionally with *ṇic* lit. 'He causes the sun to rise', c.f. *Vārttika 10*). For indeed the sun rises for him standing there in that place.

But how is it the present time here: "He tells the story of the killing of

Kaṅsa (c.f. *Vārttika 6*) "He tells the story of the binding of *Bali* " (c.f. *Vārttika* 6) When *Kaṅsa* was killed long ago and *Bali* was bound long ago?

36.15 अत्रापि युक्ता कथम्। ये तावदेते शोभनिका नामैते प्रत्यक्षं कंसं घातयन्ति प्रत्यक्षं
च बलिं बन्धयन्तीति। चित्रेषु कथम्। चित्रेष्वप्युद्गूर्णा निपतिताश्च प्रहारा दृश्यन्ते
कंसकर्षण्यश्च। ग्रन्थिकेषु कथं यत्र शब्दगडुमात्रं लक्ष्यते। तेऽपि हि तेषामुत्पत्ति-
प्रभृत्या विनाशादृद्धीर्व्याचक्षाणाः सतो बुद्धिविषयान्प्रकाशयन्ति। आतश्च सतो
36.19 व्यामिश्रा हि दृश्यन्ते।

Here too it is appropriate.

How? Those who indeed are actors (*śobhanika or śaubhika*) cause the killing of *Kaṅsa* (i.e. enact it) and causing the binding of *Bali* by re-enacting it before the eyes. How then (is the present time possible when the story is portrayed) in pictures? Also in a picture, blows raised and fallen are seen, and the tormenter of *Kaṅsa*, namely *Kṛṣṇa*.

How then in books (is the present time possible) where (the story) seems a mere superfluous excrescence, as an artificial stringing together of words? (*śabda grantha gaḍḍa matram 5.1 śabda gaḍumātram*)

For they also express success or prosperity from the birth up to final destruction and make clear matters comprehensible by reason. And for this reason they are seen mixed together with that which exists.

36.19 .... केचित्कंसभक्ता भवन्ति केचिद्वासुदेवभक्ताः। वर्णान्यत्वं
खल्वपि पुष्यन्ति। केचिद्रक्तमुखा भवन्ति केचित्कालमुखाः। त्रैकाल्यं खल्वपि
36.21 लोके लक्ष्यते। गच्छ हन्यते कंसः। गच्छ घानिष्यते कंसः। किं गतेन हतः कंस
इति ।।

Some are devotees of *Kaṅsa* some devotees of *Vasudeva* (*Kṛṣṇa*).

Also they display changes of colour indeed. Some having black faces, some having red faces. The 'Three times' (past, present and future tenses) indeed are also indicated in the world. "Go, *Kaṅsa* is slain" (present); "Go, *Kaṅsa* will be slain" future); What is the point in going, *Kaṅsa* was slain" (Past).

36.22 इति श्रीभगवत्पतञ्जलिविरचिते व्याकरणमहाभाष्ये तृतीयस्याध्यायस्य प्रथमे पादे
द्वितीयमाह्निकम्।।

Here ends the second *Āhnika* in the first *pāda* of the third *adhyāya* in the *Vyākaraṇa Mahābhāṣya* composed by the blessed Lord *Patañjali*.

Pradīpa

Pradīpa: 31.6 हेतुमति च।

कृत्रिमस्य परिभाषिकस्य प्रयोजकस्येह हेतोर्ग्रहणम्।

This here is a mention of *hetu* in an artificial and technical (sense) 'prompter of the action' (not the ordaining in ordinary popular sense as in the *sūtra tatprayojako hetuśca 1.4.55'*).

तदीयो व्यापार: प्रेषणऽध्येषणतत्समर्था चरणलक्षणो हेतुमानिह गृह्यते।

The word *hetuman* here is understood as such an activity which is characterised by sending, directing or commanding *(preṣaṇa)* solicitation, asking for instruction (*adhyeṣaṇa*) or expressing. the capacity/ability (*tat samarthacaraṇa*)

ननु सकलकारकसाध्यपाकाद्यपेक्ष: प्रयोजकस्य हेतुव्यपदेशो
न तु तदर्थावान्तरस्वसाध्यप्रेषणाद्यपेक्ष:।

Surely the designation *hetu* is for the prompter of the action with regard to the causing of cooking etc. to be accomplished by all the *kārakas,* but not with regard to the action of directing to be accomplished by itself intermediate to that purpose (of cooking etc.)

प्र० यथा काष्ठस्य पाकापेक्षं करणत्वं न तु ज्वलनापेक्षम्।

As the instrumentality of wood has regard to the cooking, but not with regard to the flaming of it.

तदपेक्षन्तु कर्तृत्वमेव। ततश्च पाकादेरेव हेतुमदव्यपदेशो युक्तो
न तु प्रेषणादे:। नैष दोष:।

But with regard to that (flaming) there is only agentship and thence for cooking etc. only the designation *hetumat* (having a cause) is appropriate not for directing, sending etc. This is not fault.

णिच्प्रकृत्या धातुनैव तस्याऽर्थस्य प्रकाशितत्वात्
प्रयोजनाभावात्तत्रैवाऽर्थे णिचोऽनुत्पादात्।

Due to its meaning being manifested by the *dhātu* along with the base by *ṇic* and due to the absence of cause there (and) from non-producing if *ṇic* in that meaning.

प्र० प्रयोज्योऽपि हेतुमच्छब्देन न गृह्यते तस्य द्रव्यत्वात्।
णिचश्च स्वभावत: करणाधिकाद्वा क्रियावाचित्वात्।
तस्मात्परिशेष्यात्पाकाद्यर्थो य: प्रेषणादिलक्षणो

लब्धपाकाद्यपेक्षहेतुव्यपदेशहेतुत्वोपलक्षितप्रयोजकसाध्यो व्यापार स एव गृह्यते।

That to be used or communicated is also not understood by the word *hetumat,* because of its substantial nature. And from the nature of *ṇic* being within the province of the governing word *karaṇa* and from its nature of expressing verbal activity. As a consequence of that meaning of *pāka* and the rest, which is characterised by directing or sending etc., that alone is understood as the activity which is to be accomplished by the prompter/impeller characterised by the nature of cause with the designation *hetu* having regard to the acquired action of cooking etc.

Pradīpa: 31.7 कथमिति।

यदा पचतीत्युक्ते प्रयोज्यसाध्य एव व्यापारो गम्यते। न प्रयोजकसाध्योऽपि तदा प्रत्ययार्थस्य करणाधिकारोपस्थापितस्य करणस्य विशेषणं हेतुमतीति संपद्यते। यदा त्वनेकार्थत्वाद्धातूनां तादर्थ्याद्वाऽधिश्रयणादिवत् प्रयोजकव्यापारोऽपि पचादिवाच्यो भवति यथा पञ्चमीर्हलैः कृषतीति तदा प्रकृतिविशेषणपक्षो भवति। तदा तु णिच्प्रत्ययो द्योतकः संपद्यत इति पक्षद्वयस्य संभवाद्दोषदर्शनाच्च प्रश्नः।

When it is stated 'He cooks', only the activity which has to be commissioned to be accomplished has not even the purpose to be accomplished then *hetumati* is produced as a qualification of the cause (sense of making); which has been caused to stand beside the governing rule as '*kāraka*' for the meaning of the *pratyaya* (*ṇic*). But when due to the many meanings of *dhātus* or having that same meaning then even the mention of the prompter like that of putting (fuel) on the fire etc. is to be expressed by *dhātu pac* etc. Just as 'He ploughs with five ploughs' (means he causes five teams to plough) then is applicable the view that *hetumati* is a qualification of the base. But then *ṇic pratyaya* is (only) illuminating meaning. Thus the question arises from this possibility and from perception of a fault.

Pradīpa: 31.13 हेतुमत इति।

हेतुमदर्थाऽभिधायिन इत्यर्थः।

"The meaning is 'expressing' (*kāraka* relationship)."

कारकोपादानमिति। mentioning of *kāraka*

कारकशब्देन प्रत्ययार्थ उच्यते स हि प्रत्ययं करोति निष्पादयति।

By the word *kāraka* is expressed the meaning of the *pratyaya* (*ṇic*). For that makes the *pratyaya* (meaningful) or brings about or accomplishes its function of being instrumental in accomplishing the action as directing etc.

Pradīpa: 31.13 प्रत्ययार्थ इति।

"The meaning of the *pratyaya* (*ṇic*)."

प्रत्ययस्यार्थः प्रयोजनं स सुष्ठु परिगृहीतः परिपूर्णो भवति, वाचकत्वात् प्रत्ययस्य। प्रकृतिविशेषणे तु प्रत्ययस्याऽनुवादकत्वाद् द्योतकत्वात्प्रयोजनमपरिपूर्णं स्यादित्यर्थः। अथवाऽर्थोऽभिधेयमुच्यते स चान्वयव्यतिरेकाश्रयव्यवस्थत्वाद् प्रेषणादिः प्रत्ययस्यैव न प्रकृतेरिति सुष्ठु परिगृहीतो व्यवस्थापितो भवति।

The meaning of the *pratyaya* is cause; that is well grasped and accomplished (perfect, a whole) because of the *pratyayas* expressing (the primary meaning directly). The meaning is that 'however when it, *hetumati,* is a qualification of the *prakṛti* (base), because of its (merely corroborative nature) illluminating or making clear (the meaning of the base, the cause would not be accomplished', Or else the meaning is said to be that expressed, and that through the nature of resorting to the method of agreement and difference, directing etc. is firmly established as the meaning of the *pratyaya* alone and not of the *prakṛti* (base).

Pradīpa: 31.15 यथा तनूकरण इति

As for example, *śnu* acts after *dhātu takṣ* in the sense of making thin, paring.

यदा विकरणार्थाः कर्त्रादय इति पक्षस्तदा तनूकरणशब्देन कर्ताऽभिधीयते तदा साधर्म्येण दृष्टान्तः। यदा तु सार्वधातुकार्थाः कर्त्रादय इति पक्षस्तदा वैधर्म्येण दृष्टान्त इति व्याख्यानम्। यथा तनूकरणं प्रकृत्यर्थो न तथा हेतुमद् व्यापार इत्यर्थः।

When the point of view is that 'the meaning of the *vikaraṇa pratyaya* is agent etc.', then by the word *tanūkaraṇa* the agent is designated ('what makes attenuated or pares'), then that is an example by (the method of) sameness of nature/homogeneousness. However, when the view is that the *sārvadhātuka pratyayas* have the meaning of agent etc. then the example is by (the method of) difference or heterogeneity. This is the exposition (here). As *tanūkaraṇa* is the meaning of the base, not so is the activity having a cause/*hetumat* (the meaning of the base). This is the meaning.

परस्तु साधर्म्येण दृष्टान्तं सार्वधातुकत्वं च कर्त्रादीनां मन्यमान आह-यदीति।

However, further thinking on the example by similarity and the *sārvadhātuka* nature of the agent and the rest he says, 'If then like that this is qualification of the meaning of the *prakṛti* base . . .

Pradīpa: 31.17 अस्त्विति।

"Let it be (qualification of the *prakṛti*/base)."

विनापि णिचा पञ्चभिर्हलैः कृषति इति प्रयोजकव्यापारावगमात्
प्रकृत्यर्थत्वं हेतुमत उपपद्यते। पचतीत्यादौ द्योतको
णिज्नास्तीति तदप्रतिपतिरिति भावः।

The sense is, even without *ṇic* from the understanding of the activity of prompter/causer (in the example) 'He ploughs with five ploughs', it is possible for *hetumat* to be the meaning of the *prakṛti.* However, the fact that "in the case of *pacati* 'He cooks' etc. there is (not applicable) *ṇic* as (merely) illuminating (the meaning of the base)" is not ascertained or understood.

Pradīpa: 31.18 उक्तः करोतीति।

"(Qualification of *prakṛti*—here *ṇic* obtains) 'He who was told, does...'."

153.2 प्रकृतिविशेषणपक्षे यथा प्रकृत्यभिहिते प्रयोजकव्यापारे
णिज्भवत्येवमुक्तप्रेषितादिशब्दाभिहितेऽपि प्राप्नोति
हेतुमद्विशेणत्वात्करोत्यर्थस्य।
प्रत्ययार्थं विशेषणपक्षे तूक्तार्थत्वाणिजभावः।

As the view of the *hetumat* as qualification of *prakṛti* (base), *ṇic* is applicable when the sense of the activity of prompter is expressed by the *prakṛti.* So when it has already been expressed by the word *preṣita* (impelled) etc. it obtains because of *karoti's* meaning as a qualification of having a cause/*hetumat.*

However, when the view is that hetumat is a qualification of the meaning of the *pratyaya,* because the meaning has already been expressed, there is absence of *ṇic.*

Pradīpa: 31.20 यत्रेति।

"Where (there is no understanding of the meaning without the word)."

यस्याऽर्थस्य द्योतनाय णिज्विधीयते स यदाशब्दान्तराऽवगतो
भवति तदा प्रयोजनाऽभावाण्णिज् न भवतीत्यर्थः।

The meaning is "that for illuminating whose meaning *ṇic* is ordained when another word is understood (which is *vācaka-Nāgeśa*) then due to the absence of cause *ṇic* is not applicable."

Pradīpa: 31.22 उभयोरिति।

"expression of both agents (by the *la* tense *pratyaya* becomes wrongly applicable)."

धातुवाच्यस्य व्यापारस्य कर्तरि लकारेणोत्पत्तव्यम्।
यदा च पचिना द्वयोरपि प्रयोज्यप्रयोजकयोर्व्यापारोऽभिधीयते णिच्प्रत्ययः
केवले स्वार्थिकत्वात् प्रयोजकव्यापारस्य द्योतकस्तदा धातुवाच्यव्यापारसाम्यात्कर्त्रोरपि
साम्यमिति द्वयोरप्यभिधानं स्यात् ततः पाचयतो
देवदत्तयज्ञदत्ताविति प्रसज्येतेत्यर्थः।

When agent of the activity to be expressed by the *dhātu,* is to be mentioned (produced) by the *la* (tense *pratyaya*), and when the activity of the two, both cause/prompter and that to be caused/prompted is expressed by *dhātu pac;* because of the *svārthika* nature (expressing the meaning of its base) when on its own, *ṇic pratyaya* is the (mere) illuminator of the activity to the prompter/causer; then because of the similarity of the action to be expressed by the *dhātu* directly, there is also similarity for the two agents. Thus three would be designation even for both. The meaning is that 'the form *pācyate-Devadatta-Yajñadattau* (*Devadatta* and *Yajñadatta* both cause to cook) would be wrongly applicable.

Pradīpa: 31.23 प्रधानकर्तेति।

"The principal agent (is expressed by the *la* (tense *pratyaya*))."

प्रकृत्यर्थोपसर्जनत्वाण्ण्यर्थस्य प्राधान्यान्तस्य कर्ताऽपि प्रधानमिति भावः।

"The priciple agent etc. ..."

The sense is because of the meaning of the *prakṛti* being subordinate (and) the principal nature of the meaning of *ṇi* its agent is also principal.

Pradīpa: 31.24 गमित इति।

Yajñadatta caused *Devadatta* to go to the village.

प्रयोजकव्यापारस्य गमिवाच्यत्वात्तस्य कर्तरि प्रयोजके क्तः
प्राप्नोतीत्यर्थः। प्रयोज्यस्य तु कर्मत्वात्तत्रैव क्त इष्यते।
तदुक्तम् अप्रधाने दुहादीनां कर्तृश्च कर्मण इति। 1.4.51, 1.335,15-16

The meaning is, because of the activity of the prompter having its nature to be expressed by *dhātu gam, kta pratyaya* obtains in the sense of its agent, as prompter/causer. However, because of the nature *karman*/ object pertains to that to be prompted/caused, there in fact *kta* is desired. That was stated (by *Bhāṣya* on *1.4.51*) when 'it should be stated *la* and the rest are applicable in the sense of subordinate object of *duḥ* (to milk) etc. (*śloka vārttika*) (and further connection with *ṇi* causative stem *la* etc. are expressers of the *karman*/object (which was) the *kartṛ*/agent.' (on *akathitam ca 1.4.61*)

Pradīpa: 31.26 व्यतिभेदयन्त इति।

'They are bursting forth together on each other simultaneously.'

प्रयोजकव्यापारस्य व्यतीहारो न तु
प्रयोज्यव्यापारस्येति द्रष्टव्यम्।

Whether it is true, it should be seen (in usage), that the reciprocity is of the activity of the prompters but not of the activity of those prompted.

Pradīpa: 32.3 भवति हीति।

ण्यर्थस्य प्राधान्यत्तद्व्यापारेणेप्सिततमत्वात्प्रयोज्यस्येत्यर्थः
प्रकृत्यर्थविशेषणेत्वे तु द्वयोरपि प्रयोज्यप्रयोजकव्यापारयोरेकधातु
वाच्यत्वाद्धातुवाच्यव्यापाराऽपेक्षया द्वयोरपि
कर्तृत्वाल्लेनाऽभिधानं प्राप्नोतीति दोष उक्तः।

The meaning is: "Because of the meaning of *ni* being principal by reason of its activity (and) because of that prompted having the nature of being that most desired to be obtained (by the agent). However, when there is the application of the qualification of the meaning of *prakṛti* (by *hetumati*) because of the nature of the two, namely the activity of the prompted and the prompter, having to be expressed by one *dhātu*, and because of the nature of agent also (being) for both with regard to the activity to be expected by the *dhātu*, a fault is stated, namely that designation by *la* (a tense *pratyaya*) obtains."

ग्रामं गमयतीति।

'He causes (him) to go to the village.'

ण्यर्शस्यैव ग्रामः प्रयोज्यश्च कर्मेति भावः

The village pertains in fact to that having the meaning of *ṇi* (because of being principal etc. *Nāgeśa*) and that to be prompted is the *karman*/ object.

Pradīpa: 32.6 षष्ठी न प्राप्नोतीति।

'The sixth case does not obtain (although desired).'

ण्यर्थस्य कर्मत्वादिति भावः सुट् तु करोतिधात्वाश्रयत्वाण्णिजुत्पत्तावपि तद्रूपसन्निधानात्सिध्यत्येवेति तन्नाऽचूचुदत्।

'The sense is, because of the meaning of *ṇi* having the nature of *karman*/object. However, an augment *suṭ* because of resort to (dependence) on the *dhātu kṛ* even when *ṇic* arises, due to its proximity to that, in fact is established as valid. (Thus it did not implel or cause to move.)

Pradīpa: 32.7 प्रयोज्ये कर्तरि इति।

"(Sixth case does not obtain) in the sense of agent to be prompted or compelled."

तस्या प्राधान्यादिति भावः।

The sense is because of its not being principal *kartṛkaraṇayostṛtīyā 2.3.18* (*anabhihite*) would be applicable.

Pradīpa: अभिषावयतीति।

He causes him to press out (the *soma*).

ण्यर्थस्योपसर्गो विशेषक इति भावः।

The sense is that the *upasarga* is a (qualifying or) attribute of the meaning of *ṇi*.

Pradīpa: 32.11 एतेषामेवेति।

"For these (*dhātus*) alone (not ending in *ṇi* that which is agent in the non-causal state has *karman* applicable in the causal when *ṇi* follows)."

ण्यर्थस्य प्राधान्यात्तेनेप्सिततमस्य प्रयोजनस्य सिद्धा कर्मसंज्ञा।
न च स्वव्यापाराऽपेक्षया स्वातन्त्र्यात्परत्वात्कर्तृसंज्ञा प्राप्नोतीति युक्तं वक्तुम्।
प्रयोज्यव्यापारस्याऽ प्राधान्यात्प्रधाना प्रधानव्यापारसंनिधौ च प्रधाननिमित्तस्य कार्यस्ययुक्तत्वात्। नियमेन तु प्राधाव्यप्रयुक्तकार्यव्यावृत्तौ गुणनिमित्तकार्यसद्भावात्कर्तृत्वं भवत्येव तदुक्तं हरिणा।
गुणक्रियां स्वातत्र्यात्प्रेषणे कर्मतां गतः।
नियमात्कर्मसंज्ञायाः स्वधर्मेणाभिधीयते।। इति 3.7.127

"The techncal name *karman* is established as valid for that prompted which is most desired to be obtained; therefore this is because of the meaning of *ṇic* being principal. And further it is not proper to say that the technical name agent obtains, because of 'independence' being subsequent with regard to its own activity.'

... Because of the activity of that to be prompted being non-principal and because of the non-suitability of the effect as cause of the principal in presence of the activity of the principal and the non-principal. However, when by a restriction there is turning away from the principal used operation and because of the existence of an operation which is a subordinate cause, agentship is in fact applicable (i.e. valid)."

That was stated by *Bhartṛhari:*

"The agent who becomes the object of the act of prompting is called by his own characteristic (agent), because he retains his indepedence with regard to his own minor or subordinate action and also because of the restriction of the name (*karman*) (to special cases)."

Pradīpa: 32.13 नासाविति।

"That (person) is not (impelled by saying go to the village)."

ग्रामः प्रकृत्यर्थस्य कर्म न तु ण्यर्थस्येत्यर्थः।

The meaning is that village is the object/*karman* of the meaning of the *prakṛti* but not of the meaning of *ṇi*.

Nāgeśa: This is essential by reason of the *sakarmaka*/transitive nature of the *dhātu gam,* because of it expecting a *karman* and because of the expectation of a *karman* for that having the meaning of *ṇi* being quietened by reason of the object (being that) to be prompted.

Pradīpa: 32.14 साधनविशिष्टामिति।

"(One impelled to do an action) which is distingusished by a *kāraka.*"

ग्रामकर्मिकां गमनक्रियां प्रयोज्यः प्रेष्यति - प्राप्नोत्यर्थः।

The meaning that 'one to be prompted impels the action of going to the village, which it has as its object' obtains.

स च प्रेष्यते प्राप्यते।

And that is obtained as 'one is impelled':

Nāgeśa questions *Kaiyaṭa's* interpretation.

Pradīpa: 32.19 कर्तृभूतपूर्वमात्रेऽपीति।

"So that sixth case be applicable even when an agent only in former time (is to be denoted)."

प्रधानचरेऽपि कर्तरीत्यर्थः।

The meaning is even when formerly he was principal agent.

Nāgeśa: "Kaiyata says this because the nature of former time is not a possibility."

Pradīpa: 32.21 सुनु अभीति।

"(Change of *ṣ* for *s* does not obtain) when *abhi* is to join with *dhātu su(nu)*"

न प्रयोजकव्यापारस्याभिमुख्यमभिशब्देन द्योत्यते

अपि तु प्रयोज्य व्यापारस्यैवेत्यर्थः।

The meaning is that 'by the word *abhi* is not illuminated the presence of the action of the prompter but rather of the activity of that to be prompted only'.

Pradīpa: 32.23 युक्तं पुनरिति।

"It is proper to again (consider the matter)."

सन्देह एव विचारनिमित्तं नोपपद्यते।
अन्वयव्यतिरेकाभ्यां भूयोदर्शनविषयाभ्यां
प्रत्ययार्थविशेषणपक्षस्यैवोपपन्नत्वादिति भावः।

The sense is that, doubt alone as the cause of deliberation is not proper, because of the nature of the view of *hetumati* as qualification of the meaning of the *pratyaya* (obtained through the method of 'similarity and difference' having as its object seeing more).

Pradīpa: 32.25 यासाविति।

"That (activity) which (softens grains of rice)."

तदर्थत्वात्कारकग्रामस्य तदनन्तरञ्च फलोत्पादादिति भावः।
तदुक्तं हरिणा - अन्तन्तरं फलं यस्याः कल्पते तां क्रियां विदुः।
प्रधानभूतां तादर्थ्यादन्यासां तु तदाख्यता।। इति वा० पद 3.8.15
तत्र यथाऽधिश्रयणादयस्तादर्थ्यात्पचिवाच्यास्तथा प्रेषणादिरपि द्योतकस्तु
णिजपेक्ष्यत इत्यर्थः। न च कारकाणामपि तादर्थ्यात्पच्यभिधेयत्वप्रसङ्गः
तेषामक्रियारूपत्वाद्धातोश्च क्रियावाचित्वात्। विक्लित्तिश्चाऽत्र
फलानन्तरव्यापारोपलक्षणम् इष्टकाः पचन्तीत्यादौ तस्या
संभवादित्याहुः।

The sense is because of village as *kàraka* having that purpose and immediately after that because of producing the fruit/result. That was stated by *Bhartṛhari* (quoted also on *3.1.22 Vā.1*).

"That moment immediately after which the result is produced, they know to be the principal or primary action, the others are so called because they have that purpose (of producing the result)." The meaning there is that just as because of activities 'putting on the fire' etc. having that purpose (of cooking etc.) are thus to be expressed by the *dhātu pac,* similarly, the activities of impelling etc. also are (merely) illuminating (i.e. secondary) with respect to the *ṇic.* [And] nor is there the possibility of the *kāraka* having the meaning of the *dhātu pac,* due to being intended for not having that meaning, [both] because of their not having the nature of verbs and because of *dhātus* expressing verbal activity. Here softening (of the rice) is a synecodoche for the result immediately following. They say this because of the impossibility of such statements as 'the bricks cook' etc."

Pradīpa: 32.26 प्र पच्यर्थः स्यादिति।

"May (all) be part of the meaning of *pac.*"

संभावने लिङ्। संभाव्यते पच्यर्थत्वं प्रेषणादेः। अत एव संशयाद्विचार्य प्रत्ययार्थविशेषणपक्षो भाष्यकारेण स्थापितः तद्दोषाणां परिहृतत्वात् पक्षान्तरे दोषाणां चापरिहारात्। अथवा प्रकृयर्थविशेषणपक्षोऽपि स्थापितः, तत्पक्षभाविनां दोषाणां सुपरिहरत्वात्। तथा हि युक्तं द्वयोः कर्त्रोर्लेनाभिधानं प्राप्नोतिति नायं दोषः प्रकृत्या प्रयोज्यव्यापारोपसर्जनस्य प्रयोजकव्यापारस्याभिधानात्तस्यैव णिचा द्योतनात् प्रधान एवं कर्तरि लो भविष्यति नाऽप्रधाने णिचा च द्योतकेन प्रधानभूतगत्यर्थत्वं निविर्तितं गमनारूपस्य प्रधानस्याऽर्थस्याभिधानादिति ण्यन्तात्प्रयोजककर्तरि लस्याऽनुत्पत्तिः। व्यतिभेदयन्त इत्यत्रापि हिंसनालक्षणः प्रधानं धात्वर्थो न तु हिंसारूप इत्यात्मने पदनिषेधाऽभावः।

'*Liṅ* (optative) is in the sense of supposition/assumed. It is (thought) possible for impelling etc. to be part of the meaning of *pac-i*.

Due to doubt, having considered (finally) the view of *hetumati* as a qualification of the *pratyaya,* it is settled/established by the *Bhāṣyakāra,* because of its faults being refuted and the faults of the other view not being refuted. Or else the view that (*hetumati*) is a qualification of the *prakṛti* is also established, because of the fault attached to that view being well refuted. For so what was said, 'designation by *la* (tense *pratyaya*) obtains for both agents'. (This) is not a fault, because of the designation of the activity of the prompter of the subordinate activity of that to be prompted; due to its alone illuminating (meaning) together with *ṇic, la* will be applicable in relation to the principal agent alone, not to the non-principal, and preventd from having the meaning to go, when formerly principal (agent) with *ṇic* as illuminator, and expressing the meaning of principal as movement. Thus after that ending in a *ṇi* there is not arising of *la* in the sense of causative agent.

'Vyati bhedayante'— here too the meaning of the *dhātu* is principal, suggesting hurting but not as its nature, there being absence of prohibition of *ātmanepada.*

Pradīpa: 32.27 अथेति।

"Now (what is the meaning of *matup*)?"

Kaiyaṭa: Although the meaning of sixth case and of seventh case is known with the nature of the meaning of *matup,* still when there (is the characteristic of having) many meanings for the word *hetu,* due to not knowing (perceiving) the meaning of *hetu,* a question arises because of *matup* which is characteristic of that (*hetu*), so is this also not preceived/known? But that exists in the sphere of *hetu* only because of (its) meaning.

32.27 कै० — हेतुरिति। What is *hetu*? What cause is the prompter? Now (it is stated as) mere efficent or instrumental cause.

32.27 हेतु कर्तेति। 'The sense is that *hetu* is the prompter.'

Pradīpa: 33.5 नावश्यमिति।

"It is not necessarily (the one who causes someone to stay by saying you may stay)."

The meaning is 'the activity of the prompter is also the exercise of capacities and because of the dependence on the existence of that for the accomplishment of the (success of) the action by the one prompted.

Pradīpa: 33.9 पृच्छतु मा भवान्।

'Ask me a question, Sir',

The questioner is the impeller, the prompter of the one to be prompted or commissioned. The question is why is not *ṇic* applicable in the sense of this activity? There is the possibility of alternatively *loṭ* or *ṇic,* because of having a single sphere (of application).

Pradīpa: 33.10 अकर्तृत्वात्।

(*Ṇic* is not applicable because of the one commanding) not being the agent.

The meaning is '*Hetu* is said to be the prompter of the agent, (the independent one who has the system within himself). And the one to be prompted here is not the agent, so the prompter does not receive the technical name *hetu.*

Pradīpa: 33.10 तूष्णीमिति।

"(He remains) silent."

The meaning is because of being devoid of activity/actionless, he does not even have the nature of being *kāraka* (in relation to the action), whence agentship which is a (mere) special form or (qualification) of that agentship, is in fact being mentioned or understood/held for that, as 'be thou the agent of the action of questioning!' Similarly, 'be thou king (and) fight!' thus kingship is understood/held. However, he who is agent (having one) to be prompted, (whose) action has begun or is a possible action, for the prompter who is *hetu*, there is no *ṇic* applicable. किं च भो इति। "And, Sir, (Should he only be agent at the present time)?"

Another having thought "By this one only, agentship for action of the present time was expressed."

He (then) impels...

2.33.12 अभिसंबन्ध इति। A connecton is made there. He did this action.

The meaning is the connection of the agent of the action of the past and future is established in past and future.

Pradīpa: 33.15 अथ कथमिति।

"Now then how, (when this one is not asking a question, does *prach* operate)?" i.e. due to the impossibility of using the word when the meaning is not present.

Pradīpa: 33.15 अभिसंबन्ध इति।

"A connection (is made there. Do this action.)"

The sense is that it is through the use of the word, even when the meaning remains in the mind, (the action) not existing outside.

Pradīpa: 33.17 न च कर्तेति।

"And thus the Agent is not (expressed)."

Because of the very nature of being held...

That was stated by *Bhartṛhari*

द्रव्यमात्रस्य तु प्रैषे पृच्छादेर्लोङ्विधीयते।

सक्रियस्य प्रयोगस्तु यदा स विषयो णिचः ।। 3.7.126

"The imperative (*loṭ*) is ordained after *dhātu* like *prach*, when just the object is prompted. When the already active object is prompted, it comes within the sphere of *ṇic* (causative *pratyaya*)."

Pradīpa: 33.17 अथापि।

"Now even if (somehow there be an agent, no fault)."

The sense is 'Even by assenting to the weak position, the rejection of *ṇic* is expressed...'

Pradīpa: 33.18 लोटोक्तत्वादिति।

"Because already expressed by *loṭ*."

From the point of view of single sphere (of application) for *ṇic* and for *loṭ* etc. when *loṭ* arises, then because of being expressed by that alone, the *ṇic* for (expressing) impelling will not be applicable.

Pradīpa: 33.19 प्रैषातिसर्गप्राप्तकालेषु कृत्याश्च। 3.3.163

"*Kṛtya pratyayas* and *loṭ* (imperative) act after *dhātus* in the sense of *ṇic* granting permission and proper time."

"(By one sitting) in a desertd place it is said..."

He shows the man's incapability in respect of ploughing.

Pradīpa: 33.21 तूष्णीमासीन इति।

'Sitting silently'

Expressing the absence of activity.

Some one, due to exceeding strength might plough with five ploughs or alternatively to deny that (possibility) it was stated, 'seated silently in a deserted place'.

In that context from understanding that he causes ploughing of the ground by five others with ploughs, when *ṇic* is present *kṛṣati* (without *ṇic*) does not obtain (though desired). The meaning is that, non-arising of *ṇic* has to be stated.

Pradīpa: 33.25 प्रतिविधानेऽपि।

"It also (occurs) in the sense of disposing/managing (the activity)."

The meaning is that, 'because many meanings of a *dhātu* (it is specifically stated that *ṇic*) occurs in indicating the exercise of that capacity in the sense of the activity of a prompter after the *dhaṫu kṛṣ* alone.

There is absence of *ṇic*, because of its meaning being revealed by the *dhātu* alone together with its subordinate accompanying word. And following the options allowed by *vibhāṣopapadena pratīyamāne 1.3.77* '*ātmanepada pratyayas*' optionally act, when the fruit of the action accruing to the agent is indicated by the *upapada* (subordinate accompanying word)", there is absence of *ātmanepada*.

However, when the *dhātu kṛṣ* occurs in the sense of ploughing (in the causative form), then in fact the form is 'He causes ploughing with five ploughs' using *ṇic* only.

Pradīpa: 34.1 यज्यादिष्विति।

"And in the case of *yaj* and the rest (no interchange of *pada*)."

Due to the *dhātu yaj's* nature of expressing a particular kind of throwing (of oblation), and because of the agentship of the priest in relation to the throwing, and because of the sacrificer's nature as prompting agent, there is a rule to avoid the possibility of *ṇic*...

Pradīpa: 34.3 नानाक्रिया इति।

"Various verbal activities (comprise the meaning of *yaj* and the rest)."

In that context by the resorting to the word *tyāga* (abandoning/donation) it is to be seen that whatever usage is different to that, is in the sense expressing throwing (of an oblation).

Pradīpa: 34.10 इह व्याकरणस्येति।

"Here (in the sentence) he composes a *sūtra* of grammar/body of rules."

The word *vyākaraṇa* occurs either in the sense of *lakṣya śabda* (word to be indicated) or *laksaṇa* . . . (the collection of indications)/*sūtra*/ rules. Thus sixth case is for the binding of the differences!

See *vārttika 18 Paś. Paś.*

vyākaraṇa (means) *lakṣya and lakṣaṇa*

also *vā. 14*

सूत्रे व्याकरणे षष्ठ्यर्थे नोपपद्यते व्याकरणस्य सूत्रम्।

Bhāṣya: If *vyākaraṇa* means *sūtra* (body of rules) then the meaning of the sixth case ending in *vyākaraṇasya sūtram* (the body of the rules of *vyākaraṇa*) cannot be justified. Because what other thing than *sūtra* could *vyākaraṇa* be than that to which *sutras* belong?

Kaiyaṭa

षष्ठ्यर्थ

... since both the words *vyākaraṇa* and *sūtra* stand for the *Aṣṭādhyāyī* there can be no *vyatireka* (genitive relation indicating separateness between them). But there is no contradiction of using them by way of general and a particular word.

सामान्यविशेषशब्दतया।

When, however, the word *vyākaraṇa* occurs in the sense of *sūtra* (body of rules) it is *lakṣaṇa* in fact, then sixth case is cause of designating a secondary thing as principal (i.e. *sūtra* as whole grammar). When there is the same case relationship व्याकरणं सूत्रं करोति। 'He makes a grammar *sūtra*', then just as मुण्डयति माणवकम् 'He shaves the youth' is valid, so similarly व्याकरणं सूत्रयति। "That (connection of the words *sūtra* and *vyākaraṇa* disappears)".

Pradīpa: 34.11 योऽसाविति।

In a sentence, by the word *sūtra* is expressed the form of the object (called) a *sūtra*/aphorism. However, when *ṇic* arises, because of going beyond the state of substantive it is possible for the word *sūtra* to be expressing the meaning of *karoti*/to make. That was stated 'a complex formation (involves) designation of the meaning of another word'. And this was expressed by resort to the distinction come from etymological formation. However, in reality, different from a *dhātu, sūtra* is a special kind of verbal noun, expressing verbal activity.

Pradīpa: 34.14 आख्यानादिति।

"After (a word expresing the name of) a story (*ṇic*)."

Ākhyānam is that which is told. Thus the formation is stated, communicated or declared.

प्रकृतिवदिति। "(The word) restored to its original form."

That which was the original form of *kaṅsavadha* and the rest, formed from *ṇic* like that (original too) is the *kāraka* relationship, that *kaṅsa* and the rest (had, should be restored to that original). The meaning is that 'just as the nature of *karman* (is applicable) for *kaṅsavadha* etc. with regard to the action of telling (a story), so likewise for *kaṅsa* and the rest also, who are the object of a incomplete tale. 'Also by extension of the condition of the original for *kaṅsa* and the rest, because of being separated (from *han* etc.). In the case of *kaṅsam aghātāyat* 'He caused *kaṅsa* to be slain' and the rest, when there is the technical name *aṅga* for *Hansa* and the rest, separated (from *vadha* etc.), *aṭ* augment and the rest are not applicable for *kaṅsa* and the rest. And because of producing *vat* (like), it is even applicable for resorting to its own original condition.

In the example, 'He unites that with (knowledge of conjuction of the moon) with *Puṣya*' there is no *karman* nature for *puṣya.* Or else *prakṛtivat* means occuring (existing) like the original, that is like the *prakṛti.*

Through resorting to 'extending both ways', being *kāraka* relation for that ending in *ṇi,* somewhere someone is accepted. By reason of the restoration to the original in the case of 'the coming of the king'/

rājāgamanam etc. elision of *n* (by 8.2.7) also ceases and (the proper form) obtained becomes *'rājānam āgamayati'* he cause the king to come'.

Pradīpa: 34.17 कंसवधमिति।

"(He tells the story of) the killing of *Kaṅsa.*"

Although here the cessation of the *ādeśa vadha* is established, because of (the formulation of *Patañjali* on *4.1.36 vā. 4*) 'when there is departure of one of the remaining connections (in an operation) there is absence of both'.

(सन्नियोगाशिष्टानामन्यतरापाये उभयोरप्यभाव:)

Nonetheless, because the cessation is not established as valid, due to the absence of having a remainder from the connection in place of the gutturals in the case of example पुष्येण योगं जानाति पुष्येण योजयति।

"He knows the (name of) the connection (of the moon) with the asterism *Puṣya*" (Where in the verbal form of *yuj* the *tālu*/palatal *j* is reverted to in this formation with *ṇic*). So it is stated "restoration to the original state (of *prakṛti*)". See *vā 11* in the *sūtra.*

Pradīpa: 34.29 किं पुनरिति।

"But (should there be the arising of *ṇic* only after these words which have become the names of tales...)?"

The meaning is of tales like *kaṅsavadha* which have had *lopa* elision of *n* etc.

"When the function of the activity of telling the story is for the purpose of seeing/visualising something."

When one situated in a forest, having approached deer playing, relates "in this very place such kinds of deer play", then application of *ṇic* in the context of telling a story is applicable for the purpose of visualising what is to be explained.

दृशि इक् कृष्यादिभ्य: वा० 8 द्योति 3.3.108

Pradīpa: 35.2 यदा हि ग्राम इति।

"For (only) when in the village does he see playing of deer."

Because of the impossibility of deer in a village, there is not application of *ṇic* for the purpose of seeing them. And this 'when it is for the purpose of seeing' has to be seen as only having 'playing of deer etc.'

as its sphere of application. However, in the context of 'the coming of the king' *rājāgamana* etc., even in the absence of application for the purpose of seeing, *ṇic* is applicable.

Pradīpa: 35.6 वा॰ 9 आरात्रिविवासमिति।

"He tells a tale until daybreak."

The meaning is 'as long or until the finishing or passing of the night, so long he tells the tale."

Nāgeśa: The sense is that *'rātri'* is the continuous period of time and the tale is the *ākhyāna* and the *karman*/object.

Because of the intransitive nature of the *dhātu vas, gatibuddhi 1.4.52* etc. applies and therefore the *karman* nature of *rātri* applies when that having a cause/*hetumat* follows.

Pradīpa: 35.8 चित्रीकरण इति।

"(*Ṇic* acts) in the sense of surprise (at reaching a place)."

Here *ṇic* is to be stated when the sense understood obtains as causing surprise or wonder.

Pradīpa: 35.10 संभावयत इति।

"Thus he thinks it is possible."

The form of this is derived from the tenth class *bhū ātmanepada,* in this sense of obtainment or attainment.

Dh.P. भू चु॰ आ॰ से॰ 1945 प्राप्तावात्मनेपदी

Pradīpa: 35.14 पुष्येणेति।

"He knows the time of the moon's conjuction with the *Puṣya* asterism."

Puṣya is the agent of the action of conjoining for that connects with the moon. In that context, *sūtra*

उभयप्राप्तौ कर्मणि 2.3.66 (कृति षष्ठी)

applies, whereby "when the agent and the object are denoted by words formed with *kṛt pratyayas* and both are employed in one sentence then the sixth case is only for the *karman*/object". Due to that restriction, in the absence of sixth case there is a third case compounded as '(पुष्यो योगक्रियायाः)'.

In that context because of the extension of 'being like the original/ *prakṛti iva,* the third case is applicable for expresseing agent. However, the *la* (tense *pratyaya*) is in fact principal, so is applicable in the sense of (principal/agent not secondary) by extended application.

Pradīpa: 35.16 प्र सामान्यकृतत्वादिति।

"(This need not be stated because *ṇic*) is taught/formed (in the sense of cause) in general."

The meaning is because of the correct forms being in fact established by the general rule alone.

Pradīpa: 35.19 देवदत्ते चेति।

"(For the nature of the cause) in *Devadatta* and (the sun is the same)."

The meaning is the nature of cause of the other is the (same) sphere (of application) as that of *Devadatta.*

Pradīpa: 36.4 परिभाषा इति।

'Reproofs'

दण्डनादिका: = verbal punishment

Pradīpa: 36.9 यदभिप्रायेष्विति।

"Since (they are) intent on (fulfilling) his intentions."

That was stated by *Bhartṛhari*

निमित्तेभ्य: प्रवर्तन्ते सर्व एव स्वभूतये।
अभिप्रायानुरोधोऽपि स्वार्थस्यैव प्रसिद्धये।। 3.7.124

"For various reasons everybody in fact acts for his own welfare. Even conforming to the wish of another is really to fulfill one's own purpose."

Pradīpa: 36.9 सज्जन्त इति।

"They are intent on"

Ātmanepada (here) because of *Patañjali's* so stating it. However, in the *Dhātu Pāṭha* it is only *parasmaipada* with *gluñcu* in the sense of movement.

Pradīpa: 36.14 चिरहत इति।

"When (*kaṅsa*) was killed long ago..."

The meaning is because of the impossibility of the quality of present time being associated with the action of prompting the killer to be sentenced to death;

Pradīpa: 36.15 शौभिका इति।

'actors' (*K.B. Lyer' T* of) *12.10.69*) 'Interpreters to the audience of the dumb actors of shadow figures.'

Kaiyaṭa: Due to the female teacher's explaining for the actors imitating *kaṅsa* and the rest.

It is intended to express in the *Bhāṣya* that by the mind of the spectators, the actor imitating *kaṅsa* is understood as *kaṇsa.*

c.f. *K. Arth. 2.27.25*

नटनर्तक प्लवकसौभिकचारणानां...

Ś. Br. 13.3.3.7.8 गन्धर्वा: युवान शोभना:

अप्सरस युववय: शोभना

Pradīpa: 36.17 ग्रन्थिकेष्विति।

"(How then) in books?"

The meaning is those who relate or recites stories.

Pradīpa: 36.17 तेऽपीति

"For they also (explain . . .by reason)."

This was stated by *Bhartṛhari*

शब्दोपहितरूपांस्तु बुद्धेर्विषयतां गतान्।
प्रत्यक्षमिव कंसादीन् साधनत्वेन मन्यते।। 3.7.5

"One thinks of *kaṅsa* and the rest, whose forms are placed before (us, i.e. represented) by words and who became the objects of the mind's eye, as being of the nature of instruments or means (for accomplishing the action), as though they were present before the eyes (in person)."

Notes

[1] यथा तनूकरणे तक्ष:।

There is some doubt as to whether it means 'like *tanūkaraṇa*' or 'unlike *tanūkaraṇa*'. See note on *Pradīpa.*

[2] स्वशब्देनोक्तत्वात्।

'because already expressed by the word itself'

c.f. उक्तार्थानामप्रयोगः 'There is non-employment of these words already expressed' *Vyādi Pari. 51.*

[3] कर्त्रोर्लेनाभिधानं प्राप्नोति।

expression of both agents obtains (though undesired) by *la.*

la is replaced by *tiṅ vibhakti pratyaya*/verbal ending

लस्य 3.4.77 तिप् तस् झि ··· महिङ् 3.4.78

Here the *ti* of *pacati*

By लः कर्मणि च भावे चाकर्मकेभ्यः। 3.4.69

"The ten tenses or mood *pratyayas* called *la* act in denoting *karman*/object and *kartṛ*/agent and after intransitive *dhātus* denote *bhāva*/abstract notion of the *dhātu* and *kartṛ* (agent)."

[4] कर्तुरीत्येव तृतीया।

'Third case alone is employed in the sense of agent.'

by कर्तृकरणयोस्तृतीया 2.3.18

'In denoting agent (*svatantraḥ kartā 1.4.54*) or instrument (*sādhakatamaṃ karaṇam 1.4.42*) when not otherwise expressed (by the verb ending) *'anabhihite' 2.3.1* the third *vibhakti pratyaya*/case is employed.'

[5] अव्यतिरिक्तो गत्यर्थः।

Not separated from the (causative) meaning 'made to go', obtains in the sense of the agent. i.e. *gam* + *ṇic* which is the base of *gamita* does contain '*gam*' which is not different from or separate from *gam* + *ṇic.*

[6] कर्तारि क्तः प्राप्नोति।

गत्यर्थ अकर्मकश्लिषशीङ्स्था

आसवसजनरूहजीर्यतिभ्यश्च 3.4.72

"The *pratyaya kta* acts in denoting the agent, act and object after verbs of motion, after intransitive *dhātus* and after the *dhātu* implying *sthā* (stand), *ās* (sit), *vas* (dwell), *jan* (be born), *ruḥ* (mount), and *jṝ* (grow old);" but in fact by

गतिबुद्धिप्रत्यवसानार्थशब्दकर्माकर्मकाणामणिकर्ता स णौ। 1.4.52

"For *dhātus* having the sense of motion, knowledge or information and eating, and for those that have a literary work as object and for intransitive *dhātus* that which was agent in the non-causal state is called *karman* in the causative state when followed by *ṇi.*"

[7] तस्मिन्नीप्सा। 'He has a desire related to him'

कर्तुरीप्सिततमं कर्म। 1.4.49

"That which is most desired to be obtained for the benefit of the agent, is the *karman*/object in relation to the action."

[8] द्वितीयाचतुर्थ्यौं न प्राप्नुत:। The second and fourth cases do not obtain.

Pradīpa: The sense is that both the village and the one prompted are *karman*/object of that *dhātu* having the *ṇi*/causative meaning.

[8] षष्ठी न प्राप्नोति।

The sense is because of the meaning of *ṇi*/causative having or expressing the nature of *karman.* However, it is because of resorting to *kṛ* there is augment *su-ṭ* even when the *pratyaya ṇi* has arisen and because of the proximity of its form, sixth case is established; for that has not impelled or caused to move.

कर्तृकर्मणो: कृति 2.3.65

"The sixth case *pratyaya* acts after a word in denoting the agent and the object when used along with a *kṛt* (*kṛd-atiṅ 3.1.93*) *pratyaya.*"

2.32.22 c.f. भावकर्मतिङ् सि 2765

द्विकर्मनानाम्

प्रयोज्यकर्मण्यन्येषां ण्यन्तानां लादयो मता:।

"For other causative *dhātus* with two objects the *la* etc. (tense *pratyayas*) are added in relation to the *prayojya* or 'subordinate' object.

[10] प्रापीति।

"When (there is) suspense at reaching (*ṇic*)."

by वा॰ 9 (on 3.3.108) संपदादिभ्य: क्विप्

उ in sense of भाव

similarly ज्ञि in वा॰ 11

[11] कंसकर्षण्य c.f. *V.1* कन्यस्य कृष्णस्य च

शब्द गड्डुमात्रम् c.f. *V.1* गडडमात्रम्

कण्ड्वादिभ्यो यक् ॥ ॥ 3 । 1 । 27 ॥

Pāṇini 3.1.27: The *pratyaya yak* acts after *kaṇḍu* and the rest (scratching/itching).

37.2 किमर्थः ककारः[1]। गुणवृद्धिप्रत्षेधार्थः। ङि्कतीति[2] गुणवृद्धिप्रत्षेधो यथा स्यात्।
नैतदस्ति प्रयोजनम्। सार्वधातुकार्धधातुकयोरङ्गस्य गुण उच्यते धातोश्चविहितः
प्रत्ययः शेष आर्धधातुकसंज्ञायां लभते न चायं धातोर्विधीयते। कण्ड्वादीनि
37.5 हि प्रातिपदिकानि।

Bhāṣya: What is the purpose of the letter *k*? (The purpose is) for the prohibition of *guṇa* and *vṛddhi*. So that the prohibition of *guṇa* and *vṛddhi* should be applicable.

This is not the purpose. *Guṇa* is stated for an *aṅga*/base followed by a *sārvadhātuka* or an *ārdhadhātuka pratyaya,* and the *pratyaya* (ordained after a *dhātu*) which is one of the remainder (of *pratyayas* other than those called *tiṅ* (verbal endings) or those having an indicatory *ś/śit*) receives the technical name *ārdhadhātuka* and this (*pratyaya yak*) is not ordained after a *dhātu,* for *kaṇḍu* and the rest are *prātipadikas*/crude bases.

37.6 कण्ड्वादिभ्यो वावचनम् ॥ 1 ॥

Vārttika 1: After *kaṇḍu* and the rest, (*yak*) (acts) optionally.

37.7 कण्ड्वादिभ्यो वेति वक्तव्यम्॥

Bhāṣya: It should be stated that (*yak*) optionally acts after *kaṇḍu* and the rest.

37.8 अवचने हि नित्यप्रत्ययत्वम् ॥ 2 ॥

Vārttika 2: For when (this option) is not stated, the *pratyaya* (*yak*) invariably/*nitya* must be applicable.

37.9 अक्रियमाणे हि वावचने नित्यः प्रत्ययविधिः प्रसज्येत॥ तत्र को दोषः।

Bhāṣya: For when the word *vā*/optionally is produced (in the *sūtra*) the invariable *pratyaya* rule would be applicable. What fault is there (in that)?

37.10 तत्र धातुविधितुक्प्रतिषेधः ॥ 3 ॥

Vārttika 3: There (in the context of the *sūtra*) is prohibition of *tuk āgama*/augment and of the *dhātu* rule.

37.11 तत्र धातुविधेस्तुकश्च प्रतिषेधो वक्तव्यः स्यात्। कण्ड्वौ कण्ड्वः। अचि श्नुधातुभ्रुवां य्वोरियङुवङौ (6.4.77) इत्युवङादेशः प्रसज्येत। इह च कण्ड्वा कण्ड्वे नोङ्धात्वोः (6.1.175) इति प्रतिषेधः प्रसज्येत।। तुक्च प्रतिषेद्धव्यः। वल्गुः

37.14 मन्तुरिति। ह्रस्वस्य पिति कृति तुक्प्राप्नोति।।

Bhāṣya: There it should be said that there is prohibition of the *dhātu* rule and of the *āgama tuk* (= *t* added to the final of what precedes).

(If *kaṇḍu* has the name *dhātu* then the following examples) *kaṇḍv-au* and *kaṇḍv-aḥ uv-an ādeśa*/subsitute would be applicable (instead of the correct *ādeśa* by *iko yaṇ aci 6.1.77*) by *aci śnu dhātu bhruvām yvor iyaṅ uvaṅau 6.4.77* "In the presence of a *pratyaya* beginning with a vowel, in the place of the *u*, of the fifth class *vikaraṇa śnu*, of the final short or long *i* or *u* of a *dhātu* and in the place of the *ū* of *bhrū*, *iy-aṅ* = *iy*) v for *i* or *ī* and *uv-aṅ* (= *uv* for *u* or *ū*) are the *ādeśas*".

And here *kaṇḍv-ā* (by the itching) and *kaṇḍv-e* (for the itch) would have been applicable to them. The prohibition of *udātta* for the *vibhakti pratyaya* by *noṅ dhātvoḥ 6.1.175* ("After the semi-vowel *ādeśas* of the *udātta ū* (feminine *pratyaya* by *ūṅ-utaḥ" 4.1.66*) or of the *udātta* final vowels of *dhātus* when preceded by a consonant, the *bha*/weak case endings beginning with a vowel do not take the *udātta*/acute accent"), (would have been applicable if *kaṇḍu* had the name *dhātu*).

And *t-uk* (*āgama*/augment) is to be prohibited (in the case of) *valguḥ* "handsome, beautiful" and *mantuḥ* (advice, fault, transgression etc. in the *kaṇḍvādi gaṇa*) *tuk āgama*/augment obtains by *hrasvasya piti kṛti tuk 6.1.71* "*T-uk* is the *āgama* for the final short vowel (of a *dhātu*) in the presence of *kṛt pratyaya* with an indicatory *it p*".

37.15 ह्रस्वयलोपौ च ।। 4 ।।

Vārttika 4: And there is a short vowel (for *kaṇḍu* etc.) and *lopa* of the *ya*.

37.16 ह्रस्वयलोपौ च वक्तव्यौ स्याताम्। वल्गुः मन्तुरिति। किमर्थमिदं न ह्रस्व एवायमन्तरङ्गत्वात्। अकृद्यकार इति दीर्घत्वं प्राप्नोति। यलोपः। यलोपश्चवक्तव्यः। कण्डूः वल्गुः मन्तुरिति। किमर्थमिदं न वलीत्येव सिद्धम्। वली-

37.19 त्युच्यते न चात्र वलादिं पश्यामः। ननु च क्वब्वलादिः।

Bhāṣya: It should be stated 'let there be a short vowel (for *kaṇḍu* etc.) and *lopa* of *ya* (*yak*). (Short vowel thus) *valguḥ, mantuḥ*.

What is the puprpose of this (statement)? Is it not already short? Because of being *antaraṅga,* the letter *ya* (= *yak*) being not a *kṛt pratyaya,* lengthening of the final vowel of the *aṅga*/stem obtains.

(Therefore short must be stated.) Further, there is *lopa* elision of *ya,* and *lopa* elision of *ya* should be stated (as in the *prātipadika* forms) *kaṇḍuḥ mantuḥ* and *valguḥ.* What is the purpose of this? Is it not established (already) by the vowel rule that when *val* (*pratyāhāra* of all consonants except *y*) follows there is *lopa* of *y* (c.f. *lopo vyor-vali 6.1.66*) "There is *lopa* elision of *v* and *y* in the presence of a *val* (any consonant except *y*)"?

When *val* follows we do not see anything beginning with a *val* (but rather *ya*) *lopa* of *y* is stated. But surely *kvip* is beginning with a *val.*

37.19 .... क्विब्लोपे कृते वलाद्यभावान्न प्राप्नोति। इदमिह संप्रधार्यम्। क्विब्लोपः क्रियतां वलि लोप इति किमत्र कर्तव्यम्। परत्वात्क्विब्लोपः। नित्यःखल्वपि क्विब्लोपः। कृतेऽपि यलोपे प्राप्नोत्यकृतेऽपि प्राप्नोति। नित्यत्वात्परत्वाच्च क्विब्लोपे कृते वलाद्यभावान्न प्राप्नोति।

37.23 एवं तर्हि प्रत्ययलक्षणेन भविष्यति। वर्णाश्रये नास्ति प्रत्ययलक्षणम्।।

Because of the absence of a (form) beginning with *val* (the *sūtra*) does not obtain. Here this should be deliberated upon whether there is to be effected *kvip-lopa*/elision or a *lopa* when *val* follows. What is to be done here? Because of the *kvip* (*lopa*) rule being subsequent (*lopo vyor vali 6.1.66*) *kvip lopa* is elided. *Kvip lopa* is also indeed a *nitya*/invariable rule/operation. Even when *ya lopa* occurs (*kvip lopa*) obtains (and) when *ya lopa* has not been effected it (still) obtains, when *kvip lopa* has been effected. Because of being a *nitya* (invariable) rule and being subsequent, and because of the absence of initial *val,* (*lopa vyor-vali 6.1.67*) does not obtain. Well then by (*pratyaya lope*) *pratyaya lakṣaṇam* (*1.1.62*) "When *lopa* elision of a *pratyaya* has taken place the *pratyaya* still exerts its influence, and the operations dependent on it take place as if it were present manifestly", (the *lopa*) will still be applicable. (But) "When there is a grammatical operation dependent upon letter (rules and causes/*nimitta*), there is no *pratyaya lakṣaṇa*". (*Paribhāṣā 21*).

38.1 अथ क्रियमाणेऽपि वावचने यदा यगन्तात्क्विप्तदैते दोषाः कस्मान्न भवन्ति। नैतेभ्यस्तदा क्विब्द्रक्ष्यते। किं कारणम्। अन्येभ्योऽपि दृश्यते। (3.2.178) इत्युच्यते न चैतेभ्यस्तदा क्विब्दृश्यते। यथैव तर्हि क्रियमाणे वावचनेऽन्येभ्योऽपि दृश्यत इत्येवमत्र क्विब्न भवत्येवमक्रियमाणेऽपि न भविष्यति। अवश्यमेतेभ्यस्तदा

38.5 क्विबेषितव्यः। किं प्रयोजनम्। एतानि रूपाणि यथा स्युरिति।।

Now even when the *vā*/optionally is expressed, when *kvip* (acts) after that ending in *yak,* then how can there not be these faults? Then, *kvip* will not be seen after these. What is the reason? Thus it is stated, *anyebhyo'pi dṛśyate 3.2.178* "The *pratyaya kvip* is seen after other *dhātus* also besides those previously mentioned, in the sense of the Agent having such a habit etc.", and so then *kvip* is not seen after these.

As in fact then, when the expression of *vā*/optionality is effected, so here the *sūtra* (*anyebhyo'pi dṛśyate 3.2.178*) is not applicable, so even (when the expression of *vā*/optionality is not being effected), (*kvip*) will not be applicable.

It is essential that the *kvip* be sought (i.e. approved) after these. What is the purpose?

So that these forms (*kaṇḍuḥ* etc) be possible (as valid forms).

38.6 तत्तर्हि वावचनं कर्तव्यम्। न कर्तव्यम्। उभयं कण्ड्वादीनि धातवश्चैव प्रातिपदिकानि च। आतश्चोभयं कण्डूयतीति क्रियां कुर्वाणे प्रयुज्यतेऽस्ति मे कण्डूरिति वेदनामात्रस्य सांनिध्ये।।

Then that expression of *vā*/optionally must be made? No, it does not have to be made. *Kaṇḍu* and the rest are both *dhātus* and *prātipadikas.* And indeed they are both for the sake of usage. '*kaṇḍū-ya-ti*', "He scratches" (*yak*) is applicable when the verb is being formed; (and) '*asti me kaṇḍūḥ*', 'I have an itch/scratch"; when there is a mere sensation (of an itch).

38.9 अपर आह।

And others say in a *śloka vārttika*:

38.10 धातुप्रकरणाद्धातुः कस्य चासञ्जनादपि।
आह चायमिमं दीर्घं मन्ये धातुर्विभाषितः[3]।।

Śloka Vārttika: "(What ends in *yak*) is called *dhātu* because of (being in the sphere of) the *dhātu adhikāra*/governing rule, and because of the (indicatory) *k* attached (to prevent *guṇa* and *vṛddhi*).

And he states this with long *ū* (of *kaṇḍū*) "I think (these) *dhātus* are optionally designated".

Pradīpa

Pradīpa: कण्ड्वादिभ्यो वावचनमिति।

To show a purpose of the letter *k* he alludes to another matter. The meaning is 'when the *kaṇḍū* and the rest are called *prātipadika* that should be stated as optional (otherwise) they are called *dhātus.*'

Pradīpa: तत्र को दोष इति।

What fault (in *yak* being *nitya*)?

The sense is that *kaṇḍū* and the rest are established as valid (*prātipadika*) forms by *kvip pratyaya* even when the *pratyaya yak* is treated as *nitya*/ invariable.

Pradīpa: तत्रेति।

"There (in the *sūtra*) is prohibition of *āgama* and the name *dhātu.*"

He says this in order to show that the desired form is not establihsed as valid by means of *kvip* (alone). When the *pratyaya kvip* is ordained after the word *kaṇḍūya* there is not the condition of being like the original, for the *lopa* in place of *a,* when *uvaṅ ādeśa* is to be effected (by 3.4.77). "When *kvi* follows the *lup* elision is not like the original,"

'उण' 'क्वौ लुप्तं न स्थानिवत्'

व्किक्तुगुपद्यात्वचडपरहासकुत्वेडक संख्यानम्।। वा॰ 2 न पदान्त 1.1.58

"Because of the prohibition of *sthānivatva* when there is *luk kvip,* penultimate vowel, *caṇ* (aorist) or shortening of a vowel of a guttural substitute." Now then, even if because of *lopa a* of *ya* being treated like the original, *sthānivat,* there were *uvañ,* still *ūṭh* will be effected in place of the *v* (by *6.3.19*). When *ūṭh* is to be effected by 'having a *v* prior to an indicated vowel', there is absence of *sthānivatva.*

Hence *uvaṅ āgama* is not applicable in place of *ūṭa* and in that context *uvaṅ* (wrongly) obtains after the word *kaṇḍū* when two things made of gold follow.

However by ओ: सुपि 6.4.83

"When *sup*/case *pratyaya* follows beginning with a vowel then the semivowel *v* is *ādeśa* for the final *ū* of a stem containing more than one syllable, if it ends in a *dhātu* ending in *ū* not preceded by a conjunct consonant forming part of the *dhātu.*"

So *yaṅ ādeśa* is stated for that not preceded by a consonant.

37.10 क्वौ किमुदाहरणम्।

कण्डूयतेरप्रत्यया

कण्डूरिति।

नैतदस्ति।

यलोपविधिं न स्थानिवत्।

कण्डूय क्विप् अन्येभ्योऽपि दृश्यन्ते 3.2.178

वरेपृक्तस्य 6.1.67 (लोप) उपदेशे 1.3.2

हलन्त्यम् 1.31.3 लशक्व 1.3.8

तस्य लोपः 1.3.9

but क्विबन्ताद्धातुत्वं न त्यजन्ति

यलोप लोपो व्योर्वलि 6.1.66

"There is *lopa* elision of *v* and *y* in the presence of (any consonant except *y* =) *val.*"

Pradīpa: 37.17 अकृद्यकार इति दीर्घत्वं प्राप्नोति।

There is अकृत्सार्वधातुकयोदीर्घः 7.4.25

"The long vowel acts in place of the final vowel of an *aṅga* in the presence of *pratyaya* beginning with a *ya* and having an indicatory *k* or *ṅ* when it is neither a *kṛt* nor *sārvadhātuka pratyaya.*"

Pradīpa: 37.22 नित्यत्वात्परत्वाच्चेति

(When *kvip* has been effected) because of being a *nitya*/invariable rule (and being *para*/subsequent).

Lopo vyor vali 6.1.66 does not obtain. This is stated 'having resorted to' the rule before *verapṛktasya 6.1.67*

"(*Lopa* of the *vi* reduced to a single consonant)", namely लोपो व्योर्वलि so that when a *val* follows there is *lopa* of the *v* (if present).

Pradīpa: 37.23 वर्णाश्रय इति

"When there is a grammatical operation dependent on letter (rules and causes) there is not *pratyaya lakṣaṇa* (operational effect)."

The resort to the letter rule *'lopo vyor vali'* means *lopa* of *v* and *y* but not resort to the *pratyaya* (e.g. *kvip*). However, when the view expressing option/*vā* is taken, due to non-production of *yak* (the form becomes established as desired).

Pradīpa: 38.2 'नैतेभ्य इति'।

"(Then *kvip* will) not (be seen) after these."

The sense is, because of ordaining *kvip* in the sense of agent and because of the meaning of agent not being understood as (applicable to) *kaṇḍūh.*

Pradīpa: 38.4 'अवश्यमिति'।

"It is essential (*kvip* be sought/approved after these)."

The sense is, *'kvip'* should be effected in the sense of abstract action/*bhāve*, because of (falling within the scope of the *vārttika 9*).

'संपदादिभ्यः क्विप' 3.3.108

Pradīpa: 38.8 वेदनामात्रस्येत्ति।

"(When there is) a mere <u>sensation</u> (of an itch) and (here) the word *vedanā* is understood as having the form of a substantive (i.e. sensation of feeling) not something to be accomplished (e.g. making known).

कमेर्णिङ् ॥ 3 । 1 । 30 ॥

Pāṇini 3.1.30: The *pratyaya ṇiṅ* acts after the *dhātu kam* (to desire).

38.13 किमर्थोऽयं णकारः वृद्ध्यर्थः। ञ्णितीति वृद्धिर्यथा स्यात्। क्रियमाणेऽपि
वै णकारे वृद्धिर्न प्राप्नोति। किं कारणम्। क्ङिति च (1.1.5) इति प्रतिषेधात्।
38.15 णित्करणसामर्थ्याद्भविष्यति।। अत उत्तरं पठति।

Bhāṣya: What is the purpose of the letter *ṇ*? For the purpose of (causing) *vṛddhi* so that (by *ata upadhāyāḥ 7.2.116*) (*ñin it-i*) "*Vṛddhi* acts in the place of the penultimate short *a* of an *aṅga*/base when in the presence of a *pratyaya* having an indicatory *ñ* or *ṇ*" and so that here there should be *vṛddhi* (of *kam*). Even when the letter *ṇ* (indicatory) is being produced, *vṛddhi* does not obtain. What is the reason? Because of the prohibition "*kṅ-it-i ca*" (*1.1.5*) "And that which otherwise would have caused *guṇa* or *vṛddhi* does not do so when it has an indicatory *k* or *ṅ*" It will be applicable (here) by force of (specific) formation (of the *pratyaya* with an *it ṅ*). Therefore he reads as follows:

38.16 णिङि णित्करणस्य सावकाशत्वाद्वृद्धिप्रतिषेधप्रसङ्गः।। 1 ।।

Vārttika 1: In respect of the presence of *ṇiṅ* (*pratyaya*) there is occasion for the prohibition on *vṛddhi* because of the producing of the indicatory *ṇ* (of *ṇiṅ*) having scope of application elsewhere.

38.17 णिङि णित्करणं सावकाशम् कोऽवकाशः। सामान्यग्रहणार्थो णकारः। क्व
सामान्यग्रहणार्थेनार्थः। णेरनिटि (6.4.51) इति। णिङि णित्करणस्य सावकाश-
त्वाद्वृद्धेः प्रतिषेधः प्राप्नोति।। ङित्करणमपि तर्हि सावकाशम्। कोऽवकाशः।
38.20 सामान्यग्रहणाविधातार्थो ङकारः। क्व सामान्यग्रहणाविधातार्थेनार्थः। अत्रैव।

Bhāṣya: In respect of *ṇiṅ pratyaya* the indicatory *ṇ* (of *ṇiṅ*) has scope of application elsewhere. What scope of application has it? The letter *ṇ* is for the purpose of inclusion on *ṇiṅ* in a general (group of *pratyayas*). Where is the purpose of 'including it with a general (group of *pratyayas*)' served? (In the *sūtra*) *ṇer-an-iṭ-i 6.4.51* "*Lopa* acts in place of the *i* of the *pratyaya ṇiṅ* (the *ṇ* and *ṅ* which are both indicatory/*it*) in the presence of an *ārdhadhātuka pratyaya* i.e. other than a *tiṅ* or a *śit pratyaya* (*ārdhadhātukaṃ śeṣaḥ 3.4.114*)".

Because of their being scope of application for the indicatory *ṇ* in *ṇiṅ* produced (here), prohibition of *vṛddhi* obtains.

Then the producing of indicatory *ṅ* also has scope of application elsewhere. The letter *ṅ* is not for preventing the application of the general reference to (*ṅ*). Where is purpose of it not preventing the application of the general reference served? Just here (namely *ṇeraniṭi 6.4.51*).

38.20 ....शक्यो-
ऽत्र सामान्यग्रहणाविधातार्थेऽन्योऽनुबन्ध आसङ्क्तुम्। तत्र ङकारानुरोधाद्वृद्धि-
प्रतिषेधः प्राप्नोति। अवश्यमत्रात्मनेपदार्थो ङकारोऽनुबन्ध आसङ्क्तव्यो ङित
इत्यात्मनेपदं[1] यथा स्यात्। एवमप्युभयोः सावकाशयोः प्रतिषेधबलीय-स्त्वात्प्रतिषेधः[2]
प्राप्नोति। एवं तर्ह्याचार्यप्रवृत्तिर्ज्ञापयति न कमेर्वृद्धिप्रतिषेधो भवतीति यदयं न
38.25 कम्यमिचमामिति मित्संज्ञायाः प्रतिषेधं शास्ति।

Here it is possible to attach another *anubandha* (indicatory letter) for not preventing the application of the general reference (*ṅ*). Therefore because of the (specific) reference to the letter *ṅ*, prohibition of *vṛddhi* obtains.

It is essential here that the letter *ṅ* be attached as *anubandha* for the puropse of *ātmanepada* (*pratyayas*) so that having an *it ṅ* there should be *ātmanepada.*

Then also, when both these have scope of application elsewhere, because of prohibition being stronger, prohibition obtains.

Well then the master's usage makes known that there is no prohibition of *vṛddhi.*

Since (the *gaṇa sūtra* in the *dhātu pāṭha*) teaches prohibition of the technical name *m-it* by stating the rule *mit sañjñā,* prohibition is not applicable for *kam-i* (*am* and *cam dhātus* in the *bhvādi gaṇa*) "*na kamyamicām*".

39.1 मित्प्रतिषेधस्य चार्थवत्त्वात् ।। 2 ।।

Vārttika 2: And (there is prohibition of *vṛddhi*) because of *m-it* prohibition having a purpose (elsewhere).

39.2 मित्प्रतिषेधस्य चार्थवत्त्वात्प्रतिषेधः प्राप्नोति। अर्थवान्मित्प्रतिषेधः कोऽर्थः। णिङन्तस्य णिचि या वृद्धिस्तस्या ह्रस्वत्वं [3] मा भूदिति। नन्वेतस्या अपि क्ङिति चेति प्रतिषेधेन भवितव्यम्। न भवितव्यम्। उक्तमेतत् क्ङिति प्रतिषेधे तन्नि-
39.5 मित्तग्रहणमिति [4]।।

Bhāṣya: And because of *m-it* prohibition having purpose (elsewhere), prohibition of *vṛddhi* obtains. Prohibition of *m-it* has a purpose (elsewhere). What is the purpose? So that the *vṛddhi* (which acts in the sense of the penultimate short *a* of an *aṅga*/base) ending in the *pratyaya ṇiṅ* when *ṇic* follows, should not become a short vowel. (c.f. '*hetu-mati ca*' *3.1.26*) (*ṇic*) '*ata upadhāyāḥ*' *7.2.116* (*vṛddhi, ñ-ṇ-it-i*) '*mitāṃ hrasvaḥ*' *6.4.92.* "The *dhātus* having an indicatory *m* (*800-873* of the *bhvādigaṇa*) retain their penultimate short vowel before the causative *ṇi*".

Surely even for this the prohibition *kṅ-it-i-ca* (*1.1.5*) ("And that which otherwise would have caused *guṇa* or *vṛddhi* does not do so, when it has an indicatory *k, g* or *ṅ*") should be applicable. It should not be applicable. This has been stated (in *Vā. 1* and *2* of *1.1.5*), "When there is prohibition of (*guṇa* or *vṛddhi*) when that having *anubandha k, g* or *ṅ* follows specific mention of *nimitta*/cause (should be made)".

39.5 .... एवं तर्हि न ण्िङन्तस्य णिचि या वृद्धिस्तस्या ह्रस्वत्वं प्राप्नोति। किं कारणम्। णिङा व्यवहितत्वात्। लोपे कृते [5] नास्ति व्यवधानम्। स्थानिवद्भावाद्व्यवधानमेव।। ण्िङ्येव तर्हि मा भूदिति। णिङि च न प्राप्नोति। किं कारणम्। असिद्धं बहिरङ्गलक्षणमन्तरङ्गलक्षण इति।। नैव वा पुनर्णिङन्तस्य
39.9 णिचि वृद्धिः प्राप्नोति। किं कारणम्।

Well then short for that *vṛddhi* acting in place of (the short *a* of that *aṅga*) ending in the *pratyaya ṇic* when *ṇic* follows, (by *mitāṃ hrasvaḥ 6.4.92*) does not obtain. What is the reason?

Because of being separated by (the presence of) *ṇiṅ pratyaya,* when *lopa* is effected (by *ṇeraniṭi 6.4.51*), there is no intervention. Because of the substitute/*ādeśa* being like the original/*sthānivat,* there is no intervention. Then when *ṇic* alone follows it should not be applicable. And when *ṇiṅ* follows it does not obtain. What is the reason? *asiddham bahiraṅgalakṣaṇam antaraṅgalakṣaṇe* "That which is *bahiraṅga* (expecting more conditions or operations) is (regarded as) not having taken effect (or as not existing). When that which is *antar-aṅga* (inner, expecting less conditions) is to take effect". (*Pari. 50*)

Nor indeed again does *vṛddhi* obtain when *ṇic* follows for that which ends in the *pratyaya ṇic.* What is the reason?

39.9 .... णिङा व्यवहितत्वात्। लोपे कृते नास्ति व्यवधानम्। स्थानिवद्भावाद्व्यवधानमेव[6]।। इदं तर्हि प्रयोजनं यत्तच्चिण्णमुलोर्दीर्घोऽन्यतरस्याम् (6.4.93) इति दीर्घत्वं तत्कमेर्णिङि मा भूदिति। किं पुनः कारणं

39.12 तत्र दीर्घोऽन्यतरस्यामित्युच्यते न ह्रस्वोऽन्यतरस्याम् मित्येवोच्येत।

Because of the intervention by *ṇiṅ* when *lopa* elision is effected there is no intervention. In fact because of *lopa* elision being *'sthānivat'* (like the original), by (*sthānivat ādeśaḥ*) "*acaḥ parasmin pūrvavidhau*" (*1.1.57*), "A substitute/*ādeśa* in the place of a vowel caused by something which follows, should be regarded as that whose place it takes when a rule would otherwise take effect on what stands prior to the original vowel", there is intervention.

This then is the purpose (of prohibition) that the lengthening which is taught by (the *sūtra*) *ciṅ-ṇamulo dīrgho 'nyatarasyām 6.4.93;* "Optionally a long vowel acts in place of the penultimate of the causative of *m-it dhātus* before *pratyaya ciṇ* (*prathama puruṣa*/third person singular of passive aorist) and before the *pratyaya ṇamul* (absolutive)", should not be applicable here for (the *a* of) *kam* (to desire) when *ṇiṅ pratyaya* follows. But again, what is the reason why there (in the *sūtras*) lengthening optionally . . . is stated and shortening optionally is not stated ?

39.12 .... यथाप्राप्तं चापि कमेर्ह्रस्वत्वमेव। तत्रायमप्यर्थो ह्रस्वग्रहणं न कर्तव्यं भवति प्रकृतमनुवर्तते। क्व प्रकृतम्। मितां ह्रस्वः (92) इति। का रूपसिद्धिः अशमि अशामि शमं शमम् शामं शामम्। वृद्ध्या सिद्धम्। न सिध्यति। नोदात्तोपदेशस्य मान्तस्यानाचमेः

39.16 (7.3.34) इति वृद्धिप्रतिषेधः प्राप्नोति। चिण्कृतोः स प्रतिषेधो न णिचि।

And also in conformity with a previous rule (i.e. regularity) there is in fact a short vowel (ordained) for *kam-i* (by *mitāṃ hrasvaḥ 6.4.92*). There also this is the meaning, that mention of the word *hrasva* need not be made (because) the original (word *hrasva*) follows on (by *anuvṛtti* from a previous *sūtra*). Where is the original *hrasva*? (In the *sūtra*) *mitāṃ hrasvaḥ 6.4.92* ("*Dhātus* having an indicatory *m* retain their penultimate short vowel before the causative *ṇi*"). What form is ordained? For example *a-śam-i* or *a-śām-i* "He was caused to be quiet". *śāmam śāmam* or *śamam śāmam* "having often become quiet". It can be obtained by *vṛddhi* (i.e. lengthening). It is not obtained. The prohibition of *vṛddhi* obtains (by the *sūtra*) *nodāttopadeśasya māntasyānācameḥ 7.3.34* ("*Vṛddhi* is not *ādeśa*/substitute for the vowel of the *dhātu* which ends in *m* (e.g. *kam*) and is *udātta* acute accented (in the *dhātu pāṭha*) in the presence of the aorist *pratyaya ciṇ* or a *kṛt pratyaya* with an indicatory *ñ* or *ṇ* but not in the case of the *dhātu cam* after *upasarga ā*"). (This is not a fault). That prohibition of *vṛddhi* is before *ciṇ* or *kṛt* with *it ñ* or *ṇ*, not when *ṇic* (causative *pratyaya*) follows.

39.16 .... इदं तर्हि। अजानि
अजानि जनं जनम् जानं जानम्। जनिवध्योश्च (35) इति वृद्धि-प्रतिषेधः प्राप्नोति।
सोऽपि चिण्कृतोरेव।। णिज्व्यवहितेषु तर्हि यङ्लोपे चोपसंख्यानं कर्तव्यं स्यात्।
शमयन्तं प्रयोजितवान् अशामि अशामि शमं शमम् शामं शामम्।
39.20 शंशमयतेः अशंशमि अशंशामि शंशमं शंशमम् शंशामं शंशामम्। किं पुनः
कारणं न सिध्यति। चिण्णमुल्परे णौ मितामङगानां ह्रस्वो भवतीत्युच्यते यश्चात्र
39.22 णिश्चिण्णमुल्परो न तस्मिन्मिदङ्गं यस्मिंश्च मिदङ्गं .नासौ णिश्चिण्णमुल्परः।

This (is the reason). (The examples are) *ajāni* or *ajāni* "He was begotten", *janaṃ janam* or *jānaṃ jānam* "having often been born". Prohibition of *vṛddhi* obtains (by the *sūtra*) *jani vidhyośca 7.3.36* ("*Vṛddhi* is not the *ādeśa*/substitute for the vowels of the *dhātus jan-i* and *vadh-i* before the passive aorist sign *ciṇ pratyaya* and *kṛt pratyayas* with indicatory *ñ* or *ṇ*"). That also (applies) only when *ciṇ* or *kṛt* (*pratyayas*) follows.

There should be made additional enumeration when (several) *ṇic* (i.e. the causative of causatives) intervene then, and when *yaṅ lopa* (intensive) has occured. *śamayantaṃ prayojitavān* i.e. *aśāmi* or *aśam-i* "He compelled the one causing quietness" and *śāmaṃ śāmam* or *śamaṃ śamam* "having compelled the one causing quietness again and again". From (the intensive) *śamśamayati śamśami* or *aśamśami* "He entirely caused the one causing to be made to appeased or extinguished". (The absolutive) *śamśamaṃ śamśamam* or *śamśāmaṃ śamśāmam* "having again and again caused the causer to be entirely appeased made to appear".

But what is the reason *hrasva* is not valid/effective? When there is *ṇi* (causative) with *ciṇ* or *ṇamul* following, it is stated there is applicable a short vowel for those *aṅgas* (i.e. *dhātus* become bases). And that which is here (an *aṅga*) ending in the causative *pratyaya ṇi* with *ciṇ* or *ṇamul* following, at that time is not an *aṅga* having an *it m/mit;* and when there is (present) an *aṅga* (base) which is *mit,* then that is not one which ends in *ṅi* with *ciṅ* or *ṅamul* following.

39.22 ....णिलोपे
तर्हि कृते चिण्णमुल्परः स्थानिवद्भावान्न चिण्णमुल्परः।। अथ दीर्घोऽन्यतरस्या-
मित्युच्यमाने यावता स्थानिवद्भावः कथमेवैतत्सिध्यति। एतदिदानीं दीर्घग्रहणस्य
39.25 प्रयोजनं दीर्घविधिं प्रत्यजादेशो न स्थानिवद स्तानिवद्भावप्रतिषेधः सिद्धो भवति।।
यदा खल्वप्यायादय अर्धधातुके वा भवन्ति तदा णिची निङ्नास्ति तदर्थं च
39.27 मित्प्रतिषेधः स्यात्।। तस्मात्प्रतिषेधः प्राप्नोति।।

Then, when *lopa* elision of *ṇi* has been effected (by *ṇer-aniṭi 6.4.51*) then *ciṇ* or *ṇamul* (remain) following (the *aṅga*). Because the *ādeśa*/substitute (here *lopa*) is regarded as the original/*sthānivat* or *ciṇ* or *ṇamul* do not follow (immediately) after (the *aṅga*).

Now when it is being stated "long/*dīrgha* optionally" in so far as there is the condition of *sthānivattva* (the *ādeśa lopa* being regarded as like the *ṇi* it replaces), how in fact (can) this be valid? Now this is the purpose of mentioning "long/*dīrgha*" (by *sūtra na-padānta* etc. *1.1.58*); in relation to a "lengthening rule (the long vowel) substitute is not *sthānivat*/like the original it replaces". Thus (by that rule) the prohibition of *sthānivattva* is established as valid. Even when indeed, by the *sūtra āyādaya ārdhadhātuke vā 3.1.31* ("The *pratyaya āya* and the rest, namely *īyaṅ* and *ṇiṅ* are optionally added, when it is desired to express onself with an *ārdhadhātuka pratyaya*"), are applicable then when *ṇic* follows, there is not *ṇiṅ,* and for that reason there should be prohibition of (the technical name) *mit* (for *kam* etc.). Therefore the prohibition obtains.

40.1 उक्तं वा ।। 3 ।।

Vārttika 3: Or it was (in fact) stated (previously).

40.2 किमुक्तम्। तद्धितकाम्योरिक्प्रकरणादिति।।

Bhāṣya: What was stated? "Because of the context being *ik* (*i, u, ṛ, ḷ* vowels only), (*guṇa* and *vṛddhi* prohibition is not applicable by *kṅiti ca 1.1.5*) for *taddhita pratyayas* (in the *sūtra taddhitesvacāmādeḥ 7.2.117*) and for *kam* (*dhātu* by *ata upadhāyāḥ 7.2.116*)" i.e. *1.1.5 Vārttika 4: taddhita kāmyor ik prakaraṇāt.*

Pradīpa

Pradīpa: 39.5 णिङन्तस्येति।

"... short for the *vrddhi* acting in place of (short *a* of an *aṇga*) ending in *ṇ* or *ṅ* the *pratyaya ṇic* (when *ṇic* follows)."

Ṇic applies for one directing, or causing the one desiring (or causing anyone to love *Ṛtus*).

Pradīpa: 39.7 णिङ्येवेति

"Then when *ṇic* alone follows (short does not obtain).."

The meaning is that, 'that *vṛddhi* which has *ṇic* as its cause should not have shortening caused by *ṇiṅ;* thus the meaning should be prohibition of *mit,* so that there is no *jñāpaka* (implied rule) from *vṛddhi* caused by *ṅic.*

Pradīpa: 39.7 णिङि चेति।

"And when *ṇiṅ* follows (it does not obtain)."

Hrasvatva/shortening (should be added) to complete the sense.

39.8 असिद्धमिति। "(That which is *bahiraṅga* (expecting more operations) is regarded as not having taken effect (when that which is *antaraṅga* (having fewer conditions) is to take effect)."

The meaning is that when 'shortening' is to be effected *vṛddhi* being *bahiraṅga* is (treated as of non-effect).

Pradīpa: 39.10 स्थानिवद्भावादिति।

"Because of *lopa* elision being *sthānivat*/like the original *sthānin* (there is intervention)."

When the context is a rule concerning a penultimate letter then by *vā. 2* (on *1.1.58*) न पदान्त (क्विलुगुपधात्व) *na padānta* there is prohibition of being like the *sthānin.* It should be stated in fact, that applies only to a *pratyaya* rule.

And similarly prohibition is not applicable when *vṛddhi* is to be effected in the example here *paṭayati* (He strings together).

Pradīpa: 39.11 किं पुनरिति।

"But again, what is the reason (lengthening is optionally stated . . .)?"

The sense is, because of the prohibition of *vṛddhi* in case of *kami.* When *ṇiṅ* follows invariable shortening alone is established, so that prohibition of *mit* is not to be effected. However, being effected, only the *jñāpaka* (is applicable) for *vṛddhi* when *ṇiṅ* follows.

Pradīpa: 39.18 उपसंख्यानं कर्तव्यं स्यात् इति।

"There should be additional enumeration (when several *ṇic's* intervene).

The meaning is 'the possibility obtains of the view that (there be additonal) optional application of *vṛddhi*'.

Pradīpa: 39.24 एतदिदानीम्।

"Now this (is the purpose of mentioning *dīrgha* (long)."

And hence the prohibition of *mit* is for preventing the optional lengthening, not a *jñāpaka*/implied rule.

Pradīpa: 39.26 यदेति।

"When indeed by *3.1.31*, *ṇiṅ* is optionally added."

(आयादय आर्धधातुके वा)

The meaning is when *ṇiṅ* is effected after *kam-i* not ending in *ṇiṅ*, then there the prohibition of *mit* would be applicable for the purpose of preventing shortening.

Notes

[1] ङिति इति आत्मनेपदं।

(अनुदात्तङित आत्मनेपदम् 1.3.12) "After a *dhātu* having an indicatory *anudātta* vowel or an indicatory *ṅ* the *pratyayas* are *ātmanepada.*"

[2] प्रतिषेधबलीयस्त्वादिति।

(When both these have scope of application elsewhere) because of prohibition, being stronger (prohibition obtains).

परि 112 निषेधश्च बलीयांसः

Kaiyaṭa : The pre-eminence in strength of the prohibition is because of the prohibition's nature of barring (even *antaranga*) rules due to its *apavāda* nature.

[3] ह्रस्वत्वं।। मितां ह्रस्व 6.4.92

[4] ङ्किति प्रतिषेधे तान्निमित्तग्रहणम् 1.1.5 वा॰ 1

[5] लोपे कृते। 'णेरनिटि' 6.4.51

[6] स्थानिवदिति।।

न तदान्तद्विर्वचनवरेय लोपस्वरसवर्णानुस्वार दीर्घजश्चावृद्धिषु 1.1.58 "A vowel *ādeśa* is not *sthānivat* in rules relating to the finals of words, to the doubling of letters, to the *pratyaya varac,* to elision of *ya,* to accent, to homogeneous letters, to *anusvāra,* to the lengthening of vowels and to the substitution of *jaś* and *car* letters."

आयादय आर्धधातुके वा ॥ 3 । 1 । 31 ॥

Pāṇini 3.1.31: The *pratyaya āya* and those that follow (namely *īyaṅ* and *ṇiṅ)* optionally act when an *ārdhadhātuka pratyaya* follows.

40.4 - कथमिदं विज्ञायते।

Bhāṣya: How is this (*sūtra* to be) understood?

40.4 .... आयादिभ्यो यदार्धधातुकं तस्मिन्नवस्थिते वायादीनां निवृत्ति-र्भवतीति। आहोस्विदायादिप्रकृतेर्यदार्धधातुकं तस्मिन्नवस्थिते वायादीनामुत्पत्ति-र्भवतीति। किं गतमेतदियता सूत्रेणाहोस्विदन्यतरस्मिन्पक्षे भूयः सूत्रं कर्तव्यम्। गतमित्याह। कथम्। यदा तावदायादिभ्यो यदार्धधातुकम् तस्मिन्नवस्थिते वायादीनां निवृत्तिर्भवतीति तदा विशेषेण सर्वमायादिप्रकर-णमनुक्रम्यायादय आर्धधातुके वेत्युच्यते। यदाप्यायादिप्रकृतेर्यदार्धधातुकं तस्मिन्नवस्थिते वायादीनामुत्पत्तिर्भवतीति

40.10 तदैकं वाक्यं तच्चेदं च। गुपूधूपविच्छिपणिपनिभ्यः आयः (28) आर्धधातुके वा। ऋतेरियङ् (29) आर्धधातुके वा। कमेर्णिङ् (30) आर्धधातुके वेति।। कश्चात्र

40.12 विशेषः।

Either, when that *ārdhadhātuka pratyaya* which acts after *āya* and the rest is present, optionally there is the cessation of *āya* and the rest, or when that *ārdhadhātuka pratyaya* which acts after bases ending in *āya* and the rest, is actually present, there is optionally arising of *āya* and the rest. Is this understood by such a *sūtra* or in the alternative view, should another *sūtra* be formed? He says it is understood. How? When (it is stated) as above "when that *ārdhadhātuka pratyaya* which acts after *āya* and the rest is present, optionally there is cessation of *āya* and the rest"; then without distinction having enumerated all the section of (*sūtras* ordaining) *āya* and the rest, the *sūtra āyādaya ārdhadhātuka vā* is uttered. Also, when (it is stated as above) "when that *ārdhadhātuka pratyaya* which acts after bases ending in *āya* and the rest is actually present, there is optionally arising of *āya* and the rest", then there is a single sentence comprising this and that (which follows).

gupū-dhūpa-vicchi-paṇi pani-bhya āyaḥ 3.1.28 (ārdhadhātuka vā) "The *pratyaya āya* acts after the *dhātus gup* (to protect), *dhūp* (to heat), *paṇi* (to contract and to praise), and *pan* (to praise) optionally when an *ārdhadhātuka pratyaya* follows".

ṛter īyaṅ 3.1.29 (*ārdhadhātuka vā*) "The *pratyaya īyaṅ* acts after the *dhātu ṛti* (to reproach), optionally when an *ārdhadhātuke vā pratyaya* follows".

kamer ṇiṅ 3.1.30 (*ārdhadhātuka vā*) "The *pratyaya ṇiṅ* acts after the *dhātu kam* (to desire) optionally when an *ārdhadhātuke vā pratyaya* follows".

What is the difference between these two interpretations?

40.13 आयादिभ्यो यदार्धधातुकमायादिप्रकृतेर्यदार्धधातुकमिति
चोभयथानिष्ट-प्रसङ्गः ॥ 1 ॥

Vārttika 1: Both the (following positions) (give rise to) an undesired contingency: "When that *ārdhadhātuka pratyaya* which acts after *āya* and the rest (is present there is cessation of *āya* etc. optionally) and (when that) *ārdhadhātuka pratyaya* which acts after the bases ending in *āya* and the rest is present, there is arising of *āya* etc. optionally.

40.15 आयादिभ्यो तदार्धधातुकमायादिप्रकृतेर्यदार्धधातुकमिति चोभयथानिष्टं प्राप्नोति।
यदि विज्ञायत आयादिभ्यो यदार्धधातुकं तस्मिन्नवस्थिते वायादीनां निवृत्तिर्भव तीति
गुप्तिः जुगोपेति चेष्टं न सिध्यति। इदं चानिष्टं प्राप्नोति गोपांचकार गोपेति
40.18 च। इदं तावदिष्टं सिद्धं भवति गोपायांचकार गोपायेति[1]॥

Bhāṣya: An *ārdhadhātuka* (*pratyaya*) which acts after *āya* and the rest 'or' an *ārdhadhātuka* which acts after the bases (ending in) *āya* and the rest; both these obtain as undesired possibilities.

If (the meaning of the *sūtra*) is understood as "when an *ārdhadhātuka pratyaya* that acts after the *pratyaya āya* and the rest is present, the optional cessation of *pratyaya āya* and the rest is applicable", the desired form *guptiḥ* (protecting) and *jugopa* (protected) do not become established as valid and these understood forms obtain *gopām cakāra* ("He protected") and *gopā* (protector).

40.18 .... अथ विज्ञायत आया-
दिप्रकृतेर्यदार्धधातुकं तस्मिन्नवस्थिते वायादीनामुत्पत्तिर्भवतीति गुप्तिः जुगोपेति चेष्टं
सिद्धं भवति। इदं चानिष्टं प्राप्नोति गोपांचकार गोपेति। इदं त्विष्टं न सिध्यति
40.21 गोपायांचकार गोपायेति।।

Now then (the *sūtra*) is understood (also to mean) "When an *ārdhadhātuka pratyaya* which acts after a base ending in *āya* or the rest is present optionally there is arising of *āya* and the rest". The desired forms *gupti* and *jugopa* become established as valid. And these undesired forms do not obtain, *gopāṃ cakāra* and *gopā*. However, these are not established: *gopāyāṃ cakāra* and *gopāya*.

40.21 .... इदं तावदिष्टं सिध्यति गोपायांचकारेति। कथम्
अस्त्वत्रायादिप्रकृतेर्यदार्धधातुकं लिट् तस्मिन्नवस्थिते वायादय आम्मध्ये पतिष्यति
40.23 यथा विकरणास्तद्वत्।। इदं तर्हीष्टं न सिध्यति गोपायेति।।

Just this form is established as valid: *gopāyāṃcakāra*. How? Let there be here the *ārdhadhātuka pratyaya liṭ* (perfect) after a base ending in *āya* and the rest. When that is present (in the mind), optionally *āya* and the rest (arise), and *ām* will fall/come in the middle like a *vikaraṇa pratyaya*. Then this desired form is not established, namely '*gopāya*'.

40.24 सिद्धं तु सार्वधातुके नित्यवचनादनाश्रित्य वाविधानम् ।। 2 ।।

Vārttika 2: However it is established that when a *sārvaradhātuka pratyaya* follows (or is determined upon in the mind), because of not having resorted to (the use of the word) *vā*, there is (automatically) *nitya*/invariable ordaining of *āya* and the rest.

40.25 सिद्धमेतत्। कथम्। अविशेषेणायादीनां वाविधिमुक्तवा सार्वधातुके नित्यमिति
वक्ष्यामि।।

Bhāṣya: This is established (already). How? Having expressed the optional rule for *āya* and the rest without a specific restriction, I shall say invariable/ *nitya* when a *sārvaradhātuka pratyaya* follows.

41.1 स्यादिबलीयस्त्वं तु विप्रतिषेधेन तुल्यनिमित्तत्वात् ।। 3 ।।

Vārttika 3: However, since the cause (of the operation) is the same, there is preeminence in strength for *sya* (*vikaraṇa*) *pratyaya 3.1.33* and the rest (over *āya*) etc. by reason of a conflict (of rule of equal force requiring the later rule to prevail).

41.2 स्यादिभिस्त्वायादीनां बाधनं प्राप्नोति विप्रतिषेधेन। किं कारणम्। तुल्यनिमित्त-
त्वात्। तुल्यं हि निमित्तं स्यादीनामायादीनां च। स्यादीनामवकाशः। करिष्यति
हरिष्यति। आदीनामवकाशः। गोपायति धूपायति। इहोभयं प्राप्नोति। गोपायिष्यति
41.5 धूपायिष्यतीति। परत्वात्स्यादयः[2] प्राप्नुवन्ति।।

Bhāṣya: By reason of a conflict (of rules of equal force requiring the subsequent to prevail) the barring of *āya* and the rest by *sya* (*vikaraṇa pratyaya*) and the rest obtains. What is the reason? Because of the cause (occasioning an operation) being the same (in both cases). For the cause (occasioning manifestation) of *sya* and the rest and *āya* and the rest is the same (namely when a *tiṅ* i.e. *sārvaradhātuka pratyaya* follows). There is scope (of application) for *sya* and the rest: *kar-i-ṣya-ti* ("He will make") and *hariṣyati* ("He will take"). There is scope (of application) for *āya* and the rest (as) *gopāyati* "He protects"; *dhūpāyati* "He fumigates or perfumes with incense". Here both obtain: *gopāyisyati* "He will protect"; *dhūpāyiṣyati* "He will perfume with incense". Because of being the subsequent (rules) *sya* and the rest (by *syatāsī lṛluṭoḥ 3.1.33* and the rest) obtain (i.e. become wrongly applicable).

41.6 न वायादिविधानस्यानवकाशत्वात् ।। 4 ।।

Vārttika 4: Or else (this difficulty does not arise) because of there not being scope (of application) for the ordaining of *āya* and the rest.

41.7 न वैष दोषः। किं कारणम्। आयादिविधानस्यानवकाशत्वात्। अनवकाशा
आयादय उच्यन्ते च ते वचनाद्भविष्यन्ति। ननु चेदानीमेवावकाशः प्रक्लृप्तो
गोपायति धूपायतीति। अत्रापि शप्स्यादिर्भवति। यद्यप्यत्रापि शप्स्यादिर्भवति न
41.10 त्वत्रास्ति विशेषः सति वा शप्यसति वा।

Bhāṣya: This is not a fault. What is the reason? Because of there being no scope (of application) for the ordaining of *āya* and the rest. *Āya* and the rest are without scope (of application) elsewhere, and they which are stated (by *sūtras*) will be applicable because of express statements in a rule. But surely, just now is not scope (of application) in fact made (in these examples)? *gopāyati* "He protects", *dhūpāyati* "He perfumes with incense". Here also *śap sya* and the rest are applicable (by *kartari śap 3.1.68* etc.)

Although here also *śap, sya* and the rest are applicable, yet there is no difference when *śap* is present or not present.

41.10 ....अन्यदिदानीमेतद्यदुच्यते नास्ति
विशेष इति। यत्तु तदुक्तमायादीनां स्यादिभिरव्याप्तोऽवकाश इति स नास्त्यवकाशः।
अवश्यं खल्वप्यत्र शप्स्यादिरेषितव्यः। किं कारणम्। रोपायन्ती धूपायन्तीति
शप्श्यनोर्नित्यम् (7.1.81) इति नुम्यथा स्यादिति।। यदि तर्ह्यनवकाशा आयादय
आयादिभिः स्यादीनां बाधनं प्राप्नोति। यथा पुनरयं सूत्रभेदेन परिहारो यदि
41.15 पुनः शपि नित्यमित्युच्येत। सिध्यति। सूत्रं तर्हि भिद्यते।।

This which is stated, namely "there is no difference" is something else. However with reference to that which was stated "the scope of *āya* etc. is not pervaded by *sya* etc." (I say) there is no scope for *āya* etc. It is essential also indeed that *śap, sya* etc. be sought. What is the pupose? So that *num āgama* (augment) be invariably applicable because of the rule *ś-ap-śyanor nityam 7.1.81.* When the *pratyaya śatṛ* acts after a verbal *aṅga* (base) ending in the *vikaraṇas ś-ap* and *śyan,* it invariably takes the augment *num* before the *napunsaka* (neuter) case ending *ś-i* (*i*) and the feminine *ī* (*nadī*).

If then *sya* etc. have no scope, the barring of *sya* etc. by *āya* etc. obtains. However, as there will be avoiding (of this problem) by dividing the *sūtra* (in two), if again it is simply stated "when *śap* follows, invariable (application of *aya* etc.)", it is established as valid. But then the *sūtra* is (to be) divided (into two).

41.16 यथान्यासमेवास्तु। ननु चोक्तमायादिभ्यो यदार्धधातुकमायादिप्रकृतेर्यदार्ध-
धातुकमिति चोभयथानिष्टप्रसङ्ग इति। नैष दोषः। आर्धधातुक इति नैषा परसप्तमी
का तर्हि। विषयसप्तमी। आर्धधातुकविषय इति। तत्रार्धधातुकविषय आयादि-
41.19 प्रकृतेरायादिषु कृतेषु यो यतः प्रत्ययः प्राप्नोति स ततो भविष्यति।

Let it be as written. But surely indeed it was stated (previously) (*Vārttika 1*) the following positions give rise to an undesired contingency: "When that *ārdhadhātuka pratyaya* which acts after *āya* and the rest (is present, there is optionally cessation (of the appearance) of *āya* and the rest)", and "(when that) *ārdhadhātuka pratyaya* which acts after the bases (ending) in *āya* and the rest, is present, the arising of *āya* etc. is optional". This is no fault because *ārdhadhātuke* is not *para saptamī* (seventh case in the sense of "when that follows, the operation is to take place on that which is immediately prior to that in the seventh case" (*1.1.66 tasminniti nirdiṣṭe pūrvasya*)). What then? *viṣaya-saptamī* "The seventh/*adhikaraṇa*/locative case in the sense of "with regard to that sphere, i.e. *ārdhadhātuka viṣaya* in the domain of *ārdha-dhātuka* (*pratyayas*). There in the domain of *ārdhadhātuka pratyayas* (in the mind), when *āya* and the rest have been formed after a base (ending) in *āya* and the rest, whatever *pratyaya* obtains after a stem will be added to that stem.

Pradīpa

Pradīpa: 40.3 आयादय:।

प्र. Having resorted to *parasaptamī*/seventh case in the sense of (action taking place of that immediately in front of) that which follows *1.1.66*, there is consideration of two views, i.e. because consideration has not begun in relation to *viṣaya* . . .

... कथमिति। having thought of the fault of both views he asks the question 'How?'.

आहोस्विदन्यतरस्यामिति।

Or else in the other alternative . . .

He thinks the word *nivṛtti* (cessation) or *utpatti* (arising), should be indicated. *Nāgeśa:* the purpose must be reflected on, because everywhere in the rule/sentence even in the absence of these they are understood. In one view, when more is to be effected in fact, and because of the *Bhāṣya* aiming at that, in some places the word *utpatti* is an optional reading.

When *āyādaya* is in fact established (already by *anuvṛtti*) there is (possible) a change of the ending to fifth case for *āyādayati*. The meaning is 'that *ārdhdhātuka pratyaya* which acts after *āya* and the rest, when that follows, *āya* and the rest do not arise after *gup* and the rest'.

Pradīpa: 40.7 यदा तावदिति।

"When (it is) just (said that *ārdhadhātuka pratyaya* which acts after *āya* and the rest . . .)"

When *āya* and the rest are ordained, without regard to the subsequent as cause of operation/*paranimitta* by means of the sentences ordaining *āya* and the rest without regard to the sentence, then by reason of that, when an *ārdhadhātuka* follows, in their view cessation is effected. Even though words are eternal, still in the context of formation of words in the science (of grammar) in some places by way of *lopa*/elision of that arisen, cessation is effected. In some places by reason of ordaining an *apavāda*/exception (*pratyaya*) the non-arising of the *utsarga*/general (*pratyaya*) is made known (e.g. *adi prabhṛtibhyaḥ śapaḥ* 2.4.72). Hence the view which supports *nivṛtti* /cessation (to be added) is not inappropriate.

Pradīpa: 40.19 यदेति।

"When (also that *ārdhadhātuka pratyaya* which acts after the base ending with *āya* and the rest and when that is established (in the mind as desired), optionally, there is arising of *āya* and the rest applicable)."

A view is: 'When this union of three *sūtras* is the remainder (to be supplied) then there is the existence of one sentence/ *ekavākyatā;* when an *ārdhadhātuka pratyaya* follows *āya* and the rest optionally arise."

If then there is 'the existence of one sentence' then when a *sārvadhātuka pratyaya* follows *āya* and the rest would not arise. This is no fault. Here alone, when it is to be stated *gup dhūp* "(act) optionally when an *ārdhadhātuka pratyaya* follows" because of a different reading, "when a *sārvadhātuka pratyaya* follows also *āya* and the rest are applicable" is thus known. However, by reason of 'being one sentence', "when an *ārdhadhātuka pratyaya* only follows" they are optionally so ordained.

Pradīpa: 40.10 'अन्यदिदानीमिति'।

Now (what is stated) is that something else is not a qualification.

The sense is that even in the absence of a distinction or qualification, because of the force of the rule (itself) it is produced by *śap.* Here, however, for the form *kāmayate* 'he desires', there is in fact a qualification because of the absence of this form without *śap.*

Pradīpa: 40.14 यथा पुनरिति।

... "But as (there will be) avoiding (of this problem) by dividing the *sūtra* (into two)."

However, that was stated by the *vārttikakāra* namely "However, it is established that when a *sārvadhātuka pratyaya* follows, (or is determined on in the mind), because of not resorting to the word *va,* there is invariable ordaining of *āya* etc."

Thus by division of the *sūtra* being stated, the refutation was expressed.

The meaning is when a division of the *sūtra* has to be effected as 'invariably when *śap* follows (*āya* etc.), such a reading/statement has to be made whereby no fault is possible'. But surely because of the *tudādi* character of vicch (*dhātu* to go) it would be formed with *ś-a vikaraṇa* but not with *śap.*

Well then, the purpose is (said to be) to imply a difference in the written text. However, the written text has to be effected as 'invariable/*nitya* when *śap* follows'.

Notes

[1] गोपायांचकार गोपायेति च। He protected, protector.

कास्प्रत्ययादाममन्त्रे लिटि 3.1.35

"The *pratyaya ām* acts after the *dhātu kās* (to cough) and those *dhātus* formed by *pratyayas* (derivative verbs) when *liṭ* (perfect) follows except in the *Veda*."

'अ प्रत्ययात्' 3.3.102

"After the *dhātus* that end in a *pratyaya* there is the *pratyaya a*, the word being feminine" - *gopā*

गोपायतीति। He protects.

He thinks 'because of the absence of any qualification'. Here there is not arising of *śap* and there is no scope of application for *āya* etc.

[2] 40.5 परत्वात्स्यादयः प्राप्नुवन्ति।

"Because of being subsequent rules, *sya* and the rest obtain. . ."

स्यतासी लृलुटोः 3.1.33

When लृ (लृङ् conditional and लृट् second future) and लुट् (first future) then स्य and तासि are respectively *vikaraṇa pratyayas* of a *dhātu*.

"The *pratyaya śap* acts after a *dhātu* when a *sārvadhātuka pratyaya* follows signifying the agent."

सनाद्यन्ता धातवः ॥ 3 । 1 । 32 ॥

Pāṇini 3.1.32: Words ending with the *pratyaya san* and the rest have the name *dhātu*.

41.21 अन्तग्रहणं किमर्थं न सनादयो धातव इत्येवोच्येत। केनेदानीं तदन्तानां भविष्यति। तदन्त[1] विधिना॥ अत उत्तरं पठति।

Bhāṣya: What is the purpose of the mention of *anta* (end) ? Could one not just say *sanādaya dhatavaḥ "pratyayas* beginning with *san* are called *dhātus*". By reason of what (rule) will there now be (the name *dhātu*) for those which end in that (*pratyaya*) ? By the *tad anta* rule (namely *yena vidhis tad antasya 1.1.72*) "A rule which is enjoined with regard to a particular attribute applies to words having that attribute at their end as well as to that attribute itself".

Therefore (the *vārttika-kāra*) speaks the following:

41.23 सनादिष्वन्तग्रहण उक्तम् ।। 1 ।।

Vārttika 1: A reply was stated (previously) *1.4.14 Vā. 1* with regard to the mention of *anta* in relation to *san* and the rest (*pratyayas*).

41.24 किमुक्तम्। पदसंज्ञायामन्तवचनमन्यत्र संज्ञाविधौ प्रत्ययग्रहणे तदन्तविधि-प्रतिषेधार्थमिति[2]। इदं चापि प्रत्ययग्रहणमयं चापि संज्ञाविधिः।।

Bhāṣya: What was stated (in *1.4.14 Vā. 1*) ? "The expressing of *anta* (ending), in the rule ordaining the technical name *pada*, namely "*sup-tiṅ-antam padam*" *1.4.14* ("That which ends in a *sup* (case nominal ending) or a *tiṅ* (verbal ending) is called *pada* (fully inflected word)" was for the purpose of prohibiting the *tadanta* ("for that ending in that") rule elsewhere when there is specific mention of a *pratyaya* in a *sañjñā sūtra* (giving a technical name to a linguistic unit). And this also is a specific mention of a *pratyaya* and also it is a *sañjñā* (technical name) rule.

42.1 किमर्थं पुनरिदमुच्यते न भूवादयो धातवः (1.3.1) इत्येव सिद्धम्। न सिध्यति। पाठेन धातुसंज्ञा क्रियते न चेमे तत्र पठ्यन्ते। कथं तर्ह्यन्येषामपठ्यमानानां धातुसंज्ञा भवति। अस्तेर्भूः ब्रुवो वचिः चक्षिङः ख्याञ् (2.4.52, 53, 54) इति। यद्यप्येते तत्र न पठ्यन्ते प्रकृतयस्त्वेषां तत्र पठ्यन्ते तत्र स्थानिवद्भा- वात्सिद्धम्। इमेऽपि तर्हि यद्यपि तत्र न पठ्यन्ते येषां त्वर्था आदिश्यन्ते ते तत्र पठ्यन्ते

41.6 तत्र स्थानिवद्भावात्सिद्धम्।

For what purpose is this stated? Is not in fact (the technical name *dhātu* already) established (by the *sūtra*) *"bhūvādayo dhātavaḥ" 1.3.1* "The words beginning with *bhū* (to be or become) and denoting action are called *dhātus*"? No it is not established. The technical name *dhātu* is formed by the recitation (of the seed forms in the *dhātu pāṭha*) and these are not recited there. How is it then that for others not being recited (in the *Dhātu Pāṭha*) the technical name *dhātu* is applicable? (As in the *sūtras*) *"aster-bhūḥ" 2.4.52 "Bhū* is the *ādeśa* (substitute) of the *dhātu as* (to be) when an *ārdhadhātuka pratyaya* is to be applied"; *bruvo vaci 2.4.53 "Vac-i* is the *ādeśa* of *brū* (to speak) when an *ārdhadhātuka pratyaya* is to be applied"; *cakṣiṅaḥ khyāñ' 2.4.54* "*Khyāñ* is the *ādeśa* of *cakṣiñ* (to perceive, to tell) when an *ārdhadhātuka pratyaya* is to be applied". Although these are not recited/ listed there nonetheless the original/*sthānin* of them is recited. There (the name *dhātu*) is established as valid because of these *ādeśas* being like the originals. Also although they are not recited (in the *dhātu pāṭha*), nonetheless those for which meanings are indicated there, are recited. There too because of being like the original/*sthānin* (meanings/*arthas* given in the *Dhātu Pāṭha* with each *dhātu*), (the name *dhātu*) is established as valid.

42.6 .... न सिध्यति। आदेशः स्थानिवद्भावतीत्युच्यते न चेम आदेशाः। इमेऽप्यादेशाः। कथम्। आदिश्यते यः स आदेश इमे चाप्यादिश्यन्ते।। एवमपि षष्ठीनिर्दिष्टस्यादेशाः स्थानिवद्भवन्तीत्युच्यते न चेमे षष्ठीनिर्दिष्टस्यादेशाः। षष्ठीग्रहणं निवर्तिष्यते[3]। यदि निवर्ततेऽपवाद उत्सर्गकृतं प्राप्नोति। कर्मण्यण् (3.2.1) आतोऽनुपसर्गे कः (3) इति केऽप्यण्कृतं प्राप्नोति। नैष दोषः आचार्यप्रवृत्तिर्ज्ञापयति नापवाद उत्सर्गकृतं भवतीति यदयं श्यनादीन्कां-
41.12 श्चिच्छितः करोति। श्नम् श्ना श्नुरिति।।

It is not established. It is said "The *ādeśa* is like the original/*sthānivat*" but these are not *ādeśas*. There also are *ādeśas*. How? That which is pointed out/*ādiśyate* in an *ādeśa* and these too are 'pointed out'.

Well then it is said "(only) the *ādeśa* of those (originals) which are mentioned in the sixth case are like the original/*sthānivat*, and these *ādeśas* are not in place of those mentioned in the sixth case.

The mention of sixth case will cease. ('*ṣaṣṭhī sthāneyogā 1.1.49*' and '*sthānivad ādeśo' nal vidhau 1.1.56*').

If it ceases, (the operation) produced by the *utsarga sūtra* causes in the case of *apavāda* in relation to *karman 3.2.1* ("*aṇ pratyaya* acts after a *dhātu* when the *karman* (object) is in composition with it as an *upapada* (subordinate word)" = (*utsarga sūtra*) and *āto' nupasarge kaḥ 3.2.3* "*pratyaya ka* acts after a *dhātu* ending in long *ā* when no *upasarga* precedes and when the *karman* (object) is in composition with it". That caused by the *apavāda pratyaya* obtains in place of *ka*. There is no fault. The usage of the Master makes known that when (there is applicable) an *upavāda sūtra* that which is caused by the *utsarga* is not applicable. Because of this situation he makes some (*vikaraṇa pratyayas*) *śyan* and the rest have an indicatory *ś* (as) *śyan śnam śnā and śnu.*

Pradīpa

Pradīpa : 42.1 सनाद्यन्ताः। भूवादय इत्येवेति।

प्र (Is not *dhātu*) in fact (established by) the *sūtra bhūvādaya* words beginning with *bhū* and denoting action are called *dhātus* ?

The sense is such because of resorting to the interpretation of the meaning as '*dhātus*', expressing becoming/*bhū*. There the meaning is 'and thence because of expressing verbal activity the technical name *dhātu* is established as valid for those ending in *san* and the rest'.

Pradīpa : 42.2 पाठेनेति।

(Technical name *dhātu* is established) by recitation (in *Dhātu Pāṭha*).

The sense is 'because of the connection each one has the word *ādi* etc. and the technical name *dhātu* is ordained after the meaning and (the form) is recited'.

The meaning is 'because of the mention there of an *ādeśa* word in place of a word used in its conventional sense, it is established there only for those which have the nature of *ādeśa* on the cessation of the original *sthānin,* so that the mention there is for them alone.

Pradīpa : 42.7 इमेऽपीति।

"These also are *ādeśas.*"

The meaning is, the mention there is of a word which is an *ādeśa* of one cause of verbal activity. Here *codayanti,* 'they impel', if by reason of being like the original the technical name *dhātu* is enjoined for *san* and the rest, then because of the absence of (applicability of *tadanta* rule), the augment *aṭ* etc. dependent on having the technical name *aṅga,* obtain for *pratyayas* alone and are desired for those *aṅgas* ending in *pratyayas*. And the *pratyaya yaṅ* is enjoined in the sense of its base/*svārthe* after a *dhātu* expressing verbal activity characterised by repetition, and *āya* etc. unqualified are enjoined in the sense of the base. Thus because of the absence of any cessation of the original', 'due to absence of *sthānivatva,* the technical name *dhātu* does not obtain.

Here it is said because of the maxim 'all are the *ādeśas* of the whole *pada'* (*1.1.20 vā. 5*). The form 'He desires to make' there is the *aṅga*/ base 'making' in the sense of *dhātu iṣ* desire.

When there is occasion for the *dhātu iṣ* occurring, the word '*cikīrṣa* is indicated as ending in *san* because the *dhātu*-nature of that ending (in a *san pratyaya*), is established as valid.

The intention of the *Bhāṣyakāra* is that when there is the possibility of the use of the word *lū* (to cut), expressing the activity of cutting distinguished by repetition, the word *lolūyate* is indicated 'He cuts intensely'. When there is occasion for *gup-i,* 'the word' *gopāya* (is indicated), 'He shuns, detests' (also *svārthe*).

Notes

[1] तदन्तविधिना। By the *tad anta* rule

येन विधिस्तदन्तस्य 1.1.72 "A rule which is enjoined with regard to a particular attribute applies to words having that attribute at their end, as well as that attribute itself."

[2] प्रतिषेधार्थमिति।

For the purpose of prohibiting (*tadanta* rule elsewhere)

पदसंज्ञायामन्तवचनं अन्यत्र संज्ञाविधौ प्रत्ययग्रहणे तदन्तविधिप्रतिषेधार्थम्। 1.4.14

वा॰ The expression of *tad anta* in any other than in the *pada* technical name rule, is for the purpose of prohibiting the *tadanta* rule (when there is mention of a *pratyaya*).

[3] षष्ठीग्रहणं निवर्तिष्यते। "The mention of sixth case will cease."

षष्ठीस्थाने योगा 1.1.49 "The sixth case implied the relation of 'instead'", i.e. that for which something is substituted.

स्थानिवदादेशोऽनल्विधौ 1.1.56

स्यतासी लृलुटोः ॥ 3 । 1 । 33 ॥

Pāṇini 3.1.33: In the presence of *lṛ* and *luṭ*, *sya* and *tāsi* acts as (*vikaraṇa pratyayas*) after a *dhātu*.

42.14 इमे विकरणाः पठ्यन्ते तत्र न ज्ञायते क उत्सर्गः कोऽपवाद इति। तत्र वक्तव्य-
मयमुत्सर्गोऽयमपवाद इति। इमे ब्रूमो यगुत्सर्गोऽपवाद शबादिः स्यादयश्च ॥

Bhāṣya: These *vikaraṇa pratyayas* are recited (but) it is not known there which is the *utsarga sūtra* (general) and which is the *apavāda* (particular *sūtra* debarring the general). There it should be stated "this is an *utsarga sūtra,* (and) this is an *apavāda sūtra*". These we will state: "*yak* is an *utsarga pratyaya*" (by) *sārvadhātuke yak 3.1.67.* "The *pratyaya yak* acts after a *dhātu* when a *sārvadhātuka pratyaya* follows, denoting the action or the object" and *śap* and the rest and *sya* and the rest are *apavāda sūtras c.f. kartari śap 3.1.69* "The *pratyaya śap* acts after a *dhātu* when a *sārvadhātuka pratyaya* following signifying the agent".

42.16 यद्येवमपवादविप्रतिषेधाच्छबादिबाधनम्।। अपवादविप्रतिषेधाच्छबादिभिः स्या-
दीनां बाधनं प्राप्नोति। शबादीनामवकाशः। पचति यजति। स्यादीनामवकाशः।
42.18 पक्ष्यते। यक्ष्यते। इहोभयं प्राप्नोति। पक्ष्यति यक्ष्यति। परत्वाच्छबादयः प्राप्नुवन्ति।।

Vārttika: If this is so, "because of the conflict (of rules of equal force requiring the subsequent to prevail) the subsequent of (two) *apavāda sūtras* bars the prior so there is debarring by *śap* and the rest".

Bhāṣya: Because of the conflict (of rules of equal force requiring the subsequent to prevail) the subsequent of two *apavāda sūtras* is debarred, and there obtains debarring by *śap* and the rest of *sya* and the rest. There is scope for *śap* and the rest in *pacati* "He cooks", *yajati* "He sacrifices". There is scope (of application) for *sya* and the rest (in) *pakṣyate* "It will be cooked" and *yakṣyate* "It will be sacrificed". Here both obtain *pakṣyati* "He will cook" and *yakṣyati* "He will sacrifice". Because of being subsequent (rules to *sya* and the rest) *śap* and the rest obtain.

42.19 अपवादो नामानेकलक्षणप्रसङ्गः।। अपवादो नाम भवति यत्रानेकलक्षणप्रसङ्गः।
तत्र भावकर्मणोर्यग्विधीयते कर्तरि शप्कः प्रसङ्गो यद्भावकर्मणोर्यकं कर्तरि शबा-
42.21 दयो बाधेरन्।। एवं तर्हि यक्शपावुत्सर्गावपवादाः श्यनादयः[1] स्यादयश्च।।

Vārttika: There is occasion for the word *apavāda* having more than one definition.

Bhāṣya: The (word) *apavāda* is such that it is possible to have more than one definition and here *yak* is ordained in the sense of *bhāva* (abstract notion of a *dhātu*) or *karman* (object), (but) *śap* (is ordained) in denoting *kartṛ* (agent). What is the contingency where *śap* and the rest in the sense of agent would debar *yak* in the sense of action/*bhāva* and object/*karman?* Well then, *yak* and *śap* are (by) *utsarga sūtras, śyan* and the rest and *sya* and the rest (by) *apavāda sūtras.*

42.22 अपवादविप्रतिषेधाच्श्यनादिबाधनम्।। अपवादविप्रतिषेधाच्श्यनादिभिः स्यादीनां
बाधनं प्राप्नोति। श्यनादीनामवकाशः। दीव्यति सीव्यति। स्यादीनामवकाशः
पक्ष्यति यक्ष्यति। इहोभयं प्राप्नोति। देविष्यति सेविष्यति। परत्वाच्श्यनादयः

42.25 प्राप्नुवन्ति।। नैष दोषः। शबादेशाः श्यनादयः करिष्यन्ते शप्च स्यादिभिर्बाध्यते
तत्र दिवादिभ्यः स्यादिविषये नास्ति शबेव नास्ति कुतः श्यनादयः। तत्तर्हि शपो
43.1 ग्रहणं कर्तव्यम्।

Vārttika: Because of a conflict (of rules of equal force requiring the subsequent rules to prevail over the earlier rules, *utsarga sūtras* here would prevail over), the *apavāda sūtras,* so *śyan* and the rest would debar (*sya* and the rest).

Bhāṣya: Because of a conflict, there obtains debarring of *sya* and the rest by *śyan* and the rest. There is scope (of application) for *śyan* and the rest: *dīvyati* "He plays" and *sīvyati* "He sews". There is scope (of application) for *sya* and the rest *pakṣyati* "He will cook" and *yakṣyati* "He will sacrifice". Here both obtain *deviṣyati* "He will play dice" and *seviṣyati* "He will sew". Because of being subsequent *śyan* and the rest obtain.

There is no fault, *śyan* and the rest will be produced as the substitutes of *śap.* Moreover *śap* is debarred by *sya* and the rest. There, after *div* and the rest, in the context of *sya* and the rest, *śap* in fact is not present, how much less *śyan* and the rest. Then should specific mention of *śap* be made?

43.1 ....न कर्तव्यम्। प्रकृतमनुवर्तते। क्व प्रकृतम्। कर्तरि शप् (3.1.68) इति।
तद्वै प्रथमानिर्दिष्टं षष्ठीनिर्दिष्टेन चेहार्थः। दिवादिभ्य इत्येवा पञ्चमी शबिति प्रथमायाः
षष्ठीं प्रकल्पयिष्यति तस्मादित्युरस्य (1.1.67) इति।

43.4 प्रत्ययविधिरयं न च प्रत्ययविधौ पञ्चम्यः प्रकल्पिका भवन्ति। नायं प्रत्ययविद्धिः।

It should not be made. The original (*śap*) follows on (from a previous *sūtra*). Where is the original? (In the *sūtra kartari śap 3.1.68*) "The *pratyaya śap* acts after a *dhātu* when *sārvadhātuka pratyaya* follows signifying the agent" That really is mentioned in the first case, but here the purpose is conveyed by sixth case indication. (No fault here). The fifth case (in the *sūtra divādibhyaḥ śyan 3.1.69*) "After *div* and the rest (acts *pratyaya śyan*)" will put the sixth case in place of the first (case indication for the *pratyaya*) *śap* because of the *sūtra tasmād-ityuttarasya 1.1.67* ("That indicated in the fifth case enjoins an operation or *ādeśa* /substitute for that (immediately) following"). This is a *pratyaya* rule and in a *pratyaya* rule fifth case words cannot effect change. This is not a *pratyaya* rule.

43.5 विहितः प्रत्ययः प्रकृतश्चानुवर्तते।। अथवानुवृत्तिः करिष्यते। सार्वधातुके यक् (3.
1.67) स्यतासी लृलुटोः च्लि लुङि च्लेः सिच्भवति कर्तरि शप् (68) स्यतासी
लृलुटोः च्लि लुङि च्लेः सिज्भवति। दिवादिभ्य श्यन् (69) स्यतासी लृलुटोः
च्लि लुङि च्लेः सिज्भवति।। अथवान्तरङ्गाः स्यादयः। कान्तरङ्गता।
43.9 लावस्थायामेव स्यादयः सार्वधातुके श्यनादयः।।

The *pratyaya* is already ordained and the base follows on (from a previous *sūtra*).

Or otherwise there will be effected *anuvṛtti* (following on from previous *sūtras* of the elements required). (As) *sārvadhātuka yak 3.1.67* (*pratyaya yak* acts after a *dhātu* when a *sārvadhātuka pratyaya* follows denoting action/*bhāva* or object/*karman*) (may require following on from previous *sūtras*). "*sya tāsī lṛluṭoḥ*" *3.1.33*; "*cli luṅi*" *3.1.43* (In the presence of the *pratyaya luṅ* (aorist sign) *pratyaya cli* acts after a *dhātu*) and "*cleḥ sic*" *3.1.44* ("*Sic* acts in the place of the *pratyaya cli*"). Similarly the *sūtra kartari śap 3.1.68* (tr. above) (may require the following same *sūtras* by *anuvṛtti*) "*sya tāsī lṛlutoḥ*" *3.1.33* ("In place of *śap, sya* and *tāsī* act when *lṛ* or *luṭ* follow"). "*cli luṅi* and *cleḥ sic* (Similarly the *sūtra*) "*divādibhyaḥ śyan 3.1.69*". ("After the *dhātus div* and the rest *śyan* acts in place of *śap*" (may require)) *syatāsī lṛluṭoḥ; clu luṅi* and *cleḥ sic.*

Otherwise *sya* and the rest (as *vikaraṇa pratyayas* with no specific meaning designated other than that of their own base/*svārthe*) are *antaraṅga* (requiring fewer operations). What is the nature of *antaraṅga* (here)? The only condition *sya* and the rest have is "when a *la* (*lṛṭ* and the rest of tense/mood *pratyayas*) follow (whereas) *śyan* and the rest have (the additional condition) "when a *sārvadhātuka pratyaya* follows (signifying action/*bhāva*, object/*karman*, or agent/*kartṛ*).

Pradīpa

Pradīpa : 42.13 स्यतासी। इमे इति।

These (*vikaraṇa pratyayas* . . .)

He asks to know the (qualities of the properties) of general/*utasarga pratyayas* and the exception/*apavāda.*

Pradīpa : 42.15 यगुत्सर्ग इति।

Yak is an *utsarga*/general *pratyaya*

The sense is that through the *anuvṛtti* of *bhāva* and *karman* because of being ordained after merely the one condition 'when a *sārvadhātuka pratyaya* follows' (it is *utsarga*).

'यगुत्सर्गो।' 3

सार्वधातुक युक् 3.1.67 (भावकर्मणोः)

"The *pratyaya yak* acts after a *dhātu* when a *sārvadhātuka* (*3.4.113*) *pratyaya* follows denoting the abstract action/*bhāva* of the object/*karman.*"

'शबादि' 4

'कर्तरि शप् 3.1.58 (सार्वधातुके धातोः)

"The *pratyaya śap* acts after a *dhātu* when *sārvadhātuka pratyaya* follows signifying the agent."

Pradīpa : 42.16 अपवादप्रतिषेधादिति।

"Because of the conflict (there is barring of *śap*) by

विप्रतिषेधे परं कार्यम् 1.4.2

"When rules of equal force prohibit each other the latter/subsequent in the order of the *Aṣṭādhyāyī* is to take effect."

The meaning is, when there is a conflict among the *apavādas* or exceptions to the *utsarga yak,* between *śap* and the rest and *sya* and the rest, because *śap* and the rest are later, *śap* and the rest would be applicable.

Pradīpa : 42.16 अपवाद इति।

Where there is the possibility of an *utsarga* characterised (*pratyaya*) and one characterised as *apavāda* there is usage of the *apavāda.*

However, the meaning is in the *yak* rule, because of the mention of *bhāva* and *karman* following on and because of there being a possibility of *yak* in the sense of agent there is not the nature of being *apavāda* for that.

Pradīpa : 43.9 लावस्थायामिति।

"When *la* (*lṛ* and the rest of the tense/mood *pratyayas* follow)."

And surely because of being subsequent, the *ādeśa* of *la* should be applied.

And there is not non-invariability/*a-nityatva* for the *ādeśas* of *la,* even when *sya* and the rest have been effected, because of the possibility of the substitutes of *la,* due to resort to the qualification ordained, that (they be) in place of *la,* which has been ordained after a *dhātu,* even within the context of the *dhātu* governing rule, as far as the conclusion of the third *adhyaya.* So then, even when the *ādeśas* of *la* have been effected, *sya* and the rest, being *antaraṅga* (having few conditions), in fact are applicable. For in that rule the sense of agent etc. is not resorted to, as having the nature of *sārvadhātuka* or qualification of the meaning, by (any) word. However, *śyan* and the rest, because of their nature of (having to resort to or) depend on that (qualification agent), are *bahiraṅga* (requiring more operations). And it is essential that this be assented to, 'when the *ādeśas* of *la* have been effected, *sya* and the rest are effected'. Otherwise, how could there be an implied rule/ *jñāpaka* for this meaning, 'the accent of a *vikaraṇa*, by reason of the ordaining *anudātta* for a *sārvadhātuka* substitute of *la* following *tāsī*, bars the accent of the *sārvadhātuka ādeśa* of *la*'?

For if, 'when a *la* follows *tāsi* is effected, and afterwards the *sārvadhātuka pratyaya*', then applies the (*vārttika 9* on *6.1.158*) *satiśiṣṭatvāt* (*la sārvadhātukasya udāttatve*) 'because of the comparatively superior strength of a subsequent acute, replacing the one previous in the process of the formation of a word, *udātta* obtains in the place of the *anudātta* accent on the substitute of *sārvadhātuka ādeśa* of *la*'.

The *jñāpaka* (implied rule) that the rule is for the purpose of an *anudātta* accent, which has not obtained (yet by rule), would not then be acceptable. However, those who say 'because of the *bahiraṇga* nature of the *ādeśas* of *la*, when there is *ekavākyatā* (being a single sentence) (applicable for the sentence ordaining *ādeśas* of *la*), and further by reason of the connection with the section (ordaining) *ātmanepada* and *parasmaipada* together with ordaining of number as well as because of the *antaraṅga* nature, it is in fact in the context of *la*'; and (so finally) because of ordaining for each *pada, sya* and the rest are applicable. It is not established by those people that the previously spoken of meaning as a *jñāpaka* is applicable for the ordaining of *anudātta* for the *sārvadhātuka ādeśa* of a *la* which follows after *tāsi*.

Notes

[1] श्यानादयः ॥

दिवादिभ्यः श्यन् 3.1.69

The *pratyaya śyan* acts after a *dhātu* of the *divādi gaṇa* when a *sārvadhātuka pratyaya* denoting the agent follows.

सिब्बहुलं लेटि ॥ 3 । 1 । 34 ॥

Pāṇini 3.1.34: *Sip* diversely acts as *pratyaya* after a *dhātu* in the presence of *leṭ* (*pratyaya* signifying the Vedic subjunctive).

43.11 सिबुत्सर्गश्छन्दसि ॥ 1 ॥

Vārttika 1: *Sip* should be ordained as a general *pratyaya* in *chandas/veda.*

43.12 सिबुत्सर्गश्छन्दसि कर्तव्यः॥

Bhāṣya: *Sip* should be made applicable as a general *pratyaya* in the *chandas.*

43.13 सनाद्यन्ते नेषत्वाद्यर्थः ॥ 2 ॥

Vārttika 2: Because of the occurence of the words *neṣatu* (let him lead) and the rest (*sip* is also applicable) in (the context of) *san* and the rest.

43.14 सनाद्यन्ते च कर्तव्यः[1]। किं प्रयोजनम्। नेषत्वाद्यर्थः। इन्द्रो नस्तेन नेषतु। गा वो नेष्टात्॥

Bhāṣya: And (*sip*) should be effected in the context of the governing *sūtra sanādyantā dhātavaḥ 3.1.32.* "Words ending with the *pratyaya san* and the rest are called *dhātus*". What is the purpose? For the sake of (the verbal forms) *neṣatu* and the rest. And *Indra nas tena neṣatu* "Let *Indra* lead us by that (path etc.)" (*ni-s*(*ip*)-(*s*) *a* (*p*)-*tu*(*loṭ*) *gā vo neṣṭāt* "May he lead your cows".

43.16 प्रकृत्यन्तरत्वात्सिद्धम् ॥ 3 ॥

Vārttika 3 : (This is) established because of being different from the base.

43.17 प्रकृत्यन्तरत्वात्सिद्धमेतत्। प्रकृत्यन्तरं नेषतिः।

Bhāṣya: This is established because of being different from the base *neṣati* ((Cl. 1. P.) to moisten, sprinkle (M.W.) but (*dhātu pāṭha nesṛ 617*) *gatau* "He goes" is a different base.)

43.18 नेषतु नेष्टादिति दर्शनात् ॥ 4 ॥

Vārttika 4 : Because of seeing (the forms) *neṣatu* and *neṣṭāt,* it is established that it is a different base (in use in the language).

43.19 नेषतु नेष्टादिति दृश्यते॥
अथ किमर्थः पकारः। स्वरार्थः अनुदात्तौ सुप्पितौ (3.1.4) इत्येष

43.21 स्वरो यथा स्यात्॥

Bhāṣya: (The forms) *neṣatu* and *neṣṭāt* are seen (in the literature). Now what is the purpose of the letter *p*? For the sake of accent. So that this (*anudātta*/grave) accent be applicable by the *sūtra* "*anudāttau sup pitau" 3.1.4* ("A *sup pratyaya* and a *pratyaya* with an indicatory *p* is *anudātta*").

43.22 पित्करणानर्थक्यं चानच्कत्वात् ॥ 5 ॥

Vārttika 5: The producing of an indicatory *p* is pointless because of the *pratyaya* not having a vowel.

43.23 पित्करणं चानर्थकम्। किं कारणम्। अनच्कत्वात्। अनच्कोऽयं तत्र नार्थः स्वरार्थेन पकरेणानुबन्धेन॥ इटि कृते साच्को भविष्यति।

Bhāṣya: The producing of an indicatory *p* is pointless. What is the reason? Because *sip* is (in fact) without a vowel. Being without a vowel, the indicatory letter *p* with which it is endowed, is not for the purpose of accent. When (the augment) *iṭ* is formed (then) it will become possessed of a vowel.

44.1 इटोऽनुदात्तार्थमिति चेदागमानुदात्तत्वात्सिद्धम् ॥ 6 ॥

Vārttika 6 : If the purpose is *anudātta* for the *iṭ āgama* (augment) then *anudātta* (accent) is already established because of (the statement) *anudātta* for the augment.

44.2 आगमानुदात्तत्वेनेटोऽनुदात्तत्वं भविष्यति॥ एवं तर्हि सबयं कर्तव्यः।

Bhāṣya: By reason of the statement about *anudātta* /grave accent for *āgamas*/ augments, the *āgama iṭ* will be *anudātta.* Well then this should be prescribed as *sap.*

44.2 ....किं प्रयोजनम्। यदव यासिसीष्ठाः। एकाज्लक्षण इट्प्रतिषेधो[2] मा भूदिति क्वायम-कारः श्रूयते॥ न क्वचिच्छ्रूयते लोपोऽस्य भविष्यत्यतो लोप आर्धधातुक इति[3]।

44.5 यदि न क्वचिच्छ्रूयते नार्थः स्वरार्थेन पकारेणानुबन्धेन॥ एवमपि कर्तव्य एव। किं प्रयोजनम्। अनुदात्तस्य लोपो यथा स्यादुदात्तस्य मा भूदिति। किं च स्यात्।

44.7 उदात्तनिवृत्तिस्वरः[4] प्रसज्येत्॥

What is the purpose? As when (it is said) here *ava yāsisīṣṭhāḥ Ṛgveda 4.1.4* "Avert/put far away (from us) the wrath of the divine *Varuṇa".* So that there should not be prohibition of *iṭ āgama* (due to being) characterised by a single vowel.

Where is the letter *a* heard? Nowhere is it heard. There will be applicable *lopa* elision of that by "*ato lopaḥ 6.4.48* (*ārdhadhātuke*)" ("*Lopa* acts in the place of the final short *a* of an *aṅga* (base) in the presence of an *ārdha-*

dhātuka pratyaya".) If it is not heard anywhere, then there is no point in the indicatory letter *p* for the purpose of indicating accent. Even so it should not be effected. What is the purpose? So that there should be *lopa* elision of that which has an *anudātta*/grave accent and there should not be elision of that having an *udātta* (acute) accent. And what would be (the significance of that) ? An accent which is caused by *anudāttasya ca yatrodāttalopaḥ 6.1.161 (udāttaḥ)* ("In place of an *anudātta* (grave accent) *udātta* (acute) accent acts when on account of it the preceding *udātta* is *lopa* elided.")

44.8 सिब्बहुलं छन्दसि णित् ।। 7 ।।

Vārttika 7: Diversely in the *chandas/veda sip* has an indicatory *ṇ*.

44.9 सिब्बहुलं छन्दसि णिद्वक्तव्यः[5]। सविता धर्म साविषत्[6]। प्र ण आयूषि तारिषत्[7]।।

Bhāṣya: It should be stated that diversely in the *chandas sip* has an indicatory *ṇ*. *Savitṛ* created or set in motion dharma). (V.S.9.5) May he prolong lives. (RV 1.25. 12;4. 39.6;10.186.1)

Pradīpa

Pradīpa: 43.11 सिब्बहुलम्। सिबुत्सर्ग इति।

प्र॰ Without having mentioned any following cause/condition *s-ip* is to be ordained after a *dhātu* in the class of *san* and the rest.

Therefore, when there is the technical name *dhātu* for that ending in that (*sip*), the forms *neṣatu* etc. are established as valid.

After the word *nī* (to lead) when *sip* follows and *guṇa* is effected when *loṭ* (imperative also) follows the form *neṣata* is derived.

Pradīpa: 43.16 प्रकृत्यन्तरत्वादिति।

This is established because of being different from the base.

Because of the reading in the *Dhātu Pāṭha* of

जेषृ 6.16 णेषृ 6.17 एषृ 6.18 प्रेषृ 6.19 गतौ भ्वादिगण

in the sense of going, the general *pratyaya* is not to be effected (here) in the sense of 'he leads'.

However, the meanings 'put far away from' *ava yasīsiṣṭhāḥ* etc. are to be effected in fact.

Pradīpa : 43.19 नेषतु नेष्टदिति दृश्यते।

नेषतु नेषतादिति Let him lead, may he lead.

दृश्यते इति भाष्ये पाठः। कालेऽपीति शेषः।

This is read in the *Bhāṣya:* 'in popular usage' is required to complete the sense.

नेष्टादिति दृश्यते इति लेखप्रमादः। The form *neṣṭād* is a scribal error.

Pradīpa : 44.2 सबयमिति।

Well then this (should be presented as) *sap.*

The sense is that just as among the *pratyayas san* and the rest, so here in fact there is option/*vā.*

Pradīpa : 44.3 यदव यासिसीष्ठा इति।

As when (it is said) 'Avert/put far away (from the wrath of *Varuṇa*)'.

Dhātu yā (*t*) to go, preceded by *upasarga ava* followed by *śap* = *liñ* (optative) *madhyama puruṣa*/second person, e.g. *ātmane.*

With *s-uṭ* and *sī-yuṭ* as augments, *iṭ* becomes the augment of that beginning with the augment *sī-yuṭ* because of the *aṇga* ending in *śap* having more than one vowel.

c.f. एकाच उपदेशेऽनुदात्तत् 7.2.10 (न इट्)

If however, *sip* is effected, then it is essential that the letter *i* be explained as for the purpose of pronunciation. Otherwise it would be heard. Then (in that context), because of the *dhātu* ending in *sip,* having only one vowel, prohibition of *iṭ* augment would be applicable. But surely, that *dhātu* here which is *anudātta* in an original teaching (namely) the word *yā* (*dhātu,* to go) does not have *ārdhadhātuka pratyaya* after it, because of being separated by *sip.* And that, after which, ending in *sip,* there is an *ārdhadhātuka pratyaya,* is not *anudātta* in an *upadeśa*? Well then, when *san* and the rest are parts (of *aṅgas*) having the name *dhātu,* because of the *sūtra sanādyantā dhātavaḥ* (for so the meaning was explained) then there is the possibility of the prohibition of *iṭ* augment, because of the mention by reference to *yāti* (to go), as having *sip* forming part of *yāti.* When, also by reason of resorting to *sthānivad bhāva* the *sūtra* is rejected, then by being *sthānivat,* prohibition of augment *iṭ,* in fact obtains, due to the *anudātta* single voweled (*dhātu*) being heard.

Pradīpa: 44.6 अनुदात्तस्येति।

"(So that there should be *lopa* elision) of that which has *anudātta*."

Without resorting to the next *sūtra dhātoḥ* (*6.1.162* 'A *dhātu* has *udātta* accent on the end syllable') this was stated. Otherwise this (comment) of the *Bhāṣya* is a resort to the reading of this very example.

Pradīpa: 44.6 उदात्तस्येति।

"(so that) there should not be (elision) of that having *udātta* accent."

Due to the *udātta* accent on the *a* of the word *sa*, with either *pratyaya* or *dhātu* accent, when there is *anudātta* for the *sārvadhātuka* substitute of *la*, (due to being so in the *upadeśa* and being *sārvadhātuka* because of *chandasi ubhayathā 3.4.117*), the accent causing cessation of *udātta* would become applicable for *aṭ* augment. However, when there is present the letter *p*, *anudātta* only is applicable (*3.1.4*).

And because of the force of the *it* letter *p* alone, the *dhātu* accent is not applicable, for the letter *a* of the word *sa* or because of the reading in this place/example. However, the word *yā* (to go) in fact is not applicable. That which is *anudātta* because if *tiṅ ṅatiṅaḥ 8.1.28*.

"A finite verb is *anudātta* when a word precedes it which is not a finite verb", is prohibited by *nipātair yayādi 8.1.30*, "the finite verb retains its accent in connection with the particles *yat*, *yādi*, etc."

Notes

[1] सनाद्यन्ते च कर्तव्यः।

c.f. सनाद्यन्ता धातवाः 3.1.32

[2] इट्प्रतिषेधो

एकाच उपदेशेऽनुदात्तात् 7.2.10

The augment *iṭ* is not added to that *pratyaya* which is connected to a *dhātu* in (the *Dhātu Pāṭha*) *upadeśa* of one vowel and *anudātta* accent.

[3] अतो लोप आर्धधातुकेति

अतो लोप 4.4.48 (आर्धधातुके) "The *a* at the end of an *aṅga*/stem is *lopa*/elided before an *ārdhadhātuka pratyaya*."

[4] 2.44.7 उदात्तनिवृतिस्वरः।।

अनुदात्तस्य च यत्रोदात्तलोप: 6.1.161 In place of an *anudātta* vowel there is *udātta* when on account of it the preceding *udātta* is elided.

[5] 44.9 णिद्वक्तव्य:। "It should be stated *sip* has an *it ṇ*"

अचो ञ्णिति 7.2.115 "Before *pratyayas* having an indicatoery *ñ* or *ṇ vṛddhi* acts as the *ādeśa* for the final vowel of the *aṅga.*"

[6] साविषत् इति। "(*Savitṛ*) created or set in motion (*dharma*)."

There is *anudātta* for the word *āva* by *tiṅ codāttavat 8.1.71* "A *gati* becomes *anudātta* when followed by an unaccented finite verb."

This is the form of *dhātu sū* to impel when *leṭ* (Vedic subjunctive) follows.

[7] तारिषत् इति। "May he extend"

(This is the subjunctive of *tṛ/tarati* (to cross over)).

कास्प्रत्ययादाममन्त्रे लिटि ॥ 3 । 1 । 35 ॥

Pāṇini 3.1.35: The *Pratyaya ām* acts after the *dhātu kās* (to cough) and those *dhātus* that are formed by *pratyayas* (derivative verbs *san,* and the rest) in the presence of *liṭ* except in the *mantra/veda.*

44.11 कास्ग्रहणे चकास उपसंख्यानम् ॥ 1 ॥

Vārttika 1: When there is mention of *kās* (there should be) additional enumeration (of the form) *cakāsa.*

44.12 कास्ग्रहणे चकास उपसंख्यानं कर्तव्यम्। चकासांचकार। च कर्तव्यम्। चकास्प्रत्ययादिति वक्ष्यामि। चकास्ग्रहणे कास उपसंख्यानं कर्तव्यम्। कासांचक्रे। सूत्रं च भिद्यते।। यथान्यासमेवास्तु। ननु चोक्तं कास्ग्रहणे चकास उप-

44.15 संख्यानमिति। नैष दोष:।

Bhāṣya: Additional enumeration should be made of the form *cakāsa* (as taking the *pratyaya ām*), as *cakāsāṃcakāra* "He shone". It should not be made. I shall state, "after *cakās* and the *dhātus* formed by *pratyayas* (acts *ām*)". When *cakās* is mentioned additional enumeration should be made of *kās* (as followed by *ām*). And the *sūtra* is split i.e. is changed. Let the *sūtra* be as written. But surely it was stated when *kās* was mentioned, 'additional enumeration of *cakās* (as followed by *ām*)'.

44.15 .... चकास्शब्दे कास्शब्दोऽस्ति तत्र कास्प्रत्ययादित्येव
सिद्धम्। न सिध्यति। किं कारणम्। अर्थवतः कास्शब्दस्य ग्रहणं न च चकास्शब्दे
कास्शब्दोऽर्थवान्।। एवं तर्हि कास्यनेकाच इति वक्तव्यम्। किं प्रयोजनम्।
44.18 चुलुम्पाद्यर्थम्। चुलुम्पांचकार दरिद्रांचकार।।

This is not a fault. When the word *cakās* is present there is the word *kās* (also present). So in fact, "after *kās* and that formed by a *pratyaya*" is established. It is not established. What is the reason? The mention of the word *kās* having meaning (is intended), and (when we say) "when the word *cakās* (is present) there is the word *kās*", *kās* does not have meaning. Well then it should be stated that "when *kās* and a *dhātu* having more than one vowel (is present *ām* acts)". What is the purpose? (For other examples of *dhātus* not formed from *pratyayas* taking *ām*). For the sake of *culumpa* and the rest *culumpāṃcakāra* "He fondles a child or calf". *daridrāṃcakāra* "He was in need or became poor".

Pradīpa

Pradīpa: 44.10 कास्प्रत्यया।

Surely here the mention of *pratyaya* is pointless. Having ordained *ām* generally by a division of the *sūtra* '*ām amantre liṭi*', I could explain the mention of *kās* as for the purpose of restriction. If it is said that "due to being established 'when ending in a *pratyaya*' because of *kās* (example only) as the example after a *dhātu* sought in the *Dhātu Pāṭha*", that is not so because of the purpose of mentioning ending in a *pratyaya*-formed *dhātu* for those 'having more than one vowel'. Therefore, after *ka* and the rest in the sense of conduct formed with *kvip, ām* does not act. And this is hinted at in *Haradatta's* book (*Padamañjari* on *Kāśikāvṛtti*): "And do not let that ending in a *pratyaya* and having one vowel in fact be (applicable) because when it is established, by mention of *kvip* only, the pointlessness of mentioning *pratyaya* is cogent". And because of happening to conflict with *Bhāṣya's* usage *gopāyāticakāra* etc.

इजादेश्च गुरुमतोऽनृच्छः ॥ 3 । 1 । 36 ॥

Pāṇini 3.1.36: The *pratyaya ām* acts when *liṭ* follows after a *dhātu* beginning with an *ik* (*i* , *u* , *ṛ*, *ḷ*) vowel and having a prosodial heavy/ *guru* vowel, excepting the *dhātu ṛcch* (to go).

44.20 गुरुमत आम्विधाने लिण्निमित्तात्प्रतिषेधः ॥ 1 ॥

Vārttika 1: When *ām* is ordained after a *dhātu* with a prosodially heavy vowel caused by *liṭ* (perfect) *pratyaya* itself, there is prohibition (of *ām*).

44.21 गुरुमत आम्विधाने लिण्निमित्तात्प्रतिषेधो वक्तव्यः। इयेष उवोष। गुणे कृते[1] इजादेश्च गुरुमतोऽनृच्छ इत्याम्प्राप्नोति।। गुरुमद् वचनमिदानीं किमर्थं स्यात्।

Bhāṣya: It should be stated that there is prohibition (of *ām*) when *ām* is ordained after a *dhātu* with a prosodially heavy syllable caused by *liṭ* (*pratyaya* itself). As *iyeṣa* "He desired" (from *iṣ icchāyām*) *uvoṣa* "He burnt" (from *uṣ dāhe*). When *guṇa* has been effected (by *puganta laghūpadhasya ca 7.3.86*) ("*Guṇa* acts in place of a short penultimate vowel of a *dhātu* that ends in a single consonant and for *ik* vowels of the causative stems which take the augment *p-uk* (*7.3.36*) in the presence of a *sārvadhātuka* or an *ārdhadhātuka pratyaya*"), *ām* obtains after the *dhātu ṛcch* beginning with an *ik* vowel and having a prosodially heavy syllable. What now should be the purpose of the expression "having a prosodially heavy syllable"?

45.1 गुरुमद्वचनं किमर्थमिति चेण्णल्युत्तमे यजादिप्रतिषेधार्थम् ॥ 2 ॥

Vārttika 2: If (it is asked) what is the point of the expression "having a heavy syllable" (the answer is) it is for the purpose of prohibiting (*ām*) for *yaj* and the rest when the first person singular substitute *ṇal* follows.

45.2 गुरुमद्वचनं किमर्थमिति चेण्णल्युत्तमे यजादीना[2] मा भूदिति। इयजाहम् उवपाहम्।

Bhāṣya: If it is said 'what is the purpose of saying 'having a heavy syllable'?', then (the answer is that) it is so that (*ām*) should not be applicable for *yaj* and the rest when the first person singular/ *ṇal uttama pratyaya ādeśa* follows. (As) *iyajāham* "I worshipped", *uvapāham* "I sowed or scattered seeds".

45.5 उपदेशवचनात्सिद्धम् ॥ 3 ॥

Vārttika 3: (This is) established because of expression in an original teaching/ *upadeśa*.

45.5 उपदेशे गुरुमत इति वक्तव्यम्।। यद्युपदेशग्रहणं क्रियत उच्छेराम्वक्तव्यः।
व्युच्छांचकारेति।।

Bhāṣya: It should be stated that "after a *dhātu* having a prosodially heavy syllable in the original teaching, if a specific mention of the original teaching is made, it should be stated that *ām* acts after (the *dhatu*) *ucch-i* (*vivāse* banishment, *uñche* gleaning). *vyucchām cakāra* "He was banished" or "shone forth".

45.7 ऋच्छिप्रतिषेधो ज्ञापक उच्छेराम्भावस्य ।। 4 ।।

Vārttika 3: The prohibition of *ṛcch-i* is a *jñāpaka* (implied rule), that for *ucch-i* there should be the *pratyaya ām.*

45.8 यदयमनृच्छ इति प्रतिषेधं शास्ति तज्ज्ञापयत्याचार्यस्तुग्निमित्ता यस्य गुरुमता
भवति तस्मादामिति।। स तर्हि ज्ञापकार्थ[4] ऋच्छिप्रतिषेधो वक्तव्यः। ननु चावश्यं
प्राप्त्यपर्थोऽपि वक्तव्यः। नार्थः प्राप्त्यर्थेन।ऋच्छत्यृताम् (7.4.11) इत्यृच्छेर्लिटि
45.11 गुणवचनं ज्ञापकं नर्च्छेर्लिट्याम्भवतीति।

Bhāṣya: The fact that the master teaches prohibition by the statement 'not after *ṛcch*' makes known that *ām* acts after that *dhātu* whose heavy syllable is caused by the *tuk* augment (by *che ca 6.1.73* "Augment *t* acts (as augment) of a preceding short vowel also when *ch* follows (in uninterrupted speech)").

Then it should be stated "the prohibition of *ṛcchi-i* is for making a *jñāpaka* (implied rule)".

The mention of *ṛcch* in the rule is meant not only for *jñāpaka* but also for its own sake. *Ṛcch* must just be liable for *ām* then only prohibition is possible. The mention of *ṛcch* is to indicate *prāpti* (obtainment) of *ām* after *ṛcch* itself.

And surely it is essential (to show) application (of *ām* after *ṛccha*) also. No purpose is served by mentioning it for the application (of *ām* after it). Because of the *sūtra* "*ṛcchatyṝtām* " 7.4.11 ("*Guṇa* acts for the vowel of *ṛcch, ṛ* and *dhātus* ending in long *ṝ*"). The express mention of '*guṇa* (for the initial vowel) when *liṭ* (perfect) follows', indicates that there is an implied rule/ *jñāpaka* that *ām* is not applicable after *ṛcchati.*

45.11 .... नैतदस्ति ज्ञापकम्। अर्त्यर्थमेतत्स्यात्। कथं पुनर्ऋच्छेर्लिटि
गुण उच्यमानोऽर्त्यर्थः शक्यो विज्ञातुम्। सामर्थ्यात्। ऋच्छिर्लिटि नास्तीति
कृत्वा प्रकृत्यर्थं विज्ञायते। तद्यथा। तिष्ठतेरित् (7.4.5) जिघ्रतेर्वा (6) इति
चङि तिष्ठतिजिघ्रती न स्त इति कृत्वा प्रकृत्यर्थं
45.15 विज्ञायते।।

This is not an implied rule/*jñāpaka.* The rule is for the sake of *dhātu ṛ* (with *ādeśa*/substitute *ṛcch*).

But how is it possible to know that 'the statement of *guṇa* for *ṛcchi* is for the sake of (the original *dhātu*) *ṛ*? By force of (specific statement). The (substitute) *ṛcchi-i* (in place of the original *ṛ*) does not occur when *liṭ* follows (because it has not an indicatory *ś*). Having formed (this conclusion) it is known that (the rule) is for the sake of the original (*dhātu ṛ*).

As for example having formed the conclusion that substitutes *tiṣṭhati* and *jighrati* do not occur when *caṇ* (reduplicated aorist of a causative stem follows) (from the observation of their presence in the *sūtras*) '*tiṣṭhater-it*' *7.4.5* ("When in the presence of *ṇi* (causative) followed by *caṅ*, short *i* is the *ādeśa* of the penultimate of the *dhātu sthā*" (in the form *sthāp 7.3.36* e.g. *atiṣṭhipat*) and '*jighrater-vā*' *7.4.6.* ("Optionally when in the presence of *ṇi* followed by *caṅ*, *i* is the *ādeśa* in place of the penultimate of the *dhātu ghrā*" (in the form *ghrāp 7.3.36* e.g. *ajighripat*); it is known that (the *sūtras*) are for the sake of the original *dhātus sthā* and *ghrā.*

.... किं पुनरर्तेर्लिटि गुणवचने प्रयोजनम्। आरतुः आरुः एतद्रूपं यथा स्यात्। किं पुनः कारणं न सिध्यति। द्विर्वचने कृते सवर्णदीर्घत्वे च यदि तावद्धातुग्रहणेन ग्रहणमृकारान्तानां लिटि गुणो भवीतीति[5] गुणे कृते रपरत्वे च अरतुः अरुरित्येतद्रूपं प्रसज्येत। अथाभ्यासग्रहणेन ग्रहणमुरत्वं[6] रपरत्वं हलादिशेषोऽत आदेः (7.4.70) इति दीर्घत्वमातो लोप इटि च (6.4.64) इत्याकारलोपः अतुः उरिति वचनमेव श्रूयेत।

But again what is the purpose in stating *guṇa* for the *dhātu ṛ* (= *arti*) when in the presence of *liṭ* (perfect)? So that these forms *āratuḥ* "They both went" *āruḥ* "They (all) went" should be applicable. But again, what is the reason (*guṇa*) is not established (here)?

When the dual is effected and there is lengthening of the homogeneous vowel (here *a*), if (*ā* can be) taken/understood by the mention of the *dhātu*, there is *guṇa*; (that) mention is the (cause of) *guṇa* for all *dhātus* ending in *ṛ* when *liṭ* follows, and when *guṇa* has been effected and *ṛ* following effected (by *uraṇ raparaḥ 1.1.51*), the forms *aratuḥ* and *aruḥ* would be applicable. Now, if *ā* is understood by the mention of *abhyāsa* (reduplicted syllable, which is prefixed), (there is) mention of (the rule) '*ur-at*' *7.4.66* ("Short *a* acts in place of the short or long *ṛ* of the reduplicated syllable") for that having the characteristic of having a *ṛ* following (by *uraṇraparaḥ 1.1.51.* "In place of *ṛ* (short or long) *aṇ* (= *a i u*) having a *r* following" and mention) of the rule '*halādiḥ śesaḥ*' *7.4.60* ("of the consonants of the reduplicative syllable, only the first is retained, the remainder are *lopa* elided"), and (mention of the *sūtra*) "*ata ādeḥ*" (*7.4.70* "A long vowel acts as *ādeśa* of the initial *a* of a reduplicated syllable in the perfect/*liṭ*") and of (the *sūtra*) *āto lopa iṭi ca 6.4.64.* "*Lopa* acts in place of the final *ā* (of a *dhātu* in the presence of an *ārdhadhātuka pratyaya* with the *āgama iṭ*, as well as when it begins with a vowel and has an indicatory *k* or *ṅ*", (*asamyogātliṭkit 1.2.5*) so that the expressions which actually would be heard are *ātuḥ* ('they both go') and *uḥ* ('they go').

45.20 .... गुणे पुनः सति गुणे कृते रपरत्वे[7] च द्विर्वचनं हलादिशेषोऽत
आदेरिति दीर्घत्वं ततः सिद्धं भवति यथाटतुः आटुरिति।। किं पुनः कारणं
सवर्णदीर्घत्वं[8] तावद् भवति न पुनरुरत्वम्। परत्वादुरत्वे भवितव्यम्। अन्तरङ्गत्वात्।
अन्तरङ्गं सवर्णदीर्घत्वं बहिरङ्गमुरत्वम्। कान्तरङ्गता। वर्णावा-
45.24 श्रित्य सवर्णदीर्घत्वमङ्गस्योरत्वम्। उरत्वमप्यन्तरङ्गम्। कथम्।

But when there is *guṇa* present, (then) when *guṇa* is effected (*ṛ* becomes *a*) and also a following *r* (is added by *1.1.51*); (there is) reduplication (by *ajāder dvitīyasya 6.1.2*); *lopa* elision of the non-initial consonants in the reduplicate (by *halādiḥ śeṣaḥ 7.4.60*) and a long vowel in place of the initial short *a* of the reduplicated syllable in the perfect (by *ata ādeḥ 7.4.70*), so that then it becomes established (as a valid form): as for example *āṭatuḥ* "They both wandered about (as religious mendicants)", *āṭuḥ* "They (all) wandered about". What is the reason there is just lengthening (of the reduplicated syllable *a*) but not (application of the *sūtra*) *ur-at 7.4.66* (*a* in place of *ṛ* or *ṝ*)? Because of being a letter *sūtra*, 'in place of *ṛ* or *ṝ a* 'should be applicable. Because of being *antaraṅga* (more inner/less operations), lengthening should be applicable. Lengthening in place of two homogeneous *ak* (*a i u ṛ ḷ*) vowels/*savarṇa dīrghatva* is *antaraṅga. A* in place of *ṛ* or *ṝ*/*urat-tva* is *bahiraṅga* (more outer/having more operations). What is the nature of *ạntaraṅga* (here) ? Having resorted to two letters or sounds, (only) the long homogeneous (sound is the one *ak* for the one before and the one after), (but) *ur-at-tva* (takes place) for an *aṅga* ('s final letter). *Urattva* is also *antaraṅga*. How?

45.24 ....वक्ष्यत्येतत्
प्रागभ्यासविकारेभ्योऽङ्गाधिकार[9] इति। उभयोरन्तरङ्गयोः परत्वादुरत्वम्। उरत्वे
कृते रपरत्वं हलादिशेषोऽत आदेरिति दीर्घत्वं परस्य रूपस्य यणादेशः सिद्धं
46.1 भवत्यारतुः आरुरिति।। अथापि कथंचिदर्तेर्लिटि गुणेनार्थः स्यात्। एवमपि न
दोषः। ऋच्छत्यृतामित्यृकारोऽप्यत्र निर्दिश्यते। कथम्। प्रश्लिष्टनिर्देशोऽयम्। ऋच्छतिऋ
46.3 ऋताम् ऋच्छत्यृतामिति।।

Patañjali will say this "*prāg-abhyāsa vikārebhyo 'ṅgādhikāraḥ*" on *6.4.1.* "The governing *sūtra aṅgasya* (forms a base) or has its scope of application as far as "*atra lopo' bhyāsasya*" *7.4.58.* (Therefore *urat 7.4.66* is not an *aṅga* rule). For both there is the nature of being *antaraṅga*; so because of being subsequent *urat* rule *prevails*. When *uratva* has been effected there is a following *r/raparatva* (and) "all non-initial consonants of the reduplicated syllable are *lopa*" / *halādiḥ śeṣaḥ 7.4.60.* There is a long vowel in place of the initial *a* of a reduplicate and the semivowel is the substitute (for the vowel) of the form of that following (the reduplicated syllable), (so the forms) *āratuḥ* ("They both went") and *āruḥ* ("They went") are established (as valid).

Now even somehow the purpose of the *sūtra* is *guṇa* for *arti* (*dhātu ṛ* to go) when *liṭ* (perfect) *pratyaya* follows, even so there is no fault. Here (in the *sūtra*) *ṛcchatyṝtām 7.4.11* ("*Guṇa* acts in the perfect of *ṛcch, ṛ* and *dhātus* ending in long *ṝ*") the letter *ṛ* (short) is also mentioned. How? This is indication of a coalescent (vowel) i.e. *ṛ* + *ṛ* = *ṝ ṛcchati-ṛ-ṝt-ām* (is formed from) *ṛcchati* (to go) *ṛ* (to go) and of those *dhātus* ending in long *ṝ*.

46.3 .... इहापि तर्हि प्राप्नोति चक्रतुः चक्रुरिति।
संयोगादिग्रहणं[10] नियमार्थं भविष्यति। संयोगादेरेवाकेवलस्य नान्यस्याकेवलस्येति।।
तदेतदन्तरेणा-
46.5 र्तेर्लिटि गुणवचनं रूपं सिद्धमन्तरेण चर्च्छिग्रहणमर्तेर्लिटि गुणः सिद्धः। स एषोऽनन्यार्थ
ऋच्छिप्रतिषेधो वक्तव्य उच्छेर्वाम्वक्तव्यः।। उभयं न वक्तव्यम्। उपदेश-
46.7 ग्रहणं न करिष्यते। कस्मान्न भवति इयेष उवोषः।

Then here also in (the forms) *cakr-atuḥ* and *cakr-uḥ* the mention of "beginning with a conjunct consonant" (by *ṛtaśca saṃyogāder guṇaḥ 7.4.10* "*Guṇa* acts for a *dhātu* ending in a short *ṛ* and beginning with a conjunct consonant, in the presence of *liṭ* (perfect)", will be for the purpose of a restriction. (*Guṇa*) only for that *dhātu* which begins with a conjunct consonant not (thus) having a vowel on its own, nor any other *dhātu* on its own (without a conjunct consonant). That expression of *guṇa* for *arti* (*dhātu ṛ*) when *liṭ* follows is established without mention of *arti* and without reference to or mention of (substitute) *ṛcch*. It is established that there is *guṇa* of *arti* in the presence of *liṭ*. This prohibition of *ṛcchi*, which has no other purpose, should be stated or it should be stated that there is *pratyaya ām* for *dhātu ucch-i*. Neither should be stated. Specific mention of 'original teaching/*upadeśa*' (i.e. *Dhātu Pāṭha*) will not be made. Why is it not applicable to *iyeṣa* "He desired" and *uvoṣa* "He burnt" ?

46.8 उक्तं वा ।। 5 ।।

Vārttika 5: Or (the reply) was stated (before).

46.9 किमुक्तम्। संनिपातलक्षणो विधिरनिमित्तं तद्विघातस्येति।।

Bhāṣya: What was stated? (*Pari. 85 P.1.1.39, Vā. 3*) "(That which is taught in) a rule (the application of) which is occasioned by the combination (of two things), does not become the cause of the destruction of that combination" (i.e. *iyeṣa* and *uvoṣa* become *gurumat* but this does not occasion *ām*).

46.10 उर्णोतेश्चोपसंख्यानम् ।। 6 ।।

Vārttika 6: There should be additional enumeration (of the prohibition of *ām*) after the *dhātu urṇu/urṇo-ti.*

46.11 ऊर्णोतेश्चोपसंख्यानं कर्तव्यम्। प्रोर्णुनाव।। न वक्तव्यम्।

Bhāṣya: Additional enumeration (of prohibition of *ām*) after *urṇo-ti* should be made. (The proper form is) *prorṇunāva* "He covered". It should not be stated.

46.12 वाच्य ऊणोर्णुवद्भावो यङ्प्रसिद्ध प्रयोजनम्।
आमश्च प्रतिषेधार्थमेकाचश्चेडुपग्रहात्[11]।।

Śloka Vārttika: It should be stated that *ūrṇu* should be treated like *dhātu ṇu* (to praise) so that *yaṇ* (intensive *pratyaya*) is established as valid; also for the prohibition of *ām pratyaya*, and (further) having one vowel like *ṇu* (there will be) prohibition of *iṭ* (*āgama*).

46.14 अथवोकारोऽप्यत्र निर्दिश्यते। कथम् अविभक्तिको निर्देशः। अनृच्छ उ
अंनृच्छो दयायासश्च (3.1.37) इति।।

Bhāṣya: Or otherwise the letter *u* is also mentioned here. How? There is indication without a *vibhakti*/case ending. So . . . *anṛccha 3.1.36 + u* (becomes by *sandhi* when the *sūtras* are considered as in *saṁhitā*), *anṛccho dayāyasaśca* (*3.1.37*) (*V.M.om.*). (So that the *sūtras* mean . . . "not after *ṛcch* and a *dhātu* ending in *u*", "After the *dhātus dayā* (to give, protect and go) and *ās* (to sit) there acts the *pratyaya ām* when *liṭ* (perfect) follows".)

Pradīpa

Pradīpa : 44.21 उवोषेति।

"He burnt."

But surely here, by virtue of the option, in उषविदजागृभ्योऽन्यतरस्याम् 3.1.38

"The *pratyaya ām* optionally acts after *uṣ* (to burn), *vid* (to know), and *jāgṛ* (to wake) when *liṭ* follows", so *ām* should be applicable.

Here they say . . . because of the absence of *guṇa* in the dual and the plural and the absence of a prosodically heavy vowel, option has scope of application, because of which, where there is a heavy vowel there invariably/*nitya ām* obtains.

"When there is a conflict of rules of equal force the subsequent prevails" (applies here) and not having resorted to the nature of the strength of a rule stating expressly the words for which it is meant, namely a *prātipadika vidhi.* The example was given by the *Bhāṣyakāra* because there, when option in fact is resorted to, it will be applicable. This does not have to be mentioned here.

Pradīpa : 45.1 गुरुमद्वचनमिति ॥

(What is the purpose of) the expression 'having a heavy syllable'.

The sense is that here also when lengthening of two *savarṇa* vowels has been effected, as *iṣatuḥ* (they all desired) because of then having a prosodially heavy syllable, everywhere after an *ik*-beginning *dhātu* with a heavy syllable, *ām* should be applied. Because of the force of expressing 'having a heavy syllable', he will resort to the (statement) 'for that *dhātu* having a heavy syllable in the context (only) of the *upadeśa/ Dhātu Pāṭha*'.

Pradīpa : 45.4 उपदेशवचनादिति ॥

"(Established) because of being expressed in an original teaching."

By *vacana* is intended 'explanation' otherwise, when there is rejection by one rule of another rule which quality would be applicable? Therefore, when there is a *nitya* rule because of resorting to *matup* when in the situation of the original teaching, the meaning is he will resort to 'having a heavy syllable (as condition)'.

Pradīpa : 45.7 उछेरिति ॥

For *dhātu ucchi* (there should be *ām*). *Dhātu ucchi vivāṣe* in sense of banishment, because of a heavy vowel not being read (the long vowel is to indicate it never takes augment *iṭ* when *kta* of past participle passive follows (*7.2.14*)).

Pradīpa : 45.13 तिष्ठतेरिति ॥

"(When *ṇi* is followed by *caṇ*, *i* is *ādeśa* of penultimate of *sthā* (to stand)."

The conclusion of this is that *ādeśas* do not occur when reduplicated aorist (*caṇ*) follows because of their presence in this *sūtra.*

The meaning is that here too when a *pratyaya* with an *it ś* follows *sthā,* having effected the *ādeśa tiṣṭha* in its place (some) indication has been made. There, 'by reason of that formed', (indicates) the word *sthā* alone is understood (as having *ādeśa* before *saṅ*).

Pradīpa : 45.16 द्विर्वचन इति ॥

"When the dual is effected . . . (lengthening of homogeneous vowel)."

Due to the *yaṅ* substituted by reason of the (exceptional) prior rule prevailing when two of equal force are in conflict, the doubling is then effected.

For so, when the rule 'being like the *sthānin*/original' applies, even for two *yaṇ ādeśa* (applies} invariably when the dual is being expressed, so the conflict (of rules of equal force) is regular.

Or else, just like *ni-nyataḥ* (they both lead), here should have *yaṇ ādeśa* because dual is prior, in fact *yaṅ* does not operate, so here too when doubling has been effected, lengthening of the *savarṇa* vowel must apply. *Yaṅ* either does not operate, or when *yaṅ* is present, because of its being like the original, there is doubling. When that has been effected there, because of its being subsequent to *yaṅ,* the substitute rule '*savarṇa* lengthening' (is applied).

Pradīpa : 45.16 यदि तावदिति ॥

If (*ā* can be understood) just (by the mention of the *dhātu* there is *guṇa* and (that mention is cause of *guṇa*) for all *dhātus* ending in *ṛ* when *liṭ* follows. The sense is that because of the condition of the one *ādeśa* being like the last of the prior and the first of the subsequent, (*antādivacca 6.1.85*) because of the designation/strategem of 'either way' (option) for both the *ādeśas* and because of being like the original/*sthānin* . . .

Pradīpa : 45.10 प्राप्त्यर्थेऽपीति ॥

The meaning is that it is for the obtainment of prohibition.

ऋच्छेर्लिटि गुणवचनं।

'In place of the vowel of *ṛcchi* the express mention of *guṇa* (for the initial vowel when *liṭ* follows)', *ṛcchi dhātu* not having a light vowel in the penultimate would not have received *guṇa* by

'पुगन्तलघूपधस्य च' 7.3.86

If *guṇa* will be applicable because of the rule even if *ām* intervenes, then 'when present' by *tasminniti nirdiṣṭe 1.1.66* this would be barred. Therefore, it is known (by *jñāpaka*) that by the enjoining of *guṇa* there is absence in fact of *ām.*

"By force of (specific statement we know *guṇa* is for *dhātu ṛ*)." The meaning of this is *dhātu ṛ* (*gati prāpanayoḥ* 'to get and attain', *936*) when *tip* and *sup* follow, then *ṛccha* is the *ādeśa* by *8.3.78,* not the *ṛcch* without an *ādeśa.*

Pradīpa : 45.13 नास्तीति।

ऋच्छिर्लिटि (The substitute *ṛcchi*) does not occur in place of *ṛ* when *liṭ* follows.

The absence of that *ādeśa ṛccha* (which occurs when *it ś* follows) is when the perfect follows.

पाघ्राध्मास्थाम्नादाण्दृश्यर्तिसर्तिशदसदां

पिबजिघ्रधमतिष्ठमनयच्छपश्यर्च्छधौशीयसीदा: 7।3।78।।

In place of पा घ्रा ध्मा स्था म्ना दाण् दृश् ऋ सृ शद् and सद्

there are पिब जिघ्र धम तिष्ठ मन यच्छ पश्य ऋच्छ धौ शीय and सीद before a

प्रत्यय beginning with an इत् श्

Pradīpa : 45.23 अन्तरङ्गत्वादिति ।।

"Because of being *antaraṅga* (having less operations), (lengthening should not be applicable)."

This statement that 'a rule relating to an *aṅga* is stronger than when a letter rule', however, is (really only applicable) in the sphere where what relates to *aṅga* and what relates to letters have the same resort/ locus, just as instrument/ *kāraka* (may refer to) a collection. *Guṇa* and *vṛddhi* are applicable because of the *yaṅ* substitute.

Here however, resorting to *liṭ* (perfect) there is short *a* by '*ur-at* ' followed by *r*. However, (with) resort to two letters, lengthening of the *savarṇa* vowel applies.

This is, when the two rules have different 'resorts'/loci.

Pradīpa : 46.1 अथापीति ।

Now even (when the purpose is *guṇa* for *ṛ* when *liṭ* follows there is no fault).

The sense is, that the *aṅga* governing rule operates until the end of the seventh *adhyāya* so that *vavraśca* etc. depending on that are established as valid.

Uddyota: Here *samprasāraṇa* of *r* and *ur-at* are effected when for it a subsequent cause points to it as *aṅga* so that then would be prohibition of *samprasāraṇam* by '*na samprasāraṇe samprāsaranam*' *6.1.37* but being like the *sthānin* is established as valid.

Pradīpa : 46.2 ऋकारोऽपीति।

The letter *r* is also (mentioned).

The sense is because of the indication of plural (in the *sūtra*).

Pradīpa : 46.3 इहापीति।

Then here also (in *cakratuḥ* . . . mention of beginning with a consonant will be for restriction).

The sense is (the mention of) *ṛ* being because of the existence of *tadanta* rules mentioning letters.

Pradīpa : 46.4 संयोगादेरिति। अकेवलस्य।

"*Guṇa* only for that *dhātu* which begins with a conjunct consonant not thus having a vowel on its own."

The meaning is for that together with another letter. And after that *dhātu* only the mention stands (applicable).

Pradīpa : 46.5 स एष इति।

"This prohibition of *ṛcchi* . . . should be stated."

The meaning is for the sake of a prosodically heavy *dhātu* which is the cause of the *āgama*.

By resorting to the *paryudāsa*/prohibition 'exception' *an-ṛcca, ām* is applicable after *uchi* because of the mention implied in relation to a *dhātu* 'like that (i.e. *ṛccha*). Otherwise, although by reason of the ordaining of *guṇa, ām* is not applicable after *ṛcchi* is known (to be so), still the prohibition *an-ṛccha* by reason of the possibility of its ordaining, is producing a *jñāpaka* applicable for the purpose spoken of.

Pradīpa : 46.6 उपदेशग्रहणमिति

"(Neither should be stated.) (There is) specific mention of original teaching."

The meaning is *gurumataḥ* is *matup* (with sense of having) being the basis for all having that nature as possessed of a heavy syllable; as for example, '*pitṛmān*' means 'having a father'. However, this is not an invariable rule, so he will explain.

Pradīpa : 46.9 सन्निपातलक्षण इति।

That taught in a rule, the application of which is occasioned by combination (of two things does not become the cause of destruction of that combination).

Liṭ 'is the cause of the combination', i.e. (requiring) *guṇa* does not become the cause of *ām* causing the destruction of that combination:

yeṣa and *uvoṣa,* through *gurumat* do not take *ām.*

न वा सनिपातलक्षणो विधिरनिमित्तं तद्विघातस्य 1.1.39 वा॰ 3

Pradīpa : 46.10 ऊर्णोतेरिति।

(Additional enumeration of prohibition of *ām*) after *urṇoti.*

The meaning is a prohibition.

Pradīpa : 46.14 उकारोपीति।

Or otherwise the letter '*u*' (is mentioned here) whereby *ām* is not applicable for *urṇoti* ending in *u.*

(When *sūtras* considered in *saṃhitā*)

Pradīpa : 46.15 अनृच्छो दयायासश्चेति।

anṛccha + *u* becomes *anṛccho.*
He shows the form of reciting one *sūtra* with *saṃhitā* (operating).
c.f. परः संनिकर्षः संहिता 1.4.109

Notes

[1] गुणे कृते।

'पुगन्तलघूपधस्य च' 7.3.86

[2] यजादीनां।। (*ām* should not be applicable for *yaj* and the rest).

लिट्यभ्यासस्योभयेषाम् ६।१।१७।।
वंच्यादीनां ग्रह्यादीनां चाभ्यासस्य सम्प्रसारणं लिटि।

"There is a *sāmprasāraṇa*/vocalisation of the semivowel of the reduplicate (*abhyāsa*) of both."

Before लिट् there is सम्प्रसारण of the अभ्यास of both sets of धातुs viz. वच् (वचिस्वपयिजादीनां किति 6.1.15) etc. and ग्रह्यादि (6.1.16) etc. इयाज॥

3 तुग्निमित्ता॥ *ām* acts after that *dhātu* whose heavy syllable is caused by *tuk* augment.

छे च 6.1.73

The implication by the mentioning of *tuk* is that all augments therefore, are excluded. Here *iṅ khām cakāra* 'He went', is applicable as valid.

4 ज्ञापकार्थ "for making an implied rule."

The mention of *ṛcch* in the rule is meant not only as a *jñāpaka* but also for its own sake. *Ṛcch* must first be liable for *ām*, then only prohibition is possible. So, the mention of *ṛcch* is to indicate *prāpti*/obtainment of *ām* after *ṛcch* itself.

5 ऋकारान्तानां लिटि गुणो। There is *guṇa* in the perfect for *ṛcch*, *ṛ*, and *dhātus*.

ऋच्छत्यॄताम् 7.4.11 ending in long *ṝ*.

रपरत्वे। When *ṛ* following applies . . .

उरण् रपर: 1.1.51 "In place of *ṛ* or *ṝ* there is *a i* or *u* with *r* following."

6 उरत्वम्॥ उरत् 7.4.66

अत अर् (1.1.51) is *ādeśa* in place of *ṛ* or *ṝ* of a reduplicate.

'हलदिशेष:' 7.4.60 of the consonants of the reduplicate only the first is retained, the rest are *lopa*/elided.

7 'गुणे कृते। पुगन्तलघूपधस्य' 7.3.86

8 'सवर्णदीर्घत्वं॥ अक: सवर्णे दीर्घ: 6.1.101

When a simple vowel (*a i u ṛ ḷ*) is followed by a homogeneous vowel, the corresponding long vowel is the one *ādeśa* for both prior and subsequent.

9 अङ्गाधिकार

प्रागभ्यासविकारेभ्योङ्गाधिकार 6.41

भाष्य। See text for translation.

[10] संयोगादिग्रहणम् ।।

ऋतश्च संयोगादेर्गुण: 7.4.10 'A *dhātu* ending in short *ṛ* and preceded by a conjunct consonant receives *guṇa* in the perfect.'

[11] एकाचश्चेडुपग्रहात् ।।

(*Yaṅ* is valid) having one vowel (like *nu* there will be prohibition of *iṭ* (*āgama*).

धातोरेकाचो हलादे: क्रिया समभिहारे यङ् 3.1.22

श्रयुक:किति 7.2.11

The augment *iṭ* is not added to a *pratyaya* with an indicatory *k* when it acts after the *dhātu* or after a single syllable *dhātu* ending in उ or ऊ, ऋ, ॠ in the *Dhātu Pāṭha.*

उषविदजागृभ्योऽन्यतरस्यात् ॥ 3 । 1 । 38 ॥

Pāṇini 3.1.38: The *Pratyaya ām* optionally acts after the *dhātu uṣ* (to burn) *vid* (to know) and *jagṛ* (to wake) when *liṭ* (perfect) follows.

46.17 विदेराम्कित् ।। 1 ।।

Vārttika 1: *Ām* having an indicatory *k* acts after *dhātu* (*vid*).

46.18 विदेराम्किद्वक्तय:[1]। विदांचकार।। न वक्तव्य:। विदिरकारान्त:। यद्य-
कारान्तो वेत्तीति गुणो न सिध्यति। लिट्संनियोगेन। एवमपि विवेदेति न सिध्यति।

46.20 एवं तर्ह्याम्संनियोगेन।।

Bhāṣya: It should be stated that *ām* having an indicatory *k* acts after *vid. vidām cakāra* "He knew". It should not be stated. (The *dhātu*) *vid* ends in the letter *a* (in the *sūtra*). If it ends with the letter *a* then the form *vetti* is not possible to be established with *guṇa* (of the penultimate vowel). (Then) in conjunction with *liṭ* (perfect, this should be stated). So also *viveda* "He knew", is not possible to be established. Well then, (only) in conjunction with the *pratyaya ām* (*vid* ends in *a*).

46.21 भारद्वाजीया: पठन्ति। विदेराम्किन्निपातनाद्वागुणत्वमिति।।

The followers of *Bhāradvāja* read:

"*Kit ām* acts after *vid* or (treating forms like *vidāncakāra* etc.) as (an irregular form), absence of *guṇa* (is justified)."

Pradīpa

Pradīpa : 46.18 विदिरकारान्त इति।

Dhātu vid ends in *a* (in the *sūtra*).

The sense is the nature of ending in *a* as (the characteristic) of *dhātu vid* in the *sūtra* is laid down as an irregular form. Another, having thought, 'in fact in the *Dhātu Paṭha vid* ends in *a* and by reason of that or (this form) of *vid* is stated', he says यदि इति if (it ends in *a* . . .)

Pradīpa : 46.19 गुणे न सिध्यतीति।

"(The form *ve-tti*) is not possible to be established with *guṇa*."

The meaning is that, because of the absence of the letter *i* (of *vid*) having the nature of being penultimate, and because of the absence of *lopa* elision of the final *a*, the form *vidati* would be derived.

Pradīpa : 46.20 आम्संनियोगेनेति।

(Well then only) in conjunction with *ām* (does *vid* end in *a*).

The meaning is by reason of the principle nature of *ām*, because of being non-ordained (as a *pratyaya* which is principal in relation to the subordinate *prakṛti*, its succession (is valid) after *vid* ending in *a*).

Notes

[1] किद्वक्तव्यः (*Vid*) should be stated as having a *k* (so preventing *guṇa* or *vṛddhi* by क्ङिति च 1.1.5 (इको गिणवृद्धी न)).

भीहीभृहुवां श्लुवच्च ॥ 3 । 1 । 39 ॥

Pāṇini 3.1.39: The *Pratyaya ām* acts optionally after the *dhātu bhī* (to fear), *hṛī* (to be ashamed), *bhṛ* (to nourish) and *hu* (to sacrifice) in the presence of *liṭ*; and when *ām* is *pratyaya* the effect is as if there were *ślu* elision (and the *dhātus* belonged to the *juhvādi gaṇa,* even for the purpose of *liṭ ārdhadhātuka pratyaya*)

46.23 श्लुवदतिदेशे किं प्रयोजनम्।

Bhāṣya: What is the purpose of the extended application being like *ślu*?

47.1 श्लुवदतिदेशे प्रयोजनं द्वित्वेत्वे ॥ 1 ॥

Vārttika 1: The purpose of the extended application of the rule as "being like *ślu*" is for the sake of reduplication and the *ādeśa* (substitute) *i* (in the reduplicate).

47.2 बिभरांचकार[1]॥

Bhāṣya: (For example) *bibharāṃcakāra* "He carried (the burden)".

Pradīpa

Pradīpa : 47.1 श्लुवदतिदेश इति।

The purpose of the extended application of the rule as 'being like *ślu* . . .

He asks this: Reduplication has to in fact be ordained anyway (because class 3), what is the point of the extended application?

By 'नलुमताङ्गस्य 1.1.63'

"For that *aṅga* whose *pratyaya* has been elided by the use of words containing *lu* (namely *lu-k ślu* and *lup*), the operations dependent on it, do not take place regarding such a base."

This being elision by *luk ślu,* prohibition of *guṇa* is not applicable.

This is prohibition of the obtainment from the *sūtra* '*pratyaya lopa pratyayalakṣaṇa*' and that obtainment is not applicable here.

Notes

[1] बिभरांचकार ।। He carried.

श्लौ 6.1.10 "For a non-reduplicate *dhātu,* there is reduplication in the presence of *ślu* (*vikaraṇa pratyaya*)."

भृञामित् 7.4.76 "Short *i* acts in place of the vowel of the reduplicates of the *dhātus bhṛñ* (*maṇ* and *o-hāṅ*) in the presence of *ślu vikaraṇa.*

कृञ्चानुप्रयुज्यते लिटि ।। 3 । 1 । 40 ।।

Pāṇini 3.1.40: After a *dhātu* ending in *ām pratyaya,* the *dhātu kṛ* (to do) is joined in the presence of the *liṭ* (*pratyaya* for the perfect).

47.4 किमर्थमिदमुच्यते। अनुप्रयोगो यथा स्यात्। नैतदस्ति प्रयोजनम्। आमन्तम-व्यक्तपदार्थकं तेनापरिसमाप्तोऽर्थ इति कृत्वानुप्रयोगे भविष्यति।। अत उत्तरं पठति।

Bhāṣya: Why is this said? So that there should be subsequent use (of an auxiliary verb). This is not the purpose. That which ends in the *pratyaya ām* is with an inarticulate word-meaning and so the meaning not being fully completed, there will be subsequent use (of an auxiliary verb). Hence he next recites what follows:

47.6 कृञोऽनुप्रयोगवचनमस्तिभूप्रतिषेधार्थम् ।। 1 ।।

Vārttika 1: The stating of *kṛñ* (as being for) subsequent use (as an auxiliary verb) is for the purpose of prohibiting *as-ti* (to be) and *bhū* (to become).

47.7 कृञोऽनुप्रयोगवचनं क्रियतेऽस्तिभूप्रतुषेधार्थम्। अस्तिभुवोरनुप्रयोगो मा भूदिति।।

Bhāṣya: The stating of *kṛñ* (as for) subsequent use (as an auxiliary verb) is for the purpose of prohibiting *as-ti* (to be) and *bhū* (to become), (in that capacity), so that there should not be additional use of *asti* and *bhū* (as auxiliary verbs).

47.9 आत्मनेपदविध्यर्थं च ।। 2 ।।

Vārttika 2: And for the purpose of a rule ordaining *ātmanepada pratyayas.*

47.10 आत्मनेपदविध्यर्थं च कृञोऽनुप्रयोगवचनं क्रियते। आत्मनेपदं यथा स्यात्।।
उच्यमानेऽप्येतस्मिन्नवश्यमात्मनेपदार्थो यत्नः कर्तव्यः।। अस्तिभूप्रतिषेधार्थेन चापि
47.12 नार्थः।

Bhāṣya: The stating of additional use (as an auxiliary verb) for the *dhātu kṛñ* is also made for the sake of the rule ordaining *ātmanepada pratyayas.* Even when this is being (here) stated, still effort has to be made specifically for the purpose of (obtaining) *ātmanepada* (endings) by *ām pratyayavat kṛño 'nuprayogasya 1.3.63* "Like the *dhātu* which takes *ām pratyaya* (if the *dhātu* be conjugated with *ātmanepada* endings) so for the *dhātu kṛ* (to do) when joined there as auxiliary, the terminations are *ātmanepada* (even when the fruit does not accrue to the agent)". But the purpose is also not for the prohibition of *asti* and *bhū* (as auxiliary verbs).

47.13 इष्टः सर्वानुप्रयोगः ।। 3 ।।

Vārttika 3: It is desired that there be subsequent use (as auxiliary verbs) for all (three).

47.14 सर्वेषामेव कृभ्वस्तीनामनुप्रयोग इष्यते। किमिष्यत एवाहोस्वित्प्राप्नोत्यपि
इष्यते च प्राप्नोति च। कथम्। कृञिति नैतद्धातुग्रहणम्। किं तर्हि। प्रत्याहारग्रहणम्।
क्व संनिविष्टानां प्रत्याहारः। कृभ्वस्तियोग इत्यतः प्रभृत्या कृञो ञका-
47.17 रात्[1]।।

Bhāṣya: Subsequent use (as auxiliaries) is desired for all (three) *kṛ, bhū* and *asti.* It is desired or does it in fact also obtain? It is desired and it obtains. How? This *kṛñ* is not just a mention of (the one) *dhātu.* What then? It is reference to a *pratyāhāra.* Where is (formed) the *pratyāhāra* (drawing together) of those contained in it? From the *sūtra kṛbhvastiyoge 5.4.50* onwards up to the letter *ñ* of *kṛño 5.4.58.*

47.18 सर्वानुप्रयोग इति चेदशिष्यमर्थाभावात् ।। 4 ।।

Vārttika 4: If (we accept the statement of additional usage) of all (as auxiliaries), (the statement of subsequent usage) need not be taught because (the word ending in *ām*) has no meaning.

47.19 सर्वानुप्रयोग इति चेदशिष्यं कृञोऽनुप्रयोगवचनम्। किं कारणम्। अर्थाभावात्।
आमन्तमव्यक्तपदार्थकं तेनापरिसमाप्तोऽर्थ इति कृत्वानुप्रयोगो भविष्यति।। इदं
तर्हि प्रयोजनं कृभ्वस्तीनामेवानुप्रयोगो यथा स्यात्पचादीनां मा भूदितिं एत-
47.22 दपि नास्ति प्रयोजनम्।

Bhāṣya: If (it is said) 'additional use of all (three *dhātus* as auxiliaries)', the expressing of additional use of *kṛñ* (as auxiliary), is a thing necessary to teach. What is the reason? Because the meaning is absent. The word ending in *ām* has an inarticulate meaning, so the meaning is incomplete; there will then be applicable subsequent use (of auxiliaries). This then is the purpose so that there should be subsequent use (as auxiliaries) of *kṛ, bhū* and *asti* only and not of *pac* (to cook) and the rest. This too is not the purpose.

47.23 अर्थाभावाच्चान्यस्य ॥ 5 ॥

Vārttika 5: Due to the other (*dhātus*) being without meaning.

47.24 अर्थाभावाच्चान्यस्य सिद्धम्। कृभ्वस्तयः क्रियासामान्यवाचिनः क्रियाविशेष-
वाचिनः पचादयो न च सामान्यवाचिनोरेव विशेषवाचिनोरेव वा प्रयोगो भवति।
48.2 तत्र विशेषवाचिन उत्पत्तिः सामान्यवाचिनोऽनुप्रयोक्ष्यन्ते॥

Bhāṣya: Due to the other (*dhātus*) being without meaning, this non-applicability of other *dhātus* is established. *Kṛ, bhū, asti* express a general or common activity; *pac* and the rest express a particular/special activity. And the usage (in the language) is not only of (*dhātus*) expressing general (action) nor only of those expressing particular (action). There, (where the forms are derived from a *dhātu* expressing particular action), the *dhātus* expressing general (action) will be employed after, in addition (as auxiliary verbs).

48.3 लिट्परार्थं वा ॥ 6 ॥

Vārttika 6: Or else it is for the sake of (when) *liṭ* (perfect) follows.

48.4 लिट्परार्थं तर्हि कृञोऽनुप्रयोगवचनं क्रियते। लिट्परस्यैवानुप्रयोगो यथा स्यादन्यपरस्य
मा भूदिति॥ किं परस्य पुनःप्राप्नोति।लट्परस्य।न लट्परस्य-
48.6 प्रयोगेण भूतकालो विशेषितः स्यात्॥

Bhāṣya: Then it is for the sake of (when) *liṭ* follows that the stating of the additional use of *kṛñ* (as auxiliary) is made; so that the additional use should be only for that which has *liṭ* following, and should not be applicable for that having any other *pratyaya* following. But for what (other *pratyaya*) following does it obtain? For a following *laṭ* (present). Past time would not be specified by means of subsequent use of that, having *laṭ* following.

48.6 .... निष्ठापरस्य तर्हि मा भूदिति। न निष्ठापरस्यानु-
प्रयोगेणपुरुषोपग्रहौ विशेषितौ स्याताम्। लुङ्परस्य तर्हि मा भूत्। न लुङ्पर-
स्यानुप्रयोगेणानद्यतनो भूतकालो विशेषितः स्यात्। लङ्परस्य तर्हि मा भूत्। न
लङ्-
48.9 परस्यानुप्रयोगेणानद्यतनः परोक्षःकालो विशेषितः स्यात्॥

Then so that it should not be applicable for that having a *niṣṭhā* (i.e. past participle passive *kta* and past participle active *k-tavat-u*) following. The persons and voice/*pada* of a *dhātu* would not be specified by the additional use (of auxiliaries) for that having *niṣṭha* following. Then, so that it should not be applicable for that having *luṅ* (aorist) following. The past-time not of the present day would not be specified by the additional use (of auxiliaries) for that having *luṅ* following. Then so that it should not be applicable for that having *laṅ* (imperfect) following. The time not of the present day and beyond the sight (of the speaker, i.e. completed action in the remote past), would not be distinguished by the additional use (of auxiliaries) for that having *laṅ* following.

48.9 .... अयं तर्हि भूते परोक्षेऽनद्यतने लङ्विधीयते हशश्वतोर्लङ् च 3.2.116) इति तत्परस्य मा भूदिति। एत-दपि नास्ति प्रयोजनम्। एकस्या आकृतेश्चरितः प्रयोगो द्वितीयस्यास्तृतीयस्याश्च न भवति। तद्यथा। गोष स्वाम्यश्वेषु चेति। न च भवति गोषु चाश्वानां च

48.13 स्वामीति।।

Well then this *laṇ* is ordained in the sense of past time not of the present day and beyond the sight of the speaker (by the *sūtra*) *"haśaśvatorlaṅ ca 3.2.116"* ("The *pratyaya laṇ* acts after a *dhātu* when the particles *ha* and *śaśvat* are connected with it and when the *dhātu* denotes past action unperceived by the speaker and before commencement of the present day"); thus (stating of additional use is) so that it should not be applicable for that having *laṇ* following (under those conditions). This also is not the purpose. Usage ascertained for one form is not applicable for a second or a third. As for example *goṣu svāmyaśveṣu ca* The lord of the cows and the horses; and so (the same rule) is not applicable (here): *goṣu cāṣvānām ca svamī* "He is lord of the cows and the horses".

48.14 अर्थसमाप्तेर्वानुप्रयोगो न स्यात् ।। 7 ।।

Vārttika 7: Or else because of the meaning being completely accomplished there would not be additional use (of auxiliaries).

48.15 अर्थसमाप्तेस्तर्ह्यनुप्रयोगो न स्यात्। आमन्तेन परिसमाप्तोऽर्थ इति कृत्वानुप्रयोगो न स्यात्।। एतदपि नास्ति प्रयोजनम्। इदानीमेव ह्युक्तमामन्तमव्यक्तपदा-

48.17 र्थकं तेनापरिसमाप्तोऽर्थ इति कृत्वानुप्रयोगो भविष्यतीति।।

Bhāṣya: Then because of the meaning being completely accomplished there would be no additional use (of auxiliaries); having made (the statement) 'the meaning is completed by ending in the *pratyaya ām*'. For now in fact having made (the statement) 'the meaning was not completed by that'

because it was stated that 'since that which ends in *ām* has an inarticulate meaning'; additional use (of auxiliaries) will be applicable.

48.18 विपर्यासनिवृत्यर्थं वा ॥ 8 ॥

Vārttika 8: Or else it is for the purpose of preventing interchange.

48.19 विपर्यासनिवृत्यर्थं तर्हि कृञोऽनुप्रयोगवचनं क्रियते। ईहां चक्रे। चक्र ईहामिति मा भूत्॥

Bhāṣya: Then the expression of additional use of auxiliaries is made to prevent inversion of the order (or auxiliaries) *īhāmcakre* "He endeavoured to obtain". So that *cakra īhām* should not be applicable.

48.21 व्यवहितनिवृत्यर्थं च ॥ 9 ॥

Vārttika 9: And for the purpose of preventing being placed apart/separated.

48.22 व्यवहितनिवृत्यर्थं च कृञोऽनुप्रयोगवचनं क्रियते। अन्वेव चानुप्रयोगो यथा स्यात्। ईहांचक्रे। व्यवहितस्य मा भूत्॥ ईहां देवदत्तश्चक्र इति॥

Bhāṣya: The stating of additional use (of auxiliaries) is also made for the sake of *kṛñ* being prevented from being separated (from the main *dhātu*); so that the additional use should only take place immediately after only as *īhāmcakre;* so that (additional use) should not be applicable for (*dhātu* and auxiliary being) separated (as) *īhām devadattaścakre* ("*Devadatta* endeavoured to obtain").

48.24 इति श्रीभगवत्पतञ्जलिविरचितं व्याकरणमहाभाष्ये तृतीयाध्यायस्य प्रथमे पा-दे तृतीयमाह्निकम्॥

Thus (ends) the third *Āhnika* in the first *pāda* of the third *adhyāya* in the *Vyākaraṇa Mahābhāṣya* composed by the blessed master *Patañjali.*

Pradīpa

Pradīpa : 47.4 किमर्थमिति।

"And *kṛñ* is used . . . Why is this said?"

Even without beginning the *sūtra,* the subsequent usage (of auxiliaries) is established as valid, having taught time, instruments for accomplishing the action, number, backward direction etc. (it is applicable) fot *kṛñ* having *liṭ* (perfect) following. For after that ending in *ām* a particular time is to be obtained/insisted on, but not another meaning. There, the subsequent usage (of an auxiliary) will not be applicable for a *dhātu* of the same meaning (as) *oṣamu-voṣa* (He heated).

Because of all meaning being manifest by the subsequent (*dhātu*) alone, there is the possibility of that ending in *ām* being meaningless. Nor (is it) even (possible) for that having a different meaning (as *īhām, papāca* 'He does strive, He cooked'). Because of not (even understanding) *sādhana*/instrument for accomplishing the action as connected with that ending in *ām*.

However, *kṛñ* expresses general (activity). The sense is that also the usage of expressing general and special (activities) is congenial to understanding a distinction of meaning (between the *dhātu* and its auxiliary).

Pradīpa : 47.4 अनुप्रयोग इति।

(So that there should be) subsequent use (of an auxiliary).

The sense is that, although all meaning is not manifest (after) that ending in *ām*, still because of the force of usage etc., it will be so (therefore) that this should be stated for the purpose of establishing as valid subsequent uses (of an auxiliary).

Pradīpa : 87.4 आमन्तमिति ।

"That which ends in *ām* (has an inarticulate word meaning)."

The sense is that, because of the force of usage etc. for the meanings previously stated, ascertainment is not possible, so for the purpose of expressing that meaning, the subsequent use (of an auxiliary) is established as valid.

Pradīpa : 47.6 कृ इति

To show this restriction, so that subsequent usage be for *kṛ*/ *karoti* only, and should not be for *bhū* and *as* he states (*Vā. 1*) *kṛño* etc.

Pradīpa : 47.9 आत्मनेपदेति।

(And for the purpose of a rule ordaining) *ātmanepada pratyayas.*

The meaning is that when subsequent usage of *kṛñ* is established as valid, repetition is for the purpose of the subsequent usage of that having extremely similar qualities, therefore *karoti* is used as an auxiliary only for that ending in *ām*, ending in *ātmanepada* and for *ātmanepada* base; thus the *sūtra*:

Pradīpa : 47.11 आम्प्रत्ययवत्कृञोऽनुप्रयोगस्य (1.3.63)

"Like the *dhātu* that takes *ām pratyaya,* if the *dhātu* takes *ātmanepada* so that this is true of *kṛ* when joined as an auxiliary. It also is *ātmanepada* (even if fruit does not accrue to the agent)." (This *sūtra*) is not to be effected produced.

Pradīpa : 47.11 अवश्यमिति।

"It is essential (effort has to be made for obtaining *ātmanepada*)."

The sense is that, because of the meaning of agent being understood even by *parasmaipada* endings, the subsequent usage would be for (a *dhātu* ending in that (*parasmaipada*).

Pradīpa : 47.15 प्रत्याहारग्रहणमिति।

"It is a reference to a *pratyāhāra.*"

And this is known because the mention of *kṛñ* here in the *sūtra* "*ām pratyayavat kṛño 'nuprayogasya' 1.3.69* (see previous note) is for the purpose of *as* and *bhū* ceasing to be applicable.

And the verb *sam-pad* will not be applicable as an auxiliary verb because of a conflict of meaning (with *kṛ bhū* and *as* having the general meaning of activity), (in spite of it coming within the province of the *pratyāhāra* beginning with *kṛñ* and ending with *ñ*).

Pradīpa : 47.19 अशिष्यमिति।

"(Subsequent usage) need not be taught because the word ending in *ām* has no meaning."

It is not even used for preventing of usage of *vidyati* (to exist/be). Due to the enumeration of all these used and to not seeing use of it as an auxiliary (in the language).

Pradīpa : 48.1 न चेति।

"And (the usage is) not (only of *dhātus* expressing generalisation in or only of those expressing action)."

The sense is, because of the absence of usage of two (verbs) having the same meaning. And for the purpose of showing the general customs/ usage, it was stated 'because of expressing general (activity)'. However, there is not ordaining of *ām* after *kṛ, bhū* and *as* expressing general (activity). A qualifying word is not able to illuminate/make visible the meaning as expressing general (activity). On the contrary, by the rejection of another qualification it is (obstructing)/inimical to that meaning.

Pradīpa : 47.4 लट्परार्थेति।

"(For what other *pratyaya* does that *it* obtain?) For a following *laṭ*"

The sense is, because of the teaching of the qualification *bhūta* 'past tense' in connection with that ending in *ām.*

Having resorted to the present . . . though in place of the past, and having past as the preceding/prior, the usage of *laṭ* should be applicable.

Pradīpa : 48.5 न लट् परस्येति।

"(Past time would not be specified by means of subsequent use) for that having *laṭ* following."

Because of the subsequent use of an auxiliary having the purpose of manifesting the meaning of that ending in *ām,* and that having *laṭ* expressing the present, which is a conflicting time, will not be used subsequently as an auxiliary.

Pradīpa : 48.11 एकस्या इति।

"(Usage ascertained) for one form (is not applicable for a second)."

This principal is well known in the *Veda* and the popular usage. For as when there are the instruments for accomplishing the action 'He ties it to the *khadira* tree' or 'He ties it to the *palāśa* tree' etc. are optional, so that with whatever means/instrument the action is undertaken, with that very one it is accomplished.

There (in that context), if sometime there is tottering or failure of the *khadira* tree then the *barbura* which is like that, and because of similarity, thinking of it as *khadira,* it is put in its place/substituted; but the *palāśa* tree is not taken hold of (grasped) on both sides. By reason of a difference in instruments of the action, (and) because of the different nature of the action, there is the possibility of not accomplishing the action undertaken.

Also in the worldly (usage), when to teach the state of 'wealth/possessions' and 'cord of possessions/wealth' the sixth case is had recourse to/treated of (in the example) 'owner/lord of cows'. Then here also, (he may say) 'and of horses'. (This is) to make that understood, that (sixth case) alone succeeds, i.e. accomplishes the aim.

Otherwise, it would (wrongly) also be applicable. Is the re-assertion of *adhikaraṇa*/locative expressed (*abhihita*) and the translation 'the (owner of) horse' and 'he stands among horses' ?

The meaning is therefore, that which is the meaning by which the word form was undertaken to be taught, is to be accomplished for that alone, not by any other word form. For then brevity of statement is possible.

Pradīpa : 48.13 स्वामीति।

स्वामीश्वराधिपतिदायादसाक्षिप्रतिभूप्रसूतैश्च (2.3.39)

"The sixth and seventh *vibhakti* case *pratyayas* act after words, when they are joined with the words *svāmin* (master), *īśvara* (lord), *adhipati* (ruler), *dāyāda* (heir), *sākṣin* (witness), *pratibhā* (surety), and *prasūta* (begotten)."

Pradīpa : 48.14 अर्थसमाप्तेवेति।

"Or because of the meaning being completely accomplished (there would not be additional use of auxiliaries)."

The sense is that, insofar as it is possible to express the meaning as a word ending in *ām*, only/so far as the meaning is established there; thus additional use of auxiliary would be applicable.

Pradīpa : 48.16 एतदपीति।

"This too is the purpose."

The *Bhāṣyakāra* says this to (show) it to be wrong.

Pradīpa : 48.18 विपर्यासनिवृत्यर्थं वेति।

"Or else it is for the purpose of preventing interchange."

When the usage of *kṛñ* is established as valid, the rule/*vārttika 8* is for the purpose of restricting place (of application). Due to the word *anu* having the meaning of afterwards, therefore, *kṛñ* is used only after that ending in *ām*, not before, nor separated by anything. Thus there is attainment of (the agreed) meaning.

Notes

[1] कृनो ञकारात्।

"Thus the *pratyāhāra* is formed beginning with *kṛ* and ending with *ñ*"

कृभ्वस्तियोगे संपद्यकर्तरि च्वि (5.4.50) to कृञो द्वितीयतृतीयशम्बबीजात् कृषौ (5.4.58)

च्लिः लुङि ॥ 3 । 1 । 43 ॥

Pāṇini 3.1.43: When *luṅ* (aorist *pratyaya*) follows the *pratyaya cli* acts after a *dhātu*

49.2 क्वायं च्लिः श्रूयते। न क्वचिच्छ्रूयत एतस्य सिजादय आदेशा उच्यन्ते। यदि न
क्वचिच्छ्रूयते किमर्थस्तर्हि च्लिरुत्सर्गः क्रियते न सिजुत्सर्ग एवं कर्तव्यः। तस्य
49.5 क्सादयोऽपवादा भविष्यन्ति।। अत उत्तरं पठति।

Bhāṣya: Where is *cli* heard? It is nowhere heard. *Sic* and the rest are stated to be the *ādeśas* (substitutes) of this.

If it is nowhere heard, what then is the purpose of making *cli* a general *pratyaya* ? Should not *sic* in fact be made the general/*utsarga sūtra* ? *Ksa* and the rest will be special/particular or *apavāda sūtras* (debarring the general rule). Therefore he reads the following (*vārttika*).

49.5 च्ल्युत्सर्गः सामान्यग्रहणार्थः ।। 1 ।।

Vārttika 1: The general *pratyaya cli* is for the purpose of a common reference.

49.6 च्लिरुत्सर्गः क्रियते सामान्यग्रहणार्थः।क्व सामान्यग्रहणार्थेनार्थः।मन्त्रे घस-
ह्वरणशवृदहाद्वृच्कृगमिजनिभ्यो लेः (2.4.81) इति। तत्रावरतस्त्रयाणां ग्रहणं
49.8 कर्तव्यं स्यात्।चङङोः सिच इति।।

Bhāṣya: The general *pratyaya cli* is made for the purpose of a common reference (point for all forms of the aorist). Where is the purpose (or common reference served) ? In the *sūtra "mantre ghasa hvara naśa vṛ dahād vṛc kṛ gami-janibhyo leḥ" 2.4.80* ("In the *mantra* (portion of the *Vedas*) there is *luk* elision of the *cli* of the aorist (and the perfect) after the *dhātus ghas* (to eat), *hvar-a* (to be crooked), *naś-a* (to destroy), *vṛ* (to choose or to cover), *daha* (to burn), *dhātus* ending in a, *vṛc* (to avoid), *kṛ* (to make), *gam-i* (to go), and *jan-i* (to be produced)"). There would have been specific mention of at least three (substitutes of *cli*), namely *caṅ, aṅ* and *sic.*

49.9 क्सविधाने चानिड्वचने च्लिसंप्रत्ययार्थः ।। 2 ।।

Vārttika 2: And it is for the sake of the recognition of the meaning of *cli*, when *ksa* is ordained without the expression of *iṭ* (*āgama*).

49.10 क्सविधाने चानिड्वचने च्लिसंप्रत्ययार्थश्चच्लिरुत्सर्गः क्रियते। च्लेरनिटः क्सः
सिद्धो भवति[1]।।

Bhāṣya: And when *ksa* is ordained without the expression of *iṭ* (*āgama*), it is for the sake of the right conception (of the meaning) of *cli*, that *cli* is made a general (*pratyaya*). *Ksa* is established as valid in place of *cli* without the *āgama iṭ*.

49.12 घस्लृभावे च ॥ 3 ॥

Vārttika 3: And when *ghas-ḷ* is substituted (an *aṅ* is substituted in place of *cli* only).

49.13 घस्लृभावे च च्लावेव कृत लृदित इत्यङ् सिद्धो भवति[2]॥

49.14 अथ चित्करणं किमर्थम्।

Bhāṣya: When the substitute *ghas-ḷ* takes place, *aṅ* taught by rule *ḷditaḥ* etc., is effected only when *cli* has been effected.

Now then what is the purpose of producing the indicatory *c* ?

49.15 च्लेश्चित्करणं विशेषणार्थम् ॥ 4 ॥

Vārttika 4: The producing of the indicatory letter *c* of *cli* is for the purpose of distinguishing.

49.16 च्लेश्चित्करणं क्रियते विशेषणार्थम्। क्व विशेषणार्थेनार्थः। च्लेः सिच् (3.1.44) इति। लेः सिजित्युच्यमाने लिङ्लिटोरपि प्रसज्येत॥ नैतदस्ति

49.18 प्रयोजनम्। लुङीत्युच्यते न च लुङि लिङ्लिटौ स्तः॥

49.19 अथेदित्करणं किमर्थम्।

Bhāṣya: The producing of the indicatory letter *c* of *cli* is done for the purpose of distinguishing (from other *pratyayas*). Where is the purpose served of distinguishing? (In the *sūtra*) '*cleḥ sic 3.1.44*' ("*sic* acts in the place of *cli*"). (If) it is being stated *leḥ sic* (*sic* in place of *liṭ*'), it would also be applicable to *liṅ* (optative) and *liṭ* (perfect). This is not the purpose. It is said that when *liṅ* (aorist) follows there is *liṅ* and *liṭ* do not occur.

Now then what is the purpose of producing an indicatory *i* (in *cli*) ?

49.20 इदित्करणं सामान्यग्रहणार्थम् ॥ 5 ॥

Vārttika 5: The producing of an indicatory *i* is for the purpose of common mention/reference.

49.21 इदित्करणं क्रियते च सामान्यग्रहणार्थम्। क्व सामान्यग्रहणार्थेनार्थः। मन्त्रे घसन्ह्वरणशवृदहाद्वृच्कृगमिजनिभ्यो लेरिति। आमः (2.4.81) इति च॥ इकारे चेदान्तीं सामान्यग्रहणार्थे क्रियमाणेऽवश्यं सामान्यग्रहणाविघातार्थश्चकारः कर्तव्यः।

49.24 क्व सामान्यग्रहणाविघातार्थेनार्थश्चकारेण। अत्रैव।।

Bhāṣya: The producing of indicatory *i* is done for the purpose of common reference. Where is the purpose of common reference served? (In the *sūtra*) *mantre ghasa hvara ṇaśa vṛ dahād vṛc kṛ gami-janibhyoḥ leḥ 2.4.80.* "In the *mantra* portion of the *Veda* there is *luk* elision of *li* (of the aorist and perfect) after the *dhātus ghas* (to eat), *hvar* (to be crooked), *ṇaś* (to destroy), *vṛ* (to choose or to cover), *dah* (to burn), *dhātus* ending in long *ā*, *vṛc* (to avoid), *kṛ* (to make), *gami* (to go), and *jani* (to be produced)" and (in the *sūtra*) *āmaḥ 2.4.81*, "There is *luk* elision in the place of that *li* (tense *pratyaya*) which acts after *ām* (of the perfect)". And now when the letter *i* is being effected for the purpose of general mention, it is essential that the letter *c* be produced for the purpose of non-hindrance/*avighāta* (of the application of the particular term) to common reference to others, where it should apply. Where is there found the letter *c* (used) with the purpose of (indicating) 'non-hindrance' to common reference? Here in this very *sūtra* just quoted, namely *āmaḥ 2.4.81.*

50.1 यत्तावदुच्यते च्ल्युत्सर्गः सामान्यग्रहणार्थ इति। क्रियमाणेऽपि वै च्ल्युत्सर्गे तान्येव
त्रीणि ग्रहणानि भवन्ति। च्लि लुङि च्लेः सिच् लेरिति।। यदेतल्लेरिति तत्परार्थं
भविष्यति। कथम्। यदेतद्गातिस्थाघुपाभूभ्यः सिचः परस्मैपदेषु (2.4.77)
50.4 इत्यत्र सिचो ग्रहणमेतल्लेरिति वक्ष्यामि।।

What is just said is that *cli* is a general/*utsarga pratyaya* for the purpose of common reference (for all forms of the aorist). Even when indeed *cli* is being formed as a general/*utsarga pratyaya*, only the three (*sūtra*) references are applicable:

cli luṇi 3.1.43; cleḥ sic 3.1.44 (*sic* in place of *cli*); and *leḥ* (*2.4.80, 81* above).

That which (is stated) as '*leḥ*' *2.4.80* 'in the place of *li*' is for the following *sūtra* (*āmaḥ*). How? This mention which I will mention of '*sicaḥ*' (in place of *sic*) in the *sūtra* "*gāti-sthā-ghu-pā-bhūbhyaḥ sicah. parasmaipadeṣu*" *2.4.77* (means) "which is in place of *li*" i.e. there is *luk* of *sic* in place of *li* after the *dhātus gā* (to go), *sthā* (to stand), *dhātu* called *ghu 1.1.20, pā* (to drink), and *bhū* (to be).

50.4 .... यदि लेरित्युच्यते धेटश्चातुः शब्द्यं प्राप्नोति। अदधत्
अधात् अधासीत्। अदधादित्यपि प्राप्नोति।। न चङो लुकि द्विर्वचनेन भवितव्यम्।
किं कारणम्। चङि (6.1.11) इत्युच्यते न चात्र चङं पश्यामः
50.7 प्रत्ययलक्षणेन। ल लुमता तस्मिन्निति प्रत्ययलक्षणप्रतिषेधः।।

If *leḥ* (in the place of *li*) is stated, then four (aorist) word forms from *dheṭ* obtain. (By "*vibhāṣa dheṭ śvyoḥ*" *3.1.49* ("*caṅ* optionally acts in place of *cli* after the *dhātu dheṭ* (to suck) and *śvi* (to grow) when in the presence of *luṅ* signifying the agent") and "*vibhāṣā ghrā dheṭ śācchāsaḥ*" *2.4.78* "There is optionally *luk* elision in place of *sic* after the *dhātus ghrā* (to smell), *dheṭ* (to drink), *śā* (*śo* to pare), *chā* (*cho* to cut), and *sā* (= *so* to destroy), when *parasmaipada* terminations are employed". Thus *adadhat* (*caṅ*) *adhāt* (*kṣa*) *adhāsīt* (*sic*) *adadhāt* also obtains. "He sucked". There should not be reduplication when *luk* elision occurs of *caṅ*. What is the reason? Thus it is stated *caṅ 6.1.11* ("For a non-reduplicate *dhātu* there is reduplication when *caṅ* (*6.1.11*) *ādeśa pratyaya* of the aorist follows"). But here we do not see *caṅ*. By virtue of the *pratyaya's* characteristic properties (even when elided) the operations dependent on it continue, if *lopa* elision has occured.

50.7 .... बहुवचने तर्हि चातु:-
शब्द्यं प्राप्नोति। अदधन् अधु: अधासिषु:। अधानित्यपि प्राप्नोति।। नैष दोष:।
आत: (3.4.110) इति जुस्भावो भविष्यति।। न सिध्यति। सिज्ग्रहण[3] तत्रानु-वर्तते।।
सिज्ग्रहणं निवर्तिष्यते।। यदि निवर्तते अभूवन्निति प्रत्ययलक्षणेन जुस्भाव:
50.11 प्राप्नोति।। एवं तर्हि लुक्सिजपवादो विज्ञास्यते।।

Then in the plural the four word (forms) obtain. *adadhan, adhuḥ,* and *adhāsiṣuḥ* ("He sucked"); *adhān* also obtains. This is no fault. Because of the *sūtra* "*ātaḥ*" *3.4.110,* ("when *sic* is elided *jus* is *ādeśa* of *jhi* after an aorist *aṅga* ending in long *ā*"), there will thus be the substitution of *jus.* This is not established. The mention of *sic* there follows on (from the previous *sūtras*).

The mention of *sic* will cease to follow on. If it ceases to follow on, then by reason of *pratyayalakṣaṇa, jus* substitute (for the form) *abhūvan* obtains. So then the *luk* will be understood as *apavāda* of *sic.*

50.11 .... यदि लुक्सिजपवादो विज्ञायते मा हि दताम्
मा हि धातामित्यत्रादि: सिचोऽन्यतरस्याम् (6.1.187) इत्येष स्वरो न प्राप्नोति।
तस्मान्नैतच्छक्यं वक्तुं लुक्सिजपवाद इति। न चेदुच्यते अभूवन्निति प्रत्ययलक्षणेन
जुस्भाव: प्राप्नोति। तस्मादात इत्यत्र सिज्ग्रहणमनुवर्त्य तस्मिं-
50.15 श्चानुवर्तमाने धटश्चातु: शब्द्यं प्राप्नोति। तस्माद्गातिस्थाघुपाभूम्य: सिच: परस्मैपदेष्वित्यत्र
सिचो ग्रहणं कर्तव्यं तस्मिंश्च क्रियमाणे तान्येव त्रीणि ग्रहणानि भवन्ति
50.17 च्व्लि लुङि च्ले: सिच् लेरिति।।

Apavāda by *luk* of *sic* is known as an *apavāda* then for the forms *mā hi dātām* ("So do not let him give") *mā hi dhātām* ("So do not let him place (it)"); here by the *sūtra ādiḥ sico 'nyatarasyām 6.1.187* ("In the *sic* aorist the first syllable may optionally have *udātta* accent"); thus this accent does not obtain. Therefore it is not possible (to say) *luk* is an *apavāda* of *sic.* If it is not stated, then (for the form) *abhūvan,* by *pratyayalakṣaṇa* the *jus* substitution obtains. 'After that (ending in) long *ā* / *ātaḥ*'. Here, the mention of *sic* is to follow on (from a previous *sūtra*) and when it is following on, the four word (forms) of *dheṭ* obtain. Therefore the mention of *sic* should be made in the rule *gāti-sthā ghu-pā-bhūbhyaḥ sicaḥ parasmaipadeṣu 3.1.44* ("there is *luk* elision of *pratyaya sic* in the *parasmaipada* after the *dhātus gā* (to go), *sthā* (to stand), *dhātus* called *ghu* (*1.1.20*), *pā* (to drink), and *bhū* (to be) . . ."), and when that is being effected those three references only are (applicable). *Cli* acts when *luṅ* follows, *sic* acts in place of *cli* and *luk* elision of *li* (after *ghas* etc.).

50.18 यदप्युच्यते क्सविधाने चानिड्वचने च्लिसंप्रत्ययार्थ इति धातुमेवात्रानिट्त्वेन
विशेषयिष्यामः। धातोरनिट इति। कथं पुनर्धातुर्नामानिट स्यात्। धातुरेवानिट्।
50.20 कथम्। अनिमित्तं वा इटोऽनिट्। न वा तस्मादिडस्ति सोऽयमनिडिति।। अथ
धातौ विशेष्यमाणे क्व योऽनिडिति विशेषयिष्यसि। किं चातः। यदि विज्ञायते
50.22 निष्ठायामनिट इति भूयिष्ठेभ्यः प्राप्नोति।

With reference to what is also said that because of (the statement previously made that) "when *kṣa* is ordained as being stated as without *iṭ āgama*, it is for the sake of a right conception of *cli*". We will distinguish the *dhātu* alone as (joined) with that not having an *iṭ āgama*/augment. Thus it is stated "after a *dhātu* not having the *āgama iṭ*". But how indeed may a *dhātu* be (called) *aniṭ* without it? A *dhātu* (certainly can be called) *aniṭ* (without the *āgama iṭ*). How? Either when it is not a cause of *iṭ* it is *"an-iṭ"*, or else this expression *"an-iṭ"* means *iṭ āgama* is not after that (*dhātu*).

Now then, when a *dhātu* is being qualified (having *iṭ*), where is that which you will distinguish as (a *dhātu*) not having the *āgama it* ? And what follows from that? If it is understood (as meaning) "When a *niṣṭhā* (past participle active and passive *ktavatu* and *kta*) follows, (we say) 'after that not having the *āgama iṭ*'; then it obtains after most (*dhātus*).

50.22 .... भूयिष्ठा हि शलन्ता इगुपधा निष्ठायाम-
निटः। अथ विज्ञायते लिटि योऽनिडिति न कुतश्चित्प्राप्नोति। सर्वे हि शलन्ता
इगुपधा लिटि सेटः।। किं पुनः कारणं धातौ विशेषयिष्यमाणे एतयोर्विशेषयोर्वि-
शेषयिष्यते न पुनर्यत्र सामान्येनेटो विधिप्रतिषेधौ। क्व सामान्येन। वलादावार्ध-
50.26 धातुके।।

For most of those ending in *śal* (*ś ṣ s* and *h*) with a penultimate *ik* (*i u ṛ ḷ*) vowel, when *niṣṭhā* follows (and therefore) have no *āgama iṭ*. Now then it is understood (to mean) that "when *liṭ* (perfect) follows "that which has no *āgama iṭ*" does not apply to any (*dhātu*)". For all end in *śal* and have a penultimate *ik* vowel when *liṭ* follows (and therefore) have the *āgama iṭ*. But what is the reason? Why, when a *dhātu* is being distinguished it will be distinguished in relation to these two qualifications (namely *śalanta* and *igupadhā*), but not when there is prohibition by the general rule of *iṭ āgama*. Where is (there common mention) in general? When *ārdhadhātuka pratyaya* follows beginning with a *val* (all consonants except *y*).

50.27 यदप्युच्यते घस्लृभावे चेत्यार्धधातुकीयाः सामान्येन भवन्त्यनवस्थितेषु प्रत्ययेषु। तत्रार्धधातुकसामान्ये घस्लृभावे कृत लृदित इत्यङ् भविष्यति।

What is also said is (*Vā.* 3) "And when the substitute *ghasḷ* (to eat) occurs, the *ārdhadhātuka pratyaya* has been effected in relation to the action of the *dhātu ghasḷ* having an indicatory *ḷ*", *aṅ* will be applicable (in place of *cli*).

Pradīpa

Pradīpa : 49.2 च्लि लुङि। क्वायमिति।

"Where is this (*cli*) heard?"

Due to its nature being barred everywhere by *ādeśas*/substitutes, there is no purpose in its use. Nor even is it seen as having the purpose of an 'operation' like for *kvip* etc.

Therefore, he asks this because the ordaining of that is pointless.

Pradīpa : 49.3 च्लिरुत्सर्ग इति।

"What then is the purpose of making *cli* a general *pratyaya*?"

The meaning is the original/*sthānin*. That is set aside by the *ādeśa*/substitute. Here *sic* is the general *pratyaya*, but the general rule is expressed by the word '*utsarga*'.

Pradīpa : 49.5 च्ल्युत्सर्गः इति।

"The general *pratyaya cli* is for the purpose of common reference."

The meaning is that the general *pratyaya* is being ordained after all *dhātus*.

Pradīpa : 49.7 तत्रावरत इति।

"There (would have been specific mention of) at least (three substitutes of *cli*)."

It is essential (mention) be made of three. However, in the case of *jana*, in the *sūtra* दीपजन (3.1.61) "When *te* (third person singular *ātmanepada*) follows on, *aṅ* is (optionally) in place of (*cli*) ordained (in the *Mantra*/*Veda*)" *2.4.80*.

If *luk* is (also) seen, then mention of a fourth should be made, thus 'at least' is stated. There, because of *dheṭ/ dhayati* (to suck) having the nature of ending in *ā* (*6.1.45*), mention should be made of *caṅ* (*3.1.49*) and *sic* (*3.1.44*) and mention of *aṅ* for the sake of *ghas naś* and *gam*. However, the meaning is for the sake of another *dhātu* there should be mention of *sic*.

Pradīpa : 49.9 क्सविधान इति।

"(It is for the sake of the meaning of *cli*) when *ksa* is ordained (without expression of *iṭ āgama*)."

The meaning is 'so that there should be applicable this qualification of *cli* without *iṭ āgama*, for in that manner if *dhātu* is qualified by the mention *aniṭ* (not having *iṭ* augment), as after it elsewhere, *iṭ* augment is not seen.'

Thus another sphere understood, 'being without *iṭ* augment', must be resorted to because of the absence of obtainment for *iṭ* (augment) for the substitutes of *luṅ* (aorist), due to being *sārvadhātuka* (*pratyayas*). And from that, there would not be applicability of *ksa* after *guha* etc. (*3.1.45* = *guhī*), because there, 'having *iṭ* (augment)' is really optionally with *iṭ* (*svarati . . . ūdito vā 7.2.44*).

Now then, also according to the view of there being an absence of *iṭ* augment, there would be lack of *iṭ* for them. Nonetheless *ksa* would be invariably/ *nitya* applicable.

However, when *cli* is being qualified, when there is not *iṭ* (augment) for it, then *ksa* becomes applicable as '*adhukṣat*'. However, when *iṭ* is applicable then *sic* applies as *agūhīt* (He hid).

Pradīpa : 49.12 घस्लृभावे वेति।

And when *ghas* is substituted (*aṅ* is in place of *cli* only).

That *ārdhadhātuka pratyaya* which acts when *liṅ* follows, acts in place of the first (when) the condition of *ghas* (substitute of *ad*) is ordained.

There, when *cli* follows when the substitute *ghas-ḷ* is (in place of that following?) *aṅ* is established as valid (*3.1.55*).

Otherwise only in the presence of *sic*, the *ghas-ḷ* condition would be applicable.

Even when '*lup*-elided' by reason of 'having a *lu*', by virtue of the effect of the *pratyaya* still operating (in spite of *1.1.63*), it is because of its accent being desired (in fact that it is applicable).

Pradīpa : 49.18 लुङीत्युच्यत इति।

"It is said that when *luṅ* follows (there *liṅ* and *liṭ* do not occur)."

The meaning is that when *luṅ* follows on by *aṇuvṛtti*, this can also be a refutation (the *Paribhāṣā 82*).

तदनुबन्ध ग्रहणं नातदनुबन्धकस्य। "When there is mention of *anubandhas* for that (term) it does not denote that which has an additional *anubandha*."

However, because of being refuted in another way by the *Bhāṣyakāra* it was not stated.

Pradīpa : 49.22 आम इति चेति।

And in the (*sūtra*) *āmaḥ 2.4.81*

'There is *luk* elision in the place of that *li* acting after *ām* of the perfect.'

The sense is there, when there is general mention, the operation is known as possible to occur.

Pradīpa : 49.24 अत्रैवेति।

"Here in this very (*sūtra* quoted, namely *āmaḥ 2.4.81*)."

The meaning is that, otherwise by the *paribhāṣā 82* (above) there would be mention of only this (*luṅ*) not of *liṭ* (perfect) and hence by *āmaḥ 2.4.81* there would not be *luk* in place of *liṭ*.

Pradīpa : 50.2 तान्येवेति।

Only the (three *sūtra*) references are applicable (*cli 3.1.43, cleḥ 3.1.44, leḥ 2.4.80*).

However, *sic* (*luṅ i*) *3.1.44* is by *anuvṛtti*. This is also to be effected with the other (*cli*). The meaning is that in the *sūtra* (*mantre ghas* etc. *2.4.80*) here those three *cli* are in fact *caṅ aṅ* and *sic* (replaced by *luk*).

Pradīpa : 50.3 वक्ष्यामिति।

"This (mention which I will make of *sicaḥ* 'in place of *sic*' in *2.4.77*, means in place of *li* (of *cli*))."

Speaking of the general/*utsarga pratyaya cli* he says ...

Pradīpa : 50.4 लेरिति वक्ष्यामिति।

"I will state (the mention) in place of *li* ..."

The meaning is that, in fact here it will follow on back from *mantre ghasa 2.4.80* and hence brevity (is achieved).

धेट्श्व्योः शब्द्यं प्राप्नोति।

"(If 'in place of *li*' is stated) then four (aorist) forms from *dheṭ* obtain."

विभाषा धेट्श्वयोः (3.1.49)

"After the *dhātus dheṭ* (to suck) and *śvi* (to swell), *caṅ* is optionally the *ādeśa* of *cli* when *luṅ* follows signifying the agent."

50.4 विभाषा घ्राधेट्शाछासः (2.4.78) सिचःपरस्मै लुक्)

"After the *dhātus ghrā* (to smell), *dheṭ* (to suck), *śā* (*śo,* to pare), *chā* (*cho,* to cut), and *sā* (*so,* to destroy), there is optionally *luk*-elision of *sic* where *parasmaipada* terminations are employed."

When here in *2.4.78,* the mention of *li* is present by *anuvṛtti* from *2.4.80,* and the *ādeśas* are effected in place of *li,* and because of being like the *sthānin*/original, and when due to the mention of them by the reference to *li, luk* is effected, doubling caused by *caṅ* obtains, so that *addhāt* would also have been applicable.

क्विलुगुपधात्व

This is no fault. Due to the prohibition of 'being like the original for that elided by *luk* by *Vā 2 on 1.1.58'* and the prohibition of the effect of the *pratyaya* meaning by न लुमताङ्गस्य (1-1-83) and (thus) from the absence of *lopa* elision of *ā.*

Pradīpa : 50.9 आत इति।

Because of the *sūtra ātaḥ 3.4.110.*

'When *sic* is elided *jus* is the *ādeśa* of *jhi* after an aorist *aṅga* ending in *ā* (there will be *jus*).'

The meaning is this will be applicable for the sake of a positive rule but not for the purpose of restriction.

Pradīpa : 50.11 एवं तर्हीति।

"So then (*luk* will be understood as *apavāda* of *sic*)."

When the *ādeśas* are not effected *luk* will be ordained in place of *li* only as the *apavāda*/exception of that; therefore with the form *abhūvan jus* will not be applicable. And the sense is that for the sake of a positive rule *ātaḥ 3.4.110* will be applicable, so that *adhuḥ* (They placed), *aduḥ* (They gave), *apuḥ* (They protected/drunk) etc. are established as valid.

Pradīpa : 50.13 तस्मादिति।

"Therefore (it is not possible to say *luk* is *apavāda* of *sic.*")

The meaning is for accomplishing the correct accent, when the *ādeśa* of *sic* is effected, (then) *luk* is to be effected.

Pradīpa : 50.19 कथमिति।

"But how (indeed may a *dhātu* really not have the augment *iṭ*)?"

For *iṭ* is ordained for *ārdhadhātuka pratyaya* (followed by a *val 7.2.35*). The sense is, that 'alone (or) due to the absence of that', is intended to indicate *an-iṭ* (without *iṭ* augment), because of understanding this as a *bahuvrīhi* in the sense of *matup*/possession.

Pradīpa: 50.20 अनिमित्तमिति।

'Without a cause' absence of *iṭ āgama* is optionally in place of *iṭ āgama.*'

The sense is, there is the condition of cause and that having a cause for the *iṭ*(*dhātu* and the augment *iṭ*) so it is not inappropriate to say it is *bahuvrīhi* in place of sixth case.

Pradīpa: 50.20 न वा तस्मादिति

'Or else (this expression *an-iṭ* means *iṭ āgama*) is not after that (*dhātu*).'

The meaning is that he will resort to interpreting it as a *bahuvrīhi* in the sense of fifth case, due to the force of the expression *aniṭaḥ.*

Pradīpa: 50.21 क्व योऽनिडिति।

"Where is that which (you will distinguish as) not having *iṭ āgama* ?"

When there is not ordaining of *cli*, the *cli vikaraṇa ksa* without resort to *iṭ āgama* should be applied.

There in this sphere, the question is, due to the absence of obtainment for *iṭ* augment, should another sphere have expectation of absence of *iṭ* augment?

Pradīpa: 50.22 निष्ठायामिति।

"(If it is understood as meaning) 'when a *niṣṭha* follows' (then after not having *iṭ āgama* it obtains after most)."

If all *ārdhadhātuka* (*pratyayas*) are understood, then after *guha* and the rest having an indicatory long *ū* (*7.2.44*) it would not be applicable thus to resort to *niṣṭhā.* And when that is resorted to, *ksa* would be invariably applicable after *guha* etc. and optionally *iṭ* is (in fact) desired.

Pradīpa: 50.22 भूयिष्ठा हीति।

"For most are (those ending in *śal* with penultimate *ik* vowel when *niṣṭhā* follows and have no *iṭ* augment)."

When *niṣṭhā* follows, because of the *an-iṭ* nature of (*dhātus*) *iṣu riṣu ruṣu sriṣu pruṣu* etc. (by *7.2.56* and *15*) *ksa* obtains (*3.1.45*).

Pradīpa: 50.25 न पुनर्यत्रेति।

"(A *dhātu* is distinguished in relation to two qualifications *śalanta* and *igupadhā*) but not where there is (prohibition by the general rule of *iṭ āgama*)."

Guha and the rest (having long *it ū* optionally taking *iṭ āgama 7.2.44*), having optional *iṭ* (after them), are divided according as they are with (that condition) or without that condition. There (in that context), for those which are *seṭ* (have *iṭ āgama* after), then *sic* will be applicable, however, after those without *iṭ* (*āgama*) *ksa*. Thus there is no fault.

Pradīpa: 50.28 आर्धधातुकसामान्य इति।

"(There), when the generic property of being *ārdhadhātuka pratyaya* (has been effected for *ghasḷ, aṅ* will be applicable in place of *cli.*"

The meaning is that he will resort to the *aṅ pratyaya,* having as its generic term *ārdhadhātuka* and distinguished by *luṅ* (aorist). If the *cli* is rejected, then (by) *mantre ghase 2.4.80,* when there is *luk* in place of *sic* by *ādeḥ* sic *6.1.187.* For the first syllable the initial of *sic* aorist *udātta* optionally obtains...

There is no fault. For there in the *Chandas* in some places there must be *udātta* for the augment *aṭ* and *āṭ* and (in) some places *tiṅ* (endings) are *anudātta.* However, where there is prohibition and a *pratyaya* accent is desired for the augments *aṭ* and *āṭ* for the *anudātta tiṅ* (respectively), that sphere is not (applicable) in the *Chandas.* And this is known because of the rejection of *cli* by *Bhāṣyakāra.*

However, in the case of *mā hi lāvit* 'for one should not cut etc.' by reason of the *sic* alone having the characteristic of an *it c* and for no other reason, the *anudātta* accent for the *āgama* will be barred. Thus for that purpose also, the attaching of an indicatory letter *cli* does not have to be produced.

Notes

[1] च्लेरनिटः क्सः सिद्धो भवति।।

Ksa is established as valid in place of *cli* without *iṭ* (augment).

शल इगुपधादनिटःक्सः (3.1.45) "After a *dhātu* that ends in *śal* consonant and has an *ik* vowel for its penultimate letter, and does not take *iṭ* (augment) (*7.2.10*), *ksa* is the substitute of *cli*."

[2] च्लावेव कृत लृदित इत्यङ् सिद्धो भवति।

When *ghas-ḷ* take place, *aṅ* taught by *ḷdita* is effected when *cli* has been effected.

लुङ्सनोर्घस्लृ (2.4.37) (आर्धधातुके) अदः

When *laṅ* (aorist) or *san* (desiderative) follow *ghas.-ḷ* is *ādeśa* of *ad* (to eat).

पुषादिद्युताद्यलृदितः परस्मैपदेषु (3.1.55)

"*Aṅ* is the *ādeśa* of *cli* after *dhātus puṣ* (to nourish) and the rest, *dyut* (to shine) and the rest, and the *dhātus* having an indicatory *ḷ* when the *parasmaipada pratyayas* follow."

[3] सिज्ग्रहणं।

"The mention of *sic* (there follows on from a previous *sūtra*)."

सिजभ्यस्तविदिभ्यश्च 3.4.109

i.e. (in those tenses marked with an indicatory *ṅ*) '*jus* is the *ādeśa* of *jhi* when it acts after an aorist in *sic* or the imperfect of a reduplicated *dhātu* or the *dhātu vid* (to know).'

च्लेः सिच् ॥ 3 । 1 । 44 ॥

Pāṇini 3.1.44: *Sic (ādeśa)* acts in place of *cli.*

51.2 किमर्थश्चकारः। विशेषणार्थः। क्व विशेषणार्थेनार्थः। सिचि वृद्धिः परस्मै-
पदेषु (7.2.1) इति। सौ वृद्धिरित्युच्यमाने अग्निः वायुरित्यत्रापि प्रसज्येत।
51.4 नैतदस्ति प्रयोजनम्। परस्मैपदेष्वित्युच्यते च चात्र परस्मैपदं पश्यामः।।

Bhāṣya: What is the purpose of the letter *c*? It is for the purpose of distinguishing. Where is the purpose served of so distinguishing? (In the *sūtra*) "*sici vṛddhi parasmaipadeṣu 7.2.1*". "When the aorist *ādeśa s* (*sic*) and the *parasmaipada* endings follow, a *vṛddhi* acts for the final of an *aṇga* ending in *i, u,* or *ṛ* (short or long), (*1.1.3*)". If it were being stated, 'when *si* follows *vṛddhi* acts' it would also become applicable for (the nouns followed by *s-u* = *sau* in seventh case) *agni-ḥ* (fire) *vāyu-ḥ* (air) etc. This is not the purpose. It is stated when *parasmaipada pratyayas* follow and here we do not see *parasmaipada pratyayas.*

51.4 .... स्वरा-
र्थस्तर्हि। चितोऽन्त उदात्तो भवतीत्यन्तोदात्तत्वं यथा स्यात्[1]। एतदपि नास्ति प्रयो-जनम्। अनच्कोऽयं तत्र नार्थः स्वरार्थेन चकारेणानुबन्धेन। इटि कृते साच्कोभविष्यति। तत्र प्रत्ययाद्युदात्तत्वेनेट उदात्तत्वं भविष्यति। न सिध्यति। आगमा

51.8 अनुदात्ता भवन्तीत्यनुदात्तत्वं प्राप्नोति।। अत उत्तरं पठति।

Then it is for the purpose of accent. So that there should be final *udātta* (by the *sūtra*) *citaḥ 6.1.63* (*antaḥ, udāṭtaḥ*) ("For an *aṅga* having a *pratyaya* or *āgama* with an indicatory *c*, there is *udātta* for the final syllable".) Therefore he states as follows. This also is not the purpose. This (*sic*) is without a vowel. Therefore there is no purpose in attaching *anubandha c* for the sake of accent. (But) it will be possessed of a vowel after *iṭ* is added. In that case acute will be there by the rule prescribing accent on the initial vowel of a *pratyaya.* It is not established as valid. *Anudātta* ordains (by the *paribhāṣā*) "*āgamas* have *anudātta* accent".

51.9 सिचश्चित्करणानर्थक्यं स्थानिवत्वात् ।। 1 ।।

Vārttika 1: The making of an indicatory *c* for *sic* is pointless because of the substitute *ādeśa* being like the original/*sthānin.*

51.10 सिचश्चित्करणमनर्थकम्। किं कारणम्। स्थानिवत्वात्। चितोऽयमादेशः स्थानिवद्भावाच्चिद्भविष्यति।।

Bhāṣya: The making of an indicatory *c* for *sic* is pointless. What is the reason? Because of (the substitute/*ādeśa*) *sic* being like the original/*sthāni* (*cli*). This is an *ādeśa* of that having an indicatory *c* which, because of the conditions of being like the original, will (also) have an indicatory *c.*

51.12 अर्थवत्तु चित्करणसामर्थ्याद्धीट उदात्तत्वम् ।। 2 ।।

Varttika 2: However (adding the *anubandha c* is) meaningful by force of making (*si*) have an indicatory *c*, for then *udātta* is applicable to the *āgama iṭ.*

51.13 नैष दोषः। अर्थवत्तु सिचश्चित्करणम्। कोऽर्थः। चित्करणसामर्थ्यादीट उदात्तत्वं भविष्यति। नाप्राप्ते प्रत्ययस्वर आगमानुदात्तत्वमारभ्यते। तद्यथैव प्रत्ययस्वरं
51.15 बाधत एवं स्थानिवद्भावादपि या प्राप्तिस्तामपि बाधेत॥

Bhāṣya: This is not a fault. Moreover the making of an indicatory *c* (for *si-c*) is meaningful. What is the meaning? For, due to the force of making (*sic*) have an indicatory *c* (in the *sūtra*) there will be *udātta* for the *āgama iṭ*. When accent essentially obtains for a *pratyaya, anudātta* is undertaken for *āgamas.* Just as indeed *anudātta* debars *pratyaya* accent, so also it would debar whatever obtains because of the condition of being like the original.

51.16 तस्माच्चित्करणम् ॥ 3॥

Vārttika 3: Therefore the making of (*sic*) have an indicatory *c* (should take place).

51.17 तस्माच्चकारः कर्तव्यः

51.18 अथेदित्करणं किमर्थम्।

Bhāṣya: Therefore the letter *iṭ c* should be produced. Now then what is the purpose of the indicatory *i* ?

51.19 इदित्करणं नकारलोपाभावार्थम् ॥ 4 ॥

Vārttika 4: The producing of an indicatory *i* is so that there should be an absence of *lopa* elision of the letter *n.*

51.20 इदित्करणं क्रियते नकारलोपो मा भूदिति। अमंस्त अमंस्थाः। अनिदितां हल उपाधायाः क्ङिति (6.4.24) इति॥

Bhāṣya: The producing of an indicatory *i* is done so that there should not be *lopa* elision of the letter *n.* (For example) *amansta* "He thought"; *amansthāḥ* "You (sg.) thought", by the *sūtra aniditām hala updhāyaḥ kṅiti 6.4.24.* "For those *aṅgas* (bases) without *iṭ i* and ending in a consonant, *lopa* acts in place of a penultimate *n* in the presence of a *pratyaya* with an *it k* or *ṅ*".

51.22 न वा हन्ते सिचः कित्करणं ज्ञापकं नकारलोपाभावस्य ॥ 5 ॥

Vārttika 5: Or else (this is) not the purpose. There is an implied rule/ *jñapaka* from the making indicatory *k* applicable for *sic* (followed by *ātmanepada pratyayas*) after the *dhātu han* (to kill) for the absence of *lopa* elision of the letter *n.*

51.23 न वैतत्प्रयोजनमस्ति। किं कारणम्। यदयं हनः सिच् (1.2.24) इति हन्तेः सिचः कित्वं शास्ति तज्ज्ञापयत्याचार्यो न सिजन्तस्य नकारलोपो भवतीति।।

51.25 नैतदस्ति ज्ञापकम्। अस्ति ह्यन्यदेतस्य वचने प्रयोजनम्। किम्। सिच्येव नलोपो यथा स्यात्परस्मिन्निमित्ते मा भूदिति। कः पुनरत्र विशेषः सिचि वा नलोपे सति

52.2 परस्मिन्वा निमित्ते।

Bhāṣya: Or else this is not the purpose. What is the reason? When this master teaches indicatory *k* for *sic* acting after *dhātu han-ti* (by the *sūtra*) '*hanaḥ sic*' *1.2.24*. "*Sic ātmanepada pratyayas* have an indicatory *k* after the *dhātu han* (to kill)", he makes known that the *lopa* elision of *n* is not applicable for that ending in *sic* (in spite of it having an indicatory *i*). This is not an implied rule/*jñapaka*. There is another purpose in stating this. What? So there should be *lopa* elision of *n* only when *sic* follows and that it should not be applicable when another cause follows. What is the difference here, whether when *sic* follows there is elision of *n* or when another cause follows there is the elision of *n*?

52.2 .... अयमस्ति विशेषः। सिचि नलोपे सति नलोपस्यासिद्धत्वा-दकारलोपो[2] न भवति। परस्मिन्पुनर्निमित्ते नलोपे सत्यकारलोपः प्राप्नोति। समानाश्रयमसिद्धं व्याश्रयं चेदम्।। ननु च परस्मिन्नपि निमित्ते नलोपे सत्यकार-लोपो न भवति। कथम्। असिद्धं बहिरङ्गलक्षणमन्तरङ्गलक्षण इति। तदेतद्धन्तेः

52.6 सिचः कित्करणं ज्ञापकमेव न सिजन्तस्य नलोपो भवतीति।।

This is the difference. When there is *lopa* elision when *sic* follows because of the *lopa* of *n* being *a-siddha*, *lopa* elision of *a* is not applicable. But when there is elision of *n* when another condition follows, the *lopa* of *a* obtains. (The *lopa*) is *asiddha* when the basis (i.e. cause of the operations) is the same but (here) the basis is different. But surely even when another condition follows, when there is *lopa* of the *n* the elision of *a* does not obtain. How? (Because of the *Paribhāṣā 50*) "That which is characterised as *bahiraṅga* is (regarded as) not having taken effect (or as not existing) when that which is characterised as *antaraṅga* (is to take effect)". This making of indicatory *k* for *sic* (added) after *han* is indeed a *jñapaka* of the fact that there is no elision of *n* (of *han*) ending in *sic*.

52.7 इदित्वाद्वा स्थानिवत्वात् ।। 6 ।।

Vārttika 6: *Sic* is possessed of the *anubandha i* because of its being like the original.

52.8 अथाप्यनेनेदितार्थः स्यादिदितोऽयमादेशः स्थानिवद्भावादिदिद्भविष्यति।।

Bhāṣya: Even if (it is argued that) this (*i*) serves the purpose of (making *sic*) *idit* let the substitute be *idit.* (Even then) it will become *idit* by '*sthānivad bhāva*'.

52.9 स्पृशमृशकृषतृपदृपः सिज्वा ॥ 7 ॥

Vārttika 7: *Sic* is optionally aorist *pratyaya ādeśa* for the *dhātus spṛś* (to touch), *mṛś* (to consider), *kṛṣ* (to plough), *tṛp* (to satisfy), and *dṛp* (to be mad).

52.10 स्पृशमृशकृषतृपदृपः सिज्वेति वक्तव्यम्[3]॥ स्पृश। अस्पृक्षत् अस्प्राक्षीत्। स्पृश॥
मृश। अमृक्षत् अम्राक्षीत्। मृश॥ कृष। अकृक्षत् अक्राक्षीत्। कृष॥ तृप।
अतृपत् अत्राप्सीत्। तृप॥ दृप। अदृपत् अद्राप्सीत्। किं प्रयोजनम्। सिज्यथा
स्यात्। अथ क्सः सिद्धः। सिद्धः शल इगुपधादनिट
52.14 इगुपधादनिटः (3.1.45) इति॥

Bhāṣya: It should be stated that *sic* optionally acts (as *ādeśa* of *cli pratyaya*) for the *dhātus spṛś* (to touch), *mṛś* (to consider), *kṛṣ* (to plough), *tṛp* (to be satisfied), and *dṛp* (to be mad).

spṛś (touch) *aspṛkṣat asprākṣīt* "He touched",

mṛś (touch mentally, reflect) *amṛkṣat amrākṣīt* "He considered",

kṛṣ (draw, drag) *akṛkṣat akrākṣīt* "He drew or ploughed",

tṛp (be content) *atṛpsat atrāpsīt* "He himself was satisfied",

and *dṛp* (be mad) *adṛpat adrāpsīt* "He was mad".

What is the purpose? So that *sic* should be applicable. Now then *ksa* is (also) established as valid. It is established (by the *sūtra*) *śala igupadhādaniṭaḥ ksaḥ 3.1.45.* "After a *dhātu* ending in *śal* (*ś ṣ s h*) and having an *ik* vowel for its penultimate letter and not taking the *āgama iṭ* (*7.2.10*) *ksa* is the *ādeśa* of *cli.*

52.15 सिजपि सिद्धः। कथम्। च्लेश्चित्करणं प्रत्याख्यायते तत्र च्लावेव झल्लक्षणे-
ऽमागमे कृते विहतनिमित्तत्वात्क्सो न भविष्यति॥ यद्येवमन्त्यस्य सिजादयः
52.17 प्राप्नुवन्ति।

Sic is also established as valid. How? The making of the *c* of *cli* an indicatory letter is set aside (*3.1.43*).

[**Vārttika 4:** *cleścitkaraṇam* (*kriyate viśeṣanārtham prayojanam*)] "The purpose of the indicatory letter *c* of *cli* is for the purpose of distinguishing", is refuted.

Bhāṣya: *naitadasti.* This is not the purpose.] There when *cli* alone follows when *am āgama* characterised by *jhal* has been effected, because *ksa* has been absent, (*ksa* will not be applicable). If so *sic* and the rest obtain in place of the final letter.

52.18 सिद्धं तु सिचो यादित्वात्।। सिद्धमेतत्। कथम्। यादिः सिच्करिष्यते सो-
ऽनेकाल्शित्सर्वस्य (1.1.55) इति सर्वादेशो भविष्यति। कि न श्रूयते यकारः।
52.20 लुप्तानर्दिष्टो यकारः।। चङ्ङोः कथम्।

However, this is established because of *sic* beginning with *y*. This is established as valid. How? *Sic* will be formed having *y* initial. It will become *ādeśa*/ substitute for the whole (of *cli*) (by the *sūtra anekāl śitsarvasya 1.1.55*) "An *ādeśa* having more than one letter and one having an indicatory *ś* acts in place of the whole of the original exhibited in the sixth case". Why is the letter *y* not heard? It is the letter *y* whose *lup* elision has been indicated. How (can that be true) in the case of *caṅ* and *aṅ*?

52.21 चङ्ङोरपि प्रश्लिष्टनिर्देशोऽयम्।च अङ् चङ्।अ अङ् अङ्।
सोऽनेकाल्शित्सर्वस्येति सर्वादेशो भविष्यति।।

Vārttika: It is established as valid because of the indication for coalescent *sandhi* for *caṅ* and *aṅ*.

Bhāṣya: This is also (established) in the case of *caṅ* and *aṅ* as the reference by coalescent (*sandhi*). Thus *ca* + *aṅ* = *caṅ*; *a* + *aṅ* = *aṅ*. (By the *sūtra anekāl śitsarvasya 1.1.55*) (trans. above) that will become the *ādeśa* of the whole of the original. How (can that be true) of *ciṅ*?

52.23 चिणोऽनित्वात्सिद्धम्। चिणोऽनित्वात्सिद्धम्। किमिदमनित्वादिति अन्त्यस्यायं
स्थाने भवन्न प्रत्ययः स्यात्। असत्यां प्रत्ययसंज्ञायामित्संज्ञा न। असत्या-
मित्संज्ञायां लोपो न। असतिऽनेकाल्। यदानेकाल्तदा सर्वादेशः। यदा सर्वादेशस्तदा
52.26 प्रत्ययः। यदा प्रत्ययस्तदेत्संज्ञा[4]। यदेत्संज्ञा तदा लोपः।।

Vārttika: It is established as valid because of *ciṇ* being without an indicatory letter *c*.

Bhāṣya: It is established as valid because of *ciṇ* being without an indicatory letter *c*. Why is this (said) "because of being without an indicatory letter"? This being in the place of the final letter would not be a *pratyaya* (but an *ādeśa*).

In the absence of the technical name *pratyaya*, there is no technical name *iṭ*. When the technical name *it* is absent there is no *lopa* elision (possible of *it*). When *lopa* is absent/non-existent, then (*ciṅ*) has more than one letter/ *anekāl*. When it has more than one letter then *iṭ* is the *ādeśa* of the whole (of the original *cli*). When it is the *ādeśa* of the whole (of the original) then it has the name *pratyaya*. When it (has the technical name) *pratyaya*, then the technical name *it* (and by the *sūtra 'cuṭū' 1.3.7*, the *c* of *ciṇ* has the name *it*). When it has the technical name *iṭ* then *lopa* elision (occurs by *'tasya lopaḥ' 1.3.9*).

एवं च तत्र[5] वार्त्तिककारस्य निर्णयः सप्रयोजनं चित्करणमिति। अपि च त्रैशब्द्यं न प्रकल्पते। अस्पृक्षत अस्प्राक्षीत्। अस्पार्क्षीदिति न सिध्यति। सिचि पुनः सति विभाषा सिच्। सिच्यपि झल्लक्षणोऽमागमो विभाषा।। यस्य खल्वप्यमा निमित्तं न विहन्यते स स्यादेव। तस्मात्सुष्ठूच्यते स्पृशमृशकृषतृपदृपः सिज्वेति।।

And thus the conclusion of the *vārttika* maker is that the producing of the indicatory *c* has a purpose. (c.f. *cleścitkaraṇam viśeṣanārtham 3.1.43 Vā. 4*). Moreover the three word (forms) are not settled. (The two forms) *aspṛkṣat asprākṣīt* "He touched" are established. (The form) *asprākṣīt* is not established as valid. But when *sic* follows there is optionally *sic.* Also when *sic* is present the *āgama am* characterised by a *jhal* letter (i.e. not having the *āgama iṭ*) is optional. That (grammatical operation) whose cause is not prevented by *am,* (that) alone would be applicable.

Therefore it is well said: *sic* optionally acts (in place of the *pratyaya cli*) for the *dhātus. spṛś, mṛs, kṛṣ, tṛp,* and *dṛp.*

Pradīpa

Pradīpa: 51.3 अग्निरिति।

If *si* were being stated, *vṛddhi* would also be applicable for nouns followed by *s* (*u*) = '*sau*', *e.g. Agni s* = *ḥ* (i.e. it cannot in fact apply to nouns).

The combination would be understood. When *si* follows and when *parasmaipada pratyayas* follow and so too here it would be applicable. '*San*' would be a common indication of the words *si* aorist substitute of *cli* and *su* (first case singular).

The sense is by the added/adventitious letter *i* the letter *s* would be indicated.

Pradīpa : 51.4 न चात्रेति।

"And here (we do not see *parasmaipada pratyayas*)."

The sense is that, because of the difference in the indication of *vibhakti* (one singular the other plural) the relation is that between limbs of a body or word or the mutual relation of different members of (the word) but not a combination.

Pradīpa: 51.4 स्वरार्थ इति।

"(Then it is) for the purpose of accent."

The meaning is that, even when there is the characteristic for *sic* of not having a vowel, because of the (rule) *Vārttika 1* on *citoḥ 6.1.163* 'a base formed by a *pratyaya* or augment with an *it c* has *udātta* on the final syllable of the base', the purpose is (there be *udātta*) for the *dhātu,* as in *mā hi kārṣṭām* 'For do not let the two make (it)'.

Pradīpa: 51.6 अनच्को यमिति।

"This (*sic*) is without a vowel."

The sense is that, in the case of examples like *mā hi karṣṭām* 'For do not let the two do', by *6.1.187* "In the *sic* aorist the first syllable may optionally be *udātta*".

आदि: सिचोऽन्यतरस्याम्। The *udātta* option should be applied, so this is not in the sphere of *cit* accent (final *udātta 6.1.163*).

Pradīpa: 51.7 उदात्तत्वं भविष्यति।

"*Udātta* will be there (by the rule prescribing *udātta* for a *pratyayas* initial vowel)." by आद्युदात्तश्च (3.1.3)

Pradīpa: 51.12 अर्थवत्त्विति।

"However, (*it c*) is meaningful (making *si* have an *it c* so then *udātta* is applicable for the *āgama iṭ*)."

Due to having the purpose of not destroying the common mention of *it c* for *cli,* the accent which obtains from being like the original/*sthāni* in such examples as *mā hi lāvīt* 'For let him not cut', would bar the (normal) *anudātta* for an augment.

The meaning is therefore, the purpose of the *it c* of *sic* is for final *udātta.*

"This is no fault (i.e. *Vā* 1 *c* of *sic* is pointless)."

The meaning is that, what was stated (in *Vā 1*) 'the making of an indicatory *c* for *sic* is pointless', is not so.

Here some say there are two exceptions to the (general) *pratyaya* accent (i.e. initial *udātta*): (1) *anudātta* for *āgamas* makes known by *jñāpaka* in the *sūtra* '*yāsuṭ parasmaipadeṣu udātta ṅicca*' *3.4.103* that only in that place (is an *āgama udātta,* everywhere else *anudātta*), and (2) the (final *udātta*) accent (indicated by) *it c* in the sixth *adhyāya 6.1.163.*

There in that context, because of the conflict of two *apavādas* (of equal force), only the *cit* accent will be applicable and there is no purpose in the indicatory *c* for *sic*. This is not so. For these two are not *apavādas*, (exceptions to the *pratyaya* accent) because of there being no possibility of that (*pratyaya* accent) for the augment of bases repeating (the meaning of) another's base and (not) for those having an *it c* like *kuṇḍinac* etc. (*2.4.70*). And this being *sthānivat*/like the original, by *kārya atideśa*/treating the *ādeśa* like the original, for the sake of operations caused by the original, (*Bhāṣya* on *1.1.59*), even though there is the quality 'being subsequent as a later *sūtra*', this is not for the (final) *udātta* indicated by the *cit* accent. And by reason of *anudātta* accent for augments without distinction ... all (other) accent is to be barred. Therefore it is established that the indicatory *c* of *sic* is for the purpose of barring that *anudātta*.

Pradīpa : 52.1 परस्मिन्निति।

"(What is the difference whether when *sic* follows there is elision of *n* or) when another follows (there is elision of *n*) ?"

The meaning is when that *sārvadhātuka pratyaya* which follows *sic* follows:

Pradīpa : 52.4 असिद्धमिति।

"(*Lopa*) is *asiddha*/of none effect (when the cause of the operations is the same, but here the basis is different)."

The meaning is that, the state of being *a-siddha*/of none effect is due to the basis of operations being outer, *sārvadhātuka pratyayas* (operations) giving it the nature of being *bahiraṅga* (requiring more operations).

That which ends in *a* in an *upadeśa* (having the name) *ārdhadhātuka* has *lopa*-elision of that (*6.4.48*). So there will not be applicable the *lopa* of the *a* of *han* (*dhātu*). And in like manner it is said there is not *lopa* of the *a* of those which have a part (already) *lopa*.

Pradīpa : 52.9 स्पृशेति।

"(*Sic* is optionally *ādeśa pratyaya* for *dhātus*) *spṛś* (to touch) etc."

After three, *ksa* obtains (*spṛś, mṛś, kṛś, 3.1.45*).

After two in the alternative, when forming part of *puṣādi gaṇa 3.1.55*, when *aṅ* (obtains), *sic* is ordained.

Pradīpa: 52.15 च्लेश्चित्करणमिति।

"The making of the *c* of *cli* an indicatory letter (for accent etc. is set aside, *Vā 4* on *3.1.43*)."

And hence because of the absence of purpose, there is no technical name *it* for the letter *c*, so when there is *cli* (and) on the option of beginning with a *jhal* (i.e. without *iṭ* augment), *am* augment is effected and *sic* (applies in place of *cli*).

Pradīpa: 52.16 अमागमे कृते।

अनुदात्तस्य चर्दुपधस्यान्यतरस्याम् (6.1.59) "The augment *a* acts optionally after the *ṛ* of those *dhātus* which are *anudātta* in the *Dhātu Pāṭha* when they end in a consonant having *ṛ* as penultimate, and are followed by a *pratyaya* beginning with a *jhal* (mute or sibilant) and not having an indicatory *k.*"

The meaning is that 'on the alternative of the absence of *am* augment, however, the mention of *ksa* for the three of them is not to be effected'.

Pradīpa: 52.1 अन्त्यस्येति।

"(If so, *sic* and the rest obtain) in place of the final (letters)."

The mention of *antya* (final) is synecdoche (part for the whole); for *caṅ* and the rest obtain in place of the first of that which follows:

अलोऽन्त्यस्य (1.1.52) "The *ādeśa* takes the place of only the final letter (of that denoted by the term exhibited in the sixth case)."

Pradīpa: 52.23 चिणोऽनित्वादिति।

"It is established as valid because of *ciṇ* being without an indicatory *c.*"

Here (in the *sūtra*): चिण् भावकर्मणोः (3.1.66) "चिण् is *ādeśa* of च्लि when the third person singular *ātmanepada* follows denoting the action/ *bhāva* or the object/ *karman.*"

Mention of *dhātu* is not expected because of which *ādeḥ parasya* (*1.1.56* 'That enjoined to come in place of what follows after a *dhātu* in the fifth case is understood to be in place of only the first letter thereof') will not be applicable (because it relates to the fifth case), as namely (*ciṇ* as *ādeśa* of *cli*), after *pad-ḷ* (to go) and after *dīpa* etc. *3.1.61*. 'In place of the first of that which follows' *1.1.54* obtains, therefore, it should be rejected by resort to the qualification enjoined.

Pradīpa: 53.1 सप्रयोजनमिति।

'The producing of indicatory *c* has a purpose.'

Due to it having been already stated (*Bhāṣya* on *Vā.* 5 on *3.1.43*, the letter *c*) is used with the purpose of non-hindrance to common reference.

The meaning is 'and when there is a purpose, there should be the technical name *it* for the letter *c* and the letter *l* is applicable as a jhal.' So thus, due to the absence of the augment *am, ksa* alone would (wrongly) be applicable.

Pradīpa: 53.3 यस्य खल्वपीति।

"That (grammatical operation) whose (cause is not prevented by *am* would be applicable."

Aṅ after *puṣ* and the rest (*3.1.55*).

For even when *am* augment is effected that takes place.

Notes

[1] स्यात् चित: (6.1.163) (अन्त: उदात्त:)

[2] 52.3 अकारलोपो। "(When there is *lopa* when *sic* follows, because of *lopa* of *n* being *asiddha*), elision of *a* is not applicable."

Asiddha/of none effect/unknown to other *sūtras* in that section of the grammar.

असिद्धवदत्राभात् (6.4.22) "The change an *aṅga* will undergo by any of the *sūtras* from here to *6.4.129* is to be considered as not to have taken effect when we apply any other *sūtra* between *6.4.23-129*."

Elision of *a* is not applicable by अतो लोप: (6.4.48) "*A* at the end of an *aṅga* is *lopa* before *ārdhadhātuka pratyaya*."

[3] सिज्वेति वक्तव्यम्। It should be stated *sic* optionally acts (after *spṛś* etc.).

शल इगुपधादनित: क्स: (3.1.45)

पुषादिद्युताद्यलृदित: परस्मैपदेषु (3.1.55) "अङ् is the *ādeśa* of *cli* after the *dhātus puṣ* (to nourish) and the rest, *dyut* (to shine) and the rest, and *dhātus* with an indicatory *ḷ* when the *pratyayas* of *parasmaipada* follow."

[4] तदेत्संज्ञा। "Then the technical name *it.*"

चुटू (2.3.7) "An initial palatal or a cerebral of a *pratyaya* has the name *it.*"

तस्य लोपः (1.3.9) "Of that *it* there is *lopa*-elision."

[5] 53.1 तत्र च्लेश्चित्करणं विशेषणार्थम् (3.1.43) वा॰ 4

The producing of the indicatory letter *c* of *cli* is for the purpose of distinguishing.

शल इगुपधादनिटः क्सः ॥ 3 । 1 । 45 ॥

Pāṇini 3.1.45: After a *dhātu* ending in a *śal* and having an *ik* vowel as penultimate, and not taking the *āgama iṭ* (by '*ekāca upadeśe'nudāttāt*' 7.2.10), *ksa* is the *ādeśa* in the place of the (aorist *pratyaya*) *cli.*

53.6 क्सविधान इगुपधाभावश्च्लेर्गुणनिमित्तत्वात् ॥ 1 ॥

Vārttika 1: When *ksa* is ordained there is absence of a *dhātu* having an *ik* vowel as a penultimate because of *cli's* being a cause of *guṇa.*

53.8 क्सविधान इगुपधस्याभावः।. किं कारणम्। च्लेर्गुणनिमित्तत्वात्। च्लिर्गुण-निमित्तं तत्र च्लावेव गुणे कृत इगुपधादिति क्सो न प्राप्नोति।।

Bhāṣya: When *ksa* is ordained there is an absence of (any) penultimate *ik* (vowel). What is the reason? Because of *cli* having the nature of being a cause of *guṇa. cli* (being a cause of *guṇa* by *pugantalaghūpadhasya ca 7.3.86*), when *cli* follows *guṇa* has been effected, therefore *ksa* does not obtain "after (a *dhātu* having) an *ik* vowel as penultimate".

53.10 न वा क्सस्यानवकाशत्वादपवादो गुणस्य ॥ 2 ॥

Vārttika 2: Or else not, because of the absence of scope for *ksa* (elsewhere) it is an exception to general/*utsarga guṇa.*

53.11 न वैष दोषः। किं कारणम्। क्सस्यानवकाशत्वात्। अनवकाशः क्सो गुणं बाधिष्यते।।

Bhāṣya: Or else this is not a fault. What is the reason? Because of there not being scope (of application elsewhere) for *ksa. Ksa* without any scope of application elsewhere, bars *guṇa.*

53.13 अनिड्वचनमविशेषणं च्लेर्नित्यादिष्टत्वात् ।। 3 ।।

Vārttika 3: The expression of *ksa* as being without *iṭ* (*āgama*) is not a qualification, because of *cli* indicated being always substituted.

53.14 अनिड्वचनमविशेषणम्। किं कारणम्। च्लेर्नित्यादिष्टत्वात्। नित्यादिष्टश्च्लिर्न
क्वचिच्छ्रूयते तत्र च्लेरनिट इति क्सो न प्राप्नोति।।

Bhāṣya: The expression (of *ksa*) as being without *iṭ* (*āgama*) is not a qualification. What is the reason? Because of *cli* being always substituted. The *cli* is not heard anywhere because of being always substituted, (so) there *ksa* does not obtain after *cli* without *āgama iṭ*.

53.16 न वा क्सस्य सिजपवादत्वात्तस्य चानिडाश्रयत्वादनिट
प्रसिद्धे क्सविधिः ।। 4 ।।

Vārttika 4: Or else not, because of the nature of *ksa* as *apavāda* of *sic* and because its basis being a *dhātu* without the *āgama iṭ*, when it is established as valid without the *āgama iṭ*, the *ksa* rule (applies).

53.18 न वैष दोषः। किं कारणम्। क्सस्य सिजपवादत्वात्।

Bhāṣya: Or else this is not a fault. What is the reason? Because of the nature of *ksa* as *apavāda* of *sic*.

53.18 .... सिजापवादः क्सः स चानिडाश्रयः।
न चापवा दविषय उत्सर्गोऽभिनिविशते। पूर्वं ह्यपवादा अभि-
53.20 निविशन्ते पश्चादुत्सर्गाः। प्रकल्प्य वापवादविषयं तत उत्सर्गोऽभिनिविशते। तत्र
तावदत्र कदाचित्सिज्भवत्यपवादं क्सं प्रतीक्षते। क्सस्य सिजपवादत्वात्तस्य
चानिडाश्रयत्वादनिट्त्वं प्रसिद्धम्। अनिटि प्रसिद्धे क्सविधिः। अनिटि प्रसिद्धे क्सो
53.23 भविष्यति।। सिजिदानीं क्व भविष्यति।

Ksa is *apavāda* of *sic* and it has (the *dhātu*) without *āgama iṭ* as its basis and the *utsarga* does not enter into the sphere of an *apavāda* (*pratyaya*). For, first the *apavāda* (*pratyaya sūtras*) enter and afterwards the *utsarga* (*sūtras*). Or having settled the sphere of the *apavāda* (*sūtras*) then the *utsarga* (*sūtra*) enters. Just there it never happens that *sic* is applied and one expects the *apavāda ksa*. Because of *ksa* being *apavāda* of *sic* and because of its nature of having a (*dhātu*) without *iṭ āgama* as its basis, the characteristic of being without *iṭ* is established. When being without the *āgama iṭ* is established, then *ksa* applies.

When being without the *āgama iṭ* is established, then *ksa* will be applicable. Now where will *sic* be applicable?

53.24 शेषे सिज्विधानम् ॥ 5 ॥

Vārttika 5: There is ordaining of *sic* in the rest (of the same).

53.25 शेषे सिज्विधानं भविष्यति। अकोषीत् अमोषीदिति॥

Bhāṣya: The ordaining of *sic* will be applicable in the rest (of the cases). *Akoṣīt* "He tore asunder"; *amoṣīt* "He stole".

Pradīpa

Pradīpa: 53.7 क्सविधान इति।

'When *ksa* is ordained (there is absence of *ik* penultimate because of *guṇa* for *cli*).'

Due to the absence of the qualification (*ik* penultimate), a fault in the rule is caused to arise.

When there is resort to former circumstances/conditions or resort to the qualifications ordained, the object aimed at is not accomplished. However, the producing of *it k* is for the purpose of distinguishing (in *sūtra*):

क्सस्याचि (7.3.72) "The *ksa* is elided before *pratyayas* beginning with a vowel."

. . . so that there be prevention of *lopa* elision in the case of *vatsa* etc. where *sa* is without *k*. च्लेर्गुणनिमित्तं The cause of *guṇa* for *cli* (being present).'

पुगन्तलघूपधस्य च (7.3.86) "*Guṇa* is *ādeśa* in place of the *ik* vowels of the causative stems taking augment *puk* (*7.3.86*) and for a short penultimate vowel of a *dhātu* which ends in a single consonant before a *sārvadhātuka* or *ārdhadhātuka pratyaya.*"

Pradīpa: 53.10 न वा क्सस्येति।

"Or else not (because of the absence of scope) for *ksa.*"

The meaning is (because of the view), 'when there is resort to the former condition (of a word) the *it k* would be pointless, and because of the *apavāda* nature of that having an *anubandha* without scope, there is barring of *guṇa* (for *cli*).'

And the purpose of *it k* is not 'distinguishing' as in the *sūtra* क्सस्याचि (7. 3.72) by which '*a* of *ksa* is elided before a *pratyaya* beginning with a vowel'. Because of the mention of *ksa* being established as valid there due to its nature as a *pratyaya* and its meaningfulness alone.

Due (to the absence of possibility of it being applicable) in the case of *vatsa* etc. because of *uṇādi pratyayas* underivable nature.

Pradīpa: 53.13 अनिड्वचनमिति।

'The expression without *iṭ* (augment) is with qualification ... because it was invariable for *cli.*'

So that 'being without the augment *iṭ*' should be a qualification of *cli,* it was stated (*Vā. 1* on *3.1.43*) that *cli* was made an *utsarga* of general *pratyayas.*

The meaning is that, because the form having an implied absence of augment *iṭ,* and because of (it being said) 'for that *sic* should invariably be (without *iṭ*)', nowhere is found the qualification of *cli* as without *iṭ* (augment), so it is not established.

Pradīpa: 53.16 न वा क्सस्येपि।

"Or else not because of *ksa's* (nature of being *apavāda* of *sic*)."

This is the sense, when the *dhātu lih* (to lick) is established as '*a-liṭ*' *sic* would not be applicable, for this is the sphere of *ksa* (only). It is not understood that *ksa* also should not be applicable, as long as it had the character of being without *iṭ* augment. In that context, when there is obtainment of *iṭ* augment for the *la* (tense *pratyaya*), only because of the prohibition of that, there is *an-iṭ* (absence of *iṭ* augment, and *ksa* itself is established as valid adequately).

So the example becomes *a-likṣat* 'he licked', (with *iṭ*). However, where there is no prohibition of *iṭ,* there *sic* alone is applicable, e.g. *akoṣīt* 'He tore asunder'.

श्लिष आलिङ्गने ॥ 3 । 1 । 46 ॥

Pāṇini 3.1.46: *Ksa* is the *ādeśa* in place of the *pratyaya cli* after the *dhātu śliṣ* when it has the sense of embracing.

54.2 किमर्थमिदमुच्यते। नियमार्थम्। श्लिष आलिङ्गन एव क्सो यथा स्यात्। इह मा भूत्। उपाश्लिषज्जतु च काष्ठं च। समाश्लिषद्ब्राह्मणकुलमिति।। अत उत्तरं पठनि।।

Bhāṣya: Why is this said? This is said for the purpose of restriction. So that *ksa* should be applicable after *dhātu śliṣ* only in the sense of embracing. Here it should not be applicable.

upāśliṣaj jatu ca kāṣṭham ca "Lac and wood stuck together";

samāśliṣad brāhmaṇakulam "He came near the *Brāhman* family".

Then he goes on to say:

54.4 श्लिष आलिङ्गने नियमानुपपत्तिर्विधेयभावात् ॥ 1 ॥

Vārttika 1: The restriction (of *ksa*) after *śliṣ* (only) in the sense of embracing is not justified because of its being a statement to be enjoined.

54.5 श्लिष आलिङ्गने नियमस्यानुपपत्तिः। किं कारणम्। विधेयभावात्। कैमर्थाक्यान्नियमो भवति। विधेयं नास्तीति कृत्वा। इह चास्ति विधेयम्। किम्। पुषादि-
54.7 पाठादङ् प्राप्तस्तद्बाधनार्थः क्सो विधेयः।

Bhāṣya: The restriction (of *ksa*) after *śliṣ* (only) in the sense of embracing has no applicability. What is the reason? Because of its being a statement to be enjoined. A rule is a restriction because its purpose is questioned, since it cannot be a statement. But here there is something to be enjoined. What? By the statement '*puṣ* (to nourish) and the rest' *aṅ* obtains. (*3.1.55*)

54.7 .... तत्रापूर्वो विधिरस्तु नियमो वेत्यपूर्व एव विधिः स्यान्न नियमः॥ किं च स्याद्यद्ययं नियमो न स्यात्। आत्मनेपदेष्वा-लिङ्गने चानालिङ्गने च क्सः प्रसज्येत। यथैव च क्सोऽङं बाधत एवं चिणमपि
54.10 बाधेत। उपाश्लेषि कन्या देवदत्तेनेति॥

To bar that, *ksa* is to be enjoined. There in that context a rule may be quite a new rule or a restriction. It would be a complete new rule rather than a restriction. And what would be wrong if this were not a restrictive rule? When *ātmanepada pratyayas* follow *ksa* would be applied whether in the sense of embracing or not in the sense of embracing. And as in fact *ksa* bars *aṅ* so also it would bar *ciṇ*.

upāśleṣi kanyā devadattena "The girl was embraced by *Devadatta* "(*ciṇ*).

54.11 सिद्धं तु श्लिष आलिङ्गने चिण्विषये ॥ 2 ॥

Vārttika 2: However, this usage is established by prescribing *ksa* after *śliṣ* in the sense of embracing except in the context of *ciṇ* (passive aorist *pratyaya*).

54.12 सिद्धमेतत्। कथम्। श्लिष आलिङ्गने चिण्विषये क्सो भवतीति वक्तव्यम्॥

Bhāṣya: This is established as valid. How? It should be stated that *ksa* is not applicable after *śliṣ* in the sense of embracing when not in the context of *ciṇ*.

54.13 अङ्विधाने च श्लिषोऽनालिङ्गने ।। 3 ।।

Vārttika 3: And when *aṅ* is ordained, (it acts) after *śliṣ* in a sense other than embracing.

54.14 अङ्विधाने च श्लिषोऽनालिङ्गने इति वक्तव्यम्।। सिध्यति। सूत्रं तर्हि भिद्यते।।
यथान्यासमेवास्तु। ननु चोक्तं श्लिष आलिङ्गने नियमानुपपत्तिर्विधेयभावादिति।

54.16 नैष दोषः।

Bhāṣya: And it should be stated that when *aṅ* is ordained (it acts) after *śliṣ* in a sense other than embracing. It is established as valid, but then the *sūtra* is divided (into two). Then let it be as written. But surely it was stated that (*ksa* acts) after *śliṣ* in the sense of embracing, (but) the restriction is not applicable because of the existence of something (yet) to be enjoined. This is not a fault.

54.17 योगविभागात्सिद्धम् ।। 4 ।।

Vārttika 4: This is established as valid through the division of the rule.

54.18 योगविभागः करिष्यते। श्लिषः। श्लिषः क्सो भवति। किमर्थमिदम्। पुषा-
दिपाठादङ् प्राप्नोति तद्बाधनार्थम्।। तत आलिङ्गने। आलिङ्गने च श्लिषः क्सो
भवति। इदमिदानीं किमर्थम्। नियमार्थम्। श्लिष आलिङ्गन एव। क्व मा भूत्।

54.21 उपाश्लिषज्जतु च काष्ठं च। समाश्लिषद्ब्राह्मणकुलमिति।।

Bhāṣya: A division of the *sūtra* will be made.

(1) *śliṣaḥ ksa* is applicable after the *dhātu śliṣ.* What is the purpose of this rule? After the *dhātus* recited as *puṣ* (to nourish) and the rest (in the *Dhātu Pāṭha*) *aṅ* obtains. It is for the purpose of debarring that.

(2) *āliṅgane* "And in the sense of embracing *ksa* is applicable after *śliṣ*". Now what (would) be the purpose (of) this? For the purpose of (making) a restriction (*ksa*) is ordained. After the *dhātu śliṣ* only in the sense of embracing. Where should it not be applicable?

upāśliṣaj jatu ca kāṣṭham ca "He joined the wood and the glue".

samāśliṣad brāhmaṇakulam "He joined a family of *Brahmaṇas*".

54.21 .... यदप्युच्यते यथैव क्सोऽङं
बाधत एवं चिणमपि बाधेतेति पुरस्तादपवादा अनन्तरान्विधीन् बाधन्ते। नोत्तरानित्येवं
क्सोऽङं बाधिष्यते चिणं न बाधिष्यते। अथवा तत्र वक्ष्यति चिण्ग्रहणस्य

54.24 प्रयोजनं चिणेव यथा स्याद्यदन्यत्प्राप्नोति तन्मा भूदिति।।

What is also said is that "as in fact *ksa* bars *aṅ* even so may *ciṇ* also be barred". (But because of the *paribhāṣā 59*) *1.1.28, M.Bh. 1.90.14 purastād apavāda anantarān vidhīn bādhante nottarān "Apavādas* that precede (the *utsarga* rules) supersede (only) those rules that stand nearest to them, not the subsequent (rules)", *ksa* will thus bar *aṅ* (but) it will not bar *ciṇ*. Otherwise there (in the *sūtra* '*ciṇ bhāvakarmanoḥ*' *3.1.66 ciṇ* is the *ādeśa* in place of *cli* (aorist *pratyaya*) in the presence of the *ta* of the *prathama puruṣa*/third person singular *ātmanepada* denoting the action/*bhāva* or the object/*karman*, he will say the purpose of the specific mention of *ciṇ* is so that there should only be *ciṇ* applicable and whatever else obtains should not be applicable.

Pradīpa

Pradīpa: 54.2 श्लिष आ किमर्थमिति।

Why is this said?

The question is, is this for the sake of a positive rule for barring *aṅ* when it obtains, because of *śliṣ* being recited in the *gaṇa* beginning with *puṣ* (*3.1.55*) (or) now is it for the purpose of restriction when *ksa* is already established as valid by the previous *sūtra*?

नियमार्थमिति। "For the purpose of restriction."

Another, having made the *sūtra* division going to be spoken of in his mind, says this is for the purpose of a restriction.

Pradīpa: 54.3 उपाश्लिषदिति।

"(The *jatu*) sealed the wood."

Here *dhātu śliṣ* occurs in the sense of immediate proximity/close contact not in the sense of embracing.

Pradīpa: 54.7 अङ् प्राप्त इति।

(After *puṣ* and the rest *aṅ* obtains) by

पुषादिद्युताद्यलृदितःपरस्मैपदेषु (3.1.55) "*Aṅ* is *ādeśa* of *cli* after *dhātus puṣ* (to nourish) and the rest, *dyut* (to strive) and the rest, and those *dhātus* having an indicatory *ḷ*, when the *parasmaipada pratyayas* follow."

The meaning is that there is barring because of *ksa* being undertaken when there is no absence of attainment of *aṅ* for *śliṣ*.

Pradīpa: 54.9 यथैवेति।

"And as in fact (*ksa* bars *aṅ* so it would bar *ciṇ*)."

When the sense (of the *sūtra*) is purely a positive rule, there is arising of another fault.

Pradīpa: 54.11 सिद्धं त्विति।

"However, (*ksa*) is established (after *śliṣ* in the sense of embracing, not in the context of *ciṇ*)."

When *ksa* is established (already) by a previous *sūtra*, this rule is to be effected for the purpose of a restriction.

Pradīpa: 54.11 अचिण्विषय इति।

"Not in the context of *ciṇ*."

With this the meaning of restriction is construed/connected in sense. Otherwise, this would be a positive rule for the purpose of barring *ciṇ* in the context of *la* (third person *ātmanepada 3.1.66*), but not for the purpose of restriction.

Pradīpa: 54.13 अङ विधान इति।

"When *aṅ* is ordained (after *śliṣ* it is in a sense other than embracing)."

And hence because of the prohibition of *aṅ* after *śliṣ* in the sense of embracing, when (it is said) '*ksa* after *śliṣ* in the sense of embracing, not in the context of *ciṇ*' (*Vā* 2), this is for the purpose of restriction. Otherwise this (rule) would be for the purpose of a (positive) rule.

Pradīpa: 54.19 श्लिष: क्स इति।

(Division of the *sūtra*): after *śliṣ*, *ksa* is applicable.

Here this is class 4 *śliṣ*, without *iṭ* augment, because of *aniṭ*, following on from the previous *sūtra*. There is absence of reference to the *śliṣ*, class 1 having *iṭ/ seṭ*, with the sense of burning, or because that *śliṣ*, has an indicatory (*k*). In that context, the *aṅ* inferred because of *śliṣ*, being in the *puṣ-ādi gaṇa* is barred by the manifestly taught *ksa*.

Pradipa: 54.23 अथ वेति

"Or else (he will say 'the purpose of mentioning *ciṇ* is so that *ciṇ* only be applicable and anything else which obtains should not be applicable')."

When a combination (of rules) is expected (to apply) the *Paribhāṣā*

पुरस्तादपवादा अनन्तरान्विधीन् बाधन्ते नोत्तरान् पोरे 59 "*Apavādas* that precede, supercede only rules that stand nearest to them, not the subsequent rules."

. . . is not applicable because of the statement of another refutation.

तत्र there *ciṇ*

चिण्भावकर्मणो: (3.1.66) "*Ciṇ* is the ādeśa of *cli* when *ta* of third person *ātmanepada* follows, denoting abstract action/*bhāva* or object/*karman.*"

णिश्रिद्रुस्रुभ्य: कर्तरि चङ् ॥ 3 । 1 । 48 ॥

Pāṇini 3.1.48: After a *dhātu* ending in *ṇi pratyaya* (*3.1.20-21-35* etc.) and after the *dhātu śri* (to serve), *dru* (to run), and *sru* (to drop) *caṅ* is the *ādeśa* of *cli* (aorist *pratyaya*) when *luṅ* follows signifying the agent.

55.2 णिश्रिद्रुस्रुषु कमेरुपसंख्यानम् ॥ 1 ॥

Vārttika 1: Additional enumeration should be made of (*dhātu*) *kami* (to desire) as among *ṇi, śri, dru,* and *sru.*

55.3 णिश्रिद्रुस्रुषु कमेरूपसंख्यानं कर्तव्यम्॥

Bhāṣya: Additional enumeration should be made of the (*dhātu*) *kam-i* (to desire) as among *ṇi, śri, dru,* and *sru.*

55.4 नाकमिष्टमुखं यान्ति सुयुक्तैर्वडवारथै:।
अथ पत्काषिणो यान्ति येऽचीकमतभाषिण इति॥

Śloka Vārttika: They do not attain *nāka* (heaven), the desired happiness by means of well harnessed chariots drawn by mares (who use the form) *acakamata.*

Now then, they walk painfully/with rubbing or sore feet, who go about speaking the form *acīkamata.*

55.6 कर्मकर्तरि च ॥ 2 ॥

Vārttika 2: And in the sense of 'object containing agent'/reflexive/*karmakartṛ*.

55.7 कर्मकर्तरि चोपसंख्यानं कर्तव्यम्। कारयति कटं देवदत्तः। अचीकरत कटः स्वयमेव। उच्छ्रयति कटं देवदत्तः। उदशिश्रियत कटः स्वयमेव।।

Bhāṣya: And additional statement should be made (of *caṅ*) in the sense of the reflexive passive/*karmakartṛ*.

kārayati kaṭam "*Devadatta* causes the mat to be made",

acīkarata kaṭaḥ svayam eva "The mat made itself (as it were)",

ucchrayati kaṭam devadattaḥ "*Devadatta* raises the mat,

udaśiśriyata kaṭaḥ svayam eva "The mat raised itself (as it were)".

55.9 न वा कर्मण्यविधानात्कर्तृत्वाच्च कर्मकर्तुः सिद्धम् ।। 3 ।।

Vārttika 3: Or else (*caṅ*) is not (to be additionally enumerated in this sense) because of not being ordained in the sense of the passive/*karman* and because of having the nature of agent/*kartṛ* it is (already) established as valid for (expressing) the reflexive passive/*karmakartṛ*.

55.10 न वा कर्तव्यम्। किं कारणम्। कर्मण्यविधानात्। न हि कश्चित्कर्मणि विधीयते यश्चङं बाधेत। कर्तृत्वाच्च कर्मकर्तुः सिद्धम्। अस्ति च कर्मकर्तरि कर्तृ-
55.12 त्वमिति कृत्वा चङ् भविष्यति।

Bhāṣya: Or else (*caṅ*) should not be effected (in this sense). What is the reason? Because of not being ordained in the sense of the passive/*karman*. For there is nothing ordained in the sense of the passive/*karman* which would bar *aṅ*. And because of having the nature of being agent/*kartṛ*, (*caṅ*) is already established as valid for (expressing) the reflexive passive/*karmakartṛ*; and having made (the statement) there is agentship/*kartṛtva* in the sense of *karmakartṛ*, *caṅ* will be applicable.

55.12 .... ननु चायं कर्मणि विधीयते चिण्भावकर्मणोः (3.1.66) इति। प्रतिषिध्येते तत्र यक्चिणौ। यक्चिणोः हेतुमण्णिश्रिब्रूञामुपसंख्यानमिति।। यस्तर्ह्यहेतुमण्णिच्। उदपुपुच्छत गौः स्वयमेव। अत्रापि यथा भारद्वाजीयाः पठन्ति यथा भवितव्यं प्रतिषेधेन। यक्चिणोः प्रतिषेधे णिश्रन्थि-
55.16 ग्रन्थिब्रूञात्मनेपदाकर्मकाणामुपसंख्यानमिति।।

But surely this is ordained in the sense of passive/*karman* (by the *sūtra*) *ciṇ bhāvakarmaṇoḥ* (*3.1.66*) "*ciṇ* is *ādeśa* in place of (the aorist *pratyaya cli*) in the presence of the *prathama puruṣa*/third singular *ātmanepada ta* in the sense of action/*bhāva* or object/*karman*". There *yak* and *ciṇ* would be prohibited. When there is prohibition of *yak* and *ciṇ* there should be additional enumeration of *ṇi* in the causative sense, and of the *dhātus śri* (to serve) and *brū* (to speak). Then, that which is non-causative *ṇic* (does have *caṅ*) after it. Here also prohibition should be applicable according to the way the followers of *Bhāradvāja* read the text.

'When there is prohibition of *yak* and *ciṇ* there should be additional enumeration of *dhātus* ending in *ṇi* (causative etc.), *śranthi* (to loosen), *granthi* (to compose), *brūñ* (to speak), and *ātmanepada* intransitive/*akarmaka dhātus* as followed by *caṅ*'.

Pradīpa

Pradīpa: 55.2 निश्रिद्रुस्रु कर्मेरिति।

"(Additional enumeration should be made) of *kam-i* (to desire)."

When *ārdhadhātuka pratyayas* follows, because of *ṇiṅ* being ordained optionally (*3.1.30*), when in the alternative *sic* obtains (this) rule/*vārttika* (has its scope).

In that context *acakamata* 'he desired' (*caṅ* aorist) is applicable. However, in the optional use of *ṇiṅ*, because of being like *san* desiderative, the form is *acīkamata.*

When these rules apply: सन्वल्लघुनि चिङ्परेऽनग्लोपे (7.4.93) "In the reduplicated aorist of the causative, the reduplicate adapts itself to that of the desiderative, when the vowel of the *dhātu* is light and the *dhātu* has not lost its end vowel, before the causative *pratyaya* (by *atolopaḥ 6.4.48*)."

सन्यतः (7.4.79) "इ is substituted for the final short *a* of the reduplicate in the desiderative."

दीर्घो लघोः (7.4.94) "In the reduplicative syllable, a prosodially short vowel is lengthened, in the reduplicated aorist of the causative, when the vowel of the *dhātu* is light and the *dhātu* has not lost its end vowel before the causative *ṇi.*"

These *sūtras* are to be stated because of the force of mention *para* (i.e. when *caṅ* follows *ṇi* is resorted to, having the meaning of a different *pada*/word because of the impossibility (of it being for another). The meaning is therefore, 'when *caṅ* follows *ṇi* (causative), that which (has a light *dhātu* vowel in that context, has for the reduplicate which follows (as if it were *saṇ* desiderative following), the operation applicable. (i.e. long *ī*).

कर्तव्यम् कमेर्णिङ् (3.1.30)

आयादव आर्धधातुके वा (3.1.31)

Pradīpa: 55.3 नाकमिष्ट सुखमिति।

"They do obtain *Nāka*/heaven, the desired happiness (by means of well-harnessed chariots . . .)."

'They attain *Nāka*/heaven, the desired pleasure, by means of well-harnessed chariots, drawn by mares', 'By whom?' it is asked, 'What form is applicable for *kam-i,* when *liṅ* follows?' and it is stated *acakamata.*

However, "those who uttered *acīkamata* walk painfully with rubbing feet. Due to forgetting the rule." This is being stated for the purpose of blame and for the purpose of honouring those who remember the rule.

However, others say 'those by whom' *akamiṣṭa* is uttered, they in fact metaphorically are spoken of by the word *akamiṣṭa* by a word of imitation. Due to it not being desired to express the difference between the act of imitation and that to be imitated, the *vibhakti*/verb ending is not effected.

'They, though going by means of well-harnessed chariots drawn by mares, do not attain happiness because of pronouncing an incorrect word. However, those who *say acīkamata,* though walking painfully with rubbing feet attain happiness.'

Pradīpa: 55.6 कर्मकर्तरि चेति।

"And in the sense of reflexive passive (*caṅ* should be stated)."

Caṅ being expressed when a *pratyaya* follows signifying agent, it does not obtain in the sense of reflexive passive, hence this *vārttika.*

Pradīpa: 55.14 उद्पुपुच्छतेति।

"(The cow) raised its tail of itself."

(The denominative), *utpucchayate* means 'the cow raises its tail there'. When, because of an implied inherent *ṇi* (causative) meaning, the transitive nature is applicable with the word cow, then *utpucchayate* 'He causes the cow to raise its tail' is applicable. But when it is desired to express the exceeding ease of the cow alone, as the agent and the past time, then there is this example.

अस्यतिवक्तिख्यातिभ्योऽङ् ॥ 3 । 1 । 52 ॥

Pāṇini 3.1.52: After the *dhātus as* (to throw), *vac* (to speak), *aṅ* is the *ādeśa* of (the aorist *pratyaya*) *cli* in the presence of *luṅ* in the sense of the agent.

55.18 अस्यतिग्रहणं किमर्थम्।

Bhāṣya: What is the purpose of the specific mention of (the form) *asyati* ?

55.19 अस्यतिग्रहणमात्मनेपदार्थम् ॥ 1 ॥

Vārttika 1: The mention of the form *asyati* is for the sake of *ātmanepada pratyayas* (being applicable).

55.20 अस्यतिग्रहणमात्मनेपदार्थं द्रष्टव्यम्। किमुच्यत आत्मनेपदार्थमिति न पुनः परस्मैपदा- र्थमपि स्यात्। पुषादिपाठात्परस्मैपदेष्वङ् भविष्यति[1]॥

Bhāṣya: It should be observed that the purpose of mentioning the form *asyati* is for the sake of *aṅ* being applicable when the *ātmanepada pratyayas* follow. Why is it stated for the sake of the *ātmanepada* (context) ? Should it not again be also for the sake of the *parasmaipada* (context) ? Because of *asyati* forming part of the *gaṇa* beginning with *puṣ* (to nourish). Due to its being recited in the *Dhātu Paṭha* in the *gaṇa* beginning with *puṣ* when *parasmaipada pratyaya* follow, *aṅ* will be applicable (anyway).

55.22 कर्मकर्तरि च ॥ 2 ॥

Vārttika 2: And (*aṅ* should be applicable) in the sense of the passive reflexive/*karmakartṛ*.

55.23 कर्मकर्तरि चोपसंख्यानं कर्तव्यम्। पर्यास्थेतां कुण्डले स्वयमेव॥ अत्रापि न वा कर्मण्यविधानात्कर्तृत्वाच्च कर्मकर्तुः सिद्धमित्येव॥

Bhāṣya: Additional enumeration should be made of *aṅ* in the sense of the reflexive passive/*karmakartṛ* e.g. *paryāsthetām kuṇḍale svayam eva* "The two earings turned round of themselves". Here also (the *Vārttika 3* on *3.1.48*) applies.

Or else (additional enumeration) is not (necessary) because of not being ordained in the sense of *karman* /passive and because of having the nature of being agent/*kartṛ*. It is established already in the sense of *karmakartṛ*.

Pradīpa

Pradīpa: 55.17 अस्यति।

"(The mention of) *asyati* (is for *ātmanepada pratyayas* because of being part of *puṣ* and the rest taking *aṅ* with *parasmaipada 3.1.55*)."

Due to *puṣ* and the rest being at the conclusion of the *divādi gaṇa*, thus including *as* (to throw).

Pradīpa: 55.19 अस्यतिग्रहणमिति।

"The mention of *asyati* . . ."

The making of the sign *vṛt* (in class 4 of the *Dhātu Pāṭha*) is for the purpose of indicating the conclusion of the *gaṇa* beginning with *rādh* but not for the purpose of concluding the group *puṣ* and the rest; for the purpose of so teaching, the Master, who has become a friend, says 'the mention . . .'

Pradīpa: 55.23 अत्रापीति

"Here too (because of being ordained in sense of *karman* and because of agentship, reflexive passive is established)." (c.f. *Vā.* 3 on *3.1.48.*)

The sense is that, because of not ordaining here any operation for *karman* resulting from substitution/extended application, and because of the absence of bar to the operation, that which is basic in itself, in fact occurs.

Notes

[1] अङ् भविष्यति। *Aṅ* will be applicable (by पुषादिद्युताद्यॢदितः परस्मैपदेषु 3.1.55).

जॄस्तम्भुम्रुचुम्लुचुग्रुचुग्लुचुग्लुञ्चुश्विभ्यश्च ॥ 3 । 1 । 58 ॥

Pāṇini 3.1.58: And optionally *aṅ* is *ādeśa* of (aorist *pratyaya*) after the *dhātus jṝ* to grow old), *stambh* (to stiffen). *mruc* and *mluc* (to steal), *gluñc* (to go), and *śvi* (to grow or swell) when the *parasmaipada pratyayas* follows.

56.2 इदं ग्लुचिग्रहणं ग्लुञ्चिग्रहणं च क्रियते। अन्यतरच्छक्यमकर्तुम्। कथम्। यदि तावद्ग्लुचिग्रहणं क्रियते ग्लुञ्चिग्रहणं न करिष्यते। तेनैव सिद्धं न्यग्लुचत् न्यग्लोचीत्। इदमिदानीं ग्लुञ्चे रूपं न्यग्लुञ्चीत्।। अथ ग्लुञ्चिग्रहणं क्रियते ग्लुचिग्रहणं न करिष्यते। तेनैव सिद्धं न्यग्लुचत् न्यग्लुञ्चीत्।। इदमिदानीं ग्लुचे रूपं
56.6 न्यग्लोचीदिति ।।

Bhāṣya: The separate mention of *gluc-i* and *gluñc-i* is made. It is possible not to have to make (mention of) either. How? If mention is just made of *gluc-i* there will not be mention made of *gluñc-i.* By reason of that alone (these forms) *nyaglucat, nyaglocīt* "He went down", are established as valid. This now is the form from *gluñc-i*: *nyagluñcīt.*

Now if the specific mention of *gluñc-i* is made the specific mention of *gluc-i* will not be made. By reason of that alone *nyaglucat* and *nyagluñcīt* are established as valid forms. This now is the form for *gluc-i : nyaglocīt.*

Pradīpa

Pradīpa: 56.2 जॄस्तम्भु। अन्यतरिदिति।

"(It is possible not to make mention of) either (*gluci* or *gluñci*)."

The sense is that because of *dhātus* having more than one meaning, here in this context a difference of meaning is not the purpose of maintaining both forms.

However, that (view) which (says) because of the force of mention of both forms, when *aṅ* follows after *gluñc-i lopa* of *n* is not applicable (thus the form was by some expressed as *nya-gluñcat*) because of conflicting with the *Bhāṣyakāra,* is not to be respected.

चिण्ते पदः ॥ 3 । 1 । 60 ॥

Pāṇini 3.1.60: *Ciṇ* is the *ādeśa* in place of (the aorist *pratyaya*) when *ta* (*ātmanepada prathama puruṣa* third singular) follows after the *dhātu pad* (to go).

56.8 अयं तशब्दोऽस्त्येवात्मनेपदमस्ति परस्मैपदमस्त्येवैकवचनमस्ति बहुवचनम्।
कस्येदं ग्रहणम्। यः पदेररस्ति। कश्च पदेरस्ति पदिरयमात्मनेपदी॥

Bhāṣya: The word *ta* is in fact *ātmanepada.* (No) it is *parasmaipada.* It is in fact singular. (No) it is plural. Of what is this a specific mention? That which is after the *dhātu padī.*

And what is after the *dhātu pad-ī* ? This *dhātu pad-ī* takes *ātmanepada vibhakti pratyaya.*

Pradīpa

Pradīpa: 56.9 पदिरयमात्मनेपदी।

> "Therefore this is a reference to the *ātmanepada prathama*/third *puruṣa* singular."

चिण्भावकर्मणोः ॥ 3 । 1 । 66 ॥

Pāṇini 3.1.66: *Ciṇ* is *ādeśa* of (aorist *pratyaya*) *cli* when *ta* (of the *ātmanepada prathama puruṣa*/third singular) follows in the sense of action/ *bhāva* or object/ *karman* after a *dhātu.*

56.11 चिणिति वर्तमाने[1] पुनश्चिण्ग्रहणं किमर्थम्। नेत्येवं तदभूद्विध्यर्थमिदम्। अथवा
वेत्येव तदभून्नित्यार्थमिदम्॥ अथवा चिणिति वर्तमाने पुनश्चिण्ग्रहणस्यैतत्प्रयोजनं
56.13 चिणेव यथा स्याद्यदन्यत्प्राप्नोति तन्मा भूदिति॥

Bhāṣya: When *ciṇ* exists by following on/ *anuvṛtti* (from *ciṇ te padaḥ 3.1.60*), what is the purpose of mentioning *ciṇ* again? (Otherwise) that (mention of *ciṇ*) which was connected with *na* (not), (would thus be from *na rudhaḥ 3.1.64.* "*Ciṇ* is not *ādeśa* of *cli* after *dhātu duḥ* (to milk) when used reflexively and when *ta* (follows)"). This *sūtra* is for the purpose of a (positive) rule (to counter the negation). Otherwise the mention of *ciṇ* in that was connected with option.

This is for making the rule invariable/*nitya.* Or otherwise, the purpose of *ciṇ* being mentioned again, when it is present by *anuvṛtti,* is so that *ciṇ* only should be applicable and so that whatever else obtains should not be applicable.

Pradīpa

Pradīpa: 56.11 अथवेति

"Otherwise (optionally it would be . . . this is for making it invariable)."

But surely here because of the absence of obtainment, due to *'na'* (not) it will not be expected, so he says 'otherwise'

वेत्येवं 2 that optionally applies . . . by

दीपजनबुधपूरितायिप्यायिभ्योऽन्यतरस्याम् (3.1.61)

"*Ciṇ* is optionally the *ādeśa* of *cli* when *te* (third person singular) *ātmanepada* follows after the *dhātus dīp, jan, budh, pūr, tāy,* and *pyāy."*

Pradīpa: 56.12 अथवेति।

"Otherwise . . . (the purpose is so that *ciṇ* only be applicable.")

Even though there is *ciṇ* optionally because of the prior (reference to *ciṇ*) in fact being made to cease by the prohibition (*3.1.60*), it will not be expected (to follow on). So he says . . . 'otherwise'.")

Notes

[1] चिणित वर्तमाने ('चिण ते पद: 3.1.60)

Ciṇ already exists by *anuvṛtti from 3.1.60*

नेत्येदमिति। न रुध: (3.1.64) "(For the purpose of the rule) *ciṇ* is not . . ."

'*Ciṇ* is not *ādeśa* of *cli* after the *dhātu rudh* (to obstruct) when used in a reflexive sense in the third person singular *ātmanepada.*'

The meaning is, the prohibition connected with this *sūtra ciṇ* would not be applicable.

सार्वधातुके यक् ॥ 3 । 1 । 67 ॥

Pāṇini 3.1.67: The *Pratyaya yak* acts after a *dhātu* when a *sārvadhātuka* (*tiṅ śit 3.4.113*) follows denoting action/ *bhāva* or object/ *karman.*

56.15 इह पश्यामः कर्मणि द्विवचनबहुवनान्युदह्रियन्ते। पच्येते ओदनौ पच्यन्त
ओदना इति। भावे पुनरेकवचनमेव। आस्यते भवता आस्यते भवद्भ्याम्
आस्यते
56.17 भवद्भिरिति। कनैतदेवं भवति।।

Bhāṣya: Here we see that in denoting object/passive/*karman* dual and plural (words) are illustrated: *pacyete odanau* "Two (portions of) rice are cooked", *pacyanta odanaḥ* "(Many portions or grains of) rice are cooked". But in the sense of abstract action/*bhāva*, there is only singular.

āsyate bhavatā "It is being seated by you",

āsyate bhavadbhyām "You two are seated",

āsyate bhavadbhiḥ "You (all) are seated".

But why does this happen?

56.17 .... कर्मानेकं तस्यानेकत्वाद्द्विवचनबहुवचनानि भवन्ति।
भावः पुनरेक एव। कथं तर्हीह द्विवचनबहुवचनानि भवन्ति। पाकौ पाका इति।
आश्रयभेदात्। यदसौ द्रव्यं श्रितो भवति भावस्तस्य भेदाद्द्विवचनबहुवचनानि
भवन्त। इहापि तर्हि यावन्तस्ते तां क्रियां कुर्वन्ति सर्वे ते तस्या आश्रया
56.21 भवन्ति तद्भेदाद्द्विवचनबहुवचनानि प्राप्नुवन्ति।।

The *karman*/object is more than one. Because of its being more than one, dual and plural (endings/*vibhakti*) are applicable. But abstract action/*bhāva* is singular only. How is it that there exist dual and plural numbers e.g. in *pākau* (two cookings), *pākāḥ* (more than two) cookings? Because of a difference in their substratum. Due to the distinction of that object on which the action rests distinction of dual and plural (*vibhaktis*) are applicable. How also then as many of them perform that action so many will become its substratum. Due to that distinction dual and plural numbers obtain.

56.21 .... एवं तर्हीदं तावदयं प्रष्टव्यः किमभिस-
मीक्ष्यैतत्प्रयुज्यते पाकौ पाका इति। यदि तावत्पाकविशेषानभिसमीक्ष्य यश्चौदनस्य
57.2 पाको यश्च गुडस्य यश्च तिलानां बहवस्ते शब्दाः सरूपाश्चतत्र युक्तं

बहुवचनमेकशेषश्च। तिङभिहिते चापि तदा भावे बहुवचनं श्रूयते। तद्यथा। उष्ट्रासिका आस्यन्ते। हतशायिकाः शय्यन्त इति। अथ कालविशेषानभिसमीक्ष्य यश्चाद्यतनः पाको चश्च ह्यस्तनो यश्च श्वस्तनस्तेऽपि बहवः शब्दाः सरूपाश्च तत्र युक्तं बहुवचनमेकशेषश्च। तिङभिहिते चापि तदा भावेऽसारूप्यादेकशेषो न भवति।
57.7 आसि आस्यते आसिष्यते।।

So then this (following) has just to be asked having regard to what are these forms *pākau* and *pākāḥ* used? If (he says that) they are used with reference to kinds of cooking, namely that which (may be) the cooking of rice, also that which (may be) cooking of *jagari*, or that which (may be the cooking) of sesamum seeds, these words are many and of the same form (namely *pāka*). There the plural is appropriate and one (of those *pāka* words, only) is retained.

And also when *tiṅ* (verb endings) are ordained then the plural (*vibhakti*) are heard in the sense of the action. As for example *uṣṭrāsikā āsyante* "Those sitting on camels are (in fact) seated", *hataśāyikāḥ śayyante* "those who had stopped lying down are being made to sleep".

Now with reference to distinctions of time, that which is today's cooking and which is yesterday's and which is tomorrow's, (they too) are many words and the same form *'pāka'*. Therefore there the plural is proper and one (only) is retained and the abstract action is expressed by *tiṅ* (verbal endings). Then because of dissimilarity of the forms the one (only) is not retained: *āsi* "He was seated", *āsyate* "He is being seated", *āsiṣyate* "He will be seated".

57.7 .... अस्ति खल्वपि विशेषः कृदभिहितस्य भावस्य तिङभिहितस्य च। कृदभिहितो भावो द्रव्यवद्भवति। किमिदं द्रव्यवदिति। द्रव्यं क्रियया समवायं गच्छति। कं समवायम्। द्रव्यं क्रियाभिनिर्वृत्तौ साधनत्वमुपैति।
57.10 तद्वच्चास्य भावस्य कृदभिहितस्य भवति। पाको वर्तत इति। क्रियावन्न भवति।

There is indeed also a distinction between an abstract action expressed by a *kṛt pratyaya* and one expressed by a *tiṅ*. An action expressed by a *kṛt pratyaya* is like a substance. What is this (being) "like a substance"? The substance attains inseparable concomitance/conjunction with the verbal activity. What inseparable concomitance (does it attain)? When there is accomplishment of the action the substance acts as a means for the accomplishment of an action, and like that becomes applicable for that action expressed by a *kṛt pratyaya* e.g. *pāko vartate* "The cooking proceeds". Being like the verbal activity is not applicable.

57.11 किमिदं क्रियावदिति। क्रिया क्रियया समवायं न गच्छति। पचति पठतीति। तद्वच्चास्य कृदभिहितस्य न भवति। पाको वर्तत इति।। अस्ति खल्वपि विशेषः

कृदभिहितस्य भावस्य तिङभिहितस्य च। तिङभिहितेन भावेन कालपुरुषोपग्रहा अभिव्यज्यन्ते कृदभिहितेन पुनर्न व्यज्यन्ते।। अस्ति खल्वपि विशेषः कृदभिहितस्य

57.15 भावस्य तिङभिहितस्य च। तिङभिहितो भावः कर्त्रा संप्रयुज्यते कृदभिहितः पुनर्न संप्रयुज्यते। यावता किंचित्सामान्यं कश्चिच्च विशेषो युक्तं यदयमपि विशेषः स्याल्लि-

57.17 ङ्गकृतः संख्याकृतश्चेति ।।

What is this 'being like the verbal activity' ? An action does not attain inseparable concomitance with (another) action: *pacati pathati* "He cooks, recites". And like that, for (the action) enjoined with a *kṛt pratyaya* (inseparable concomitance) is not applicable (with another action). *pāko vartate* "The cooking proceeds".

There is indeed another distinction between that action expressed by a *kṛt pratyaya* and that expressed by a *tiṅ pratyaya.* With an action/*bhāva* expressed by a *tiṅ pratyaya* time, person and mood/*pada* are manifested but (they) are not manifested with an action expressed by a *kṛt pratyaya.*

There is also (another) distinction between that action expressed by a *kṛt pratyaya* and that expressed by a *tiṅ pratyaya.* The action expressed by a *tiṅ* (*pratyaya*) is connected with the agent but that expressed by a *kṛt pratyaya* is not connected (with the agent).

Inasmuch as there is something common and something special it is proper that that specific feature formed with gender and formed with number also should be there.

57.18 इदं विचार्यते भावकर्मकर्तारः सार्वधातुकार्था वा स्युर्विकरणार्था वेति। कथं च सार्वधातुकार्थाः स्युः कथं वा विकरणार्थाः। भावकर्मवाचिनि सार्वधातुके यग्भवति कर्तृवाचिनि सार्वधातुके शब्भवतीति सार्वधातुकार्थाः। भावकर्मणोर्यग्भवति सार्वधातुके

57.21 कर्तरि शब्भवति सार्वधातुक इति विकरणार्थाः कश्चात्र विशेषः।

This is to be considered, whether action/*bhāva* object/*karman* and agent/*kartṛ* be the meanings of *sārvadhātuka pratyayas* or of *vikaraṇa pratyayas,* and how they could be the meanings of the *sārvadhātuka pratyayas* or how they could be the meanings of the *vikaraṇa pratyayas*? When a *sārvadhātuka pratyaya* expressing the agent follows, *śap pratyaya* is applicable. Thus the meanings of *sārvadhātuka pratyayas* (are shown). In the sense of action and object *yak* is applicable when a *sārvadhātuka* follows. Thus the meanings of the *vikaraṇa pratyayas* (are shown); and what is the distinction here?

57.22 भावकर्मकर्तारः सार्वधातुकार्थाश्चेदेकद्विबहुषु नियमानुपपत्तिरतदर्थ-त्वात् ।। 1 ।।

Vārttika 1: If action/ *bhāva*, object/ *karman* and agent/ *kartṛ* are the meanings of *sārvadhātuka pratyayas,* then the restriction to the senses of singular dual and plural (for the *tiṅ vibhakti pratyaya*) is inapplicable because of their not having (just) that meaning.

57.24 भावकर्मकर्तारः सार्वधातुकार्थाश्चेदेकद्विबहुषु नियमस्यानुपपतिः। किं कारणम्। अतदर्थत्वात्। न हि तदानीमेकत्वादय एव विभक्त्यर्थाः। किं तर्हि। भावकर्म
57.26 कर्तारोऽपि।। सन्तु तर्हि विकरणार्थाः।।

Bhāṣya: If action, object and agent are the meanings of *sārvadhātuka pratyayas,* then the restriction in the sense of singular dual and plural (for the *tiṅ vibhakti*) has no applicability. What is the reason? Because of their not having (just) that meaning. For then singular and the rest are not alone the meanings of the *vibhakti pratyayas.* What then (are the others) ? (They are) also action/ *bhāva* object/ *karman* and agent/ *kartṛ.* Then let them be the meanings of the *vikaraṇa pratyayas.*

57.27 विकरणार्था इति चेत्कृताभिहिते विकरणाभावः ।। 2।।

Vārttika 2: If (we say they are) the meanings of the *vikaraṇa pratyayas,* when *kṛt pratyaya* is enjoined there (will) be an absence of *vikaraṇa* (*pratyayas*).

57.28 विकरणार्था इति चेत्कृताभिहिते विकरणो न प्राप्नोति। धारयः पारय इति।। किमुच्यते कृताभिहित इति न लेनाप्यभिधानं भवति। अशक्यं लेनाभिधानमाश्रयितुम्। पक्षान्तरमिदमास्थितं भावकर्मकर्तारः सार्वधातुकार्था वा स्युर्विकरणार्था
58.3 वेति यदि च लेनाप्यभिधानं स्यान्नेदं पक्षान्तरं स्यात्।

Bhāṣya: If (we say) these are the meanings of *vikaraṇa pratyayas,* when a *kṛt pratyaya* is enjoined a *vikaraṇa* does not obtain e.g. in *dhārayaḥ* '(someone) holding', '*pārayaḥ* '(someone) ferrying'.

Why is it said "when a *kṛt pratyaya* is expressed"? Does not expression take place by a *la* (*pratyaya*) signifying the ten tenses and moods? It is not possible to resort to expression by a *la* (tense or mood *pratyaya*). The alternative views stand as (the statement) 'action/ *bhāva,* object/ *karman* and agent/ *kartṛ* may be the meanings of *sārvadhātuka pratyayas* or the meanings of *vikaraṇa pratyayas*'. But if there were expression by a *la* (tense *pratyaya*) the alternative words would not be possible.

58.3 .... कथमशक्यं यदा भवा-नेवाह लः कर्मणि च भावे चाकर्मकेभ्यः (3.4.69) इति। एवं वक्ष्यामि लः

58.5 कर्मणो भावाच्चाकर्मकेभ्य इति यस्मिंस्तर्हि ले विकरणा नश्रूयन्ते कस्तत्र भावकर्मकर्तृनभिधास्यति। क्व च नश्रूयन्ते। य एते युग्विकरणाःश्लुविकरणाश्च।

58.7 अत्राप्युक्ते कर्तृत्वे लुग्भविष्यति।

How is it not possible when you sir say, *laḥ karmaṇi ca bhāve cākarmakebhyaḥ 3.4.69* "(tense and mood *pratyayas* called) *la* act in denoting the object/*karman* and the agent/*kartṛ* and after intransive/*akarmaka dhātus* they denote the action/*bhāva* and the agent". Thus I shall say, "*la* (*pratyayas*) act after (a *vikaraṇa pratyaya* denoting) object/*karman* and the agent/*kartṛ* and after intransitive *dhātus* denoting action/*bhāva* and agent". Then when *vikaraṇa pratyayas* are not heard when a *la* follows, what will express action/*bhāva*, object/*karman* and agent/*kartṛ*? But when are they not heard? In the case of these which are (called) *luk vikaraṇas* and *ślu vikaraṇa pratyayas.* Here also when agentship is expressed *luk* elision will be applicable.

58.7 .... यस्मिंस्तर्हि ले विकरणा नैवोत्पद्यन्ते कस्तत्र भावकर्मकर्तृनभिधास्यति। क्व च नैवोत्पद्यन्ते। लिङ्लिटोः। तस्मान्नैतच्छक्यं वक्तुं न लेनाप्यभिधानं भवतीति। भवति चेदभिहिते विकरणाभाव इत्येव।। एवं तर्हीदं स्यात्। यदा भावकर्मणोर्लस्तदा कर्तरि विकरणा यदा कर्तरि लस्तदा भावक-

58.11 र्मणोर्विकरणाः।।

Then when the *vikaraṇa pratyayas* in fact do not arise, when a tense *pratyaya* is present, what there will express action, object and agent? And when do they in fact not arise? When *liṅ* (optative) and *liṭ* (perfect) follow. Therefore it is not possible to state this, 'not even by a *la* (tense *pratyaya*) is there expressing applicable'. If it is applicable, it is when it is expressed. Then indeed, there is the absence of a *vikaraṇa pratyaya.*

Then let this be (stated). When there is a *la* (tense *pratyaya*) in the sense of action/*bhāva* and *karman*/object, then the *vikaraṇa pratyaya* is in the sense of agent/*kartṛ*. When the *la* (tense *pratyaya*) is present in the sense of agent, then the *vikaraṇa pratyaya* is present in the sense of *bhāva* or *karman.*

58.11 .... इदमस्य यद्येव स्वाभाविकमथापि वाचनिकं प्रकृतिप्रत्ययौ प्रत्ययार्थं सह ब्रूत इति न चास्ति संभवा यदेकस्याः प्रकृतेर्द्वयोर्नानार्थयोर्युगपदनुसहायीभावः स्यात्। एवं च कृत्वैकपक्षीभूतमेवेदं भवति सार्वधातुकार्था एवेति।। ननु चोक्तं भावकर्मकर्तारः सार्वधातुकार्थाश्चैकद्विबहुषु नियमानुपपत्तिरतदर्थत्वादिति

58.15 नैषः दोषः।

If this in fact arises from its own nature, or even if it is founded on express statement, according to the maxim "The *prakṛti* (base) and the *pratyaya* together express the meaning of the *pratyaya*", there is no possibility there could be simultaneously companionship of two different meanings for one base/*prakṛti*. And therefore, this which has become the single view is applicable. Only the *sārvadhātuka pratyayas* have (these) meanings and not the *vikaraṇa pratyayas*.

But surely it was stated "if action/*bhāva*, object/*karman* and agent/*kartṛ* are the meanings of *sārvadhātuka pratyayas* there is inapplicablity of a restriction in relation to the sense of singular, dual and plural because of not having that meaning"? This is no fault.

58.16 सुपां कर्मादयोऽप्यर्थाः संख्या चैव तथा तिङाम्।

Vārttika: *Karman* (object) and the rest are also the meaning of the *sup* (noun endings/*vibhakti pratyaya*) and number in fact likewise of the *tiṅ* (verbal *vibhakti pratyayas*).

58.17 सुपां तिङां च संख्या चैवार्थः कर्मादयश्च।

Bhāṣya: Number is in fact the meaning of *sup* (noun endings) and *tiṅ* (verbal endings) and so are *karman*/object and the rest.

58.18 प्रसिद्धो नियमस्तत्र

Vārttika: A restriction is well established there.

58.19 प्रसिद्धस्तत्र नियमः।

Bhāṣya: A restriction is well established there.

58.20 नियमः प्रकृतेषुः॥

Vārttika: The restriction is in relation to original (meanings).

58.21 अथवा प्रकृतानर्थानपेक्ष्य नियमः। के च प्रकृताः। एकत्वादयः। एकस्मि-
न्नेवैकवचनं न द्वयोर्न बहुषुः। द्वयोरेव द्विवचनं नैकस्मिन्न बहुषुः। बहुष्वेव
58.23 बहुवचनं नैकस्मिन्न द्वयोरिति॥

Bhāṣya: Or else the restriction is with regard to the original meanings. What are the original meanings? Singular in the sense of one only not in the sense of two or many. Dual is in the sense of two only not in the sense of one or many. Plural is in the sense of many only, and not in the sense of one or two.

58.24 भावकर्मणोर्यग्विधाने कर्मकर्तर्युपसंख्यानाम् ॥ 3 ॥

Vārttika 3: When *yak* is ordained in the sense of action/*bhāva* and object/*karman* there should be additional enumeration (of *yak*) in the sense of the reflexive passive/*karmakartṛ*.

58.25 भावकर्मणोर्यग्विधाने कर्मकर्तर्युपसंख्यानं कर्तव्यम्। पच्यते स्यवमेव। पठ्यते स्वयमेव। किं पुनः कारणं न सिध्यति।

Bhāṣya: When *yak* is ordained in the sense of *bhāva* (action) and *karman* (object) additional enumeration should be made of *yak* in the sense of the reflexive passive/*karmakartṛ*.

pacyate svayam eva "It cooked itself",

paṭhyate svayam eva "It recited itself".

But what is the reason it is not established as valid?

59.1 विप्रतिषेद्धाद्धि शपो बलीयस्त्वम् ।। 4 ।।

Vārttika 4: For, because of a conflict (of rules of equal strength requiring the subsequent to prevail) *śap* has pre-eminence in strength (i.e. is more powerful).

59.2 विप्रतिषेधाद्धि शपो बलीयस्त्वं प्राप्नोति। शपोऽवकाशः। पचति पठति।
यकोऽवकाशः। पच्यत ओदनो देवदत्तेन। पठ्यते विद्या देवदत्तेन। इहोभयं
59.4 प्राप्नोति। पच्यते स्वयमेव पठ्यते स्वयमेव। परत्वाच्शप्प्राप्नोति।।

Bhāṣya: For, because of a conflict (of rules of equal force requiring the subsequent to prevail) pre-eminence of its strength obtains for *śap*. There is scope (of application) for *śap* (in the forms) *pacati* "He cooks", *paṭhati* "He recites". There is scope for *yak*: *pacyate odano devadattena* "The rice is cooked by *Devadatta*",

paṭhyate vidyā devadattena "The knowledge is taught or mentioned by *Devadatta*". Here both obtain.

pacyate svayam eva "The rice cooks itself",

paṭhyate svayam eva "The knowledge teaches itself".

Because of being the subsequent (*sūtra*) *śap* obtains.

59.5 योगविभागात्सिद्धम् ।। 5 ।।

Vārttika 5: (*Yak*) is established as valid through separating the *sūtra* (into two).

59.6 योगविभागः करिष्यते। चिण्भावकर्मणोः। सार्वधातुके यग्भावकर्मणोः।
ततः कर्तरि। कर्तरि च यग्भवति भावकर्मणोः।।

Bhāṣya: A separation of the *sūtra* (in two parts) will be made. *Ciṇ* acts (in place of *cli*) when *ta* of *ātmanepada prathama puruṣa* follows in the sense of action/*bhāva* and object/*karman*. *Yak* acts when a *sārvadhātuka pratyaya* denoting *bhāva* and *karman* follows.

Then (also) in the sense of agent/*kartṛ*. And *yak* is applicable in the sense of agent as well as in the sense of *bhāva* and *karman*.

59.8 यथैव तर्हि कर्मणि कर्तरि यग्भवत्येवं भावे कर्तरि प्राप्नोति।
एति जीवन्तमानन्दः। नास्य किंचिद्रुजति रोग इति।।

As in fact then *yak* is applicable in the sense of agent/*kartṛ* and object/*karman*, so it also obtains in the sense of *bhāva* (action) and agent, e.g. *eti jīvantam ānandaḥ* "Bliss lasts to the end of the life", *nāsya kiñcidrujati rogaḥ* "The disease does not affect him at all".

59.9 .... द्वितीयो योगविभागः करिष्यन्ते।
चिण्भावे। ततः कर्मणि च चिण्भवतीति। ततः सार्वधातुके यग्भवति भावे
च कर्मणि च। ततः कर्तरि। कर्तरि च यग्भवति। कर्मणीत्यनुवर्तते भाव इति
59.12 निवृत्तम्। ततः शप्। शप् च भवति कर्तरीत्येव। कर्मणीत्यपि निवृत्तम्।।

A second separation of the *sūtra* (in two parts) will be effected. Then from that (*sūtra*) there is 'in the sense of *karman*/object'. And *ciṇ* is applicable 'in the sense of *karman*'. Then *yak* is applicable when a *sārvadhātuka pratyaya* follows in the sense of *bhāva* and *karman*. Then 'in the sense of agent'. And *yak* is applicable in the sense of agent/*kartṛ*. The word *karman* follows on from the previous *sūtra* (but the word) *bhāva* ceases to follow on. Then the rule is '*śap*' and '*śap* is applicable only in the sense of agent'; 'in the sense of *karman* (object)' also ceases to follow on.

59.12 .... एव-
मप्युपसंख्यानं कर्तव्यं विप्रतिषेधाद्धि श्यनो बलीयस्त्वं प्राप्नोति। श्यनोऽवकाशः।
दीव्यति सीव्यति। यकोऽवकाशः। पच्यत ओदनो देवदत्तेन। पठ्यते विद्या देव-
59.15 दत्तेन। इहोभयं प्राप्नोति। दीव्यते स्वयमेव। सीव्यते स्वयमेव। परत्वाच्श्यन्प्रा-
प्राप्नोति। ननु चैतदपि योगविभागादेव सिद्धम्। न सिध्यति। अनन्तरा या प्राप्तिः
सा योगविभागेन शक्या बाधितुम्। कुत एतत्। अनन्तरस्य विधिर्वा भवति
प्रतिषेधो वेति। परा प्राप्तिरप्रतिषिद्धा तया प्राप्नोति। ननु चेयं प्राप्तिः परां प्राप्तिं
59.19 बाधेत। नोत्सहते प्रतिषिद्धा सति बाधितुम्।।

So also additional enumeration should be made (of *karma kartari*). For due to a conflict (of rules of equal strength requiring the subsequent to prevail) the pre-eminence in strength of *śyan* obtains. There is scope (for the application) of *śyan* (in) *dīvyati* "He plays (dice etc.)", *sīvyati* "She sews". There is scope (for the application) of *yak* in *pacyate odano devadattena* "The rice is cooked by *Devadatta*", *paṭhyate vidyā devadattena* "The knowledge is taught by *Devadatta*", Here both obtain *dīvyate svayam eva* "(The game) plays itself (as it were)", *sīvyate svayam eva* "(The cloth) sews itself (as it were)". Because of being the subsequent (rule) *śyan* obtains. But surely this is also established (validly) through separating the rule (in two parts). No it is not established as valid (in this way). It is possible to bar that (rule) obtaining which is contiguous (immediately adjoining) by separating the rule (into two parts). Why is this statement made? Either rule or prohibition is applicable for that which is immediately following. A following (rule) which obtains (and is) not prohibited by reason of that obtains. But surely this obtaining would bar a following obtaining. It is not possible that an existent prohibited rule should be barred (again).

59.19 .... एवं तर्हि शबादेशाः श्यनादयः
करिष्यन्ते शप् च यका बाध्यते तत्र दिवादिभ्यो यग्विषये शबेव नास्ति कुतः
श्यानादयः। तत्तर्हि शपो ग्रहणं कर्तव्यम्। प्रकृतमनुवर्तते। क्व प्रकृतम्। कर्तरि
शप् (3.1.68) इति। तद्वै प्रथमानिर्दिष्टं षष्ठीनिर्दिष्टेन चेहार्थः। दिवादिभ्य इत्येषा
पञ्चमी शबिति प्रथमायाः षष्ठीं प्रकल्पयिष्यति तस्मादित्युत्तरस्य (1.1.67)
इति। प्रत्ययविधिरयं न च प्रत्ययविधौ पञ्चम्यः प्रकल्पिका भवन्ति।

59.25 नायं प्रत्ययविधिः। विहितः प्रत्ययः प्रकृतश्चानुवर्तते।।

59.26 अथवा

So then *śyan* and the rest will be made the *ādeśas* (substitutes) of *śap* and *śap* will be barred by *yak*. There in the context of *yak*, after the *dhātus div* and the rest *śap* does not occur, much less *śyan* and the rest. Then should that specific mention of *śap* be made? It should be made. The original word follows on. Where is the original? (In the *sūtra*) *kartari śap 3.1.68*. That is indeed indicated in the first case, but here the purpose is (revealed) by sixth case indication. The fifth case (in the *sūtra*) *divādibhyaḥ śyan 3.1.69* ("After *dhātus div* and the rest *śyan* acts"), he will put in the sixth case, in place of the first case *śap*. Because of (the *sūtra*) *tasmād ityuttarasya 1.1.67* ("After that indicated in the fifth case an operation is for the initial of that which immediately follows"). This is a *pratyaya* rule and in a *pratyaya* rule (other cases) being in place of the fifth case is not applicable. This is not a *pratyaya* rule. The *pratyaya* has been enjoined, the original following on from the previous *sūtra*.

60.1 भावकर्मणोरित्यननुवृत्त्यैव सिद्धे सत्यनुवृत्तिर्यको भावाय।

Vārttika: When (*yak*) is already established in the sense of action/*bhāva* and object/*karman* without *anuvṛtti* in fact (already by *la karmaṇi*) *ca bhāve cākarmakebhyaḥ 3.4.69* the following on is for the sake of the application of *yak* in the sense of *karmakartṛ*.

60.2 इह सार्वधातुके यगित्यन्तरेण् भावकर्मणोरित्यनुवृत्तिं सिद्धम्। सोऽयमेवं सिद्धे सति यद्भावकर्मणोरित्यनुवर्तयति तस्यैतत्प्रयोजनं कर्मकर्तर्यपि यथा स्यात्।।

Bhāṣya: Here (*yak*) is already established by (the *sūtra*) *sārvadhātuka yak* even without the following on of *bhāvakarmaṇoḥ* (in the senses of action and object). When this is thus already established as valid, the fact that he causes *bhāva karmaṇoḥ* to follow on (from *3.1.66)* is meant so that (*yak*) should be applicable in the sense of the reflexive passive/*karmakartṛ* 'object containing agent'.

60.4 कर्तरीति च योगविभागः श्यनः पूर्वविप्रतिषेधावचनाय।।

Vārttika: And (there should be) a separating of the rule (into two parts) as *kartari* (*kartari śap 3.1.68*) (in the sense of agent) so that there is not (required) the expressing of *pūrvavipratiṣedha* (conflict of two rules, the preceding rule superceding the latter, so that *yak* acts in place) of *śyan.*

60.5 कर्तरीति योगविभागः कर्तव्यः श्यनः पर्वूविप्रतिषेधं मा वोचमिति।।
अथवा कर्मवद्भाववचनसामर्थ्याद्यग्भविष्यति। अस्त्यन्यत्कर्म्मवद्भाववचने प्र-
60.7 योजनम्। किम्। आत्मनेपदं यथा स्यात्। वचनादात्मनेपदं भविष्यति।

Bhāṣya: And a separation of the rule (into two parts) should be effected. (First part) *kartari* ("in the sense of agent *yak* acts"), so that I should not have to say, *pūrvavipratiṣedha* (There is a conflict of two rules, where the preceding rule supercedes the latter, so that *yak* comes in place) of *śyan.* Or otherwise through the force of the expression 'being like the *karman/* object' *yak* will be applicable. There is another purpose in the expression of the rule being like the *karman.* What is the purpose ? So that *ātmanepada pratyayas* will be applicable. The *ātmanepada pratyaya* endings will be applicable because of express statement.

60.7 .... चिणतर्हि
यथा स्यात्। चिणपि वचनाद्भविष्यति। चिण्वद्भावस्तर्हि यथा स्यात् नैकं
60.9 प्रयोजनं योगारम्भं प्रयोजयति। तत्र कर्मवद्भाववचनसामर्थ्याद्यग्भविष्यति।।

Then so that *ciṇ* should be applicable. *Ciṇ* will also be applicable from an express statement (in a *sūtra*) as *ciṇ bhāvakarmanoḥ 3.1.66.*

Then so that 'being like *ciṇ*' should be applicable. The undertaking of a rule does not aim at just one purpose. There, because of being like the *karman*/object *yak* will be applicable.

60.10 अथवाचार्यप्रवृत्तिर्ज्ञापयति भवति कर्मकर्तरि यगिति यदयं न दुहस्नुनमां यक्चिणौ (3.1.89) इति यक्चिणोः प्रतिषेधं शास्ति।।

Or else the master's usage makes known '*yak* is applicable in the sense of reflexive passive/object containing agent/*karmakartṛ*. This (is what we infer because) he teaches prohibition of *yak* and *ciṇ* (*3.1.62*) by the *sūtra na duha snunamām yak ciṇau 3.1.89.*

The *pratyayas yak (3.1.67)* and *ciṇ* (*3.1.62*) do not act in the reflexive voice of the *dhātus duḥ* (to milk), *snu* (to fall in drops), and *nam* (to bow).

Pradīpa

Pradīpa: 56.15 इह पश्याम इति

Here we (shall) see (*liṅ* denoting the object, dual and plural are illustrated)."

When the action of *dṛś* (to see) has the meaning of the sentence about to be expressed as its object, as for example 'See, the deer runs', here the nature of *karman*/object (is applicable) for the action of running of the agent, deer.

Pradīpa: 56.17 केनैतदिति।

"(In denoting *karman,* dual and plural; in denoting *bhāva* singular is applicable). By reason of what (is this applicable)?"

Here the verb is declared to be principal. And that verbal activity, because of its nature of being 'something to be accomplished' (denotes) 'action without or divorced from particular differences'.

That was stated (by *Bhartṛhāri*).

विवृत्तभेदा सर्वैव क्रियाऽऽख्यातेऽभिधीयते।
श्रुतेरशक्या भेदानां प्रविभागप्रकल्पना।।

"It is (in general) as divorced from (particular) differences, that all actions are expressed as verbs. From the mere hearing (of the word) it is impossible to distinguish the differences (between actions)."

In that context, just as when the *la* (tense *pratyaya*) is expressing agent and *karman,* because of the difference of means of accomplishing the action, in the dual and plural, so there is the possibility of expressing abstract action. Now one view is, when there is dependence on number (dual and plural), as the means of accomplishing the action to be expressed by one word, then *pākau* (two cooking) *pākaḥ* (three or more cooking) obtain here as the forms. So, because of the means of accomplishing the action not being expressed by *ghañ* (*pāka* = *pac* + *ghañ* - *3.3.10 bhāve*), the question is by reason of what is it applicable?

Pradīpa: 56.17 कर्मानेकमिति।

"The object is more than one . . ."

The substance which is the container of the powers of the object is more than one. The difference between the power and that having the power/powerful, is not conveyed by the word. This also is the case (when it is stated for example) 'The rice is cooked', there is the same case relationship for the word 'rice' expressing the substance having the power, with that declared as expressing the power, (namely the verb).

Pradīpa: 56.18 भाव: पुनरिति।

"But abstract action is (one only) . . ."

"The characteristic of absence of difference, the unity of non-difference, (is the nature) of abstract action/*bhāva.* However, not for the abstract action which is to be expressed by the verb with singularity of number. Due to non-objective/non-substantial nature of that, and because of the abstract action to be expressed by the verb not being a substance.

Pradīpa: 56.19 आश्रयभेदात् इति।

"Due to a difference in resort, i.e. that to which they are annexed."

Due to the diffence of resort (reasons for) *jagari,* sesamum etc., even the one action of cooking resorted to . . . is split (into many). The sense is the nature of substance is designated by *ghañ* etc. so that the difference of number is the resort, and so the nature of the (substance) of things is not impeded.

Pradīpa: 56.20 इहापीति।

"Here too then, just as they perform that action so they all become supports of another . . ."

Due to the difference in resort, even for the abstract action to be expressed by the verb let there also be a difference.

The meaning is, hence there is the possibility (undesired) of a difference in number.

Pradīpa: 57.1 पाकविशेषानिति।

"(If just having observed) different kinds of cooking . . ."

Some explain the word *pāka* as a means of expressing the object. The meaning is, particular kinds of cooking, *jagari* etc. However, this is not proper. Due to the difficulty of obtaining *ghañ* in the sense of *karman/* object when not a technical name (*7.3.19*). Therefore the meaning here is, because of the difference arising from the different types of resort, he says different kinds of cooking. Otherwise, because of the mention of technical name being rejected, even when not a name, in expressing the *karman* (object) *ghañ* is applicable.

Pradīpa: 57.3 उष्ट्रासिका आस्यन्ते इति।

"Those sitting on the camels sit down . . ."

The meaning is here, because of the differences among the resting places for camels, there are many kinds of different seats used, and because of the same case relationship with that, due to the difference in the states to be expressed by the verb, the plural (is employed), *āsyante* 'they are seated'.

And even without the use of the word *iva*/like there is understanding of the word *iva*. This is the meaning of that (sentence) 'of whatever kind the camels are, with the many kinds of seats, such kinds are effected by *Devadatta* and the rest'. 'You are seated'/ *bhavad-bhir āsyate.*

Here, however, because of the absence of cause, from the understanding of a difference of that resorted to, (and) because of a difference in resting place/resort, the difference is not perceived, so singular only is applicable. For example, 'among the *Palāsā* trees the *Tāmra* (copper red) is red-coloured.

And everywhere there is not understanding of a difference in that resorted to, because of a difference in resort, (and) because in examples like 'He cooks the pots' there is in fact an understanding of the difference of cooking.

However, some desire *la* (tense *pratyaya*) in the sense of *karman*/object, as 'Those seated on camel seats are seated', because of the abstract action characterising the sitting of the camels, having the nature of *karman*/object. As for example 'While (milking of cows goes on, the milker sleeps, . . . and) is fallen asleep'. [Thus] however, when there is another intention, it is in fact applicable. Thus the plural is effected by the *Bhāṣyakāra* in the context of ordaining a *la* (tense *pratyaya*) when even the sense of *bhāva*/abstract action is present.

Pradīpa: 57.5 तेऽपि बहव इति।

"Those too will be many (words, and with the same form, so plural and only one remaining is proper)."

The sense is, only because of the nature of the difference in time.

Pradīpa: 57.5 तत्र युक्तमिति।

"There (is same form, so plural and only one meaning is) proper."

The sense is that, when there is 'one remaining' by reason of the science (of grammar) applying its rule, due to the nature of one expressing the meaning of many or (even) without 'one remaining being undertaken', because of the one having the meaning of many, it (naturally in fact) acts in place of the many having the same forms.

Pradīpa: 57.6 तिङभिहित इति।

"(And also) when *tiṅ* is enjoined (then it is in the sense of abstract action)."

The sense is, for one *tiṅ*/verb ending word has no capacity in the elucidation of the states of more than one time, as in fact different words are employed for the elucidation of the different times, places and actions.

Pradīpa: 57.8 द्रव्यवदिति।

"(An action enjoined with a *kṛt pratyaya*) is like a substance/substantive."

What is (meant) by the nature of being a substance is, that which is well known like pot etc.; the condition 'like that' with the supposition of a connection with gender, number and case/*sādhana*. In that context, when there is connection with the characteristics of a substance, there is expectation of accomplishment and lack of accomplishment, and the condition of being the object with which anything is comprehended, the subject of comparison.

Pradīpa: 57.11 क्रिया क्रिययेति।

"A verb does not attain (inseparable concomitance) with a verb."

Surely a verb is in fact connected with a verb with the condition of agent and *karman*/object (in the examples) 'He exists (as) he cooks', 'See the deer runs'.

In that context, the nature of agent and object is not incompatable with the abstract action/*bhāva* to be expressed by the verb. For, as in fact there is (always) expectancy of the verb *bhū* (to be), for it (there is) agency. And meaning (is applicable) with its own form. Thus agency in (becoming)/coming into existence is proper/valid. So, then also, *karman,* because of its nature as the fruit of action, is principal. Thus too, the nature of object/*karman* is also proper for it.

However, *karaṇa*/instrument and the rest without being secondary in connection with the whole self, are not proper. Thus because of 'being principal' being completely incompatable, they are not suitable for it, namely (abstact action).

Well then, it was intended to say (a verb) does not attain concomitance with the form/nature of instrument and the rest (of the *kārakas*). But surely, due to the nature of a verb being something to be accomplished, how can there be the condition of *karman*/object or agent in relation to another verb? Owing to the difference of sphere (of reference) there is no fault, because of the possibility of a connection between the condition of that to be accomplished and the means of accomplishing. That was stated by *Bhartṛhāri*

तत्र यं प्रति साध्यत्वमसिद्धा तं प्रति क्रिया।
सिद्धा तु यस्मिन् साध्यत्वं न तमेव पुनः प्रति।। 3.8.49

"There, (that) in relation to which act something is to be accomplished, in relation to that it is not accomplished. However, that in which something is accomplished, in relation to that in fact it is not to be accomplished again."

मृगो धावति पश्येति साध्यसाधनरूपता।
यथा विषयभेदेन सरणस्योपपद्यते ।। 3.8.51 ।।

"In the sentence 'See, the deer runs', it is quite appropriate there be the nature of that to be accomplished, for the act of running is in accordance with the difference of sphere (of reference)."

Pradīpa: 57.13 कालेति।

"(By an action enjoined by *tiṅ* verbal *pratyayas*), time (person and *pada* are manifested)."

The purpose of that in connection with the word *puruṣa* is so that the inner (self) and the outer world (senses body etc.) be expressed.

'उपग्रहः' Many kinds; having the nature of being for the sake of oneself (*ātmane*), for the sake of others (*parasmaipada*), etc.

Pradīpa: 57.15 कृदभिहित इति

"(The action enjoined by a *tiṅ* is connected with an agent, but that) enjoined by a *kṛt pratyaya* (is not so connected)."

But surely even for an (abstract) action enjoined by a *kṛt pratyaya,* there is connection (applicable) with an agent, as for example 'the manifestation of the *Brāhmaṇas*'. In that context they say 'It is not joined with an agent to be expressed by a single word', as for example *pacati* (He cooks), where the agent is to be expressed (directly by the *tiṅ*). Just so (in the case of *pākaḥ*) 'cooking' (with *kṛt ghañ*), due to the elucidation only of a pure/unqualified abstract action. Otherwise the established form for the abstract action is expressed by *ghañ* etc. Here there is absence of connection with the agent in (that) form. However, with the form of the *dhātu* to be treated, having the nature of (being) to be accomplished, connection with the agent is applicable. Otherwise by implication, (being expressed elliptically), the abstract action is connected with the agent when *kṛt pratyayas* follow, (as in) *pākaḥ*. However, when *tiṅ pratyayas* follow, (as in the example) *pacati,* it is connected with (the agent), with the principal having the nature of being accomplished. In that context, when *kṛt pratyayas* follow the meaning is here, 'there is no connection with the principal agent'.

Pradīpa: 57.18 इदं विचार्यत इति।

"(This) is to be deliberated/considered: (Would *bhāva, karman* and *kartṛ* be meanings of *sārvadhātuka* or *vikaraṇa pratyayas*)?"

The meaning is that matter which goes diversely (in the mind)/*vicarati* is deliberated on (i.e. is considered/moves hither and thither (in the mind)) leads to variety/manifoldness.

Hence the resort to the method of agreement and difference taught in the *śāstra* (science of grammar) etc. is purposeful for raising up or scattering of the parts of words. And those two, the methods of sameness and difference, do not differ respectively even one from the other, due to the understanding of (*luk*) with the agent, even without a *sārvadhātuka pratyaya.* As for example 'Go to the village' (*kartṛ*), 'you sat' (*bhāva*), 'a mat was made' (*karman*) (*akāri*).

As even without *vikaraṇa pratyayas,* there is understanding of agent etc. (e.g.) 'May he cut the field' (*laviṣiṣṭa*). Even when there is absence of both, (*vikaraṇa* and *sārvadhātuka*), it is applicable *ajāgarbhavān* 'You awoke'. However, in some places, in the vicinity of both, there is the understanding of agent etc. (He cooks and it is cooked). In that context, due to the absence of conviction/certainty the deliberation is made. What view is to be resorted to which does not conflict with the *śāstra*/science of grammar?

Pradipa: 57.22 एकद्विबहुषु इति।

"(If *bhāva, karman* and *kartṛ* are the meanings of a *sārvadhātuka pratyaya*, the restriction) in that sense of singular, dual and plural, (becomes inapplicable because of not having that meaning)."

The meaning is, the restriction which (would state) 'the singular is only in the sense of unity and no other meaning', is not proper, because of the agent etc. also having that meaning.

बहुषु बहुवचनम् 1.4.21

"In expressing plurality the plural *vibhakti pratyaya* is employed."

द्वयेकयोर्द्विवचनैकवने 1.4.22

"In expressing duality and unity, the dual and singular *vibhakti pratyayas* are respectively employed."

Pradīpa: 57.25 अतदर्थत्वादिति।

"(Singular etc. inapplicable) . . . because of not having that meaning."

The sense is, due to the force of circumstances the determination/limitation of the sense of the words is resorted to; those do not in fact have the sense of unity etc.

However, the meaning is also, though (meaning) agent etc. . . .

Pradīpa: 57.27 कृताऽभिहित इति

"(If we say they are the meanings of the *vikaraṇas*) when a *kṛt pratyaya* is enjoined (there is absence of *vikaraṇas*)."

In some places in fact, when a *kṛt* follows a *vikaraṇa* is enjoined, not everywhere. Thus only when effected (according to the *sūtra*) 'a *kṛt* acts in the sense of agent' (*3.4.67*) is the meaning of agent indicated, and by reason of that alone, due to the nature of agent having been expressed, a *vikaraṇa* expressing that does not obtain, and hence in the case of *dhārayaḥ* (holding) *3.1.138* etc. when *śap* is not present (but *śa* is) *guṇa* would not be applicable.

Pradīpa: 57.28 धारय पारय इति।

"Holding, ferrying across."

अनुपसर्गाल्लिम्पविन्दधारिपारिवेद्युदेजिचेतिसातिसाहिभ्यश्च 3.1.138 (शः)

"The *pratyaya śa* acts after the following *dhātus* when used without an *upasarga: limp, vind,* and the causatives *dhāri, pāri, udeji, sāti,* and *sāhi.*"

कर्तरि कृत् 3.4.67 "The *pratyayas* called *kṛt* act in the sense of agent."

कर्तरि शप् 3.1.68 "The *pratyaya śap* acts after a *dhātu* when a *sārvadhātuka pratyaya* follows signifying the agent."

सार्वधातुकार्धधातुकयोः 7.3.84 "*Guṇa* acts in place of the *ik* vowel of an *aṅga* in the presence of *sārvadhātuka* and *ārdhadhātuka pratyayas.*"

Pradīpa: 58.1 न लेनापीति।

"(When it is said 'when a *kṛt* is enjoined') is not enjoining applicable with a *la* (tense *pratyaya*)?"

The meaning is that, even though the *sūtra* '*laḥ karmaṇi ca*' (*3.4.69*) (there is designation of agent etc. by the substitutes of *la*), so there too, where a *vikaraṇa* is not obtaining, why is it not undertaken? There it is stated from the *sūtra laḥ karmaṇi* etc. *3.4.69.* It is not in fact possible that the nature of the *vikaraṇa's* meaning will be that of agent etc.

Pradīpa: 58.4 एवं वक्ष्यामीति।

"This I will say (*la pratyaya* acts after one denoting object or agent . . .)."

The meaning is, I will explain . . .

लः कर्मणीति। "*La* (tense *pratyayas*) act in denoting object (and agent after transitive *dhātus,* action and agent after intransitive *dhātus*)."

The meaning is, he will explain (*la* acts) after an existing *vikaraṇa* in the sense of *karman* . . .

In that context the *vikaraṇa* is expressing *karman;* by the word *karman* the '*bhāsya* expressed' (this). But surely how is the latter *la* a cause of *sārvadhātuka pratyaya* thus explained? Well then we say, 'when letter *la* has been effected with reference to a *sārvadhātuka*'. Thus because of resorting to seventh case in the sense of *viṣaya*/in the context, when the *vikaraṇa* has been effected by the *sūtra laḥ karmaṇi ca* etc., because of the *vikaraṇa* expressing *bhāva, karman,* and *kartṛ, la* following is valid, so there is no fault from this explanation.

Pradīpa: 58.7 अत्राप्युक्त।

"Here also (when agentship is expressed *luk* will be applicable)."

The meaning is, it is admitted by means of the elision of the *vikaraṇa;* the base alone is expressing agent etc.

Pradīpa: 58.7 यस्मिंस्तर्हि इति।

"Then when a *la* (is present the *vikaraṇa pratyayas* in fact do not arise. . .)."

The meaning is: and hence because of the non-arising of the *vikaraṇa* there is possibility of non-validity for the *ādeśa*/substitute, or due to the force of the ordaining 'when a *la* is present the *vikaraṇa pratyaya* in fact do not arise'.

Pradīpa: 58.11 इदमस्येति।

"(If) this is (in fact arising) from (its own nature, then it is also founded on express statement)."

This is the meaning, where two words are to be expressed, the agent and the object are means of accomplishing the action, there due to the absence of contradiction, a difference of operation/effect connected with that is proper.

However, in one word, when teaching a distinct meaning for the *vikaraṇa* and the *sārvadhātuka pratyayas* having opposed meanings, due to the absence of assistance, and not being able to help each other, there would not in fact be use (for them). For so the agent is expressed as distinguished by the verb, as *pacati* he cooks'.

The *karman* distinguished by the verb is 'It is cooked'. However, it is not possible by one (verb) to teach two means of action as distinguished by that verb.

Pradīpa: 58.13 एकपक्षी भूतमिति।

"(And thus having made the statement), this which has become the single view, is applicable . . ."

The meaning is there is only one view, namely, the *sārvadhātuka pratyayas* have the meaning *karman* etc. and with regard to the (prior previous) division, there is indication of the *pratyaya cvi.*

Pradīpa: 58.18 प्रसिंद्धौ नियम इति।

"The restriction is well established (there)."

The meaning is a restriction on meaning. Due to the indication of a different meaning for *karman* etc. this is not a restriction on the *pratyaya* established by authority. In that context singular is in the sense of unity only; thus the meaning of unity etc. is restricted. However, the *pratyaya* is not, because if there is another meaning for it, it is not opposed to *karman* etc.

Pradīpa: 58.21 अथवेति।

"Otherwise (the restriction is with regard to meanings of the original bases)."

The meaning is, because of the force of ordaining *karman* etc. the restriction is only with regard to numerals of the same kind.

Pradīpa: 58.24 कर्मकर्तरीति।

"(Additional enumeration of *yak*) in the sense of reflexive passive."

Due to the non-barring of the operation for its own resort, by the extended application 'being like the *karman* (of reflexive passive)' when there is obtainment of the *vikaraṇa* as resort of agent, this *vārttika* is stated.

Pradīpa: 59.1 विप्रतिषेधाद्धि।

"Because of conflict (of rules of equal force, *śap* being stronger, obtains . . .)."

When the view of the extended application, i.e. supposition of original in place of substitute for the sake of a rule of the grammatical *śāstra,* when *śap* has greater strength.

However, when looking upon the *ādeśa* as original for the sake of the operations caused by the original, *yak* alone in fact has greater strength.

कर्तरि शप् 3.1.66 "*Śap* acts when a *sārvadhātuka* in sense of agent follows."

59.9 आनन्द भावे 3.3.18 "*Pratyaya ghañ* acts after a *dhātu* in the sense of abstract action."

रोग इति

। रूजार्थानां भाववचनानामज्वरे 2.3.54 "The object of *dhātus* having the sense of *ruj* (to afflict) with the exception of the causative *jvaraya* (to be feverish), take sixth case when the *dhātu* expesses a condition (i.e. when the subject is an abstract noun)."

Pradīpa: 59.6 करिष्यते चिण्भावकर्मणोः 3.1.66

"*Ciṇ* is *ādeśa* of *cli* when *ta* of third person singular *ātmanepada* follows denoting abstract action or object."

The meaning is, when there is mention of *ciṇ* by *anuvṛtti* the repeated mention of *ciṇ* is for the purpose of additional ordaining of a rule, so that *ciṇ* will be applicable in the sense of the reflexive passive.

Due to greater strength of *śyan* it obtains by दिवादिभ्यः श्यन् (3.1.69) '*pratyaya śyan* acts after *dhātus div* etc. when a (*sārvadhātuka pratyaya*) follows denoting the agent."

Pradīpa: 59.16 ननु चेति।

"But surely (this is also established by separating the rule into two) ?"

The sense is that all that is obtaining will be barred by dividing the rule in two.

Pradīpa: 59.18 परा प्राप्तिरिति।

"A following (rule) obtaining (obtains as not prohibited by that)."

The meaning is, because of being more powerful, due to being a subsequent rule/*paratva.*

Pradīpa: 59.18 ननु चेयमिति।

"And surely this (obtaining would bar the following rule obtaining)."

The meaning is, a division of the *sūtra* into two obtaining, there will (in fact) be barring by reason of a conflict of rules (of equal force on occasions requiring) the prior (rule to prevail).

Pradīpa: 59.19 नोत्सहत इति।

"It is not possible to (bar a prohibition, already existing)."

The meaning is, owing to appropriateness of resorting to the conflict of rules principle, the obtainment of a separation of the *sūtra* into two is lacking in strength/has no force.

Pradīpa: 60.2 इहेति

"Here (with regard to the *sūtra sārvadhātuka yak*, the following on of *bhāva* and *karman* is established)."

The meaning is even though there is the sense of agent stated in the general statement, 'when a *sārvadhātuka pratyaya* follows/(signifying the agent) *yak* acts/is applicable', due to enjoining an exception/ *apavāda* to *śap* and the rest, *yak* will be applicable in the sense of *bhāva* (action) and *karman* (object) and because of greater effort, *bhāva* and *karman* follow on (from the previous *sūtra 3.1.66*).

So *yak* will also be applicable in the sense of reflexive passive.

Pradīpa: 60.4 कर्तरीति चेति।

"(And there should be a separating of the rule into two (at first) (in the sense of agent) (so that there is not expressing of prohibition of the prior *śyan*)."

Here too, in the explanation he says a separation is to be made (into two *sūtras* . . . as first in the sense of agent . . .

Otherwise due to the effort to obtain *bhāva* and *karman* as following on by *anuvṛtti* there would be a barring of *śap* as immediately contiguous but not of *śyan* and the rest. However, by the separating of the rule (into two), they too are barred.

Pradīpa: 60.6 यग्भविष्यति

Yak will be applicable by. . .

कर्मवत्कर्मणा तुल्यक्रियः 3.1.87 "The *la* (tense *pratyaya*) signifying the agent, when the action affecting the agent is like the action which affects the *karman*/object, (i.e. reflexive) is treated as if it were a *la* signifying the *karman*/object. . . "

Pradīpa: 60.7 वचनादात्मनेपदं भविष्यति

"Due to statement (in a *vārttika*), *ātmanepada* will be applicable"

आत्मनेपदवचनं नियमार्थम् 1.3.12 वा॰ 1

"The expressing of *ātmanepada* is for the purpose of a restriction."

कर्तरि कर्मव्यतिहारे 1.3.14 (आत्मनेपदम्)

"In denoting the agent, when reciprocity of action is to be expressed, the *ātmanepada pratyayas* are employed (i.e. in the reflexive passive)."

Ātmanepada follows on by *anuvṛtti* (so) here *kartari* (will follow on) due to the separation of the *sūtra* into two.

And in that context because of the mention of *karman* follows on (from *3.1.66*), even without exended application, *ātmanepada* will be applicable.

Pradīpa: 60.8 चिणपीति।

"*Ciṇ* will also be applicable because of express statement."

चिण्भावकर्मणोः 3.1.66

Pradīpa: 60.8 नैकमिति।

"Not just one (purpose does the undertaking of the rule aim at)."

The meaning is that otherwise it would have to be stated in the *sūtra* that . . . *sya sic sīyuṭ* etc. *6.4.62.* 'When the agent has action similar to one object, the *dhātus* are treated optionally in the same way as in the third person of the passive aorist in *ciṇ* and when so treated have the *āgama iṭ*).

यसोऽनुपसर्गात् ॥ 3 । 1 । 71 ॥

Pāṇini 3.1.71: The *Pratyaya śyan* optionally acts after the *dhātu yas* (to strive) when it is without an *upasarga* and when a *sārvadhātuka pratyaya* denoting the agent follows.

60.13 अनुपसर्गादिति किमर्थम्। आयस्यति प्रयस्यति।। अनुपसर्गदिति शक्यमक-
र्तुम्। कथमायस्यति प्रयस्यति। संयसश्च (3.1.72) इत्येतन्नियमार्थं भविष्यति।
60.15 संपूर्वादेव यसो नान्यपूर्वादिति।।

Bhāṣya: What is the purpose of saying "not after an *upasarga*"? (Here there is no option), *āyasyati* "He works hard or exerts himself", *prayasyati* "He endeavours or strives after". It is possible not to (have) to make the statement "not after an *upasarga*". How (then can we obtain the forms) *āyasyati* and *prayasyati* (with no option)? Because of the *sūtra samyasaśca 3.1.72.* "*śyan pratyaya* acts optionally after the *dhātu yas* (to strive) when preceded by the *upasarga sam* and when a *sārvadhātuka pratyaya* denoting an agent follows". This will be for the purpose of restriction (of the option to the *upasarga sam* before *yas*). After *yas* preceded by *sam* only, not preceded by any other (*upasarga*) (there will be this option).

Pradīpa

Pradīpa: 60.12 यमोऽनु।

The sense in this is a restriction with its sphere (*dhātu yas* together with an *upasarga* is equivalent to *yas* receives *śyan*) only preceded by *upasarga sam*.

Thus by reason of this *śyan*, it would not be applicable after *yas* alone (without any *upasarga*). This is set aside (by the *sūtra*).

So he says, 'not preceded by any other (*upasarga*)'.

रुधादिभ्यः श्नम् ॥ 3 । 1 । 78 ॥

Pāṇini 3.1.78: The *pratyaya śnam* acts after the *dhātus* of the class beginning with *rudh* (to obstruct) when a *sārvadhātuka pratyaya* follows in the sense of agent.

60.17 किमर्थः शकरः। सार्वधातुकार्थः शित्सार्वधातुकमिति सार्वधातुकसंज्ञा सार्व-
धातुकमपिदिति ङित्वं ङितीति गुणप्रतिषेधो यथा स्यात्[1]। भिनत्ति छिनत्तीति।
नैतदस्ति प्रयोजनम्। सार्वधातुकार्धधातुकयोरङ्गस्य गुण उच्यते यस्माच्च प्रत्यय-विधि
स्तदादि प्रत्ययेऽङ्गसंज्ञ[2] भवति यस्माच्चात्र प्रत्ययविधिर्न तत्प्रत्यये परतो
60.21 यच्च प्रत्यये परतो न तस्मात्प्रत्ययविधिंः॥

Bhāṣya: What is the purpose of the letter *ś*? For the sake of obtaining the technical name *sārvadhātuka* (for the *sūtras*) *tiṅ śit sārvadhātukam 3.4.113* ("The verbal endings/ *tiṅ* and those *pratyayas* having an indicatory *ś* have the name *sārvadhātuka*"). *sārvadhātukam apit 1.2.4* ("A *sārvadhātuka pratyaya* not having an indicatory *p* is like *ṅit* (having an indicatory *ṅ*)"). Because of having an indicatory *ṅ* (there applies the *sūtra*) *kṅiti ca 1.1.5* ("And that which otherwise would have caused *guṇa* or *vṛddhi*, does not do so, when it has an indicatory *k, g,* or *ṅ*"), so that prohibition of *guṇa* should be applicable, e.g. in the forms *bhinatti* "He splits", *chinatti* "He cuts".

This is not the purpose. It is stated *sārvadhātukārdhadhātukayoḥ 7.3.84* (*aṅgasya, guṇaḥ*) "There is *guṇa* of an *ik* vowel of an *aṅga* when a *sārvadhātuka* or an *ārdhadhātuka pratyaya* follows". And *yasmāt pratyayavidhis tadādi pratyaye'ṅgam 1.4.13* "That word form after whatsoever a *pratyaya* is enjoined (be it *dhātu* or *prātipadika*) having that as its beginning is called *aṅga* in relation to the *pratyaya* which follows".

Here, that after which a *pratyaya* is enjoined is not followed by a *pratyaya* and for that which is followed by a *pratyaya*, a *pratyaya* is not enjoined.

60.21 .... इदं तर्हि प्रयोजनमार्धधातुकसंज्ञा मा
भूदिति। किं च स्यात्। वलादिलक्षण इट् प्रसज्येत[3]॥ एतदपि नास्ति प्रयोजनम्।
वलादिरार्धधातुकस्याङ्गस्येडुच्यते। यस्माच्च प्रत्ययविधिस्तदादि प्रत्ययेऽङ्गसंज्ञं
भवति यस्माश्चात्र प्रतययविधिर्न तत्प्रत्यये परतो यच्च प्रत्यये परतो न तस्मात्प्रत्य-
यविधिः॥

61.2 अत उत्तरं पठति।

Then this is the purpose so that "the technical name *ārdhadhātuka* should not be applicable", and what would be (wrong)? For that characterised by an initial *val* (consonant) *iṭ āgama* would be applicable.

This also is not the purpose. It is stated that *iṭ āgama* is enjoined for an *ārdhadhātuka pratyaya* beginning with a *val*(consonant) which is added to an *aṅga* by *ārdhadhātukasyeḍvalādeḥ 7.2.35* and (by the *sūtra yasmāt pratyayavidhis tadādi pratyaye'ṅgam 1.4.13*) "that after whatsoever a *pratyaya* is ordained (be it *dhātu* or *prātipadika*) having that as its beginning has the technical name *aṅga*"; and here that after which a *pratyaya* is enjoined is not followed by a *pratyaya* and after that which is followed by a *pratyaya* no *pratyaya* is enjoined. Then he goes on to say . . .

61.3 श्नमिशित्करणं प्वादिह्रस्वार्थम् ॥ 1 ॥

Vārttika 1: In *śnam* the producing of *ś* is for the purpose of a shortening of *pū* (to purify) and the rest.

61.4 श्नमि शित्करणं क्रियते प्वादीनां शिति ह्रस्वत्वं यथा स्यात्[1]। पृणति मृणतीति॥

Bhāṣya: The producing of indicatory *ś* in *śnam* is done so that there should be a shortening of the vowel of *pū* and the rest (by the *sūtra*) *pvādīnām hrasvaḥ 7.3.80*. "A shortening is *ādeśa* in place of the vowel of *pū* and the rest when a *pratyaya* having an indicatory *ś* follows", e.g. *pṛṇati* 'He protects of fills'; *mṛṇati* 'He crushes'.

61.5 न वा धात्वन्यत्वात् ॥ 2 ॥

Vārttika 2: Or else not, because of being different *dhātus*.

61.6 न वा कर्तव्यम्। किं कारणम्। धात्वन्यत्वात्। धात्वन्तरं पृणिमृणी॥
यत्तर्हि न धात्वन्तरम्। यत्र भूम्यां वृणसे। नैष श्नम्। श्न एद्ध्रस्वत्वम्॥

Bhāṣya: Or else it should not be done. What is the reason? Because of being different *dhātus*. *pṛṇi* and *mṛṇi* are different *dhātus*. What about those that are not different *dhātus* e.g. *yatra bhūmyām uṛṇase* "On what ground thou choosest". This is not *śnam*. For *śna* there is shortening of the *pratyaya* vowel (i.e. *kriyādi gaṇa* Class 9).

61.7 ....यदि श्नो
ह्रस्वत्वं स्वरो न सिध्यति। वृणसे। अदुपदेशाल्लसार्वधातुकमनुदात्तं भवतीत्येष
स्वरो न प्राप्नोति। तस्माच्श्नमेषः। यदि श्नम् श्नसोरल्लोप (6.4.111) इति लोपः
61.10 प्राप्नोति। उपधाया इति वर्ततेऽनुपधात्वान्न भविष्यति। न स शक्य उपधाया
इति विज्ञातुम्। इह हि दोषः स्यात्। अङ्क्तः अञ्जन्ति। तस्माच्श्न एव ह्रस्वत्वम्।

61.12 स्वरः कथम्।

If the shortening is of *śna* the accent is not established as valid. *vṛṇase* "thou choosest". (Here) the *anudātta* accent does not obtain.

Therefore this *śnam.* If it is *śnam* then *lopa* elision obtains (by the *sūtra*) *śnasoral lopaḥ 6.4.111* "In the presence of a *sārvadhātuka pratyaya* with an indicatory *k* or *ṅ* the *a* of *śnam* and *as* (to be) is *lopa* elided". "In place of the penultimate" follows on from the *sūtra ūd upadhāyā gohaḥ 6.4.89.* Because of (the *a* of *śnam*) not being penultimate, *lopa* will not be applicable. That *lopa* cannot be understood as that *upadhāyāḥ* (of a penultimate). For here there would be a fault *aṅktaḥ* "The two apply ointment"; *añjanti* "They apply ointment". Therefore *vṛṇase* can be derived by shortening for *śna* alone. How is the (correct) accent (obtained)?

61.13 बहुलं पित्सार्वधातुकं छन्दसि ।। 3 ।।

61.14 सार्वधातुकस्य बहुलं छन्दसि पित्वं वक्तव्यम्[5]। पितश्चापित्वं दृश्यतेऽपित्तश्च
पित्त्वम्। पितस्तावदपित्वम्। मातरं प्रमिणीमि जनित्रीम्। अपितः पित्वम्। शृणोत
ग्रावाणः।। तत्तर्हि ह्रस्वत्वं वक्तव्यम्। अवश्यं छन्दसि ह्रस्वत्वं वक्तव्यम्।
61.17 उपगायन्तु मां पत्नयो गर्भिणयो युवतय इत्येवमर्थम्।।

Vārttika 3: Diversely a *sārvadhātuka pratyaya* has an indicatory *p* in the *chandas.*

Bhāṣya: It should be stated that a *sārvadhātuka pratyaya* diversely has an indicatory *p* in the *chandas/Veda.* And so, not having an indicatory *p* is seen (in the case) of that enjoined with an indicatory *p* and having an indicatory *p* (in the case) of that enjoined without an indicatory *p.* (First) then, (an example of) absence of *it p* for that enjoined with *it p.*

mātaram pramiṇīmi janitrīm "destroy the mother (who is) a real mother". (c.f. *A.V. 6.110.3)*

An example if *it p* for that enjoined without an *it p śṛṇota grāvāṇaḥ* "Hear O *ye soma* pressing stones!" (c.f. *T.S.I.3.13.1, M.S.I.3.1, Kāṭhaka S.3.9)*

Then that shortening (of *śnā*) should be stated? It is essential that it should be stated. There is shortening in the *Chandas* for the sake of examples such as *upagāyantu mām patnayo garbhiṇayo yuvatayaḥ* "Let wives, pregnant women and young women sing to me".

61.18 विशेषणार्थस्तर्हि। क्व विशेषणार्थेनार्थः। श्नान्नलोपः (6.4.23) इति। नान्नलोप
इत्युच्यमाने यज्ञानाम् यत्नानामित्यत्रापि प्रसज्येत। दीर्घत्वे[6] वृत्ते न भविष्यति।
61.20 इदमिह संप्रधार्यम्। दीर्घत्वं क्रियतां नलोप इति किमत्र कर्तव्यम्। परत्वान्नलोपः
स्यात्। तस्माच्छकारः कर्तव्यः।। अथ क्रियमाणे शकार इह कस्मान्न भवति।

61.22 विश्नानाम् प्रश्नानामिति। लक्षणप्रतिपदोक्तयोः प्रतिपदोक्तस्यैवेति।।

Then (*ś*) is for the purpose of distinguishing (from other *pratyayas*). Where is the purpose of distinguishing served? (In the *sūtra śnān nalopaḥ 6.4.23*). (If it were) being stated "after that ending in *na*" (*lopa* of the *n*) of the (sixth case plural of) *yajñānām* (of sacrifices) and *yatnānām* (of efforts) would be applicable. When lengthening has been effected this (*lopa* rule) will not be applicable (anyway); the final of the *anga* before the sixth case plural *nām* (having the *āgama n-uṭ*). Here this should be considered whether lengthening should be effected (or) *lopa* of *na*. If this is the case then what is to be done? Because of being the subsequent *sūtra, lopa* of *na* should be applicable. Therefore the letter *ś* should be produced (to prevent that).

Now then when *ś* is being produced how is it not applicable here? *viśnānām* (of lusters), *praśnānām* (of questions). (*Paribhāṣā 105*)

lakṣaṇa pratipadoktayoḥ pratipadoktasyaiva grahaṇam "When a question arises as to which of two words be accepted, that arrived at by certain modifications/*lakṣàṇokta* or that directly expressed/*pratipadokta,* the latter should be preferred.

Pradīpa

Pradīpa: 60.18 भिन्नतीति।

(He splits).

The meaning is that indicatory *ś* is effected so that there should not be *guṇa* connected with the technical name *aṅga* for the word *'bhi'*.

Pradīpa: 60.19 यस्माच्चेति।

"And (that word form) after which a *pratyaya* is enjoined (be it a *dhātu* or *prātipadika*) having that as its beginning, is called *aṅga* in relation to the *pratyaya* that follows."

The meaning is 'after the word *bhid'*. For only after what has the nature of *rudh* and the rest, not however, after the word *bhi* which is only a part, there is ordaining of the *pratyaya* (*śnam*).

Pradīpa: 61.4 पृणतीति।

"He protects or fills."

The *dhātus pṛ* and *mṛ* are recited in the *Kryādi Gaṇa*(9th Class). After them by transposition (of *vikaraṇa*), *śnam pratyaya* acts.

Pradīpa: 61.6 धात्वन्तरमिति।

"*(pṛṇi* and *mṛṇi) are different dhātus."*

The meaning is that they are in the *tudādi* (sixth class).

Pradīpa: 61.7 वृणस इति।

"Thou choosest."

After the *kryādi gaṇa* (class 9) *dhātu vṛ* (in the sense of choose) with transposition of *vikaraṇa, are śnam* and *thās* (*madhyama puruṣa ekavacana*).

Pradīpa: 61.8 श्न इति।

"(This shortening is) of *śnā*."

The sense is this is peculiar to the *Chandas/Veda.*

Pradīpa: 61.9 स्वरो

"(*Anudātta*) accent (does not obtain), by

तास्यनुदात्तेन्ङिददुपदेशाल्लसार्वधाकमनुदात्तमह्निवङोः (६।१।१८६)

"The *la* (tense *pratyaya*), personal endings and their *ādeśas* (*3.2.124-126*) are, when they are *sārvadhātuka* (*3.4.113* etc.) *anudātta* after the characteristic of the periphrastic future/*tāsi*, after a *dhātu* which in the *Dhātu Pāṭha* has an *anudātta* vowel or an *iṭ ṅ* (with the exception of the *dhātus hnu* and *iṅ*) as well as after what has a final a in the *Dhātu Pāṭha*."

Pradīpa: 61.10 उपधाया 3

"In place of the penultimate" (follows on from the Sutra ऊदुपधाया गोहः 6.4.89)

"For the penultimate *'o'* of the *guṇated aṅga goḥ* (from *guḥ*) there is substituted *ū* before a *pratyaya* beginning with a vowel." e.g. निगूहति.

Pradīpa: 61.11 अङ्क इति।

(The two apply ointment)

श्नान्नलोपः (6.4.23)

"After the *na* of *śnam* there is *lopa*-elision of the following *n* of a *dhātu*."

असिद्धवदत्राभात् (6.4.22)

"The change an *aṅga* will undergo by application of any of the rules from this *sūtra* up to *6-4-129* (*bhāṣya*) is to be considered as of none effect/unknown to any other rule in this section."

Due to the *lopa* of *ñ* of *añj* etc. by *6.4.23* being *asiddha* by *6.4.22*, there is absence of penultimate (vowel to be lengthened).

Pradīpa: 61.15 प्रमिणीमीति।

"I destroy (the mother. . .)."

मीनातेर्निगमे (7.3.81) "There is shortening for the *dhātu min* in the *Veda/ nigma* before a *pratyaya* with an indicatory *ś*."

Due to *mip* (*uttama puruṣa eka parasmai*) being (considered as without *it p*) (व्यत्ययो बहुलम् 3.1.85) when *it ṅ* then follows by सार्वधातुकमपित् (1.2.4) there is *ī* (by ई हल्यघोः (6.4.113))

Pradīpa: 61.20 परत्वादिति।

"Due to being the subsequent (*sūtra, lopa* of *na* should be applicable)."

That lengthening which (would be applicable by) *supi ca* (*6.3.102* 'Before a *sup*/case ending beginning with a *yañ pratyaya* the final *a* of a nominal stem is lengthened'), does not take place because of the force of the *Paribhāṣā*

संनिपातलक्षणो विधिरनिमित्तं तदविघातस्य 85

"That taught in a rule occasioned by the combination of two things does not become the cause of the destruction of that combination."

Pradīpa: 61.20 परत्वादिति।

"However that which was stated elsewhere ('Due to the lengthening caused by *nāmi 6.4.3* being subsequent *supi ca* should be applicable' is not in conflict with the *sannipāta, paribhāṣā*" by reason of the resort (for the operations) not being invariable')."

Pradīpa: 61.22 लक्षणेति।

"That arrived at by certain modifications of rules... or directly expressed."

When a question arises as to which of two words, that arrived at by certain modifications of rules or that directly expressed (*prātipadokta*) the later should be preferred.

The sense of *lakṣanokta* is so called because of its nature as interpreter of signs of inferring or expressing indirectly, but *prātipadokta* is so called because of its explicitness of being evidence of immediate perception.

Notes

[1] गुणप्रतिषेधो यथा स्यात्
"So that there would be prohibition of *guṇa*."
क्ङिति च (1.1.5)
सार्वधातुकमपित् (1.2.4)
तिङ्शितार्धधातुकम् (3.4.113)
[2] अङ्गसंज्ञं भवति। "The technical name *aṅga* will be applicable."
सार्वधातुकार्धधातुकयोः (7.3.84)
पुगन्तलघूपधस्य च (7.3.86)
यास्मात्प्रत्ययविधिस्तदादि प्रत्ययेऽङ्गम् (1.4.13)
See text.
[3] इट् प्रसज्येत। "*Iṭ* augment would be applicable." by
आर्धधातुकस्येड्वलादेः "*Iṭ* is the augment of an *ārdhadhātuka pratyaya* beginning with *val* (any consonant except *y*)."

[4] प्वादीनां शिति ह्रस्वत्वं यथा स्यात्

So that there should be a short vowel for *pū* etc. when that with an *it ś* follows by प्वादीनां ह्रस्वः (7.3.80)

[5] पित्त्वं वक्तव्यम्।

" '*p*' is to be stated (therefore *anudātta*) ", by अनुदात्तौ सुप्पितौ (3.1.4)

[6] दीर्घत्वे

"When lengthening (is effected)". by नामि (6.4.3)

"The long vowel acts in place of the final of *aṅga* before the sixth case plural *nām* (with *āgama nuṭ* by ह्रस्वनद्यापो नुट् 7.1.54)."

तनादिकृञ्भ्यः उः ॥ 3 । 1 । 79 ॥

Pāṇini 3.1.79: The *pratyaya u* acts after the *dhātus* of the *gaṇa* beginning with *tan* and after the *dhātu kṛ* (to make) when a *sārvadhātuka pratyaya* follows signifying the agent.

61.24 अथ किमर्थं करोतेः पृथग्ग्रहणं क्रियते न तनादिभ्य इत्येवोच्येत। अन्यानि तनोत्यादिकार्याणि मा भूवन्निति। कानि। अनुनासिकलोपादीनि[1]। दैवरक्ताः किंशुकाः।
62.1 अनुनासिकाभावादेवानुनासिकलोपो न भविष्यति॥

Bhāṣya: Now why is a separate mention of *kṛ/karoti* made, and (why is it) not stated just "after the *dhātus tan* and the rest, the *pratyaya u* acts? So that the other operations of grammar (linked with) *tan* and the rest should not be applicable (to *kṛ*). Which? *Lopa* elision of the nasal and the rest.

daivaraktāḥ kiṅśukāḥ "divine red coloured (Butera Frondosa) blossoms".

Due to the absence of a nasal, the *lopa* of a nasal will not be applicable in fact.

62.1 .... इदं तर्हि तनादिकार्यं मा भूत् तनादिभ्यस्तथासोः (2.4.79) इति। ननु च भवत्येवात्र ह्रस्वादङ्गात् (8.2.27) इति। तनैव यथा स्यादनेन मा भूदिति। कश्चात्र विशेषस्तेन वा सत्यनेन वा।
62.4 तेन सति सिज्लोपस्यासिद्धत्वाच्चिण्वद्भावः[2] सिद्धो भवति।

This is the reason, so the grammatical operations for *tan* and the rest then should not be applicable (for *kṛ*) (namely) *tanādibhyastathāsoḥ 2.4.79* "After the *dhātus tan* and the rest there acts optionally *luk* elision of *sic* when the *ātmanepada pratyayas ta* and *thas* of the third i.e. *prathama* and the second i.e. *madhyama* persons follows". Now surely in fact here elision is applicable (by) *hrasvād aṅgāt 8.2.27.*

("The *s* of the aorist *sic* is *lopa* elided before a *pratyaya* beginning with *jhal* consonant when it is preceded by an *aṅga* ending in a short vowel".) *Kṛ* is separately mentioned by reason of that alone so that elision may not be applicable, (and) by this it should not be applicable. What is the distinction here: by reason of that (rule) or by reason of this (rule)? If (elision) takes place by reason of that, the elision of *sic* being non-effective/*asiddha*, the state of being like *ciṇ* becomes effective.

62.4 ....अनेन पुनः सति चिण्वद्भावो न स्यात्। अनेनापि सति चिण्वद्भावः सिद्धः। कथम्। विभाषा लुक्।

62.6 यदा न लुक्तदा तेन लोपः। तत्र सिज्लोपस्यासिद्धत्वाच्चिण्वद्भावः सिद्धो भवति।।

If however (elision) takes place there would not be the state of being like *ciṇ* (*6.4.62*). The state of being like *ciṇ* is established as valid even when (elision) takes place by reason of this. How? Optionally there is *luk* elision. When there is no *luk*, then by that (rule) there is *lopa* elision there; because of the *sic lopa* elision being non-effective, the state of being 'like *ciṇ*' becomes of effect (as a rule).

62.7 तनादित्वात्कृञः सिद्धं सिज्लोपे च न दुष्यति।
चिण्वद्भावेऽत्र दोषः स्यात्सोऽपि प्रोक्ता विभाषया।।

Śloka Vārttika: Due to having the nature of (being part of) *tan* and the rest (the *pratyaya u*) is established as valid for *kṛñ* (*dhātu*) and when there is *lopa* elision of *sic* this is not a fault. Here, when there is the state of 'being like *ciṇ*', there would be a fault but that is also stated optionally.

Pradīpa

Pradīpa: 62.5 विभाषा लुक्।

"Optionally there is *luk* elision."

But surely that (rule) of 'non-obtainment', *hrasvād aṅgāt 8.2.27* is that by which *luk lopa* is barred. Then how could *lopa* be applicable (at all) in the 'absence of *luk* view'? This is no fault where on one view *luk* takes place, there is barring of *lopa.* But it is not taking place!

Notes

[1] 'The operations like elision of the nasal etc.' by

अनुदात्तोपदेशवनतितनोत्यादीनामनुनासिकलोपो झलि क्ङिति (6.4.37)

"The final nasal of those *dhātus* which in the *Dhātu Pāṭha/ upadeśa* have an *anudātta dhātu* vowel, as well as of *van* and the rest and *tan* and the rest is *lopa*-elided in the presence of a *pratyaya* beginning with a *jhal* (any consonant except semivowels and nasals) when this has an indicatory *k* or *ṅ.*"

[2] 62.4 चिण्वद्भावः। "The state of being like *ciṇ* (becomes effective)."

स्यसिच्सीयुट्तासिषु भावकर्मणोरुपेदेशेऽज्झनग्रगदृशां वा चिण्वदिट्च (6.4.62)

"In the presence of the *pratyaya sya* (second future and conditiona) *sic* (s. aorist) *sīyuṭ* (benedictive) and *tāsi* (periphrastic future), when they are employed in the impersonal (*bhāva*) and passive (*karman*) voices, *dhātus* ending in a vowel in the *upadeśa* (*Dhātu Pāṭha*), as well as the *dhātu han, grah,* and *dṛś* are treated optionally in the same way as the *prathama*/third person singular of passive aorist in *ciṇ* and receive the *āgama iṭ*"

धिन्विकृण्व्योर च ॥ 3 । 1 । 80 ॥

Pāṇini 3.1.80: The *pratyaya u* acts after the *dhātus dhinv-i* (to please) *kṛnv-i* to hurt) when a *sārvadhātuka pratyaya* follows signifying the Agent; and in these *dhātus a* is the *ādeśa* of the final *i*.

62.10 क्वायमकारः श्रूयते। न क्वचिच्छ्रूयते लोपोऽस्य भवत्यतो लोप आर्धधातुक
इति। यदि न क्वचिच्छ्रूयते किमर्थमत्वमुच्यते नलोप एवोच्येत। नैवं शक्यम्।
लोपे हि सति गुणः प्रसज्येत। अत्वे पुनः सत्यकारलोपस्य स्थानिवद्भावाद्गुणो न
62.13 भवति[1]।।

Bhāṣya: Where is the letter *a* heard? It is not heard anywhere. *Lopa* elision of it is applicable in the presence of an *ārdhadhātuka pratyaya* (by the *sūtra*) *ato lopah 6.4.48* ("*Lopa* acts in place of the final short *a* of an *aṅga* in the presence of an *ārdhadhātuka pratyaya*") If it is nowhere heard what is the purpose of starting short *a* 1.8 "*Guṇa* (and why not just) *lopa* elision of *n* stated? It is not thus possible. For when *lopa* elision takes place then *guṇa* would be applicable (by the *sūtra pugantalaghūpadhasya ca 7.3.86*). "*Guṇa* is the *ādeśa* in place of the *ik* (*i u ṛ ḷ*) vowels of the causative stems which take *p* (*7.3.36*) and for the short penultimate vowel of a *dhātu* ending in a single consonant". But when short *a* is effected because of *lopa* elision of *a* being like the original/*sthānivad bhāva, guṇa* is not applicable (because *a* is already *guṇa*).

62.13 .... ननु च लोपेऽपि सति न धातुलोप आर्धधातुके (1.1.4) इति
प्रतिषेधो भविष्यति। आर्धधातुकनिमित्ते लोपे स प्रतिषेधो न चैष
आर्धधातुकनिमित्तो लोपः। अपि च प्रत्याख्यायते स योगः।
तस्मिन्प्रत्याख्याते गुणः स्यादेव
62.16 तस्मादत्वं वक्तव्यम्।।

But surely even when *lopa* elision takes place prohibition will be applicable (by the *sūtra*) *na dhātulopa ārdhadhātuke 1.1.4* "The *guṇa* and *vṛddhi ādeśas* (which otherwise would have presented themselves) do not take place when such an *ārdhadhātuka* (*3.4.114*) *pratyaya* follows, which causes *lopa* elision of a portion of the *dhātu*". That prohibition (is applicable) when the *lopa* elision is caused by an *ārdhadhātuka pratyaya* and this *lopa* is not caused by an *ārdhadhātuka pratyaya*. And also that rule is being rejected. When that is rejected *guṇa* would in fact be applicable. Therefore a short *a* should be stated.

62.17 अथ किमर्थं[2] नुमनुषक्तयोर्ग्रहणं क्रियते न धिविकृव्योरित्येवोच्यते। धिवि-
कृव्योरित्युच्यमानेऽत्वे कृतेऽनिष्टे देशे नुम्प्रसज्येत। इदमिह संप्रधार्यम्। अत्वं
क्रियतां नुमिति किमत्र कर्तव्यम्। परत्वान्नुमागमः। अन्तरङ्गमत्वम्। कान्तरङ्ग-
62.20 ता।

Now what is the reason that specific mention is made of (the two *dhātus*) having the *āgama n-um* closely attached? (Why) is it not (simply) stated "in the case of *dhātus dhiv-i* and *kṛv-i* (*7.1.58*)"?

(If) it were being stated (that *u* acts) for *dhiv-i* and *kṛv-i* when the nature of short *a* is present the *num* (*āgama*) would be applicable in an undesired place. Here this is to be considered (carefully) whether a short *a* be effected (or) *num āgama*. What is to be done here? Because of being the later rule *num* augment applies first. (But) the application of short *a* is *antaraṅga* (inward). What is the nature of this *antaraṅga*?

62.20 .... प्रत्ययोत्पत्तिसंनियोगेनात्वमुच्यत उत्पन्ने प्रत्यये प्रकृतिप्रत्य-
यावाश्रित्याङ्गस्य नुमागमः। नुमप्यन्तरङ्गः। कथम्। वक्ष्यत्येतन्नुम्विधावु- पदेशिवद्वचनं
प्रत्ययविध्यर्थमिति-

62.22 उभयोरन्तरङ्गयोः परत्वान्नुमागमः। तस्माद्धिविकृव्योरिति वक्तव्यम्।

The short *a* is stated simultaneously with the arising of the *pratyaya u*. (But) when the *pratyaya* has arisen, having resorted to both the base/*prakṛti* and the *pratyaya, num* acts as the *āgama* for an *aṅga*. *Num āgama* is also *antaraṅga*. How? He will say this (in *7.1.58 Vā.1*). "In a *num* augment rule that expressing 'being like the *pratyaya* used in an original teaching/*upadeśa* (= *dhātu pāṭha*)' is for the sake of a *pratyaya* rule (not for the *prakṛti*)". When both are *antaraṅga*, because of being subsequent the *num āgama* rule (applies first). Therefore *dhivi kṛvyoḥ* should be stated.

Pradīpa

Pradīpa: 62.14 आर्धधातुकनिमित्त इति।

"(Prohibition is applicable) when (the lopa elision is) caused by an *ārdhadhātuka pratyaya*."

The sense is, due to resorting to *dhātu-lopa* as a *bahuvrīhi* (meaning) 'having (a portion of a) *dhātu* elided.

न चैष "And this (*lopa*) is not (caused by an *ārdhadhātuka pratyaya*)."

Due to the nature of the rule 'when, (of) two things which are taught together, one disappears, then the other disappears as well'. *Pari 86* सन्नियोगशिष्टानामन्यतरापाय उभयोरप्यपाय:

there is no possibility of the condition of cause and that having a cause.

Pradīpa: 62.18 अत्वे कृते इति।

"When a short *a* is effected (there *num* would be applicable in an undesired place)."

The meaning is that it would be after the letter *a*.

Pradīpa: 62.20 उत्पन्ने प्रत्यय इति।

But when the *pratyaya* has arisen *num* acts as *āgama* for an *aṅga*.

The sense is when the ordaining of *num* is after the *adhikāra aṅga* (i.e. within its province) (*6.4.1*).

Notes

[1] गुणो न भवति *Guṇa* is not applicable (because of a *lopa* being *sthānivat* by. . .) अच: परस्मिन्पूर्वविधौ (1.1.57)

An *ādeśa* in place of a vowel caused by something which follows, should be regarded as like that whose place it takes when a rule would otherwise have taken effect on what stands prior to the original vowel.

[2] किमर्थ नुम् उच्चते इदितो नुं धातो: (7.1.58)

"Why is *num* (augment) stated by 'The *āgama num* is added after the vowel of a *dhātu* having an indicatory *i* in the *Dhātu Pāṭha*' (*7.1.58*)?"

[3] प्रत्ययविध्यर्थमिति। "For the sake of *pratyaya* rule (not for the *prakṛti* rule)."
नुम्विधावुपदेशिवद्वचनं प्रत्ययविध्यर्थम् (7.1.58) वा० 1

हलः श्नुः शानज्झौ ॥ 3 । 1 । 83 ॥

Pāṇini 3.1.83: The *pratyaya śānac* is *ādeśa* in place of *śnā* after a *dhātu* ending in a consonant when *hi* follows (of the imperative).

62.24 किमर्थः शकारः। शित्सार्वधातुकमिति सार्वधातुकसंज्ञा सार्वधातुकमपिदिति ङित्वं ङितीति प्रतिषेधो यथा स्यात्[1]॥ कुषाण पुषाणेति॥ अत उत्तरं पठति।

Bhāṣya: What is the purpose of the letter *ś*? So that the technical name *sārvadhātuka* be applicable by (*tiṅ-śit sārvadhātukam 3.4.113*). "verbal *pratyaya tiṅ* and those having an indicatory *ś* have the technical name *sārvadhātuka*". Then by *sārvadhātukam apit 1.2.4* "A *sārvadhātuka pratyaya* not having an indicatory *p* is like that having an indicatory *ṅ*", *śnā* and *śānac* therefore have the nature of possessing an indicatory *ṅ*, so that there should be prohibition (of *guṇa* and *vṛddhi* by) *kṅiti ca* (*1.1.5*) "In the presence of that having an indicatory *k*, *g* or *ṅ* there is not *guṇa* or *vṛddhi* of an *ik* vowel", e.g. *kuṣāṇa* "Do thou tear asunder or draw out"; *puṣāṇa* "Do thou nourish or be nourished".

Therefore he states the following:

63.1 श्नाविकारस्य शित्करणानर्थक्यं स्थानिवत्वात् ॥ 1 ॥

Vārttika 1: The producing of an indicatory *ś* for the substitute *vikaraṇa pratyaya/vikāra śnā* is pointless because of being an *ādeśa* like the original/ *sthānivat* (i.e. like *śap*).

63.2 श्नाविकारस्य शित्करणमनर्थकम्। किं कारणम्। स्थानिवत्वात्। शितोऽयमादेशः स्थानिवद्भावाच्छिद्भविष्यति॥

Bhāṣya: The producing of an indicatory *ś* for the *ādeśa/vikāra śnā* is pointless. What is the reason? Because of being like the original/ *sthānivat*. This is an *ādeśa* of that having an indicatory *ś* and because of its nature being like the original it will have an indicatory *ś*.

63.4 अर्थवत्तु ज्ञापकं सार्वधातुकादेशेऽनुबन्धास्थानिवत्वस्य ॥ 2 ॥

Vārttika 2: However it does have a purpose (to indicate) an implied rule/ *jñāpaka* "an *anubandha* (indicatory letter) does not have the nature of being like the original, in the case of the *ādeśa* of a *sārvadhātuka pratyaya*".

63.5 अर्थवत्तु श्नाविकारस्य शित्करणम्। कोऽर्थः। ज्ञापकार्थम्। किं ज्ञापकम्। एतज्ज्ञापयत्याचार्यः सार्वधातुकादेशेऽनुबन्धा न स्थानिवद्भवन्तीति॥ किमेतस्य
63.7 ज्ञापके प्रयोजनम्।

Bhāṣya: However, the making of indicatory *ś* for the *ādeśa* of *śnā* has a purpose. What is the purpose? It is for the purpose of an implied rule/ *jñāpaka.* What is to be made known (as an implied rule)? This is what the master makes known, "When there is an *ādeśa* of a *sārvadhātuka pratyaya* the indicatory letters do not become like the original/*sthānivat.* What is the purpose in making this known as a *jñāpaka*?

63.8 प्रयोजनं हितातङोरपित्वम् ।। 3 ।।

Vārttika 3: The purpose is so that there should be absence of an indicatory *p* for *hi* and *tātaṅ.*

63.9 हेः पित्वं न प्रतिषेध्यम्[2]। पितोऽयमादेशः स्थानिवद्भावात्पित्स्यात्। सार्व-
धातुकादेशेऽनुबन्धा न स्थानिवद्भवन्तीति नायं पिद्भविष्यति।। तातङि
च ङकारो नोच्चार्यो भवति[3]। पितोऽयमादेशः स्थानिवद्भावात्पित्स्यात्।
सार्वधातुकादेशेऽनुबन्धा
63.12 न स्थानिवद्भवन्तीति नायं पिद्भविष्यति।।

Bhāṣya: There should not be prohibition of *hi* having an indicatory *p.* This *śānac* is *ādeśa* of that have an indicatory *p* and because of being like the original/*sthānivat* (like *śap*) it would have in indicatory *p.* but because of the *jñāpaka* "when an *ādeśa* is in place of a *sārvadhātuka pratyaya* the indicatory letters are not 'like the original'", this will not be possessed of an indicatory *p.*

And the letter *ṅ* in *tātaṅ* is not one to be pronounced (as part of the *ādeśa*). This *adeśa* being in place of that having an indicatory *p* due to the condition of being like the original should have an indicatory *p* (itself). But by the *jñāpaka* "when the *ādeśa* acts in place of a *sārvadhātuka pratyaya* the indicatory letters are not like those of the original", this will not be possessed of an indicatory *p.*

63.13 तबादिषु चाङित्त्वम् ।। 4 ।।

Vārttika 4: And when the *ādeśas tap* and the rest occur they do not have indicatory *ṅ.*

63.14 तबादिषु चाङित्त्वं प्रयोजनम्। शृणोत ग्रावाणः। ङित इम आदेशाः स्थानि-
वद्भावान्ङितः स्युः। सार्वधातुकादेशेऽनुबन्धा न स्थानिवद्भवन्तीति नेमे ङितो
63.16 भवन्ति।।

Bhāṣya: And when the *ādeśas tap* and the rest occur, the purpose is that (they too) should not have an indicatory letter *ṅ*, e.g. *śṛṇota grāvāṇaḥ* "Hear O ye *soma* pressing stones". These *ādeśas* being in place of that having an indicatory *ṅ* because of their 'condition of being like the original' would have an indicatory *ṅ* also. (By the *jñāpaka*) "When the *ādeśa* acts in place of a *sārvadhātuka pratyaya* the indicatory letters are not 'like the original'", these then are not possessed of an indicatory *ṅ*.

63.17 तस्य दोषो मिप आदेशे पिदभावः ॥ 5 ॥

Vārttika 5: Its fault is the absence of indicatory *p* when there is an *ādeśa* of *mip*.

63.18 तस्यैतस्य लक्षणस्य दोषो पित आदेशे पितोऽभावः[4]। अचिनवम् असुनवम्
अकरवम्। पितोऽयमादेशः स्थानिवद्भावात्पिद्भवति। सार्वधातुकादेशेऽनुबन्धा न
स्थानिवद्भवन्तीति नायं पित्स्यात्॥ अत्यल्पमिदमुच्यते मिप आदेश इति। ति-
63.21 प्सिब्मिपामादेशा इति वक्तव्यम्[5]। वेद वेत्थ॥

Bhāṣya: The fault of this rule is the absence of an indicatory *p* when the *ādeśa* acts in the place of *mip*. *tas-thas-tha-mip-ām-tām-tam-tāmaḥ 3.4.101*. The *ādeśas tam, tām, ta,* and *am* act respectively in the place of the *pratyayas tas, thas, tha* and *mip* of any *la* having an indicatory *ṅ*), e.g.

acinavam "I collected or arranged in a heap",

asunavam "I pressed out (the *soma*)",

akaravam "I did".

This *ādeśa* of that having an indicatroy *ṅ*, because of being like the original has an indicatory *p*. (By the *jñāpaka*) "when the *ādeśa* acts in place of *sārvadhātuka pratyaya* the indicatory letters are not 'like those of the original' ". This would not have an indicatory *p*. This is stated, namely "The *ādeśa* of *mip* is too small (a statement)". It should be stated that "the *ādeśa* of *tip, sip,* and *mip* (have an indicatory *p*)", e.g.

veda "He knows",

vettha "Thou knowest".

63.22 विदेर्वसोः शित्वम् ॥ 6 ॥

Vārttika 6: For the *ādeśa vasu* (acting in the place of *śatṛ*) after the *dhātu vid* (to know) there is the nature of having an indicatory *ś*.

63.23 विदेरुत्तरस्य वसोः शित्वं वक्तव्यम्[6]। शितोऽयमादेशः स्थानिवद्भावाच्छि-
द्भवति। सार्वधातुकादेशेऽनुबन्धा न स्थानिवद्भवन्तीति नायं शित्स्यात्।

Bhāṣya: It should be stated that there is the nature of having an indicatroy *ś* for the *ādeśa vasu* (in the place of *śatṛ*) because of the 'condition of being like the original' has an *it* (itself). (By the *jñāpaka*) "when an *ādeśa* acts in palce of *sārvadhātuka pratyaya* the *anubandhas* do not become like those of the original" this would not have an indicatory *ś*.

64.1 कित्करणाद्वा सिद्धम् ॥ 7 ॥

Vārttika 7: Or else it is established as valid because of making it have an indicatory *k*.

64.2 अथवावश्यमत्र सामान्यग्रहणाविघातार्था ककारोऽनुबन्धः कर्तव्यः। क्व सामान्य-
ग्रहणाविघातार्थेनः। वसोः संप्रसारणम् (6.4.131) इति। तेनैव यत्नेन
64.4 गुणो न भविष्यति॥

Bhāṣya: Or else it is essential here that the indicatory *k* be produced for the purpose of non-hindrance to the general mention (of *vasu*). Where is the purpose served of not hindering the general mention? (In the *sūtra*) *vasoḥ samprasāraṇam 6.4.131* ("There is vocalisation of the semi-vowels/*samprasāraṇam* of *vasu* (*ādeśa* of *śatṛ*) final of a *bha aṅga*"). By the same effort *guṇa* will not be applicable.

64.5 अस्य ज्ञापकस्य सन्ति दोषाः सन्ति प्रयोजनानि। समा दोषा भूयांसो वा। तस्मा-न्नार्थोऽनेन
ज्ञापकेन। कथं यानि प्रयोजनाति। तानि क्रियन्ते न्यास एव। एवमपि
64.7 भवेत्पित्करणसामर्थ्यात्पित्कृतं स्यान्ङित्करणसामर्थ्यान्ङित्कृतम्।

There are demerits and merits for this *jñāpaka* (implied rule). The demerits are equal or (even) more (than the merits). Therefore there is no purpose in this *jñāpaka*. What are the merits? Those are stated in the written/literal text only.

Th.ıs may it be that because of the force of making an indicatory *p*, something having an indicatory *p* would be formed, and because of the force of making an indicatory *ṅ*, something having an indicaotry *ṅ* would be formed.

64.7 .... यत्तु खलु पिति ङित्कृतं प्राप्नोति ङिति च
पित्कृतं केन तन्न स्यात्। तस्माद्वक्तव्यं पिन्न ङिद्भवतीति ङिच्च न पिद्भवतीति।
न वक्तव्यम्। एवं वक्ष्यामि। सार्वधातुकं ङिद्भवति पिन्न। एवं तावत्पितो ङित्वं
प्रतिषिद्धम्। ततो संयोगाल्लिट्किद्भवतीति ङिच्च पिन्न भवति। एवं ङित्तः पित्वं
प्रतिषिद्धम् ॥ 1 ॥

However, how may that not be (applicable) which being caused by that having (*anubandha*) *ṅ* obtains (i.e. wrongly applies) when that having (*anubandha*) *p* follows, and that which being caused by that having *anubandha p* obtains when that having *anubandha ṅ* follows?

Therefore it has to be stated "That having an *it p* does not become one having an *it ṅ* and that having an *it ṅ* does not become that having an *it p*". It has not to be stated. Thus I will say "a *sārvadhātuka pratyaya* has an *it ṅ* and not an *it p*". Thus there should just be prohibition of having *it ṅ* for that having an *it p*. Thence by the (*sūtra*) *asaṃyogāllit kit 1.2.5* "The *pratyayas* of the *liṭ* (perfect) not coming after conjunct consonant are as if they had an indictory *k*", and that having an *it ṅ* and that having an *it ṅ* does not become that having an *it p*". Thus is prohibited the state of having *it p* for that having an *it ṅ*.

Pradīpa

Pradīpa: 63.13 तबादिष्विति।

"When the *ādeśas tap* etc. (occur they are without an *it ṅ*)."

तप्तनप्तनथनाश्च (7.1.45)

"Also *tap* and *tanap* (the *it p* indicates the preceding vowel of an *aṅga* is strengthened or if weak not shortened), *tana* and *thana*, are *ādeśas* for *ta* (of second person *parasmaipada* of imperative in the *Veda*)."

Thus in the examples: *sṛṇota* (for *sṛṇuta*) 'Do you hear'.

Those which are ordained as *ādeśas* of *tiṅ* (verb endings) having *it ṅ* are *tap* and the rest.

Pradīpa: 64.6 एवमपीति।

"Thus too (it may be that because of making an *it p* something having an *it p* would be formed...)".

The meaning is, 'The reason for *it p* is *anudātta* accent (*3.1.4*), (as in) 'let it be'/*bhavatu*, 'May you speak'/*brutāt bhavān* and (for) *it āgama*/ augment', and the reason for *it ṅ* is prohibition of *guṇa* and *vṛddhi*.

Pradīpa: 64.9 पित्रेति।

सार्वधातुकमपित् (1.2.4)

"A *sārvadhātuka pratyaya* not having an *it p* is like that having an *it ṅ*"

The *p* expression *apit* is resort to *prasajya-pratiṣedha*, the negative form of an applicable positive statement, i.e. not having an *it p*. The meaning is, being possessed of *it p* and not being possessed of *it ṅ*. And as great as is the obtainment due to a division of the rule of having an it *ṅ sārvadhātuka pratyaya*, that (is the extent it is) prohibited.

Pradīpa: 64.10 असंयोगादिति

There by the *sūtra asaṃyogāt* etc.

असंयोगाल्लिट्कित् (1.2.5) see text.

Here having an *it ṅ/ṅit* and having an *it p/pit* follows from previous *sūtras 1.2.1* and *1.2.4*.

Therefore that having an *it ṅ* does not have an *it p*; the *pit* nature obtaining for *tātaṅ* by being like the one original/*sthānivat*, is prohibited.

Notes

[1] ङितीति प्रतिषेधो यथा स्यात्।
So that there should be prohibition when that having an *it ṅ* follows.
तिङ्शित् सार्वधातुकम् (3.4.113)
सार्वधातुकमपित् (1.2.4)
क्ङिति च (1.1.5) (इको गुण वृधी न)
[2] प्रतिषेध्यम्।
"(There should not be) prohibition (of *pit* for *hi* which is already stated", by सेर्ह्यपिच्च (3.4.87) "For the *loṭ*/imperative, *hi* (*madhyama puruṣa* second person singular *parasamai*) is *ādeśa* of *si*, and this has not the indicatory *p* of *sip*."

[3] तातङि च ङकारो तुह्योस्तातङं भवति।

"And the letter *ṅ* in *tātaṅ* is not one to be pronounced (as part of the *ādeśa*)."

63.11 तुह्योस्तातङाशिष्यन्यतरस्याम् (7.1.35)

"*Tātaṅ* is optionally *ādeśa* in place of the *pratyayas tu* and *hi* (in turn *ādeśas* of *tip* and *sip*) of the imperative/*loṭ* when benediction/*āśiḥ* is meant."

[4] पितोऽभाव:। "The fault is absence of *it* (for the *ādeśa* of *mip*)."

63.19 तस्थस्थमिपां तांतंताम: (3.4.101)

"The *ādeśas tām tam ta* and *am* act respectively in place of the *tiṅ pratyayas tas thas tha* and *mip* of any *la* (tense *pratyaya*) having an indicatory *ṅ*."

[5] तिप्सिब्मिपामादेशा इति वक्तव्यम्।

"It should be stated that the *ādeśas* of *tip sip* and *mip* (have an *it p*)."

For example, in the formation of *vid:* by विदो लटो वा (3.4.83) "The nine *pratyayas* of the perfect (*ṇalatus*) etc. are optionally added in the present/ *laṭ* also after *dhātu vid.*"

[6] विदेरुत्तरस्य वसोः शित्वं वक्तव्यम्।

"It should be stated that there is that nature of having a *it ś* for the *ādeśa* of *vasu* (in place of *śatṛ*, following the *dhātu vid.*"

विदेः शतुर्वसुः (7.1.36) "*Vasu* is *ādeśa* for the present participle *pratyaya satṛ* after the *dhātu vid* (to know)."

छन्दसि शायजपि ॥ 3 । 1 । 84 ॥

Pāṇini 3.1.84: In the *Chandas/Veda śāyac* is also the *ādeśa* of *śnā* after *dhātus* ending in a consonant when *hi* (of the imperative) follows.

---

64 13 शायच्छन्दसि सर्वत्रेति ॥ 1 ॥

Varttika 1: Everywhere in the *Chandas śāyac* (acts as *ādeśa*).

64.14 शायच्छन्दसि सर्वत्रेति वक्तव्यम्। क्व सर्वत्र। हौ चाहौ च। किं प्रयोजनम्।
महो अस्कभायत् यो अस्कभायत् उद्गृभायत
उन्मथायतेत्यर्थम्।। Cf. RV 5.15.16 AV 20.132.4

Bhāṣya: It should be stated that everywhere in the *chandas śāyac* (acts as *ādeśa*). Where is everywhere? When *hi* follows and when *hi* does not follow. What is the purpose (of the rule)? (e.g.)

mahī askabhāyat "The earth supported",

Yo askabhāyat "Which caused (the earth) to support",

ud gṛbhāyata "Do thou lift up", Cf. RV 7.104.18

unmathāyata "Do thou shake".

That is the purpose.

Pradīpa

Pradīpa: 64.15 अस्कम्भायदिति।

'(The earth) supported.'

Skambhu is a *sautra dhātu* (i.e only mentioned in *sūtras* not in *Dhātu Pāṭha*). When *laṅ*/imperfect follows (there is then) *tip, śāyac* in place of *vikaraṇa śnā* and *aṭ* augment.

a-ṭ skambha āya ti-p

Cf. AV 4.1.4 (तुङ्लङ्लृङ्क्ष्वडुदात्तः 6.4.71)

and *i lopa by* (इतश्च 3.4.100)

व्यत्ययो बहुलम् ॥ 3 । 1 । 85 ॥

Pāṇini 3.1.85: (In the *Chandas* there is) diversely an interchange (of the various *vikaraṇas śap* and the rest which have been previously ordained under special circumstances).

64.17 योगविभागः कर्तव्यः। व्यत्ययो भवति स्यादीनामिति[1]। आ॒ण्डा शुष्ण॑स्य॒
भेद॒ति। भिनत्तीति प्राप्ते। स च न मरति। म्रियत इति प्राप्ते॥ ततो बहुलम्।
बहुलं छन्दसि विषये सर्वे विधयो भवन्तीति। सुपां व्यत्ययः तिङां व्यत्ययः।
64.20 वर्णव्यत्ययः।

Bhāṣya: A separation of the rule (into two parts) should be made. There is interchange of *sya* and the rest. *āṇḍā́ śúṣṇasya bhédati* (*Ṛgveda 8.40.11*) "*Indra* breaks the eggs of this hisser (demon)", when *bhinnati* obtains (Cl. 7 with *śnam*).

There the rule *bahulam* (diveresly) is to be read. In the context/sphere of the *Chandas/Veda* all rules are diversely applicable. There is interchange of *sup* (nominal *vibhakti pratyaya*), interchange of *tiṅ* (verbal *vibhakti pratyaya*), interchange of letters.

64.20 ....लिङ्गव्यत्ययः। कालव्यत्ययः। पुरुषव्यत्ययः। आत्मनेप- दव्यत्ययः।
परस्मैपदव्यत्यय इति॥ सुपां व्यत्ययः। युक्ता मा तासीद्धुरि दक्षिणायाः। दक्षिणायामिति
प्राप्ते॥ तिङ्गां व्यत्ययः। चषालं ये अश्वयूपाय तक्षति। तक्षन्तीति प्राप्ते॥
वर्णव्यत्ययः। त्रिष्टुभौजः शुभितमुग्रवीरम्। सुहितमिति प्राप्ते। लिङ्गव्य-
64.24 त्ययः। मधोर्गृह्णाति।

'And He does not die.' RV 1.191.10 *marati* when *mriyate* obtains. Interchange of gender, (*pratyayas*), interchange of time, interchange of person, interchange of *ātmanepada pratyayas* and interchange of *parasmaipada pratyayas.*

1) Interchange of *sup* (nominal *vibhakti pratyaya*):

yuktā mātāsīd dhurì dakṣiṇāyāḥ Ṛg 1.164.9.

"Yoked was the mother to the boon cow's car pole" (G) when (the form) *dakṣiṇāyām* is applicable.

2) Interchange of *tiṅ* (verbal *vibhakti pratyaya*):

caṣālam yé aśvayupāya takṣati Ṛg. 1.162.6.

"Those who carve the knob to deck the horses stake" (G) when *takṣanti* obtains

(3) Interchange of letters:

triṣṭubhaujaḥ śubhitam ugravīram c.f. *T.S. 4.412.2*

"A powerful man beautified/embellished with the vigour of the *tṛṣṭubh*" (v.l. *śudhitam*) when *suhitam* (very fit, beneficial, salutary, suitable) obtains.

4) Interchange of gender:

madhor gṛhṇāti "He takes of the honey".

64.24 .... मधोस्तृप्ता इवासते। मधुन इति प्राप्ते। कालव्यत्ययः।
श्वोऽग्नीनाधास्यमानेन। श्वःसोमेन यक्ष्यमाणेन।आधाता यष्टत्येवं प्राप्ते[2]।।
65.2 पुरुषव्यत्ययः। अधा स वीरैर्दशभिर्वि यूयाः। वियूयादिति प्राप्ते।। आत्मनेपद-
व्यत्ययः। ब्रह्मचारिणमिच्छते। इच्छतीति प्राप्ते।। परस्मैपदव्यत्ययः। प्रतीपमन्य
65.4 ऊर्मिर्युध्यति। युध्यत इति प्राप्ते।।

madhos tṛptā ivāsate "He remains as it were satisfied from the honey" when *madhunaḥ* obtains.

5) Interchange of time :

svo'gnīn ādhāsyamānena śvaḥ soména yakṣyamāṇena

(c.f. *Kāthaka S. 8.12 agnim for agnīn, ityadheyam* c.f. *H.Ś.S.3.2 somena yaksyamāṇa adabhāno natrum naksatram sūrkeṣedityekesam*).

"Tomorrow with that *soma* which will be being sacrificed", when indeed *ādhātā* and *yaṣṭā* obtain respectively (*pratyaya luṭ* after a *dhātu* by *3.3.15*).

6) Interchange of persons:

ádhā sá vīráirdaśábhir-víyūyāḥ Ṛg. 7.104.15

"May he be deprived of his ten sons" when *viyūyāt* obtains.

7) Interchange of *ātmanepada pratyayas:*

brahmacārinam icchate "He wants a *brahmacāri*" (young *brahmaṇa* student of the *Veda)* when *iccati* obtains. *Atharva Veda 2.5.17*

8) Interchange of *parasmaipada pratyaya:*

prātīpam ánya ūrmir yúdhyati M.S.4.4.1

"Another wave fights/moves against the stream" when *yudhyate* obtains.

65.5 सुप्तिङुपग्रहिलिङ्गनराणां कालहलच्स्वरकर्तृयङां च।
व्यत्ययमिच्छति शास्त्रकृदेषां सोऽपि च सिध्यति बाहुलकेन।।

Śloka Vārttika: (The) creator of the science/*sāstra* desires the transposition of these: *sup* (noun endings), *tiṅ* (verb endings), *upagraha* (*pada* or voice) (*parasmaipada* and *ātmanepada pratyaya*), *liṅga* (gender), *nara* (person), and of time/*kāla*, consonants/*hal*, vowels/*ac*, accent/*svara*, causes/*kartṛ* etc., *kārakas* modifiers (*vikaraṇas* beginning with) *yak* (*3.1.67*) and endings in *aṅ* (*3.1.86*) and (all) that is accomplished by (the use of the word) *bahulam* (diversely, manifoldness).

Pradīpa

Pradīpa: 64.24 मधुन इति प्राप्ते इति।

'When *madhunaḥ* obtains (as the regular classical form).'

This means the word *madhu* (honey), the milk of the immortals, expressing 'either of the two', always neuter.

Pradīpa: 64.5 उपग्रह।

Literally seizure, adding, alternation *pada* or voice of a *dhātu.*

All arrangement of the substitutes of *la* with the sense of the base (*svārthe*) etc.

Here following from the understanding that *parasmaipada* and *ātmanepada* are expressed indirectly by the word *upagraha.*

Notes

[1] स्यादीनामिति Interchange of *sya* etc.

स्यतासी लृलुटोः (3.1.33)
by "When (*lṛṅ* conditional *lṛṭ* second future) and *luṭ* (first/periphrastic future) follow *sya tāsi* respectively are the *vikaraṇa pratyayas* after a *dhātu.*" The meaning is the *sya, tāsi,* and all that follows.

प्राप्ते "When *ādhātā* 'will be placing', *yaṣṭā* 'will be sacrificed' obtain..."

अनद्यतने लुट् (3.3.15) "The *pratyaya luṭ* (first future) acts after a *dhātu* in the sense of what will happen but not in the course of the present day."

लिङ्याशिष्यङ् ॥ 3 । 1 । 86 ॥

Pāṇini 3.1.86: The *pratyaya aṅ* acts in the *Chandas/ Veda* (as a modifier/*vikaraṇa*) when *pratyayas* of the benedictive follow.

65.8 अयमाशिष्यङ्विधीयते। तस्य किं प्रयोजनम्।

Bhāṣya: This ordains *aṅ* when the benedictive follows (i.e. *pratyaya āsir-liṅ*). What is its purpose?

65.9 आशिष्यङः प्रयोजनं स्थागागमिवचिविदयः ॥ 1 ॥

Vārttika: The purpose of (ordaining the *vikaraṇa pratyaya*) *aṅ* when the benedictive *pratyaya* follows (is so that the *dhātus sthā gā gami vaci* and *vidi* (only might receive it).

65.10 स्था। उप स्थेषं वृषभं तुग्रियाणाम्। स्था॥ गा। अञ्जसा सत्यमुप गेषम्[2]।
गा॥ गमि। यज्ञेन प्रतिष्ठां गमेयम्। गमि॥ वचि। मन्त्रं वोचेमाग्नये। वचि॥
65.12 विदि। विदेयमेनां मनसि प्रविष्टाम्॥
शकिरुहोश्चेति वक्तव्यम्। शकेम त्वा समिधम्। अस्रावन्तीमा रुहेमा
65.14 स्वस्तये॥

Bhāṣya: Thus *sthā upá sthesam uŕṣabham tugriyānām* (v.l. *steyam*) "May I stand near the bull of the *Bhujyus* or *Tugras*" (c.f. *tugrāt ghaṅ 4.4.115*) c.f. *V.S. 2.8 vasumat īmagne te chāyām ua sthesam M.S. 4.1.14 vasumatas te chāyām upasthesam ityagnivai vasumān agnereva chāyām upatiṣṭhate.*

gā añjásā satyam upá geṣam "May I arrive at truth quickly" *V.S.5.5. T.S.1.2.10.2 gami yayñéna pratiṣthă gamèyam* "May I by sacrifice attain the resting point/foundation" (to go) *T.S. 1.6.11.7*

vaci (to speak) *T.S. 1.6.2.4 mántram vocema agnáva* "May I utter the *mantra* for *Agni*". *T.S.1.6.2.4. R.V. 1.74.1.2*

vid-i vídeyam énām mánasi právistḥām (to know) *A.V. 19.4.2.2* "May I know that which has entered into the mind".

and it should be stated that *aṅ* acts as *vikaraṇa pratyaya* for the *dhātus śaki* and *ruhi.*

śakéma tvă samidham "May we/I have power to kindle thee". *R.V. 1.94.3*

ásravantīm ăruhema svastáye R.V. 10.63.10 "The heavenly ship free from defect will be ascending for happiness.".

65.15 दृशेरक् पितरं च दृशेयं मातरं च ।। 2 ।।

Vārttika 2: After (*dhātu*) *dṛśi* the *pratyaya ak* acts (in the line) *pitáram cá dṛśéyam mātáram cá dṛ́śeyam (R.V. 1.24.1)* "May I see both father and mother".

65.16 दृशेरग्वक्तव्यः[3] पितरं च दृशेयं मातरं च दृशेयमित्येवर्थम्।।

65.17 इह उपस्थेयामेत्याडपि[4] वक्तव्यो न ह्यङैव सिध्यति।। न वक्तव्यः। सार्व-
धातुकत्वात्सलोप आर्धधातुकत्वादेत्वं तत्रोभयलिङ्गत्वात् सिद्धम्[5]।।

65.19 इति श्रीभगवत् पतञ्जलिविरचिते व्याकरणमहाभाष्ये तृतीयस्याध्यायस्य प्रथमे
पादे चतुर्थमाह्निकम्।।

Bhāṣya: It should be stated that *ak* acts after the *dhātu dṛś-i* (in the line '*pitaram ca dṛśeyam mātaram ca dṛśeyam*' *R.V. 1.24.1* "that I may see my father and mother". Thus is the purpose (of the *vārttika* seen).

Here also is the example *upastheyama* "May we stand near" (where) *iṭ āgama* also is to be stated, for the valid form is not established just with *aṅ*. It is not to be stated. Because of being a *sārvadhātuka pratyaya,* there is a *lopa* of *s* and because of being *ārdhadhātuka, e ādeśa* (is applicable). In that context because of having both natures *sārvadhātuka* and *ārdhadhātuka*) the desired form is established.

Thus ends the fourth *āhnika* in the first *pāda* of the third *adhyaya* in the *vyākaraṇa mahābhāṣya* composed by the Blessed Master *Patañjali.*

Notes

[1] तुग्रियाणाम् (Bull of the) *Tugras,* of
तुग्रात् घञ् (4.4.115)
"*Pratyaya ghañ* acts in the *Chandas* in the sense of who stays there."

[2] गेषम् May I arrive (at the truth).
v-l, geyam (Kielhorn)

[3] दृशेरगिति।
"It should be stated *ak* acts after *dhātu dṛś* (to see)."
दृशोऽरङि गुण: (7.4.16)
"*Guṇa* is *ādeśa* of the vowels of *dhātus* ending in *ṛ* or *ṝ* as well as of *dṛś* (*dhātu* to see) in the presence of the *pratyaya aṅ.*"
क्ङिति च (1.1.5)
"And that which otherwise would have caused *guṇa* does not do so when it has an *it k, g* or *ṅ.*"

[4] 65.17 उपस्थेयामेति। "May we stand near."
Upa-sthā (optative) *liṅ mas*
yā-suṭ with *sa-lopa* by
लिङ सलोपोऽनन्त्यस्य (7.2.79) Having resorted to *aṅ, lopa* of *ā* by
आतो लोप इति च 6.4.64 आर्धधातुके किति and by अतो येय: (7.2.80)
"*Iy* acts in place of *yās* being part of a *sārvadhātuka pratyaya* acting after what ends in short *a.*"
aṭ has to be made *āgama* of *mas,* otherwise when (*y* is elided by *6.1.66* there would be the wrong form *upasthema*).

[5] उभयलिङ्गत्वात्सिद्धम्। Because of having two natures (*sārvadhātuka* and *ārdha-dhātuka*) the desired form is established.
लिङ सलोपोऽनन्त्यस्य (7.2.79) "The *s* which is not final in a *sārvadhātuka liṅ* (potential *pratyaya*) is *lopa* elided."
i.e. the *s* of *āgamas yāsuṭ* and *sīyuṭ*.
एर्लिङि (6.4.67)
"*E* is *ādeśa* in place of the *a* of a *ghu (dhātu, dā, dhā, mā, sthā, pā, jahāti,* and *sā* (= *so*) in the benedictive mood *parasmaipada*", e.g. *deyāt* 'May he give'.
छन्दसि उभयथा (3.4.117)
"In the *Chandas/Veda,* the *ārdhadhātuka* and the *sārvadhātuka pratyayas* occur in both ways one for the other."

कर्मवत्कर्मणा तुल्यक्रियः ॥ 3 । 1 । 87 ॥

Pāṇini 3.1.87: (The agent), when the action affecting the Agent is similar to the action which affects the object, is treated as if it were object.

66.2 वत्करणं किमर्थम्। स्वाश्रयमपि यथा स्यात्। भिद्यते कुशूलेनेति। अकर्म-
काणां भावे लो भवतीति भावे लो यथा स्यात्।। कर्मणेति किमर्थम्। करणाधि-
करणाभ्यां तुल्यक्रियः कर्ता यः स कर्मवन्मा भूत्। साध्वसिश्छिनत्ति साधु
स्थाली
66.5 पचति।।

Bhāṣya: What is the reason for making *vat* (like) (attach to *karman*)? So that there may also be (the grammatical operation) relating to (the original) itself e.g. *bhidyate kuśulena* "The granary splits by itself".

So that there may be a *la* in the sense of the impersonal action (of the *dhātu*) because *la* in the sense of abstract action/*bhāva* is applicable for intransitive (*dhātus*).

What is the reason for saying *karmaṇā* (equal, similar) with = to the object? So that the agent whose action is similar to that of the instrumental/*karaṇa* or locative/*adhikaraṇa* should not be treated as if it were object/*karmavat* (e.g.) *sādhvasiśchinatti* "A sword cuts well"; *sādhu sthālī pacati* "(in) the pot (rice) cooks well".

66.5 .... तुल्यक्रिय इति किमर्थम्। पचत्योदनं देवदत्तः। तुल्यक्रिय
इत्यप्युच्य-मानेऽत्र प्राप्नोति। अत्रापि हि कर्मणा तुल्यक्रियः कर्ता। न तुल्यक्रिय-
ग्रहणेन समानक्रियत्वमभिसंबध्यते। किं तर्हि। यस्मिन्कर्मणि कर्तृभूतेऽपि तद्वत्क्रिया
लक्ष्यते
66.8 यथा कर्मणि स कर्मणा तुल्यक्रियः कर्ता कर्मवद् भवतीति।।

What is the purpose of saying *tulyakriyaḥ* (having similar action)? To explain e.g. *pacaty odanam devadattaḥ* "*Devadatta* cooks the rice". Here *Devadatta* is not *tulyakriyaḥ* even when *tulyakriya* (having similar action to that affecting the object) is mentioned, (*karmavat*) obtains here. For here too, the agent has action similar to that of the object *tulyakriyaḥ*. By the mention of *tulyakriya* 'the same action" is not to be referred to. What then? That agent having an action similar to the object, being (orginally) an object has become an agent, and in whom the same action as in the object is served, is treated as an object. Even when the object/*karman* has become the agent/*kartṛ* the action is indicated as like that; in like manner, the Agent whose action is similar to the action which exists in the object/*karman* is *karmavat* (treated as if it were a *la* denoting object).

66.9 कर्मवदकर्मकस्य कर्ता ।। 1 ।।

Vārttika 1: The agent of an intransitive (*dhātu*) is treated as if it were an object/*karmavat.*

66.10 अकर्मकस्य कर्ता कर्मवद् भवतीति वक्तव्यम्। किं प्रयोजनम्। सकर्मकस्य कर्ता कर्मवन्मा भूदिति। भिद्यमानः कुशूलः पात्राणि भिनत्ति।। तथा।।

Bhāṣya: It should be stated that the Agent of an intransitive *dhātu* is treated as if it were an object/*karmavat.* What is the purpose? So that the Agent of a transitive (verb/*dhātu*) should not be *karmavat* e.g. *bhidyamānāḥ kuśūlaḥ pātrāṇi bhinatti* "While the granary is splitting to itself it splits the drinking vessels'. So also...

66.12 कर्म दृष्टश्चेत्समानधातौ ।। 2 ।।

Vārttika 2: And if (the agent) is seen an an object (this should be) when the same *dhātu* is used (that it should be treated as an object)

66.13 कर्म दृष्टश्चेत्समानधाताविति वक्तव्यम्। इह मा भूत्। पचत्योदनं देवदत्तः राध्यत्योदनः स्वयमेव।। तथा

Bhāṣya: It should be stated that the agent is treated as object when the same *dhātu* is used, so that it should not be applicable here: *pacaty odanam devadattaḥ* "*Devadatta* cooks the rice", and *rādhyaty odanaḥ svayam eva* "It accomplishes (the cooking) of itself". So also...

66.15 कर्मस्थभावकानां कर्मस्थक्रियाणां च ।। 3 ।।

Vārttika 3: And (the Agent is *karmavat*) for those *dhātus* having their verbal activity situated in the object or those having the abstract action situated in the object.

66.16 कर्मस्थभावकानां कर्मस्थक्रियाणां वा कर्ता कर्मवद् भवतीति वक्तव्यम्। कर्तृस्थभावकानां कर्तृस्थक्रियाणां वा कर्ता कर्मवन्मा भूदिति।।

Bhāṣya: It should be stated that the agent is as if an object/*karman* for those *dhātus* having their verbal activity situated in the object or those having the abstract action situated in the object, so that (the agent) of those *dhātus* whose state stands within the agent or whose action is confined to the agent, should not be *karmavat* (like object).

66.18 यत्तावदुच्यते कर्मकस्य कर्त्ता कर्मवद् भवतीति वक्तव्यमिति न वक्तव्यम्
वक्ष्यत्येतत्सकर्मकाणां प्रतिषेधोऽन्योऽन्यमाश्लिष्यत इति।। यदप्युच्यते कर्म
दृष्टश्चेत्स-
66.20 मानधाताविति वक्तव्यमिति न वक्तव्यम्। धातोरिति वर्तते।

What (has been) just said (in the *Bhāṣya* on *Vārttika 1*) "It should be stated that the agent of an intransitive *dhātu* is treated as if it were a *la* denoting object" is not to be stated. He will say this: "prohibition of transitive *dhātus*" e.g. 'they were joined to each other' *Vā 11*. Moreover, what also was just said (in the *bhāṣya* on *Vārttika 2*), "It should be stated that if (the agent) is seen (as if it were a *la*) denoting object (this should only be) when the *dhātus* are the same" should not be stated, because the word *dhātoḥ* "after a *dhātu*" follows on.

66.20 .... धातोः[1] कर्मणः
कर्तुरयं कर्मवद् भावोऽतिदिश्यते। तत्र संबन्धादेतद्गन्तव्यं यस्य धातोर्यत्कर्म
तस्य चेत्कर्ता स्यादिति। तद्यथा। धातोः कर्मण्यणभवतीति। तत्र संबन्धादेतद्गम्यते
यस्य
66.23 धातोर्यत्कर्मेति। इह मा भूत्। आहर कुम्भं करोति कटमिति।।

The application of 'being like an object'/*karmavat* is extended for the agent which is the object of a *dhātu*. There, from the connection it should be understood that *karmavadbhāva* takes place, if the *karman* is the agent of that *dhātu* of which it is the object. As for example, "After a *dhātu* a *pratyaya* acts when the object is in composition with it as an *upapada*" (*karmaṇyan 3.2.1*). There, from that connection it is understood that *karmavadbhāva* takes place if the *karman* is the agent of the *dhātu* of which it is the object. So that *karmavat* should not be applicable here: *āhara kumbham, karoti kaṭam* "Bring the pot. He makes the mat".

66.23 .... यदप्युच्यते
कर्मस्थभावकानां कर्मस्थक्रियाणां वा कर्ता कर्मवद्भावतीति वक्तव्यं
कर्तृस्थभावकानां कर्तृस्थक्रियाणां वा कर्ता कर्मवन्मा भूदिति न वक्तव्यम्।
कर्मस्थया क्रिययायां कर्तारमुपमिमीते न च कर्तृस्थभावकानां कर्तृस्थक्रियाणां
वा कर्मणि क्रि-
67.2 यायाः प्रवृत्तिरस्ति।।

What is stated (in *Bhāṣya* on *Vārttika 3*) "It should be stated that the agent is as if it were an object/*karmavat* for those *dhātus* having their verbal activity situated in the object or those having the abstract action or state situated in the object and that (the agent) for those *dhātus* whose abstract action or state stands within the agent or whose action is confined to the agent, should not be *karmavat*/like an object", that should not be stated. One measures the agent by the activity situated in the object and there is not applicability of the activity as being in the object for those (*dhātus*) whose abstract state stands in the agent or whose action is confined to the agent.

67.3 किं पुनः कर्मकर्तरि कर्माश्रयमेव भवत्याहोस्वित्कर्त्राश्रयमपि किं चातः। यदि
कर्माश्रयमेव चङ्शप्कृद्विधयो न सिध्यन्ति। चङ्। अचीकरत[2] कटः स्वयमेव
शप्। नमते[3] दण्डः स्वयमेव। कृद्विधिः भिदुरं[4] काष्ठं स्वयमेव।। अथ क-
67.6 र्त्राश्रयमपि सिद्धमेतद्भवति। किं तर्हीति।

But when there is the reflexive passive/*karmakartṛ*, is (the grammatical operation) depending on the object only applicable or also (the grammatical operation) depending on the agent? What follows from that? If there is resort to the object only, the rules (enjoining) *caṅ, śap* and *kṛt* are not established as valid.

caṅ (reduplicated aorist): *acīkarata kaṭaḥ svayam eva* "The mat made itself",
śap (*vikaraṇa pratyaya* for the first conjugation etc.): *namate daṇḍaḥ svayam eva* "The stick bends itself",
kṛt rule: *bhiduram kāṣṭhām svayam eva* "The wood is splitting of itself".
If this resort also to agent is there, it is established as valid. What then?

67.7 आत्मनेपदशबादिविधिप्रतिषेधः ।। 4 ।।

Vārttika 4: Prohibition of the rules relating to *ātmanepada* and *śap* (*vikaraṇa*) and the rest should be stated.

67.8 आत्मनेपदं विधेयं शबादीनां च प्रतिषेधो वक्तव्यः।। उभयं क्रियते न्यास एव।।
67.10 किमर्थं पुनरिदमुच्यते।।

Bhāṣya: *Ātmanepada* and *śap* are to be prohibited. Both statement and prohibition are actually (already) made in the text itself.

Why is this stated again?

67.11 कर्मकर्तरि कर्तृत्वं स्वातंत्र्यस्य विवक्षितत्वात् ।। 5 ।।

Vārttika 5: Due to the desire to express independence, the agentship exists in the reflexive passive.

67.12 कर्मकर्तरि कर्तृत्वं स्वातन्त्र्यस्य विवक्षितत्वात्। स्वातन्त्र्येणैवात्र
कर्ता विवक्षितः।। किं पुनः सतः स्वातन्त्र्यस्य विवक्षाहोस्विद्विवक्षामात्रम्।

Bhāṣya: In the reflexive there is agentship. Why? Because of the independence (of the agent) being intended to be expressed. Here the agent is intended to be independent alone. But it is the desire to speak of an already existing independence or merely the desire to speak in general?

67.13 .... सत
इत्याह। कथं ज्ञायते। इह भिद्यते कुशूलेनेति न चान्यः कर्ता दृश्यते क्रिया
67.15 चोपलभ्यते। किं च भो विग्रहवतैव क्रियायाः कर्त्रा भवितव्यं न पुनर्वातातपकाला
अपि कर्तारःस्युः। भवेत्सिद्धं यदि वातातपकालानामन्यतमः कर्ता स्यात्। यस्तु
खलु निवाते निरभिवर्षे ऽचिरकालकृतः कुशूलः स्वयमेव भिद्यते तस्य नान्यः
कर्ता
67.18 भवत्यन्यदतः कुशूलात्॥

He says "on an existing" (indepedence). How is (this) known? Here (in the example) *bhidyate kuśūlena* "the granary splits itself" and no other agent is seen and the action (verb) is understood. Can that alone having a body become the performer of action and would not the wind, heat and time also be agents? It can be established if any one of wind, heat and time would be the agent. However, if the granary in the place not being affected by wind, not being affected by rain, and not being affected by long time elapsed, splits itself there is no other agent, other than the granary (itself).

67.18 .... यद्यपि तावदत्रैतच्छक्यते वक्तुं यत्रान्यः कर्ता नास्तीहि
तु कथं न स्यात् लूयते केदारः स्वयमेवेति यत्रासौ देवदत्तो दात्रहस्तः समान्तो
विपरिपतन्दृश्यते। अत्रापि यासौ सुकरता नाम तस्या नान्यः कर्ता भवत्यन्यदतः
67.21 केदारात्॥ अस्ति प्रयोजनमेतत्। किं तर्हीति।

Although just here it is possible to say "there is no other agent" how could it not be so here (in the expression) *lūyate kedāraḥ svayameva* "the meadow mows itself" where (in fact) "you *Devadatta* with sickle in hand" are seen running around on all sides? Here also that which is called (the quality of) easiness, has no other agent applicable other than the meadow. This is the purpose. What then?

67.22 तत्र लान्तस्य कर्मवदनुदेशः ॥ 6 ॥

Vārttika 6: The prescription of *karmavat* for that which ends in *la* (should be made).

67.23 तत्र लान्तस्य कर्मवदनुदेशः कर्तव्यः। लान्तस्य कर्ता कर्मवद्भवतीति वक्तव्यम्॥

Bhāṣya: The prescription of *karmavat* for that which ends in *la* sould be made.

67.25 इतरथा हि कृत्यक्तखलर्थेषु प्रतिषेधः॥ 7 ॥

Vārttika 7: Otherwise prohibition (of *karmavat*) should be stated when the *pratyayas kṛtya* and *kta* and those having the meaning of *khal* follow.

67.26 अक्रियमाणे हि लग्रहणे कृत्यक्तखलर्थेषु[5] प्रतिषेधो वक्तव्यः स्यात्। कृत्य। भेत्तव्यः कुशूल इति कर्म। स यदा स्वातन्त्र्येण विवक्षितस्तदास्य कर्मवद्भावः स्यात्। तस्य प्रतिषेधो वक्तव्यस्तस्मिन्प्रतिषिद्धे ऽकर्मकाणां भावे कृत्या भवन्तीति भावे

68.3 यथा स्यात्।

Bhāṣya: For when mention of *la* is not being made, it should be stated that there be prohibition when a *kṛtya* or *kta pratyaya* or one having the meaning of *khal* follows.

kṛtya (e.g.) *bhettavyaḥ kuśūlaḥ* "The granary is to be split".

Thus (the *pratyaya kṛtya* denotes) passive/*karman* (of *dhātu bhid*). When that is intended to be independent there would obtain the state of being like an object/*karmavat.* Prohibition of that should be stated so that *kṛtya pratyayas* are applicable in the sense of abstact action or state of *dhātus.*

68.3 .... भेत्तव्यं कुशूलेनेति। कृत्य।। क्त। भिन्नः कुशूल इति कर्म। स यदा स्वातंत्र्येण विवक्षितस्तदास्य कर्मवद्भावः स्यात्। तस्य प्रतिषेधो वक्तव्यस्त-

68.5 स्मिन्प्रतिषिद्धे कर्मकाणां भावे क्तो भवतीति क्तो यथा स्यात्। भिन्नं कुशूले-नेति। क्त।। खलर्थः। ईषद् भेदः। कुशूल इति कर्म। स यदा स्वातन्त्र्येण विव-क्षितस्तदास्य कर्मवद्भावः स्यात्। तस्य प्रतिषेधो वक्तव्यस्तस्मिन्प्रतिषिद्धेऽकर्मका-

68.8 णां भावे खल्भवतीति भावे यथा स्यात्।

Prohibition of that should be stated so that when there is prohibition in the sense of abstract action or state of intransitive *dhātus, kta* should apply (as) *kta* is applicable in the sense of the action or state of (*dhātus*): *bhinnam kuśūlena* "the granary was split by itself". (The end of the) *kta* (example).

Pratyayas having the meaning of *khal* (e.g.) *īṣad bhedaḥ kuśūlaḥ* "The granary was slightly split". (A *pratyaya* in the sense of *khal* denotes) the object/*karman.* When it is intended to be independent, then there should be the state of 'being like an object/*karmavat*' for that (agent). Prohibition of that should be stated; (but) even when there is prohibition in the sense of abstract action or state of transitive *dhātus, khal* should (still) be applicable in the sense of abstract action or state of (intransitive *dhātus*).

68.8 .... ईषद्भेदं कुशूलेनेति।। तत्तर्हि लग्रहणं कर्तव्यम्। न कर्तव्यम्। क्रियते न्यास एव। लिङ्याशिष्यङ् (3.1.86) इति

68.10 द्विलकारको निर्देशः।।

The granary was of itself slightly split. Then should mention of *la* (tense/mood *pratyaya* denoting the object) be made? It should not be made. It is (already) made in the text itself, (because of the *sūtra*) *liṅyāśiṣyaṅ 3.1.86* is indicating two letters *l.*

68.11. सिद्धं तु प्राकृतकर्मत्वात् ।। 8 ।।

Vārttika 8: However it is established that *la* denotes the object because of being originally *karman* (object).

68.12. सिद्धमेतत्। कथम्। प्राकृतकर्मत्वात्। प्राकृतमेवैतत्कर्म यथा कटं करोति
शकटं करोतीति।। कथं पुनर्ज्ञायते प्राकृतमेवैतत्कर्मेति।

Bhāṣya: This is established. How? Because this was orginally an object. This 'object' is in fact the original base (as) for example *kaṭam karoti* "He makes a mat". How is it known that this *karman* (object) is the original base?

68.14 आत्मसंयोगे कर्मकर्तुः कर्मदर्शनात् ।। 9 ।।

Vārttika 9: Due to seeing the object of the reflexive passive when (the word) *ātman* (is used) in connection with the *karmakartṛ.*

68.15 आत्मसंयोगे कर्मकर्तुः कर्म दृश्यते। क्व। हन्त्यात्मानम्ँ। हन्यत आत्मनेति।
विषम उपन्यासः। हन्त्यात्मानमिति कर्म दृश्यते कर्ता न दृश्यते। आत्मना
68.17 हन्यत इति कर्ता दृश्यते कर्म न दृश्यते।।

Bhāṣya: The object of the object containing agent/reflexive passive is seen where there is connection with *ātman.* Where? *hanty-ātmānam* "He kills himself", *hanyate ātmanā* "He is killed by himself".

Unsuitable example! (In the example) *hanty-ātmānam,* the object is seen but the agent is not seen. (In the example) *ātmanā hanyate,* the agent is seen but the object is not seen.

68.18 पदलोपश्च ।। 10 ।।

Vārttika 10: And *lopa* elision of a word (is to be seen).

68.19 पदलोपश्चात्र द्रष्टव्यः। हन्त्यात्मानमात्मा। आत्मना हन्यत आत्मेति।। कः
पुनरात्मानं हन्ति को वात्मना हन्यते। द्वावात्मानावन्तरात्मा शरीरात्मा च। अन्त-रात्मा
तत्कर्म करोति येन शरीरात्मा सुखदुःखे अनुभवति। शरीरात्मा तत्कर्म
68.22 करोति येनान्तरात्मा सुखदुःखे अनुभवति।।

Bhāṣya: And here should be seen *lopa* elision of a word. *hanty ātmānam ātmā* "One's own self kills himself", *ātmanā hanyate ātmā* "One's own self is killed by himself". But who kills the self or who is killed by the self? There are two selves, the inner self and the bodily self. The inner self performs that action whereby the corporeal self experiences pleasure and pain. The corporeal self performs that action whereby the inner self experiences pleasure and pain.

68.23 सकर्मकाणां प्रतिषेधोऽन्योऽन्यमाश्लिष्यत इति ।। 11 ।।

Vārttika 11: There is prohibition of (*karmavat*) for transitive/*sakaramaka dhātus* (e.g.) *anyo'nyam āślisyataḥ* "They embraced each other".

68.24 सकर्मकाणां प्रतिषेधो वक्तव्यः। किं प्रयोजनम्। अन्योऽन्यमाश्लिष्यतः
अन्योऽन्यं संस्पृशतः। अन्योऽन्यं गृह्णीत इति।।

Bhāṣya: It should be stated that there is prohibition of (*karmavat*) for transitive *dhātus.* What is the reason?

anyo'nyam āśliṣyataḥ "They joined to/ embraced each other",

anyo'nyam samspṛśataḥ "They touch each other",

anyo'nyam gṛhṇītaḥ "They seize one another".

68.26 तपेर्वा सकर्मकस्य वचनं नियमार्थम् ।। 12 ।।

Vārttika 12: Or else the statement (of *karmavat*) regarding the transitive (*dhātu*) *tapi* is for the purpose of (making) a restriction.

68.27 तपेर्वा सकर्मकस्य वचनं[7] नियमार्थं भविष्यति। तपेरेव सकर्मकस्य नान्यस्य
सकर्मकस्येति।। तस्य तर्ह्यन्यकर्मकस्यापि प्राप्नोति। उत्तपति सुवर्णं सुवर्णकारः।
69.2 उत्तप्यमानं सुवर्णं सुवर्णकारमुत्तपति।

Bhāṣya: Or else the statement (of *karmavat*) regarding (*dhātu*) *tapi* being for the purpose of (making) a restriction *karmavatva* obtains only for *tapi* when transitive, not for any other transitive *dhātus.* For then it (*karmavat*) obtains also for (*tap-i*) with another object e.g. *uttapati suvarṇam suvarṇakāraḥ* "The goldsmith thoroughly heats the gold"; *uttapyamāṇam suvarṇam suvarṇakāram uttapati* "He affects/heats the goldsmith who is heating the gold".

69.3 तस्य च तपः कर्मकस्यैव ।। 13 ।।

Vārttika 13: And (the agent) of that (*tap*) only which has the word *tapas* as object is *karmavat.*

69.4 तस्य च तपः कर्मकस्यैव कर्ता कर्मवद्भवति नान्यकर्मकस्येति। किमिदं तप
इति। तपेरयमौणादिकोऽस्कारो भावसाधनः। कः प्रकृत्यर्थः कः प्रत्ययार्थः।
स एव संतापः। कथं पुनः स एव नाम प्रत्ययार्थः स्यात्स एव प्रकृत्यर्थः। सामान्य-
तपेरवयवतपिः कर्म भवति। तद्यथा। स एतान्पोषानपुष्यद्गोपोषमश्वपोषं रैपोषमिति
सामान्यपुषेरवयवपुषिः कर्म भवति। एवमिहापि सामान्यतपेरवयवतपिः
69.9 कर्म भवति।।

Bhāṣya: And the agent only of the *tap* which has the word *tapas* as its object, becomes "like an object"/*karmavat.* This is not so for the object of any (other) word. What is this (word) *tapas*? This is the *uṇādi pratyaya as* after the *dhātu tap-i* (which is) the means of bringing about the sense of abstract action or state (of the *dhātu*). What is the meaning of the base/*prakṛti*? What is the meaning of the *pratyaya*? That is in fact the same as usual namely "becoming very hot/affliction, self mortification". But how could that in fact really be the meaning of the *pratyaya* (when) that is in fact the meaning of the base/*prakṛti*? The specific *tap-i* which is a part, is the object of the action of *tap-i* in general, as for example: *sa etān poṣān apuṣyad, gopoṣam, aśvapoṣam raipoṣam* "He nourished these (ones) nourishing, nourishing cows, nourishing horses and increasing riches" (said of *Kṛṣṇa* in *M.Bh.*) Thus the specific *puṣ-i* which is a part of the object of the general (*dhātu*) *puṣ-i.* So here also the *tap-i* which is a part (of a compound) is applicable as the object of *tap-i* in general.

69.10 दुहिपच्योर्बहुलं सकर्मकयोः ।। 14 ।।

Vārttika 14: The agent is diversely (like an object/*karmavat*) for the *dhātus duh-i* and *pac-i* when they are transitive/*sakarmaka.*

69.11 दुहिपच्योः सकर्मकयोः कर्ता बहुलं कर्मवद् भवतीति वक्तव्यम्। दुग्धे गौः पयः
तस्मादुदुम्बरः स लोहितं फलं पच्यते। बहुलवचनं किमर्थम्। परस्मैपदार्थम्।
69.13 यद्येवं नार्थो बहुलवचनेन। न हि परस्मैपदमिष्यते।।

Bhāṣya: It should be stated that the agent of the *dhātu duh-i* and *pac-i,* when they are transitive is diversely treated like an object (e.g.) *dugdhe gauḥ payaḥ* "The cow itself milks its milk"; *tasmād udumbaraḥ sa lohitam phalam pacyate* "Therefore that *udumbara* tree (ficus glomerata) ripens its own fruit". What is the purpose of the expression 'diversely'? For the purpose of *parasmaipada pratyaya.* If so there is no purpose in the expression 'diversely'. For *parasmaipada pratyayas* are not desired.

69.14 सृजियुज्योः श्यंस्तु ।। 15 ।।

Vārttika 15: The Agent of the *dhātus sṛj-i* and *yuj-i* (is diversely) treated like the object, moreover there is *śyan* (in place of *yak vikaraṇa*)

69.15 सृजियुज्योः सकर्मकयोः कर्ता बहुलं कर्मवद्भवतीति वक्तव्यम्। श्यंस्तु भ-
वति[8]।। सृजेः श्रद्धोपपन्ने कर्तरि कर्मवद्भावो वाच्यश्चिणात्मनेपदार्थः। सृज्यते
मालाम्। असर्जि मालाम्। युजेस्तु न्याय्ये कर्मकर्तरि यकोऽभावाय। युज्यते ब्रह्म-
69.18 चारी योगम्।

Bhāṣya: It should be stated that the agent of the *dhātus sṛj-i* and *yuj-i* when transitive is treated like an object/*karmavat*. Moreover *śyan* is applicable (in place of *yak vikaraṇa*)

When the agent of the *dhātu sṛji* is endowed with faith there is the condition of being like an object/*karmavat* to be stated for the purpose of being 'like *ciṇ*' and *ātmanepada pratyayas* (e.g.) *sṛjate mālām* "The garland is created of itself"; *asarji mālām* "The garland was created of itself". Moreover when the proper *karmakartṛ* (reflexive passive) of the *dhātu yuj-i* is applicable it is for the sake of the absence of the *yak vikaraṇa: yujyate brahmacārī yogam* "The *brahmacārin* absorbs himself in *yoga* meditation".

69.19 करणेन तुल्यक्रियः कर्ता बहुलम् ।। 16 ।।

Vārttika 16: The agent whose action is similar to that done by the instrument, diveresely becomes like an object.

69.20 करणेन तुल्यक्रियः कर्ता बहुलं कर्मवद्भवतीति वक्तव्यम्। परिवारयन्ति
कण्टकैर्वृक्षम्। परिवारयन्ते कण्टका वृक्षमिति।।

Bhāṣya: It should be stated that the agent whose action is similar to that of the instrument is diveresely stated as like an object.

parivārayanti kaṇṭakair vṛkṣam "They compass the tree with thorns",

parivārayanti kaṇṭakā vṛkṣam "The thorns themselves encompass the tree".

69.22 स्रवत्यादीनां प्रतिषेधः ।। 17 ।।

Vārttika 17: Prohibition of (being like an object/*karmavat* for the agent) of the *dhātus sravati/sru* and the rest.

69.23 स्रवत्यादीनां प्रतिषेधो वक्तव्यः।स्रवति कुण्डिकोदकम्। सवति कुण्डिकाया
उदकम्। स्रवन्ति वलीकान्युदकम्। स्रवति वलीकेभ्य उदकमिति।।

Bhāṣya: Prohibition should be stated (of being like an object for the agent) of the *dhātus sravati/sru* and the rest e.g.

sravati kuṇḍikodakam "The small waterpot let flow the water",

sravati kuṇḍikāyā udakam "The water flows from the waterpot",

sravanti valīkāny udakam "The thatched reeds flow to the water",

sravati valīkebhya udakam "The water flows from the reeds".

69.24 .... स तर्हि प्रतिषेधो वक्तव्यः। न वक्तव्यः तुल्यक्रिय इत्युच्यते क्रियान्तरं चात्र गम्यते। इह तावत्स्रवति कुण्डिकोदकमिति विसृजतीति गम्यते। स्रवति कुण्डिकाया उदक-मिति निष्क्रामतीति गम्यते।स्रवन्ति वलीकान्युदकमिति विसृजन्तीति गम्यते।

70.2 स्रवति वलीकेभ्य उदकमिति पततीति गम्यते।

Then should the prohibition be stated? It should not be stated. It is said *tulyakriyaḥ* (an agent whose) action is similar becomes *karmavat* and here another action is understood.

Just here (in the sentence) *sravati kuṇḍikodakam* "the waterpot lets the water flow" *sravati* is understood as *visṛjati* 'pours forth'. In the sentence *sravati kuṇḍikāyā udakam* "The water flows from the pot of itself", *sravati* is understood as *niṣkrāmati* "It goes out". In the sentence *sravanti valīkāny udakam* "The reeds (let) the water flow", *sravati* is understood as *visṛ-janti* "they pour forth". In the sentence *sravati valīkebhya udakam* "The water flows from the reeds", *sravati* is understood as *patati* 'It falls down'.

70.3 भूषाकर्मकिरतिसनां चान्यत्रात्मनेपदात् ।। 18 ।।

Vārttika 18: And (prohibition) of the agent being like the object for *dhātus* having the sense of *buṣā*/as the act of adorning, *kṝ* (to scatter) and *san* (desiderative *pratyaya*) ending *dhātus* other than *ātmanepada.*

70.4 भूषाकर्मकिरतिसनां च प्रतिषेधो वक्तव्योऽन्यत्रात्मनेपदात्। भूषयते कन्या स्वयमेव। अबुभूषत कन्या स्वयमेव। मण्डयते कन्या स्वयमेव। अममण्डत कन्या स्वयमेव।। किरति। अवकिरते हस्ती स्वयमेव। अवाकीर्ष्ट हस्ती स्वय-

70.7 मेव।। सन्। चिकीर्षते कटः स्वयमेवः अचिकीर्षिष्टः कटः स्वयमेव।।

Bhāṣya: And prohibition should be stated (of the agent being like an object/*karmavat*) for *dhātus* conveying the sense of the act of adorning, *kṝ* (to scatter) and *dhātus* ending with the *pratyaya san* (desiderative) other than the *ātmanepada* e.g.

bhūṣayate kanyā svayam eva "The girl adorns herself."

abubhūṣata kanyā svayam eva "The girl adorned herself."

maṇḍayate kanyā svayam eva "The girl decorates herself",

amamaṇḍata kanyā svayam eva "The girl decorated herself."
kirati (e.g.)
avakirate hastī svayam eva "The elephant besmears itself",
avākīrṣṭa hastī svayam eva "The elephant smeared itself",
san (e.g.)
cikīrṣate kataḥ svayam eva "The mat desires to make itself",
acikīrṣiṣṭa kataḥ svayam eva "The mat desired to make itself",

Pradīpa

Pradīpa: 66.2 वत्करणमिति।

"(What is the reason for) making *vat*/like (attach to *karman*)?"
The sense is even without *vat* from the use of the word in the sense of having an object (designed for an object...dependent on something else).

Pradīpa: 66.2 स्वाश्रयमिति।

"(So that there may also be the grammatical operation) relating to (the original) itself."

If there were not the producing of *vat,* the technical name *karman* would be understood as belonging to the agent. And thence, because of the absence of the designation intransitive/*akarmaka, la* (tense *pratyaya*) would not be applicable in the sense of the abstract action. However, when *vat* is produced, the operations of the *karman* are extended for the agent, but the operation relating (only) to itself is not (abandoned/rejected) or prohibited and the *la* (tense *pratyaya*) is established as valid in the sense of abstract action. So because of the agent not being designated by the *ādeśa* of *la* (*tiṅ* verb endings etc.), the third case is applicable (*kartṛ-karaṇayo-stṛ-tī-yā 2-3-18*).

Pradīpa: 66.3 लो यथा स्यात्।

So that there may be *la* (in the sense of impersonal action)...

लः कर्मणि च भावे चाकर्मकेभ्यः (3.4.69)

"The tense or mood *pratyayas* called *la* are applicable in denoting the object/*karman* and the agent *kartṛ*; and after intransitive/*akarmaka dhātus* they denote the abstract action/*bhāva* as well as the agent."

कर्तृकरणयोस्तृतीया (2.3.18) (अनभिहिते)

"In denoting the agent (स्वतंत्र कर्ता 1.4.54) or the instrument (साधकतमं करणम् 1.4.42) the case/*vibhakti pratyaya* is applicable."

Pradīpa: 66.3 कर्मणेति किमिति।

"What is the reason for saying *karmaṇā* (equal/similar with) to the action?"

The sense is the verbal activity is to be expressed by the *dhātu* in fact united/inherent in the agent and object. In the context the agent (it is said) cannot possibly be having the same action/equal with the action which is in the agent, because the action situated in the object alone will be resorted to.

Pradīpa: 66.4 साध्वसिश्छिनत्तीति।

"The sword cuts well."

Surely the activity of instrument is not expressed by the *dhātu*. When however, it is expressed then only there is agentship, but not the nature of being an instrument etc. And the nature of resorting to a different case/means of accomplishing the action, other than agent and object is not proper for the verb. This is no fault. Although the activity of instrument is not to be expressed by *dhātus,* nonetheless they perform the activity relating to themselves, the instrument etc. accomplishing the principal verbal activity. In the context, it is essential regard should be had to a different condition (situation) as resort for the agent (namely) the nature of having an action similar/*tulya-kriyatva* as stated. The agent having an action similar to the action connected with another condition (situation/state) and hence the conditions of instrument etc. would (all) be resorted to as like the condition of *karman*/object. And the principal activity is established for agent and object only, but not the intermediate/secondary activity as well, because of the condition of that, being everywhere only in relation to the action/*kārake* (*1.4.23*). Although its agency is in relation to its own activity, nonetheless for the purpose of opposing (preventing/refuting) the mention of similarity of action, established in a thing designating instrument etc., and obtained with regard to the pincipal action, the word '*karmaṇā*' has in fact to be produced (in the *sūtra*). Although there is no nature to be expressed by the *dhātu* for the activity of instrument etc., nonetheless here in the *sūtra* because of the nature to be expressed by a *dhātu* not depending on resorting to a word, there would be in fact the possiblity of joining with /depending on an existent thing/substance (as opposed to an action).

Pradīpa: 66.4 साधु स्थाली पचतीति।

'(In) the pot (rice) cooks well."

When there is the nature of being the location for a pot, whatever the verbal action, with its nature of being the fitness for holding etc., is like, so like that in fact would the nature of being like the object in relation to agentship.

Pradīpa: 66.5 तुल्यक्रिय इति किमर्थमिति।

"What is the purpose of saying 'having similar action *tulyakriya*'?" He will explain the word *karmaṇā* as being the third case by the supplying of the word *tulya*. And the question is, 'Is the similarity for the agent due to having similarity of action?'

Otherwise the question is, 'Even when action is being performed is there unwarrantable stretching of the rule when mention is made of *tulya*/being similar?'

Pradīpa: 66.5 पचत्योदनिमिति।

"(*Devadatta*) cooks the rice."

The sense is that, the third case may also be understood in the sense of together with/*saha;* therefore the agent which is (set forth) is regarded as together with the object. For the purpose of preventing intransitive verbs, there would be hearing of *karman* (in the *sūtra*) so it would not be applicable to *āste* 'He sits', *śete* 'He lies'.

Pradīpa: 66.6 अत्रापीति।

"For here too (the agent has action similar to that of the object)."

The sense is that because of the word *tulya* having the nature of expressing similarity and because of the verbal activity here having the nature of that to be accomplished by the agent and the object.

Pradīpa: 66.6 समानक्रियत्वमिति।

"(By mention of *tulyakriya*) the same action (is not to be referred to)."

The meaning is commonness of action and this is obtained only by the mention of 'similar action'. Otherwise he would say *'Karmavat-karmaṇā'* alone (without *tulyakriya*).

Pradīpa: 66.7 यस्मिन्निति।

"(That agent having an action similar to the object) when (it was originally an object has become an agent and in whom the same actions as in the object is observed, is treated like an object/*karmavat*)."

The meaning is that resort is made to the word *tulya* as expressing likeness.

Pradīpa: 66.7 कर्तृभूत इति।

"(When what was an object) has become an agent."

Due to *cvi* being optionally ordained, here it is absent. The meaning is 'turned into an agent'.

Otherwise optionally, due to the refutation (of normal meaning) of *bhū* for the (class 10 meaning in *ātmanepada*) in the sense of attaining, and due to *ṇic* being optional, there is this form. The meaning is therefore, agentship is obtained. In the context of the usage of 'occurrence', the word *kartṛ* occurs in the sense of agentship/nature of agent. And due to the difference in the condition of agent and object, even for one verbal activity, a different resort and similarity is valid/regular.

Pradīpa: 66.8 कर्मणेति।

"(Having an action similar to) the object."

The meaning is (similar to) the action situated in the object. Due to the total difference between that to be accomplished and the means of accomplishing and because of the impossibility of equality, the action situated in the object is expressed by the word *karman*/object.

For, due to being contained in that, it is applicable as for example 'The platforms cry out' (means, men on them do so to drive away birds etc.).

In the context 'He cooks rice', here, because of the total difference between the actions of agent and object and the absence of similarity there is absence of being 'like the object' *karmavat.*

Here in the example 'The fields mow themselves as it were', they are characterised as a two-fold place of abode. Just as, that which is like an action situated in the condition of the object, so is that in fact also situated in the condition of agent. (Here), there is being like an object/*karmavadbhāva.*

Pradīpa: 66.11 भिद्यमान इति।

"While (the granary) is splitting of itself (it splits the drinking vessels)."

Even the place of abode of the drinking vessels is two-fold, as well as for the granary. So 'being like an object' obtains (for them too).

Pradīpa: 66.12 कर्मदृष्ट इति।

"(If the agent) is seen as an object, this should be when the same *dhātus* are used."

The meaning is, if in the same *dhātu* the agent is seen with the nature of object, the 'being like the object' is applicable, however, when in one *dhātu* there is the object and in another the agent then *karmavat bhāva* must not be applied.

Pradīpa: 66.13 पचत्योदनमिति।

"(*Devadatta*) cooks the rice."

As is that action which is characterised by softening of the grains of rice in relation to the nature of the object for the rice, so also is the action in relation to the nature of the agent.

Due to *'rādhyati'* (cooking) expressing the 'softening' there is not simultaneous use of the two sentences/phrases.

However, there is mention of two sentences, to teach the similarity of the action situated in the object. Otherwise, even when in the same *dhātu,* how is similarity of action shown by the commentators? If it is, then the nature of object for the field is in the *dhātu lunāti.* 'The field causing mowing of itself, as it were'. (In that situatation) *karmavad bhāva* (wrongly) would not be applicable. Here some say, *lunāti* has in fact become *lāvi* with *ṇic* following (causative), thus (having the nature of being the same *dhātu.* Others say, in the *lāvayati* (he causes to mow) both agentship and object-nature occur, so there is no fault.

Pradīpa: 66.15 कर्मस्थभावकानामिति।

"(The agent is *karmavat* for those *dhātus*) having the impersonal action situated in the object..."

Impersonal action is the meaning of *dhātus* whose means of accomplishment and action to be accomplished are without motion.

However, verbal activity is (characteristic of *dhātus*) whose means of accomplishment and action to be accomplished is with motion.

And where there is seeing of a particular action performed, that situated in that is called *kriyā* (verbal action).

And hence in 'the king sees himself' and 'the elephant mounts of itself', there is absence of *karmavad bhāva.*

Pradīpa: 66.19 सकर्मकाणामिति।

"(He will say 'The prohibition) of transitive *dhātus* "(They were joined to each other" etc.')"

The meaning is 'They were joined to each other' is surely an example. However, this is not for the purpose of teaching prohibition of being *karmavat* in the sphere distinguished by reciprocity, exchanges of blows etc.

Pradīpa: 66.23 आहर कुम्भमिति।

"Bring the pot."

Even without giving scope for the *Samartha paribhāṣā* (*2.1.1.*), a form is in fact applicable. The mention is to show the desired established form.

Pradīpa: 67.1 कर्तारमिति।

"(One measures) the agent by the activity situated in the object/ *karman.*"

The meaning is the verbal activity which is situated in the agent.

Pradīpa: 67.3 किं पुनरिति।

"But (when there is the reflexive passive, is (the grammatical operation) depending on the object only applicable or that depending on the agent also)?"

The question is, is the operation relating to itself prevented by the extended application, or not?

Although this is in order that there should hereby be made complete ascertainment also for the operation relating to itself; nonetheless for producing another fault again it is (to be) pondered/investigated.

Pradīpa: 67.8 उभयमिति।

"Both (statement and prohibition are already made in the text)."

The agent which is agent alone there, due to the absence of *parasmaipada* there has *ātmanepada* applicable. Here, when *kartari śap 3.1.68* applies and becomes divided (the first part meaning) 'When in the sense of agent *sārvadhātuka* follows... there is barring of *śap* and the rest by *yak*'.

As the extension of the operation, this is optionally resorted to. And (only) that which is not contrary is applicable in relation to its own resort but not that which is contrary. Thus, there is absence of *śap* etc. and *parasmaipada*.

Pradīpa: 67.11 स्वातन्त्र्यस्येति।

"Due to the desire to express independence (the agentship exists in the reflexive passive)."

'The rice is cooked of itself as it were', expresses the *dhātu pac* as merely softening (the grains) and there is agentship in fact for the rice. 'The field is cut (of itself). *Lunāti*/ to cut expresses a two-fold place of abode and so the agentship of the field.

Pradīpa: 67.14 क्रिया चेति।

"(The granary splits itself and no other agent is seen) and the verbal activity (is understood).." The meaning is the action of dissolution.

Pradīpa: 67.15 किं च भो इति।

"Sir, can (that alone having a body become the performer of action...)?"

The sense is, in the absence of a cause. Due to the absence of an operation called dissolution, it is essential it should be (brought about) by some cause or other like the wind etc.

Pradīpa: 67.18 अन्यदत इति।

"(If the granary is not affected by the wind etc. splits itself) there is no other (agent than the granary itself)."
The sense is that, due to the inappropriateness of imagining another unseen cause when the logical cause is the action of dissolution of the granary alone.

यत्रासौ देवदत्तः दात्रहस्तः समन्ततो विपरिपतन्दृश्यते।

Where *Devadatta* with sickle in hand is seen running around.

(c.f. बृह् उप॰ 4.3.19 तद्यथा। अस्मिन्नाकाशे श्येनो वा सुपर्णो वा विपरिपत्य श्रान्तः संहत्य। पक्षौ संलयायैव ध्रियते।

"As a hawk or falcon flying in the sky becomes tired and stretching its wings is bound for his nest (so does the *puruṣa* run for this state, where, falling asleep, he craves no desire and sees no dream).")

Here also, for that which is called (the quality of) easiness, no other agent is applicable than the meadow.

The meaning is, it is characterised by a two-fold place of abode. The sense is otherwise *Devadatta* would even cut a mountain.

Pradīpa: 67.23 लान्तस्य कर्मेति।

"(The prescription of *karmavat*) for that ending in *la* (should be made)."

The meaning is, that agent which is to be expressed by that ending in *la* is in fact the operation of that ending in *la* (and) becomes *karmavat* (like the object).

Therefore, the *kṛtya pratyayas* etc., due to extended application being ordained in the sense of *karman,* are not applicable in the sense of reflexive passive, but in the sense of abstract/impersonal action/ *bhāva.*

And hence, because of the nature of agent having been expressed by these, there are two *vibhaktis* for agent, sixth and third, by कृत्यानां कर्तरि वा (2-3-71) e.g. The granary is to be split itself, *bhetavya kuśūlasya,* or *kuśūlena.* And here *bhidyate kuśūlaḥ/* 'The granary is split', second case is not applicable.

Hence the purpose of mentioning *kta*/past participle passive, is not seen (2.3.69). Here 'Milk is milked by the cow itself.' Thus is seen said.

For so due to being intransitive because of the rule.

गत्यर्थकर्मकश्लिषशीङ्स्थासवसजनरुहजीर्यतिभ्यश्च ३।४।७२।।

It should be applicable only in the sense of agent with *kta* as:

भिन्नः कुशूलः स्वयमेव।

'The granary was split of itself' in the sense of agent. And so *kta* will be illustrated with 'a morsal of food stuck fast of itself (in the throat)', because of the statement 'It should be stated, for the reflexive passive of *grasa* (a mouthful) after *dhātus si* (to bind/get stuck).'

Pradīpa: 68.11 सिद्धमिति।

"It is established however (that *la* denotes the object because of (the base) being originally object/*karman.*"

The meaning is this, object is only the original/natural (object), but not that resulting from substitution/*atideśa.*

Pradīpa: 68.14 आत्मसंयोग इति।

"(Due to seeing the object of the reflexive passive when the word) *ātman* (is used) in connection (with the *karmakartṛ*/reflexive passive)."

The meaning is, it is intended the self be expressed by the division of (what is) in fact one substance by the nature of object and the nature of agent.

That was stated by *Bhartṛhari.*
एकस्य बुद्ध्यवस्थाभिर्भेदे च परिकल्पिते।
कर्मत्वं करणत्वं च कर्तृत्वं चोपजायते।।
वा॰ पद 3.7.104

"By means of a different condition of mind/ *buddhi,* difference is imagined for one (thing). The nature of being an object or an instrument or an agent is thus produced."

Pradīpa: 68.15 कर्म दृश्यत इति।

"(Of the reflexive passive) the object is seen (when in connection with *ātman*)." The meaning is, 'the nature of *karman*/object' is seen.

Pradīpa: 68.16 विषम उपन्यास इति।

"An unsuitable example..."

This is the sense: in the example, due to the nature of the difference of (the word) *ātman* taught, the nature of object is appropriate. However, here in the examples 'The field is cut', 'The rice is cooked' etc., when the word itself/ *svayam* is not used, then when it is not intended to express differences of the *ātman;* due to the absence of the nature of object, agentship only occurs in the sense of the two-fold place of abode for 'fields etc. (because of which) the substitution of *karmavat/* being like the object is in fact to be effected.

And in the examples 'The stick bends' etc., when there is prohibition of *yak* and *ciṇ* in the sense of the nature of the original object *'śap* and *caṅ* would not be applicable, and in the example 'By the granary it is split', because of the transitive nature of the *dhātu, la* would not be applicable in the sense of impersonal action (after it).

Pradīpa: 68.16 कर्म दृश्यत इति।

"The object is seen (but the agent is not seen)."

Ātmānam is the object to be expressed as ending in the second case.

कर्ता न दृश्यत इत्। "The agent is not seen."

The sense is, because of not producing a particular kind of agent, even when the *la* (tense *pratyaya*) arises, it is in the sense of agent, as *hanti* 'He kills'.

Pradīpa: 68.17 कर्ता दृश्यत इति।

"The agent is seen."

The sense is, due to the absence of action without him, so it should be stated by means of the Self.

Pradīpa: 68.17 कर्म न दृश्यत इति।

"The object is not seen."

The sense is, here because of the nature of the object being difficult to be demonstrated for another different form a particular (kind of) agent.

Pradīpa: 68.18 पदलोपश्चेति।

"And *lopa* elision of a word (is to be seen)."
The meaning is, due to the nature of the meaning being understood, there is not usage of the word.
However, that which is illustrated by commentators 'The meadow mows itself as it were', there the word *svayam*/itself is used for teaching the nature of agent. So the meadow alone, by teaching the absence of another different agent, acts. However, this is not an example of *karmavat bhāva* because of the word *svayam* existing in the sense of third case, namely 'by himself',

68.18 पदलोपश्चेति।

"Because of the existence of the original nature of *karman* for the meadow, when there is the nature of the agent for the self."

Pradīpa: 68.20 द्वावात्मानाविति।

"There are two selves (the inner self and the bodily self)."
Here is explained the *sūtra*
णेरणौ यत् कर्म णौ चेत् स कर्तानाध्याने (1.3.67)
"After a *dhātu* ending in the *pratyaya ṇi* (causal) the *ātmanepada* is employed, provided that when the object is non-*ṇi*/non-causal in sense it becomes agent in the causal, and when it does not mean to remember with regret, even when the fruit of the action does not accrue to the agent."
Hence in fact it is to be ascertained.

Pradīpa: 68.23 आश्लिष्यत इति।

"They embraced (each other)."

Due to the perception in the object, of the conjunction of the fruits of an action, here the nature of the action situated in the object is to be seen.

c.f. कर्तरि कर्म व्यतिहारे (1.3.14)

"In denoting the agent, when reciprocity of action is to be expressed the *pratyayas* of the *ātmanepada* are employed."

Pradīpa: 68.26 तपेर्वेति।

"Or else (statement of *karmavat* regarding the transitive *dhātu*) *tap* (is for a restriction)."

The sense is that, by a separation of the rule into two there is formed a restriction on *dhātu tap.*

Surely here, in the example *3.1.88* 'The ascetic practices austerities', there is not for the agent an action similar to the action situated in the object... due to the nature of the meaning of *tap* being (either) pain, when the nature of the agent is for *tapas* (austerity) like fasting etc., or however when the agency is for the ascetic becaused of the meaning of earning (merit etc.).

This is no fault.

Due to similarity of the action characterised as heating or tormenting the body, even though there are two states, the tormenting of the body and the earning (of merit), really they are for the ascetic from whence the activity arises.

Pradīpa: 69.5 कः प्रत्ययार्थ इति।

"What is the meaning of the *pratyaya?*"

When the *la* (tense *pratyaya*) arises in the sense of object (passive as 'By the assetic austerities are performed...' तापसेन तपस्तप्यते) it is seen that the nature of the meaning of the *pratyaya* is for the form of the action, which has the meaning of the base alone. And due to the condition of that to be accomplished/*sādhya* and the means of accomplishing/ *sādhana* relating to the verb and the object (respectively), the difference must be (evident). However, here due to the absence of difference, the meaning for the base and *pratyaya* is not applicable. Otherwise the sense is, due to the rule *tapaḥ karma-kasyaiva 3.1.88.* Agent of *tap* is *karmavat* only when the object is the word (*tapas* itself). There is resort to the nature of object for the meaning of the base only and that is contradictory or (contrary to law).

Pradīpa: 69.8 अवयवतपिरिति।

"The *tap* which is a part (of a compound) (is applicable as object of *tap-i* in general)."

The meaning is that the special *tap* is that *tapas* characterised by knowledge.

Pradīpa: 69.11 दुग्धे गौरिति।

"The cow itself milks (its milk)."

The meaning is, the cow releases its milk, due to *duh-i* having two objects (*vārttika* on *1.4.51*).

Even when the nature of similar action is situated in the object, because of being transitive when it does not obtain, there is this *vārttika*. Here 'The fuit is ripened' when it is desired to express the agency of the tree when (in fact it is) totally unobtaining, there is this *vārttika*.

However, others say (*pac-i*), 'here in the context of *pac*', because of the impossibility of fruit ripening without ripening of the tree there are two objects, the tree is the unexpressed object; and when there is the desire to express the agency of it alone, then this *karmavad bhāva* (applies). And in such a kind of context only *karmavad bhāva* is desired, not in the case of 'He cooks rice' etc.

Pradīpa: 69.16 चिणात्मनेपदार्थ इति।

"For the purpose of being like *ciṇ* and (receiving) *ātmanepada pratyaya*"

The meaning is *yak* only is barred with *śyan* not *ciṇ* However, when there is *śyan*, there is initial *udātta* for the base but when there is *yak* ... when there is *anudātta* for a *sārvadhātuka* substitute of *la*, *udātta* for *yak* only applied. Thus here, in relation to accent there is a distinction between *śyan* and *yak*.

सृज्यते मालमिति। "The garland is created (of itself)."

The meaning is, by faith he brings about/accomplishes the garland.

Pradīpa: 69.17 असर्जि मालमिति।

"The garland was created (of itself)."

The meaning is he accomplished the garland (by faith).

Pradīpa: 69.17 यकोऽभावायेति।

"(Reflexive passive in *yaj* is) for the sake of absence of *yak vikaraṇa.*"

The meaning is, due to coalescent *a* it is for the sake of barring of *yak.*

Pradīpa: 69.17 युज्यत इति।

"(The *brahmacārin*) absorbs himself (in *yoga*/meditation).

The meaning is *yoga* engages the *brahmacārin*, i.e. joins or unites him. Thence when it is intended to express the agency of the *brahmacārin* 'The *brahmacārin* absorbs himself in *yoga*' become applicable.

Pradīpa: 69.19 करणेनेति।

"(The agent whose action is similar to that done) by the instrument (is diversely *karmavat*)."

Due to the mention of *bahulam* (diversely) it is not applicable in the examples 'The sword cuts well' etc. .

Pradīpa: 69.23 स्रवति कुण्डिकेति।

"The small water-pot allows (the water) to flow."

Due to the similarity of action in this sense 'water going out' and 'it causes water to go out', obtaining as 'being like the object'/*karmavad* it is in fact barred.

Pradīpa: 69.26 विसृजतीति गम्यत इति।

(*Sravati*) is understood as *visṛjati* 'it pours forth'.

And as in the world it is said, 'It is pitiable nothing flows' and *visarga* is called 'giving', therefore, there is absence of similarity of action.

Pradīpa: 70.3 भूषाकर्मेति।

"(Prohibition of *karmavat* for *dhātus*) having the sense of the act of adorning."

The word *karma* (here) expresses action. And the fruit of 'adorning' is called bright, handsome. Seen in relation to the object thus, the adorning is situated in the object. And the mention of *bhūṣā* (adorning) is for the sake of that not ending in *ṇi* (causative), because the prohibition being establihsed of *yak* and *ciṇ* by what is going to be stated for those ending in *ṇi*. Therefore, 'the girl adorns herself' and 'the girl adorned herself' are valid forms.

70.6 अवकिरत इति। (The elephant) smears itself or pours water on itself.

Someone smears the elephant with soil/pollen etc. In that context the elephant is intended to be expressed as with the agency owing to the ease of the action.

Pradīpa: 70.7 चिकीर्षत इति।

"(The mat) desires to make itself (as it were)."

Here, with regard to the action of making, there is the action situated in the object. However, desire is in the agent only, and due to (that) meaning there is predominance for *dhātu kṛ* because of desire having that as its purpose.

Notes

[1] c.f. कर्तरि कर्मव्यतिहारे 1.3.14

66.20 धातोरिति। "After a *dhātu.*"

धातोरेकाचो हलादेःक्रियासमभिहारे यङ् (3.1.22) See text.

धातोः कर्मण इति। "(*Karmavat* is extended for the agent which is) after the object of a *dhātu.*"

The meaning is for the agent after a *karman*/object (of a *dhātu*)

[2] 67.4 अचीकरतेति "(The mat) made itself."

Even when *yak* and *ciṇ* are prohibited, *caṅ* and *śap* relating to their own resort, do not obtain.

णिश्रिद्रुस्रुभ्यः कर्तरि चङ् (3.1.48)

"After a *dhātu* ending in *ṇi* (*3.1.20, 21, 25, 26* etc.) and after the *dhātus śri* (to serve), *dru* (to run), and *sru* (to drop), *caṅ* is the *ādeśa* of *cli,* when *liṅ* follows signifying the agent."

यक्चिणोः प्रतिषधे हेतुमण्णिश्रिब्रूञामुपसंख्यानम् (3.1.89) वा॰ 1

"When there is prohibition of the use of *pratyayas yak* and *ciṇ* in the reflexive passive, there should be additional enumeration of *dhātus* taking *ṇa* and *dhātus sri* and *brūñ.*"

[3] 67.5 नमते। "(The stick) bends (of itself)."

कर्तरि शप् (3.1.68) "*Śap* acts after a *dhātu* when a *sārvadhātuka pratyaya* follows signifying the agent."

यक्चिणोः प्रतिषेधे ··· आत्मनेपद अकर्मकानाम् उपसंख्यानम् (3.1.81) वा॰ 2

"When there is prohibition of the use of the *pratyaya yak* and *ciṇ* in the reflexive passive, there should be additional enumeration of *ātmanepada* and intransitive *dhātus.*"

[4] भिदुरमिति। "(The wood) is splitting (of itself)."
कर्तरिकृत् (3.4.67)
"The *pratyayas* called *kṛt* act in the sense of agent."
विदिभिदिच्छिदेःकुरच् (3.2.162)
"The *pratyaya kurac* acts in the sense of agent having such a habit etc. after the *dhātus vid* (to know), *bhid* (to divide), and *chid* (to pierce)."
kurac does obtain in the sense of agent. The rule 'the agent of that ending in a *la* is *karmavat*' is not just now established because it has been stated that a *kṛt* rule is not established as valid.

[5] 67.16 कृत्यक्तखलर्थेषु प्रतिषेधः। "Prohibition of *karmavat* when *kṛtya pratyayas*, *kta* and those having the meaning *khal* follow."
तयोरेव कृत्यक्तखलार्थाः।। (3.4.70) (भावे कर्मणि)
"The *pratyayas* called *kṛtya* and the *pratyaya kta* and those having the sense of *khal* have only the sense of impersonal action and object."

[6] 68.15 हन्त्यात्मानम्। "He kills himself."
c.f. हन्ता चेन्मन्यते हन्तुं हतश्चेन्मन्यते हतम्।
उभौ तौ न विजानीतो नायं हन्ति न हन्यते।।
कठ उप॰ 1.2.19
"If the killer thinks (of it) in terms of killing, and if the killed thinks (of it) as killed, both of them do not know. It does not kill, nor is it killed."
आत्मना हन्यत आत्मेति।
The self is killed by the Self.
c.f. उद्धरेदात्मनाऽत्मानं नात्मानमवसादयेत्।
आत्मैव ह्यात्मनो बन्धुरात्मैव रिपुरात्मनः।।
गीता 6.5
"Let a man raise himself by himself, let him not lower himself; for, he alone is the friend of himself, he alone is the enemy of himself."
बन्धुरात्माऽऽत्मनस्तस्य येनात्मैवात्मना जितः।
अनात्मनस्तु शत्रुत्वे वर्ततात्मैव शत्रुवत्।। 6.6
"To him who has (conquered) himself by himself, his own self is the friend of himself, but to him who has not (conquered) himself, his own self stands in the place of an enemy like the external (foe)."

[7] 68.27 वचनं। तपस्तपः कर्मकस्यैव (3.1.88)
"The agent of *dhātu tap* (to heat) becomes like the object/*karmavat* only when the object is the word *tapas* itself."

[8] 69.16 श्यंस्तु भवति
दिवादिभ्यः श्यन् (3.1.69)

"*Pratyaya śyan* acts after a *dhātu* of the *div-ādi gaṇa* when a *sārvadhātuka pratyaya* follows", signifying the agent.

श्रद्धोपपन्न इति।

"(When the agent of *dhātu sṛj*) is endowed with faith (there is *karmavat* condition)."

The meaning is when the agent is endowed with faith.

न दुहस्नुनमां यक्चिणौ ॥ 3 । 1 । 89 ॥

Pāṇini 3.1.89: The *pratyaya yak* (*3.1.67*) and *ciṇ* (3.1.62) *acaḥ karmakartari* do not act in the reflexive passive voice of the *dhātu duh* (to milk) *sru* (to flow) and *nam* (to bow).

70.9 यक्चिणोः प्रतिषेधे हेतुमण्णिश्रिब्रूञामुपसंख्यानम् ॥ 1 ॥

Vārttika: When there is prohibition of *yak* and *ciṇ* there should be additional enumeration of *dhātus* ending in the causative *ṇi*, and or *śri* and of *brū*.

70.10 यक्चिणोः प्रतिषेधे हेतुमण्णिश्रिब्रूञामुपसंख्यानं कर्तव्यम्। णि। कारयते कटः स्वयमेव।
अचीकरत कटः स्वयमेव। णि। श्रि। उच्छ्रयते दण्डः स्वयमेव। उदशिश्रियत दण्डः
स्वयमेव।। श्रि। ब्रूञ्। ब्रूते कथा स्वयमेव। अवोचत्त कथा
70.13 स्वयमेव।।
भारद्वाजीयाः पठन्ति। यक्चिणोः प्रतिषेधे णिश्रन्थिग्रन्थिब्रूञात्मनेपदाकर्मकाणा-
70.15 मुपसंख्यानमिति।।

Bhāṣya: When there is prohibition of *yak* and *ciṇ* additional enumeration should be made of *dhātus* ending in the causative *ṇi*, of *śri* and of *brū*.

ṇi (e.g.)

kārayate kaṭaḥ svayam eva "The mat is caused to make itself",

acīkarata kaṭaḥ svayam eva "The mat was caused to make itself",

(end of *ṇi* example).

śri (e.g.)

ucchrayate daṇḍaḥ svayam eva "The stick is raised of itself",

udaśiśriyata daṇḍaḥ svayam eva "The stick was raised of itself",

(end of *śri* example).

brūñ (e.g.)

brūte kathā svayam eva "The story is told of itself",

avocata kathā svayam eva "The story was told of itself",

(end of *brūñ* example).

The followers of *Bhāradvāja* read "when there is prohibition of *yak* and *ciṇ* there should be additional enumeration of *ṇi* ending *dhātus* of *dhātus śranth-i* (to be loosened), *granth-i* (to fasten) and *brūñ* (to speak) and of *ātmanepada* and intransitive *dhātus.*

Pradīpa

Pradīpa: 70.9 न दुहस्नु यकचिणोरिति।

(When there is prohibition) of *yak* and *ciṇ* ...

In the context where *ātmanepada* has been ordained, those *dhātus* which are indicated as intransitive when the sense of the causative *ṇi* is implied, become transitive. Then, because of the nature of being like the object, when *yak* and *ciṇ* obtained they would be prohibited. As 'horses move to and fro/shake feet etc.)'.

विकुर्वते सैन्धवाः (The meaning is they bound leap or gallop.)

When another causes them to leap or gallop, then there is the nature of being object for them. Again when there is the intention to express agency/due to (its indicating) extreme ease (of performance), *yak* and *ciṇ* are not applicable (here), 'the horses leap/gallop or themselves (as it were)', 'The horses leapt of themselves',

उत्पुच्छयते गौः

Here too, 'The cow raises its tail (of itself)', because of the meaning of *ṇi*/causative being implied due to being 'like the object', there is obtainment for *yak* and *ciṇ*.

Pradīpa: 70.12 ब्रूते कथेति।

"The story is told (of itself)."

The speaking, due to its nature as the fruit of illuminating the word, is situated in the object.

कुषिरजोः प्राचां श्यन्परस्मैपदं च ॥ 3 । 1 । 90 ॥

Pāṇini 3.1.90: The *pratyaya śyan* acts after *dhātus kuṣ* (to pull) and *rañj* (to colour) in the reflexive passive voice, according to the opinion of the Eastern Grammarians and these *dhātus* take *parasmaipada pratyayas.*

70.17 कुषिरजोः श्यन्विधाने सार्वधातुकवचनम् ॥ 1 ॥

Vārttika 1: Mention (should be made) of *sārvadhātuka* when *śyan* is ordained for the *dhātus kuṣ-i* and *raj.*

70.18 कुषिरजोः श्यन्विधाने सार्वधातुकग्रहणं कर्तव्यम्।

Bhāṣya: Mention should be made of *sārvadhātuka* when *śyan* is ordained for *kuṣ-i* and *raj* (*dhātus*).

70.19 अवचने हि लिङ्लिटोः प्रतिषेधः ॥ 2 ॥

Vārttika 2: For if mention is not made, prohibition of *liṅ* (optative) and *liṭ* (perfect) (has to be stated).

70.20 अक्रियमाणे हि सार्वधातुकग्रहणे लिङ्लिटोः प्रतिषेधो वक्तव्यः स्यात्।

Bhāṣya: For it would have to be stated that there is prohibition of *liṅ* and *liṭ* when mention of *sārvadhātuka pratyayas* is not being made.

70.21 चुकुषे पादः स्वयमेव। ररञ्जे वस्त्रं स्वयमेव। कोषिषीष्ट पादः स्वयमेव। रङ्क्षीष्ट वस्त्रं स्वयमेव॥ क्रियमाणेऽपि सार्वधातुकग्रहण इह प्राप्नोति। कतीह कुष्णानाः[1] पादाः। श्यना च स्यादीनां बाधनं प्राप्नोति॥ कोषिष्यते पादः स्वयमेव। रङ्क्ष्यते वस्त्रं स्वयमेव। अकोषि पादः स्वयमेव। अरञ्जि वस्त्रं स्वय-

71.2 मेव॥

cukuṣe pādaḥ svayam eva "The foot withdrew itself",

rarañje vastram svayam eva "The cloth coloured itself",

koṣiṣīṣta pādaḥ svayam eva "May the foot draw itself out",

raṅkṣīṣta vastram svayam eva "May the cloth colour itself".

Even when the mention of *sārvadhātuka pratyaya* is being made it obtains here *katīha kuṣṇānāḥ pādāḥ* "How many feet are there withdrawing (themselves)?" The *pratyaya cānaś* acts after a *dhātu* in expressing habit, standard of age and ability.

The *tiṅ* (verbal *pratyayas*) and *pratyayas* with an indicatory *ś* have the name *sārvadhātuka.*

And the barring of *sya* and the rest by *śyan* obtains.

koṣiṣyate pādaḥ svayam eva "the foot will withdrw of itself",

raṅkṣyate vastram svayam eva "The cloth will colour itself",

arañji vastram svayam eva "The cloth coloured itself."

71.3 यत्तावदुच्यते सार्वधातुकग्रहणं कर्तव्यमिति न कर्तव्यम्। प्रकृतमनुवर्तते।
क्व प्रकृतम्। सार्वधातुके यक् (67) इति। यदि तदनुवर्तते पूर्वस्मिन्योगे किं
71.5 समुच्चयः। ले च सार्वाधातुके चेति। आहोस्विल्लग्रहणं सार्वधातुकविशेषणम्।
किंचातः। यदि समुच्चयः कतीह भिन्दानाः कुशूला इत्यत्रापि प्राप्नोति। अथ
लग्रहणं सार्वधातुकविशेषणं लिङ्लिटोर्न सिध्यति।। बिभिदे कुशूलः स्वयमेव।
भित्सीष्ट
71.8 कुशूलः स्वयमेवेति।।

As to that which was just said "a mention of *sārvadhātuka* should be made", it is not (in fact) to be made. The original word follows on from a previous *sūtra.* Where is the original? (In the *sūtra*) *sārvadhātuke yak 3.1.67.* If that follows on from a previous rule, is it the connecting (of two words by *ca*/ and)? (As) "when a *la* (tense/mood *pratyaya*) follows and when a *sārvadhātuka pratyaya* follows". Or else is the mention of *la* a qualification of *sārvadhātuka*? And what follows from that? If it is a connecting, *śyan* wrongly obtains here *katīha bhindānāḥ* "Here how many granaries are splitting (of themselves)?" If the mention of *la* /(tense/mood *pratyaya*) is a qualification of *sārvadhātuka,* (then the prohibition of *śyan*) when *liṭ* (perfect) follows is not established as valid. (e.g.)

bibhide kuśūlaḥ svayam eva "The granary split itself",

bhitṣīṣta kuśūlaḥ svayam eva "May the granary split of itself".

71.8 .... अस्तु लग्रहणं सार्वधातुकविशेषणम्। ननु चोक्तं लिङ्लिटोर्न
सिध्यति।। लिङ्लङ्ग्रहणमपि प्रकृतमनुवर्तते। क्व प्रकृतम्। कास्प्रत्ययादा-
71.10 ममन्त्रे लिटि (35) लिङ्याशिष्यङ् (86) इति। एवं च कृत्वा सोऽप्यदोषो
भवति यदुक्तं कतीह कुष्णानाः पादा इति प्राप्नोतीति। अत्रापि लविशिष्टं सार्व-
71.12 धातुकग्रहणमनुवर्तते।।

Let the mention of *la* be the qualification of *sārvadhātuka.* But surely it was stated "when *liṅ* or *liṭ* follows it is not established as valid". The original mention of *liṅ* and *liṭ* also follows on from previous *sūtras.* Where is the original ? (In the *sūtras*) *kās-pratyayād āmamantre liṭi 3.1.35* ("The *pratyaya* *ām* acts after the *dhātu kās* (to cough) and those *dhātus* formed by *pratyayas* when *liṭ* (perfect) follows except in the "*mantra/veda*" and *liṅyāśiṣyaṅ 3.1.86* ("The *pratyaya aṅ* acts in the *Chandas/Veda* when the *pratyayas* of the *āśir-liṅ* (benedictive) follow"). And thus having made (this statement), that also which was stated (previously) is applicable without fault; thus obtains *kutīha kuṣṇānāḥ pādāḥ* "How many feet are drawing themselves out?" Here the mention of *sārvadhātuka* qualified by *la* (tense/mood *pratyaya*) follows on from a previous *sūtra*.

71.13 यदप्युच्यते श्यना च स्यादीनां बाधनं प्राप्नोति यक्प्रतिषेधसंबन्धेन श्यनं
वक्ष्यामि। न दुहस्नुनमां यक्चिणौ (89) ततः कुषिरजोः प्राचां यक्चिणौ न
भवतः। ततः श्यन्परस्मैपदं येति।। यथैव तर्हि यको विषये श्यन्भवत्येवं चिणो-
71.16 ऽपि विषये प्राप्नोति। अकोषि पादः स्वयमेव। अरञ्जि वस्त्रं स्वयमेवेति।।

As to what also (was) said "and barring of *sya* and the rest by *śyan* obtains", I will state *śyan* by the connection with prohibition of *yak*. *na dahasnunamāṅ yakciṇau 3.1.89* (The *pratyaya yak* (*3.1.67*) and *ciṇ* (*3.1.62*) do not act in the reflexive passive voice of the *dhātus duh* (to milk) *snu* (to fall in drops) and *nam* (to bow)". Then in the opinion of the Eastern Grammarians *yak* and *ciṇ* are not applicable after *kuṣ* and *raj*. Then *śyan* (is applicable) and there are *parasmaipada pratyayas* (after it).

As in fact then *śyan* is applicable in the context of *yak*, it also obtains in the context of *ciṇ*.

akoṣi pādaḥ vastram svayam eva "The foot was withdrawn of itself",

arañjivastram svayam eva "The garment was coloured of itself".

71.16 .... एवं
तर्हि द्वितीयो योगविभागः करिष्यते। न दुहस्नुनमां चिण्भवति। ततो यक्। यक् च
न भवति दुहस्नुनमाम्। ततः कुषिरजोः प्राचां यग्न भवति। ततः श्यन्परस्मैपदं
च।। अथवानुवृत्तिः करिष्यते। स्यतासी लृलुटोः (33) च्लि लुङि (43)
71.20 च्लेः सिज्भवति। कर्तरि शप् (68) स्यतासी लृलुटोः च्लि लुङि च्लेः सिज्भवतीति।।
दिवादिभ्यः श्यन् (69) स्यतासी लृलुटोः च्लि लुङि च्लेः सिज्भवतीति। कुषिरजोः
प्राचां श्यन्परस्मैपदं च स्यतासी लृलुटोः च्लि लुङि च्लेः सिज्भवतीति।। अथवा-
71.23 न्तरङ्गाः स्यादयः कान्तरङ्गता लकारावस्थायामेव स्यादयः सार्वधातुके श्यन्।।

Well then the second separation of the rule (into two parts) will be made. (1) *ciṇ* is not applicable for the *dhātus duh, sun* and *nam* (in the reflexive passive) (2) and *yak* is not applicable for *dhātus duh, sun* and *nam*. Then in the opinion of the Eastern Grammarians *yak* is not applicable after the *dhātus kuṣ-i* and *raj*. Then *śyan* (is applicable) and *parasmaipada pratyayas* (follow it).

Otherwise (words) following on from previous *sūtras* will be effected (i.e.) *syatāsī lṛluṭoḥ 3.1.33* (when *lṛ* and *luṭ* follow and *tāsi* acts as the *vikaraṇa* after *dhātus*".) *Cli luṅi 3.1.43* ("In the presence of *luṅ cli* acts after a *dhātu*)", *cleḥ sic 3.1.44* ("In place of *cli sic* acts as the *ādeśa*"). Thus *kartari śap 3.1.68* ("The *pratyaya śap* acts after a *dhātu* when a *sārvadhātuka pratyaya* follows signifying the agent") *syatāsī lṛluṭoḥ 3.1.33, cli luṅi* (*3.1.43*), ("*Cli* acts when *luṅ* follows") and by *cleḥ sic, sic* is applicable in place of *cli* (which in turn acts in place of *śap*). (By the *sūtra*) *divādibhyaḥ śyan 3.1.69* ("After the *dhātus div* and the rest *śyan* acts as *ādeśa* in place of *śap* when a *sārvadhātuka pratyaya* follows signifying the agent"); (for the future and conditional tenses) *syatāsī lṛluṭoḥ* (follow on, and for the formation of the aorist by) *cli luṅi* and *cleḥ, sic, sic* is applicable (after these *dhātus*). "In the opinion of the Eastern Grammarians *śyan* acts after the *dhātus kuṣ* and *raj* (in the reflexive passive) and there are the *parasmaipada pratyayas* after them" when *lṛ* and *luṭ* follow *sya* and *tāsī* are the *vikaraṇas* and when the aorist *luṅ* follows *cli* is *pratyaya* (in place of *śap*) and is applicable as *ādeśa* in place of *cli*.

Otherwise *sya* and the rest are *antaraṅga* (more inner/requiring fewer operations). What is the nature of *antaraṅga* ? *Sya* and the rest are applicable when there is only (one) condition, namely that the *la* (tense/mood *pratyaya* be) following, (but) *śyan* (has the other condition as well) 'when a *sārvadhātuka pratyaya* follows (signifying the agent)'.

Pradīpa

Pradīpa: 70.17 कुषिरजो:।

"(Mention should be made of *sārvadhātuka* when *śyan* is ordained) for *kuṣ* and *rañj*."

When *yak* obtains, *śyan* is ordained. Therefore when *śyan* follows by the *sūtra*

ञ्नित्यादिर्नित्यम् (6.1.197)

"What is derived with a *pratyaya* having it *ñ* or *n* (as *śyan*), has *udātta* invariably on the first syllable."

And *num* augment is invariable by

शप्श्यनोर्नित्यम् (7.1.81)

"When *pratyaya śatṛ* acts after an *aṅga* ending in *vikaraṇas śap* and *śyan*, it invariably takes augment *num* before the neuter case ending *śī* (*ī* and the feminine ending *ī* (*nadī*)."

कुष्यन्ती जंघा
"The shanks are being drawn out (or weighed?)."

Pradīpa: 70.17 सार्वधातुकवचनमिति।

"Mention (should be made) of *sārvadhātuka*."

The meaning is when *sārvadhātuka* is stated as the sphere, then *śyan* and *parasmaipada* are applicable.

Pradīpa: 70.23 श्यना चेति।

"Barring of *sya* etc. by *śyan* obtains."

The sense is because of the nature of being ordained as a special (or *apavāda*) *pratyaya*.

Pradīpa: 70.13 यक्प्रतिषेधसंबन्धेनेति।

"(I will state *śyan*) by the connection with prohibition of *yak*."

Therefore, where there is prohibition of *yak* obtaining, there *śyan* and *parasmaipada* are applicable, nowhere else. Thefore they are not applicable in the sphere of *sya* and the rest.

Pradīpa: 70.23 लकारावस्थायामेवेति।

"(*Sya* and the rest are applicable when there is) only (one condition) that the *la* (tense *pratyaya*) be following.

when the *ādeśas* of *la* have not in fact been effected, those ordained as special *pratyayas sya* and the rest are applicable, 'before'. Because of conflict of *śyan* with them, due to the nature of being barred, the remaining (secondary) injunction (for) *parasmaipada* also is not applicable.

Notes

[1] 70.23 कुष्णाना इति।
"(How many feet are) withdrawing themselves (or being balanced)?"
ताच्छील्यवयोवचनशक्तिषु चानश् (3.2.129)
"The *pratyaya cānaś* acts after a *dhātu* in expressing habit, standard of age and ability."
Here *śyan* obtains, and *parasmaipada* he thinks is propounded as a matter of secondary importance.
तिङ्शित्सार्वधातुकम् (3.4.113)

"The *tiṅ*/verbal *pratyayas* and those having an *it ś (e.g. cānaś)* have the name *sārvadhātuka*.

धातोः ॥ 3 । 1 । 91 ॥

Pāṇini 3.1.91: After a *dhātu* (acts a *pratyaya* to the end of the third *adhyāya*)

70.24 आ कुतोऽयं धात्वधिकारः। किं प्राग्लादेशात्[1]। आहोस्विदा तृतीयाध्यायपरिसमाप्तेः।

Bhāṣya: Up to where is this *dhātu* governing *sūtra* applicable? Is it as far as the *ādeśas* of *la* ?

Or else up to the conclusion of the third *adhyāya* ?

72.1 धात्वधिकारः प्राग्लादेशात् ॥ 1 ॥

Vārttika 1: The *dhātu* governing rule is applicable up to the substitutes of *la.*

72.2 प्राग्लादेशाद्धात्वधिकारः॥

Bhāṣya: The *dhātu* governing rule is applicable up the *ādeśas* of *la.*

72.3 लादेशे हि व्यवहितात्वादप्रसिद्धः॥ 2 ॥

Vārttika 2: For when the *ādeśas* of *la* follow because of *vikaraṇas* intervening (between *la* and the *dhātu*) it is not established (as validly present).

72.4 अनुवर्तमाने हि लादेशे धात्वधिकारे व्यवहितत्वादप्रसिद्धः स्यात्। किं च स्यात्।

Bhāṣya: For when the *adeśas* of *la* follow on from previous *sūtras* in the sphere of the *dhātu* governing rule, because of (*vikaraṇas*) intervening the word would not be established as validly present and what would happen?

72.6 आद्ये योगे न व्यवाये तिङः स्युः

Vārttika a: In the first rule (after *lasya 3.4.77*) *tiṅ* (verbal *pratyayas 3.4.78*) would not be applicable when (*vikaraṇas*) intervene.

72.7 आद्ये योगे[2] विकरणैर्व्यवहितत्वात्तिङो न स्युः। पचति पठतीति॥ इदमिह संप्रधार्यम्। विकरणाः क्रियन्तामादेशा इति किमत्र कर्तव्यम्।

Bhāṣya: In the first rule (3.4.78), because of being separated by *vikaraṇa pratyayas* the *tiṅ* (verbal *pratyayas*) would not be applicable after *dhātu*.

pacati "He cooks", *paṭhati* "He recites".

This here should be reflected upon. Whether the *vikaraṇa pratyayas* be produced or the *ādeśas*? What is to be done here?

72.8 .... परत्वादादेशाः।
नित्या विकरणाः[3]। कृतेष्वप्यादेशेषु प्राप्नुवन्त्यकृतेष्वपि प्राप्नुवन्ति। नित्यत्वा-
द्विकरणेषु कृतेषु विकरणैर्व्यवहितत्वादादेशा न प्राप्नुवन्ति। अनवकाशास्तर्ह्यादेशाः।।
सावकाशा आदेशाः। कोऽवकाशः। य एते लुग्विकरणाः श्लुविकरणाश्च
72.12 लिङ्लिटौ च।।

Because of being subsequent rules the *ādeśas* (should prevail). Because of being invariable rules the *vikaraṇas* (would prevail). Even when the *ādeśas* have been effected they obtain and also when they have not been produced (*vikaraṇas*) obtain. When because of being invariable the *vikaraṇas* are effected, *ādeśas* do not obtain due to being separated by *vikaraṇas*. Then the *ādeśas* do not have scope of application. The *ādeśas* do have scope of application. What scope? (In the context of) these *luk* and *ślu vikaraṇa pratyayas* and when *liṅ* (optative) and *liṭ* (perfect) follow.

72.13 न स्यादेत्वं टेष्टितां यद्विधत्ते।

Vārttika b: The substitution of *e* which he ordains in place of the *ṭi* portion of those la (tense/mood *pratyayas*) having an indicatory *ṭ* would not be applicable.

72.14 यच्च टित्संज्ञानामेत्वं विधते[4] तच्च विकरणैर्व्यवहितत्वान्न स्यात्।

Bhāṣya: And that substitution of *e* which he ordains in place of the *ṭi* portion of those *la* (tense/mood *pratyayas*) having the technical name *ṭit* (having an indicatory *ṭ*) and due to being separated by *vikaraṇa pratyayas*, would not be applicable.

72.15 एशः शित्वं।

Vārttika c: The *ādeśa eś* has to be formed having an indicatory *ś*.

72.16 एकारश्च शित्कर्तव्यः[5]। किं प्रयोजनम्। शित्सर्वस्येति सर्वादेशो यथा स्यात्।
अक्रियमाणे हि शकारे तस्मादित्युत्तरस्यादेशःपरस्य (1.1.67,54) इति
72.18 तकारस्यैत्वे कृते द्वयोरेकारयोः श्रवणं प्रसज्येत।

Bhāṣya: And the *ādeśa e* should be formed having an indicatory *ś*. What is the reason? So that *e* having an *it ś* be *ādeśa* of the whole (of the original/*sthānin* in the sixth case) by the *sūtra anekāl śit sarvasya 1.1.55* "An *ādeśa* of more than one letter or having an indicatory *ś* acts in place of the whole of that original/*sthānin* ending in the sixth case". For if it were not being produced with an indicatory *ś*, (because of the *sūtras*) *tasmādityuttarasya 1.1.67* "When there is indication in the fifth case, a grammatical operation is for that following" and *ādeḥ parasya 1.1.54* "The operation is for the first letter of that which immediately follows (that in the fifth case)". When a letter *e* is (thus) effected in place of the letter *t* (being the first letter of *ta*) the hearing of two '*e*'s, would be applicable.

72.18 .... निवृत्ते पुनर्लादेशे धात्वधिकारे-ऽलोऽन्त्यस्य विधयो[6] भवन्तीत्येकारस्यैकारवचने प्रयोजनं नास्तीति कृत्वान्तेरणापि
72.20 शकारं सर्वादेशो भविष्यति।।

But when the *dhātu* governing rule ends when *ādeśas* of *la* (tense/mood *pratyayas* begin), the *ādeśa* rules are applicable (according to the *sūtra*) *alo'ntyasya 1.1.52* ("An *ādeśa* acts in place of only the final letter of that indicated in the sixth case"). But since there is no purpose in enjoining the letter *e* in place of the letter *e*, even without the letter *ś* it will therefore act as *ādeśa* in place of the whole (of the original/*sthānin*.)

72.21 यच्च लोटो विधत्ते

Vārttika d: And what (*ādeśas*) he enjoins for *loṭ* (imperative) (would not be applicable).

72.22 तच्च विकरणैर्व्यवहितत्वान्न स्यात्। किं पुनस्तत्। लोटो लङ्वत् एरुः सेर्ह्यपिच्च वा छन्दसि (3.4.85-88) इति।।

Bhāṣya: And that would not be applicable because of being separated by *vikaraṇas*. But what again is that? (The *sūtras*) *loṭo laṅvat* (*3.4.85*) "The personal endings of the imperative are like those of the imperfect". *eruḥ* (*3.4.86*) ("In place of the *i* of the imperative there is *u*"). *serhy apic-ca 3.4.87* ("*Hi* is the *ādeśa* for *si* of *loṭ* and this has not the indicatory *p* of *sip* i.e. it is *udātta*) and *vā chandasi 3.4.88* ("In the *Veda* the *ādeśa hi* is optionally treated as not having an indicatory *p*").

72.24 यच्चाप्युक्तं लङ्लिङोस्तच्च न स्यात्।

Vārttika e: And that which was stated (previously when *laṅ* or *liṅ* follow, too would not be applicable.)

72.25 किं पुनस्तत्। नित्यं ङितः इतश्च तस्थस्थमिपां ताम्तम्तामः लिङः सीयुट् यासुट् परस्मैपदेषूदात्तो ङिच्च (99-103) इति। तस्मात्प्राग्लादेशाद्धात्वधिकारः।।

Bhāṣya: What again is that? (the *sūtras*) *nityam ṅitaḥ 3.4.99,* "There is always *lopa* elision of the *s* of the *uttama puruṣa*/first person *pratyayas* that act in the place of that *la* (tense/mood *pratyaya*) having an indicatory *ṅ*".

itaśca 3.4.100 "And there is *lopa* elision of the *i* of that *parasmaipada pratyaya* which is *ādeśa* of a *la* having an indicatory *ṅ*"

tas thas tha mip ām tām tam tāmaḥ 3.4.101 "The *ādeśas tām, tam, ta* and *am* respectively act in the place of the *tiṅ pratyaya tas, thas, tha* and *mip* of any *la* having an indicatory *ṅ*". *liṅaḥ sīyuṭ 3.4.102* "The personal endings of the potential and the benedictive have the *āgama sīyuṭ* and *yāsuṭ parasmaipadeṣūdātto ṅicca 3.4.103,* "When the *parasmaipada pratyayas* of the potential follow then *yāsuṭ udātta* is their *āgama* and the termination is regarded as having an *it ṅ*".

Therefore the *dhātu* governing rule is applicable as far as the *ādeśas* of *la.*

73.2 यदि प्राग्लादेशाद्धात्वधिकारोऽकारः[7] शित्कर्तव्यः। किं प्रयोजनम्। शित्सर्व-
स्येति सर्वादेशो यथा स्यात्। अनुवर्तमाने पुनर्लादेशे धात्वधिकारे तस्मादित्युत्तरस्यादेः
परस्येति थकारस्यात्वे कृते द्वयोरकारयोः पररूपेण[8] सिद्धं रूपं स्यात्
73.5 पेच यूयम् चक्र यूयमिति। ननु च निवृत्तेऽपि लादेशे धात्वधिकारेऽलोऽन्त्यस्य
विधयो भवन्तीत्यकारस्याकारवचने प्रयोजनं नास्तीति कृत्वान्तरेणापि शकारं
73.6 सर्वादेशो भविष्यति॥

If the *dhātu* governing rule governs as far as the *ādeśas* of *la,* the letter *a* (of the perfect) should be made to have an indicatory *ś*. What is the purpose? So that, (according to the *sūtra anekāl śitsarvasya 1.1.55* "An *ādeśa* of more than one letter or having an indicatory *ś* acts in place of the whole of the original indicated in the sixth case"), it would thus be *ādeśa* of the whole of the original/*sthānin* (i.e. *tha* here). Again, when there is the following of the *dhātu* governing rule in the sphere of *ādeśas* of *la,* afer *a* is substituted in place of the *th,* the forms (for instance) *peca* "You cooked", *cakra* "You made", will be formed by effecting *pararūpa* (substitute) in place of both the *akāras* (letter *a*'s) and (because of the *ṣūtras*) *tasmād ity uttarasya 1.1.67* and *ādeḥ parasya 1.1.54 e* is in place of *tha* (i.e. only the first letter of that). But surely even when the *dhātu* governing rule ceases to follow on in the context of the *ādeśas* of *la* by the *sūtra alo'ntyasya.* "The *ādeśa* acts in the place of only the final letter of the *sthānin* indicatd in the sixth case"; *a* would be substituted in place of the final *a.* But since there is no purpose in enjoining a letter *a* in place of letter *a,* the *ādeśa* will be in place of the whole (of the *sthānin*) even without the indicatory letter *ś.*

73.7 .... अस्त्यन्यदकारस्याकारवचने प्रयोजनम्। किम्। वक्ष्यत्ये-
तदकारस्याकारवचनं समसंख्यार्थमिति[9]॥ आर्धधातुकसंज्ञायां[10] धातुग्रहणं कर्तव्यं
धातोः परस्यार्धधातुकसंज्ञा यथा स्यात्। इह मा भूत् वृक्षत्वम् वृक्षतेति।
73.10 तस्माल्लादेशे धात्वधिकारोऽनुवर्त्यः।

Bhāṣya: There is another purpose in enjoining the letter *a* in place of the letter *a*. What? We will state this "the expressing of *a* in place of *a* is for the purpose of the same number (of *ādeśas* and *sthānins*) (*3.4.82 Vā.4*).

When the technical name *ārdhadhātuka* (is defined by *sūtra ārdhadhātukam śeṣaḥ 3.4.114* ("The remainder of the *pratyayas* other than *tiṅ* and those with an indicatory *ś* acting after a *dhātu* are called *ārdhadhātuka*"), mention has to be made of the word *dhātu*, so that the technical name *ārdhadhātuka* would be for that which follows after a *dhātu/dhātoḥ*, and (so that) it should not be applicable here *vṛkṣa-tvam, vṛkṣatā* (*tva/ta taddita pratyayas* following after a *kṛt* not a *dhātu*) "the state or notion of a tree". Therefore the *dhātu* governing rule is to follow on in the context of the (statement of) substitutes for *la*.

73.11 ननु चोक्तमाद्ये योगे न व्यवाये तिङः स्युरिति। नैष दोषः। आनुपूर्व्यात्सि-
द्धमेतत्। नात्राकृतेष्वादेशेषु विकरणाः प्राप्नुवन्ति। किं कारणम्। सार्वधातुके
विकरणा उच्यन्ते। न चाकृतेष्वादेशेषु सार्वधातुकत्वं भवति। ये तर्हि नैतस्मिन्वि-
शेषे विधीयन्ते। के पुनस्ते। स्यादयः[11]। तत्रापि विहितविशेषणं धातुग्रहणम्।

73.15 धातोर्विहितस्य लस्येति॥

But surely it was stated (in the *Vārttika*) "In the first rule (after *lasya 3.4.77*) *tiṅ* (verbal *pratyayas 3.4.78*) would not be applicable when (*vikaraṇa pratyayas*) intervene". This is not a fault. This is established as valid in due order. Here, when the *ādeśas* have not been effected, the *vikaraṇas* do not obtain. What is the reason? The *vikaraṇa pratyayas* are stated (to act) when a *sārvadhātuka pratyaya* follows. And when the *ādeśas* have not been effected the *sārvadhātuka* nature is not applicable. What about those then which are not ordained in the context of this specific condition? But which are they? *Sya* and the rest. There too the mention of *dhātu* (is necessary) as a qualifier of that which is ordained. *lasya* (*3.4.77*) *dhātoḥ* "In place of the *la* (tense/mood *pratyaya*) which has been ordained after a *dhātu* (act the *ādeśas tiṅ* etc.)".

73.15 .... यद्येवं विन्दतीति णलादयः प्राप्नुवन्ति[12]।
धातुनात्र विहितं विशेषयिष्यामो विदिना चानन्तर्यम्। धातोर्विहितस्य लस्य
विदेरनन्तरस्येति॥ इह तर्हि अजक्षिष्यन् अजागरिष्यन्नित्यभ्यस्ताज्झेर्जुस्भव-तीति[13]
जुस्भावः प्राप्नोति। अत्रापि धातुना विहितं विशेषयिष्यामोऽभ्यस्तेनानन्तर्यम्।
धातोर्विहित-

73.19 स्याभ्यस्तादनन्तरस्येति॥

If so, the *ādeśas ṇal* and the rest obtain (for the form) *vindati* ("He finds"). And here we shall specify "that which is ordained with a *dhātu* and in immediate sequence after the *dhātu vid*". 'In place of the *la* ordained immediately adjoining after the *dhātu vid* (*ṇal* is substituted)'.

Here then (in the examples) *a jakṣ-i-ṣyan* "They would have eaten", *ajāgariṣyan* "They would have woken", the application of *jus* obtains because of the rule that *jus* acts in place of *jhi* after a reduplicated *dhātu*.

Here too we shall qualify *vihita* "enjoined" with a "a *dhātu*" and the word *ānantaryam* "immediately adjoining" with a reduplicated (*dhātu*)". In place of that (*la*) which is enjoined after a *dhātu* and immediately adjoining a reduplicated *dhātu*".

73.19 .... आतः (3.4.110) इत्यत्र कथं विशेषयिष्यसि।
यदि तावद्धातुग्रहणं विहितविशेषणमाकारग्रहणमानन्तर्याविशेषणम् अलुनन्नित्यत्रापि
प्राप्नोति। अथाकारग्रहणं विहितविशेषणं धातुग्रहणमानन्तर्यविशेषणम्। अपिबन्नित्यत्रापि
प्राप्नोति[14]। अस्तु तर्हि धातुग्रहणंविहितविशेषणमाका रग्रहणमानन्तर्यविशेषणम्। ननु
चोक्तमलुनन्नित्यत्रापि प्राप्नोतीति। नैष दोषः। लोपे कृते
73.24 न भविष्यति।

"When *sic* is *luk* elided *jus* is *ādeśa* of *jhi* after an aorist *aṅga* ending in long *ā*". How will you distinguish here (in the *sūtra ātaḥ*) *3.4.110*? If just the mention of *dhātu* is the qualification of that enjoined and the mention of long *ā* is a qualification of that (which is) immediately adjoining, *jus* obtains here too (in the form) *a-lunam*". "They cut", (because of the *vikaraṇa śn-ā*) which is enjoined, and the mention of *dhātu* is a qualification of that which is immediately adjoining, (so) *jus* obtains here also in the form *apiban* "They drank" (from *dhātu pā*).

Then let there be mention of *dhātu* as the qualification of that which is enjoined (and) the mention of the letter *ā* as a qualification of that which is immediately adjoining the (*dhātu*). But surely it was stated (*jus*) obtains here too (in the form) *alunan* ? This is no fault. When *lopa* elision has been effected, (*jus*) will not be applicable.

73.24 ....नात्र लोपः प्राप्नोति। किं कारणम्। ईत्वेन बाध्यते। नात्रेत्वं
प्राप्नोति। किं कारणम्। अन्तिभावेन बाध्यते। नात्रान्तिभावः प्राप्नोति। किं
कारणम्। जुस्भावेन बाध्यते। नात्र जुस्भावः प्राप्नोति। किं कारणम्। लोपेन
बाध्यते। लोप ईत्वेनेत्वमन्तिभावेनान्तिभावो जुस्भावेन जुस्भावो लोपेनेति[15] चक्र-
74.1 कमव्यवस्था प्रसज्येत। नास्ति चक्रकप्रसङ्गः।

Bhāṣya: Here *lopa*/elison does not obtain. What is the reason? It is prevented by reason of the long *ī* being present. But here long *ī* does not obtain. What is the reason? It is prevented by reason of there being *Anti* (the substitute for jhi/3rd pl. parasmaipada). But here the condition for *anti* does not obtain. What is the reason?

It is prevented by reason of *jus* being present. But here *jus* does not obtain. What is the reason? It is barred by *lopa*. *Lopa*, by the state of long *ī* being present. The state of long *ī* by the condition for *anti*. The condition for *anti* by reason of *jus* being present. The reason for *jus* being present by virtue of *lopa*. Thus the 'wheel condition'/circularity would obtain. But there is no expectation for this circularity.

74.1 .... न ह्यव्यवस्थाकारिणा शास्त्रेण भवि-
तव्यम्। शास्त्रेण नाम व्यवस्थाकारिणा। न चात्रहलदिना मुहूर्तमपि शक्यमव स्थातुम्।
तावत्येवान्तिभावेन भवितव्यम्। अन्तिभावे कृते लोपः। लो-
74.4 पेन व्यवस्था भविष्यति।। यदप्युच्यत एशः शित्त्वमिति। क्रियते न्यास एव।।
74.5 कानि पुनरस्य योगस्य प्रयोजनानि।

For the science (of language) should not be producing irregularity. Indeed the science (of language) should be producing regularity. But here it is not possible for that beginning with a consonant to stay even for a moment. First in fact there should be the application of *anti*. When the *anti* has been effected *lopa* elision. By means of *lopa* there will be regular (derivation) of the proper form. As to that which is stated, namely "*eś* should have an indicatory *ś*" it is in fact already done in the text.

But what again is the purpose of this rule ?

74.6 प्रयोजनं प्रातिपदिकप्रतिषेधः ।। 3 ।।

Vārttika 3 : (One) purpose is the prohibition of (acting after *a*) *prātipadika*.

74.7 प्रातिपदिकप्रतिषेधः प्रयोजनम्। धातोस्तव्यदादयो[16] यथास्युः प्रातिपदिकान्मा
भूवन्निति।। नैतदस्ति प्रयोजनम्। साधने तव्यदादयो विधीयन्ते साधनं च क्रियायाः।
क्रियाभावात्साधनाभावः। साधनाभावादसत्यपि धात्वधिकारे प्रातिपदिका-
74.10 त्तव्यदादयो न भविष्यन्ति।

Bhāṣya: Prohibition of (acting after) a *prātipadika* is the one purpose. So that *tavya* and the rest should not act after a *dhātu* and should not act after a *prātipadika*. This is not the purpose. *Tavya* and the rest are ordained in the sense of that which is the instrumental means and the instrumental means is for the accomplishment of verbal activity. Due to absence of a verbal action, there is absence of an instrument for accomplishing it. Even when no *dhātu* governing rule exists, *tavyat* and the rest will not be applicable after a *prātipadika*.

74.11 स्वपादिषु ।। 4 ।।

Vārttika 4 : Another purpose is in relation to the (*dhātus*) *svap* and the rest.

74.12 स्वपादिषु तर्हि प्रयोजनम्। स्वपिति। स्वपिति मा भूत्।।

Bhāṣya: Then there is another purpose in relation to (the *dhātus svap* and the rest, (e.g.) *svap-iti* "He sleeps". So that is should not be (the *samprasāraṇa* form) *supa-ti.*

74.13 अङ्गसंज्ञा च ।। 5 ।।

Vārttika 5 : And (a purpose is for forming) the technical name *aṅga.*

74.14 अङ्गसंज्ञा च प्रयोजनम्। यस्मात्प्रत्यविधिस्तदादि प्रत्ययेऽङ्गम् (1.4.13) इति धातोरङ्गसंज्ञा सिद्धा भवति।।

Bhāṣya: And one purpose is (the formation of) the technical name *aṅga.* The technical name *aṅga* is established as valid "after a *dhātu*" (by the *sūtra yasmātpratyayavidhistadādi pratyaye'ṅgam 1.4.13* "After whatsoever there is a *pratyaya* enjoined (be it *dhātu* or *prātipadika*), the word form having that as its beginning is called an *aṅga* in relation to the *pratyaya* which follows".

74.16 कृत्संज्ञा च ।। 6 ।।

Vārttika 6 : And (one purpose is for forming) the technical name *kṛt.*

74.17 कृत्संज्ञा च प्रयोजनम्। धातुविहितस्य प्रत्ययस्य कृत्संज्ञा सिद्धा भवति[17]।।

Bhāṣya: And one purpose (is for forming) the technical name *kṛt.* The technical name *kṛt* is established as valid for a *pratyaya* enjoined after a *dhātu* (by the *sūtra kṛd-a-tiṅ 3.1.93*).

74.18 उपपदसंज्ञा च ।। 7 ।।

Vārttika 7 : And (another is for forming) the technical name *upapada.*

74.19 उपपदसंज्ञा च प्रयोजनम्। तत्रैतस्मिन्धात्वधिकारे सप्तमीनिर्दिष्टमुपपदसंज्ञं भवतीत्युपपदसंज्ञा सिद्धा भवति।।

Bhāṣya: And (another) purpose (is for forming) the technical name *upapada.* The technical name *upapada* is established as valid by saying that "there in this sphere of the *dhātu* governing rule whatsoever is indicated in the seventh case has the technical name *upapada*".

74.21 कृदुपपदसंज्ञेतावत्र प्रयोजयत:। अधिकारादिप्येते सिद्धे।। स्वपादिषु तर्ह्यङ्गसंज्ञा च प्रयोजनम्।

The use of *kṛt* and *upapada* as technical names does not become the purpose. These two are established as valid. due to (their being their own) governing *sūtras.*

Then the purpose is (the forming of) the technical name *aṅga* and in relation to *svap* and the rest.

74.23 धातुग्रहणमनर्थकं यङ्विधौ धात्वधिकारात् ।। 8 ।।

Vārttika 8 : The mention of *dhātu* is pointless because of the *dhātu* governing rule expressed in the *sūtra* ordaining *yaṅ*.

74.24 धातुग्रहणमनर्थकम्। किं कारणम्। यङ्विधौ धात्वधिकारात्। यङ्विधौ[18]
धातुग्रहणं प्रकृतमनुवर्तते।। तच्चावश्यमनुवर्त्यम्।

Bhāṣya: The mention of *dhātu* (in the *sūtra*) is pointless. What is the reason? Because of the *dhātu* governing rule in the *sūtra* ordaining *yaṅ*. The original mention of *dhātu* in the *sūtra* ordaining *yaṅ* follows on. And it is essential that it should follow on.

75.1 अनधिकारे ह्यङ्गसंज्ञाभावः ।। 9 ।।

Vārttika 9 : For if there was no governing rule (there would be) the absence of the technical name *aṅga*.

75.2 अनधिकारे हि सत्यङ्गसंज्ञाया अभावः स्यात्। करिष्यति हरिष्यतीति[19]।।
यदि तदनुवर्तते चूर्णचुरादिभ्यो णिज्भवति[20] धातोश्चेति
धातुमात्राण्णिच्प्राप्नोति।।

Bhāṣya: For when there does not exist a governing rule (*dhātoḥ*) there would be absence of the technical name *aṅga* e.g. (in forms) *kariṣyati* "He will make", *hariṣyati* "He will take".

If that (word) *dhātoḥ* follows on (from *3.1.22*) *ṇic* which is applicable after the *prātipadika cūrṇa* (etc.) and after the *dhātu cur* (to steal) and the rest, because of (saying) *dhātoḥ ṇic*, obtains after all *dhātus*.

75.4 हेतुमद्वचनं तु ज्ञापकमन्यत्राभावस्य ।। 10 ।।

Vārttika 10 : However the mention of *hetumat* (that having the nature of being cause) is also an implied rule/*jñāpaka* for (expressing) the absence of (*ṇic*) elsewhere.

75.5 यदयं हेतुमति च (3.1.26) इत्याह तज्ज्ञापयत्याचार्यो न धातुमात्राण्णिज्भव-
तीति।। इह तर्हि कण्ड्वादिभ्यो यग्भवति धातोश्चेति धातुमात्राद्यक्प्राप्नोति।

Bhāṣya: When he *says hetumati ca 3.1.26* (The *pratyaya ṇic* acts after a *dhātu* when the operation of a causer is to be expressed), the master makes known that *ṇic* is not applicable after all *dhātus*.

Here then (by the *sūtra*) *kaṇḍvādibhyo yak 3.1.27* ("*Yak* acts after *kaṇḍū* and the rest") (if we say) *dhātoh* then *yak* obtains after all *dhātus.*

75.7 कण्ड्वादिषु च व्यपदेशिवद्वचनात् ॥ 11 ॥

Vārttika 11 : And because of the rule expressing a special designation in relation to *kaṇḍū* and the rest (*yak* does not act after all *dhātus*).

75.8 यदयं कण्ड्वादिभ्यो यग्भवतीत्याह तज्ज्ञापयत्याचार्यो न धातुमात्राद्यग्भवतीति॥ अथवा कण्ड्वादिभ्यो धातुग्रहणेनाभिसंभन्त्स्यामः। कण्ड्वादिभ्यो धातुभ्य इति।

Bhāṣya: When he says this *"kaṇḍvādibhyo yak" 3.1.27 "Yak* acts after *kaṇḍū* and the rest" the master makes known that *yak* is not applicable after all *dhātus.* Otherwise we will connect the word *'kaṇḍvādibhyo'* (after *kaṇḍū* and the rest) with the mention of *dhātu.* Thus 'after the *dhātus kaṇḍū* and the rest'.

Pradīpa

Pradīpa: 71.23 धातोः।

"Due to the admission of the nature of *svarita* accent (1.3.11), the nature of this as a governing *sūtra* is known but not the particular limit (of its application).

Pradīpa: 71.24 आ कृत इति

Up to where . . . ?

Now then, even when there is a *svarita* accent, a governing *sūtra* is not (necessarily) applicable. This is the exlanation. Nonetheless, due to being hardly visible or difficult to be expressed, it is not known where is the *svarita* admitted/declared as for the purpose of conditioning the *dhâtu* governing rule('s province).

Pradīpa: 72.7 विकरणैरिति।

"(*Tiṅ* after a *dhātu* would not be applicable because of being separated) by *vikaraṇa pratyayas.*" Here the *vikaraṇas sya* etc. are intended, not *śap* etc. due to their nature of depending on a *sārvadhātuka* (following); (and thus) because of the absence of obtainment, when an *ādeśa* of *la* is not effected.

However, when the view taken is *sārvadhātuka* being *viṣaya saptamī*/ seventh case in the sense of 'in that context' (i.e. when in the mind they are intended), there is obtainment of *śap* etc.

Pradīpa: 72.18 द्वयोरेकारयोरिति।

"(The hearing of two) *e* sounds (would be applicable.)"

The sense is, although there is the *ādeśa ay* in the place of one *e*, nontheless by way of hearing the *ādeśa* there is possibility of hearing that ('original) also.

Pradīpa: 73.4 थकारस्यात्व इति।

"(When the letter *a* is effected) in place of (only the first letter of) *tha*."

Surely, when *'pac + tha'* is the situation, due to being a subsequent rule, *iṭ* augment obtains. This is no fault. The letter *a* is invariable. It obtains when *iṭ* is effected and when not effected. However, *iṭ* (augment) is variable because when *a* is effected, due to (absence of) beginning with *val* (consonant), it does not obtain. Although by reason of the obtaining of another word, there is variableness for the letter *a*, nonetheless because of the possibility of it, whether effected or not effected, there is in fact invariability for it. And the variableness produced by the obtainment of another word here (referred to), is not (in fact) anywhere resorted to in the science of grammar.

Pradīpa: 74.3 तावत्येवेति।

"First there should in fact (be the application of *anti*)."

The meaning is, when in fact the word the pratyaya *jhi* has been effected (and) the *vikaraṇa* not effected.

The sense is due to the rule expressing 'being like the (original) *jha* etc. used in the *upadeśa* (*3.4.78*)'. Here should be application of *ant* as *ādeśa* in place of *jha* also at the time (inner or less operations) of the original (teaching)/*upadeśa*.

Pradīpa: 74.7 प्रातिपदिकान्मा भूवन्निति।

"(And) so they should not act after a *prātipadika*."

The sense is like the words *dvitīya* etc. *dvi* (*prātipadika*) *tīya* + *āp* (*taddhita*).

Pradīpa: 74.8 साधन इति।

"(*Tavya* etc. are ordained) in the sense of instrumental means."

When there arises the means of accomplishing the action to be expressed by the base it is *antaraṅga* (inner or less operations), while the means of accomplishing the action to be expected by another word is *bahiraṅga* (so) *tavya* and the rest will not be applicable.

The sense is: however, *dvitīya* etc. being ordained after a *prātipadika* only, because of the force of the rule/expression "In relation to the means of accomplishing the action/*sādhana*, when it has regard to the action to be expressed by another word, (it is *bahiraṅga*)", are applicable.

Pradīpa: 74.11 स्वपादिष्विति।

"(Another purpose is in relation to *dhātus*) *svap* etc."

Those *apabhraṁśa prākṛt* forms which express action like *anavayati* etc. should not have *tavya* etc. after them. Or they are not *dhātus*, because of their nature of having been rejected from having the technical name *dhātu* by recitation (in the *Dhātu Pāṭha* list).

The meaning is that, hence when *svapiti* (he sleeps) is in the form to be used, and the *apabhraṁśa* usage is *supati*, after that there should not be arising of the *pratyaya* (*tavya*) etc.

Pradīpa: 74.13 अङ्गसंज्ञेति

"(A purpose is for forming) the technical name *aṅga*."

The meaning is, if there were not a *dhātu* governing rule, due to the nature of a combination of *dhātu* and *upasarga* expressing a particular kind of action, when there is ordaining of a *pratyaya*, the technical term being for that alone, there is the possibility of *āṭ āgama* etc. (for it) in the wrong form '*prāsthita*' who has set off etc. (when short *a* is required).

Pradīpa: 74.19 तत्रैतस्मिन्निति।

"There in the sphere (of the *dhātu* governing rule), that in the seventh case (is called *upapada*/dependent word.")

= तत्रोपपदं सप्तमीस्थम् (3.1.92)

"When in the sphere of this *dhātu* governing rule, (there, is the *upapada*)."

For that this is the valid inference of meaning in connection with that word, not otherwise (with other words).

Pradīpa: 75.5 यदयमिति।

"When he says this (*hetumati ca . . .*)"

The meaning is, if *ṇic* were to be applicable after all *dhātus* without distinction, then even being ordained in the sense of *hetumati* 'having a cause', (would be in the sense of *kṛ* (in making)). So thus would be established 'in sense of making'. But there again *ṇic* would not be ordained.

However, the mention of *cur-ādi* (tenth class) would not be an implied rule for the purpose of saying 'after a *prātipadika* with the sense of the *dhātu*" (i.e. *svārthe*).

Pradīpa: 75.7 व्यपदेशिवद्वचनादिति।

"(And) because of the rule expressing a special designation (in relation to *kaṇḍu* etc. *yak* does not act after all *dhātus*)."

The designation *dhātu* exists. Those having this designation namely *pac* etc. recited in the *Dhātu Pāṭha* with which *kaṇḍū* etc. are equal. With *it k* for *yak* because of inferring their nature as *dhātus.*

This is the meaning of that: If *yak pratyaya* were applicable after all *dhātus,* then the mention of *kaṇḍvādi* would be pointless. Because of *yak* (being ordained) after all *dhātus* (mentioned), it is established for them also because of their express verbal activity.

Pradīpa: 75.9 अथवेति।

"Otherwise (we will connect after *kaṇḍu* and the rest with the mention of *dhātu*)."

The sense is, by reason of the same case relation, connection of them both is possible due to the inappropriateness of a resort to "conjuctive sense/being joined by 'and'".

Even for the purpose of the technical name *ārdhadhātuka,* this *dhātu* governing rule is not applicable. Due to the meaning of an ordained qualification being for the following on of that appropriated (for that use) in the *yaṅ* rule alone, and due to the cessation of the technical name *ārdhadhātuka* being established in the case of *jugupsate* (*3.1.5 san*) *tubhyām* (*4.1.2 svaujas... = tu + bhyām*) etc. before and after the sphere of *dhātoḥ.* Or else due to a second mention of *dhātu* following on from the *sūtra.* शमिधातोः संज्ञायाम् (3.2.14) (अच्)

Notes

[1] प्राग्लादेशात्। So he asks up to where?

"As far as the *ādeśas* of *la.*"

तिप् तस् झि सिप् थस् थ मिप् वस् मस् त आताम् झ थास् आथाम् ध्वम् इट् वहि महिङ् (3.4.78)

[2] 72.7 आद्यं योग इति।

"In the first rule (after *lasya 3.4.77*)", namely *3.4.78.*

[3] 72.1 नित्या विकरणाः "Invariable *vikaraṇas.*"

स्यतासी लृलुटोः (3.1.33)

"*Sya* and *tāsi* are the *vikaraṇas* of *lṛ* (*lṛṅ* conditional and *lṛṭ* second future) and *luṭ* (first future), after a *dhātu.*"

[4] 72.14 टित्संज्ञानामेत्वं विद्यते। "That substitution of *e* he ordains in place of the *ṭ* of those having the name *it ṭ*"

टित आत्मनेपदानां टेरे (3.4.79)

"The *ādeśa e* acts in place of the last vowel with the consonant that follows of the *ātmanepada ādeśas* of that *la* having an indicatory *ṭ*"

[5] 72.16 एकारश्च शित्कर्तव्यः।

"And the letter *e* is to be effected as having an *it ś.*"

लिटस्तझयोरेशिरेच् (3.4.81)

"*Eś* and *irec* are the *ādeśas* of *ta* and *jha* respectively in the perfect tense *ātmanepada.*"

शित्सर्वस्येति

"Having an *it ś* is *ādeśa* of the whole."

अनेकाल् शित्सर्वस्य (1.1.55)

"An *ādeśa* of more than one letter or having an *it ś* acts in place of the whole of that in the sixth case."

[6] 72.19 विधयो
अलोऽन्तस्य (1.1.52)

"See text.

[7] 73.2 अकार इति।

"(If that *dhātu* governing rule governs as the *ādeśa* of *la* the) letter a (should be made to have an *it ś*)."

परस्मैपदानां णलतुसुस्थलथुसणल्वमाः (3.4.82)

"In place of the *parasmaipada pratyayas* the following are the *ādeśas* in the perfect tense:

णल् (अ) अतुस् उस् थल् (थ) अथुस् अ णल् (अ) व म"

That *a* which is ordained in place of *śas.*

[8] 73.4 पररूपेण।

"By reason of the 'form of the following' (*a* would be the established form)."

अतो गुणे (6.1.97)

"When a short *a* not final in a *pada* is followed by a *guṇa* letter, then in place of both, the prior and the subsequent, the single *ādeśa* is the form of the subsequent." (i.e. *guṇa*)

[9] 73.8 समसंख्यार्थमिति।

"The expressing of *a* is for the purpose of the same number (of *ādeśas* and *sthāninaḥ*)."

अकारवचनं समसंख्यार्थम् (3.4.82) वा॰ 4

also यथासंख्यमनुदेशःसमानाम् (1.3.10)

[10] आर्धधातुकसंज्ञाया

when *ārdhadhātuka* is defined by आर्धधातुके विकरणा उच्यन्ते

सार्वधातुके यक् (3.1.67) see text.

[11] 73.14 स्यादयः
स्यतासी लृलुतोः (3.1.33) see text.

[12] 73.15 प्राप्नुवन्ति। *Ṇal* etc. obtain.

विदो लटो वा (3.4.83)

"The nine *pratyayas* of the perfect optionally act in the present tense also after the *dhātu vid* (to know)."

[13] 73.17 झेर्जुस्भवति इति।

"*Jus* obtains because of the rule that *jus* acts in place of *jhi.*"

जक्षित्यादयः षट् (6.1.6)

"The six *dhātus* beginning with *jakṣ-i* have the name *abhyasta*/reduplicates."

सिजभ्यस्तविदिभ्यश्च (3.4.109)

"*Jus* acts as the *ādeśa* of *jhi* after *sic* (aorist) or the imperfect of a reduplicated *dhātu/abhyasta* or the *dhātu vid* (to know) in the case of those *la* (tense/mood *pratyayas*) which have an indicatory *ṅ.*"

[14] 73.22 अपिबन्नित्यत्रापि प्राप्नोति।

"*(Jus)* also obtains here in the form *apiban.*"

c.f. ५२२ पाघ्राध्मास्थाम्नादाणदृश्यर्तिसर्तिशदसदां
पिब्जिघ्रधमतिष्ठमनयच्छपश्यर्च्छधौशीयसीदा :।७।३।७८।।
पादीनां पिबादयःस्युरित्संज्ञकशकारादौ प्रत्यये परे।

In place of पा घ्रा ध्मा स्था म्ना दाण् दृश् ऋ सृ शद् and सद्

there are पिब जिघ्र धम तिष्ठ मन यच्छ पश्य ऋच्छ धौ शीय and सीद before a

प्रत्यय beginning with an इत् श्

पिबादेशोऽदन्तस्तेन न गुणः। पिबति।।

The *ādeśas* act in the presence of that having an indicatory *ś.*

[15] 73.27 लोपेनेति। "(The *jus*) by *lopa* elision (would be applicable)."

श्नाभ्यस्तयोरातः (6.4.112)

"In the presence of a *sārvadhātuka kit* or *ṅit pratyaya* beginning with a vowel the long *ā* of *śnā* (*vikaraṇa* of the ninth class) and the reduplicated stems are *lopa* elided."

ई हल्यघोः (6.4.113)

"In the presence of a *sārvadhātuka kit* or *ṅit pratyaya* beginning with a consonant the *a* of *śnā* and of the reduplicates is replaced by *i* when the *dhātu* is *dā* or *dhā* (i.e. *ghu*)."

झोऽन्तः (7.1.3)

"*Ant* is the *ādeśa* in place of the *jh* of a *pratyaya.*"

लङः शाकटायनस्यैव (3.4.111)

"In the opinion of *Śākaṭāyana* only, *jus* is the *ādeśa* of *jhi* in the imperfect of the *dhātus* which end in long *ā.*"

[16] 74.7 धातोस्तव्यदादयो।

"(So that) *tavya* and the rest should act after a *dhātu.*"

(3.1.96)

"The *kṛtya pratyayas tavyat, tavya* and *anīyar* act after a *dhātu* (in the sense of *bhāva* or *karman*)."

[17] 74.17 भवति। "(Technical name *kṛt*) becomes (established)."

by कृदतिङ्

"(From *3.1.92* to the end of the third *adhyāya* in the province of a *dhātu* governing rule, any *pratyaya*) other than *tiṅ* (verbal *pratyaya*) is called *kṛt.*"

[18] 74.24 यङ्विधौ "In the *yaṅ* rule."

i.e. धातोरेकाचो हलादेः क्रियासमभिहारे यङ् (3.1.22)

[19] 75.2 हरिष्यति "He will take."

c.f. स्यतासी लृलुटोः (3.1.33)

सार्वातुकार्धधातुकयोः (7.3.84) (इकः गुणः अङ्गस्य)

[20] 75.3 णिज्भवति। "*Ṇic* is applicable" by

सत्यापपाशरूपवीणातूलश्लोकसेनालोमत्वचवर्मवर्णचूर्णचुरादिभ्यो णिच् (3.1.25)

तत्रोपपदं सप्तमीस्थम् ॥ 3 । 1 । 92 ॥

Pāṇini 3.1.92: There (in the third *adhyāya* in the sphere of the *dhātu* governing rule) the word mentioned in the seventh (*adhikaraṇa*/locative) case is called *upapada.*

75.11 स्थग्रहणं किमर्थम्। तत्रोपपदं सप्तमीतीयत्युच्यमाने यत्रैव सप्तमी श्रूयते तत्रैव स्यात्।
स्तम्बेरमः कर्णेजपः[1]। यत्र वैतेन शब्देन निर्देशः क्रियते। शप्तम्यां जनेर्डः
75.13 (3.2.97) इति। इह न स्यात्। कुम्भकारः नगरकारः[2]।

Bhāṣya: What is the purpose of mentioning *stha* (standing or being situated in)? If just so much is being stated: "There the word in the seventh case is called *upapada*" (omitting *stha*), it would (mean) only where the seventh case is heard. There only would (*upapada* technical name) be applicable (e.g.) *stamberamaḥ* "an elephant, who sports in a cluster of grass"; *karṇe japaḥ* "a salnderer, who whispers in the ear".

Or else where there is indication by the word *saptamī* (seventh case) (there is the technical name *upapada*) (e.g.) *saptamyām janerḍaḥ 3.2.97* ("The *pratyaya ḍa* acts after a *dhātu jan* (to be produced) with past signification, when a word in composition with it is in the seventh case..."). Here in *kumbhakāraḥ* "potter" *nagarakāraḥ* "city maker" the (technical term *upapada*) would not be applicable.

75.13 ....स्थग्रहणे पुनः क्रियमाणे यत्र च सप्तमी
श्रूयते यत्र च न श्रूयते यत्र चैतेन शब्देन निर्देशः क्रियते यत्र
75.15 चान्येन सप्तमीस्थमात्रे सिद्धं भवति।। अथ तत्रग्रहणं किमर्थम्।

But when mention is made of *stha,* when the seventh case is heard and when it is not heard, when there is indication made by this word (*saptamī*) and where (it is made) by another word, the (*upapada* technical name) becomes applicable to whatever is mentioned in the seventh case (*adhikaraṇa*/locative) *saptamīstha.*

Now then what is the purpose of the mention of the word *tatra.*

75.16 तत्रग्रहणं विषयार्थम् ॥ 1 ॥

Vārtika 1: The mention of *tatra* (there) is for the purpose of restricting the sphere of application of the rule.

75.17 विषयः प्रतिनिर्दिश्यते। तत्रैतस्मिन् धात्वधिकारे यत्सप्तमीनिर्दिष्टं तदुपपदसंज्ञं
भवतीत्युपपदसंज्ञा सिद्धा भवति।।

Bhāṣya: The sphere is referred to. There, in the sphere of application of the *dhātu* governing rule, "whatever is indicated in the seventh case has applicable the technical name *upapada*". Thus the technical name *upapada* becomes established as valid.

75.19 उपपदसंज्ञायां समर्थवचनम् ।। 2 ।।

Vartika 2: When there is the technical name *upapada* there is the mention of *samartha* (having the same grammatical construction) (with the main word).

75.20 उपपदसंज्ञायां समर्थग्रहणं कर्तव्यम्। समर्थमुपपदं प्रत्ययस्येति वक्तव्यम्। इह
मा भूत्। आहर कुम्भं करोति कटमिति।। क्रियमाणे चापि समर्थग्रहणे महान्तं
75.22 कुम्भं करोतीत्यत्रापि प्राप्नोति। न वा भवितव्यं महाकुम्भकार इति।

Bhāṣya: When there is the technical name *upapada,* mention should be made of *samartha* having the same syntactical relation (with the main word). It should be stated 'an *upapada* having the same syntactical relation (as the main word) is for (the sake of) the *pratyaya*'. Here it should not be applicable *āhara kumbham karoti kaṭam* "Bring the pot, he makes a mat". (*Karmaṇy aṇ 3.2.1*)

75.22 .... भवितव्यं
यदैतद्वाक्यं भवति महान्कुम्भो महाकुम्भः महाकुम्भं करोतीति महाकुम्भकारः।
76.2 यदा त्वेतद्वाक्यं भवति महान्तं कुम्भं करोतीति तदा न भवितव्यं तदा
च प्राप्नोति। तदा मा भूदिति। यत्तावदुच्यते समर्थग्रहणं कर्तव्यमिति।।
न कर्तव्यम्।
76.4 धातोरिति वर्तते।

And even when mention of having syntactical relation is being made here also, (in the sentence) *mahāntam kumbham karoti* "He makes a big pot", (*kṛt* derivation obtains).

Or else it should not be *mahākumbhakāraḥ* "the great potter".

It should be when the underlying sentence is *mahākumbham karoti* "He makes a great pot". *mahākumbhakāraḥ* "the great potter". Then *mahākumbhakāraḥ* should not be derived and there it obtains. Then it should not obtain. As to that which is just now stated, 'mention should be made of having syntactical relation'it should not be made because *dhātoḥ* (*3.1.91*) "after a *dhātu*" follows on.

76.4 .... धातोः कर्मण्यणभवति। तत्र संबन्धादेतद्गन्तव्यं यस्य
धातोर्यत्कर्मेति।। यदप्युच्यते क्रियमाणे चापि समर्थग्रहणे महान्तं कुम्भं करोतीत्यत्रापि
प्राप्नोतीति। उपपदमिति महतीयं संज्ञा क्रियते संज्ञा च नाम यतो न लघीयः।
कुत एतत्। लघ्वर्थं हि संज्ञाकरणम्। तत्र महत्याः संज्ञायाः करण एतत्प्रयो-

जनमन्वर्थसंज्ञा यथा विज्ञायेत। उपोच्चारि पदमुपपदमिति। यच्चात्रोपोच्चारि न तत्पदं यच्च पदं न तदुपोच्चारि। यावता चेदानीं पदगन्धोऽस्ति पदविधिरियं भवति।

73.10 पदविधिश्च समर्थानां भवति[3]। तत्रासामर्थ्यान्न भविष्यति।।

After a *dhātu*, *aṇ pratyaya* acts when the object is in composition as an *upapada*". There because of the connection this should be understood "*aṇ* is added to that *dhātu* (accompanied by an object) to which that object is related". (*3.2.1*)

Also that which was said "and even when mention is being made of having syntactical relation" (the *kṛt* derivation) obtains here (in the sentence) *mahāntam kumbham karoti* "He makes the great pot". (I say) this word *upapada* is formed as a "great technical term", (whereas) in fact a technical term is that than which there is nothing briefer. Why is this so? For the making of a technical term is the purpose of brevity. In that context the purpose of making a great technical name is so that it should be known as a term significant in itself. A word uttered near to (the main word) is *upapada*. And since that which is here uttered near to is not a *pada*, and that which is a *pada* is not uttered near to (the main word); and since this is the mere smell of *pada*, this becomes a *pada* rule. And a *pada* rule is applicable for words which are syntactically connected. (*2.1.1.*)

There because of not having syntactical relation (the *pada* rule) will not be applicable.

76.11 अथ च्व्यन्त उपपदे किमणा भवितव्यम्। अकुम्भं कुम्भं करोति कुम्भीकरोति मृदमिति। न भवितव्यम्। किं कारणम्। प्रकृतिविवक्षायां च्विर्विधीयते। तत्सापेक्षम्। सापेक्षं चासमर्थं भवति।। न तर्हीदानीमिदं भवति इच्छाम्यहं काशकटीकार-

76.14 मिति। इष्टमेवैतद्गोनर्दीयस्य।।

Now when a *cvi* ending word is the word uttered near, is the *pratyaya aṇ* to be applicable? (For instance) 'he makes a pot which was not a pot' (i.e.) *kumbhī karoti,* that is to say (he makes) clay (a pot)? It should not be applicable. What is the reason? *cvi* is ordained when it is desired to speak of the base/*prakṛti*. That has expectancy and that which has expectancy cannot be syntactically related.

Then this (*kṛt* derivation) should not be applicable here. *icchāmy aham kāśakaṭīkāram* "I seek for one who makes grasses into mats". This is in fact desired (as applicable) by *Gonardīya.*

76.15 निमित्तोपादानं च ।। 3 ।।

Vārttika 3: And (there should be) mention of *upapada* conditon.

76.16 निमित्तोपादानं च कर्तव्यम्। निमित्तमुपपदं प्रत्ययस्येति वक्तव्यम्।

Bhāṣya: And mention should be made (of *upapada*) as a condition. It should be stated that the *upapada* is a cause or condition for a *pratyaya.*

76.17 अनुपादाने ह्यनुपपदे प्रत्ययप्रसङ्गः ॥ 4 ॥

Vārttika 4: For when there is no mention of condition *pratyaya* would be applicable or contingent, even when there is no *upapada* (subordinate word in construction).

76.18 अक्रियमाणे हि निमित्तोपादानेऽनुपपदेऽपि प्रत्ययः प्रसज्येत। निर्देश इदानीं किमर्थः स्यात्।

Bhāṣya: For when no mention is being made of condition, a *pratyaya* would be applicable even when there is no *upapada.*

Now what would be the purpose of the special mention of *upapada*?

76.20 निर्देशः संज्ञाकरणार्थः ॥ 5 ॥

Vārttika 5: The special mention is for the purpose of making a technical name.

76.21 यदोपपदे प्रत्ययस्तदोपपदसंज्ञा वक्ष्यामीति। तत्तर्हि निमित्तोपादानं कर्तव्यम्। न कर्तव्यम्।

Bhāṣya: When a *pratyaya* (is ordained) in relation to an *upapada* then I shall state the technical name *upapada.*

Then should mention be made of the condition? It should not be made.

76.23 तत्रवचनमुपपदसंनियोगार्थम् ॥ 6 ॥

Vārttika 6: The mention of *tatra* (there) is for the purpose of simultaneous conjunction with the *upapada.*

76.24 तत्रवचनं क्रियते तदुपपदसंनियोगर्थं भविष्यति। कर्मण्यण्विधीयते तत्र चेत्प्रत्ययो भवतीति। ननु चान्यत्तत्रग्रहणस्य प्रयोजनमुक्तम्। किम्। तत्रग्रहणं
76.26 विषयार्थमिति। अधिकारादप्येतत्सिद्धम्॥

Bhāṣya: The expressing of *tatra* is made so that there will be simultaneous conjunction with *upapada.* The *pratyaya aṇ* is ordained (after a *dhātu*) when the object is an *upapada* (and it is an *upapada*) if a *pratyaya* is ordained when it is a word uttered nearby).

But surely another purpose was stated for mentioning *tatra* (there). What? The mention of *tatra* is for the purpose of (indicating) the sphere (of application of the rule, namely in the same sphere as the *dhātu* governing rule, the remainder of the third *adhyāya*). This is also established by the governing rule.

Pradīpa

Pradīpa: 75.11 तत्रोपपदं। स्थग्रहणमिति

What is the purpose of mentioning *stha* ?

The question is, due to being closely linked with the word *saptamī*, will those indicated be understood as seventh case indications in the *sūtras* ?

Pradīpa: 75.11 यत्रैव सप्तमीति।

(It would mean), only where the seventh case (is heard), if it were arisen from the principal meaning, because of the irregular nature of mentioning the secondary (meaning), the technical name *upapada* would only be applicable for the seventh case (word actually indicated as such). This is due to the prohibition of the *tadanta* rule, when there is mention of *pratyaya* in a technical name rule. However, because of the scope for the *samartha paribhāṣā* (*2.1.3*) there is a 'compound' and there would be applicability of the *tadanta* rule.

Pradīpa: 75.12 यत्र वेति।

"Or else (where there is indication by the word *saptamī*.")

The meaning is, when the mention of the actual word form *saptamī* (is taken as the meaning), then it would only be applicable in cases where present, like सप्तम्यां जनेर्डः (3.2.97), for the purpose of establishing such forms as उपसरज 'born of the first conception', but would not be applicable in the case of 'कुम्भकार' etc.

Pradīpa: 75.13 स्थग्रहण इति।

"(But) when mention is made of *stha* . . ."

The meaning is: however, when there is mention of *stha*, because of the ordaining of the technical name (*upapada*) for the implied special use of the seventh case in the *sūtras.* it is established as valid.

Pradīpa: 75.15 अथ तत्रग्रहणमिति।

"Now (what is the purpose of) mentioning the word *tatra* ?"

The question is, 'because of *dhātoḥ'* (after a *dhātu*) following on (from *3.1.91*) will the technical name *upapada* be applicable in the province of the very *dhātu* governing rule ?

Pradīpa: 75.17 तत्रैतस्मिन्निति।

"There in this (sphere of application of the *dhātu* governing rule)."

The sense is, by the mention of the word *tatra,* there is clear understanding as referred to this governing rule. Otherwise the question is, due to the technical name *upapada* being after the governing rule will it not be applicable to the *dhātu* governing rule right here ?

"If the *adhikāra sūtra* were to be resorted to, with every *sūtra* there would be cumbrousness/needless multiplication of causes."

The answer is 'However, when there is mention made of the word *tatra* due to completion (satisfaction), by that one sentence only, the technical name is ordained, so that there will be the gaining of brevity'.

Pradīpa: 75.19 समर्थवचनमिति।

"There is the mention of *samartha*/having the same grammatical construction."

Here when the meaning of the *prātipadika* is triple/three-fold, characterised as the meaning of its own base/*svārtha,* a thing, or gender (2.3.46), then without the *vibhakti*/case ending there will not be applicable *upapada* in *karman, adhikaraṇa* (locative) etc.

Thus it is essential it should arise with a *vibhakti* ending. And hence because of being a *pada* rule, there is in fact scope for the *samartha paribhāṣā.* The sense is that in the view of there being four-fold meaning or five-fold meaning, because of the *prātipadika* expressing only *karman* etc. and due to the absence of a *pada* rule and also because of there not being scope for the *samartha paribhāṣā,* the express mention of *samartha* has to be made.

Pradīpa: 75.21 आहार कुम्भमिति।

"Bring the pot."

When *kumbha* is *upapada, aṇ* would be applicable after *dhātu kṛ* (by *karmaṇyaṇ 3.2.1*). However, due to the absence of syntactical relation/grammatical agreement, three would not be an *upapada* compound.

Pradīpa: 75.21 महान्तं कुम्भमिति।

"He makes a big pot."

The sense is, there is grammatical agreement of *kumbha* joined with *mahati*, with the *dhātu kṛ* (to make).

And if there were to be a *pratyaya* (*aṇ*), then when a compound was effected of the word *kumbha* with the word *kāra*, due to becoming one meaning in the sense of 'making', there would not be a compound with the word *mahat*. Due to there also not being the nature of (*sup* ending) for a combination ending in a *sup*, when there is an *upapada* compound, even when there is cessation of the mention of *sup*, for that ending in the sixth case, and finally due to 'ending in first case' following on, there is no compounding.

Pradīpa: 76.8 न तत्पदमिति।

"Since that which is 'uttered near to' is not a *pada* . . . "

The sense is, because of its being a combination of words.

Pradīpa: 76.9 यच्च पदमिति।

"And that which is a *pada* (is not uttered near the main word)."

(In relation to) this word *mahāntam* and this word *kumbham*, athough there is a word/*pada* and it is uttered near, nonetheless because of expectation (of another word to complete the sense) due to absence of grammatical agreement together, there is no cause for the arising of the *pratyaya aṇ*. Due to making this a term whose meaning is intelligible in itself, 'a word uttered near', in fact there is seventh case indication. Due to the absence of the nature 'being uttered near', for the meaning of the *pratyayas* qualifying the meaning of the bases and their qualifying (words), the technical name *upapada* is not applicable.

Pradīpa: 76.9 पदविधिरिति।

"(This) becomes a *pada* rule."

The sense is, due to the nature of the *pratyaya* rule being cause of *pada* (technical name).

Pradīpa: 76.11 अथ च्व्यन्त इति।

"Now when a *cvi* ending word (is the word uttered near. . .)"

Here in some places when there is expectation (of another word to complete the sense) the *pratyaya* is not applicable, as *mahāntam putram icchati* 'He desires a great son'.

In some places, however, it is applicable, as *mānavakam muṇḍayati* 'He shaves the young man' (*3.1.21*) where *ṇic* acts in the sense of making.

The question arises from the doubt regarding that. And even when there is indeclinable nature for that ending in *cvi,* he thinks of that as having the nature of object due to the non-completion of becoming substantive.

Pradīpa: 76.12 प्रकृतिविवक्षायामिति।

"(*Cvi*) is ordained, when it is desired to speak of the base."

When it is desired to express the non-difference of the base and its modification, *cvi* is ordained. In that context it is essential, the modification be considered as qualification (distinction) of the base. When that is not so considered, it is due to the absence of *cvi.* The meaning is, "And hence as here 'He makes the great pot' *aṇ* is not applicable so also मृदं कुम्भीकरोति 'He makes what was not a clay pot a clay pot' etc."

Here, however, कुशान्कटीकरोति 'He makes (grass) into *kuśa* grass mats', by (reason of a desired rule) *aṇ* is applicable (i.e. of *Patañjali*).

When that arises in conjuction with a *kṛt pratyaya,* after the *kuśa,* there is a sixth case for that, and thus fifth case compound. That rule says that 'By reason of compound form alone', being desired (by *Patañjali iṣṭi*) due to being the accepted form, the sentence is applicable as काशानां कटीकार: 'The maker of *kuśa* grass mats'.

Pradīpa: 76.18 निर्देश इति।

"Now what would be the purpose of special mention?"

The sense is, due to the understanding of seventh case being ('indication *upapada*') as *karmaṇi* 'when *karman*/object is *upapada*', when it in fact exists as object, the *pratyaya* will be applicable.

Pradīpa: 76.20 निर्देश संज्ञाकरणार्थ इति।

"The special mention is for the purpose of making a technical name (for *upapada*)."

The sense is, just as it is stated there is nasalisation for the sake of (indicating) technical name *it* (for a vowel), so too without any regard to meaning, the *sūtra* gives indication of the technical name *upapada* with the seventh case as in *karmaṇi* etc.

However, when there is regard to meaning in the seventh case, there would be (wrongly) applicable *karman* as the signification of the *pratyaya* *aṇ* as in the *sūtra* धः कर्मणि ष्ट्रन् (3.2.181) 'The *pratyaya ṣṭran* acts in denoting the object after the *dhātu dhā* to feed'.

And so that nature of being *upapada* is not understood, and when there is no expectation of meaning, the meaning would be '*aṇ*' is applicable after a *dhātu* after that in the seventh case and the object has the technical name *upapada.* Thus there would not be understanding of *karman*/object as having the nature of cause for the arising of the *pratyaya.*

Pradīpa: 76.23 तत्रवचनमिति।

"The mention of *tatra* (is for purpose of simultaneous conjunction with *upapada.*"

Due to the mention of *tatra* the meaning is obtained. There alone when not present the *pratyaya* is applicable not when present. If it is said 'How can this be?' It is said the word *pratyaya* follows on here from *3.1.1.* And this is the meaning "In that context the technical name *upapada* is applicable to that (indicated) in the seventh case, and there when the *upapada* is present the *pratyaya* is applicable".

Notes

[1] 75.12 कर्णेजपः। "A slanderer who whispers in the ear."

स्तम्बकर्णयोरमिजपोः (3.2.13)

"The *pratyaya ac* acts after the *dhātu ram* (to sport) and *jap* to whisper) when the *sup* (case) inflected words *stamba* (a clump of grass) and *karṇa* (ear) are in composition with them respectively."

[2] 75.13 नगरकारः। "City maker."

कर्मण्यण् (3.2.1)

"The *pratyaya aṇ* acts after a *dhātu* when the object is in composition with it as an *upapada.*"

[3] 76.10 भवति। "(A *pada* rule) is applicable (for words syntactically connected)."

समर्थपदविधिः (2.1.1)

"A rule which relates to complete words (not *dhātus* or *pratyayas* from which words are formed) is to be understood to apply only to those words the sense of which are connected."

कृदतिङ् ॥ 3 । 1 । 93 ॥

Pāṇini 3.1.93: (In the sphere of the *dhātu* governing rule) any *pratyaya* other than *tiṅ* (tense *pratyaya*) is called *kṛt.*

77.2 अतिङिति किमर्थम्। पचति करोति।। अतिङिति शक्यमकर्तुम्। कस्मान्न भवति पचति करोतीति। धातोः परस्य कृत्संज्ञा प्राक्च लादेशाद्धात्वधिकारः[1]।।

77.4 एवमपि स्थानिवद्भावात्कृत्संज्ञा प्राप्नोति।

Bhāṣya: What is the purpose of (saying) 'other than *tiṅ*' (tense *pratyaya*)? (So that) (e.g.) *pacati* "He cooks" *karoti* "He makes" (should not be called *kṛt* ending). It is possible not to have to say *atiṅ* (other than *tiṅ*). Why is *kṛt* not applicable (in the case of) *pacati* "He cooks" and *karoti* "He makes"? The technical name *kṛt* is applicable for that (*pratyaya* acting) after a *dhātu* and the *dhātu* governing rule extends as far as the substitutes of *la* (tense/mood *pratyayas*).

Even then because of the condition of being like the original the technical name *kṛt* obtains.

77.4 ....अथातिङित्युच्यमाने यावता स्थानिवद्भावः कथमेवैतत्सिध्यति प्रतिषेधवचनसामर्थात्। अथवा तिङ्भाविनो लकारस्य कृत्संज्ञाप्रतिषेधः ।। किं च स्याद्यद्यत्र कृत्संज्ञा स्यात्। कृत्प्रातिपदिकमिति प्रातिपदिक-

77.7 संज्ञा स्यात्प्रातिपदिकादिति स्वाद्युत्पत्तिः प्रसज्येत[2]। नैष दोषः।

Inasmuch as there is the condition of being like the original/*sthānivat,* when it is being stated "when there is a *pratyaya* other then *tiṅ*", how in fact is this established?

Due to the force of stating prohibition, or else the prohibition of the technical name *kṛt* is for *la* (tense/mood *pratyaya*) which is about to be (replaced by) *tiṅ* (verbal *pratyayas*).

And what would be (wrong) if here there was the technical name *kṛt*? (That ending in) *kṛt* would have the technical name *prātipadika* and after a *prātipadika* would be applicable the arising of *su* and the rest. This is not a fault.

77.7 .... एकत्वादिष्वर्थेषु स्वादयो विधीयन्ते[3] ते चात्र तिङोक्ता एकत्वादय इति कृत्वोक्तार्थत्वान्न भविष्यन्ति।। टाबादयस्तर्हि तिङन्तान्मा भूवन्निति। स्त्रियां टाबादयो विधीयन्ते न च तिङन्तस्य स्त्रीत्वेन योगोऽस्ति।। अणादयस्तर्हि तिङन्तान्मा भूवन्निति। अपत्यादि-

77.11 ष्वर्थेष्वणादयो विधीयन्ते[4] न च तिङन्तस्यापत्यादिभिर्योगोऽस्ति।।

Su and the rest are ordained in the sense of unity/singularity etc. and the rest have been expressed (already) by the *tiṅ pratyayas.* Thus, because the meaning has already been expressed (*su* and the rest) will not be applicable.

Then *kṛt sañjñā* should be given to *tiṅ* so that *tap* and the rest are ordained in expressing femininity and there is no connection of femininity with that ending in *tiṅ.*

Then so that *aṇ* and the rest (*3.2.1*) etc. should not be applicable for (verbs) ending in *tiṅ* (verbal *pratyayas*). *Aṇ* and the rest are ordained in the sense of *apatya* (his) offspring etc. and those words ending in *tiṅ* (verbal *vibhakti pratyayas*) are not enjoined with the sense of "offspring" etc.

77.11 .... अथापि कथंचिद्योगः स्यात्। एवमपि न दोषः। आचार्यप्रवृत्तिर्ज्ञापयति न तिङन्तादणादयो भवन्तीति यदयं क्वचित्तद्धितविधौ तिङ्ग्रहणं करोति। अतिशायने तमबिष्ठनौ तिङश्च (5.3.55, 56) इति। इह तर्हि पचति पठतीति ह्रस्वस्य पिति कृति तुक् तुम्भवतीति

77.15 तुक्प्राप्नोति[5]। धातोरिति वर्तते।।

If somehow or other the rule should be applicable, even so there is no fault. The master's usage makes known that *aṇ* and the rest are not applicable after that ending in a *tiṅ* (tense/*pratyaya*) inasmuch as he makes mention of *tiṅ* sometimes (in the *taddhita* rules) e.g. *atiśayane tamabiṣṭhanau 5.3.55* ("When the sense is that of surpassing, there act the *pratyayas tamap* and *iṣṭhan* after a *prātipadika,* the word retaining its own meaning/*svārthe*") and *tiṅaśca 5.3.56* ("So also after a finite verb/*tiṅ anta* acts the *pratyaya tamap* when surpassing is meant").

Then here in the forms *pacati* "He cooks" *paṭhati* "He recites" (by the *sūtra*) *hrasvasya piti* (*kṛti*) *tuk* obtains ? (*6.1.71*) ("In the presence of a *kṛt pratyaya* with an indicatory *p, t-uk* is the *āgama* of the final of that which ends in a short vowel"). The word *dhātoḥ* 'after a *dhātu*' follows on.

77.15 .... एवमपि चिकीर्षतीत्यत्र प्राप्नोति। अत्रापि शपा व्यवधानम्। एकादेशे कृते नास्ति व्यवधानम्। एकादेशः पूर्वविधौ स्थानिवद्भावतीति स्थानिव-

77.17 भावाद्व्यवधानमेवेति।

Even then it obtains here (in the form) *cikīrṣati* "He desires to make". Here too, because of being separated by *śap* (there is no *tuk āgama*). But when the single *ādeśa* is effected, there is no intervention. The single *ādeśa* is like the original/*sthānivat.* When a rule would otherwise take effect on what is prior to the original vowel/*pūrvaviddhau* (*1.1.57*) and because of the condition of being like the original, there is in fact intervention.

77.18 इति श्रीभगवत्पतञ्जलिविरचिते व्याकरणमहाभाष्ये तृतीयस्याध्यायस्य प्रथमे पादे पञ्चममह्निकम्।।

Thus ends the fifth *āhnika* in the first *pada* of the third *adhyāya* in the *Vyākaraṇa Mahābhāṣya* composed by the Blessed Master *Patañjali.*

Pradīpa

Pradīpa: 77.4 कृदतिङ्। स्थानिवद्भावादिति।

"Because of the condition of being like the original/*sthānivat* (technical name) *kṛt* obtains."

लस्य (3.4.77)

"In place of *la* (the tense/mood *pratyayas tiṅ* etc.) act."

The prohibition of 'other than *tiṅ'* is able to bar the technical name *kṛt* for a *tiṅ* only in its own place of abode, not however, (if) attached to the substitution teaching/*sthānivat sūtras.*

The sense is, this derives from the expression 'if the rule is applicable for that which is contiguous' or else the prohibition is applicable.

Pradīpa: 77.5 प्रतिषेधेति।

"(Due to the force of strong endings) the prohibition."

The sense is 'otherwise the prohibition would be pointless.'

Pradīpa: 77.9 टाबादय इति।

"*Ṭāp* and the rest."

The sense is that, just as there is arising of singular etc. as causes of number, resorted to by the means of accomplishing the action so indeed *ṭāp* etc. would be resorted to for gender in those (means) of . . .

Pradīpa: 77.1 स्त्रियामिति।

"(*Ṭāp* etc. are ordained) in expressing femininity."

स्त्रियाम् (4.1.3)

"When feminine nature is intended to be indicated, the *pratyayas* which follow are to act."

The sense is, due to the natural power of a word, there is employment of number as the basis of the means of accomplishing action, but the use of gender is not for that ending in a *tiṅ* (verbal *pratyaya*).

Pradīpa: 77.16 एकादेश इति।

"But when the single *ādeśa* (is effected there is intervention).

Surely having barred 'being like the original' because of being the later rule, 'being like the last/ *antavat* should apply'.

This is no fault. Due to the expressing that as desired (by an *iṣṭi* of *Patañjali*) for the word which follows, 'being like the original' is in fact the bar of 'being like the final'.

Surely when there is the prohibition of 'not a *tiṅ*' due to its ending in a *prātipadika* (by *kṛttaddhita-samāsaśca 1.2.46*), there (wrongly) obtains the *lopa* elision of *n* of *paceran* (optative of *pac*) 'May they cook'.

झस्य रन् (3.4.105)

"*Ran* is the *ādeśa* of *liṅ* (optative and benedictive *jhas*.")

Due to the force of expressing the letter *n* (in this rule), the above (*lopa* of *n*) will not be applicable.

Here then विचीयात् 'One may discern . . ."

Due to the *y* letter having the nature of *kṛt*, long vowel does not (wrongly) obtain. This also is not a fault. The prohibition of *sārvadhātuka* makes known अकृत्सर्वधातुकयोर्दीर्घः (7.4.25) that *akṛt* i.e. 'not a *kṛt*' prohibition, is not a prohibition of *tiṅ* (*3.4.113*).

For if it were, then in the case of *sunuyāt* 'one may press out some', *cinuyāt* 'one may collect', etc. also when a *sārvadhātuka* follows there will not be lengthening by reason of the prohibition of *kṛt*, and thus the separate prohibition of *kṛt*, and thus the separate prohibition of *sārvadhātuka pratyayas* would be pointless.

Notes

[1] 77.3 लादेशाद्धात्वधिकारः।

धातोः (3.1.91)

The *dhātu* governing rule extends as far as substitutes.

तिप्तस्झि सिप्थस्थ मिप्वस्मस् तातांझ थासाथांध्वंइड्वहिम्हिङ् (3.4.78)2

[2] 77.7 प्रसज्येत

"After a *prātipadika* would be applicable (the arising of *sic* etc.)."

कृत्तद्धितसमासाश्च 1.2.46

"The forms ending in *kṛt pratyayas* or *taddhita pratyayas* or *samāsas* (compounds) are also called *prātipadikas.*

ङ्याप्प्रातिपदिकात् (4.1.1)

"From this point forward as far as the end of the fifth *adhyāya,* whatever is ordained, acts after that which ends with the feminine *pratyayas* ङी or आप् or after a nominal stem/*prātipadika.*"

[3] 77.8 विधीयन्ते "(*Su*) etc. are ordained (in the sense of unity etc.)."

बहुषु बहुवचनम् (1.4.21)

"In expressing multiplicity the plural *pratyaya* acts."

द्व्येकयोर्द्विवचनैकवचने (1.4.22)

"In expressing duality and unity the dual and the singular *pratyayas* act."

[4] 77.11 विधीयन्ते

"(*Aṇ* and the rest) are ordained (in the sense of *apatya* . . . etc.)."

तस्यापत्यम् (4.1.92)

"The *pratyaya aṇ* (*4.1.83*) and those that follow it denote 'the descendant of that (person)'."

[5] 77.15 तुक्प्राप्नोति

ह्रस्वस्य पिति कृति तुक् (6.1.71)

"For the final of a *dhātu* ending in a short vowel the augment *tuk* (= *t*) acts when a *kṛt pratyaya* having an indicatory *p* follows."

धातोरिति।

"(The word) *dhātoḥ* (after a *dhātu*)" follows on from the *sūtra*

धात्वादे: ष: स: (6.1.64)

वासरूपोऽस्त्रियाम् ॥ 3 । 1 । 94 ॥

Pāṇini 3.1.94: (In the sphere of the *dhātu* governing rule) a special/ *apavāda pratyaya* which is to debar a general one not being of the same form, optionally debars it, but not so in the case of feminine *pratyayas* (which always debar the general/ *utsarga pratyayas 3.3.94* etc.)

78.2 कथमिदं विज्ञायते। स्त्रियामभिधेयायां वासरूपो न भवतीति। आहोस्वित्स्त्रीप्रत्यये-
ष्विति। किं चात:। यदि विज्ञायते स्त्रियामभिधेयायामिति लव्या लवितव्य अत्र वासरूपो
न प्राप्नोति[1]। अथ विज्ञायते स्त्रीप्रत्ययेष्विति व्यावक्रोशी व्यावक्रुष्टिरिति न
78.5 सिध्यति[2]॥

Bhāṣya: How is this (*astriyām*) to be understood? Is it to be understood as "when feminine is being expressed a *pratyaya* of dissimilar form is not optionally applicable"?

Or else is it to be understood as "when the feminine *pratyaya* follows a dissimilar *pratyaya* does not optionally apply"? What follows from that? If it is understood to mean "when feminine is being expressed", here (in the forms) *lavyā, lavitavyā* "to be cut down" *vāsarūpo* does not obtain.

Now (if) it is understood to mean "when the feminine *pratyayas* follow", then (the forms) *vyāvakruṣṭih* "mutual abuse or impercation" (*H. car., P.3.3.43, 5.4.14, 7.3.6*) and *vyāvakruṣṭiḥ* (id.) are not established as valid (because they are formed before *3.3.94* 'feminine' *adhikāra*).

78.5 .... एवं तर्हि नैवं विज्ञायते स्त्रियामभिधेयायां नापि स्त्रीप्रत्ययेष्विति। कथं तर्हि।
स्त्रीग्रहणं स्वरयिष्यते। तत्र स्वरितेनाधिकारगतिर्भवति स्त्रियामित्यधिकृत्य ये प्रत्यया विहितास्तेषां
प्रतिषेधो विज्ञास्यते॥

78.8 किमर्थं पुनरिदमुच्यते।

Well then it is understood to mean neither "when feminine nature is being expressed" nor "when the feminine *pratyayas* follow". How then? The mention *strī*/feminine will be pronounced with a *svarita* accent (to indicate a governing rule). There, by reason of the *svarita* accent there is understanding of it as a governing *sūtra.* Thus it will be known that the prohibition is for those *pratyayas* which have been ordained having placed it at the head of a governing *sūtra strīyāḥ* (in the sense of feminine nature).

But what is the reason this is stated?

78.8 असरूपस्य वावचनमुत्सर्गस्य बाधकविषये निवृत्त्यर्थम् ।। 1 ।।

Vārttika 1: The optional statement of a *pratyaya* of dissimilar form is so that the general rule should not be debarred in the context of a rule that cancels it.

78.9 असरूपस्य वावचनं क्रियत उत्सर्गस्य बाधकविषये ऽनिवृत्तिर्यथा स्यात्। तव्यत्तव्यानीयर उत्सर्गास्तेषामजन्ताद्यपवादः[3]। चेयम्। चेतव्यमिति यथा स्यात्। नैतदस्ति प्रयोजनम्। अजन्ताद्यद्विधीयते हलन्ताण्ण्यद्विधीयते[4] एतावन्तश्च

78.12 धातवो यदुताजन्ता हलन्ताश्च। उच्यन्ते च तव्यदादयस्ते वचनाद्भविष्यन्ति।।

Bhāṣya: The exression of option for *pratyayas* of dissimilar form is made so that there should be no ceasing to be valid of the general *utsarga sūtra* in the context of debarring. For instance the general/*utsarga pratyayas* are *tavyat, tavya* and *anīyar* and the *pratyaya yat* that acts after a *dhātu* ending in a vowel is their *apavāda* (exception) *3.1.97* e.g. *ceyam* "to be collected". (*vāsarūpo* is to be stated) so that *cetavyam* also should be derived.

This is not the purpose. *Yat* is ordained after a *dhātu* ending in a vowel (*3.1.97*). *Ṇyat* is ordained after a *dhātu* ending in a consonant (*3.1.124*) and *dhātus* which are vowel ending or consonant ending (are intended here). *Tavyat* and the rest (*3.1.96*) are also stated. They will apply because of the statement (of the rule).

78.13 ....एवं तर्हि ण्वुल्तृचावुत्सर्गो तयोः पचादिभ्योऽजपवादः[5]। पचतीति पचः। पक्ता पाचक इत्यपि यथा स्यात्।। एतदपि नास्ति प्रयोजनम्। वक्ष्यत्येतदजपि सर्वधातुभ्यो वक्तव्य इति।। एवं तर्हिण्वुल्तृजच उत्सर्गास्तेषामिगुपधात्कोऽपवादः विक्षिपः विलिखः। विक्षेप्ता विक्षेपक इत्यपि यथा स्यात्।। अस्ति प्रयोजनमेतत्।

78.16 किं तर्हीति।

Well then *ṇvul* and *tṛc* are *utsarga pratyayas* (*3.1.133*) and the *pratyaya ac* (*3.1.134*) after *pac* (to cook) and the rest is an *apavāda pratyaya. pacati=pac aḥ* "One who cooks".

Vāsarūpo is stated so that the forms *paktā* (*tṛc*) "who cooks" and *pācakaḥ* (*ṇvul*) "cooking or a cook" also should be derived.

This too is not the purpose. He will say this "It should be stated that *ac* also acts after all *dhātus*".

Well then *ṇvul tṛc* and *ac* are general/ *utsarga pratyayas* (and) in place of those *ka* acts as the special/ *apavāda pratyaya* after *dhātus* having a penultimate *ik* (*i u ṛ ḷ*) vowel.

After a *dhātu* with a penultimate *ik* vowel and after *jñā* (to know), *prī* (to please) and *kṝ* (to scatter) the *pratyaya ka* (*a*) acts (*3.1.135*) (e.g.) *vikṣipaḥ* "scatterer" *vilikhaḥ* "writing, writer" *vāsarūpo* is stated so that the forms *vikṣeptā* (*tṛc*) "a scatterer, disperser" and *vikṣepakaḥ* (*id.*) also should be derived. This is the purpose. What then?

78.17 तत्रोत्पत्तिवाप्रसङ्गो यथा तद्धिते ।। 2 ।।

Vārttika 2: There is occasion for the optional arising (of a *pratyaya*) as in the case of a *taddhita pratyaya.*

78.18 तत्रोत्पत्तिर्विभाषा प्राप्नोति यथा तद्धिते।। अस्तु। यदा विक्षिपः विलिखः इत्ये-
तत्र तदा विक्षेप्ता विक्षेपक इत्येतद्भविष्यति। यद्येतल्लभ्येत कृतं स्यात्। तत्तु न
लभ्यम्। किं कारणम्। यथा तद्धित इत्युच्यते तद्धितेषु च सर्वमेवोत्सर्गापवादं
78.21 विभाषा। उत्पद्यते वा न वा।।

Bhāṣya: There optional arising (of a *pratyaya*) obtains as in the case of a *taddhita pratyaya.*

Be it so. When the forms *vikṣipaḥ* "scatterer" and *vilikhaḥ* "writing or painting" do exist then the (alternative forms) *vikṣeptā* (*tṛc*) "scatterer" and *vikṣepakaḥ* (*ṇvul*) *id.* exist.

If this was to be found so it would be alright. However it is not to be found so. What is the reason? It is stated "just as in the case of a *taddhita pratyaya*". And in the case of a *taddhita pratyaya* following, all special/ *apavāda* and general/ *utsarga pratyayas* are optionally applicable. (The *pratyayas*) either arise optionally or else they do not arise.

78.22 सिद्धं त्वसरूपस्य बाधकस्य वावचनात् ।। 3 ।।

Vārttika 3: However it is established as valid by expression of option for the barring of *pratyayas* of dissimilar form.

78.25 सिद्धमेतत्। कथम्। असरूपस्य बाधकस्य वावचनात्। असरूपो बाधको वा
बाधको भवतीति वक्तव्यम्। सिध्यति।सूत्रं तर्हि भिद्यते।। यथान्यासमेवास्तु।

79.2 ननु चोक्तं तत्रोत्पत्तिवाप्रसङ्गो यथा तद्धित इति। नैष दोषः। अस्ति कारणं येन
तद्धितेषु विभाषोत्पत्तिर्भवति। किं कारणम्। प्रकृतिस्तत्र प्रकृत्यर्थे वर्ततेऽन्येन
शब्देन प्रत्ययार्थोऽभिधीयते। इह पुनर्न केवला प्रकृतिः प्रकृत्यर्थे वर्तते न चान्यः
79.5 शब्दोऽस्ति यस्तमर्थमभिद्धीतेति कृत्वानुत्पत्तिर्न भविष्यति॥

Bhāṣya: This is established as valid. How? By expression of option for the barring of a *pratyaya* of dissimilar form. It should be stated that (the *pratyaya* of) dissimilar form that bars, is optionally barring. It is established as valid. But then the *sūtra* is split (into two).

Let it be as it is composed. But surely it was stated (*Vārttika 2*) "There is occasion for the optional arising (of a *pratyaya*) as in the case of a *taddhita pratyaya* following". This is no fault. There is a reason why in the case of *taddhita pratyayas,* optional arising (of *pratyayas*) is applicable. What is the reason? The base occurs there in the sense of the base and by another word the meaning of the *pratyaya* is expressed. But here the *prakṛti* does not exist in the sense of the base and there is no other word which could express that meaning of the *pratyaya.* Therefore the non-arising of a *pratyaya* will not be applicable.

79.5 .... अथवा समयः कृतो
न केवला प्रकृतिः प्रयोक्तव्या न च केवलः प्रत्यय इति[6]। एतस्मात्समयादनुत्प-
त्तिर्न भविष्यति। ननु च य एव तस्य समयस्य कर्ता स एवेदमप्याह। यद्यसौ
तत्र प्रमाणमिहापि प्रमाणं भवितुमर्हति। प्रमाणमसौ तत्र चेह च। सामर्थ्यं त्विह
द्रष्टव्यं शब्दानां प्रयोगे न चानुपत्तौ सामर्थ्यमस्ति। तेनानुत्पत्तिर्न भविष्यति।
कथं तर्हि तद्धितेष्वनुत्पत्तौ सामर्थ्यं भवति। अन्येन प्रत्ययेन सामर्थ्यम्। केन।
79.11 षष्ठ्या ॥

Or otherwise a conventional rule is formed thus "the base/*prakṛti* is not be used alone nor is the *pratyaya* (to be used) alone"

On account of this conventional rule, non-arising will not obtain. But surely he alone who is the maker of this rule says this is also applicable. If that one is the authority there, he deserved to be made the authority here also. He is authority there and here. The capacity of a word (to express its sense) is to be seen in the use of words, and the capacity (to express the same meaning) does not exist when there is no arising (of a *pratyaya*). Therefore non-arising will obtain.

How then does the capacity (to express meaning) exist in the case of *taddhita* (derivation) even when there is non-arising (of a *pratyaya*)? The capacity is due to another *pratyaya.* Which? By reason of the sixth case/genitive.

79.11 .... अथवा रूपवत्तामाश्रित्य वाविधिरुच्यते न चानुत्पत्ती रूपवती। तेनानुत्पत्तिर्न भविष्यति।। एवमपि कुत एतदपवादो विभाषा भविष्यति न पुनरुत्सर्ग इति। न चैवास्ति विशेषो यदपवादो विभाषा स्यादुत्सर्गो वा। अपि च सापेक्षोऽयं निर्देशः क्रियते वासरूप इति न चोत्सर्गवेलायां किंचिदपेक्ष्यमस्त्यपवादवेलायां

79.15 पुनरुत्सर्गोऽपेक्ष्यते।

Or otherwise the statement of option is made with reference to the nature of having form, and non-arising has no form. Therefore non-arising does not obtain.

So too, how then is it that the *apavāda* (special) *pratyaya* will be applicable optionally but not the general/*utsarga pratyaya*? In fact there is not a distinction as to whether the *apavāda* should be optional or the *utsarga*. And also this reference *vāsarūpaḥ* is made as requiring (another word to complete the sense). And thus at the time/occasion of the general/*utsarga pratyaya* there is no expectancy (to complete the sense), but at the time of the special/*apavāda pratyaya* the *utsarga pratyaya* is required (to complete the sense).

79.15 .... तेन यो रूपवानन्यपूर्वको बाधकः प्राप्नोति स वा बाधको भवि-ष्यति। कः पुनरसौ। अपवादः।। यदि यो रूपवानन्यपूर्वको बाधकः प्राप्नोति स वा बाधको भवतीत्युच्यते क्विबादिषु समावेशो न प्राप्नोति। ग्रामणीः ग्रामणाय इति[7]। न ह्येते रूपवन्तः। एतेऽपि रूपवन्तः। कस्यामवस्थायाम्। उपदेशाव-

79.19 स्थायाम्। यद्येवम्

Therefore that (*pratyaya*) which has a form and is preceded by another, obtains as barring (it). That barring will be optional barring. What is that? The special/*apavāda pratyaya*. If it is said that which has a form and is preceded by another (*pratyaya*), obtains as optional barring, inclusion of *kvip* etc. does not obtain. e.g. *grāmaṇīḥ* (with *kvip* by *3.2.61*). "the leader or chief of a village" or (with the *utsarga pratyaya aṇ* by *karmaṇy aṇ 3.2.1* ("The *pratyaya aṇ* acts after a *dhātu* when the object is in composition with it as an *upapada*") *grāmanāyaḥ*. For these do not have form. Even these have form. In what state? In the state of the original teaching. If so...

79.20 अनुबन्धभिन्नेषु विभाषाप्रसङ्गः ॥ 4 ॥

Vārttika 4: There is occasion for option in the case of (*pratyayas* with) different indicatory letters.

79.21 अनुबन्धभिन्नेषु विभाषा प्राप्नोति। कर्मण्यण् (3.2.1) आतोऽनुपसर्गे कः (3) इति कविषयेऽणपि प्राप्नोति।।

Bhāṣya: Option wrongly obtains when there are *pratyayas* having different indicatory letters (e.g.) *karmaṇy aṇ 3.2.1* "The *pratyaya aṇ* acts after a *dhātu* when the object is in composition with it (as an *upapada*)" and by *āto'nupasarge kaḥ 3.2.3* "The *pratyaya ka* acts after a *dhātu* that ends in long *ā* when there is an *upasarga* preceding it". Thus in the sphere of *ka aṇ* also obtains.

79.23 सिद्धमनुबन्धस्यानेकान्तत्वात् ॥ 5 ॥

Vārttika 5: This is establiahsed as valid because of the indicatory letter's nature of not forming a part of that to which it is attached.

79.24 सिद्धमेतत्। कथम्। अनुबन्धस्यानेकान्तत्वात्। अनेकान्ता अनुबन्धाः॥
अथवा प्रयोगेऽसरूपाणां वाविधिर्न्याय्यः।

Bhāṣya: This is established as valid. How? Because of the indicatory letter's nature of not forming part (of that to which it is attached). *anekāntā anubandhāḥ* (*Pari. 4*) "The *anubandhas* (indicatory letters) are no part (of that to which they are attached)". Otherwise it is proper to ordain option for (such *pratyayas*) which are dissimilar in actual use.

79.26 प्रयोगे चेल्लादेशेषु प्रतिषेधः ॥ 6 ॥

Vārttika 6: If it is proper to state option for such *pratyayas* which are dissimilar in actual usage, there is prohibition in relation to the *ādeśas* of *la* (tense *pratyayas*).

79.27 प्रयोगे चेल्लादेशेषु प्रतिषेधो वक्तव्यः। ह्योऽपचदित्यत्र[8] लुङपि प्राप्नोति।श्वः
पक्तेत्यत्र[9] लृडपि प्राप्नोति॥ नैष दोषः। आचार्यप्रवृत्तिर्ज्ञापयति न लादेशेषु वास-
80.2 रूपो भवतीति यदयं हशश्वतोर्लङ् च (3.2.116) इत्याह।अथवा प्रयोगेऽसरू-
पाणां वाविधौ न सर्वमिष्टं संगृहीतमिति कृत्वा द्वितीयः प्रयोग उपास्यते। कोऽसौ।
80.4 उपदेशो नाम। उपदेशे चैते सरूपाः।

Bhāṣya: If it is proper to state option for such *pratyayas* which are dissimilar in actual usage, then there is prohibition in relation to the *ādeśas* of *la* (tense *pratyayas*) to be stated (e.g.) *hyo'pacat* "Yesterday he cooked". Here *luṅ* (aorist) also obtains. *śvaḥ paktā* "Tomorrow he will cook". Here *Lṛṭ* also obtains.

This is not a fault. The master's usage makes known that in the case of the *ādeśas* of *la* (the present rule) "an *apavāda* debars an *utsarga pratyaya* of dissimilar form optionally/*vāsarūpo*" is not applicable, since he says this '*haśaśvatorlaṅ ca*' *3.2.116,* ("And the *pratyaya laṅ* acts after a *dhātu* when the particles *ha* and *śaśvat* are in connection with it, and when the verb denotes past action unperceived by the speaker, and before the commencement of the present day"). Or since that statement 'the optional rule is for *pratyayas* of dissimilar form in actual use', does not cover all the desired cases, the second usage is resorted to. What is that? It is also called an original teaching. And these (*la kāras*) are of the same form in the *upadeśa* (original teaching).

80.5 ननु चोक्तमनुबन्धभिन्नेषु विभाषाप्रसङ्ग इति। परिहृतमेतत्। कथम्। सिद्धमनुबन्धस्यानेकान्तत्वादिति।
अथैकान्ते दोष एव। एकान्ते च न दोषः। आचार्यप्रवृत्तिर्ज्ञापयति नानुबन्धकृतमसारूप्यं
भवतीति यदयं ददातिदधात्योर्विभाषा शं शा-

80.8 स्ति।।

But surely is was stated "there is occasion for option the case of *pratyayas* with different indicatory letters." This has been avoided. How ? (*Vā* 5) "(This is) established as valid because of the indicatory letters' nature of not forming a part (of that to which it is attached)". But the fault is in forming a part (of that to which it is attached). There is no fault in forming part (of that to which it is attached). The master's usage makes known (*Pari 8*). *nānubandhakṛtam asārūpyam "Pratyayas* which when without indicatory letter (have the same form, must) not (be considered) to differ in form when different indicatory letters (have been attached to them". This is (the implied rule/*jñāpaka* which he makes known when) he teaches *śa* optionally by *dadātidadhātyorvibhāṣā 3.1.139* "The *pratyayas śa* optionally acts after the *dhātu dā* (to give) and *dhā* (to hold), when without an *upasarga* (otherwise *ṇa* acts)".

80.8 ....अथवासरूपो बाधको वा बाधको भवतीत्युच्यते। अपवादो नामानुबन्धभिन्नो
वा भवति रूपान्यत्वेन वा। तेनानेनावश्यं किंचित्त्याज्यं किंचित्तु संग्रहीतव्यम्।
तद्यदनुबन्धकृतमसारूप्यं तन्नाश्रयिष्यामो यत्तु रूपान्यत्वेनासारूप्यं तदाश्रयिष्यामः।।
अथवासरूपो बाधको वा बाधको भवतीत्युच्यते सर्वश्चासरूपस्तत्र प्रकर्षगतिर्विज्ञा-

80.12 स्यते। साधीयो योऽसरूप इति।

Or it is said "a dissimilar form barring becomes applicable as optionally barring". The special *apavāda pratyaya* really either has a different indicatory letter or a different form (from the general/*utsarga*). By reason of that it is essential that something be abandoned, but something has to be retained. That dissimilarity which is brought about by the (presence merely of the) indicatory letter/*anubandha* we shall not accept but that dissimilarity which is by reason of the form itself being different we shall accept. Or, it is said "a dissimilar form barring is applicable as optionally barring", and all are dissimilar in form. Therefore excess will be understood. That which is more dissimilar will be accepted.

80.12 ....कश्च साधीयः। यः प्रयोगे च प्राक्च प्रयोगात्।। अथवासरूपो
बाधको वा बाधको भवतीत्युच्यते न चैवं कश्चिदपि सरूपः।

80.14 त एवं विज्ञास्यामः क्वचिद्ये ऽसरूपा इति। अनुबन्धभिन्नाश्च प्रयोगे सरूपाः।।

80.15 अथ कथमिदं विज्ञायतेऽस्त्रियामिति। किं स्त्रियां न भवतीति। आहोस्वित्प्राक्स्त्रिया भवतीति। कश्चात्र विशेषः।

And what is more dissimilar? That which exists (as dissimilar) both in use and before use. Or it is said "a dissimilar form barring is applicable optionally barring" and thus in that way nothing at all is of similar/same form. Thus we shall know that those which are of dissimilar form somewhere (are to be accepted), and those which have different indicatory letters (yet) in use are of the same form.

Now then how is this word *astriyām* understood? Does (it mean) "not applicable in the feminine"? Or else "as far as the word *astrī* it is applicable"? And what is the distinction here ?

80.17 स्त्रियां प्रतिषेधे क्तल्युट्तुमुन्खलर्थेषु विभाषाप्रसङ्गः ।। 7 ।।

Vārttika 7: When the prohibition is effected in the feminine there is occasion for option in the presence of the *pratyayas kta, lyuṭ, tumun* and those having the sense of *khal.*

80.18 स्त्रियां प्रतिषेधे क्तल्युट्तुमुन्खलर्थेषु विभाषा प्राप्नोति। क्त। हसितं छात्रस्य शोभनम्। घञपि प्राप्नोति[10]। ल्युट्। हसनं छात्रस्य शोभनम्। घञपि प्राप्नोति। तुमुन्। इच्छति भोक्तुम्। लिङ्लोटावपि प्राप्नुतः[11]। खलर्थः। ईषत्पानः सोमो भवता।

80.21 खलपि प्राप्नोति।। एवं तर्हि स्त्रियाः प्रागिति वक्ष्यामि।।

Bhāṣya: When the prohibition is effected in the feminine, option obtains in the presence of the *pratyaya kta, lyuṭ, tumun* and *pratyayas* having the sense of *khal.*

kta (e.g.) *hasitam chātrasya śobhanam* "splendid is the laughing of the student". *ghañ* also obtains.

lyuṭ (e.g.) *hasanam chātrasya śobhanam* "splendid is the laughter of the student". *ghañ* obtains.

tumun (e.g.) *icchati bhoktum* "He desires to eat".

liṅ and *loṭ* also obtain.

Having the sense of *khal* (e.g.) "You easily drink *soma*".

khal also obtains.

Well then I shall say as far as "*striyām* (*ktin* 3.3.94) etc.

80.22 स्त्रियाः प्रागिति चेत्क्तवायां वावचनम् ।। 8 ।।

Vārttika 8: When it is stated 'as far as '*striyām*' the expression of option in relation to *pratyaya ktvā* (should be made).

80.23 स्त्रियां प्रागिति चेत् क्त्वायां वावचनं कर्तव्यम्। आसित्वा भुङ्क्ते आस्यते भोक्तुमित्यपि यथा स्यात्।

Bhāṣya: If (it is stated) as far as *striyām* (*3.3.94*) etc. the expresson of option in relation to *pratyaya ktvā* should be made (e.g.) *āsitvā bhuṅkte* "Having sat he eats". So that *āsyate bhoktum* "He sits to eat" also should be derived.

80.24 कालादिषु तुमुनि ।। 9 ।।

Vārttika 9: When time and the rest are in composition, there is (option) in relation to the *pratyaya tumun*.

80.25 कालादिषु तुमुनि वावचनं कर्तव्यम्। कालो भोक्तुम्। कालो भोजनस्येत्यपि यथा स्यात्[12]।।

Bhāṣya: When the word *kāla* (time) and the rest are in composition, expression of option should be made in relation to the *pratyaya tumun* (e.g.) *kālo bhoktum* "It is time to eat". So that also should be applicable *kālo bhojanasya* "It is time for eating".

80.1 अर्हे तृज्विधानम् ।। 10 ।।

Vārttika 10: There is ordaining of the *pratyaya tṛc* in the sense of worthy or fitness (with regard to the agent).

81.2 अर्हे तृज्विधेयः। इमेऽर्हे कृत्या विधीयन्ते ते विशेषविहिताः सामान्यविहितं तृचं[13] बाधेरन् ।।

Bhāṣya: *Tṛc pratyaya* is to be enjoined in the sense of fit(ness).

These *kṛtya pratyayas* are enjoined in the sense of fitness (with regard to the agent) and they being specially enjoined would bar the generally enjoined *utsarga pratyaya tṛc*.

81.3 .... नैष दोषः। भावकर्मणोः कृत्या विधीयन्ते कर्तरि तृच्कः प्रसङ्गो यद्भावकर्मणोः कृत्याः कर्तरि तृचं बाधेरन्।। एवं तर्ह्यर्हे कृत्यतृज्विधानम्। अर्हे कृत्यतृचो विधेयाः। अयमर्हे लिङ्विधीयते स विशेषविहितः
81.6 सामान्यविहितान्कृत्यतृचो बाधेत।।

This is no fault. The *kṛtya pratyayas* are enjoined in the sense of abstract action or state/*bhāva* and in the sense of object/*karman tṛc pratyaya* (is enjoined) in the sense of agent/*kartṛ*. What occasion could be there for *kṛtya pratyaya* (enjoined) in the sense of *bhāva* and *karman* referring to *tṛc* (enjoined) in the sense of *kartṛ*?

Well then, there is enjoining of the *pratyayas kṛtya* and *tṛc* in the sense of fitness (with regard to the agent). In sense of fitness *kṛtya* and *tṛc pratyayas* are to be enjoined. This *liṅ* is enjoined in the sense of fitness. This is specially enjoined, as *apavāda pratyayas* would bar the generally enjoined (*utsarga*) *pratyayas kṛtya* and *tṛc*.

Pradīpa

Pradīpa: 78.2 कथमिति।

"How is this *striyām* to be understood ?"

He asks this having the following doubt: 'Optionally would it be in the sense of feminine' (nature) that is seventh case indicating 'signification of a word'? There would be prohibition optionally of (a *pratyaya* of the same form) when feminine only was being expressed.

Those *pratyayas* are ordained having pronounced the statement 'in the sense of femininity' *vāsarūpo* is not applicable or is it ?

Pradīpa: 78.3 लव्येति

"To be cut down." (here *vā sarūpo* does not obtain).

The meaning is invariable barring obtains of *tavya* etc. by *yat.*

Pradīpa: 78.4 व्यवक्रोशीति।

"(The form)' mutual abuse '(is not established)."

The meaning is that barring of *kt-in* obtains by *ṇac* according to –

Pradīpa: 78.5 स्त्रियां क्तिन् (3.3.94)

"In expressing abstract action etc. by a word in the feminine gender, the *pratyaya ktin* acts after a *dhātu.*"

The meaning is, among those *utsarga* and *apavāda pratyayas,* which are in the province of this feminine governing *sūtra 3.3.94,* the barring is of the *utsarga pratyayas* only.

Pradīpa: 78.18 अस्त्विति।

"Be it so...)"

The sense is, when there is absence of barring (setting aside), due to the *utsarga* not having to be annulled.

Pradīpa: 78.19 यद्येतदिति।

"If this (were to be found so, it would be alright, but it is not . . ."

The sense is, due to the *utsarga* rules being set aside by the *apavāda* rules, even in the alternative of an absence of *apavāda* (*pratyayas*), (*apavādas* prevail) because of the *utsarga* not occurring.

In that context just as by the *sūtra* अत इञ् (4.1.95) "The *pratyaya iñ* acts after a *prātipadika* which ends in a short *a* in denoting a descendant.

In the alternative 'optionally with *iñ, aṇ* is not applicable'. However, a sentence/phrase is in fact (the alternative). So here too, in the alternative of absence of *apavāda pratyayas,* the base alone would express the meaning agent etc. As for example in the case of *agnicit* etc. when *lopa kvip* etc. has been effected.

Pradīpa: 78.22 सिद्धं त्विति।

"However, it is established as valid. . ."

When there is optional barring, where in the alternative there is not barring of the *apavāda* (*pratyaya*), there due to absence of barring, the *utsarga* arises.

Pradīpa: 79.3 अन्येनेति।

". . . by another (word the meaning of the *pratyaya* is expressed.")

The meaning is, 'by the word *apatya* (descendant) etc. (the meaning of the *pratyaya* expressed)' in the sense of the offspring of *Dakṣa* etc.

Pradīpa: 79.4 इह पुनरिति।

"But here (the *prakṛti* does not exist). . ."

"The base alone does not express the whole of its own meaning, how much less will it express the meaning agent etc. For so, when (it is stated) a combination of *prakṛti* (base) and *pratyaya* is being used by 'the methods of the same and the different' it is said 'the base (is seen to) occur in the sense of the base, while the *pratyaya* occurs in the sense of the *pratyaya.* But a base with an unproduced *pratyaya* does not (make known) any meaning. Now then, although the words agent etc. are used as (is said) 'the agent of (*dhātu*) *kṣip* (to throw)', nonetheless even having regard to the verbal activity of *kṛ* (to make), agency may be understood but not in fact with regard to the agency of *kṣip* (to throw), due to the force of that (distinction) barring, even though *bahiraṅga* (with more operations), it is optionally applicable.

Pradīpa: 79.7 य एवेति

"He alone who is (the author of this rule says this)."

The sense is 'Let there be this barring of the conventional rule.'

Pradīpa: 79.9 सामर्थ्यमिति।

"The capacity of a word (to express) the same meaning (is to be seen in the use of words.)"

The meaning is that words are employed for the elucidation of meaning, and when there is non-arising of a *pratyaya* it is not possible for it to cause the meaning to be known.

In the previous refutation, it was stated there is no capacity for a base alone (even) in expressing the whole of its meaning. Further on, however, it is stated there is no usage in fact, due to a conventional rule of (a base) alone (never being allowed).

Pradīpa: 79.10 कथं तर्हीति।

"How then (does the capacity to express meaning) exist in the case of *taddhita* derivation when there is no arising of a *pratyaya*?"

The meaning is, when there is non-arising of a *taddhita pratyaya* for a base alone (without *pratyaya*) due to a conventional rule, the correct form does not obtain.

Pradīpa: 79.10 अन्येनेति।

"(The capacity is by reason of) another (*pratyaya*)."

The usage for a base not alone (i.e. not without a *pratyaya*) is the (sense) of sixth case as 'the offspring of *Dakṣa*'. Here however, when there is non-arising of a *kṛt pratyaya* the *dhātu* would in fact be alone, and due to a conventional rule there is absence of usage for that (state).

Pradīpa: 79.11 अथवेति।

"Or else (the statement of option is made of option with reference to the nature of having form)."

By the word *asarūpa,* 'a different form' is expressed. The meaning is 'And the different nature of the form of that is applicable with regard to the *utsarga* of that having form'. Thus it is asserted in that very alternative, but there is no arising of that without form.

Pradīpa: 79.13 चैवास्तीति।

"But in fact there is no (distinction as to whether the *apavāda* should be optional or the *utsarga*)."

When the *utsarga* is optional it is called *prāpta vibhāṣā* 'optional permission of an operation which otherwise without such permission would not take place at all' but when the *apavāda* is optional it is called *aprāptivibhāṣā* 'optional prescription of what otherwise is obligatory'. Thus there is not distinction.

Pradīpa: 79.14 अपवादवेलायामिति।

"But at the time of the *apavāda pratyaya* (the *utsarga* is required)."

As long as the *utsarga* is not expected to be with the nature of that to be barred, so long there is not in fact application of the *apavāda pratyaya.*

Pradīpa: 79.18 उपदेशावस्थायामिति।

"In the situation of an original teaching (they have form)."

The meaning is, that because of the convention of analogy (lit. proximity) there is resort to (conception of) the absence of form in the situation of the original teaching.

Pradīpa: 80.2 यदयमिति।

"When he teaches *śa* optionally (in the case of *ādeśas* of *la*), the present rule does not apply." (Since he says this '*haśaśvator laṅ ca*'.)

Due to being of dissimilar form, there is common applicability of *laṅ* (imperfect) with *liṭ* (perfect) by परोक्षे लिट् (3.2.115) (भूते, अनद्यतने) "The *pratyaya liṭ* acts after a *dhātu* in the sense of the past, before the commencement of the current day and not perceived by the narrator."

By the ordinary ordaining of *liṅ* the meaning is not in fact established thus. The meaning is, however, 'he makes known (by *jñāpaka*) that ordained does not have comon applicability for the *lakāras.*

Pradīpa: 80.2 अथवेति।

"Or (since the optional rule for *pratyayas* of dissimilar form, does not cover all desired cases, the second usage is resorted to)."

Pradīpa: 80.4 सरूपाः

"These are of the same form."

All the ten *lakāras* are of dissimilar form in the first stage of *upadeśa* e.g. *laṭ*, *liṭ*, etc. However, in the second stage of *upadeśa* they are all *sarūpa* because each one is simply *la*.

Pradīpa: 80.14 क्वचिद्ध इति।

"(Thus we shall know that) those which are of similar form somewhere (are to be accepted)." सरूपाः should be changed to असरूपाः the meaning in actual usage.

Due to statement 'in an *upadeśa* there is dissimilarity of form for everything', in fact the mention of dissimilar form (in this rule) would be pointless.

Pradīpa: 80.15 कथमिति।

"Then how (is this word *astriyām* to be understood)?"

When in fact it is already applicable amongst those ordained within the province of the feminine/*strī* governing rule *3.3.94*, what is the point of prohibition? Further on in fact, the rule *Vāsarūpo* is applicable for the *strī* governing rule. The question is, how is the *vāsarūpo* rule applicable up to the *strī* governing rule and prevented by the governing rule ?

Pradīpa: 81.3 कर्तरि तृच्

"*Tṛc* acts in the sense of agent."

तयोरेव कृत्यक्तखलर्थाः

"The *pratyayas* called *kṛtya* and the *pratyaya kta* and those that have the sense of *khal* have (only) those two senses, abstract action/*bhāva* and object/*karman*."

कर्तरि कृत् (3.4.67)

"The *pratyayas* called *kṛt* act in the sense of agent/*kartṛ*.

Pradīpa: 81.5 लिङ्विधीयते।

"*Liṅ* (is enjoined in the sense of fitness)."

लिङ् यदि (3.3.168)

"The *pratyaya liṅ* (optative) acts after a *dhātu* when the word is in composition, and the words *kāla* etc. occur in construction."

Pradīpa: 81.6 कृत्यतृचो

"(Would bar the *utsarga*) *kṛtya* and *tṛc*."

कृत्याः (3.1.95)

"From this *sūtra* up to *sūtra ṇvul tṛcau 3.1.133* all the *pratyayas* ordained will have the name *kṛtya*."

Notes

[1] प्राप्नोति। by अचो यत् (3.1.97)

"The *pratyaya yat* acts after a *dhātu* that ends in a vowel."

तव्यतव्यानीयरः (3.1.96)

"The *pratyaya tavyat, tavya* and *anīyar* act after *dhātus*."

[2] 78.5 सिध्यते कर्मव्यतिहारे णच्स्त्रियाम्

"The *pratyaya ṇac* acts after a *dhātu* in denoting reciprocity of the action and the word so formed is in the feminine gender."

स्त्रियामित्यधिकृत्येति।

"Having placed *striyām* at the head as a governing *sūtra* (it will be known the prohibition is for those *pratyayas* which have been ordained)."

[3] 78.10 अजन्ताद्यदपवाद।

"(*Utsarga tavyat* etc. and *yat*) after a *dhātu* ending in a vowel is (their) *apavāda*."

c.f. तव्यत्तव्यानीयरः (3.1.96) and अचो यत् (3.1.97)

[4] 78.11 हलन्ताण्ण्यद्विधीयते।

"*Ṇyat* is ordained," (after a *dhātu* ending in a consonant and one ending in *ṛ*).

by ऋहलोर्ण्यत् (3.1.124).

[5] 78.13 अजपवादः

"*Ṇvul* and *tṛc* are *utsarga pratyayas* and *ac* is *apavāda*."

ण्वुल्तृचौ (3.1.33)

"The *pratyayas ṇvul* and *tṛc* act after all *dhātus* expressing the agent."

नन्दिग्रहिपचादिभ्यो ल्युणिन्यचः (3.1.134)

"The *pratyayas lyu, ṇini* and *ac* act respectively after *nandi* and the rest, *grahi* and the rest, and *pac* and the rest."

[6] 79.6 केवलः प्रत्यय इति। "(The base is not to be used alone) nor is *pratyaya* to be used alone."

सिद्धं तूभयनियमात् भाष्य (3.1.2) वा० 2 See text.

[7] 79.17 ग्रामणीः ग्रामणाय इति। "Leader of chief of the village."

सत्सूद्विषद्रु हदुहयुजविदभिदच्छिदजिनीराजामुपसर्गेऽपि क्विप् (3.2.61) (सुपि)

"The *pratyaya kvip* acts after the following *dhātus* when in composition with a word ending in a *sup*/case, namely, *sad* (to sit), *sū* (to bring forth), *dviṣ*, (to hate), *druh* (bear malice), *duh* (to milk), *yuj* (to join, to concentracte the mind), *vid* (to know, to become, to consider), *bhid* (to divide), *chid* (to cut), *ji* (to conquer), *nī* (to lead), and *rāj* (to shine)."

[8] 79.27 ह्योऽपचदित्यत्र। "Yesterday he cooked . . ."

When imperfect/*laṅ* follows, there is the *pratyaya t* without a vowel (from *tip*) by इतश्च (3.4.100)

However, when aorist/*luṅ* follows the form being *apākṣīt* with the augment *ī*, due to the difference in form there is occasion for common applicability of form.

अनद्यतने लङ् (3.2.191) (भूते)

"*Pratyaya laṅ* acts after a *dhātu* employed in the sense of past time before the commencement of the present day."

लुङ् (3.2.110)

"*Pratyaya luṅ* acts after a *dhātu* in the sense of past time."

The meaning is *kvip* etc. are not taken due to their not having any form when in actual use.

[9] 80.1 पक्तेत्यत्र "(Tomorrow) he will cook there."

(*Lṛṭ* also obtains).

अनद्यतने लुट् (3.3.15)

"The *pratyaya luṭ* acts after *dhātu* in the sense of future time not in the course of the present day."

लृट् शेषे च (3.3.13) (भविष्यति, क्रियायाम्, क्रियार्थायाम्, धातोः)

"The *pratyaya lṛṭ* acts after a *dhātu* in the remaining cases, where simple future is to be indicated and also where there is in construction with it another verb denoting an action performed for the sake of a future action."

[10] 80.19 घञपि प्राप्नोति। "*Ghañ* also obtains."

नपुंसके भावे क्तः (3.3.114)

"The *pratyaya kta* acts after a *dhātu* when the name of an action is expressed in the neuter gender."

भावे (3.3.18)

"The *pratyaya ghañ* acts after a *dhātu* when mere action is denoted."

ल्युट् च (3.3.115) (नपुंसके भावे)

"And *lyuṭ pratyaya* acts after a *dhātu* when the name of an action is expressed in the neuter gender."

[11] 80.20 लिङ् लोटावपि प्राप्नुतः। "*Liṅ* and *loṭ* also obtain."

समानकर्तृकेषु तुमुन् (3.3.158)

"The *pratyaya tumun* acts after a *dhātu* when another *dhātu* meaning to wish is in construction, provided that the agent of both the *dhātus* is the same."

इच्छार्थेषु लिङ् लोटौ (3.3.157)

"The *pratyaya liṅ* (optative) and *loṭ* (imperative) act after a *dhātu* when another *dhātu* having the sense of wishing is in construction with it."

By the *sūtra* लिङ् *liṅ* in fact is applicable. "The *pratyaya liṅ* acts after a *dhātu* when *dhātus* meaning to wish are in construction with it and the agent of both *dhātus* is the same." However, in *3.3.157,* due to the indication of *liṅ* and *loṭ* together, here too combined indication is effected. Due to the restriction *liṅ ca 3.3.159,* it is possible to say '*loṭ* will not be applicable'.

But surely, due to the difference in meaning, *tumun* in the sense of abstract action and *liṅ* and *loṭ* in sense of agent and object, whence is 'the state of barring that to be barred' ? This is no fault. There is ordaining of *liṅ* and *loṭ* in the sense of abstract action also. So with regard to that (situation) the state of barring that to be barred is desired.

[12] 80.21 खलपि प्राप्नोति। "*Khal* also obtains,"

By आतो युच् "The *pratyaya yuc* acts after *dhātu* ending in long *ā* (when *īṣad, dur,* and *su* are combined as *upapadas* in the sense of easily done or with difficulty)."

ईषद्दुः सुषु कृच्छ्राकृच्छ्रार्थेषु खल् (3.3.126)

"The *pratyaya khal* acts after a *dhātu* when *īṣad, dur,* and *su* are combined with it as *upapadas* in the sense of hard and difficult or light and easy."

[13] 80.24 आस्यते भोक्तुमित्यपि यथा स्यात्।

"So that 'He sits to eat' should also be applicable."

समानकर्तृकयोः पूर्वकाले (3.4.21)

"When two actions have the same agent the *pratyayas ktvā* acts after that *dhātu* which takes place in a time prior to that of the other."

समानकर्तृकेषु तुमुन्।

"The *pratyaya tumun* acts after a *dhātu* when another *dhātu* meaning to wish is in construction, provided that the agent of both the *dhātus* is the same."

Due to their having same spheres, (here) it is understood, because of the purpose of eating only a slightly earlier time, for sitting down there is occasion for the state of barring that to be barred. *Ktvā* occurs in the sense of abstract action and there in fact is here arising of a *la-kāra*.

Also the sameness of meaning exists.

In that context this is the conclusion that 'The *vāsarūpa* rule applies even beyond the sphere of the *strī adhikāra*'.

'The *pratyayas kṛtyas* and the *pratyaya tṛc,* act after a *dhātu* when fitness as regards the agent is implied, as well as the *pratyaya liṅ*'. Here however, by reason of the reference to *kṛtya* and *tṛc* the *a-nitya*/variable nature of *vāsarūpo* rule is made known, i.e. non-uniform *pratyayas* rule is not universally valid, these had to be stated specifically.

[14] 81.3 तृच्। "*Apavādas* would bar the *utsarga tṛc.*"

ण्वुलतृचौ

"The *pratyayas ṇvul* (*aka*) and *tṛc* (*tṛ*) act after all *dhātus* expressing the agent."

कृत्याः ॥ 3 । 1 । 95 ॥

Pāṇini 3.1.95: From this *sūtra* as far as *Ṇvultṛau Sto* 3.1.133 all the *pratyayas* will be called *kṛtya.*

81.8 कृत्यसंज्ञायां प्राङ्ण्वुल्वचनम् ॥ 1 ॥

Vārttika 1: When the name *kṛtya* (is stated), a statement that (it is applicable) as far as the *ṇvul* rule should be made.

81.9 कृत्यसंज्ञायां प्राङ्ण्वुल इति वक्तव्यम्। किं प्रयोजनम्। ण्वुलः कृत्संज्ञा मा भूत्॥

Bhāṣya: It should be stated that when the technical name *kṛtya* (is enjoined it is applicable) as for as *ṇvul* (*ṇvultṛcau 3-1-133*).

What is the purpose? So that the technical name *kṛtya* should not be applicable to *ṇvul.*

81.11 अर्हे कृत्यतृज्वचनं तु ज्ञापकं प्राङ्ण्वुल्वचनानर्थक्यस्य ॥ 2 ॥

Vārttika 2: However the rule (enjoining) *kṛtya* and *tṛc* in the sense of fitness is an implied rule/*jñapaka* (making known) the pointlessness of expressing "as far as *ṇvul*".

81.12 यदयमर्हे कृत्यतृचश्च (3.3.169) इति तृज्ग्रहणं करोति तज्ज्ञापयत्याचार्यः प्राङ्ण्वुलः
कृत्यसंज्ञा भवतीति॥ एवमपि ण्वुलः कृत्यसंज्ञा प्राप्नोति। योगापेक्षं
81.4 ज्ञापकम्॥

Bhāṣya: Since he makes specific mention of *tṛc pratyaya* (by) this (*sūtra*) *arhe kṛtyatṛcaśca 3.3.169* "The *pratyaya kṛtya* and the *pratyaya tṛc* act after a *dhātu* when fitness with regard to the agent is implied (as well as the *pratyaya liṅ*)". The master makes known that the technical name *kṛtya* is applicable as far as (but excluding) the *pratyaya ṇvul.*

So too the technical name *kṛtya* obtains after *ṇvul.* A *jñāpaka* concerns only that particular rule to which it refers.

Pradīpa

Pradīpa: 81.8 कृत्याः। कृत्संज्ञायामिति। वा॰ 1

"When the technical name *kṛtya* is stated . . ."

Thus by '*kṛtyāḥ*' the *sūtra* of such a kind he states . . .

ण्वुल् "(As far as) *ṇvul* . . . "

ण्वुलतृचौ (3.1.133)

Pradīpa: 81.13 योगापेक्षमिति

"(A *jñāpaka*) concerns only that partiuclar rule to which it refers."

The meaning is that the technical name governing rule *kṛtya* applies as far as this *ṇvul-tṛcau 3.1.133.*

This will be inferred by reason of the mention *tṛc* (in *arhe kṛtya tṛccaśca 3.1.169*).

तव्यत्तव्यानीयरः ॥ 3 । 1 । 96 ॥

Pāṇini 3.1.96: The *pratyayas tavyat, tavya* and *anīyar* act after *dhātus.*

81.16 केलिमर उपसंख्यानम् ॥ 1 ॥

Vārttika 1: Additional enumeration of the *pratyaya kelimar.*

81.17 केलिमर उपसंख्यानं कर्तव्यम्। पचेलिमा माषाः। पक्तव्याः। भिदेलिमाः सरलाः। भेत्तव्याः॥

Bhāṣya: Additional enumeration should be made of the *pratyaya kelimar* (e.g.) *pacelimā māṣāḥ* "Beans soon to be cooked/being soon cooked ripening quickly", *pak-tavyāḥ* "to be cooked", *bhidelimāḥ saralāḥ* (M.W.) "broken pine trees", *bhetavyāḥ* "they are to be broken".

81.19 वसेस्तव्यत्कर्तरि णिच्च ॥ 2 ॥

Vārttika 2: The *pratyaya tavyat* also acts after the *dhātu vas-i* in the sense of agent and the *pratyaya* has an *it ṇ.*

81.20 वसेस्तव्यत्कर्तरि वक्तव्यः। णिच्चासौ भवतीति वक्तव्यम्[1]। वसतीति वास्तव्यः॥

Bhāṣya: It should be stated that *tavyat pratyaya* acts after the *dhātu vas-i* in the sense of agent. And it should be stated that (*tavyat*) becomes *ṇit*, possessed of *ṇ anubandha* also. *vasati* "He dwells" = *vāstavya* "left on any spot", (as a worthless remainder; also applied to *Rudra*, to whom the leavings of the sacrifice belong) *TS.VS.* settled, resident an inhabitant (*Bh. R.* etc.).

81.21 तद्धितो वा ।। 3 ।।

Vārttika 3: Or (it should be regarded) as a *taddhita* (form).

81.22 तद्धितो वा पुनरेष भविष्यति वास्तुनि भवो वास्तव्यः ।।

Bhāṣya: Or rather it is a *taddhita* (derivative). *vāstavyaḥ* means "being in a dwelling".

Pradīpa

Pradīpa: 81.22 वास्तुनि भव इति।

"*Vāstavyaḥ* means being in a dwelling."

Due to forming a part of *digādi* (*4.3.54*) *yat pratyaya* (applies).

दिगादिभ्यो यत् (4.3.54)

"The *pratyaya yat* acts in the sense of who stays here after the *prātipadikas dik* etc."

He thinks that somehow there should be minute enumeration of all the invariable words.

As was spoken by *Bhartṛhari*

उपादायापि ये हेयास्तानुपायान् प्रचक्षते।
उपायानां च नियमो नावश्यमवतिष्ठते ।। 2.38

"(Grammarians) propound means (for the understanding of language) which, once grasped can be abandoned. And there is nothing necessarily absolute in regard to the means."

Here in the example *avāstavya* (unsubstantial, unreal). Here is no difference in relation to accent. The final *udātta* which is ordained by

कृत्योकेष्णुच्चार्वादयश्च (6.2.160)

"After the negative particle, words formed with *kṛtya pratyayas* (*3.1.95*), by *uka* and *iṣṇuc* and the words *cāru* etc. have *udātta* on the final.

That is in fact by the *sūtra*

ययतोश्चातदर्थे (6.2.156)

"Words formed with *pratyayas ya* and *yat* when not denoting 'useful for that' have *udātta* on the last syllable after the particle *nañ* negating the attribute."

Notes

[1] 81.20 वक्तव्यम्। "It should be stated (that *tavyat* becomes possessed of *p*)."

अत उपधायाः (7.2.116)

"In place of the penultimate *a* of an *aṅga*, *vṛddhi* acts in the presence of a *pratyaya* having an indicatory *ñ* or *ṇ*."

अचो यत् ॥ 3 । 1 । 97 ॥

Pāṇini 3.1.97: The *pratyaya yat* acts after a *dhātu* that ends in a vowel.

82.2 अज्ग्रहणं किमर्थम्। अजन्ताद्यथा स्याद्धलन्तान्मा भूदिति। नैतदस्ति प्रयोजनम्। हलन्ताण्ण्यद्विधीयते[1] स बाधको भविष्यति।। यथैव तर्हि ण्यद्यतं बाधत एवं तव्य- दादीनपि बाधेत[2]। अज्ग्रहणे पुनः क्रियमाणेऽजन्ताद्यद्विधीयते हलन्ताण्ण्यदेतावन्तश्च धातवो हलन्ताश्चोच्यन्ते च तव्यदादयस्ते वचनाद्भविष्यन्ति। नैत-

82.6 दस्ति प्रयोजनम्। वासरूपेण तव्यदादयो भविष्यन्ति।

Bhāṣya: What is the purpose of mentioning *ac* (vowels) ? So that (*yat*) should be applicable after vowel ending *dhātu* and not after a consonant ending *dhātu*. This is not the purpose. *Ṇyat pratyaya* is ordained after a consonant ending *dhātu*. That will be barring *yat*.

As in fact then *ṇyat* bars *yat*, so it would also bar *tavyat* and the rest (*tavyattavyānīyaraḥ 3.1.96*).

When however specific mention is being made of *ac*, *yat* is enjoined after *dhātus* ending in a vowel and *ṇyat* after consonant ending (*dhātus*), and whatever *dhātus* are there are there, they either end in vowels or end in consonants, and *tavyat* and the rest are ordained. They will obtain because of their being stated. This is not the purpose. By reason of the rule "*vāsarūpo'striyām 3.1.94.* ("An *apavāda pratyaya* optionally bars an *utsarga* of dissimilar form but not so in the case of feminine *pratyayas* which always bar *utsarga pratyayas*") *tavya* and the rest will be applicable.

82.6 .... इदं तर्हि प्रयोजनमजन्तभूत-
पूर्वमात्रादपि यथा स्यात्। लव्यम्। पव्यम्। आर्धधातुकसामान्ये गुणे कृते यि प्रत्ययसामान्ये च वान्तादेशे कृते हलन्तादिति ण्यत्प्राप्नोति[3]। तथा दित्स्यम् धित्स्यम् आर्धधातुकसामान्येऽकारलोपे कृते हलन्तादिति ण्यत्प्राप्नोति[4]। अज्ग्रहण-
82.10 सामर्थ्याद्येव भवति।।

This then is the purpose, so that (*yat*) should be applicable also after (a *dhātu*) which formerly ended in a vowel (e.g.) *lavyam* "It is to be cut", *pavyam* "It is to be purified".

When *guṇa* has been effected in the presence of *ārdhadhātuka pratyayas* in general and when the *ādeśa* for those that end in *v* (*av* for o *āv* for *au*) have been effected in the presence of the general *pratyayas* beginning with *y*, the *pratyaya ṇyat* obtains after that ending in a consonant.

Similarly (in the forms) *ditsyam* "what one is willing to give", *dhitsyam* "what one is willing to put, place or bestow", when *lopa* elision of an *ārdhadhātuka pratyaya* following has been effected then *ṇyat* obtains after that ending in a consonant.

Because of the force of mentioning *ac* (vowels), *yat* alone is applicable.

82.11 यति जनेरुपसंख्यानम् ।। 1 ।।

Vārttika 1: In (the domain of) *yat* and additional enumeration of *jan* should be made.

82.12 यति जनेरुपसंख्यानं कर्तव्यम्। जन्यं वत्सेन। अत्यल्पसिदमुच्यते। तकिशसिचतियतिजनीनामुपसंख्यानमिति वक्तव्यम्। तकि
82.14 तक्यम्। शसि शस्यम्। चति चत्यम्। यति यत्यम्। जनि जन्यम्।

Bhāṣya: Additional enumeration should be made of the *dhātu jan-i* in the domain of *yat* (e.g.) *janyam vatsena* "to be born with a calf".

Very little is being stated here. It should be stated "there is additional enumeration of the *dhātus tak-i, śas-i, yati* and *jan-i* (in the domain of *yat*)" e.g.

tak-i, takyam "to be shrunk", diseases accompanied by skin eruption,

śas-i śasyam "to be cut down or slaughtered",

cat-i catyam "to be hidden",

yat-i yatyam "to be striven for",

jan-i janyam "to be born".

82.15 हनो वा वध च ॥ 2 ॥

Vārttika 2: Optionally after *han*, and *vadha* is (*ādeśa* of *han*).

82.16 हनो वा यद्वक्तव्यः। वध इत्ययं चादेशो वक्तव्यः। वध्यः। घात्यः[5]॥

Bhāṣya: It should be stated that optionally *yat* acts after *han.* And it should be stated that *vadha* is the substitute/ *ādeśa* of *han* e.g. *vadhyaḥ* "to be killed", *ghātyaḥ id.*

82.17 तद्धितो वा ॥ 3 ॥

Vārttika 3: Or (it should be regarded as) a *taddhita* (form).

82.18 तद्धितो वा पुनरेष भविष्यति। वधमर्हति वध्यः[5]॥ यदि तद्धितः समासो न प्राप्नोति।

Bhāṣya: Or this (form *vadhya*) will be regarded as a *taddhita* (derivative) e.g. *vadham arhati* = *vadhyaḥ* "deserving or fit to be killed".

If it is a *taddhita* form, a compound/ *samāsa* does not obtain.

82.19 . . . असिवध्यः मुसलवध्य इति। यति पुनः सति साधनं कृतेति वा पादहारका-
द्यर्थमिति समासः सिद्धो भवति॥ यदि पुनरसिवधशब्दादुत्पत्तिः स्यात्। असिवध
मर्हतीति। नैवं शक्यम्। स्वरे हि दोषः स्यात्। असिवध्यः एवं स्वरः प्रस-
82.22 ज्येत। असिवध्यः इति चेष्यते॥

(E.g.) *asi vadhyaḥ* "deserving to be killed by a sword", *musalavadhyaḥ* "deserving to be killed by a club". If however *yat* is applied, a *samāsa* becomes established as valid (by) "*sādhanam kṛteti vā pādahārakādyartham*" *2.1.33 Vā. 2* "Or (the rule should be phrased as) *sādhanam kṛta* 'a word standing for any *sādhana* operator (is composed/compounded) with a semantically connected case inflected word ending in a *kṛt pratyaya*' for the sake of (compounds) like *pādahāraka* "taken away from the feet".

But if arising of the *pratyaya yat* after the word *asivadha* (with the meaning *asivadhyam arhati*) "deserving killing by the sword" is understood, (then the sentence) *asivadham arhati* "He deserves to deserve to be killed by the sword" (would be valid). It is not possible in that way. For there would be a fault with regard to accent *asivadhyáḥ*. Thus we would have a *svarita* accent applicable, and the form *asivadhyáḥ* is desired.

Pradīpa

Pradīpa: 82.11 यति जनेरिति। वा॰ 1

"In the domain of *yat*, additional enumeration of *jan* should be made."

The ordaining of *yat* after *jan* is for the purpose of accent by

यतोऽनावः (6.1.213)

"Whatever is formed with the *pratyaya yat* has, if it is a two-syllable word, *udātta* on the first syllable, with the exception of *nāvyaḥ* from *nau*."

However, it is established as valid also with *ṇyat* or as जन्यम् due to the prohibition of *vṛddhi* by

जनिवध्योश्च (7.3.35)

"*Vṛddhi* is not substituted for the vowels of *jan* and *vadhi* before the aorist sign *ciṇ* and the *kṛt pratyayas* with an indicatory *ñ* and *ṇ*."

Pradīpa: 82.18 यदि तद्धित इति।

"If it is *taddhita* form, a *samāsa* does not obtain."

Due to the absence of a rule for compounding with that...

Pradīpa: 82.19 पादहारकाद्यर्थमिति।

"(A *sādhaka* ending in a *kṛt* is) for the sake of forms like 'taken away from the feet/*pāda hāraka*'."

साधनं कृतेति पादहारकाद्यर्थम् (2.1.33) वा॰ 2

82.21 स्वरे हि दोष इति।

See text.

For there would be a fault with regard to accent, *svarita* accent would have been applicable after the word *asivadha* (deserving death by sword) when *yat* follows by

तित्स्वरितम् (6.1.185)

"A *pratyaya* with an *it t* is *svarita* (circumflex).

However, in compound with that ending in a *kṛt pratyaya*, the word *vadhya* is applicable as having initial *udātta*, by reason of the accent being that of the original word in a compound having a *kṛt pratyaya* in its last member.

And *yat* does not obtain after the word *asivadha* because of *vadha* being recited on its own in the list *daṇḍa* etc. and because of the *tadanta* rule not (applying here).

Pradīpa: 82.22 चेष्यते।

('*Asi vadhyaḥ*' is the desired form).

यतोऽनावः (6.1.213)

"Whatever is formed by the *pratyaya yat* if a two-syllable word has *udātta* on the first syllable, with the exception of *nāvyaḥ* (*nau*)."

गतिकारकोपपदात् कृत् (6.1.139) (प्रकृतिस्वरम्)

"In a *tatpuruṣa* compound, a word ending in a *kṛt pratyaya* preserves its original accent, when preceded by an indeclinable/*avyaya* called *gati* (*1.4.60*) or a noun directly related to the action of the verb/*kāraka* or any word which gives occasion for compounding as a subordinate word situated near/*upapada* (*3.1.92*)."

Notes

1 82.3 यद्विधीयते। "*Yat* is ordained after a vowel."

by ऋहलोर्ण्यत् (3.1.124)

"The *pratyaya ṇyat* acts after a *dhātu* that ends in *ṛ* long or short or in a consonant."

2 82.4 तव्यदादीनपि बाधेत्। "It would also bar *tavyat* etc."

तव्यतव्यानीयारः (3.1.96) "See text.

3 82.7 ण्यत्प्राप्नोति। "*Ṇyat* obtains."

सार्वधातुकार्धधातुकायो: (7.3.84)

"*Guṇa* acts in place of final *ik* (*i u ṛ ḷ*) vowel of an *aṅga* (here) in the presence of *sārvadhātuka* and *ārdhadhātuka pratyayas* beginning with a vowel."

वान्तोयि प्रत्यये (6.1.79)

"The substitute of *av* and *āv* for *o* and *au* also takes place in the presence of a *pratyaya* beginning with a *y*."

ऋहलोर्ण्यत् (3.1.124)

"The *pratyaya ṇyat* acts after a *dhātu* that ends in *ṛ* long or short or a consonant."

[4] 82.9 ण्यत्प्राप्नोति।

"*Ṇyat* obtains (after that ending in a consonant)."

अतो लोपः (6.4.48)

"The *a* standing at the end of a stem is *lopa*-elided in the presence of an *ārdhadhātuka pratyaya.*"

[5] 82.16 घात्यः। "To be killed."

ऋहलोर्ण्यत् (3.1.124)

हनस्तोऽचिण्णलोः (7.3.32)

"*T* is *ādeśa* in place of *n* of the *dhātu han* in the presence of a *pratyaya* with an indicatory *ñ* or *n* which causes also the *vṛddhi* of the penultimate *a*, but the *ādeśa* does not occur before the aorist sign *ciṇ* nor before the personal ending *ṇal* of the perfect."

हो हन्तेर्ञ्णिन्नेषु (7.3.54)

"A guttural is the *ādeśa* for the *h* of *han* in the presence of a *pratyaya* with an indicatory *ñ* or *ṇ* and before *n.*"

[6] 82.18 वध्यमर्हति वध्यः। "Deserving or fit to be killed."

दण्डादिभ्यो यः (5.1.66)

"After the word *daṇḍa* and the rest in the *karman* (accusative), the *pratyaya ya* acts in the sense of who deserves that."

Pradīpa says *yat pratyaya,* the reading in *kāśikā* and implies the *vṛtti* reading is in conflict with the *bhāṣya* (*Uddyota*).

गदमदचरयमश्चानुपसर्गे ॥ 3 । 1 । 100 ॥

Pāṇini 3.1.100 : The *pratyayas yat* acts after *dhātus gad* (to speak), *mad* (to be mad), *car* (to go, eat) and *yam* (to restrain) when those *dhātus* do not take any *upasarga.*

83.2 अनुपसर्गाच्चरेराङि चागुरौ ॥ 1 ॥

Vārttika 1: (*Yat pratyaya* acts) after the *dhātu car-i* without an *upasarga* and when preceded by the *upasarga āṅ* except when meaning teacher.

83.3 अनुपसर्गाच्चरेरित्यत्राङि चागुराविति वक्तव्यम्। आचर्यो देशः। अगुराविति किमर्थम्। आचार्य उपनयमानः।।

Bhāṣya: It should be stated that (the *pratyaya yat* acts) after the *dhātu car-i* without an *upasarga* and also when preceded by the *upasarga āṅ* but not in the sense of teacher/*guru.* (e.g.) *ācaryo deśaḥ* "an approachable country". Why (is it said) "but not in the meaning of teacher"? *ācārya upanayamānaḥ* "The spirutual preceptor/*guru* leading or drawing the boy to himself (in the initiation ceremony/*upanayana*).

अर्यः स्वामिवैश्ययोः ॥ 3 । 1 । 103 ॥

Pāṇini 3.1.103 : The word *arya* is laid down as an irregular form/ *nipātana* when meaning Lord and a *vaiśya.*

83.6 स्वामिन्यन्तोदत्तत्वं च ॥ 1 ॥

Vārttika 1: And in the sense of lord/*svāmin* (*arya*) has final *udātta* accent.

83.7 स्वामिन्यन्तोदात्तत्वं च वक्तव्यम्। आर्यः स्वामी ।।

Bhāṣya: And it should be stated that in the sense of lord/*svāmin* (*arya*) has final *udātta* accent. *āryaḥ svāmī* "Lord".

अजर्यं संगतम् ॥ 3 । 1 । 105 ॥

Pāṇini 3.1.105 : The word *ajaryam* (imperishable) is laid down as an irregular form/ *nipātana,* and when qualifying the word *saṅgatam* (friendship) expressed or understood.

83.9 संगतमिति किं प्रत्युदाह्रियते। अजरः कम्बलः। अजरिता कम्बल इति। किं पुनः कारणं कर्तृसाधनः प्रत्युदाह्रियते न भावसाधनः प्रत्युदाहार्यः। एवं तर्हि

Bhāṣya: What is adduced as the counter example for *saṅgatam*?

ajaraḥ kambalaḥ "an undecaying blanket",

ajaritā kambalaḥ "an undecaying blanket".

But what is the reason a counter example is to be adduced with the agent *kāraka* or *sādhana* and a counter example is not to be adduced with *bhāva* (abstract action) as *sādhana* ? Well then . . .

83.11 अजर्यं कर्तरि ।। 1 ।।

Vārttika 1: The word *ajaryam* (occurs) in the sense of agent.

83.12 अजर्यं कर्तरीति वक्तव्यम्। तत्तर्हि वक्तव्यम्। न वक्तव्यम्।

Bhāṣya: It should be stated that the word *ajaryam* (occurs) in the sense of agent. Then should that be stated (in the *sūtra*)? It need not be stated.

83.12 .... गत्यर्थानां क्तः कर्तरि विधीयते[1] तेन योगादजर्यं कर्तरि भविष्यति। गत्यर्थानां वै क्तः कर्मण्यपि विधीयते तेन योगादजर्यं कर्मण्यपि विधीयते प्राप्नोति। जीर्यतिरकर्मकः। भावे तर्हि प्राप्नोति। संगतग्रहणमिदानीं किमर्थं स्यात्। कर्तृविशेषणं संगतग्रहणम्। संगतं चेत्कर्तृ भव-

83.16 तीति। तद्यथा। हृषेर्लोमसु (7.2.29) इति लोमानि चेत्कर्तृणि भवन्ति

The *pratyaya kta* is ordained for *dhātus* having the meaning of motion in the sense of agent. Therefore, due to connection with that rule, *ajaryam* will be applicable in the sense of agent.

Indeed *kta* is also ordained in the sense of *karman* (object) for *dhātus* having the same sense of motion. Therefore, because of that rule, *ajaryam* also obtains in the sense of object/*karman*. The *dhātu jṝ* is intransitive. Then it obtains in the sense of abstract action or state/*bhāve.* Now what would be the purpose of mentioning the word *saṅgata* ? The mention of *saṅgatam* is as a qualification of the agent. If the agent is 'a friendship' then it is applicable, as for example (the *sūtra*) "*hṛṣer lomasu*" *7.2.29.* "The participial *pratyaya* optionally has *iṭ āgama* after the *dhātu hṛṣ* when the word *loman* or its synonym is in construction with it". Thus if there are hairs which are agents.

Pradīpa

Pradīpa: 83.9 किं प्रत्यदाह्रियत इति।

"What is ordained as the counter example (for *sangatam*)?"

The word *ajarya* obtains in the sense of abstract action/*bhāva* because of the rule

तयोरेव कृत्यक्तखलार्थाः (3.4.70)

"The *pratyaya* called *kṛtya* and the *pratyaya kta* and those having the sense of *khal* have only those two senses, abstract action/*bhāva* and object/*karman*."

Thus imperishable by reason of friendship. And what is desired is friendship in the sense of agent. Thus *ajaryam* is an honourable friendship. Hence he asks, what is the counter excample?

Pradīpa: 83.9 अजर इति।

"Undecaying (blanket)," ordained as the counter example (for *saṅgatam*)?

This *pratyaya* is irregularly laid down in the sense of agent.

The sense is, to avoid deficiency in the base, the counter example is to be shown only as agent.

Pradīpa: 83.14 गत्यर्थानामिति।

"(*Kta*) for (*dhātus*) having the sense of motion."

Although *saṅgamanam* going together is a sense of *saṅgata* in the sense of abstract action that is here ordained for *kta*, nonetheless the *pratyaya kta* is seen in the sene of agent for *dhātus* having the sense of motion, e.g., *Devadatta* has gone to the village (*gataḥ*).

Hence because of the close proximity of *ajaryam* to a *dhātu* having the sense of movement, he considers this a *nipātana*/irregular form in the sense of agent.

Pradīpa: 83.14 जीर्यतिरकर्मक इति।

"The *dhātu jṝ* is intransitive.

Even when for that *dhātu* having an *upasarga* there is the transitive nature, because of being laid down irregularly without an *upasarga* it should be known there is intransitive nature. And by reason of resorting to the absence of anything as object, intransitive.

However, by reason of *kāla*/time etc. there is in fact transitive nature for everything (in creation).

Pradīpa: 83.15 संगतग्रहणमिति।

"(What is the purpose of) mentioning the word *saṅgata*?"

The questions is (asked) because there is not the possible same case relationship between *gam* (expressing) 'of abstract action' and *jṝ* (decaying, expressing) 'by abstract action'.

कर्तृविशेषणमिति।

"As a qualification of the agent."

The sense is there would be a difference in the case relation of these two words.

Pradīpa: 83.16 लोमानि चेदिति।

"If hairs are agents." (!)

And so for example *hṛṣṭam* or *hṛṣitam* (*lomābhiḥ* 'with hair standing on end'), even when there is a different case relationship it is optionally applicable. Therefore (*yat*) should be stated in the sense of agent. Otherwise, because of the inapproriateness of resorting to non-agreement in case, by abandoning (the requirement of) same case relationship, optionally it is established the *pratyaya* is in fact applicable in the sense of agent.

Notes

[1] 82.14 विधीयते। "*(Kta* is also) ordained (in the sense of *karman.*)"

गत्यर्थकर्मकश्लिषशीङ्स्थासवसजनरुहजीर्यतिभ्यश्च (3.4.72)

"The *pratyaya kta* acts in denoting the agent as well as the action *bhāva* and the object after *dhātus* implying motion, after intransitive *dhātus* and after *dhātus śliṣ* (to embrace), *śī* (to lie), *sthā* (to stand), *ās* (to sit), *vas* (to dwell), *jan* (to produce), *ruh* (to grow), and *jṝ* (to grow old)."

वदः सुपि क्यप्च ॥ 3 । 1 । 106 ॥

Pāṇini 3.1.106 : After the *dhātu vad* (to speak) governing a case *sup* inflected word as its *upapada* and not having an *upasarga* preceding, the *pratyaya kyap* also acts.

83.18 वदः सुप्यनुपसर्गग्रहणम् ॥ 1 ॥

Vārttika 1: There is specific mention of (*kyap* acting) after the *dhātu vad* without an *upasarga* in the presence of a *sup*/case *pratyaya*.

83.19 वदः सुप्यनुपसर्गग्रहणं कर्तव्यम्। इह मा भूत्। प्रवाद्यम् अपवाद्यमिति।। तत्तर्हि
वक्तव्यम्। न वक्तव्यम्। अनुपसर्ग इति[1] वर्तते। एवं तर्ह्यन्वाचष्टेऽनुपसर्ग इति
वर्तते इति। नैतदन्वाख्येयमधिकारा अनुवर्तन्त इति। एष एव न्यायो यदुता-
84.2 धिकारा अनुवर्तेरन्निति।।

Bhāṣya: Mention should be made of (*kyap* acting) after the *dhātu vad* without an *upasarga*. So that (*kyap*) should not be applicable here (in the form) *pravādyam* "to be spoken forth", *apavādam* "to be censured, to be excepted".

Then should that be stated? It should not be stated. The expression "without an *upasarga*" follows on (from *gadamadacarayamaścānupasarge 3.1.100*). Well then he states that *anupasarge* "without an *upasarge*" follows on. It is not to be stated that the governing rules (all) follow on (from previous *sūtras*). (For) this is in fact a general principle that governing rules should follow on (from previous *sūtras*).

Pradīpa

Pradīpa: 84.1 नैतदिति।

See text. "This is not to (be stated that governing rules all follow on)."

It is essential a distinction be stated where there is a cutting off of the governing rule, or knowledge of a particular limit imposed or resort to the principle of the 'lion's backward glance' (a retrospective glance, while at the same time proceeding forwards).

The meaning is, however, that in such etc. due to the absence of purpose it should not be stated.

Notes

[1] 83.20 "अनुपसर्ग इति"

गदमदचरयमश्चानुपसर्गे (3.1.100)

भुवो भावे ॥ 3 । 1 । 107 ॥

Pāṇini 3.1.107 : After the *dhātu bhū* (to be) in construction with a *sup*/ case inflected word as *upapada* and when without an *upasarga,* the *pratyaya kyap* acts to denote abstract action or state / *bhāva.*

84.4 भावग्रहणं किमर्थम्। कर्मणि मा भूदिति। नैतदस्ति प्रयोजनं भवतिरयमकर्मकः। अकर्मका अपि वै धातवः सोपसर्गाः सकर्मका भवन्ति तेन अनुभव्यमामन्त्रणमित्यत्रापि प्राप्नोति। एतदपि नास्ति प्रयोजनम्। अनुपसर्ग इति वर्तते। उत्तरार्थं तर्हि भावग्रहणं कर्तव्यम्। हनस्त च (108) भावे यथा स्यात्। श्वहत्या
84.8 वर्तते। क्व मा भूत्। श्वघात्यो वृषल इति॥

Bhāṣya: What is the purpose of the mention of action or state/ *bhāva*? So that it should not be applicable in the sense of object/ *karman.* This is not the purpose. This *dhātu bhū* is intransitive. Even intransitive *dhātus* indeed, with *upasargas,* become transitive/ *sakarmaka* (e.g.) *anubhavyam āmantraṇam* "The greeting/welcome is to be experienced". Therefore it obtains here too.

This is not the purpose. The expression "without an *upasarga*" follows on from "*gadamadacarayamaścānupasarge*" *(3.1.100)*. Then the mention of *bhāva* is made for the sake of the subsequent *sūtras,* so that *sūtra* "*hanasta ca*" (*3.1.108*) should be applicable in the sense of abstract action or state (e.g.) *śvahatyā vartate* "The killing of a dog occurs". Where should it not be applicable? *śvaghātyo vṛṣalaḥ* "The rogue is a dog killer".

Pradīpa

Pradīpa: 84.4 भवतिरयमकर्मक इति।

"*Dhātu bhū* is intransitive."

Surely the meaning obtaining is transitive? This is no fault. Due to the mention here being of the first *dhātu* (in the *bhvādi gaṇa*) having the sense of pure being भू सत्तायाम्।

Surely it obtains in the sense of the object of time etc. He thinks, 'Due to it not being used in the sense of the object of time etc., it will not therefore, be applicable (in that sense)'.

अत्रापि अचो यत् (3.1.97)

अत्र इति 2 गदमदचरयमश्चानुपसर्गे (3.1.100)

See text.

हनस्त च ॥ 3 । 1 । 108 ॥

Pāṇini 3.1.108 : After the *dhātu han* (to kill) when in construction with a *sup*/case inflected word as its *upapada* and when without an *upasarga*, the *pratyaya kyap* acts in denoting state or condition/ *bhāva* and the letter *t* is *ādeśa* of its final *n*.

84.10 हनस्तश्चित्स्त्रियां छन्दसि ॥ 1 ॥

Vārttika 1: In the *Chandas/Veda* when forming a feminine noun (*kyap pratyaya*) having an indicatory *c* acts after the *dhātu han* and *t* is the *ādeśa* for the final *n*.

84.11 हनस्त चेत्यत्र चित्स्त्रियां छन्दसि वक्तव्यः[1]। तां भ्रूणहत्यां निगृह्यानुचरणम्।
अस्यै त्वां भ्रूणहत्यायै चतुर्थं प्रतिगृहाण। स्त्रियामिति किमर्थम्। आघ्ने ते दस्युहत्याय।
84.13 छन्दसीति किमर्थम्। दस्युहत्या श्वहत्या वर्तते॥

Bhāṣya: It should be stated that in the *Chandas/Veda* when forming a feminine word, (*kyap pratyaya*) having an indicatory *c* acts after the *dhātu han* and *t* is the *ādeśa* for the final *n*. (E.g.)

tām bhrūṇahatyām nigṛhyānucaraṇam "The pursuing (occurs) having (first) arrested her while killing an embryo".

asyai tvām bhrūṇahatyāyai caturtham pratigṛhāṇa "Do thou take hold of her who kills an embryo for the fourth time.

What is the purpose of saying "when (forming) a feminine word"? E.g.

āghnate dasyuhatyāya "for the purpose of striking for the fight with the *Dasyus*".

What is the purpose of saying "in the *Chandas/Veda*"?

dasyuhatyā śvahatyā vartate "There occurs killing of the *Dasyus* (and) killing of a dog".

Pradīpa

Pradīpa: 84.12 दस्युहत्यायेति।

"(For the purpose of striking) for the fight with the *Dasyus.*

In the *Chandas* only this ends in *kyap* in the neuter. However, in the (classical) language it is only feminine.

Notes

[1] 84.11 वक्तव्यः: "(Having an *it c*) should be stated."

चित्तः (6.1.163)

"A stem formed by a *pratyaya, āgama* or *ādeśa* having an *it c* has *udātta* on the final syllable."

एतिस्तुशास्वृदृजुषः क्यप् ॥ 3 । 1 । 109 ॥

Pāṇini 3.1.109 : The *pratyaya kyap* acts after the *dhātus i* (to go), *stu* (to praise), *śās* (to govern), *vṛ* (to choose), *dṛ* (to respect) and *juṣ* (to please).

84.15 क्यबिति वर्तमाने[1] पुनः क्यब्ग्रहणं किमर्थम्। क्यबेव यथा स्याद्यदन्यत्प्राप्नोति
तन्मा भूदिति। किं चान्यत् प्राप्नोति। ण्यत्। ओरावश्यके ण्यतः स्तौतेः क्यप्पूर्ववि-
प्रतिषिद्धमिति वक्ष्यति स पूर्वविप्रतिषेधो न पठितव्यो भवति। अथवा हनस्त-
84.18 श्चित्स्त्रियां छन्दसि चोदितः[2] स न वक्तव्यो भवति।।

Bhāṣya: When the *pratyaya kyap* is already present by following on (from *vadaḥ supi kyap ca 3.1.106*) what is the purpose of mentioning *kyap* again? So that *kyap* alone should be applicable (and) so that whatever else obtains should not be applicable. And what else obtains ? The *pratyaya ṇyat.* He will say "by prior prohibition (of the subsequent *pratyaya*), *kyap* acts in place of *ṇyat* after the *dhātu stu* (to praise) in the sense of necessity, (it being a) *dhātu* ending in *u*" (*3.1.125 Vā. 3*). And that 'prior prohibition' should not be read.

Otherwise what was stated (*3.1.108 Vā.1*) "In the *Chandas/ Veda* when forming a feminine word, (*kyap pratyaya*) having an indicatory *c* acts after the *dhātu han* and *t* is the *ādeśa* for the final *n*", should not be stated.

84.19 क्यब्विधौ वृञ्ग्रहणम् ।। 1 ।।

Vārttika 1: In the context of the *kvyap* rule, there should be mention of the *dhātu vṛñ* (to cover).

84.20 क्यब्विधौ वृञ्ग्रहणं कर्तव्यम्। इह मा भूत् वार्या ऋत्विज इति।।

Bhāṣya: In the context of the *kyap* rule, mention should be made of the *dhātu vṛñ* (to cover), so that it should not be applicable here. *vāryā ṛtvijaḥ* "Priests to be chosen/choice priests".

85.1 अञ्जेश्चोपसंख्यानं संज्ञायाम् ।। 2 ।।

Vārttika 2: And additional enumeration (of the *pratyayas kyap*) after the *dhātu añj-i* (to anoint), when (forming) a name.

85.2 संज्ञायामञ्जेश्चोपसंख्यानं कर्तव्यम्। आज्यम्।। यदि क्यब्वृद्धिर्न प्राप्नोति तस्माण्ण्यदेष:।

Bhāṣya: Additional enumeration should be made (of the *pratyaya kyap*) acting after the *dhātu añj-i* (to anoint), when forming a name e.g. *ājyam* "clarified butter".

If *kyap* acts, then *vṛddhi* does not obtain. Therefore this is *ṇyat*.

85.3 .... यदि ण्यदुपधालोपो न प्राप्नोति तस्मात्क्यबेवेष:। ननु चोक्तं वृद्धिर्न प्राप्नोतीति। आङ्पूर्वस्यैष प्रयोगो भविष्यति। यद्येवमवग्रह: प्राप्नोति। न लक्षणेन

85.5 पदकारा अनुवर्त्या:। पदकारैर्नाम लक्षणमनुवर्त्यम्। यथालक्षणं पदं कर्तव्यम्।

It *ṇyat* acts, then *lopa* elision of the penultimate does not obtain, therefore this is *kyap*.

But surely it was stated *vṛddhi* does not obtain. This usage will be regarded as the *dhatu añj-i* preceded by the *upasarga āṅ*. If so, separation of the component parts/ *avagraha* obtains.

A word/*pada* must be made/formed according to the rules (of grammar).

The authors of the *pada* (*pāṭha*) are not to be followed by (= instead of/ before) a rule (of grammar). Indeed a rule (of grammar) should be follwed by the author of the *pada* (*pāṭha*).

Pradīpa

Pradīpa: 84.17 अथवेति।

"Otherwise (what was stated . . . should not be stated)."

To show the difference of this *kyap* from the previous *kyap* mention (again) is made of *kyap*.

Therefore the previous *kyap* applies in the *chandas* in the feminine and having an *it c.*

Pradīpa: 84.19 क्यब्विधाविति।

"In the context of the *kyap* rule (there should be mention of *vṛñ* (to cover))."

''ईडवन्दवृशंसदुहां ण्यतः'' (6.1.214)

"The *udātta* accent on the first syllable of *īḍ, vand, vṛ, śams,* and *duh* when they are followed by the *pratyaya ṇyat.*"

Due to ordaining of initial *udātta* by this *sūtra* this is known as applicable for this word *vārya.* However, in that context due to close proximity with the two *dhātus īḍ* and *vand* which are both *ātmanepadi dhātu vṛn/vṛnoti* is understood.

(Cl. 5 *vṛñ* 1509 *sambhaktau*) bestowing, favoring, honouring.

Pradīpa: 85.3 तस्माण्ण्यदेव।

"(If *kyap* acts *vṛddhi* does not obtain) therefore this is *ṇyat.*"

Surely there is a difference of accent. When *kyap* is present there, a *pada*/word has an initial *udātta.* When *ṇyat* follows there is final *svarita.* This is no fault. Due to initial *udātta* being ordained by *Phit sūtra 26* "An invariaby neuter noun, with the exception of one ending in *is,* is initial *udātta.*

Pradīpa: 85.2 ण्यदुपधालोपो।

"If *ṇyat* acts, *lopa* of the penultimate does not obtain."

अनिदितां हल उपधायाः क्ङिति (6.4.24)

"For a *dhātu* ending in a consonant preceded by *n,* this not being one added because of having an *it i* (*8.1.58*), the *n* is elided when a *pratyaya* with an indicatory *k* or *ṅ* follows."

न लक्षणेनेति।

"(The author of the *Pada Pāṭha*) is not (to be followed = given way to) by a rule (of grammar)."

'Eternality' in fact is only true for the *saṃhitā* text (of *Ṛg Veda*). However, for the distinctions of the *pada* text there is human origin (i.e. *Pada Pāṭha* rules or conventions).

And so where there is no certainty as to meaning, there a separation is not made (between *upasarga* and *dhātu* etc., for example as here *ā* + *añj* + *ya* of *ājya*). That was stated: *hari-drur anavagṛhyate* "(*Soma*) moving in the yellow is not intercepted." (1)

Due to doubt it is said (in the *Pada Pāṭha*), is the word here, *hari* ending in *i* or is it ending in *t* (i.e. *harit*)?

Notes

[1] 84.15 वर्तमाने। "When present by *anuvṛtti* . . ."

from वदः सुपि यप् च see text.

[2] 84.18 चोदितः। And it was stated in *3.1.108 Vā.1*

"नस्तश्चिन् स्त्रियां छन्दसि" see text.

ई च खनः ॥ 3 । 1 । 111 ॥

Pāṇini 3.1.111 : The *pratyaya kyap* acts after the *dhātus khan* (to dig), and long *ī* is the *ādeśa* for the final of the *dhātu*.

85.7 दीर्घोच्चारणं किमर्थं न इ च खन इत्येवोच्येत। का रूपसिद्धिः खेयम्। आद्गुणेन सिद्धम्। न सिध्यति। षत्वतुकोरसिद्ध एकादेश इत्येकादेशास्यासिद्धत्वात्तुक्प्रसज्येत[1]। नैतदस्ति। पदान्तपदाद्योरेकादेशो सिद्धो न चैष पदान्तपदाद्योरेकादेशः।

85.10 तस्मादि च खन इत्येव वक्तव्यम्।।

Bhāṣya: What is the reason for expressing long *ī*, and why should not '*i ca khanaḥ*' in fact be stated? What is the word formation of *kheyam* 'to be dug'? It is established as a valid form by *ād-guṇaḥ* (*6.1.87*) "After a short or long *a* in the presence of any vowel *guṇa* (*a, e* or *o 1.1.2*) is the one *ādeśa* for the one before and the one after"? It is not established as valid. The single *ādeśa* is of none effect/unknown/*asiddha* in relation to change of *s* to *ṣ*/ *ṣātva* and the *āgama t-uk*. Due to 'the single *ādeśa's* nature of being *a-siddha, tuk āgama* would be applicable (for the *i*).

This is not so. A single *ādeśa* is considered to be *a-siddha* "of none effect", when it is in place of the final of the prior word/*pada* and the initial of the following *pada*. And this is not a single *ādeśa* in place of the final of one *pada* and the initial of another.

Therefore (the *sūtra*) should be stated in the form *i ca khanaḥ*.

Notes

[1] 84.1 प्रसज्येत। "(*Tuk āgama*) would be applicable."

षत्वतुकोरसिद्धः (6.1.86)

"The substitution of a single *ādeśa* (for the one before and the one after) is to be considered as of none effect when otherwise *s* would have been replaced by *ṣ* or when the *āgama tuk* (*t*) is to be added."

ह्रस्वस्य पिति कृति तुक् (6.1.71)

"*T* (*tuk*) is the *āgama* of the final short vowel of a *dhātu* when a *kṛt pratyaya* follows with an indicatory *p*."

भृञोऽसंज्ञायाम् ॥ 3 । 1 । 112 ॥

Pāṇini 3.1.112 : The *pratyaya kyap* acts after the *dhātus bhṛñ* (to bear) when not used as a name.

85.12 असंज्ञायामिति किमर्थम्। भार्या।

Bhāṣya: What is the reason for saying "when not used as a name"? *bhāryā* a female supported or dependent on another, a female mercenary, wife.

85.13 भृञः संज्ञाप्रतिषेधे स्त्रियामप्रतिषेधोऽन्येन विहितत्वात् ॥ 1 ॥

Vārttika 1: When there is prohibition of (*kyap* acting) after the *dhātu bhṛñ* to form a name, there is non-prohibition in the feminine because of its being enjoined by another (*sūtra*)

85.14 भृञः संज्ञाप्रतिषेधे स्त्रियामप्रतिषेधः अनर्थकः प्रतिषेधोऽप्रतिषेधः।

Bhāṣya: When there is prohibition of (*kyap* acting) after the *dhātu bhṛñ* to form a name, there is non prohibition in the feminine. *Apratiṣedha* is meaningless, it means prohibition.

85.14 .... किं कारणम्। अन्येन विहितत्वात्। अन्येन लक्षणेन स्त्रियां क्यब्विधीयते। संज्ञायां समजनिषदनिपतमनविदषुञ्शीङ्भृञिणः (3.3.19) इति।। प्रतिषेध इदानीं किमर्थः

85.17 स्यात्।

Bhāṣya: What is the reason? By another rule *kyap* is enjoined (in the feminine). *sañjñāyām samajaniṣadanipatamanavidaṣuñśībhṛñiṇaḥ 3.3.99* "The *pratyaya kyap* acts after the following *dhātus* in forming a word in the feminine denoting a name and it is *udātta* accented, namely *samaj, niṣad, man, vid, ṣuñ, śīñ, bhṛñ* and *iṇ*". What now would be the purpose of the prohibition ?

85.18 प्रतिषेधः किमर्थ इति चेदस्त्रीसंज्ञाप्रतिषेधार्थः ।। 2 ।।

Vārttika 2: If it is asked what is the purpose of the prohibition, then the reply is 'it is for the purpose of prohibiting a non-feminine name'.

85.19 प्रतिषेधः किमर्थ इति चेदस्त्रीसंज्ञास्ति यदर्थः प्रतिषेधः स्यात्। भार्या नाम क्षत्रियाः ।।

Bhāṣya: If it is said "what is the purpose of the prohibition?" The purpose of that is so that a non-feminine name should be prohibited. *bhāryā nāma kṣatriyāḥ "Bhārya* is the name of soldiers, mercenaries or warrior class/ *kṣatriya.*

85.21 सिद्धं तु स्त्रियां संज्ञाप्रतिषेधात् ।। 3 ।।

Vārttika 3: However it is established as valid because of the prohibition in the feminine in the sense of name.

85.22 सिद्धमेतत्। कथम्। स्त्रियां संज्ञाप्रतिषेधो वक्तव्यः। संज्ञायां समजनिषदनिपतमनविदषुञ्शीङ्भृञिणः। ततो न स्त्रियां भृञ इति। सिध्यति। सूत्रं तर्हि भिद्यते।। यथान्यासमेवास्तु।

Bhāṣya: This is established a valid. How? It should be stated that there is prohibition in the sense of name in the feminine. By *sañjñāyām samaja-niṣada nipatamana-vida-ṣuñ-śīṅ-bhṛñ-inaḥ 3.3.99, "The pratyaya kyap* acts after the following *dhātus* in forming a word in the feminine denoting a name and is *udātta,* namely *sam-aj* (to bring or collect together), *ni-ṣad* (to sit or lie down), *ni-pāt* (to fly or fall down, to befall), *man* (to think), *vid* (to know), *ṣuñ* (to press out), *śuṅ* (to lie, to sleep), *bhṛñ* (to bear) and *iṇ* (to go)", Then not after *bhṛñ* in the feminine. This is established. The *sūtra* then is split (into two parts). Let it be as it is composed.

86.1 .... ननु चोक्तं भृञः संज्ञाप्रतिषेधे स्त्रियामप्रतिषेधोऽन्येन विहितत्वादिति। नैष दोषः। भावे इति तत्रानुवर्तते कर्मसाधनश्चायम्। अथवा य एते संज्ञायां विधीयन्ते तेषु नैवं विज्ञायते संज्ञायामभिधेयायामिति।। किं तर्हि।

86.4 प्रत्ययान्तेन चेत्संज्ञा गम्यत इति।

But surely it was stated (in *Vā.* 1) "When there is prohibition (of *kyap*) after the *dhātu bhṛñ,* to form a name, there is non-prohibition in the feminine because of its being enjoined by another (*sūtra*)". This is no fault. There the word *bhāve* (abstract action or state) follows on (from *'vrajayajor bhāva kyap' 3.3.98*) "The *pratyaya kyap* acts after the *dhātu vraj* (to go) and *yaj* (to worship) with *udātta* accent, in forming a word in the feminine denoting action/state", and this *pratyaya* has *karman*/object as the means of accomplishing the action.

Otherwise among those that are enjoined in the sense of name it is not understood when a name is to be expressed. What then? If the name is understood by reason of ending in a (particular) *pratyaya.*

86.5 उपर आह।

Bhāṣya: Another says . . .

86.6 संज्ञायां पुंसि दृष्टत्वान्न ते भार्या प्रसिध्यति।

Vārttika a: Because of seeing (*kyap* used) in the masculine name, your *bhāryā* (form) is not established as valid.

86.7 संज्ञायां पुंसि दृष्टत्वात्तव भार्याशब्दो न सिध्यति।

Bhāṣya: Because of seeing (*kyap* used) in forming a masculine name, your word *bhāryā* (form) is not established as valid.

86.8 स्त्रियां भावाधिकारोऽस्ति तेन भार्या प्रसिध्यति ।। 1 ।।

Vārttika 1: There is the governing rule *bhāve* (in the sense of abstract action or state) in the feminine (and) by reason of that *bhāryā* is established as a valid form.

86.9 भाव इति तत्र वर्तते[1] कर्मसाधनश्चायम्।।

Bhāṣya: There the word *bhāve* (action or state) follows on (from *vrajayajor bhāve kyap 3.3.98*) "The *pratyaya kyap* acts in forming a word in the feminine denoting action or state after the *dhātus vraj* (to go) and *yaj* (to worship) with *udātta* accent", and also there is the instrument of the action *karman* (object).

86.10 अथवा बहुलं कृत्याः संज्ञायामिति तत्स्मृतम्।

Vārttika b: Otherwise it is rememberd, 'diversely the *kṛtya pratyayas* are applicable in the sense of name'".

86.11 अथवा कृत्यल्युटो बहुलम् (3.3.113) इत्येवमत्रापि ण्यद्भविष्यति।

Bhāṣya: Otherwise by *kṛtyalyuṭo bahulam 3.3.113* "The *kṛtya pratyayas* (*3.1.95*) and the *pratyaya lyuṭ* are diversely applicable and have other senses than those taught before", thus here *ṇyat* will also be applicable.

86.12 यथा यत्यं यथा जन्यं यथा भित्तिस्तथैव सा ।। 2 ।।

Vārttika 2: As for example (the form) *yatyam* (to be striven for), as (the form) *janyam* (to be born), as also (the form) *bhitti* (breaking, splitting a wall) so indeed that (wife/*bhāryā*).

88.13 समश्च बहुलम् ।। 4 ।।

Vārttika 4: And diversely (*kyap* acts) after *bhṛ* after an *upasarga sam.*

86.14 समश्चबहुलमुपसंख्यानं कर्तव्यम्। संभृत्या एवं संभाराः। संभार्या एवं संभाराः।।

Bhāṣya: And additional enumeration should be made (of *kyap* acting after *bhṛñ*) after the *upasarga sam,* diversely. *sambhṛtyo* (to be collected, maintained, nourished) indeed is the same as *sambhārāḥ* "bringing together, collecting, maintaining, maintenance, support, nourishment". (And) *sambhāryāḥ* "to be maintained, nourished, dependants", is in fact (the same as) *sambhārāḥ.*

Pradīpa

Pradīpa: 85.12 भृञो संज्ञायाम् असंज्ञायामिति किमर्थमिति।

"What is the reason for (saying) when not used as a name?"

The question occurs because even though that being effected is prohibited the desired (form) is not established as valid.

भार्येति। "Female supported by another, wife."

This is the name (wife), the lady of the house. In the absence of *kyap* there is *ṇyat pratyaya.*

Pradīpa: 85.14 अनर्थक इति

"(*Apratiṣedha*) is meaningless." (it means prohibition).

The sense is: This prohibition is of that *dhātu bhṛñ* obtaining, because of immediate succession (after it), not however, because of that obtaining from another rule intervening.

Pradīpa: 85.16 प्रतिषेध इदानीमिति।

"What now (would be the purpose of) the prohibition?"

The sense is, due to the force of the ordaining a prohibition, even without another rule there will be prohibition of *kyap* obtaining.

Pradīpa: 85.17 अस्त्रीसंज्ञेति।

"(For prohibiting) a non-feminine name *saṃjñā* is agreed together/ assigned.

Here the word *saṃjñā* is a means of accomplishing the action (called) the object.

Pradīpa: 85.23 ततो न स्त्रियामिति।

"Then not (after *bhṛñ*) in the feminine."

By the word *strī* is meant she who has breasts and long hair. Otherwise there would not be the division of spheres into rule and prohibition. Therefore, the sphere of (operation) of the rule is the word *bhartya,* one who is to be maintained, dependent, support, wages. However, the popular word *strī* is the sphere of the prohibition.

Pradīpa: 86.2 भाव इति तत्रेति।

"There the word *bhāva* (follows on)."

व्रजयजोर्भावे क्यप् (3.3.98)

"The *pratyaya kyap* acts after the *dhātus vraj* (to go) and *yaj* (to worship) *udātta* accented, in forming a word in the feminine denoting action."

Pradīpa: 86.3 संज्ञायामिति।

"(These are enjoined) in the sense of name."

The word *saṁjñā*/name is not understood as object (which is) means for accomplishing the action. What then? The abstract action (is understood) as means for accomplishing the action (*sādhana*). If by that ending in a *pratyaya* is meant the *rūdhi*/popular or conventional meaning, after that is the *pratyaya.* And indeed by the word *bhṛtya* mistress of the house/*gṛhini* is not expressed. So there is no occasion for *kyap.*

Pradīpa: 86.6 संज्ञायामिति।

"Because of seeing *kyap* used in the (masculine) name."

Bhāryaḥ is a name of *kṣatriyas,* and here because of the prohibition '*a-saṃjñāyām'* (not in sense of name) has scope of application (elsewhere) and because there is occasion for *kyap* in forming a feminine name by another *sūtra,* the word *bhārya* is not established (as valid) and so it is stated.

The reply is 'In the *strī*/feminine section, due to the mention of *bhāva* following on and the absence of *kyap* in the sense of *karman*/object, *ṇyat* alone is applicable.

Pradīpa: 86.12 यथेति।

"As for example (*yatyam*. . .)."

The meaning is that, just as after a vowel ending *dhātu, yat* is being ordained and because of the statement diversely/*bahulam,* in some places it is applicable after a consonant ending word, and just as in the context of *aṇ, ktin* is in fact applicable with the example *bhitti,* so when there is occasion for *kyap* with *bharya, ṇyat* is applicable.

सा० 3 अचो यत् (3.1.97)

षद् भिदादिभ्योऽङ् (3.3.104)

"The *pratyaya an* acts after those *dhātus* that have an indicatory *ṣ* and after *bhid* etc. when the word to be formed is feminine."

भिदा विदारणे (3.3.104) वा० 1

"The word *bhidā* occurs in the sense of tearing asunder, splitting."

Notes

[1] 86.9 वर्तते। "(*Bhāva*) follows on."

व्रजयजोर्भावे क्यप् (3.3.98)

See translation above.

संज्ञायां समजनिषदनिपतमनविदषुञ्शीङ्भृञिणः (3.3.99)

"The *pratyaya kyap* acts after the following *dhātus* in forming a word in the feminine denoting an appellative and is *udātta*, namely, *samaj, niṣad, nipat, man, vid, sun, śīṅ, bhṛn*, and *iṇ*"

राजसूयसूर्यमृषोद्यरुच्यकुप्यकृष्टपच्याव्यथ्याः ॥ 3 । 1 । 114 ॥

Pāṇini 3.1.114 : The words *rājasūya, sūrya, mṛṣodya, rucya, kupya, kṛṣṭa, pacya* and *avyathya* are laid down irregularly *nipātanas* formed by the *pratyaya kyap*.

86.16 सूर्यरुच्याव्यथ्याः कर्तरि ॥ 1 ॥

Vārttika 1: The words *sūrya, rucya* and *avyathya* (are formed by the *pratyaya kyap*) in the sense of agent.

सूर्य रुच्य अव्यथ्य इति कर्तरि निपात्यन्ते।। किं निपात्यते। सूर्यः।

Bhāṣya: The words *sūrya* (the sun), *rucya* (bright, pleasing, a lover) and *avyathya* (unshakeable) *Ṛv. 2.35.5 Ait. Br.* etc. (snake), are laid down as irregular forms/*nipātanas* (with the *pratyaya* acting) in the sense of agent. What is laid down as an irregular form ? *sūryaḥ*.

86.17 सूसर्तिभ्यां सर्तेरुत्वं सुवतेर्वा रुडागमः।

Vārttika : After the *dhātus sū* or *sṛ* (the *pratyaya kyap* acts), short *u* being the *ādeśa* for the *a* of *sar* (from *sṛ*) or *r* the *āgama* of *sū*.

86.19 सरणाद्वा सुवति कर्मणीति सूर्यः। सूर्य॥ रुच्य। रोचते सौ रुच्यः॥ न व्यथतेऽव्यथ्यः॥

Bhāṣya: *Sūrya* is (derived from *sṛ*) because of moving/*saraṇa* or (from *sū*) as that which impels into action/*karmaṇi*. *Sūrya* (is thus derived, meaning the sun). *rucya* (is derived from the *dhātu ruc* in the sense of) "he who pleases" *rocate* 'a lover (?). *rucya* (is explained). *avyathyaḥ* (is derived from the *dhātu vyath* in the sense of that which) does not tremble or fall/*vyathate* 'unshakeable'.

86.21 कुप्यं संज्ञायाम् ॥ 2 ॥

Vārttika 2 : The word *kupya* (is formed by *kyap*) in the sense of a proper name.

86.22 कुप्यं संज्ञायामिति वक्तव्यम्। गोप्यमन्यत्।

Bhāṣya: It should be stated that the word *kupya* (is formed by *kyap*) in the sense of a name ("a base metal, other than gold and silver"). The other (form) is *gopyam* ("to be preserved or protected").

86.23 कृष्टपच्यस्यान्तोदात्तत्वं च कर्मकर्तरि च ॥ 3 ॥

Vārttika 3 : For the word *kṛṣṭa pacya* there is the characteristic of final *udātta* accent and (it is formed by *kyap*) in the sense of the reflexive passive/ object containing agent/*karmakartṛ*.

86.24 कृष्टपच्यस्यान्तोदात्तत्वं च कर्मकर्तरि चेति वक्तव्यम्। कृष्टे पच्यन्ते स्वयमेव॥ कृष्टपच्याश्च मे। अकृष्टपच्याश्च मे। यो हि कृष्टे पक्तव्यः कृष्टपाक्यः स भवति॥

Bhāṣya: It should be stated that there is the characteristic of final *udātta* accent for the word *kṛṣṭa-pacya* and (it is formed by the *pratyaya kyap*) in the sense of the reflexive passive/*karmakartṛ*.

kṛṣṭe pacyante svayam eva "They which ripen of themselves in clutivated ground", "sown or ripening after ploughing (as rice etc.) cultivated ground (as plants)". *VS. 18.14, Taṇḍya Br. Bh.P.7.12.18.*

kṛṣṭapacyāśca me akṛṣṭapacyāśaca YV.18.14 "And plants (seeds) which ripen of themselves are mine. And the seeds which do not ripen of themselves are mine". For that which is to be ripened in cultivated soil that is *kṛṣṭapākyaḥ*.

प्रत्यपिभ्यां ग्रहेः ॥ 3 । 1 । 118 ॥

Pāṇini 3.1.118 : After the *dhātu grah-i* (to seize) preceded by the *upasarga prati* and *api*, the *pratyaya kyap* acts.

87.2 प्रत्यपिभ्यां ग्रहेश्छन्दसि ॥ 1 ॥

Vārttika 1: The *pratyaya kyap* acts after the *dhātu grah-i* preceded by the *upasargas prati* and *api* in the *Chandas/Veda.*

87.3 प्रत्यपिभ्यां ग्रहेच्छन्दसीति वक्तव्यम्। मत्तस्य न प्रतिगृह्यमनृतं हि मत्तो वदति। तस्मान्नापिगृह्यम् प्रतिग्राह्यम्।अपिग्राह्यमित्येवान्यत्र।।

Bhāṣya: It should be stated that (the *pratyaya kyap* acts) after the *dhātu grah-i* preceded by the *upasarga prati* and *api* in the *Chandas/Veda* e.g.

mattasya na pratigṛhyam anṛtam hi matto vadati "(Whatever) an intoxicated person (says) should not be accepted. For the intoxicated man does speak the unacceptable truth (of a drunkard)".

tasmān nāpigṛhyam "Therefore his mouth does not have to be closed (or his speech should not be accepted)".

Elsewhere (in the classical *sanskṛta* the forms are) in fact *pratigrāhyam* "to be taken, accepted, accetable" and *apigrāhyam* "(impers. with abl.) the mouth to be closed (before a bad smell etc.)" or "to be seized by force" (*Uddyota*).

अमावस्यदन्यतरस्याम् ॥ 3 । 1 । 122 ॥

Pāṇini 3.1.122 : The word *amāvasya* is optionally laid down as an irregular form/ *nipātana.*

87.6 कस्यायमनुबन्धः। प्रधानस्य। यदि प्रधानस्य अमावस्या एवं स्वरः प्रसज्येत अमावस्या इति चेष्यते। तथामावास्याग्रहणेनामावस्याग्रहणं न प्राप्नोति।। एवं तर्हि निपातनस्य।यदि तर्हि निपातनान्यप्येवंजातीयकानि प्येवंजातीयकानि भवन्ति श्रोत्रियंश्छन्दो-

87.9 ऽधीते (5.2.84) इति व्यपवर्गाभावाञ्न्नित्याद्युदात्तत्वं न प्राप्नोति। एवम् तर्हि

Bhāṣya: For which (part of the word is) the indicatory letter (*n* of *vun* by *4.3.30*)? For the principal (part) (i.e. the *pratyaya*). If it is for the principal (part), the accent would be applicable (by *6.1.197*) thus, "*ámāvasyā*" and in fact "*amāvasyā*" is desired.

In that manner, by reason of the mention of the word *amāvāsyā* the mention of *amāvasyā* does not obtain.

Thus (then the accent) is for a form laid down irregularly/*nipātana.* If so, then even in irregular forms/*nipātana* of such a kind (as in the *sūtra*) '*śrotriyanśchando'dhīte*' *5.2.84,* the word *śrotriyan* is irregularly formed, meaning "who has studied the *Chandas/Veda*". Initial *udātta* accent, caused by having an indicatory *ñ* or *n,* does not obtain because of the lack of difference.

87.10 अमावसोरहं ण्यतोर्निपातयाम्यवृद्धिताम् तथैकवृत्तिता तयोः
स्वरश्च मे प्रसिध्यति।।

Śloka Vārttika: I put down irregularly the absence of *vṛddhi* for *amāvasya* followed by *ṇyat pratyaya,* so that the one state of existence of the two (words) and the proper accent is established as valid for me.

Pradīpa

Pradīpa: 87.6 अमावस्यात। प्रधानस्येति।

"(The indicatory letter) is for the principal part of the word."

Due to its nature of being ordained there is predominance for the *pratyaya.* It is therefore stated, the *pratyaya yat* is irregularly laid down.

एवं स्वर इति।

"Thus the accent (would be wrongly aplicable to *amāvasya.*")

So by यतोऽनावः (6.1.213)

"Whatever is formed by the *pratyaya yat* has if it is a two-syllable word, the *udātta* accent on the first syllable, with the exception of *nāvyaḥ* (from *nau*)." There would be initial *udātta* for the second member of the compound and in fact *svarita* is desired.

गतिकारकोपपदात्कृत् (6.2.139)

"In a *tatpuruṣa samāsa* a word ending in a *kṛt pratyaya* preserves its original accent when preceded by an indeclinable/*avyaya* called *gati (1.4.80)* or a noun in direct relation to the action *kāraka* or any word which gives occasion for compound/*upapada 3.1.92.*

Pradīpa: 87.7 चेष्यते।

"And *amāvasyā* is desired."

by तित्स्वरितम् (6.1.185)

"A *pratyaya* having an indicatory *t* has the *svarita*/circumflex accent."

अमावास्याग्रहणेति।

"By reason of mention of the word *amāvāsyā* (the mention of *amāvasyā* does not obtain) due to its nature as a different word.

अमावास्याया वा (4.3.30)

"The *pratyaya vun* acts optionally after the word *amāvāsya* in the sense of born therein."

The sense is this is because of the word *amāvāsya* ending in *ṇyat* and the word *amāvasya* ending in *yat*.

Pradīpa: 87.7 एवं तर्हीति।

"Thus the accent is for the *nipātana* form."

The meaning is, ending in the *pratyaya yat* is not irregularly laid down. Surely when that with an *it t* follows, he will enjoin mention of a *pratyaya*. And having thought, when a part has been removed in a *nipātana* being resorted to, it is not established as valid, he says. . .

यदि तर्हीति।

"If so then (even in the *nipātanas* initial *udātta* does not obtain)."

एवं जातीयकारीति।

"(*Nipātanas*) of such a kind (as *śrotrīyān*) . . ."

The meaning is having some part removed.

Pradīpa: 87.9 आद्युदात्तत्वं

"Initial *udātta*.

ञ्नित्यादिर्नित्यम् (6.1.197)

"Whatever is derived with a *pratyaya* having an indicatory *ñ* or *n* has the *udātta* accent invariably on the first syllable."

Pradīpa: 87.10 अमावसोरिति।

"For *amāvasya* (I put down irregularly absence of *vṛddhi*)."

The indication in the dual is a resort to (showing) the difference between *vṛddhi* effected and not effected.

निपातयामिति।

"I put down irregularly" ('for one of the two' is to be supplied).

Pradīpa: 87.11 एक वृत्तितेति।

"The one state of existence (of the two words is established)."

One *taddhita* formation is established as valid for both forms. Because of the *paribhāṣā* 'that changed in one part is not different because of that.'

परि० 37 - एकदेशविकृतस्यानन्यत्,

For so when *ṇyat* follows regularly according to rule for the word *amāvāsya* its original nature has long *ā*, but its modified nature has a short *a*.

छन्दसि निष्टर्क्यदेवहूयप्रणीयोन्नीयोच्छिष्य-
मर्यस्तर्याध्वर्यखन्य-खान्यदेवयज्यापृच्छ्यप्रतिषीव्यब्रह्मवा-
द्यभाव्यस्ताव्यो-पचाय्यपृडानि ॥ 3 । 1 । 123 ॥

Pāṇini 3.1.123 : In the *Chandas/Veda* the following words are laid down as irregular forms/ *nipātana niṣṭarkya* (to be opened by unscrewing), *devahūya* (invocation of God), *praṇīya* (to be led on), *unnīya* (to be led upwards), *ucchiṣya* (to be left), *marya* (mortal), *staryā* (to be laid low), *dhvarya* (to be bent or thrown down), *khanya* (coming from excavation or ditches), *khānya* (being digged out), *devayajya* (worship of the Gods), *apṛcchya* (to be enquired of), *pratiṣīvya* (to be sewed on), *brahmavādya* (rivalry in sacred knowledge), *bhāvya* (future, about to be, what ought to be), *stāvya* (to be praised), and *upacāyyapṛḍa* (having a fee of gold connected with the sacrificial fire).

87.15 निष्टर्क्य इति किं निपात्यते। निष्टर्क्ये कृतेराद्यन्तविपर्ययश्छन्दसि कृताद्यर्थः। यथा कृतेस्तर्कुः कसेः सिकता हिंसेः सिंहः॥

Bhāṣya: What is irregularly laid down (in the formation of) *niṣṭarkya*? In the form) *niṣṭarkya* (to be opened by unscrewing or twisting), the initial and the final letters of *kṛt-i* (to cut) are reversed in the *Chandas/Veda* for the sake of *kṛt* and the rest. For instance from *kṛt-i* there is also *tarkuḥ* "spindle" (*Pān. G.1.15/16 c.f. G.K. atraktos* Lat. torqueo) from *kas-i* (to go, shine), *sikatā* (sand), from *hins* (to hurt), *sinha* (lion).

87.17 अपर आह।

Another says . . .

87.18 निष्टर्क्ये व्यत्ययं विद्यान्निसः षत्वं निपातनात्।
णयदायादेश इत्येतावुपचाय्ये निपातितौ ॥ 1 ॥

Śloka Vārttika 1: In the word *niṣṭarkya* one should know there is the inversion of *t* for *k* and the cerebral *ṣ* in place of (*s* of) *nis* is substituted irregularly. *Ṇyat* and *ay ādeśa* are put down irregularly in the form *upacāyya.*

87.20 निष्टर्क्यं चिन्वीत पशुकामः॥

Bhāṣya: (e.g.) *niṣṭarkyam cinvīta paśukāmaḥ* "One desiring cattle should pile up that to be loosened by untwisting".

87.21 ण्यदेकस्माच्चतुर्भ्यः क्यप्चतुर्भ्यश्च यतो विधिः।
ण्यदेकस्माद्यशब्दश्च द्वौ क्यपौ ण्यद्विधिश्चतुः ॥ 2 ॥

Śloka Vārttika 2: *Ṇyat pratyaya* (is enjoined) after one (*dhātu*), *kyap* after four, and *yat* is enjoined after four (*dhātus*). *Ṇyat* (again) after one and (there is) the word *ya*; two *kyaps* and four *ṇyats* (finally) are enjoined.

ण्यदेकस्मात्। निष्टर्क्यः। चतुर्भ्यः क्यप्। देवहूयः प्रणीयः उन्नीयः उच्छिष्यः।

88.1 चतुर्भ्यश्च यतो विधिः। मर्यः स्तर्या ध्वर्यः खन्यः।

Bhāṣya: *ṇyat pratyaya* (is enjoined) after one (*dhātu*). Thus *niṣṭarkya* (to be opened by unscrewing or untwisting). *kyap* after four. (Thus) *devahūyaḥ* (invocation of the God), *praṇīyaḥ* (to be led on), *unnīyaḥ* (to be led upwards), *ucchiṣya* (to be left). *Yat* is enjoined after four. (Thus) *maryaḥ* (mortal), *staryā* (to be laid low), *dhvaryaḥ* (to be bent down), *khanyaḥ* (coming from excavations).

88.1 .... ण्यदेकस्मात्। खान्यः। यशब्दश्च। देवयज्या। द्वौ क्यपौ।
आपृच्छ्यः प्रतिषीव्यः। ण्यद्विधिश्चतुः। ब्रह्म-वाद्यः भाव्यः स्ताव्यः उपचाय्यपृडम्॥
उपपूर्वाच्चिनोतेरायादेशो निपात्यते न हि
88.4 ण्यतैव सिध्यति। हिरण्य इति च वक्तव्यम्। उपचेयपृडमेवान्यत्र॥

1. "*ṇyat* after one" *khānyaḥ* (that is being digged out).
2. "and the word *ya*" *devayajyā* (worship of the Gods).
3. "two *kyaps*" *āpṛcchyaḥ* (to be enquired for),

   pratiṣīvyaḥ (to be sewed on).
4. "four *ṇyats* are (finally) enjoined":

   brahmavādyaḥ (rivalry in sacred knowledge),

   bhāvyaḥ (future),

   stāvyaḥ (to be praised),

   upacāyyapṛḍam (having a particular sacrificial fire/having a fee of gold).

'*Ay*' *ādeśa* is irregularly laid down after the *dhātu ci/ cino-ti* preceded by the *upasarga upa*. For (the form) is not established as valid by *ṇyat* only. And it should be stated "in the sense of gold". Elsewhere in fact the form is: *upaceyapṛḍam* "to be collected or heaped up".

Pradīpa

Pradīpa: 87.15 कृताद्यर्थ इति।

"(Final letters of *kṛt-i* etc. are reversed) for the sake of *kṛta* and the rest."

For the purpose of that letter *k* which is the initial of the *dhātu* (i.e. the word) *kṛta*. The meaning is so that the final be in the place of the initial and the initial in the place of the final *kṛtādyartha* is stated to show that the occurring of the first in place of the last forms, mutually applies not the occurring of a form with other letters.

ऋहलोर्ण्यत् ॥ 3 । 1 । 124 ॥

Pāṇini 3.1.124 : The *pratyaya ṇyat* acts after the *dhātus* that end in *ṛ* (short or long) or in a consonant.

88.6 पाणौ सृजेर्ण्यद्विधिः ॥ 1 ॥

Vārttika 1: When *pāṇi* is an *upapada* (subordinate word standing near in a compound), *ṇyat* is ordained for the *dhātu sṛj.*

88.7 पाणौ सृजेर्ण्यद्विधेयः। पाणिसर्ग्या रज्जुः ॥

Bhāṣya: When *pāṇi* (is *upapada), ṇyat* is to be enjoined after the *dhātu sṛj.* e.g. *pāṇisargyā rajjuḥ* "twisted with hands, rope".

88.8 समवपूर्वाच्च ॥ 2 ॥

Vārttika 2: (And *ṇyat* acts after *sṛj*) with the *upasargas sam* and *ava* preceding.

88.9 समवपूर्वाच्चेति वक्तव्यम्। समवसर्ग्यः॥

Bhāṣya: And it should be stated that (*ṇyat* acts after *sṛj*) with the *upasargas sam* and *ava* preceding: *samavasargyaḥ* "to be let go of or abandoned".

88.10 लपिदभिम्यां च ॥ 3 ॥

Vārttika 3: And *ṇyat* acts after *lap-i* and *dabh-i.*

88.11 लपिदभिम्यां चेति वक्तव्यम्। अपलाप्यम् अवदाभ्यम्।

Bhāṣya: And it should be stated that (*ṇyat*) acts after the *dhātus lap-i* and *dabh-i.* e.g. *apalāpyam* "to be explained away", outwitted, concealed", *avadābhyam* "to be deceived".

Pradīpa

Pradīpa: 88.7 विधेयः

"(*ṇyat*) is to be enjoined."

ऋदुपधाच्चाक्लृपिचृतेः (3.1.110)

"And after *dhātūs* having a penultimate short *ṛ* the *pratyaya kyap* acts with the exception of *dhātus kḷp* (to be capable) and *kṛt* (to hurt)."

Pradīpa: 88.11 लपि दभिभ्यां।

"And after *lap* and *dabh.*"

पोरदुपधात् (3.1.98)

"The *pratyaya yat* acts after a *dhātu* which ends in a labial letter preceded by a short *a.*"

ओरावश्यके ॥ 3 । 1 । 125 ॥

Pāṇini 3.1.125 : The *pratyaya ṇyat* acts after a *dhātu* that ends in *u* (short or long) when the sense is that of necessity.

88.13 कथमिदं विज्ञायते। आवश्यक उपपदे। आहोस्विदावश्यके द्योत्य इति। कश्चात्र विशेषः।

Bhāṣya: How is this *sūtra* (to be) understood ? Whether *ṇyat* is ordained with the word *āvaśyake* as an *upapada* or when the sense of necessity is to be indicated?

And what is the difference here ?

88.15 आवश्यक उपपद इति चेद् द्योत्य उपसंख्यानम् ॥ 1 ॥

Vārttika 1: If *āvaśyake* is (an *upapada*) there should be additional enumeration of it as the sense to be expressed by suggestion/ *dyotye*.

88.16 आवश्यक उपपद इति चेद् द्योत्य उपसंख्यानं कर्तव्यम्। लाव्यम्। पाव्यम्। अस्तु तर्हि द्योत्ये।

Bhāṣya: If *āvaśyake* is (mentioned) in the sense of *upapada* then additional enumeration should be made of it as the sense to be expressed by suggestion/ *dyotye*. e.g. *lāvyam* "to be cut", *pāvyam* "to be purified".

Let it be in the sense to be expressed (by suggestion) / *dyotye*.

88.18 द्योत्य इति चेत्स्वरसमासानुपपत्तिः ॥ 2 ॥

Vārttika 2: If it is the sense to be expressed (by suggestion), the accent for a compound is not applicable.

88.19 द्योत्य इति चेत्स्वरसमासानुपपत्तिः। अवश्यपाव्यम् अवश्यापाव्यम्॥ नैष दोषः। मयूरव्यंसकादित्वात्समासो विस्पष्टादिवत्स्वरो भविष्यति॥

Bhāṣya: If it is the sense to be expressed (by suggestion), the accent for a compound is not applicable, e.g. *avaśyalāvyam* "necessarily to be cut", *avaśyapāvyam* "necessarily to be purified".

This is not a fault. It will be a compound because of its nature of (forming part of the *gaṇa*) *mayūra-vyansaka* ("cunning like a peacock") and the rest and will have an accent applicable like that of *vispaṣṭa* (very clear) and the rest.

88.21 ओरावश्यके ण्यतः स्तौतेः क्यप्पूर्वविप्रतिषिद्धम् ॥ 3 ॥

Vārttika 3: By reason of the prior (rule being more powerful), in mutual conflict *kyap* acts after the *dhātu stauti* (to praise) in place of the *pratyaya ṇyat* in the sense of necessity.

ओरावश्यके ण्यतः स्तौतेः क्यब्भवति पूर्वविप्रतिषिधेन। ओरावश्यके ण्यद्भवतीत्यस्यावकाशः।

Bhāṣya: By reason of the prior (rule being more powerful) in the case of mutual conflict, *pratyaya kyap* is applicable after the *dhātu stu* (ending in short *u*) instead of the *pratyaya ṇyat* in the sense of necessity. There is scope of application for this *pratyaya ṇyat* (after other *dhātus* ending in short or long *u* by this *sūtra*) *orāvaśyake 3.1.125* (in the forms)...

89.1 .... अवश्यलाव्यम् अवश्यपाव्यम्। क्यपोऽवकाशः। स्तुत्यः। इहोभयं प्राप्नोति। अवश्यस्तुत्यः। क्यब्भवति पूर्वविप्रतिषेधेन।। स तर्हि पूर्वविप्रतिषेधो वक्तव्यः। न वक्तव्यः। उक्तं तत्र क्यबिति वर्तमाने पुनः

89.4 क्यब्ग्रहणस्य प्रयोजनं क्यबेव यथा स्याद्यदन्यत्प्राप्नोति तन्मा भूदिति।।

avaśyalāvyam "necessarily to be cut", *avaśyapāvyam* "essential to be purified".

There is scope of appilcation for the *pratyaya kyap* in forms like *stutyaḥ* (to be praised).

Both obtain here in the form *avaśyastutyaḥ* "necessarily to be praised". *kyap* applies here by reason of the prior one being more powerful in the case of mutual conflict.

Then should that application of the prior rule be stated? It should not be stated. It was stated there (*Bhāṣya on 3-1-109*). "When *kyap* is present (by following on from *3.1.106*), (what is) the purpose of again mentioning *kyap* ?" So that *kyap* alone should be applicable (and) whatever else obtains that is not to be applicable.

Pradīpa

Pradīpa: 88.13 कथमिति।

"How (is this *sūtra* to be understood)?"

The question is, is the *pratyaya* (applicable) when there is an *upapada* expressing directly the meaning of necessity or with a *pratyaya* when the sense of necessity is being thereby merely suggested ?

Pradīpa: 88.19 अनुपपत्ति:।

"Accent for a compound is not applicable."

उपपदमतिङ् (2.2.19)

"An *upapada* (तत्रोपपदं सप्तमीस्थम् 3.1.92) which does not end with a *tiṅ* (tense *pratyayas 3.4.78*) is invariably compounded with that with which it is in construction, the compound thus formed being called a *tatpuruṣa samāsa.*"

गतिकारकोपपदात्कृत् (6.2.139) (प्रकृतिस्वरम्)

"In a *tatpuruṣa,* a word ending in a *kṛt pratyaya* preserves its original accent, when preceded by an indeclinable called *gati* (*1.4.60*) or a noun directly related to the action of the verb/*kāraka* or any word giving occasion for compounding/*upapada 3.1.92.*"

Pradīpa: 88.19 अवश्यलाव्यमिति।

"Necessity to be cut."

In the sense of two *pūpa* cakes etc. Sometimes in worldly usage it is seen in some places even for the meaning of 'gone or past/*gata*'. He thinks this is due to having no regard to brevity.

Pradīpa: 88.20 समासो।

"(It will be) a compound (because of forming part of *gaṇa mayūravyansake.*"

मयूरव्यंसकादयश्च (2.1.72)

"And the words *mayūra-vyaṃsaka* (cunning like a peacock) and the rest are *tatpuruṣa* compounds."

Pradīpa: 88.20 विस्पष्टादिवदिति।

"(And will have an accent) like that of *vispaṣṭa* etc."

विस्पष्टादीनि गुणवचनेषु (6.2.24)

"The words *vispaṣṭa* and the rest preserve their accent when followed by a word denoting a quality or an adjective in a compound."

As for example *vispaṣṭa kaṭukam* 'very clear and sharp'.

Here due to being part of *mayūravyaṃsaka* etc. when the compound is effected there is applicable the original accent of the prior word.

So the meaning is, even in the examples *avaśyatavyam* (it has to be "To be praised."

एतिस्तुशास्वृदृजुष क्यप् (3.1.109)

"After the *dhātus i* (to go), *stu* (to praise), *śās* (to govern), *vṛ* (to choose), *dṝ* (to respect), and *juṣ* (to please), acts the *pratyaya kya.*"

आनाय्योऽनित्ये ॥ 3 । 1 । 127 ॥

Pāṇini 3.1.127 : The word *ānāyya* is laid down as an irregular form/*nipātana*, when meaning impermanent.

89.6 दक्षिणाग्नाविति वक्तव्यम्। आनेयोऽन्यः॥

Bhāṣya: It should be stated in the sense of Southern fire/*dakṣināgni*. Otherwise (the form) is *āneyaḥ* "to be brought near" (is derived).

89.7 आनाय्योऽनित्य इति चेद्दक्षिणाग्नौ कृतम् भवेत्।
एकयोनौ तु तम् विद्यादानेयो ह्यन्यथा भवेत्।

Śloka Vārttika : If *ānāyya* has the sense of 'impermanent', then it would be formed in denoting the *dakṣināgni* (southern fire). However that should be understood in the sense of having one source/origin (i.e. the *garhapatya* fire), otherwise the form would be *āneyaḥ*.

Pradīpa

Pradīpa: 89.7 आनाय्यो नित्य इति चेदिति।

"If *ānāyya* has the sense of impermanent . . .

There is a possibility of it also applying in the sense of pot etc., should be supplied.

Pradīpa: 89.7 भवेदिति।

"It would be (formed in denoting the *Dakṣināgni*)."

संभावनेऽलमिति चेत् सिद्धाप्रयोगे (3.3.154) (लिङ्)

"*Pratyaya liṅ* acts after a *dhātu* when the *expectation* (of a person or thing *being able or competent to do* or suffer the action denoted by the *dhātu* is implied (or expressed by any other word used along with them), except *alam.* For due to being irregularly laid down, the popular (conventional) meaning of the word is resorted to."

Pradīpa: 89.8 एकयोनांविति।

"In the sense of having one source."

The meaning is, that which is taken from the *Garhapatya* fire with the *Āhavanīya* fire has one source (and) (is called *dakṣiṇāgni*).

However, in the sense or context of what is taken from a *vaisya's* home, the word *ānāyya* is not applicable.

पाय्यसान्नाय्यनिकाय्यधाय्या मानहविर्निवास-सामिधेनीषु ॥ 3 । 1 । 128 ॥

Pāṇini 3.1.129 : The word *pāyya, sānnāyya, nikāyya* and *dhāyya* are laid down as irregular forms meaning "a measure", "an oblation to fire", "a dwelling", and "a sacrificial prayer" respectively.

89.11 पाय्य निकय्ययो: किं निपात्यते।

Bhāṣya: What is the irregular formation (in the words) *pāyya* and *nikāyya,* ?

89.12 पाय्यनिकाय्ययोरादिपत्वकत्वनिपातनम् ॥ 1 ॥

Vārttika 1: The irregular formation in the words *pāyya* and *nikāyya* is the initial *p* (for *m* of *dhātu mā*) and *k* (for *c* of *ci*).

89.13 पाय्यनिकाय्ययोरादिपत्वमादिकत्वं च निपात्यते।। मेयम् निचेयमित्येवान्यत्र।।

Bhāṣya: The irregular formation in the words *pāyya* and *nikāyya* is the initial *p* (of *pāyya*) and the initial *k* (of *kāyya*).

Elsewhere in fact the forms are *meyam* "to be measured" and *niceyam* "to be piled up".

क्रतौ कुण्डपाय्यसंचाय्यौ ॥ 3 । 1 । 130 ॥

Pāṇini 3.1.130 : The word *kuṇḍapāyya* and *sañcāyya* are laid down irregularly/*nipātanas,* meaning "sacrifice".

89.15 कुण्डपाय्ये यद्विधि: ॥ 1 ॥

Vārttika 1: The *pratyaya yat* is enjoined (if forming) the word *kuṇḍapāyya.*

89.16 कुण्डपाय्ये यद्विधेय:। कुण्डपाय्य: क्रतु: ॥

Bhāṣya: The *pratyaya yat* is to be enjoined in (forming) the word *kuṇḍapāyya. kuṇḍapāyya* is a sacrifice.

Pradīpa

Pradīpa: 89.16 यद्विधेय इति।

"*Yat* is to be enjoined."

Therefore initial *udātta.*

यतोऽनाव: (6.1.213)

"Whatever is formed by the *pratyaya yat* has, if it is a two syllable word, the *udātta* accent on the first syllable with the exception of *nāvyaḥ* (from *nau*)."

गतिकारकोपपदात्कृत् (6.2.139)

"In a *tatpuruṣa samāsa,* a word ending in a *kṛt pratyaya* preserves its original accent when preceded by an indeclinable called *gati* (*1.4.60*) or a noun in direct relation in the verb *verb/kāraka* or any word giving occasion for compounding/ *upapada.*"

And by reason of the accent of the original for that having a *kṛt pratyaya* forming its second member, that exists. And it should also be known that *yuk* augment is irregularly laid down.

अग्नौ परिचाय्योपचाय्यसमूह्या: ॥ 3 । 1 । 131 ॥

Pāṇini 3.1.131 : The word *paricāyya, upacāyya* and *samūhya* are laid down as irregular forms *nipātanas* when they are the names of fire.

89.18 समूह्य इत्यनर्थकं वचनं सामान्येत कृतत्वात् ॥ 1 ॥

Vārttika 1:

The word *samūhya* is pointless because it has already been formed by the general (sutra).

89.19 समूह्य इति वचनमनर्थकम्। किं कारनम्। सामान्येन कृतत्वात्। सामान्ये-
नैवात्र ण्यद्भविष्यति। ऋहलोर्ण्यत् (3.1.124) इति।। वह्यर्थं तर्हि निपातनं
90.2 कर्तव्यम्। वहेर्ण्यद्यथा स्यात्।

Bhāṣya: The word *samūhya* is pointless. Why? Because it has already been formed by the general (sutra). By the general (*sūtra*) alone *ṇyat* will be applicable. *ṛhalor ṇyat 3.1.124* "The *pratyaya ṇyat* acts after *dhātus* that end in *ṛ* (short or long) or in a consonant". Then an irregular form should be laid down for the sake of the meaning of the *dhātu vah-i*. So that *ṇyat* should be applicable after *vah-i*.

90.3 वह्यमिति चेदूहेस्तदर्थत्वात्सिद्धम् ।। 2 ।।

Vārttika 2: If (the irregular form is meant) for *vah-i,* then it is estalished by *ūhi* because it has the (same) sense.

90.4 ऊहिरपि वह्यर्थे वर्तते। कथं पुनरन्यो नामान्यस्यार्थे वर्तते। कथमूहिर्वह्यर्थे
वर्तते। बह्वर्था अपि धातवो भवन्तीति।। अस्ति पुनः क्वचिदन्यात्राप्यूहिर्वह्यर्थे
वर्तते।
90.6 अस्तीत्याह।

Bhāṣya: *ūhi* also occurs in the sense of *vah-i*. But is it in fact possible that one occurs in the sense of the other ?

How does *ūh-i* occur in the sense of *vah-i* ?

Even so *dhātus* have many meanings..

However does *uh-i* occur somewhere else also in the sense of *vah-i* ? It does, says he.

90.7 ऊहिविग्रहाच्च ब्राह्मणे सिद्धम् ।। 3 ।।

Vārttika 3: Because of the resolution (of the compound *samūhya* into) *sam* and *ūh-i,* this form is established in the *Brāhmaṇas.* It is established as valid.

90.8 ऊहिविग्रहाच्च ब्राह्मणे सिद्धमेतत्। समूह्यं चिन्वीत पशुकामः पशवो वै पुरीषं
पशूनेवास्मै तत्समूहति।।

Bhāṣya: Because of the resolution (of *samūhya*) into *sam* and *ūh-i* (is found) in the *Brāhmaṇas,* this (form) is established as valid.

samūhyam cinvīta paśukāmaḥ

paśavo vai purīṣam paśūn

evāsmai tat samūhati

"One desirous of cattle should pile up the *samūhya* fire. Cattle indeed (provide) dung. For him in fact (fire) gathers together the cattle."

Pradīpa

Pradīpa: 90.7 ऊहि विग्रहादिति।

"(Because of the resolution of the compound *samūhya*) into *sam* and *ūhi*."

The meaning is the etymology or interpretation made of the word *samūhya* in the *Brāhmaṇa* is (formed) by *ūhi* with the meaning the same as *vahi*.

चित्याग्निचित्ये च ॥ 3 । 1 । 132 ॥

Pāṇini 3.1.132 : The word *citya* and *agnicitya* are also laid down as irregular forms/ *nipātana*.

90.11 अग्निचित्या भावेऽन्तोदात्तः ॥ 1 ॥

Vārttika 1: The word *agnicitya* has final *udātta* when denoting state/condition.

90.12 अग्निचित्येति भावऽन्तोदात्तो भवति। अग्निचयनमेवाग्निचित्या।।

Bhāṣya: The word *agnicitya* has final *udātta* when denoting condition. The word *agnicitya* means the same as *agnicayana* "arranging the sacred fire place".

ण्वुल्तृचौ ॥ 3 । 1 । 133 ॥

Pāṇini 3.1.133 : The *pratyayas ṇvul* and *tṛc* act after all *dhātus* in expressing the agent.

90.14 किमर्थश्चकारः। स्वरार्थः। चितोऽन्त उदात्तो भवतीत्यन्तोदात्तत्वं यथा स्यात्। नैतदस्ति प्रयोजनम्। एकाजयं तत्र नार्थः स्वरार्थेन चकारेणानुबन्धेन। प्रत्यय–

90.16 स्वरेणैव सिद्धम्।।

Bhāṣya: What is the purpose of the letter *c*? It is for the purpose of accent. So that the final *udātta* should be applicable (by the *sūtra*) *citaḥ 6.1.163.* ("A stem formed by a *pratyaya, āgama* or *adeśa* having an indicatory *c* receives *udātta* accent on the final syllable"). This is not the purpose. The *pratyaya* has (only) one vowel so there is no purpose in having an indicatory *c* for accent. (Final *udātta*) is in fact (already) established as valid by the (general) accent.

90.16 .... विशेषणार्थस्तर्हि। क्व विशेषणार्थेनार्थः। अप्तृन्तृजिति। तृ इत्युच्य-माने मातरौ मातरः पितरौ पितरः अत्रापि प्रसज्येत। स्वसृनप्तृग्रहणं नियमार्थं

90.18 भविष्यति। एतयोरेव योनिसंबन्धयोर्नान्येषां योनिसंबन्धनामिति।

Then it is for the purpose of distinguishing. Where is the purpose of distinguishing served? (In the *sūtra*) *ap-tṛn-tṛc . . . (6.4.11).*

If *tṛ* (without *c*) were being stated *dīrgha* (long) would be applicable for the forms *mātarau* (two mothers), *mātaraḥ* (mothers), *pitarau* (two fathers), *pitaraḥ* (three or more fathers).

The specific mention of *svasṛ* and *naptṛ* will be for the purpose of á restriction. For only these two blood relations, not for any other blood relations (the penultimate vowel is lengthened).

90.18 .... सामान्य-
ग्रहणाविघातार्थस्तर्हि। क्व सामान्यग्रहणाविघातार्थेनार्थः।। अत्रैव। यदेतत्तृन्तृ न्तृचोर्ग्रहणमेतत्तृ इति वक्ष्यामि। यदि तृ इत्युच्यते मातरौ मातरः। पितरौ पितरः अत्रापि प्रयज्येत। स्वसृनप्तृग्रहणं नियमार्थं भविष्यति। एतयोरेव योनिसंबन्धयो-
90.22 र्नान्येषां योनिसंबन्धानामिति।।

Then it is for the purpose of not hindering the general mention (of the *pratyaya*). Where is the purpose of not hindering the general mention of the *pratyaya* served? Here in the very *sūtra* referred to *aptṛntṛc 6.4.11.* That which (here) is a mention of *tṛn* and *tṛc* I shall express as *tṛ*. If *tṛ* (is stated) then also in the forms *mātarau, mātaraḥ, pitarau* and *pitaraḥ* (*dīrgha*) would become applicable. The mention of *svasṛ* and *naptṛ* will be for the purpose of restriction. "Only for these two blood relations and not for any other blood relations".

91.1 ण्वुलि सकर्मकग्रहणम् ।। 1 ।।

Vārttika 1: When *ṇvul* follows (there should be) mention of (coming after a) transitive (*dhātu*).

91.2 ण्वुलि सकर्मकग्रहणं कर्तव्यम्। इह मा भूत्। आसिता शयितेति ॥

Bhāṣya: In the case of *ṇvul*, mention should be made of a transitive (*dhātu*), so that it should not be applicable here. *āsitā* "He is a sitter", *śayitā* "He is one who sleeps or rests" (*tṛc* only).

91.3 न वा धातुमात्राद्दर्शनाण्ण्वुलः ॥ 2 ॥

Vārttika 2: Or else (it should) not be (applicable) because *ṇvul* is seen (to act) after all *dhātus.*

91.4 न वा वक्तव्यम्। किं कारणम्। धातुमात्राण्ण्वुल्दृश्यते इमेऽस्यासकाः।
इमेऽस्य शायकाः। उत्थिता आसका वैश्रवणस्येति॥

Bhāṣya: Or else it should not be stated. What is the reason ? Because *ṇvul* is seen after all *dhātus.*

ime'syāsakāḥ "These are his seats",

ime'sya śayakāḥ "These are his places for lying (?)",

utthitā āsakā vaiśravaṇasya "Those seated (near) *vaiśravaṇa (Kubera)* have arisen".

91.6 तृजादिषु वर्तमानकालोपादानमध्यायकवेदाध्यायाद्यर्थम् ॥ 3 ॥

Vārttika 3: In the case of *tṛc* and the rest, mention (should be made) of the present time for the sake of the forms *adhyāyaka vedādhyāya* and the rest.

91.7 तृजादिषु वर्तमानकालोपादानं कर्तव्यम्। किं कारणम्। अध्यायकवेदाध्याया-
द्यर्थम्। अध्यायकः वेदाध्यायः। अधीतवत्यध्येष्यमाणे वा मा भूदिति॥

Bhāṣya: Mention should be made of the present time in the case of *tṛc* and the rest. What is the reason? For the sake of the forms *adhyāyaka* and *vedādhyāya* and the rest. *adhyāyaka* "teacher (especially of sacred knowledge)", *vedādhyāya* "one who repeats or is constantly repeating the *Veda*". So that (the forms *adhyāyaka* and *vedādhyāya*) should not be used when one has already studied or when one is going to study.

91.9 न वा कालमात्रे दर्शनादन्येषाम् ॥ 4 ॥

Vārttika 4: Or else (it is not applicable) because of others being seen in the sense of all times.

91.10 न वा वक्तव्यम्। किं कारणम्। कालमात्रे दर्शनादन्येषाम्। कालमात्रे ह्यन्ये-ऽपि प्रत्यया दृश्यन्ते। चर्चापारः। शमनीपारः।

Bhāṣya: Or else it should not be stated. What is the reason? Because of others being seen in the sense of all time. For other *pratyayas* are also seen in the sense of all time.

Pradīpa

Pradīpa: 90.16 सिद्धम्।

"Established as valid (by the general *pratyaya* accent)."

आद्युदात्तश्च (3.1.3)

See text.

अप्तृन्तृजिति।

"(The purpose of distinguishing is served in the *sūtra*) *aptṛn-tṛc* etc."

अप्तृन्तृच्स्वसृनप्तृनेष्टृत्वष्टृक्षत्तृहोतृ पोतृप्रशास्तॄणाम् (6.4.12)

"In the strong cases/*sarvanāmasthāna* (*1.1.42,43*) with the exception of the vocative singular/*sambuddhi*, the penultimate vowel is lengthened for *ap*, for stems formed by *tṛn* and *tṛc pratyayas* and for the nouns *svasṛ, naptṛ, neṣṭṛ, kṣatṛ, potṛ,* and *praśāstṛ*.

Pradīpa: 89.20 मातराविति।

"Two mothers."

The sense is *mātṛ* etc., are irregularly laid down as ending in the *pratyaya tṛn* of *tṛc* by the *uṇādi sūtra*.

नप्तृनेष्टृ 2.95

Pradīpa: 90.21 स्वसृनप्तृग्रहणमिति।

"Mention of *svasṛ* and *naptṛ* (will be for the purpose of restriction)."

The mention of *naptṛ* is for the purpose of restriction but the word *svasṛ* because of ending in *tṛn pratyaya* is for the purpose of ordaining positive rule only.

It is established for the letter *c* that it is for not hindering the general mention (of *tṛ*). Also because of the existence of a purpose here also.

तुश्छन्दसि (5.3.59) (इष्ठन् ईयसुनौ)

the *Chandas* after a *prātipadika* endning in *tṛ*."

तुरिष्ठेमेयस्सु (6.4.154)

"The *pratyaya tṛ* is *lopa*-elided before the *pratyayas iṣṭhan, imanic* and *īyasun*."

Pradīpa: 91.8 वेदाध्याय।

"One who respects/recites the *Veda* constantly."

by कर्मण्यण्

"The *pratyaya aṇ* acts after a *dhātu* when the object is in composition with it as an *upapada*."

नन्दिग्रहिपचादिभ्यो ल्युणिन्यचः ॥ 3 । 1 । 134 ॥

Pāṇini 3.1.134 : After the *dhātus nanda* and the rest, *grah-i* and the rest and *pac* and the rest, act the *pratyayas lyu* (*ana*), *ṇini* (*in*) and *ac* (*a*) respectively.

91.13 अजपि सर्वधातुभ्यः ॥ 1 ॥

Vārttika 1: *ac pratyaya* also (acts) after all *dhātus*.

91.14 अजपि सर्वधातुभ्य वक्तव्यः। इहापि यथा स्यात्। भवः शर्वः। न तर्हीदानीमिदं पचाद्यनुक्रमणं कर्तव्यम्। कर्तव्यं च। किं प्रयोजनम्।

Bhāṣya: It should be stated that ac *pratyaya* also (acts) after all *dhātus*. So that it should be applicable here too in the forms *bhāvaḥ* "coming into existence, birth, becoming being", *śarvaḥ* "name of a God who kills people with arrow (*śaru*)".

Now then, should not there be made this list proceeding in order, of *pac* and the rest ? It should be made also. What is the purpose ?

91.16 पचाद्यनुक्रमणमनुबन्धासज्जनार्थमपवादबाधनार्थं च ॥ 2 ॥

Vārttika 2: There is the proceeding methodically in making a list of *pac* and the rest for the purpose of attaching indicatory letters and (also) for the purpose of barring an *apavāda pratyaya.*

91.17 अनुबन्धासज्जनार्थं तावत्। नदट् नदी। चोरट् चोरी। अपवादबाधनार्थम्।
जारभरा। श्वपचेति।।

Bhāṣya: First, just for the purpose of attaching indicatory letters (e.g.) *nada-ṭ* (in the feminine therefore take *ī*): *nadī* (river), *cora-ṭ* (fem *ī*) *corī* "female thief".

For the purpose of debarring an *apavāda pratyaya* (e.g.) *jāra-bharā* "adulteress", *śvapacā* "(woman) who cooks dogs, low caste".

Pradīpa

Pradīpa: 91.17 चोरी।

"Female thief."

टिड्ढाणञ्द्वयसज्दघ्नञ्मात्रच्तयप्ठक्ठञ्कञ्क्वरप: (4.1.15) (अत: स्त्रियाम् ङीप्)

"The *pratyaya ṅīp* acts in the feminine, after the *prātipadikas* (nominal stems) ending in short *a*, if the *pratyaya* with which it ends has an indicatory *t* or if the *pratyaya* be *ḍha* or *aṇ* or *añ* or *dvayasac* or *daghnac* or *mātrac* or *tayap* or *ṭhak* or *ṭhañ* or *kañ* or *kvarap.*"

Pradīpa: 91.18 श्वपचेति।

"(woman) who cooks dogs."

Karmaṇyaṇ 3.2.1 is barred. In the alternative also it is applicable because of the word *śvapāka* being recited in *nyaṅkvādi-gaṇa.*

न्यङ्क्वादीनां च (7.3.53)

"The guttural acts in the place of the original in *nyaṅku* etc."

इगुपधज्ञाप्रीकिरः कः ॥ 3 । 1 । 135 ॥

Pāṇini 3.1.135 : After a *dhātu* ending in a consonant but preceded by *i, u* or *ṛ* (long or short) or *ḷ*, and after the *dhātus jñā* (to know), *prī* (to please), *kṝ* (to scatter) acts the *pratyaya ka* (*a*).

91.20 इगुपधेभ्य उपसर्गे कविधिर्मेषाद्यर्थः ॥ 1 ॥

Vārttika 1: The *pratyaya ka* is to be enjoined after *dhātus* with a penultimate *ik* vowel when an *upasarga* (precedes) for the sake of the words *meṣa* and the rest.

91.21 इगुपधेभ्य उपसर्गे को विधेयः। किं प्रयोजनम्। मेषाद्यर्थः। मेषः देवः सेवः॥

Bhāṣya: The *pratyaya ka* is to be enjoined after *dhātus* with a penultimate *ik* vowel, when an *upasarga* precedes. What is the purpose? For the purpose (of distinguishing from forming *meṣa* etc. which are in *pac* etc. 3.1.134 formed by *ac*) and the rest. *meṣaḥ* "ram, sheep", *devaḥ* "God", *sevaḥ* "apple" (in this sense probably from Persian Seb.), "*jujube*" (= *badara*).

92.1 न वा बुधादीनां दर्शनादनुपसर्गेऽपि ॥ 2 ॥

Vārttika 2: Or else (*ka*) is not (enjoined) because of seeing the words *budha* and the rest even not preceded by an *upasarga*.

92.2 न वा वक्तव्यः। किं कारणम्। बुधादीनामनुपसर्गेऽपि को दृश्यते। बुधः भिदः युधः सिव इति॥ कथं मेषः देवः सेव इति। पचादिषु पाठः करिष्यते॥

Bhāṣya: Or else (*ka*) is not to be stated. What is the reason? The *pratyaya ka* is seen (as the final) of *budha* and the rest even without an *upasarga*. (e.g.)

budhaḥ "awakened wise or learned man",

bhidaḥ "split? (f.) splitting",

yudhaḥ "fought, son of *Ugrasenā* (*VP*)",

sivaḥ "one who sews or stitches, a sewer, stitcher".

How are the words *meṣaḥ, devaḥ* and *sevaḥ* (formed) ? A listing will be made in (the *gaṇa*) *pac* and the rest.

Pradīpa

Pradīpa: 92.3 पचादिषु।

"Listing will be made in *pac* etc."

नन्दिग्रहिपचादिभ्यो ल्युणिन्यचः (3.1.134)

See text

पाघ्राध्माधेट् दृशःशः ॥ 3 । 1 । 137 ॥

Pāṇini 3.1.137 : The *pratyaya śa* acts after the *dhātus pā* (to drink), *ghrā* (to smell), *dhmā* (to blow), *dheṭ,* (to suck), and *dṛś* (to seek) when an *upasarga* precedes.

92.5 जिघ्रः संज्ञायां प्रतिषेधः ॥ 1 ॥

Vārttika 1: There is prohibition (of *śa*) after *jighra* when a name (is expressed).

92.6 जिघ्रः संज्ञायां प्रतिषेधो वक्तव्यः। व्याजिघ्रतीति व्याघ्रः॥ इह केचिच्छस्यैव प्रतिषेधमाहुः केचिज्जिघ्रभावस्य। किं पुनरत्र न्याय्यम्। शस्यैव प्रतिषेधी न्याय्यः।

92.8 जिघ्रभावे हि प्रतिषिद्धे केन शे आकरलोपः स्यात्।

Bhāṣya: It should be stated there is prohibition (of *śa*) after *ghrā* when a name (is expressed) (e.g.) *vyājighrati* "It scents or smells at", *vyāghraḥ* "tiger".

Here some state prohibition of *śa* only, some of *ādeśa jighra.* But what is right here?

The prohibition of *śa* alone is right. For if the *ādeśa jighra* is prohibited by what means could there be *lopa* elision of *a* when *śa* follows ?

Pradīpa

Pradīpa: 92.7 केचिदिति।

"Some say (prohibition of *śa* . . .)"

The sense is *jighra* is in fifth case, i.e. after *jighra,* the *a* being for pronunciation, when there is this substitution by this *vārttika.*

Some say 'of the *jighra* substitute', i.e. some think *jighra* in the *vārttika* is sixth case ending (meaning 'in the place of').

पाघ्राध्मास्थाम्नादाणदृश्यर्तिसर्तिशदसदां पिबजिघ्रधमतिष्ठमनयच्छपश्यर्च्छधौशीयसीदाः (7.3.78) (शिति)

"In the presence of the present sign, *it ś,* the following *ādeśas* act in place of the original/*sthānin dhātus pib* for *pā, jighra* for *ghrā, dham* for *dhmā, tiṣṭh* for *sthā, mān* for *mnā, yacch* for *dā* (*dān*), *paśy* for dṛś, *ṛcch* for *r, dhau* for *sṛ śīy* for *śad* and *sīd* for *sad.*"

Pradīpa: 92.8 केन शे आकारलोप इति।

"By what means (could there be) *lopa* elision of *a* when *śa* follows?"

आतो लोप इटि च ६।४।६४

"The final *ā* of a *dhātu* is *lopa* elided in the presence of an *ārdhadhātuka pratyaya* with the *āgama iṭ* as well as when it begins with a vowel and has an indicatory *k* or *n.*"

The sense is, due to *ārdhadhātuka* being a governing *sūtra* here.

आतश्चोपसर्गे (3.1.136)

"And also after a *dhātu* ending in a long *ā* where there is an *upasarga* along with it, acts the *pratyaya ka.*"

Śnā bhyastayor-ātaḥ 6.4.112 in fact does not obtain here.

अनुपसर्गाल्लिम्पविन्दधारिपारिवे-द्युदेजिचेतिसातिसाहिभ्यश्च ॥ 3 । 1 । 138 ॥

Pāṇini 3.1.138 : The *pratyaya śa* acts after the following *dhātus* without an *upasarga, limp* (to smear), *vind* (to find), (and the causatives) *dhār-i* (to hold, bear), *pāri* (to bring over, be capable) *vedi* (to make known), *ud-ej-i* (to cause to tremble or shake), *cet-i* (to cause to attend), *sāt-i* (to give or cause to give pleasure) and *sāh-i* (to forbear).

92.11 अनुपसर्गान्नौ लिम्पेः ॥ 1 ॥

Vārttika 1: The *pratyaya śa* acts after the *dhātu limp* when preceded by the *upasarga ni.*

92.12 अनुपसर्गान्नौ लिम्पेरिति वक्तव्यम्। निलिम्पा नाम देवाः ॥

Bhāṣya: It should be stated that (the *pratyaya śa*) acts after the *dhātu limp* when *upasarga ni* precedes. (e.g.) *nilimpaḥ* "name of a class of supernatural beings/Gods". *TS. AV.* a troop of *Maruts T.Ar.*

92.13 गवि च विन्देः संज्ञायाम् ॥ 2 ॥

Vārttika 2: And (the *pratyaya śa* acts) after the *dhātu vind-i* whenthe word *go* (is *upapada*) in expressing a name.

92.14 गवि चोपपदे विन्देः संज्ञायामुपसंख्यानं कर्तव्यम्। गोविन्द इति। अत्यल्पमिदमुच्यते गवीति। गवादिष्विति वक्तव्यम्॥ गोविन्दः अरविन्दः[1]॥

Bhāṣya: Additional enumeration should be made of (the *pratyaya śa* acting) after the *dhātu vind-i* when the word *go* is subordinate word in compound/ *upapada.*

Too little is said, (when it is said) "When *go* is an *upapada*". It should be stated "When *go* and others (are *upapadas*)". e.g. *govindaḥ* "acquiring or procuring cows or cattle", *Kṛṣṇa* (or *Viṣṇu*) *M.Bh., aravindaḥ* "having petals like spokes, a lotus", m. the Indian crane, L. Copper, L.

Notes

[1] *Uddyota - aravindaḥ* is in the *ardharcādi gaṇa* (though not quoted by *Kāś.*).

अर्धर्चाः पुंसि च (2.4.31)

Therefore both masculine and neuter.

ज्वलितिकसन्तेभ्यो: णः ॥ 3 । 1 । 140 ॥

Pāṇini 3.1.140 : After the *dhātus* beginning with *jval* (to burn brightly, shine) and ending with *kas* (to go) without an *upasarga*, the *pratyaya ṇa* optionally acts.

92.17 तनोतेर्ण उपसंख्यानम् ॥ 1 ॥

Vārttika 1: Additional enumeration (should be made) of *ṇa* (as acting) after the *dhātu tan-o-ti* (*tan* to extend.)

92.18 तनोतेर्ण उपसंख्यानं कर्तव्यम्। अवतनोतीत्यवतानः।

Bhāṣya: Additional enumeration (should be made) of *ṇa* (as acting) after the *dhātu tan-o-ti; avatanoti* "He stretches or extends downwards overspreads". Thus (the form) *avatānaḥ* m. "unbending of a bow" (N. of the verse *VS. 14.54-63 Sbr.;* a cover (spread over climbing plants) *M.Bh 2.355; R.V.16.28,* of a man, *Pān. 2.1.47 Sch.*)

शिल्पिनि ष्वुन् ॥ 3 । 1 । 145 ॥

Pāṇini 3.1.145 : The *pratyaya ṣvun (aka)* acts after a *dhātu* when the agent so expressed denotes an artificer (artisan or artist).

92.20 नृतिखनिरञ्जिभ्य इति वक्तव्यम्। इह मा भूत्। ह्वायक इति।

Bhāṣya: It should be stated that (the *pratyaya ṣvun*) acts only after the *dhātus nṛt-i* (to dance), *khan-i* (to dig) and *rañj-i* (to be dyed or coloured).

So that it should not be applicable here: *hvāyakaḥ* "calling, invoking, challenging".

प्रुसृल्वः समभिहारे वुन् ॥ 3 । 1 । 149 ॥

Pāṇini 3.1.149 : After the *dhātus pru* (to spring up), *sṛ* (to run, flow, go) and *lū* (to cut) the *pratyaya vun* acts when repetition is meant.

93.2 प्रसृल्वः साधुकारिणि वुन्विधानम् ॥ 1 ॥

Vārttika 1: There is enjoining of the *pratyaya vun* after the *dhātus pru, sṛ* and *lū* in the sense of doing (something) well.

93.3 प्रसृल्वः साधुकारिणि वुन्विधेयः। सकृदपि यः सुष्ठु करोति तत्र यथा स्याद्बहुशो यो दुष्टु करोति तत्र मा भूदति॥

Bhāṣya: The *pratyaya vun* is to be enjoined after the *dhātus pru, sṛ* and *lū* in the sense of doing (something) well.

So that *vun* should be applicable for who does (something) well even though only once; and *vun* should not be applicable for he who does badly even though many times.

93.5 इति श्रीभगवत्पतञ्जलिविरचिते व्याकरणमहाभाष्ये तृतीयस्याध्यायस्य प्रथमे पादे षष्ठमाह्निकम्॥ पादश्च समाप्तः॥

Bhāṣya: Thus ends the sixth *āhnika* in the first *pāda* in the third *adhyāya,* of the *Vyākaraṇa Mahābhāṣya* composed by the blessed master *Patañjali.*

And the (*pratyaya*) *pāda* is (now) completed.

PART THREE

APPENDIX

Technical Notes

1.2 अधिकारोऽयम्। प्रत्ययशब्दः सन्ज्ञात्वेनाधिक्रियते।

म० भा० 2.1.2 – अधिकारेणेयं प्रत्ययसंज्ञा क्रियते।

With (by) an *adhikāra* (function) this technical term *pratyaya* is formed.

adhikāra m. authority, government, rule, administration, jurisdiction (in Grammar) government; governing rule (the influence of which over any number of succeeding rules is called *anuvṛtti*[1]).

Here *pratyaya's* influence extends for three whole *adhyayās* much the largest *adhikāra sūtra* in the *Aṣṭādhyāyī* governing 1820 *sūtras.* The word follows or is taken as undertsood in every following rule up to a particular limit.

अधिकारः प्रतियोगं तस्या निर्देशार्थ इति योगे योगे उपतिष्ठते।

"The *adhikāra* (antidote or remedy) for the sake of the direction is present in every rule."

परिभाषा पुनरेकदेशस्था सती सर्वं शास्त्रमभिज्वलयति प्रदीपवत्।

P.2.1.1 M.Bh.1.139.6

"But the *paribhāṣā* being in one place like a lamp enlightens or illumines the whole *śāstra* (here the *Aṣṭādhyāyī*)"

See also *Mahābhāṣya* on *1.3.11, 1.4.49* and *4.1.83.*

The word or words which repeat in subsequent rules is (believed to be) shown by *Pāṇini's* characterizing it with a *svarita* accent.

स्वरितेनाधिकारः 1.3.11

"In the *sūtras* when a word is marked with a *svarita* accent by that an *adhikāra* is understood."

The word repeated in the following *sūtras* is stated to be *adhikāra.*

The *śabda Kaustabha* defines *adhikāra* as:

एकत्रोपात्तस्यान्यत्र व्यापारः अधिकारः

"It appears in one place, its employment is elsewhere."

Sometimes the whole is repeated e.g. प्रत्ययः (3.1.1) अङ्गस्य (6.4.1) समासान्ताः (5.4.68), while on some occasions a part only is repeated.

The repetition goes on up to a particular limit which may be stated as in असिद्धवदत्राभात् (6.4.22) प्राग्रीश्वरान्निपाताः (1.4.56)

Many times the limit is not stated by *Pāṇini* but is to be understood by virtue of a counteracting word occuring later on. On other occasions, the limit is defined by means of a convention स्वरितत्वप्रतिज्ञा declaration of the state of having a *svarita* accent therefore, being *adhikāra,* by the ancient tradional interpretors पाणिणीया:.

This *adhikāra* or governance has its influence of three kinds:

(1) अधिकारगति, by being valid or present in all the rules which come under its sphere of influence, e.g. स्त्रियाम् (4.1.3), अङ्गस्य (6.4.1)

(2) अधिककार्य, by showing additional properties, e.g. the word *apādāna* being applied to cases where there is no actual separation as in सांकाश्यकेभ्य: पाटलिपुत्रका अभिरूपतरा:

(3) अधिककार, by showing additional force such as setting aside even subsequent rules if opposing c.f. *Mahābhāṣya* on *1.3.11.*

Or it has its influence in three ways:

(1) Generally by proceeding ahead in subsequent rules like the stream of a river प्रवाहवच्चापि अधिकारस्त्रिधा मता:।।

(2) Sometimes by jumps like a frog omitting a rule of more, माण्डूक्यप्लुतमेव्।

(3) Rarely by proceeding backwards with a lion's glance, सिंहावलोकितं चैव

c.f. वाक्पद. 2.79 प्रतिपाद्येषु शब्देषु व्याकरणशास्त्रस्याधिकार:।

अभिधेयेऽर्थे शब्दस्याधिकार:।।

c.f. *kāśikā* on 3.1.1. "आ पञ्चमाध्याय परिसमाप्तेर्यानित उर्ध्वमनुक्रमिष्याम: प्रत्ययसंज्ञास्ते वेदितव्या: प्रकृत्युपपदोपाधिविकारागमान् वर्जयित्वा"

म० भा० 3.1.1 । 2.1.2 सा प्रकृत्युपपदोपाधीनामपि प्राप्नोति तस्या: प्रतिषेधो वक्तव्य:।

'That *saṃjñā*/technical name obtains also for *prakṛti, upapada* and *upādhi.* A prohibition should be stated of that."

प्रकृति। गुप्तिज्किदभ्य: सन् (3.1.5)

The *pratyaya san* acts after (the *dhātus* called *prakṛti* = base) *gup tij* and *kid.*

Prakṛti making or placing before or at first, the original or primary substance; (in grammar) the crude or elementary form of a word, base, root, an uninflected word.

(1) material cause c.f. 'तदर्थं विकतेः प्रकृतौ''।
प्रकृतिरुपादानकारणं तस्यैव उत्तरमवस्थान्तरं विकृतिः। का० 5.1.12.

"After a word signifying product or modification of the primitive/original (*pratyaya cha* (= *īya*)) acts in the sense of the elementary or primitive form (useful) for the purpose of that." (e.g. अङ्गारीयाणि काष्ठानि 'word serviceable form making charcoal'.) *Prakṛti* is material cause, *vikṛti* is produced from taking the form of the elementary or primitive, a later-stage or development of that.

(2) Original as opposed to modified *vikṛti*. The original base of a word which is used in language by the addition of *pratyayas*.

There are three kinds mentioned:धातु, प्रातिपदिक अङ्ग *Pāṇini's* term for *prakṛti*

1.3 शृङ्गारप्रकाशः शास्त्रप्रक्रियाव्यवहारे प्रकृतिप्रत्ययविभागवात्पनया शब्दार्थभावनाया प्रत्ययात् प्रथममुपादानकारदामिव या उपादीयते तां प्रकृतिरिति व्यपदिशन्ति।।

"By means of the fiction of a separation between *prakṛti*/base and *pratyaya*/affix in the usage/works of the *śāstras* (especially grammar) when meditating on the meaning of words as it were, the first material cause (arising) from the *pratyaya* which is received, that is *prakṛti*." So they teach.

म० भा० or शिव सूत्रः ऋलृक्

अपशब्दो ह्यस्य ५८० प्रकृतिः। न चापशब्दः प्रकृतिः।

न ह्यपशब्दा उपदिश्यन्ते न चानुपदिष्टा प्रकृतिरस्ति।

"For the original/*prakṛti* word is itself a bad word. No bad word can ever be the original or *prakṛti*. As 'bad-words' are never taught enunciated, and untaught words can never be called *prakṛti* (original)."

कृत्प्रकृतिर्धातुः म० भा० 6.2.239 *Vā.* 2

"There original of the '*kṛt*' (ending word) is *dhātu*." (c.f. P. 1.4.109)
"परः संनिकर्षसंहिता"। पदप्रकृतिः संहिता।

पदप्रकृतीनि सर्वचरणानां पार्षदानि।[2] निरुक्त 1.17

"*Saṃhitā* is the closest conjunction by means of a euphonic combination (*Pāṇini 1.4:109*). *Saṃhitā* is based on the 'original' form of words (= *R.P. 3.105* except order of words reversed). The phonetic treatises of all schools are based on the original form of words."

म० भा० 3.1.1. । 1.3

1.3 उपपद। स्तम्बकर्णयो रमिजपोः (3.2.13)

"The *pratyaya ac* acts after the *dhātu ram* (to sport) and *jap* (to whisper when the *sup*/case *pratyaya* ending words/ *upapadas stamba* (clump of grass) and *karṇa* (ear) are in composition with them respectively."

Upapada n. a word standing near or accompanying another to which it is subordinate (either a subordinate word in a compound (but not in a *bahuvrīhī* compound) generally forming the first member, as a discriminative appellation at the end of proper names, as *varman, śarman* etc. or a preposition particle etc. prefixed to a verb or noun, or a secondary word of any kind which is governed by or limits the general idea contained in the principal word. *Pāṇini 3.1.92* etc. *V. Prāt* . . .

In *Pāṇini's* grammar the term *upapada* is applied to such words as are put in the locative case/ *adhikaraṇa* in his rules prescribing *kṛt pratyayas* from *3.1.90* to *3.4.* end.

1.3. c.f. तत्रोपपदं सप्तमीस्थम् (3.1.92)

"There (in the third *adhyāya* governed by *dhātoḥ 3.1.91* the word implied by a term exhibited in the seventh/ *adhikaraṇa kāraka*/ case is called *upapada* (subordinate in a compound)."

'potter' e.g. कर्मणि in कर्मण्यम् 3.2.1

'The *pratyaya aṇ* acts after a *dhātu* when the *karman*/object is in composition with it."

(कुम्भं करोति) कुम्भकारः

kumbham karoti	= *kumbha-kāraḥ*	(principal
upapada	subordinate	word
in *karman*	'potter'	takes
pot - He makes		*aṇ*)

The word is also used in the sense of an adjoining word connected in sense, e.g.,

युष्मद्युपपदे समानाधिकरणे स्थानिन्यपि मध्यमः 1.4.105

"When the *sarvanāma* (pronoun) *yuṣmad* understood or expressed is the adjoining attendant word in agreement with the verb then there is the *tiṅ pratyaya*/verbal termination of the middle/second person."

as also – प्रहासे च मन्योपपदे मन्यतेरूत्तम एकवच्च। 1.4.106

"When joke is implied in relation to the action, the *dhātu*/verb denoting this is used in the middle/second person only when the word *'manya'* (to think) is the adjoining/attendant word of such a verb and the *pratyaya* of the *dhātu manya* must be of the *uttama*/best — first person singular."

c.f. also *Kāśika* on – तुमुनण्वुलौ क्रियाया क्रियार्थायम् 3.3.10

क्रियार्थायां क्रियायामुपपदे धातोर्भविष्यति काले तुमुन्ण्वुलौ भवतः।

"The *pratyaya tumun* and *ṇvul* acts after a *dhātu* in the sense of a future time when the word in the construction/*upapada* is (another) verb denoting an action performed for the sake of (future) action."

c.f. also इतरेतारान्योऽन्योपपदाच्च 1.3.16

"And after the verbs which take the words *itaretara* (each other) and *anyonya* (one another) as *upapada* (dependent qualifying words) the *ātmanepada pratyayas* are not used, though reciprocity of action be denoted."

मिथ्योपपदात्कृञोऽम्यासे 1.3.71

"After the causative '*kṛ*' (to do, make) the *ātmanepada* is used when it has the word *mithya* (incorret) as an *upapada* (dependent word) and is employed in the sense of repeated wrong (utterance) even when the fruit of the action does not accrue to the agent." e.g. पदं मिथ्या कारयति "He repeatedly pronounces the word with the wrong accent."

उपपदमतिङ् 2.2.19

"An *upapada* (or attendant word) which does not end with a *tiṅ pratyaya*/ tense affix (3.4.78) is invariably compounded with that with which it is in construction. The compound thus formed is *tatpuruṣa.*" e.g. कुम्भकारः 'one who makes pots'.

गतिकारकोपपदात्कृत्। 6.2.139 (प्रकृतिस्वरम्)

"In a *tatpuruṣa* a word ending in a *kṛt pratyaya* preserves its original accent, when preceded by an indeclinable called *gati* (*1.4.60*) or a noun standing in (intimate) relation to a verb (*kāraka*) or any word which gives occasion for compounding (*upapada*)."

उपाधि। हरतेर्दृतिनाथयोः पशौ। 3.2.25

"When (the qualification is 'an animal as agent') the *pratyaya iṇ* acts after the *dhātu hṛ* (to take), the *upapadas,* (objects in composition with it) being the words *dṛti* (leather bag) and *nātha* (master)."

दृतिहरिः dog (carrier of skin)

नाथहरिः (that carries its master) a beast.

Upādhi m. that which is put in the place of another thing, substitute (*R.*) that which may be taken or has the name or appearance of another, appearance, disgrace, anything defining more closely, attribute, limitation, qualification.

म० भा० उपदेशेऽजनुनासि इत् 1.3.2

न हि उपाधेरुपाधिर्भवति, विशेषणस्य वा विशेषणम्

"For there is not an attribute of an attribute, or a qualification of a qualification."

विकार। आगम – म० भा० 3.1.1 वा० 4

2.12 विकारागमेषु च परविज्ञातात् ॥ 4 ॥

विकारागमेषु च परविज्ञानात्प्रत्ययेसंज्ञा न भविष्यति।

"The technical term *'pratyaya'* will not be applicable to *vikāra* (modifying words) or *āgamas* (augments) because of the understanding that a *pratyaya* always follows (the base)."

Vikāra m. change of form or names, alteration or deviation from a natural state, transformation, modification, derivative of a word *Nir.*, modification of word base or a *pratyaya* caused generally by the addition of *pratyayas.*

c.f. प्रकृतेरवस्थान्तरं विकारः का on 4.3.134 तस्य विकारः।

Vikāra (means) 'the change of condition of the original'. So a *pratyaya* acts after a word in the sixth case in construction, in the sense 'a modification thereof' (*tasya vikāra*).

e.g. (मनिन्) अश्मनो विकारः = आश्मनः 'stony', modification of stone,

c.f. also लोपागमा वर्णविकारज्ञो हि सम्यग्वेदान् परिपालयिष्यति म० भा० आह्निक1

"For a man will be able to preserve the *Vedas* if he knows (the technical) elision of letters, addition of letters and changes of letters (in the process of the formation of words)", i.e. often *ādeśa*/substitute.

M.Bh. 3.1.1/2.2.9 Example.

Hanasta ca 3.1.108 —"After the *dhātu han* (to kill) when in construction with a case inflected word as its *upapada* without *upasarga* acts the *pratyaya kya* denoting condition and *t* is the substitute/*vikāra* of its final."

Āgama m. arrival, appearance, acquisition of knowledge, traditional doctrine, handed down or fixed by tradition, addition

Nir. 1.4. यस्यागमादर्थपृथक्त्वमिह विज्ञायते

"(A conjunctive particle is) that by whose addition separateness of notions is indeed recognised," a grammatical augment, a meaningless syllable or less inserted in any part of a radical word. *Prāt. Pāṇ.*

An adventitious word element, hence it differs from *ādeśa,* the substitute which wholly takes the place of the original (or *ādeśin*). Out of the several *āgamas* mentiond by *Pāṇini* those that are marked with a mute ट् are prefixed, those that are marked with क् are affixed (आद्यन्तौ टकितौ 1.1.46), while those marked with म् are placed immediately after the last vowel of the word (मिदचोऽन्त्यातपर: 1.1.47).

The augments become part and parcel of the word to which they are added, and the characteristics of which they possess.

यदागमास्तद्गुणीभूतास्तदग्रहणेन गृह्यन्ते परि॰ 11

"That to which an augment is added denotes, because the augment forms part of it (not merely itself but it denotes also) what result from its combination with that augment."

आगमानां। आगमिधर्मिवैशिष्ट्यम् परि॰ 11

"For the augments there is endowment with the distinguishing property or attributes of the base to which augment is added."

These grammarians who hold the view that words are unproduced and eternal explain the addition of an augment as only the 'substitution of a word with an augment in the place of a word without an augment.'

c.f. आदेशास्तर्हीमे भविष्यन्ति अनागमकानां सागमका:

म॰ भा॰ 1.1.1 दाधा ध्वदाप् 1.1.46 आद्यन्तौ टकितौ

The term *āgama* is defined as:

अन्यत्र विद्यमानस्तु यो वर्ण: श्रूयतेधिक:।
आगमम्यमानतुल्यत्वात्स आगम इति स्मृत:। Comm. on तै प्राति 1.2.3

"But that letter existing elsewhere which is heard as an addition, because of being equal to that which is come near is remembered as *āgama.*"

म॰ भा॰ 3.1.1 । 2.2.9 Example:

त्रपुजतुनोः षुक् 4.3.138

The *pratyaya aṇ* with the augment *ṣuk* acts in the sense of its modification after the words *trapu* and *jatu.*

PARA

para, far, previous, former, following, succeeding, final, last, enemy, supreme or absolute being, universal.

पर

(1) Subsequent, as opposed to पूर्व or prior, the word is frequently used in grammar in connection with a rule or operation prescribed later on in a grammar treatise.

c.f. विप्रतिषेधे परं कार्यम् 1.4.2

(2) Occuring after (something) प्रत्ययः परश्च 3.1.1

(3) The word पर is sometimes explained in the sense of इष्ट or desired, on the analogy of the meaning श्रेष्ठ possessd by the word. This sense is given to the word पर in the rule विप्रतिषेधे परं कार्यम् 1.4.2 with a view to apply it to earlier rules in cases of emergency.

c.f. विप्रतिषेधे परं यदिष्ट तदभवति म० भा० 1.1.3 वा०

परशब्दः इष्टवाची म० भा० 1.2.5, 1.4.2 वा, 2.1.69.

Summary

of the views of the *Munitraya* on *Pratyaya* as revealed in the *Pratyayapāda*

Only *Patañjali* specifically interprets the meaning of *pratyaya* although there is no evidence to suggest his interpretation differs from that of *Pāṇini* or *Kātyāyana.*

As we have seen the *Bhāṣya* on the eighth *vārttika* of *3.1.1* concludes by treating the term *pratyaya* as etymologically significant conveying the sense both of that which causes meaning to be known as *kartṛsādhana,* agent instrumental in conveying meaning and that whose meaning is made known only as part of the *prakṛti, karmasādhana,* object instrumental for the meaning being manifest, according to the need.

This view enables the fundamental relationship of *prakṛti* and *pratyaya* to be maintained as that between the known and the unknown, the causes and that having cause, while allowing for certain *pratyayas* which do not convey meaning directly but rather reflect the meaning of the *prakṛti,* namely the so-called *atyantasvārthika* and *dyotaka pratyayas,* relative to which the *paribhāṣa anirdiṣṭārthāḥ* applies. *Bhattoji Dīkṣita* argues[1] that the objection raised specifically against attributing meanings to *atyantasvārthika pratyayas* such as the *ka* of *avika* etc. is not valid since the whole separation of *prakṛti* meanings and *pratyayas* meanings is in the last analysis based on an assumption that components have separable meaning. Whatever the nature of the *pratyaya* be it directly agent of meaning or object reflecting the meaning of the *prakṛti,* the true unit of communication is the *pada* within the cosmos of the *vākya* which alone according to *Bhartṛhari* expresses the *sphoṭa,* the expression of the one reality, the *śabadabrahman.*

We would argue from the evidence in the *pratyayapāda* that there is no fundamental discrepancy between the views of the *munitraya* that would lead one to question *Patañjali's* formulation outlined above as accurately presenting the intention of *Pāṇini* himself, since the whole analysis into *dhātu* or *prātipadika* and *pratyaya,* with *sphoṭa* as the impulse or explosion in consciousness, assumes that every element in the cosmos of the sentence has a function ultimately connected with bringing forth the meaning.

The very fact that *Pāṇini* makes direct mention of *uṇādi patyayas* and bothers to give *nipātana* forms implies that he was understanding the fundamental function of the *pratyaya* is to convey meaning whether directly or indirectly through the *prakṛti.*

Conclusion

After a review of the nine types (including *Uṇādi*) of *pratyaya* in the *Aṣṭādhyāyī* in our introduction and the translation of the *key Pratyaya Pāda* in the *Mahābhāṣya,* we may reasonably ask what is the wider context of this concept. In other words how does it relate to *śabdabrahman*—the 'Word', besides which the various concepts of grammar are finally attempts to distinguish the indefinable, as we saw in the seventh verse of the Māṇḍūkyopaniṣad.

> अदृष्टमव्यवहार्यमग्राह्यमलक्षणमचिन्त्यमव्यपदेश्यमेकात्मप्रत्ययसारं
> प्रपञ्चोपशमं शान्तं शिवमद्वैतं चतुर्थं मन्यते।
>
> "They consider the fourth to be that which is not conscious of the internal (subjective) world, nor of the external (objective) world, nor conscious of both the worlds, nor is it a concrete consciousness, nor usual worldly consciousness, nor devoid of consciousness, which is unseen, beyond empirical dealings, beyond grasp (intangible), devoid of qualifications, beyond thinking and beyond description; essentially of the nature of consciousness (*pratyayasāram*) as the Self alone (*ekātma*) in which all phenomena cease; which is peaceful, auspicious and non-dual."
>
> स आत्मा स विज्ञेयः
>
> "That is the Self, and that is to be known."

Bhartṛhari says:

> न सोऽस्ति प्रत्ययो लोके यः शब्दानुगमादृते।
> अनुविद्धमिव ज्ञातं सर्वं शब्देन भासते।। *(V.P. 1.123/1)*
>
> "There is no (cognition)/consciousness/*pratyaya* in the world in which the 'Word' does not figure. All knowledge is as it were intertwined with the Word."

The same Word is described as (becoming manifest) in the context of St. John's Gospel 1:14 "The Word became flesh and dwelt among us". We may consider, for coming at that unity, the concepts 1) *sphoṭa* 2) *dhātu* and 3) *pratyaya.* The exlosion in consciousness first manifests at the level of *Buddhi.* In the pre-*buddhi* stage, the word *śabdatattva* is used by *Bhartṛhari,* according to Iyer's interpretation. This Ultimate Reality is the *Brahman* or the 'Word'. *Bhaṛthari* also uses the word *śabdatattva* when he refers to that principal in everybody, which is manifested by the sound. It is the *sphoṭa* which is manifested by the sounds. Thus, the *śabdatattva* within, at one stage is *sphoṭa.* This inner principle, which is manifested by the sound is said to be the integrated Word, the expressive element वाचक प्रकाशक and as it is eternally associated with the integrated meaning, the two may be taken together. That would mean that the integrated word and the integrated meaning, differentiated in the mind (only) and facing each other are rather two sides of the same coin, constituting the *sphoṭa.*

(*K.A.S. Ayer "V.P. Some Problems"*, p.47)

We may usefully relate the concepts to the four states of speech परा, पश्यन्ती, मध्यमा and वैखरी. परा is consciousness and knowledge *cit* चित् in substance. It has no movement, and no vibration. It is still and beyond experience. It is said to be the source of all energy within the individual, physically located in the navel. This is also known as *amṛtakalaśa* अमृतकलश pitcher of nectar. This is the bliss in its substance, which keeps giving life force to the individual. It is nothing less than the portion of consciousness available to the man, the *śabdabrahman* शब्दब्रह्म. ॐ *Om,* the Word embodied in each individual as his very Self, तुरीय.

पश्यन्ती is the poised state of action. Here mind and *prāṇa* प्राण are said to be joined together, where vibrations manifest. It is like standing at the middle of a crossing, where everything is under comprehension. In the region of the heart, the पश्यन्ती is said to hold within itself the *svarāḥ* स्वरा: sounds which are sixteen in number and they are known as the sixteen *kalāḥ* कला: or aspects of the universal force. These *svarāḥ* स्वरा: sounds emanate from this centre.

अ आ इ ई उ ऊ ऋ ॠ ऌ ॡ ए ऐ ओ औ अं अ:

These are different aspects of *śakti* शक्ति power of the Absolute seen as *aiśvarya* ऐश्वर्य *dharma* धर्म *śrī* श्री *jñāna* ज्ञान *vairāgya* वैराग्य *vīrya* वीर्य *yaśaḥ* यश: *mādhurya* माधुर्य etc.

Sphoṭa स्फोट an explosion in consciousness may be viewed as the impulse or desire at this stage initiating the development of the sound or *śabda* शब्द. When the sound has arisen to meet one of the possibilities and it has arisen only in the mental realm, then it is said to be called madhyamā मध्यमा. This may be linked with the development of the seed form *dhātu* धातु. Just as at the level of *paśyantī, Nāgoji Bhaṭṭa* tells us, there is perception of *prakṛti* and *pratyaya* as totally distinct as pure *svarāḥ* (on *M.Bhā. 1.3.24*), so at the level of *madhyamā*, the middle or intermediary stage may be perceived where the *dhātu* is said to develop internally in the presence of a *pratyaya śap* etc. All words or sound arise from *Om* ॐ, which is the seed of all seeds, the *dhātu* of all *dhātus*. From it other *dhātus* are formed and from them yet other secondary *dhātus*. The formation of the physical language is said to reflect this subtle process. It too has seed forms which are derived from *Om* ॐ.

The *dhātu* forms cannot be used in a sentence, since they are too general and non-specific in meaning. To give a particular definition in time and space they are modified by the *pratyaya*. Hence the *dhātu* which contains all possibilities of action, always requires the presence of a *pratyaya* for manifestation, whether it be at the simple seed stage or developed to *guṇa* or *vṛddhi*, as for example *cit* चित् becomes the *prātipadika* प्रातिपदिक *citta* चित्त *cet* (*aṅga*) चेत् (अङ्ग) becomes *cetana* चेतन and *cait* चैत् (*vṛddhi aṅga*) वृद्धि अङ्ग becomes *caitanya* चैतन्य 'consciousness'

When the sound is manifest as physical sound through mouth and tongue, it is expelled and vibrates in open space. Then it is called *vaikharī* वैखरी. When a सुप् *sup* or a *tiṅ pratyaya* is added the *dhātu* धातु or *prātipadika* becomes minifest as *pada* (*P.1.4.14*) *suptiṅantam padam* सुप्तिङन्तं पदम्. Most of the wordly communication is materialised in the *vaikharī* वैखरी state, and sometimes in *madhyamā* मध्यमा. The spiritual activites of meditation, reflection, *japa* जप, repetition of *mantra* मन्त्र etc. comprehend and make use of *madhyamā* मध्यमा and *paśyantī* पश्यन्ती. When union is made and the being is himself, then he is in *parā* परा. As Saint John tells us "And the Word was made flesh and dwelt among us and we beheld His glory, the glory as of the only begotten of the father, full of Grace and Truth". (St. John 1:14)

If this thesis is correct, then indeed *pratyaya* प्रत्यय has a crucial role to play in language, and therefore, in life, serving as साक्षात्कार making manifest or instrumental for realisation. The realisation may be the understanding that all concepts are ultimately part of नाम and रूप not only inseparably intertwined but only meaningful in relation to the 'Word'.

I would in conclusion suggest that it is most meaningful to view the concept *pratyaya* as 'throwing light on itself', self-expressive (आत्मप्रत्यायक) or as 'causing to bring forth the meaning inherent in the stem परप्रत्यायक'.

Just as in any syllable no consonant can sound except by virtue of the vowel, which gives it life and just as the "True light lighteth every man that cometh into the world" (St. John 1:9), so every word is illumined by virtue of its *pratyaya* प्रत्यय and *aṅga* अङ्ग being united as one, to manifest the meaning which may lead ultimately to the realisation of the unity of the Self.

पतञ्जलि - प्रत्याययतीति . . . प्रत्ययः। म० भा० 3.4.8

न केवला प्रकृतिः प्रयोक्तव्या न केवलः प्रत्ययः प्रत्ययार्थस्य प्राधान्यम्।

म० भा० 1.2:64 वार्त्तिक 5.

Precis of Mahābhāṣya

On Pāṇini 3.1.1

Pratyayaḥ.

The technical name *Pratyaya*/affix governs as a technical name from here to the end of the fifth *Adhyāya*

General Summary

Vā. 1: No prohibition need be stated on the term *Pratyaya* applying to *prakṛti upapada* or *upādhi* when *pratyaya* is the governing rule.

Vā. 2: . . . Because the cause is meant for that which is possessed of a cause elsewhere.

Vā. 3: . . . Or else it is established, because in relation to the chief thing there is sure knowledge of the operation.

Vā. 4: And in relation to the *vikāra* and *āgama* also the term *Pratyaya* does not apply because of the understanding that *Pratyaya* is *para* (subsequent).

Vā. 5: . . . And because the sixth case indication is connected with those (*vikāras* and *āgamas*).

Vā. 6: However the ordaining of *Pratyaya* is not justified.

Vā. 7: Therefore, it is justified there by the mention of the fifth case.

Vā. 8: Or else the rule *Pratyaya* exists because of a need to resort to meaning.

Bhā.: What causes meaning to be understood or what is caused to be understood (with its base/*prakṛti*) is *pratyaya.*

Vārttika Summary

"The technical name *pratyaya* governs as a technical name from this *sūtra* until the end of the fifth *adhyaya.*"

Kātyāyana's first *vārttika* deals with the doubt as to whether the elements other than *pratyaya,* namely *prakṛti* (base) *upapada* and *upādhi,* might receive the name and the operations associated, and thus prohibition of it applying, would have to be specifically stated. This is not necessary.

The second *vārttika* explains why. It is due to the natural distinction which does not have to be prescribed, between the cause and that for which the cause(s) exists . . . seen in life too. Cause(s) and that caused complement each other with their distinct function.

The third *vārttika* presents another natural distinction, the *pratyaya* as principal and all other factors as secondary to it. Although unknown there is sure knowledge of the operation in relation to the chief factor. However, this characteristic of being 'unknown' and principal applies to *vikāras* or *adeśas* and *āgamas*.

Therefore, the fourth *vārttika* states how they cannot receive the name *pratyaya*. It is because *pratyayas* are understood always to be subsequent to the *prakṛti*.

The sixth *vārttika* points out the practical way this distinction is shown, namely through the sixth case being attached to both *vikāras* and *āgamas*.

The natural corollary is stated in the seventh *vārttika* that the ordaining of the *pratyaya* is inapplicable in the context of *vikāras* and *āgamas* being enjoined.

However, the seventh *vārttika* shows how equally precisely it is indicated where *pratyaya* is applicable; that is, where there is the fifth case indication, the *pratyaya* acts after that.

Finally *Kātyāyana* gives an alternative way to distinguish *pratyaya* from *prakṛti* etc. at that level of meaning. In the last analysis it is the conveying of meaning that distinguishes *pratyaya* from *vikāras* etc. This *Pāṇini* implies by using a word that means 'that which makes known'.

Bhāṣya Summary

Patañjali introduces the first *vārttika* by illustrating the different functions *prakṛti* etc. and stating the consequence of having the name *pratyaya*, namely *paratva aṅga* technical name etc. In the second he gives a characteristically vivid wordly example to bring home the universality of distinction, between cause and that having a cause, between name and that having a name. *Devadatta* is he who sits on the horse not the horse! A further most helpful distinction is added between that which is known, *prakṛti* etc. and that unknown yet to be revealed, the *pratyaya* conveying the meaning.

In explaining the third *vārttika Patañjali* brings alive the meaning with the example of many people waiting to see the King and we hear echoes of *Bṛhadāraṇyakopaniṣad 4.3.37* "यथा राजानमायान्तम्... इदं ब्रह्म आयाति" "Just as when a king is coming . . . they say 'Here he comes', . . . (the elements say) 'Here comes *Brahman*'."

He further explains the nature of '*pradhānam*' as that not previously taught. However, this does not serve to distinguish *pratyaya* from *vikāras* and *āgamas*, so the next three *vārttikas* are shown to be essential for that purpose. Thus although *vikāras* and *āgamas* are not previously taught they are not prescribed as being *para* (subsequent) (*Vā. 4*). In the *bhāṣya* on *vārttikas* 3,6,7 and 8 he takes the *sūtras* '*hanasta ca*' (*3.1.108*) and '*trapujatunoḥ ṣuk*' (*4.3.138*) as a typical pedagogical device to illustrate the distinction between *pratyaya* and *vikāras* and *āgamas.*

In the *bhāṣya* on the seventh *vārttika* we also see the use of the powerful tool of reasoning, the *jñapaka,* to show how *kyap pratyaya* cannot be intended to act after all *dhātus.*

In his *bhāṣya* on the last *vārttika Patañjali* develops the discussion in such a way as to suggest the *vārttika* itself is a shorthand note representing the conclusion of the discussion *Patañjali* himself witnessed. In it he presents a solution to the problem as to how *pratyaya* can be a term whose meaning is intelligible in itself, applicable to *pratyayas* which cause meanings to be known and to those whose meaning is held within *prakṛti* which they simply reflect. The *pratyaya* is thus either the Agent instrumental in conveying meaning or the object instrumental for the meaning, according to need.

On Pāṇini 3.1.2

Paraṣca.

And a *pratyaya* is subsequent.

General Summary

Bhāṣya concludes 'So that the *pratyaya* should only be subsequent is in fact the reason for the *para* (subsequent) rule.

Vā. 1: The statement of *para* is pointless because operations in connection with 'being subsequent/*para*' are indicated by the fifth case.

Vā. 2: It was stated in connection with *vikāras* and *āgamas,* the technical name *pratyaya* is not justified.

Bhā. : Therefore, *pratyaya* is established as valid by mention of the fifth case.

Vā. 3: Or the *para* rule is for the purpose of the elision of those subsequent *pratyayas* which are completely unseen as subsequent.

Vā. 4: Or else the *para* rule is for the purpose of being a general rule restricting the use of the term *pratyaya.*

Vā. 5: The restriction with reference to use should be made because of examples of *pratyayas* not being seen when the meaning of the *prakṛti* is expressed by the *prakṛti* itself.

Vā. 6: . . . And because *dvayasac* and the rest are seen to be used alone.

Vā. 7: And when (mention is made of the *para* when) there is expression of the word *vā* (optionally) it is for the purpose of the non-production of *san* etc.

Vā. 8: And it was stated that the expression of *vā* has no purpose there because of *san* always being applicable.

Vā. 9: When there is restriction of *pratyaya* there is absence of restriction on *prakṛti.*

Vā. 10: When there is restriciton on the *prakṛti* there is no restriction on the *pratyaya.*

Vā. 11: But it is established because of both restrictions.

Bhā. : 'A *pratyaya* is to be used only following a *prakṛti* and a *prakṛti* is to be used only having a *pratyaya* following.'

Vārttika Summary

The *Vārttikakāra* begins by pointing out that the sense of *pratyaya* always having to be subsequent/*para* to the *prakṛti* has already been conveyed as the meaning of the fifth case by '*tasmād-ityuttarasya*' (*1.1.67*)

In the second *Vārttika Kātyāyana* points out that the function of the rule cannot be to distinguish *pratyaya* from *vikāras* and *āgamas* because as was stated in *Vā. 6-7* on *3.1.1* that purpose was achieved through fifth case indication.

The third *Vārttika* suggests the purpose of the rule is so that zero-*pratyayas* like *kvip* etc. should be elided in a subsequent position (for the sake of operations like augment *tuk* by '*hrasvasya piti kṛti tuk*' *6.1.71.*)

In the fourth *Vārttika* the wider function of the rule is revealed as in general acting to restrict all *pratyayas* from being anything other than subsequent.

We are now in the fifth *Vārttika* given the reason why such a restriction rule is necessary: because irregular examples are found in the language of people using the *prakṛti* on its own as if it were a valid *pada,* as for example *dvayasac* etc. (*Vā. 6*).

The seventh *Vārttika* unexpectedly suggests another reason for the rule, which is to allow the option stated in *3.1.7* to apply to *san pratyaya, vā* (optionally) following a *dhātu,* the alternative being a sentence, so that *san* would not arise.

In the eighth *vārttika* we see why *Kātyāyana* has introduced the problem of *vā* and *san* at this stage. Once it is stated that even *vā* has no such purpose in *Vā. 9* on *3.1.7.* We are only left with the purpose of restriction for the *para* rule.

The ninth *Vārttika* points out the consequence of the restriction being limited to the *pratyaya,* namely by implication the *prakṛti* would be able to stand on its own without a *pratyaya.*

In the tenth *Vārttika* the opposite possibility is stated that the restriction be placed on the *prakṛti* only and so the undesired consequence would be for *pratyayas* to be used alone, not following a *prakṛti.*

Finally *Kātyāyana* concludes therefore, the rule is for the purpose of a double restriction, *pratyaya* only after *prakṛti* and *prakṛti* only having a *pratyaya* following.

Bhāṣya Summary

Patañjali introduces the first *Vārttika* by first showing how specific positions other than subsequent, namely prior or middle, are ordained, so that *para* may be to restrict those not having a fixed place, like the calf which may precede or follow its mother. We see here *Patañjali's* typical style of *pūrvapakṣa's* view being answered by the *siddhāntin.*

In this discussion of the first *Vārttika* the *pūrvapakṣa* presents an inaccurate statement by treating *6.3.97* as an example of fifth case serving the function of *para.* This prepares the way for another view that the rule is to cover those cases where the fifth case rule does not apply, as the *vikāras* and *āgamas,* so introducing the next *Vārttika,* upon which he does not comment, but instead tells us what was said in *Vārttika 6* on *3.1.1,* in this second *Vārttika.*

On the third *Vārttika Patañjali* presents first the view that the purpose of zero-*pratyayas* like *kvip* being required to be subsequent is, so that the operations dependent on *it k* or *ṇ* may be applicable. Then this is refuted by showing an implied rule/*jñāpaka,* namely, the very adding of these indicatory letters to *pratyayas* which are to be totally elided, implies when *it k* or *ṇ* follow the operations be applicable.

He explains the nature of the restriction in *Vārttika 4,* and introduces the next by asking if there is anything undesired which prompts a general restriction.

On *Vārttika 5, Patañjali* provides us with the essential examples of *prakṛtis* being seen without *pratyayas,* as *babhruḥ* when it should be *babhravyaḥ* etc.

While the first example of *pratyayas* occuring without *prakṛti* is given in *Vārttika 6* itself, it is *Patañjali* who provides the rest implied, with the appropriate sentence, as well as mentioning the special case of *bahu.*

On the question of *vā* (optionally) in *Vārttika 7* the *Bhāṣyakāra* explains, that though 'optionally' is to connect with *para,* logically there is not anyting else that could connect. More important still, it is not desired there be any option for technical names.

On *Vārttika* 8 he explains it will be stated in *Vā. 9* on *3.1.7* that *Kātyāyana* concludes that *vā* is pointless in that *sūtra.* He then introduces the last three *Vārttikas* by asking what is the distinction between the *para* restriction applying to a *pratyaya* and *prakṛti.* Finally he shows the force of mentioning *para* when the meaning is conveyed by the fifth case is to show a *pratyaya* must only follow the *prakṛti* and *prakṛti* only occur with a *pratyaya* subsequent.

On Pāṇini 3.1.3

Ādyudattasca.

And a *pratyaya* has initial *udātta* (acute accent).

General Summary

Bha. : The rule is stated so there be initial *udātta* only.

Vā. 1: The purpose of the statement of there being initial *udātta* in conjunction with the technical term *pratyaya* is so that whatever is given the technical name *pratyaya* also has initial *udātta.*

Vā. 2: For when there is no conjunction, there is the characteristic of initial *udātta* for that after which that *pratyaya* is ordained and characteristic of *anudātta* for the final of the same.

Vā. 3: This difficulty does not arise, because the initial *udātta* for the *prakṛti,* indicated that there is no mention of the initial of that (*pratyaya* which helps form it).

Vā. 4: And because of the force of the rule of *udātta* for the *prakṛti* there is absence of accent for the *pratyaya.*

Vā. 5: Or the rule is for the purpose of *anudātta* accent for *āgamas.*

Vā. 6: Nor is this rule valid because of the rule of *anudātta* for *āgamas* (augments).

Vā. 7: For when there is not a specific rule for *Āgama* to be *anudātta* there is the characteristic of initial *udātta* for the actual initial of *sīyuṭ* (*āgama*).

Bhā. : There is a *jñāpaka* '*āgamas* are as if non-existent'.

Vā. 8: Or the rule is for the sake of the situation where there is elision for that word having initial *udātta*.

Vā. 9: Nor is the rule necessary because of the (*lopa*) rule being characterised as *bahiraṅga*.

Vā. 10: For when there is not statement of *antaraṅga* rule there is an over-application of the rule in relation to *it ñ n* and *k*.

Vā. 11: Instead of the characteristic of initial *udātta* for a *pratyaya*, final *udātta* for a *dhātu* is to be applied.

Vā. 12: Instead of the *anudātta* accent in connection with that having an indicatory *p*, the *svarita* accent in connection with that having an indicatory *t* is applicable when the feminine *pratyaya ṭāp* follows.

Vā. 13: And instead of an *anudātta* accent ordained in connection with that having an *it p*, *udātta* accent ordained in connection with that having an *it c* prevails, when the feminine *pratyaya cāp* follows.

Vā. 14: Nor is *vipratiṣedha* applicable, because initial *udātta* is taught in conjunction with the technical name *pratyaya*.

Vā. 15: When *tāp* follows the one subsitute for the one before and the one after will be with a *svarita* accent.

Vā. 16: When *cāp*, feminine *pratyaya*, follows because of having an indicatory *c* there will be final *udātta*.

Vārttika Summary

Kātyāyana explains in the first *vārttika* why the rules for *pratyaya's* accent should be given and not in the accent section at *6.1.158* to the end; it is so that initial *udātta* should apply simultaneously with the technical name *pratyaya*.

In the second *vārttika* he explains the consequences of not simultaneously ordaining the accent with the technical name, namely the '*tadādeḥ tadantasya*' *paribhāṣā* would apply, so that instead of the *pratyaya* having an initial *udātta* the word form ending in that *pratyaya* would receive the accent on its initial syllable.

The third *vārttika* points out that the rule ordaining initial *udātta* for *prakṛtis* formed by *pratyayas* with *it ñ* or *n* is an implied rule, that for those formed by any other *pratyayas* the *prakṛti* does not have such an accent.

The fourth *vārttika* deals with the other aspect of the *paribhāṣā* . . . *tad-antasya,* the requirement that if for the beginning of that ending with a *pratyaya* there should be *udātta,* it follows that for the end of such a word there would be *anudātta* accent. This is barred by the *jñāpaka,* derived from there being a rule for final *udātta* of a *dhātu,* which of course would not be necessary if the *pratyaya* were *anudātta.*

Kātyāyana suggests in the fifth *vārttika* another possible purpose for the rule being in conjunction with the name *pratyaya,* that *āgamas* as a result be *anudātta.* However, this is not a real possibility for the seventh *vārttika* states that such a rule for *anudātta* augments has already been stated.

The other view is put in the seventh *vārttika,* that without specifically starting a rule *āgama anudātta* there would have been *udātta* for the *ī* of *sīyut.*

Another possible reason for the rule being in conjunction with *pratyaya* is stated in *Vārttika* eight, as establishing *udātta* before the vowel is *lopa*-elided, so that there may be *udātta* in place of *anudātta* by *6.1.161.*

However, this last purpose is not required, if it is realised that *lopa* rules are *bahiraṅga* in relation to *antaraṅga svara* (accent) rules, according to *vārttika* nine.

The tenth *vārttika* explains that the *antaraṅga paribhāṣā* implied in the last *vārttika* will prevent unwarrantable stretch of the general rule in relation to *it ñ n* and *k.*

The eleventh *vārttika* now points out another exception to the general initial *udātta* for a *pratyaya* when final *udātta* for a *dhātu* is ordained by *dhātoḥ 6.1.162.*

In the next two *vārttikas Kātyāyana* is concerned with exceptions to *3.1.4* '*anudāttau suppitau*', directly, whereas in the previous *vārttika* this was implied. In the twelfth he shows that the *svarita* accent bars *anudātta* resulting from *it p,* when *ṭāp* follows if the *pratyaya* has an *it ṭ.*

The thirteenth *vārttika* serves to underline the fact that the *udātta* accent connected with *it c* will bar the *anudātta* arising from *it p* only when *cāp* follows.

Having presented the *pūrvapakṣa* in the last *vārttikas, Kātyāyana* now states in the fourteenth that it is not necessary (being based on *vipratiṣedha*) because initial *udātta* is taught simultaneously with the name *pratyaya* by this very *sūtra.*

In the penultimate *vārttika* it is said that *vārttika 12* was also incorrectly based on *vipratiṣedha* because *svarita* is simply the one *ādeśa* for *svarita* and *anudātta* containing both.

Finally in *vārttika* sixteen, it is stated why more specifically *vārttika 13* is incorrectly based on *vipratiṣedha* because the very purpose of the letter *c* of *cāp* is to prescribe *udātta*.

Bhāṣya Summary

Patañjali introduces the first *vārttika* by asking in general why initial *udātta* need be stated. If in fact final and middle *udātta, anudātta* and *svarita* are specifically prescribed elsewhere, then it would appear no rule is required for initial *udātta* since they are the remainder/*śeṣa*. However, where no specific rule applies prescribing accent in a fixed place then this rule is required to ensure that such *pratyayas* only have initial *udātta,* and not any of the other possibilities.

This having been clarified, *Patañjali* introduces the sublter problem, as to why these two rules on *udātta* and *anudātta* accent on *3.1.3-4* are introduced here, simultaneously with the technical name *pratyaya,* when they could easily have been stated in the sixth *adhyāya* first *pāda,* with the other accent *sūtras* and by the device of *anuvṛtti* achieved greater brevity. As it is the words of these two *sūtras* will effectively have to be repeated in *6.1.*

Since the first two *vārttikas* are complimentary, *Patañjali* makes his comments after the second. The consequences of no simultaneous conjunction with *pratyaya,* would be the operation of the *paribhāṣā* here stated, and often elsewhere, by *Patañjali* '*a pratyaya* denotes. . . a word form which begins with that to which it has been added and ends with the *pratyaya*'. He then draws a vital distinction between the form in process of being produced and the completed form. Just as the pot being produced does produce operations like carrying water, so accent prescribed with *pratyaya* is totally disconnected from operations referred to in the *paribhāṣā.*

In his discussion of *vārttika* three, *Patañjali* explains the implied rule/*jñapaka* referred to which states that a *prakṛti's* initial will be *anudātta,* when not followed by *pratyayas* with *it ñ* or *n* (*6.1.197*) so that the *paribhāṣā* is not relevant for the initial anyway.

The second half of the *Paribhāṣā* . . . '*tadantasya*' is also now shown not to be applicable. In discussing this fourth *vārttika* the *Bhāṣyakāra* shows that by the prescription of final *udātta* for a *dhātu* (*6.1.162*) and a *prātipadika* (*Phiṭ 1*) it is an implied rule that *prakṛti udātta* final is applicable where *pratyaya* is *anudātta.*

Turning to *āgamas, Patañjali* explains the fifth *vārttika* as saying, by having simultaneous connection of *udātta* initial with *pratyaya,* augments will necessarily be *anudātta.*

The *Bhāṣya* on the sixth *vārttika,* having first quoted the 'rule' of *anudātta* for augments, takes one example, the augment *iṭ* joined to *tāsi* after *dhātu lū* to form *lavitā. Patañjali* considers the two rules in turn, initial *udātta* and augment *iṭ,* agreeing that both are variable but that initial *udātta* is *antaraṅga* (requiring fewer operations). Then what of *sīyuṭ* being *udātta* ?

Nonetheless some specific statement is needed to show *āgamas* are *anudātta* *sīyuṭ* etc. would (otherwise) receive the *udātta* intended for the *pratyaya* they precede. So *Patañjali* in his discussion on *vārttika* seven, deals at length with the implied rule/*jñāpaka* inferred from *3.4.103,* that other than *yāsuṭ* mentioned in that *sūtra* as *udātta,* all others must of necessity be *anudātta.* However, the problem remains as to whether they are to be regarded as existing. Unless they are treated as non-existent for *pratyaya* rules they will receive the accent and not the *pratyaya.* This too can be implied from the *sūtra 3.4.103,* because of the rule being expressed less briefly than is possible.

On the eighth *vārttika Patañjali* explains how by *udātta* initial being stated simultaneously with the name *pratyaya,* this enables the *udātta* resulting from the elision of a preceding *udātta* to replace an *anudātta* (by *6.1.161*). However, that would seem to be barred by *6.4.1, 48* because of being *para.*

The *paribhāṣā* suggested by *vārttika* nine is clearly stated by *Patañjali* 'That which is *bahiraṅga* is as of non-effect, when that which is *antaraṅga* is to take effect'. Thus the *lopa* rule is *bahiraṅga* in relation to the accent rule.

In the *bhāṣya* on the tenth *vārttika,* two examples are given *autsī* and *kansikī* to illustrate the necessity for the *antaraṅga paribhāṣā.* To prevent over-application of *paratva* in relation to elision of that with *it ñ n* or *k, Patañjali* points out this apparent conflict does not exist, because *apavāda sūtras* like *6.1.197,* always operate first. So in the case of *kansikī* the problem is avoided by stating *udātta* for the initial of the *pratyaya* and *lopa* for the final of the *prakṛti.* In the case of *ātreyī* the *paribhāṣā* is essential, and the initial *udātta* not needed.

Patañjali explains why *vārttika* eleven speaks of *dhātu* being final *udātta* instead of the *pratyaya* initial *udātta,* namely because of a conflict of rules requiring the subsequent to prevail. So in fact '*dhātoḥ*' *6.1.162* applies.

In the *bhāṣya* on the twelfth *vārttika,* again *vipratiṣedha* (conflict of rules of equal strength requiring the subsequent to prevail) is given as the reason the *svarita* acts in place of the *anudātta* caused by *it p* when *ṭāp* follows; as in *kāryam.*

Similarly the *bhāṣya* on the thirteenth *vārttika* speaks of *udātta* caused by *it c* acting in place of the *pit anudātta,* when in the presence of *cāp*; as in *āmbaṣṭhyā* by reason of *vipratiṣedha.*

The last two *vārttikas* are now shown to be wrongly based on *vipratiṣedha.* Instead *vārttika* fourteen suggests, and the *bhāṣya* explains, when there is simultaneous conjunction of initial *udātta* with the name *pratyaya,* the next stage in the formation of the words is the final *udātta,* prescribed for a *dhātu* which acts in place of it as the remainder.

The conflict apparent between the *pit* accent and the *tit* accent is not real. Instead, the fifteenth *vārttika* says, the single *ādeśas* for the prior and the subsequent is *svarita. Patañjali* discusses these two alternative '*ekādeśa*' or ordaining of *svarita* accent in place of the *anudātta.* When both are concluded to be *anitya* (variable), *svarita* prevails because of being subsequent. Similarly when both are agreed to be *antaraṅga, svarita* again prevails, for the same reason. However, when (it is acknowledged) the *svarita* is effected, because of the near relationship between *anudātta* and *svarita,* the latter containing the former, the one substitute for both must be *svarita.*

Finally *Patañjali* explains why there is in fact no *vipratiṣedha* between *pit* and *cit,* because of the very force of creating an *it c* being to ordain final *udātta* accent.

On Pāṇini 3.1.5

Guptijkidbhyaḥ san.

San pratyaya acts after the *dhātu gup, tij* and *kit.*

General Summary

Vā. 1: The *it* letter in *gup-a* etc. is for the purpose of *ātmenepada*

Bhā. : . . . By force of producing *it* letters.
Or a sign made in a part will be distinctive of a whole.

Vārttika Summary

Kātyāyana simply explains that the *a* in *gup-a* etc. is to indicate *ātmanepada.*

Bhāṣya Summary

Patañjali in his discussion of the *vārttika,* first puts the *pūrvapakṣa* view that due to *san* intervening, *1.3.62* will apply and there will be *ātmanepada* for what was originally so, not because of the *it a* (*anudātta*). However, in the case of these *dhātus* neither *pada* is seen before *san,* so by the force of the *it a* only *ātmanepada* applies.

He now explains with a typical graphical illustration that, just as a mark on one part of a cow stands for the whole cow but not for the whole herd of cows, so the *a* of *gup* etc. indicates all formations with *san* will receive *ātmanepada* but not those with *ṇi* (causative) etc.

On Pāṇini 3.1.6

Mānbadhdānśānbhyodīrghaścābhyāsasya.

The *pratyaya san* acts after the *dhātu mān, badha, dān* and *śān* and there is a long vowel for the reduplicative syllable.

General Summary

Vā. 1: When long is ordained for the reduplicative syllable there is occasion for lengthening the letter *a*.

Vā. 2: Or there is no difficulty because of an *apavāda sūtra* not barring the *utsarga* in the case of a modification in the reduplicative syllable. *Bhā* reads the *sūtra* as 'And the lengthening of the modified reduplicative syllable.'

Vārttika Summary

In the first *vārttika Kātyāyana* focuses on the possibility of the lengthening referred to in the *sūtra* wrongly applying to the *a* of *mān* etc. in the reduplicative syllable.

The second *vārttika* is a reply to this *pūrvapakṣa* explaining that, contrary to the general rule that *apavādas* bar *utsargas,* in the case of operations modifying the reduplicative syllable, this does not apply, so the problem does not arise.

Bhāṣya Summary

Patañjali explains the *pūrvapaksa* in the first *vārttika.* One does not expect *i* in the reduplicative syllable (by *'sanyataḥ' 7.4.79,* because of not being short *a*) but a reduplicative syllable is expected (by *'sanyanoḥ' 6.1.9*), therefore long *ā* would obtain.

In the explanation of the second *vārttika* he first says that the *i* rule will not bar the lengthening in this *sūtra* because of the exceptional *paribhāṣā* referred to. Modifications are then suggested in the *sūtra* to clarify and to shorten, namely *ī* instead of the word *dīrgha* = *acaḥ* (of a vowel), or add the word *itaḥ* so that the *sūtra* specifically states lengthening 'of an *i*'. Rather than change the text he returns to the *paribhāṣā* soulution given in the second *vārttika.* Finally *Patañjali* offers a characteristically ingenious linguistic solution, namely the word in the *sūtra* is really *ābhyāsasya,* so means '(lengthening) of the modified reduplicative syllable'.

On Pāṇini 3.1.7

Dhātoḥ karmaṇaḥ samānakartṛkādicchāyām vā.

Optionally the *pratyaya san* acts in the sense of desire after a *dhātu* expressing the object desired and having the same agent of action as the desirer.

General Summary

Vā. 1: Due to the mention of *karman* in the *san* rule the mention of *dhātu* is pointless.

Vā. 2: If you say the *karman* is the *dhātu* together with an *upasarga* because of an *upasarga* being a qualification of *karman,* (in reality) *karman* is (a *dhātu*) without an *upasarga.*

Vā. 3: For when the *karman* is together with an *upasarga,* even in the context of the governing *sūtra dhātoḥ* there is no rule for *san* because of the *dhātu* not being the *karman*/object.

Vā. 4: And there is not occasion for *san* acting after a word ending in a *sup*/case ending because of *kyac* and the rest having the nature of *apavāda* rules.

Vā. 5: Or because of not expressing the meaning desired.

Vā. 6: And the mention of the object having the same agent is pointless, because of the ordaining of the *pratyaya* when 'desire is being expressed'.

Vā. 7: (*San*) is not known to occur after that which is not *karman* and which has not the same agent as that of the one desiring the *karman.*

Vā. 8: However, for the purpose of determining the *aṅga* (reference should be made to either *karman* or *dhātu*).

Vā. 9: And the word *vā* (optionally) is pointless because of the invariable nature of *san* in that context.

Vā. 10: Optionally *san* should be ordained after that ending in the *pratyaya tumun,* and for that *tumun* the operation of *luk* elision should be stated.

Vā. 11: Optionally *san* acts after the *uttama* (first) person of *liṅ* (optative).

Vā. 12: Additional enumeration (should be made of *san*) in relation to nonsentient beings in the sense of fear or apprehension (of the speaker).

Vā. 13: Or else the distinction is not applicable because of the same nature of the cause. For the understanding arises from the use of *icchā* (desire).

Vā. 14: This usage is established because of simile.

Vā. 15: Or else the usages are established because of everything having consciousness.

Śloka Vārttika : *Śaiṣika pratyayas* after *śaiṣika pratyayas, matup arthīya pratyayas* after *matup arthīya pratyayas,* are not desired; *pratyayas* of the same form are not desired to follow after one another, neither is *san* desired after *san.*

Vārttika Summary

In the first *vārttika Kātyāyana* begins as it were to question the function of each word in the *sūtra,* starting wth *dhātu* being unnecessary, because the mention of *karman* necessarily implies a *dhātu.*

The second *vārttika* brings out the consequences of leaving out mention of *dhātu,* namely an inability to show that *karman* is not an *upasarga* but a *dhātu* without an *upasarga.*

The third *vārttika* explains a further undesired consequence were *dhātoḥ* omitted, namely in spite of there being a governing *sūtra* (available by reverse *anuvṛtti*) it could not be the *karman* so *san* itself would be applicable.

The fourth *vārttika* serves to refute another possible function of mentioning *dhātoḥ,* i.e. to prevent *san* acting after a *sup* ending word, by saying that in fact *kyac* etc. are *apavādas* of *san,* so this possibility does not exist.

The simplest solution is given in the fifth *vārttika,* namely that *san* after a *sup* ending word would not express the intended meaning.

Another suggested amendment in the *sūtra* would be to specify the *karman* having the same agent as the *dhātu.* This is shown in the sixth *vārttika* to be pointless, because the ordaining of *san* in sense of desire implies that.

The seventh *vārttika* explains further, that *san* does not in fact occur without the conditions 'having an object/*karman*' and 'having the same agent as the desire'.

Kātyayāna introduces a new concept in the eighth *vārttika,* suggesting one purpose of the word '*dhātoḥ*' is for determining the measure of the *aṅga.*

Turning to the word *vā* in *vārttika* nine, he says it is pointless because *san* is invariably applicable.

The tenth states *san* as optionally acting after the ending in *tumun,* in turn being *luk* elided.

Similarly in the eleventh *vārttika*, another addition to the *sūtra* is made whereby *san* also optionally acts after the first person *liṅ*.

The twelfth is additional enumeration in relation to non-sentient beings.

The previous *vārttika* is replaced by this wider view in the thirteenth, that the distinction between sentient and non-sentient is not real, since one may understood both as arising from desire.

The wider view, he says in the fourteenth, is possible by use of simile. Or finally the varying usages may be justified, because in fact everything has consciousness.

Bhāṣya Summary

Patañjali not only introduces the first *vārttika* but by his example focuses the mind on the main problem to be discussed, namely distinguishing *dhātu* from *upasarga*, so that *aṭ* augment is added directly to the *dhātu* and not the combination of *dhātu* and *upasarga*.

After explaining the first *vārttika*, he introduces the next by pointing to the consequence of having no reference to '*dhātoḥ*' in the *sūtra*. The *dhātu* together with its *upasarga* would have to be treated as the object, hence *san* would wrongly obtain after the combination, and not just after the *dhātu* as desired.

This error arises from the proximity of the *upasarga* to the *dhātu*, as a qualification of it. However, the reality is the *karman* as *dhātu* has no *upasarga*. The *bhāṣya* on *vārttika* two then adds that this fact needs to be known (if the error is to be avoided).

In his paraphrase of the third *vārttika Patañjali* clarified why *san* could not be applicable, even when specific mention is made of '*dhātoḥ*' as a governing *sūtra*. If *dhātu* plus *upasarga* is treated as *karman*, clearly *dhātu* alone cannot be so regarded. The earlier argument that the presence of '*dhātoḥ*' is to prevent taking the *upasarga* in combination with *dhātu* as object is now treated as not the real purpose. Instead it is argued the mention of '*dhātoḥ*' is to prevent *san* acting after a *sup*/case ending word as *kyac* etc.

On the fourth *vārttika Patañjali* simply adds that the implication of *kyac* etc. being *apavādas* of *san* is that they will necessarily bar it in the context of *subanta* words, so this cannot be the purpose of '*dhātoḥ*'.

An alternative solution proposed in the fifth *vārttika*, which makes the previous *vārttika* apparently redundant, is the obvious general point that *san* acting after a *sup* ending word should not express the meaning intended of 'desire'. Having called this a last resort argument, *Patañjali* uses this aspect of meaning to refine the previous *vārttika*. *San* may not be possible after a *sup* in the sense of desire for oneself, but it may be for another, as for example desiring a son for the king where in fact *kyac* etc. apply. Here he says *Pāṇini* should have indicated that *san* like *tumun* requires having the same agent as one condition. However, where *tumun* is applicable, like 'He desires to sit' etc. *san* will not apply. Again when *pratyaya lyuṭ* actually applies in cases like 'He wants a place to sit', *san* is ruled out because there is not present the special quality that he himself wants to do that action. Even desiring a seat or friendship for another, might be wrongly expressed if the notion of an implied mention of '*dhātoḥ*' were accepted.

This need to express the agent as being the same for the *dhātu* as for the 'object', in the sixth *vārttika* he points out as unnecessary when desire is being expressed, and so *Patañjali* adds '*san* is ordained when desire is being expressed as (necessarily the same agent is involved)'.

In the *bhāṣya* on the seventh *vārttika* is explained the corollary of what has been said, that, when desire is expressed *san* is ordained, but not after anything else but the *karman,* nor after that not having the same agent. Thus if desire is not being expressed *san* will not arise.

Reference to either *dhātoḥ* or *karman, Patañjali* explains in the eighth *vārttika,* is so that there be knowledge of the determining limits of an *aṅga* upon which operations are to take place. Of these, *dhātu* is the more important, for in relation to it, measure of the *aṅga* is known, and the name *ārdhadhātuka* established for *san.* He then quotes *vārttikas 1-3* on this *sūtra* as the *pūrvapakṣa's* view and presents an alternative view on *vā. 3* by suggesting *karmaṇaḥ* is ending in 'sixth case signifying a part' so the phrase means 'after that *dhātu* which is a part of a *karman*'. However, that would not allow for a *san* after a simple *dhātu.* Though that may appear to be overcome by saying there is 'representation of a secondary thing as the principal', that would mean that *kyac* etc. apply in cases like 'He desires a great son' but in fact they (*san* or *kyac*) cannot apply because there is no syntactical connection (between the great and the desire; rather there is expectancy of a word to complete the sense).

Turning to the word *vā,* in the ninth *vārttika bhāṣya* there is agreement that it is pointless here, because *san* is invariably applicable when there is integration and invariably not applicable when there is non-integration. It seems the option must connect with the technical name *pratyaya,* but option should never apply for technical names. Therefore it is pointless.

In the first of the *vidhi vārttikas* (ordaining a specific rule) *Patañjali* adds the example, showing optional application of *san* in place of *tumun luk.* Similarly in the *bhāṣya* on the eleventh he merely adds the necessary example, where *san* optionally acts in place of a *luk liṅ* (optative).

Patañjali modifies the twelfth *vārttika,* by leaving out the word '*acetana*' (non-sentient) as too restrictive. Instead, he says, there should be additional enumeration of *san* simply in the sense of fear or apprehension, to include examples like 'The dog fears he will die'.

The *bhāṣya* on the thirteenth *vārttika,* is concerned to show by examples how it is that, in fact, in the case of the man *Devadatta,* the insentient bank and the sentient dog, the understanding of 'desire arises from observation of behaviour' from which we infer the desire arises in all three kinds of action.

Another solution presented in *vārttika* fourteen is to treat use of desiderative for insentient things, as 'simple', which *Patañjali* explains as *iva*/as it were, so that even though simile properly may not apply for verbs, we can say 'desires as it were'.

Patañjali after agreeing with the fifteenth *vārttika,* that *san* is valid in all these various usages, because of everything having consciousness, goes on to give several examples 'The goblets creep . . .' etc.

The *bhāṣya* turns now to the word *icchā* (desire) to clarify meaning, since there are three *iṣ dhātus. San* comes only after that *iṣ* which takes the *ādeśa ch,* and not where it means 'seek' (Cl. 6). The *nipātana icchā* has the sense of being for the object of desire (*3.3.101*). After discussing various possibilities in relation to the example '*grāmam gantum icchati*' he concludes *grāmaḥ* is *karman* of *dhātu gam* and both *grāma* and *gam* are the *karman* of *dhātu iṣ,* which clarifies how *icchā* (*dhātu iṣ*) can have another *dhātu* as its object.

However, the desiderative of the desiderative cannot be formed with *san,* because the meaning having been expressed by one *san,* another is not used. This is because, given words are for comprehension of meaning, there is no employment of linguistic units to convey meanings which have already been expressed.

In the example '*eṣitum-icchati/eṣiṣiṣati*', because two different meanings of the *dhātu* are being used, and for one, *iṣ* is 'the means of action' while the *pratyaya* conveys 'present time' for the other, the means is external and *pratyaya* conveys all time.

In contrast the *tumun* constructions, 'He desires to desire to make' etc. need to be prohibited for *san,* except in the case of *svārthe san* e.g. *jugupsiṣate.*

The *śloka vārttika* expresses this, as a more general rule, 'like *pratyayas* do not follow each other in the same word in the case of the '*śaiṣika-s matubārthikas* and *san* ending words.'

On Pāṇini 3.1.8

Supa ātmanaḥ kyac (dhātoḥ, karmaṇaḥ icchāyām, vā).

The *pratyaya kyac* acts optionally in the sense of wishing for oneself, after a word ending in *sup*/case *pratyaya* expressing the *karman* (object wished for or desired) connected with the wisher himself.

Kātyāyana's first *vārttika* is of considerable general significance in relation to compounding in *saṃskṛta;* for he states that even though there be the same case relation between word, compounding will not occur if there are more than two words involved.

The next *vārttika* states that, where there are more than two words involved (as in the example *mahāntam putram icchati* ('He desires a great son') the second *vibhakti* is not justified (for *putra,* since on its own it is not the *karman*/object) of *iṣ* (to desire).

The other two *vārttikas* are specific: the first is a prohibition of *kyac* acting after words ending in *m* (like *kim*) and indeclinables. The second ordains *kyac* after the word *go,* words with simple vowels orther than *a* and those ending in *n.*

Bhāṣya **Summary**

Patañjali begins by considering the possible functions of the *it c* of *kyac.* Having shown it is not for accent, nor for distinguishing (because of '*tadanubandha*' — *pari 82*) but for the unobstructed general mention in '*naḥ khye*' *1.4.15.*

In considering the purpose of '*ātmanaḥ*' in the *sūtra,* having first put the view that it is to express the sense of one's own desire, he then suggests that it ends in the sixth case in the sense of agent, so with *icchā* can also express 'one's own desire for another'. However, the retort is, the word *ātman* connects with *sup* not *icchā.* Further if *ātman* is retained, how to explain examples of desire for another in the *Vedic* example of the 'malicious wolves'? Here even without use of a third word it is clear there, desire is for another, since no one desires evil for himself. In the classical language the possibility of following this analogy is avoided, by mention of *ātman,* and made known as valid in the *Veda* by specific menton in *7.4.37.*

Turning to the purpose of *sup, Patañjali* first shows it is not to prevent *kyac* coming after a *prātipadika* since *1.4.15* specifically states a restriction, so that the rule will be applicable when there is production after a *prātipadika.* Nor is the purpose to prevent *kyac* after a *dhātu,* since *san* being stated after a *dhātu* bars others, since it has not scope elsewhere in the sense of desire for another. The reference to *ātman,* here implies the same agent there, and meaning for oneself. The last possible purpose, to prevent *kyac* coming after a phrase, serves to introduce the first *vārttika*. By reference to the *parabhāṣā 'pratyaya grahane . . .'* he explains how a phrase or sentence like 'He desires a great son' cannot be *subantam*.

Patañjali explains where integration of words having the same case relationship is not possible, namely in relation to *samāsa* rules and *pratyaya* rules with example like 'He desires a great son'. He explains that because of there being more than one word to join with, in examples like 'The servant of a prosperous king,' we cannot stay there is syntactical relation with a sixth case word, since a phrase or sentence cannot end in a *sup*. Similarly in the example 'Son of the prosperous *Upagu*,' there can be no syntactical connection between *apatyam* and *ṛddhasya* because of dissimilar cases. He concludes as introduction to the next *vārttika*, 'it should be stated compounding is not possible when a qualifying word occurs'.

Patañjali connects the second *vārttika* indirectly with an implied example 'He desires a great son', saying the son here is not the *karman*/expressed by second case of *dhātu iṣ*. He rejects this view, because then any of the case endings would be equally applicable. Equally, second case must be applicable for *mahat* etc. because it is in the same case relationship.

He then returns to the previous theme of the cause of non-integration being the qualifying words. This does not have to be qualified by 'except in the case of *muṇḍa* etc.' because the real reason for non-integration is inability of that formed with *pratyaya* to communicate the meaning conveyed by a sentence. The corollary is, there will be compounding when the ability to convey intended meaning is there, as 'He shaves the youth'.

The *bhāṣya* now turns to the *kārakas* connected with a *kyajanta* word. *Bhāva* and *kartṛ* are clear, but how can *iṣ* have *karman* as part of its own meaning and still be transitive requiring another *karman*? The object/*karman* of comparison is inherent in *dhātu iṣ* and it is transitive by means of the object to be compared. Even in the case of *muṇḍayati māṇavakam* two objects exist, the general inherent in the *dhātu* and the specific makes it transitive. So *karoti* being inherent has no connection syntactically with *muṇḍa* and *māṇavaka* specific objects, so *asāmarthyam* is not applicable. However, in expressing 'He desires the youth (to be) shaved' they are both connected with the *dhātu iṣ*. Here no integration occurs because there is 'expectancy', 'He desires shaving in relation to the youth'. Only because of the express rule *3.1.21* is integration possible for some specific words which have expectancy. Alternatively, we can say *muṇḍa* etc. are *dhātus* expressing verbal activity (*kṛ* understood). Or a sentence and denominative *pratyaya* are mutually exclusive alternatives. Adding *kyac* has implied 'making'. Otherwise we return to the previous view, that there is integration simply because of causing the intended meaning to be understood.

Finally, *Patañjali* considers whether *kyac* should be applicable to express the sentence with the past participle passive of *iṣ* '*iṣṭa*' or the present indicative passive *iṣyate* and concludes the meaning of the sentence could never be expressed by the *pratyaya* and hence not be applicable.

The *bhāṣya* simply provides the suitable examples to illustrate the *vārttika* prohibiting integration of *m* ending words and indeclinables in the context of *kyac,* and likewise for the rule for *kyac* after *go,* words with simple vowels and those ending in *n.*

On Pāṇini 3.1.9

Kāmyac-ca

The *pratyaya kāmya-c* acts/is (applicable) in the sense of desire for oneself after a (word) ending in a *sup*/case *pratyaya* (expressing) the object/*karman* (desired).

Bhāṣya asks the purpose of the *it c* ; *Vārttikakāra* says there is no purpose in *k* being called *it.*

Bhāṣya suggests the purpose is to prevent *guṇa* in *agnicit-kāmyati* or if not for *samprasāraṇam* of *yaj* in *upayaṭ-kāmyati.* There are really two *c's* or finally it is in conformity with Vedic usage where *samprasāraṇa* does not occur.

On Pāṇini 3.1.10

Upamānād ācāre.

The *pratyaya kyac* optionally acts in the sense of conduct after a word ending in a *sup*/case *pratyaya* denoting the object of comparison.

This has only one *vārttika* increasing the scope of *kyac* to location of comparision as well as object.

Bhāṣya gives two appropriate examples:

प्रासादीयति कुट्याम्, He imagines himself in a palace when in a hut.

कुटीयति प्रसादे, He imagines himself in a hut when actually in a palace.

Neither appear in any other context (the latter not even in *kāśikā*)

On Pāṇini 3.1.11

Kartuḥ kyaṅ salopaśca.

The *pratyaya kyaṅ* optionally acts in the sense of conduct after a word ending in a *sup*/case *pratyaya* denoting the *karman*/object of comparison for the agent and there is *lopa* elision of the final *s*.

General Summary

Bhā. : Introduces by illustrating the distinction between that of primary importance in the *sūtra kyaṅ* and the rule of secondary importance, elision of *s*, like begging for alms and bringing *Devadatta* (if there)!

Vā. 1 : Gives optional *lopa* of *s* and *bhāṣya* gives the example of *payas*.

Vā. 2 : Says the elision of *s* of *ojas* and *apsaras* is invalid. *Bhāṣya* introduces a further view that only *s* of *apsaras* is in fact elided. *Ojayamānam* is Vedic usage.

Vā. 3 : States that *kvip* optionally acts after *galbha, klība* and *hoḍa* in the sense of conduct.

Bhā. : *Bhāṣya* explains the purpose of the *vārttika* so that periphrastic perfect can be formed. Another (*vārttika*) says *kvip* should be stated as following all *dhātus* in the sense of conduct.

A full enumeration of *galbha* etc. should be made for purpose of indicatory letter indicating *ātmanepada*.

On Pāṇini 3.1.12

Bhṛśādibhyo bhuvyacver - lopaśca halaḥ.

The *pratyaya kyaṅ* in the sense of becoming (what the thing previously was not) acts after the *prātipadikas bhṛśa* etc., which do not end with the *pratyaya cvi* and there is *lopa* of the final consonant.

Vārttika Summary

Kātyāyana's first *vārttika* is an explanatory addition to the *sūtra* specifically stating the implication of mentioning *cvi,* that *kyaṅ* too acts in the sense of 'becoming what a thing previously was not after *bhṛśa* etc." Having said this, of course, prohibition of *cvi* in the *sūtra,* he declares meaningless. The next *vārttika* is simply for clarification, since we know *cvi* is ordained in the sense of 'becoming' after *bhū* by *5.4.50.* Similarly the fourth *vārttika* reiterates that *kyaṣ* is applicable when *ḍāc* follows by *3.1.13.*

The fifth *vārttika* quotes a current view that in relation to *bhṛśa* etc. an *upasarga* qualified the *pratyaya* (*kyaṅ*) and states this will result in the wrong accent. Similarly if it is accepted that they are 'together with an *upasarga*', produces a wrong form in relation to the augment *at.*

Bhāṣya Summary

In the introduction to the first *vārttika, Patañjali* applies the distinction he used in the previous *sūtra* treating *kyaṅ* as of primary importance and consonant elision of secondary importance. He simply provides an example from the *Veda* for the *vārttika.* For clarification he simply adds on the second *vārttika* that this means *kyaṅ* is ordained in the sense of 'becoming . . . '. He then states the corollary of the third *vārttika,* that because of its meaning being expressed after *bhū* by *cvi, kyaṅ* will not be applicable. He introduces the fourth *vārttika* by showing this implies *kyaṅ* would not act after *ḍāc,* hence the need for the *vārttika.*

Having quoted the *sūtra* referred to, he advocates no change in the *sūtra.* Instead a most helpful distinction is made on the basis of *paribhāṣā 74* '*nañ-ivayukta*' . . ., whereby we understand the addition of negative or the particle of comparison as denoting something different yet similar like 'bring a non-*brāhmaṇa*'. So we may understand *a-cvi* not ending in *cvi,* but like it in meaning 'becoming . . .'.

The *bhāṣya* then quotes a list of words from *bhṛśa gaṇa* with *upasargas,* asking whether these qualify the meaning of the *pratyaya kyaṅ* or the *prakṛtis manas* etc. This doubt prompts the next *vārttika,* upon which *Patañjali* explains, 'there wrongly would be absence of *udātta* accent by *8.1.28,* if the *upasarga* qualifies the meaning of the *pratyaya.* So, let the *upasarga* qualify the *prakṛti.* In which case he implies on the sixth, augment *aṭ* would wrongly precede both *su* and *manas* etc. Moreover the same fault applies when *lyap* and reduplication occur. Then restriction should be made to the one case where it does apply after *sam-grāmayati.* To achieve the correct accent for *bhṛśa* etc., it will have to be stated there is 'being like a part of what follows', but only in relation to accent rules, otherwise the accent with *aṭ* etc., would be wrong.

The final problem is the function of the *upasarga.* If there cannot be usage of an element for expressing what *kyaṅ* has already expressed, then *āṅ* of *śyenāyate* cannot express conduct. However, in the case of *abhi* etc. *manas,* the words are indicated with *upasarga* to remove doubt. Elsewhere with *ṇiṅ* even where there are several *upasargas* the same operates.

On Pāṇini 3.1.13

Lohitādiḍājbhyaḥ kyaṣ.

The *pratyaya kyaṣ* acts in the sense of becoming what the thing previously was not after the words *lohita* etc. and after those that end with the *pratyaya ḍāc.*

Vārttika Summary

In the first *vārttika Kātyāyana* states a restriction on the *sūtra. kyaṣ* acts only after the word *lohita* and those words ending in *ḍāc.* The rest he says in the second *vārttika* are found in *bhṛśa* and the rest.

Bhāṣya Summary

Patañjali's introduction to the first *vārttika* begins by showing that *it k* cannot be for prohibiting *guṇa* or *vṛddhi* because *lohita* etc. are *prātipadikas* not *dhātus,* nor is it for general mention, since no words end in *n* (*1.4.15*) nor a consonant (*6.4.49,50*), nor ordained after patronymic (*6.4.151-2*) nor is *k* needed in '*kyācchandasi*' (*3.2.170*). Finally, it is stated that the purpose is so that the letter *y* not a *kṛt,* causes lengthening, *kṅiti* being in *anuvṛtti,* and the various Vedic exceptions being due. (Shortening here being peculiar to the *Veda*).

In the case of the *it ṣ,* after showing that it cannot be for distinguishing, because neither *ātmane* nor *parasmaipada* are seen in the context of *1.3.90,* nor can it be for common mention in *3.2.170,* if we accept that it applies to only three forms.

On the first *vārttika* he simply provides the implied two *ubhaya pada* examples. Finally on the second *vārttika* he explains why those other than *lohita* are to be read in *bhṛśa gaṇa.* And, being followed by *kyaṅ* having an *it ṅ, ātmanepada* only would be applicable.

On Pāṇini 3.1.14

Kaṣṭāya kramaṇe.

The *pratyaya kyaṅ* in the sense of undertaking moral crookedness acts after the word *kaṣṭa* (trouble or evil) when the latter has the fourth *sup*/case *vibhakti* in construction.

Vārttika Summary

Kātyāyana simply expands the scope of the *sūtra* to have *kyaṅ* acting after *sattra* etc.

Bhāṣya Summary

Patañjali explains the irregular form *kaṣṭāya* as indicating that *kyaṅ* acts after *kaṣṭa* in the sense of *sampradāna* 'undertaking to do wickedness'.

On the *vārttika* he provides the implied examples, and also gives an alternative version of the *vārttika*, stating after *sattra* etc. and adding with sense of the fourth case and undertaking moral crookedness, so *kyaṅ* does not apply to other words like *kuṭilāya* nor for any other case relation like *kaṣṭam*.

Finally he explains that *kaṣṭāya* is not in fact a *nipātana* but fourth case in the sense of 'being intended for that' (evil).

On Pāṇini 3.1.15

Karmaṇo romanthatapobhyām varticaroḥ.

The *pratyaya kyaṅ* acts after the words *romantha* and *tapas* when they are objects of the action of repeating and performing respectively.

Vārttika Summary

Kātyāyana simply states that in spite of *kyaṅ* acting, *parasmaipada pratyayas* act after *tapas*.

Bhāṣya Summary

Patañjali explains the meaning of *romantha* as churning round and vomiting forth or swallowing down and emitting but not for creatures without jaws. This need not be stated because *kyaṅ* is not recognised to express that meaning.

On the *vārttika* he provides the example and explains *tapasyate*. . . as peculiar Vedic usage.

On Pāṇini 3.1.16

Bāṣpoṣmabhyāmudvamane.

The *pratyaya kyaṅ* acts in the sense of emitting after the words *bāṣpa* and *uṣna* as *karman* of the action.

Bhāṣya Summary

Patañjali simply adds '*kyaṅ* also acts after *phena*' and provides the example *phenāyate*.

On Pāṇini 3.1.17

Śabdavairakalahābhrakaṇvameghebhyaḥ karaṇe.

The *pratyaya kyaṅ* acts in the sense of making, after these words as the action, namely *śabda, kalaha, abhra, kaṇva,* and *megha.*

Vārttika Summary

The two *vārttikas* give three more words after which *kyaṅ* acts in the sense of making, namely *sudina* and *durdina* in the first, and *nīhara* in the second.

Bhāṣya Summary

Patañjali effectively starts with his own *vārttika,* listing six other words *aṭā* etc. after which *kyaṅ* acts in the sense of making, followed by the derivative forms. Likewise for the two *vārttikas* he provides the examples.

On Pāṇini 3.1.18

Sukhādibhyaḥ Kartṛvedanāyām.

The *pratyaya kyaṅ* acts after the words *sukha* etc., in the sense of the feeling or experience of the agent.

Bhāṣya Summary

Patañjali explains the point of the reference to the agent in the *sūtra* is to exclude the cases where it is not the agent's feeling. Even if we construe '*kartuḥ*' as sixth case in the sense of agent, so we might say it applied where feeling of the agent is for another, he construes feeling as connected primarily with *sukha* etc. which pertains to the agent, so there is no question of it applying to the feeling for another.

On Pāṇini 3.1.19

Namovarivaścitraṅaḥ kyac.

The *pratyaya kyac* optionally acts, in the sense of making after these words, as the object of the action, namely *namas, varivas,* and *citra.*

Vārttika Summary

The *pūrvapakṣa* view is presented in the first *vārttika,* that second case is not valid here after *namas. Kātyāyana* counters the view that *namas* ought to govern the fourth case by *2.3.16,* by stating that this *namas* is a different *prakṛti* and therefore second case is established for it.

The third *vārttika* states that meanings should be given for *kyac* after *namas* etc.

Bhāṣya Summary

On the first *vārttika Patañjali* simply explains what is implied by the *vārttika*, that one expects *namas* to govern fourth case, because of seeming to be the same as the *prātipadika* in *2.3.16*. He explains on the second *vārttika*, that the word *namas* quoted in *2.3.16* is meaningful in its own right, but *namas* in this *sūtra* has no meaning on its own, only as part of *namasyati*. Or rather we can say according to *Pari. 94* a *kāraka vibhakti*, being stronger than an *upapada vibhakti*, second case will necessarily be applicable not fourth.

After giving meanings and examples referred to in the third *vārttika*, he also supplied the meanings for *3.1.20* in reverse order, the *sūtra* itself not being discussed by him nor by *Kātyāyana*. The purpose of express mention cannot however be to express verbal activity, since that is known from *3.1.32*. In contrast to *tavya* etc. which are *sādhana* always needing a *sādhya* (verbal activity), *kyac* etc. are *sādhya*. As it is understood from the relationship 'father', 'son should obey' so it is understood that *tavyat* etc. are *sādhana* for accomplishing the activity of the *dhātu*. *Kyac* (ending) words are *dhātus* without meanings indicated. We can however, say the meaning is *karaṇa* (in the sense of making) or activity in general as this follows from *3.1.17*.

On Pāṇini 3.1.21

Muṇḍamiśraślakṣṇalavaṇavratavastrahalakalakṛtatūstebhyo ṇic.

The *pratyaya ṇic* acts in the sense of making after these words, namely *muṇḍa, miśra, ślakṣṇa, lavaṇa, vrata, hala, kala, kṛta* and *tūsta*.

Vārttika Summary

Kātyāyana states the reason for *hali* and *kali* having a final *a* in the *sūtra* is to prevent *sanvadbhāva*.

Bhāṣya Summary

Having introduced the *vārttika*, by asking why the *nipātana* forms *hala* and *kala* occur in the *sūtra, Patañjali* gives the reduplicated Aorist forms. In his typical pedagogical style, first taking the *pūrvapakṣa* against the *vārttika*, he shows how in fact both the *vṛddhi* and the *lopa* rules concerned are *anitya* by (*Pari. 43*) 'A rule for which a difference of word form obtains when another rule obtains is *anitya*' and therefore *vṛddhi* being the subsequent rule applies first, from which it becomes clear that only *vṛddhi* of *a* will allow the needed '*aglopa*' to prevent *sanvadbhāva*. So the *vārttika* is confirmed.

On Pāṇini 3.1.22

Dhātor-ekāco halādeḥ kriyāsamabhihāre yaṅ

The *pratyaya yaṅ* acts after the *dhātu* which has one vowel and begins with a consonant, in the sense of repetition of any act or intensity.

Vārttika Summary

Kātyāyana's pūrvapakṣa view in this first *vārttika* is as in *3.1.7 Vā. 1-3* that the mention of *dhātu* is pointless. Similarly the second *vārttika* is a reiteration of the principal stated on *Vā. 6-7* that specific mention of one vowel and beginning with a consonant is pointless, because of the meaning intended only being convyed with such conditions.

The third *vārttika* expands the rule to include *yaṅ* acting after *ūrṇu* in spite of having more than one vowel and not beginning with a consonant.

The next *vārttika* expands the scope further to six more *dhātu sūci* etc. which either have more than one vowel or do not begin with a consonant, with *ūrṇu* also included.

The fourth *vārttika* deals with conflict betwen *loṭ* and *yaṅ* expressing repetition of action explaining that *loṭ* prevails because of being the later rule.

The last view is rejected by the fifth *vārttika* stating there is no conflict because of a difference of meaning, *loṭ* is in the sense of *karman* or *kartṛ, yaṅ* is *svārthe.*

The sixth *vārttika* relates to *3.1.23,* and points out that mention of *nitya* is pointless due to absence of the sense of repetition and lack of agreement on specific meaning for the two rules *3.1.23-4*

Finally *yaṅ* is stated as not acting after the *dhātus* of *3.1.24* in the sense of repetition or intensity.

Bhāṣya Summary

Patañjali begins by explaining the meaning of the word *samabhihāra* formed with the *dhātu hṛ* preceeded by *upasargas sam* and *abhi* followed by *ghañ pratyaya* may mean the act of seizing flowers etc., but this is only one of many verbal activities that the one general activity of *hṛ* may convey. So *pac* may involve many activities *adhiśrayana* etc., but he who performs all of them can be said to cook intensely or again and again.

He then introduces the first *vārttika* by saying the mention of *dhātu* is to prevent *yaṅ* after a *dhātu* together with an *upasarga.* On which, having first quoted what the *vārttika* implies, namely *vā. 1-3* on *3.1.7,* he concludes, similarly because of mention of '*kriyāsamabhihāre*' reference to *dhātu* is pointless. However, if 'repetition of the action' is taken as together with an *upasarga,* then there can be no ordaining of *yaṅ* even in context of *dhātu* governing rule, unless there is this mention of *dhātu* in the *sūtra.*

Patañjali introduces the second *vārttika* by giving the example *īkṣate bhṛśam* to show why mention is made of having one vowel and beginning with a consonant.

Discussing the second *vārttika,* having quoted the *pūrvapakṣa vā. 6-7* on *3.1.7,* he says similarly here it may be argued "having one vowel and beginning with a consonant may be pointless since *yaṅ* in the sense of '*kriyāsamabhihāre*' only acts after such *dhātus*".

Moreover since there are examples of the intensive meaning being expressed after such *dhātus* without *yaṅ,* and cases of *yaṅ* acting after *dhātus* of more than one vowel and beginning with a vowel, it should be ordained. In other words, the next two *vārttikas* become essential to specify those exceptions, *ūrṇu* with *pra, sūci* etc. for which all the full forms are given. In addition the *śloka vārttika* treats *ūrṇu* like *nu* so that *yaṅ* may act after it, and so that *ām* of the periphrastic perfect and augment *iṭ* be prohibited.

He agrees with the fourth *vārttika,* there being scope for both *yaṅ* and *loṭ.* When there is a conflict *loṭ* prevails, being subsequent, but even repetition may also be expressed by *yaṅ,* in combination with *loṭ.*

Similarly on the fifth *vārttika* he makes the modifications based on observed usage, that though *yaṅ* should apply because of being *antaraṅga* it optionally does and then in its absence *loṭ* acts.

He explains the sixth *vārttika* by simply showing that only one usage occurs, with *yaṅ.* There being no alternative, stating *nitya* is pointless.

Finally he shows by the examples on the seventh that repetition or intensity can only be expressed by *vākya* in the case of *dhātus* in *3.1.24.*

On Pāṇini 3.1.25

Satyāpapāśarūpavīṇātūlaślokasenālomatvacavarmavarṇacūrṇacurādibhyo ṇic.

The *pratyaya ṇicz" "* acts after the words *satya pāśa, rūpa, vīṇā, tūla, śloka, senā, loma, tvaca, varma, varṇa, cūrṇa,* and *dhātus cur etc.*

Vārttika Summary

In this first *vārttika Kātyāyana* points out that the augment *āpuk* has been added to *satya* in the sense of *kṛ* to obtain *satyāpa.* In the second he adds that *ṇic* also comes after *artha* and *veda* with the augment *āpuk.*

Bhāṣya Summary

On the first *vārttika Patañjali* simply adds what is implied, that *satyāpa* is a *nipātana* form.

Having given the full forms on the second, he considers variations on *āpuk* augment because *ṭi lopa* of *āpuk* also obtains, but concludes that *lopa* will not apply because of the rule itself. The alternative is augment *ak* which for the same reason would prevent *lopa.*

On Pāṇini 3.1.26

Hetumati ca.

The *pratyaya ṇic* acts after a *dhātu* when the sense of having a cause is to be expressed.

Vārttika Summary

In this first *vārttika Kātyāyana* explains the purpose of the seventh case in '*hetumati*' as for understanding the meaning of the *pratyaya ṇic* just 'in the sense of having a cause', just as *3.1.76* says '*śnu* acts after *dhātu takṣ* 'in the sense of paring. . .'

The second *vārttika* states that *hetu* is known to be in the sense of mere efficient cause because of the way it is used in connection with *bhikṣā* etc. However, the next sub-*vārttika* states the exception that *ṇic* does not act in this sense after *kṛṣi* etc. The third *vārttika* expresses why, there is not arising of *ṇic* after *kṛṣi* etc. because of their having a variety of verbal activities connected with them.

The sub-*vārttika* having stated there is no interchange of *pada* in the case of *yaj* etc. in the fourth *vārttika* he explains the reason is because they have a variety of verbal activities connected with them.

The fifth gives an additional sense of *ṇic* after *sūtra* etc. in the sense of making or doing that. In the sixth, not only another sense is given, that of 'he relates to that' when *ṇic* acts after a story ending in a *kṛt*, but that is *luk* and the word restored to its original form and case relationship.

The seventh is a prohibition of *ṇic* in that sense after the word *ākhyāna.* However, the eighth ordains *ṇic* when the purpose of telling the story is for visualising something.

The ninth *vārttika* ordains *ṇic* when expressing a continuous period of time up to a specific limit and *lopa* of *aṅ.* The tenth says *ṇic* acts when there is surprise at reaching somewhere.

In the eleventh we learn that *ṇic* acts in the sense of knowledge of the conjunction of an asterism.

Or else the twelfth states *ṇic* is taught in the sense of cause in general.

The thirteenth shows that even if it is stated, one is not the prompter because actually the prompter is an independent one, this is in fact a statement of one in truth free from doubt. The fourteenth says, in both cases the inclination to do something is irrespective of anything.

Finally in the fifteenth he says this is equivalent to saying *hetu* is prompter of one who does something.

Bhāṣya Summary

Patañjali introduces the first *vārttika* by distinguishing the two possible meanings of *hetumati*, one 'when the sense of having a cause is to be expressed,' by the *pratyaya*, the other based on interpreting seventh case in the sense of 'with regard to', (*ṇic* acts after that *dhātu/prakṛti* which occurs 'with regard to having a cause').

Having explained the meaning of the first *vārttika*, he deals with the problem of using *3.1.76* to explain the meaning of seventh case in *hetumati* that this implies a qualification of the meaning of *prakṛti.*

Even if the qualification of *prakṛti* may be implied the point is *ṇic* will not be applicable if the meaning has already been expressed by the *prakṛti*, as *uktaḥ karoti.* The problem of *la* having to express two agents does not occur if *ṇic* qualifies the *pratyaya*, because *la* expresses principal agent and third case subordinate agent, as *pacayatyodanam devadatto yajñadattena.* Here in fact *karman* does not obtain by *1.4.52* because that *sūtra* restricts its scope to the elements mentioned, thus excluding *pac* etc. Next he points out in relation to *2.3.12* the impelling does not require *ṇic* not therefore preventing the choice of second and fourth case, because the impelling is distinguished by a *kāraka*, as *grāmam grāmāya gacchati.* Similarly the objection is that sixth case would not apply as desired by 2.3.35 for *edhodaka*, but in fact it is the object of *kṛ* and not of *kāri*, which contains the non-causative form within itself as it were. Again in relation to *bhedika* etc. the purpose of mentioning *kṛt* in *2.3.65* was so that sixth case is applicable even when an agent in a former time is denoted. Lastly in relation to *8.3.65* a change of *s* to *ṣ* is not prevented because the action is urged on after the change caused by the *upasarga* has taken place in the non-causal state.

Patañjali now turns to the meaning of *pac* etc. and concludes it is not only the softening of the grains but that impelling or asking form part of the meaning *pāci.* The sense of *hetumat* is 'He whose agent is the cause'.

On the second *vārttika* he provides the sentence to illustrate and raises the central issue how *bhikṣā* etc. without consciousness can impel etc. However, just as one sitting silently may impel action by his mere presence so we say *bhikṣā* or *kariso'gniḥ* may be said to impel.

Turning to why the imperative does not require *ṇic* he points out this is because the one commanding is not the agent, for that is expressed by *loṭ pratyaya.* Ordering etc. already being expressed by *lot ṇic* only applies to express a second impelled agent.

On the sub-*vārttika* he explains there is absence of *ṇic* exceptionally in spite of the implication that 'He ploughs' means 'He causes ploughing . . .'. The fourth *vārttika* having provided the reason for the *kṛṣyādi* exceptions being there, having a variety of meanings, *Patañjali* states another meaning of *kṛṣi* is 'the managing activities associated with ploughing'.

On the same pattern the next sub-*vārttika* states the fact that there is no interchange of *pada* for *yaj* etc., *Patañjali* giving the necessary example. The fourth *vārttika* then provides the reason, again because of the variety of activities associated with *yaj* etc. So *Patañjali* points out *yaj* can also mean renunciation or abandoning.

The *bhāṣya* on the fifth *vārttika* explains how when the *vākya* requires sixth case for *vyākaraṇasya* etc. but with *ṇic* second case. This is because there is first *sāmarthyam* between *kṛ* expressed by *ṇic* and *vyākaraṇa.*

On the sixth *vārttika* he simply provides the explanatory example.

The *bhāṣya* on *vārttika* seven having explained with the example, extends *ṇic* after all narrations of action not just names of tales.

The *bhāṣya* on the eighth apart from explaining that *kṛt luk* etc. occur here too, implies that the visualising evoked in the listener of deer etc., only requires *ṇic* when what is described is beyond the ordinary range of sight.

Still in the context of tales and *kṛt luk* etc., *Patañjali* simply gives the two possible sentences.

In order to express amazement *ṇic* and the same *kṛt luk* etc. occur, as expressed by the tenth *vārttika* and *bhāṣya.* Again on the eleventh, *Patañjali* simply adds that *kṛt luk* etc. occur and provides the examples showing knowledge of conjunction of an asterism.

The *bhāṣya* on the twelfth *vārttika,* to illustrate what is meant by causal in general, says that "the cause in *Devadatta* is not different to that in the sun; but no-one 'prompts the sun', surely ?"

The rejoinder on the thirteenth is that the prompters are similar, for the inclination to proceed for their own welfare applies irrespectively. *Patañjali* develops this discussion on the fourteenth *vārttika* illustrating how students, servants, artisans etc., though they serve, all act for the sake of their own welfare. If so then each is intent or its own purpose, *Patañjali* says on the fifteenth.

So in the example of one setting out from *Ujjayinī* he apparently causes the sun to arise at *Mahiṣmatī.*

Patañjali turns to the problem of time in the telling of stories etc., in plays, pictures or books. How is the present time possible ? In fact all three times are depicted as well as all colours etc. All matters are made comprehensible by reason.

On Pāṇini 3.1.27

Kaṇḍvādibhyo yak.
The *pratyaya yac* acts after *kaṇḍu* etc.

Vārttika Summary

Yak is stated as optional after *kaṇḍu* etc. in the first; the second giving the reason because otherwise it would be *nitya.*

The third, by stating that the *dhātu* rule and *tuk* augment do not apply, indicates how it cannot be invariable/*nitya.* The fourth states a further operation: shortening of the vowel and *lopa* of *ya.*

Bhāṣya Summary

Patañjali introduces the first *vārttika* by showing the *it k* cannot be to prevent *guṇa* or *vṛddhi* of a *dhātu* since these *kaṇḍu* etc. are *prātipadikas.* So *vā. 1* states they are also optionally called *dhātus.*

On two he asks, what fault would there be in *ya* being *nitya* ?

He explains on the third, it would mean *6.4.77* wrongly applying, as well as *6.1.77.*

On the last *vārttika* he says statement of short is because being *antaraṅga* and not *kṛt,* otherwise lengthening applies. *Lopa* is stated because *ya* is outside the scope of *6.1.66.* By *1.1.62* we expect *pratyaya lakṣaṇa* but *1.1.21* says nowhere there is a grammatical operation dependent on letters.

Kvip by *3.2.178* is essential for the forms *kaṇḍū* etc. However, *vā* is not needed because *kaṇḍū* etc. are both *dhātus* and *prātipadikas.* The first for *kaṇḍūyati* etc. the latter for *kaṇḍūḥ* etc.

Another view is *kaṇḍū* etc. ending in *yak* are *dhātus* because of being within the sphere of the governing rule and because of *it k* (to prevent *guṇa* and *vṛddhi* of a *dhātu*). The stating of *kaṇḍū* with long *ū* is a clue to *dhātu* being an optional designation.

On Pāṇini 3.1.30

Kamer-ṇiṅ.

The *pratyaya ṇiṅ* acts after the *dhātu kam.*

Vārttika Summary

The first *vārttika* points out the possibility of prohibition of *vṛddhi* by virtue of *it ṅ* because *it ṅ* has scope elsewhere. Moreover, the second states, prohibition of *it ṅ* (which prevents *vṛddhi*), also has scope elsewhere.

The third gives the solution as having already been stated, namely there is no *ik* vowel whose *vṛddhi* could be prohibited.

Bhāṣya Summary

The introduction simply explains the function of *it ṅ* is to cause *vṛddhi* of *a*, by *7.2.116*, but it appears that is barred by *it ṅ 1.1.5*.

Explaining the first *vārttika Patañjali* specifies the scope of *ṇi* as *6.4.51* but he says *it ṅ* also has scope in that *sūtra* to prevent non-application of general mention. Because this could be achieved by another *it* letter and because the other function of indication *ātmanepada* is weaker, then prohibition still obtains. However, the *gaṇa sūtra* makes known by implication that there is no prohibition of *vṛddhi.*

On the second *vārttika Patañjali* explains where is the scope for prohibition of *mit* namely *6.4.92*. As no specific mention of *nimitta* is made, *1.1.5* does not annual this. However, shortening does not obtain by *6.4.92*, because of *sthānivat-lopa ṇi* intervening. For the same reason *vṛddhi* does not obtain. Another reason for the prohibition is cited to prevent lengthening by *6.4.93* . . . Prohibition of *vṛddhi* does not in fact apply by *8.3.34* when *ṇic* follows. Nor is the reason *7.3.36*, since that also applies only when *ciṇ* or *kṛts* follows. Nor is it relevant to the causative of the causative, for when that ending in *ṇit* has *ciṇ* or *ṇamul* following, the *aṅga* is not *mit* and vice versa. Finally prohibition of a long vowel *ādeśa* is made by *1.1.58*, so that not intervening, *ciṇ* follows. when *ṇiṅ* is not applied by *3.1.31* and *ṇic* follows, then prohibition of *mit* obtains.

Finally *Patañjali* explains what is implied by the third *vārttika* namely a reference to *vā. 4* on *1.1.5*, because of the context being *ik*, *vṛddhi* cannot apply to *kam* and hence prohibition is not possible.

On Pāṇini 3.1.31

āyādaya ārdhadhātuke vā

The *pratyaya āya* and those that follow (namely *īyan* and *ṇiṅ*) optionally act when an *ārdhadhātuka pratyaya* follows.

Vārttika Summary

The first *vārttika* presents two possible undesired meanings of the *sūtra*, the first speaks of cessation of *āya* etc. optionally when an *ārdhadhātuka* acts after the *pratyayas āya* etc., the second, arising of *āya* etc. when an *ārdhadhātuka pratyaya* acts after the *prakṛtis* ending in *āya* etc.

By the very fact of not using the word *vā*, the second *vārttika* states, *āya* etc. are invariably ordained when an *ārdhadhātuka* follows.

The third *vārttika* says *sya* etc. prevail over *āya* etc. because of being the later of rules of equal force in conflict.

The fourth dismisses the last because of *āya* etc. not having scope of application elsewhere.

Bhāṣya Summary

The introduction spells out the two possible views of the *sūtra* given in the first *vārttika*. Either this *sūtra* is understood after all three previous *sūtras* or it is understood as a supplement to each.

The *Bhāṣya* on the first provides the examples showing the desired forms which do not arise and the undesired that do arise following either interpretation. The second establishes *gupti* and *jugopa* and avoids *gopāyaṃcakāra*, but does not establish *gopāyācakāra* and *gopāya*. However, the penultimate is valid when *liṭ* follows (in the mind), *ām* operates as *meaning.*

Patañjali explains the second *vārttika* as meaning *nitya* when a *sārvadhātuka* follows.

Where both *āya* etc. and *sya* etc. obtain as *gopāyiṣyati*, *Patañjali* explains in the third, the latter would be expected to prevail.

This is not a problem because of requiring scope and due to '*ato guṇe*' *6.1.97*, the presence of *śap* makes no difference.

To avoid another possibility of *āya* etc. without scope barring *sya* etc., a division of the *sūtra* into two is proposed.

The two undesired possible interpretations are finally avoided by explaining *ārdhadhātuka* as having seventh case in the sense of 'with regard to that sphere'. So in the sphere of *ārdhadhātuka* (held in the mind) when *sya* etc. have been formed after a *prakṛti* ending in *āya* etc., whatever *pratyaya* obtains after a stem will be added to that stem.

On Pāṇini 3.1.32

Sanādyantā dhātavaḥ

Words ending with the *pratyaya san* etc. have the name *dhātu*.

Vārttika Summary

Although there is specific mention of a *pratyaya* and it is a *saṃjñā* rule, the prohibition of the *tadanta* rule by *vā. 1* on *1.4.14* does not apply because of stating *anta.*

Bhāṣya Summary

Patañjali explains in the introduction the reason for mention of *anta* is so *1.1.72* may apply.

On the first *vārttika* he explains the reference to *1.4.14 vā. 1* indicating the *anta* in this rule conveys the same meaning as in *1.4.14*.

The name *dhātu* is established elsewhere by *1.3.1* even for those not actually recited in the *Dhātu Pāṭha* because *ādeśas* of those recited there. Not however, for *sananta* etc., hence this *sūtra.* These are not *ādeśas* even if they are 'pointed out', since the sixth case ending word is not what they replace.

Finally he mentions there is an implied rule, that when an *apavāda* is applicable the *utsarga pratyaya* is not applicable, so *śyam* etc. with *it ś* in place of *śap.*

On Pāṇini 3.1.33

Syatāsī lṛluṭoḥ.

In the presence or *lṛ* and *luṭ*, *sya* and *tāsi* act as *vikaraṇa-pratyayas* after a *dhātu.*

Vārttika Summary

The first (possible) *vārttika* states *śap* bars the *apavāda pratyayas* before it by *vipratiṣedha.*

The second points out the possibility of the word *apavāda* having more than one meaning.

The third shows that for the same reason *śyan* etc. *utsarga pratyayas* would bar *sya* etc. *apavāda pratyayas.*

Bhāṣya Summary

The introduction states the need to distinguish among the *vikaraṇa pratyayas* which are *utsargas* and which *apavādas. Yak* is *utsarga, śap* etc. and *sya* etc. *apavādas*.

In cases like *pakṣyati* both *śap* and *sya* obtain so by *vipratiṣedha śap* would have prevailed.

We may understand *śap* also as *utsarga* ordained in the sense of *kartṛ*, whereas *yak* is in the sense of *bhāva* and *karman*. The rest are *apavādas*.

Due to being subsequent, *śyan* would seem to bar *sya* etc. but in fact *śyan* is *ādeśa* of *śap*, and *śap* is barred by *sya*.

Special mention of *śap* need not be made here, for we may undersand the first case in the sense of sixth case for it by *anuvṛtti*, because that is implied by use of fifth case in *3.1.67* etc. according to *1.1.67*. The final priority of *sya* etc. over *śap* can be achieved by *anuvṛtti* or by recognising that *sya* is *antaraṅga* in relation to *śyan* etc. *bahiraṅga*, since they require the additional condition of having a *sārvadhātuka* following.

On Pāṇini 3.1.34

Sib-bahulaṃ Leṭi

Sip diversely acts as a *pratyaya* after a *dhātu* in the sense of *leṭ* (Vedic subjunctive)

Vārttika Summary

The first states *sip* is an *utsarga pratyaya*. Due to the occurrence of *neṣatu* etc. The second says *sip* is inferred to also be applicable in the context of *san* etc. The third says this is valid because of being different from the base *neṣati* etc. as contrasted to the forms *neṣṭāt* etc. seen in use, pointed out in the fourth.

The sixth states that *it p* is pointless because of the actual *pratyaya s(ip)* having to vowel.

Moreover, the seventh points out, if it is claimed the purpose is *anudātta* for the *āgama*, that has already been stated.

Lastly the seventh *vārttika* points out that diversely *sip* also has an *it ṇ* in the *Chandas*.

Bhāṣya Summary

Patañjali provides the examples from the *Veda* for the second *vārttika* and provides the different base referred to in the third.

Introducing the fourth he points out *it p* would signify *anudātta* for the *pratyaya* by *3.1.4*.

He introduces the sixth by suggesting it could be for *anudātta* augment. Instead he then proposes *śap* instead of *sip*, although the *a* will in fact be *lopa* by *6.4.48*. the purpose, he reveals on the sixth, is so there be *lopa* of that having *anudātta* vowel, so that *6.1.161* does not apply.

Finally he provides the example from the *Veda* for the last *vārttika*.

On Pāṇini 3.1.35

Kās-pratyayād-ām-amantre liṭi.

The *pratyaya ām* acts after the *dhātu kās* and those *dhātus* that are formed by *pratyayas* in the presence of *liṭ*, except in the *Veda*.

Vārttika Summary

As well as mentioning *kās*, the form *cakās* should be enumerated, as followed by *ām*.

Bhāṣya Summary

Patañjali having given the derived form *cakāsāmcakāra* and discussed alternatives to the *vārttika*, rejects stating *cakās* instead of *kās* because of the included *kās* not being meaningful and proposes replacing '*pratyayād*' in the *sūtra* by the words 'after a *dhātu* having more than one vowel.'

On Pāṇini 3.1.36

Ajādeśca gurumato'nṛcchaḥ.

The *pratyaya ām* acts when *liṭ* follows after a *dhātu* beginning with an *ik* vowel and having a *guru* vowel, except the *dhātu ṛcch*.

Vārttika Summary

The first is a prohibition of *ām* when the *guru* vowel is caused by *liṭ*.

The second explains the reason for '*gurumato*' is to prohibit *ām* for *yaj* ete., when *ṇal uttama* (first) person follows.

The third says the *sūtra* is established by stating 'in an *upadeśa/Dhātu Pāṭha*'.

The fourth states that the very prohibition of *ām* after *ṛcch* is an implied rule 'after *ucch-i*, also having the augment *tuk*, there should be *ām*.'

The fifth returns to the first and says this has already been stated (in *Vā. 3* on *1.1.39*).

The sixth simply states *ām* should also not act after *ūrṇu.*

Finally the *śloka vārttika* says *ūrṇu* should be treated like *nu* so that *yaṅ* is established and so that *ām* and *iṭ āgama* are prohibited.

Bhāṣya Summary

Patañjali having given the examples *iyeṣa* etc. explains how the *guru* vowel is effected by *7.3.86.* On the second he simply gives the necessary examples, and similarly with the third.

In discussing the fourth, having explained the *jñāpaka* by reference to *tuk* by *6.1.73,* he concludes after long debate that *ṛcch* also would obtain *ām,* since *6.4.11* is not a *jñāpaka* for that referring to *ṛ* with *ādeśa ṛcch* etc, that neither prohibition of *ṛcchi* should be stated nor *ām* be stated for *ucchi* because all has alredy been stated. On the fifth *vārttika* he explains what was stated, namely: That rule which is occasioned by the combination of two things does not become the cause of the destruction of that.

On the sixth he provides the examples and then says it need not be stated, because of the *śloka vārttika* (?)

Finally an alternative solution to the *vārttika* is given to deal with the exception *ūrṇu,* so that an *u* without case ending is in the *sūtra,* so that it means 'nor after *ṛcch* or an *u*-ending *dhātu.*'

On Pāṇini 3.1.38

Uṣavidajāgṛbhyo'nyatarasyām.

The *pratyaya ām* optionally acts after the *dhātu uṣ, vid* and *jāgṛ,* when *liṭ* follows.

Vārttika Summary

After the *dhātu vid, ām* should be considered as having an *it k.*

Bhāṣya Summary

Having given the derived form, *Patañjali* rejects the *vārttika* since prevention of *guṇa* is prevented by *vid-a* ending in *a* in conjuction with *ām.*

Followers of *Bhāradvāja* give another solution to accept the *vārttika* or regarding absence of *guṇa* as justified by treating the forms as *nipātanas.*

On Pāṇini 3.1.39

Bhīhrībhṛhuvāṃ śluvacca.

The *pratyaya ām* acts optionally after the *dhātus bhī, hrī, bhṛ* and *hu* in the presence of *lit;* and when *ām* acts it is as if there were *ślu* elision and the *dhātus* belonging to the *juhvādi gaṇa* even for the presence of *liṭ ārdhadhātuka pratyaya.*

The purpose of the extended application/*śluvat* is for reduplication and *ādeśa i.*

Bhāṣya Summary

Patañjali simply provides the example, *bibharāṃcakāra.*

On Pāṇini 3.1.40

Kṛñcānuprayujyate liṭi.

After a *dhātu* ending in *ām pratyaya,* the *dhātu kṛ* is joined in the presence of *liṭ.*

Vārttika Summary

The first states that the specific mention of *kṛ* is for the purpose of prohibiting *as* and *bhū* being auxiliary verbs. The second adds it is also for *ātmanepada.*

The third counters the first by saying it is desired that all three be Auxiliary.

Due to *ām* having no meaning, the fourth states, the statement of additional usage need not be taught. Moreover other *dhātus* are not applicable because of not having (general) meaning, the fifth explains.

The sixth suggests another possible reason for *kṛñ* etc., namely that it only applies when *liṭ* follows.

Another view is presented in the seventh, that it would not be applicable because the meaning has been completely expressed.

The eighth homes in on the real purpose, namely to prevent interchange, and the ninth states also for preventing *dhātu* and auxilliary being separated.

Bhāṣya Summary

Patañjali introduces by explaining that since *ām* has an inarticulate meaning, so that the meaning is not completely expressed, subsequent use of an auxiliary is necessary.

On the second he explains *1.3.63* is also needed for *ātmanepada*. Then on the third he explains *kṛñ* as a *pratyāhāra* of all three *5.4.50-58.*

The fourth he says, implies the purpose is so that the three are auxiliaries and not *pac* etc.

On the fifth he explains the distinction between the former expressing general activity and the latter particular activity. Hence the former may be used after the latter.

The implication of the sixth is that some other like *laṭ* obtain is not possible, because of not expressing past time. Similarly *niṣṭhā*, *luṅ*, and *laṅ* are shown not to obtain, nor even *laṅ* under the conditions of *3.2.116*. Usage ascertained for one form is not applicable for another.

Contrary to the statement in the seventh *vārttika* he says that since *ām* has inarticulate meaning additional use of auxiliary will be applicable.

On the eighth he states it is to prevent inversion of *ihām cakre* etc.

Finally the purpose is so there be not additional use for the *dhātu* and auxiliary being separated.

On Pāṇini 3.1.43

Cliḥ luṅi.

When *luṅ* (aorist *pratyaya*) follows, the *pratyaya cli* acts after a *dhātu*.

Vārttika Summary

The first states that *cli* is for the purpose of common reference.

In the second we are told the absence of *iṭ āgama* on the *ādeśa kṣa* is to indicate the meaning of *cli* (as an *utsarga*/general *pratyaya*).

The third explains that the *ādeśa aṅ* is in place of *cli* when *ādeśa ghasḷṛ* occurs.

In the fourth the view is put that *it c* is for the purpose of distinguishing, while the fifth says *it i* is for the purpose of common reference.

Bhāṣya Summary

Patañjali introduces the first *vārttika* by pointing out that *cli* in fact is never heard, so we may ask why is not *sic* the *utsarga*? On the first he quotes *2.4.80* as where *cli* is for common reference, instead of specific mention of *caṅ, aṅ* and *sic.*

On the second he simply clarifies that it means the purpose of *ksa* being stated, as without *it,* is to establish *cli* as the *utsarga,* since only on the assumption of it being so would *3.1.45* need to prohibit *it ksa.*

On the third, he just gives reference to the *sūtras* implied, namely *2.4.37* and *3.1.55.*

Patañjali disagrees with the fourth, showing that *3.1.44* does not show *cli* serving the purpose of distinguishing.

On the fifth, having quoted the *sūtra*, showing common mention is the function of the *it i*, he states the real purpose of *it c* is for the non-hindrance to common reference, seen in *2.4.81.* After lengthy detailed discussion, he agrees that the *utsarga* function of *cli* is only revealed in *2.4.80, 81* and *3.1.43, 44* that *luk* is *apavāda* of *sic.* In the context of *ksa* being without *i* augment *3.1.45*, in fact all *dhātus* ending in *śal* and having a penultimate *ik* vowel when *liṭ* follows would have *it i*, but in fact the *it* is augment of a *valādi pratyaya* which is *ārdhadhātuka*, hence the common mention applies.

On Pāṇini 3.1.44

Cleḥ sic.

Sic ādeśa acts in place of *cli.*

Vārttika Summary

The first states that the *it c* of *sic* is pointless because of being like the original *cli.* However, the second indicates it is for the purpose of *udātta iṭ āgama.* Hence the third, rejecting the first, says *it c* should be effected.

The fourth says *it i* is to prevent *lopa* of *n.* This is countered by the fifth which says this is not the purpose, but the *it k* for *sic* after *han* is *jñāpaka* for no *lopa* of *n.* However, the sixth points out *sic* has an *it i* already from the original *cli.*

The seventh tells us that *sic* is optionally *ādeśa* for *spṛś* etc. Another says this is valid by coalescent *sandhi* of *caṅ* and *aṅ*, also valid because of *ciṇ* itself not having an *it c.*

Bhāṣya Summary

The introduction shows the purpose is not for distinguishing nor for *udātta* since *sic* has no non-*it* vowel.

On the first he points out the context is *6.1.163.* The *c* being available by *sthānivatva* from *cli*, the second has a special purpose to indicate *udātta* for *iṭ* augment which would normally be *anudātta* as an *āgama.*

On the fourth *Patañjali* gives the necessary examples and quotes the *sūtra* *6.4.24.*

After putting a counter view, he accepts the fifth giving *Pari. 50 'asiddhan bahiraṅga ...'* in support.

On the seventh, again having provided the examples, he quotes *3.1.45* wherey *ksa* is established. Similarly *sic* is said to obtain by *Vā. 4* on *3.1.43.* He says it is established if we assume a non-indicated *lup* elided *y* for *sic* by the device of coalescent *sandhi.* We can say even *caṅ* is of more than one letter, and so replaces the whole of *cli* by *1.1.55.* On the last he explains *ciṇ* is really an *ādeśa,* hence no *lopa,* and being *anekāl* replaces the whole of *cli.* Then *c* is *it* by *1.3.7.*

He concludes by agreeing with the seventh *vārttika.*

On Pāṇini 3.1.45

Śala igupadhādaniṭaḥ ksaḥ.

'After a *dhātu* ending in *ś ṣ s* or *h* and having an *ik* vowel penultimate, not taking *it* (augment) *kas* is *ādeśa* of aorist *vikaraṇa cli* when *liṅ* follows.

Vārttika Summary

Vā. 1 : When *ksa* is ordained there is no *ik* penultimate because of *guṇa* for *cli.*

Vā. 2 : Or because of absence of scope for *ksa* (it is) *apavāda* of *guṇa.*

Vā. 3 : The expression 'without *iṭ* augment' is without qualification, because *cli* being indicated as invariable.

Vā. 4 : Or else not, because *ksa* is *apavāda sic.* When (a *pratyaya*) without *iṭ* (augment) *ksa* is established then *ksa* is ordained.

Vā. 5 : In the rest of the cases *sic* will be ordained.

Bhāṣya Summary

Patañjali explains the first implies that because *cli* is a cause of *guṇa, ksa* does not obtain. On the second he adds *ksa* being without scope elsewhere bars *guṇa.*

Since *cli* is not heard, he explains on the third, *ksa* does not obtain after it, without *āgama iṭ.*

On the fourth he explains that *ksa* as *apavāda* of *sic,* when the *dhātu* is established as without *iṭ āgama* connected, *ksa* will be applicable.

On the last he simply provides examples.

On Pāṇini 3.1.46

Śliṣa āliṅgane.

Ksa is *ādeśa* of the aorist *vikaraṇa cli* after the *dhātu śliṣ* when meaning to embrace when *luṅ* follows.

Vārttika Summary

Vā. 1 : The restriction is not appropriate because of something positive to be enjoined.

Vā. 2 : *Ksa* is established after *śliṣ* in the sense of embracing not in the context of *ciṇ*.

Vā. 3 : When *aṅ* is ordained it acts after *śliṣ* in a sense other than embracing.

Vā. 4 : It is established through dividing the rule:
(i) after *śliṣ*,
(ii) after *śliṣ ksa* is applicable.

Bhāṣya Summary

Introducing the first *Patañjali* suggests this is a restrictive *sūtra*, but then agrees with the second, there is something to be enjoined. *By 3.1.55*, *aṅ* obtains.

However, if this were not restrictive, *ātmanepada* would be applicable and *ksa* would wrongly bar *ciṇ*.

On the third, a division of the *sūtra* is turned down, but taken up by *vārttika* four, upon which he explains the first is for barring *aṅ* and the second for ordaining *ksa* after *śliṣ*, only in the sense of embracing.

Finally *ksa* only bars *aṅ* not *ciṇ* by *Pari 59* or by specific mention of *ciṇ* in *3.1.66*.

On Pāṇini 3.1.48

Ṇiśridrusrubhyaḥ kartari caṇ.

After a *dhātu* ending in *ṇi* (causative etc.) and after the *śri dru* and *sru*, *caṇ* is *ādeśa* of aorist *vikaraṇa cli* when *liṅ* follows signifying the agent.

Vārttika Summary

Vā. 1 : Additional enumeration of *kam-i* (to desire).

Vā. 2 : Additional enumeration of *ciṇ* in the sense of reflexive passive.

Vā. 3 : Or else not, because not ordaining in the sense of *karman* and because *kartṛ* (agentship) it is already established for reflexive passive.

Bhāṣya Summary

On the first *vārttika Patañjali* contributes an amusing *śloka* about the proper form of *kam acakamata.*

On the second he provides the examples of *karmakartṛ.*

On the third he simply explains that, having made the statement 'there is agentship in the sense of *karmakartṛ*', *caṇ* will apply.

When there is prohibition of *yak* and *ciṇ* there should be additional enumeration of *ṇi* in the sense of causative *śri* and *brū.*

Bharadvāja followers and *sranthi, granthi* in place of *śri* and mention *ātmanepada* in transitive *dhātus* also.

On Pāṇini 3.1.52

Asyativaktikhyātibhyo'ṅ.

After the *dhātus as, vac,* and *khyā aṅ* is the *ādeśa* of the aorist *vikaraṇa cli* when *liṅ* follows signifying the agent.

Vārttika Summary

Vā. 1 : The mention of *asyati* is for the sake of *ātmanepada pratyaya.*

Vā. 2 : (*Aṅ*) is applicable in the reflexive passive.

Bhāṣya Summary

Patañjali explains the reference to *ātmanepada* in the first *vārttika asyati* is part of *puṣādi 3.1.35.*

On the second having given the examples he quotes *Vā. 3* on *3.1.48* as in fact sufficing.

On Pāṇini 3.1.58

Jṝstambhumrucumlucugrucuglucugluñcuśvibhyaśca.

Optionally *aṅ* is *ādeśa* of *cli,* after the *dhātus jṝ, stambh, mruc, mluc, gluc, gluñc,* and *śvi* when the *parasmaipada pratyayas* follow and *luṅ* (aorist) expressing the agent.

Bhāṣya Summary

Mention of both *gluci* and *gluñci* seems unnecessary. Since on their own they establish two of the desired forms, but for the third their separate mention is necessary.

On Pāṇini 3.1.60

ciṇ te padaḥ.

Ciṇ is *ādeśa* of aorist *vikarṇa cli* (to form the aorist passive), when the word *ta* (*ātmanepada prathama puruṣa*/third person singular) follows after the *dhātu pad*, when *lup* (in the sense of agent follows).

Bhāṣya Summary

Patañjali establishes this as a reference to *padi-i* taking *ātmanepada.*

On Pāṇini 3.1.66

ciṇ bhāvakarmaṇoḥ

Ciṇ is *ādeśa* of the aorist *vikarṇa cli,* when *ta* (of *ātmanepada* third singular) follows, in the sense of abstract action or object, when *luṅ* signifying the agent follows.

Bhāṣya Summary

Ciṇ is mentioned again so that *ciṇ* only be applicable or to make the rule *nitya.*

On Pāṇini 3.1.67

Sārvadhātuke yak.

Yak pratyaya acts after a *dhatu* when a *sārvadhātuka (tiṅ śit 3.4.113)* follows, denoting action or object.

Vāttika Summary

Bhā. : Discusses the singular in denoting *bhāva* and all three numbers denoting *karman.* Are *bhāva* (action) *karman* (object) and *kartṛ* (agent), meanings of the *sārvadhātuka* or the *vikaraṇa pratyayas?*

Vā 1: If *bhāva, karman* and *kartṛ* are meanings of *sārvadhātuka pratyayas* then restriction in the sense of singular dual and plural is inapplicable because of not having that meaning.

Vā 2: If the meanings are of *vikaraṇas* when a *kṛt* is enjoined there is no *vikaraṇa* (therefore no meaning).

Bhā. : After presenting various views, 'meanings only are applicable for *sārvadhātuka pratyayas* (Not for *vikaraṇas*)' is accepted.

Vā. a : *Karman* etc. are meanings of *sup*/case *vibhakti,* (and) number of *tiṅ*/verbal *pratyayas.*

Vā. b: A restriction is well established.

Vā. c: Or else the restriction is in regard to the original base.

Vā. 3: When *yak* is ordained in the sense of *bhāva*/action or *karman*/ object there shoule be additional enumeration of it in the sense of reflexive passive.

Vā. 4: Due to a conflict of rules, the subsequent *śap* prevails, being the stronger.

Vā. 5: Correct forms established dividing the *sūtra* into two.

Bhā. : Or the master's usage ... makes known that *yak* is applicable in sense of reflexive passive...

Bhāsya Summary

Patañjali begins his discussion by showing examples of *karman* only in dual and plural but *bhāva* only in singular. This is due to a difference in their substratum.

By various examples he shows the plural is appropriate and one of the forms *pāka* etc. retained. Similarly with *tiṅ* the plural is heard in the sense of *bhāva*. Again the plural and one form retained is appropriate for verbal nouns whether past, present or future, whereas in expressing *bhāva* by *tiṅ* endings each time requires a different form.

Moreover there is a distinction between *bhāva* expressed by a *kṛt* which is like a substance, attaining inseparable concomitance with the verbal activity and *bhāva* expressed by तिङ्, which is like a verbal activity not having inseparable concomitance with another action. Further, *tiṅ bhāva* manifests time, person and *pada,* not manifested by *kṛt bhāva.* Moreover, *tiṅ bhāva* connects with the agent while *kṛt bhāva* does not.

He turns to consider whether *bhāva, karman* and *kartṛ* are the meanings of *sārvadhātukas* or *vikaraṇa pratyayas.*

On the first, he explains that *vibhaktis* would also have to mean *bhāva* etc.

However, if *vikaraṇas* express meaning, he states on the second, then not only would *kṛts* fail to, so too would the *lakāras.*

By 3.4.69 *la* after a *vikaraṇa bhāva* etc. are expressed but when there is *luk* or *ślu vikaraṇas* are not heard.

When *liṅ* or *liṭ* follow there is no *vikaraṇa,* so the *la* alone expresses these meanings. Since there can be only one meaning for one *prakṛti* he concludes by accepting that only the *sārvadhātukas* have meaning, not the *vikaraṇas.*

He explains the significance or restriciton in relation to number, in the sense of one only etc.

Having given the examples for *yak* and for when *śap* obtains instead, because of *paratva* on the third and fourth, he gives the *sūtra* division proposed by the fifth whereby *ciṇ* acts when *ta* follows and *yak* when a *sārvadhātuka* follows, both being in the sense of *bhāva* and *karman; yak* also is in the sense of agent. A second separation of the *sūtra* is proposed.

Additional enumeration is needed of *yak* in the sense of *karmakartṛ* because *śyan* would prevail by *vipratiṣedhe.* However, it is not possible that an existent prohibited rule be barred again.

Śyan is simply *ādeśa* of *śap* which in turn will be barred by *yak. Śap 3.1.68,* in the first case is treated as sixth case, when in *anuvṛtti* because of *1.1.67.*

He explains the next *vārttika* without addition.

On the last he adds the *yak* will be in the place of *śyan* by force of 'being like the *karman*'. Or else we may infer from *3.1.62* that *yak* is (otherwise) applicable in the sense of the reflexive passive.

So here also the sense is that in conveying one meaning there is a *sārvadhātuka* and in (conveying) the other a *vikaraṇa pratyaya* will be applicable.

On Pāṇini 3.1.71

Yaso'nupasargāt.

The *pratyaya śyan* optionally acts after the *dhātu yas* (to strive), when it is without an *upasarga* and when a *sārvadhātuka pratyaya* follows signifying the agent.

Bhā. : Discusses the point of saying 'not after an *upasarga*'. It need not be stated because by *3.1.72* we can understand 'after *yas*'.

Bhāṣya Summary

Patañjali says 'not after an *upasarga*' need not be stated, because by *3.1.72,* we can understand 'after *yas* precedd by *sam* only not by any other *upasarga*' will the option apply.

This is a rule ordaining *śyan* optionally.

On Pāṇini 3.1.78

Rudhādibhyaḥ śnam.

Pratyaya śnam (seventh class *vikaraṇa*) acts after the *dhātus* of the class beginning with *rudh* when a *sārvadhātuka pratyaya* follows signifying the agent.

Vārttika Summary

Bhā. : What is the purpose of *it ś* ? Not for the name *sārvadhātuka.*

Vā. 1 : *Ś* is for shortening of *pū* etc.

Vā. 2 : Or else not so because *dhātus pṛ,* and *mṛṇi* are different.

Bhā. : Shortening of *śnā* (*vikaraṇa*).

Vā. 3 : Diversely a *sārvadhātuka pratyaya* has an *it p* in the *Chandas.*

Bhā. : *Ś* is for preventing *n lopa.*

Bhāṣya Summary

He introduces the first *vārttika* by showing *it ś* cannot be for the name *sārvadhātuka.* The conditions of *1.4.13* do not apply, a *pratyaya* not following so *7.3.84* will not operate. Similarly he shows it cannot be for prohibition of *ārdhadhātuka* name, since that too relates to *aṅga* dependent on there being a *pratyaya* following, whereas *śnam* is infixed within the *dhātu.*

On the first *vārttika* he simply explains the reference to *6.3.80* with examples.

On the second, this is shown to apply to *śnā* of class 9 not *śnam,* although *anudātta* does not obtain.

Having given the Vedic examples for the third, he states it is essential shortening be stated in the *Chandas* (of *śnā*).

Ś serves the purpose of distinguishing in *6.4.23.* The *ś* should be produced for preventing *lopa* of *n.*

Finally he quotes *Pari. 105,* to explain why the rule does not apply to genitive plurals of *viśna* and *praśna.*

On Pāṇini 3.1.79

Tanādi-kṛñ-bhya uḥ.

The *vikaraṇa u* acts as a *pratyaya* after the *dhātus* of the *gaṇa* beginning with *tan* and after *kṛ* (to make) when a *sārvadhātuka pratyaya* follows signifying the agent.

Bhāṣya Summary

The special mention of *kṛ* is explained as being so that other operations of *tan* etc. like *lopa* of the nasal etc. should not apply to *kṛ*.

As a result *sic* is not optionally *luk* by *2.4.79,* but *lopa* by *8.2.27.* Being like *ciṇ* by *6.4.62,* is established either because *luk* of *sic* is only optional or because *lopa* of *sic* by *8.2.27,* is *asiddha* in relation to *6.4.62.*

On Pāṇini 3.1.80

Dhin-vi kṛṇ-vyora ca.

'The *vikaraṇa pratyaya u* acts after the *dhātus dhin-v-i* (to please) *kṛnvi* (to hurt) when a *sārvadhātuka pratyaya* follows signifying the agent, and in these *dhātus a* is the *ādeśa* of the final *i.*

Bhā. : Letter *a* is not actually heard, because *lopa,* but being *sthānivat* prevents *guṇa.*

Bhāṣya Summary

The augment *a* is needed to prevent *guṇa* by *7.3.86,* it being *sthānivat lopa* by *6.4.48,* nor subject to *1.1.4.*

Due to *num āgama* by *7.1.58,* and short *a* being *antaraṅga, num* applies first being the later rule so the rule should leave out the nasals.

On Pāṇini 3.1.83

Halaḥ śnaḥ śānag-jhau.

The *pratyaya śanac* is *ādeśa* in place of the *vikaraṇa pratyaya śnā* after a *dhātu* ending in a consonant when *hi* (of the imperative) follows.

Vārttika Summary

Bhā. : What is the purpose of *it ś*?

Vā. 1 : *Ś* for the *ādeśa* of *śnā* is pointless because of being *sthānivat.*

Vā. 2 : Purpose is a *jñāpaka* to indicate *anubandhas* are not *sthānivat.*

Vā. 3 : The purpose is so there by absence of *it p* for *hi* and *tātaṅ*.

Vā. 4 : The *ādeśa tap* etc. do not have an *it ṅ*.

Vā. 5 : The fault of the rule is absence of *it p* for a *mip ādeśa*.

Vā. 6 : *It ś* for the *ādeśa vasu* after *vid*.

Vā. 7 : Or (*vasu*) is established as (generally valid) by making it have an *it k*.

Bhāṣya Summary

The first *vārttika* is introduced by showing the *it ś* of *śnā* is so it may be called *sārvadhātuka* by *3.4.113* and thus, as if having an *it ṅ* to prevent *guṇa* by *1.1.5*.

The third is explained as meaning there should not be prohibition of *hi* having an *it p*. By the *jñāpaka* neither *hi* nor *tātaṅ* will have an *it p*.

Similarly on the fourth it is stated by the same *jñāpaka tap* etc. do not have *it ṅ*.

The fifth is expanded to include *ādeśas* of *tip* and *sip* as well as *mip* having an *it p* with examples. By the same *jñāpaka*, this would have been absent, as in the sixth, *ś* has to be stated as an *it* for the *vasu ādeśa*. Otherwise by the seventh *it k* for *vasu* will allow general mention in *6.4.131* and prevent *guṇa*.

However, he concludes the demerits of the *jñāpaka* may be greater than the merits of the text as written.

By *1.2.5* we understand that having an *it ṅ* does not become that having an *it p*.

On Pāṇini 3.1.84

Chandasi śāyaj-api.

In the *chandas*, *śāyac* is also the *ādeśa* of *śnā vikaraṇa* after *dhātus* ending in a consonant when *i* (of the imperative) follows.

Vārttika Summary

Vā. : Everywhere in the *Chandas śāyac* acts (even when other than *hi* follows).

Bhāṣya Summary

Examples from the *Chandas* to show *śānac* applies even when *hi* does not follow.

On Pāṇini 3.1.85

Vyatyayo bahulam.

In the *Chandas,* diversely transposition (of *vikaraṇas*) *śap* and the rest.

Vārttika Summary

Bhā. : A separation of the rule (into two parts) should be made.

Vā. 1 : Transposition/interchange (of *sya* and the rest).

Vā. 2 : In the *Chandas* all rules are diversely applicable; interchange of *sup, tiṅ,* letters, gender, time, person, *ātmanepada* and *parasmaipada pratyayas . . .*

Bhāṣya Summary

Separation of the rule into two is proposed. Firstly there is interchange of *vikaraṇas sya* etc., secondly in the context of the *Veda* all rules are diversely applicable. Examples are then given of interchange of *sup,* of *tiṅ,* of letters, of gender, of time, of person, of *ātmanepada* and *parasmaipada pratyayas.*

In addition to these the *śloka vārttika* mentions accent, cases and the *vikaraṇas* from *yaṅ 3.1.67* to *aṅ 3.3.83.*

On Pāṇini 3.1.86

Liṅyā śiṣyaṅ

The *pratyaya aṅ* acts in the *Chandas* (as a *vikaraṇa*) when *pratyayas* of the benedictive follow.

Vārttika Summary

Vā. 1 : The purpose of the rule ordaining *aṅ* when benedictive follows is that *sthā, gā, gami, vac* and *vid* only might receive it.

Bhā. : Also for *śak* and *ruhi.*

Vā. 2 : After *dṛś, pratyaya ak* acts.

Bhāṣya Summary

Examples are given for the first *vārttika* from the *Veda.* On the second an additional example is given *upastheyam,* where there is *lopa* because of being *ardhadhātuka* and *e ādeśa* is applied because of also having the name *ārdhad-hātuka.*

On Pāṇini 3.1.87

Karmavatkarmaṇā tulyakriyaḥ.

(The agent), when the action affecting the agent is similar to the action which affects the object, is treated as if it were object.

Vārttika Summary

Bhā. : Explains each term in the *sūtra.*

Vā.1 : The agent of an intransitive *dhātu* is treated as if it were an object/ *karmavat.*

Vā.2 : If the agent is seen as an object this should be when the same *dhātu* is used.

Vā.3 : The agent is *karmavat* for those *dhātus* having their verbal activity situated in the object or those having the abstract action situated in the object.

Vā.4 : Prohibition of the rules relating to *ātmanepada* and *śap vikaraṇa* and the rest should be stated.

Vā.5 : Due to the desire to express independence the agentship exists in the reflexive passive.

Vā.6 : Prescription of being *karmavat* (should be made) for that which ends in *la* (tense *pratyayas*).

Vā.7 : Otherwise prohibition of *karmavat* should be stated when the *pratyayas kṛtya* and *kta* and those having the meaning of *khal* follow.

Vā.8 : However, it is established that *la* denotes the object because of (the base) orginally being *karman*/object.

Vā.9 : (This is known) due to seeing the objects of the reflexive passive when (the word *ātman* is used) in connection (with the *karmakartṛ*)

Vā.10 : *Lopa* elision of a word (is to be seen).

Vā.11 : There is prohibition of (*karmavat*) for transitive *dhātus*, e.g. *anyonyam āśliṣyataḥ* (they joined each other).

Vā.12 : Or else the statement (of *karmavat*) regarding the transitive (*dhātu*) is for the purpose of making a restriction.

Vā.13 : And the agent of that *tap* only which has the word *tapas* as object is *karmavat.*

Vā.14 : The agent is diversely (like on object/*karmavat*) for the *dhātus* *duh-i* and *pac-i* when they are transitive/*sakarmaka.*

Vā.15 : The agent of *dhātus sṛj* and *yuj* is diveresely treated like an object. However, there is *śyan* in place of *yak vikaraṇa.*

Vā.16 : The agent whose action is similar to that done by the instrument diversely becomes like an object.

Vā.17 : Prohibition (is to be stated) of being like an object for the agents of the *dhātus sru* and the rest.

Vā.18 : And prohibition should be stated of the agent being like the object for *dhātus* conveying the sense of the act of adorning, the *dhātu kṛ* (to scatter) and *san* (desiderative *pratyaya*) ending *dhātus* other than in the *ātmanepada.*

Bhāṣya Summary

The *vat* of *karmavat* is so the operations relate to itself and so the *la* in the sense of *bhāve.*

Karmaṇā/'similar to the object' is stated so that the instrumental or locative be not treated as if *karmavat.*

'*Tulyakriya*' is 'that agent having an action similar to the object; being originally an object has become an agent and in whom the same action as the object is observed, who is treated as an object.'

On the first *vārttika* the example is given, showing that the agent of an intransitive *dhātu* (not a transitve) will be *karmavat.*

On the third the corollary is given, so that the agent of those *dhātus* whose *bhāva* stands within the agent or whose action is within the agent are not *karmavat.*

'When *dhātus* are the same' *Vā. 2* need not be stated, because 'after a *dhātu*' is in *anuvṛtti.* '*Karmavad-bhāva*' takes place only if the *karman* is the agent of the *dhātu* of which it is the object.

Similarly *Vārttika 3* is not required because one measures the agent by the activity situated in the object and that does not apply for those *dhātus* whose *bhāva* or action is confined to the agent.

If there is resort to the object only and not the agent in the reflexive passive, the rules enjoining *caṅ*, *śap*, and *kṛt* would not be established as valid.

On the fifth it is explained that an existing independence is intended to be expressed, as in the absence of wind etc. the granary splits itself. Similarly to express ease of cutting agentship is attributed to the meadow.

The prohibition of *karmavat* for *kṛtya* etc. is explained with the examples so that they are instead seen to be applicable in the sense of *bhāva* of *dhātus.* Mention of *la* need not be made because *3.1.86,* indicates two *l's.*

Having thus explained the seventh, the eighth and ninth are treated together, the latter answering how it is known that *karman* is the original base by the example of *ātman* connected with *karmakartṛ.*

The tenth explains the implication of *lopa,* that really the inner self and the corporal self are distinct.

Having given examples for the eleventh, on the twelfth he explains the restriction as being necessary when another object obtains.

For the thirteenth, explanation is given of *tapas* derived by *uṇādi* as and *dhātu tap-i.* It is shown how specific *tap* can be the object of the general action *tap-i.*

On the fourteenth it is stated that if the point of 'diversely' is to allow *parasmaipada* in fact they are not desired.

The *Bhāsya* on the fifteenth explains the condition for *karmavat* in relation to *sṛj-i* is that the agent be endowed with faith, so, it is like *ciṅ* receiving *ātmanepada.* The purpose in relation to *yuj-i* is for the absence of *yak.*

Having given the examples for the sixteenth and seventeenth, it is explained why prohibition should not be stated in the latter, because a similar action is understood.

Finally on the eigteenth simply the examples are provided.

On Pāṇini 3.1.89

Na duhasnunamāṃ yakciṇau.

Vikaraṇa pratyaya yak and *ciṇ* do not act in expressing the reflexive passive voice for the *dhātus duh, snu* and *nam.*

Vārttika Summary

Vā. 1 : When there is prohibition of *yak* and *ciṇ* there should be additional enumeration of the causative/*ṇi* ending *dhātus* of *śri* and *brū.*

Bhā. : Provides the necessary examples. Followers of *Bhāradvāja* mention *śranth* (in place of *śri*) *ātmanepada* and intransitive *dhātus.*

On Pāṇini 3.1.90

Kuṣirajoḥ prācāṃ śyanparasmaipadaṃ ca.

'*Vikaraṇa pratyaya śyan* acts after the *dhātus kuṣ* and *rañj* in the reflexive passive voice, (according to the opinion) of the Eastern Grammarians and they take the *parasmaipada pratyayas*

Vārttika Summary

Vā. 1 : Mention should be made of *sārvadhātuka* when *śyan* is ordained for *kuṣ* and *rañj.*

Vā. 2 : Otherwise prohibition of *liṅ* and *liṭ* (has to be stated)

Bhā. : *Sārvadhātuka* is present by *anuvṛtti.* Separation of the rule into two parts is proposed.

Bhāṣya Summary

Having provided the examples relating to the first two *vārttikas* it is explained where *śyan* obtains when mention of a *sārvadhātuka* occurs, and similarly where the barring of *sya* etc. by *śyan* obtains.

Both ways of achieving mention of *sārvadhātuka* from *3.1.67* whether through *ca* or *la,* a qualification of it, have undesired effects. However, accepting the latter alternative it is shown that in fact *liṅ* and *liṭ* are established as valid by *anuvṛtti* from *3.1.86* and *35* respectively.

Śyan is stated by connection with the prohibition in *3.1.89* of *yak* with *parasmaipada.* It thus also obtains in the context of *ciṇ.*

Another division of the *sūtra* into two is proposed:

(1) *ciṇ* is not applicable for *duh* etc. in reflexive passive;

(2) *yak* is not applicable for *duh* etc.;

(3) *yak* is not applicable for *kuṣi* and *raj* according to Eastern Grammarians, so that *śyan* is applicable with *parasmaipada.*

Otherwise it is indicated how this can be achieved by *anuvṛtti.*

Finally, the solution is given in *sya* etc. being *antaraṅga,* they are in fact applicable when there is only one condition, namely *la* following, whereas *śyan* has the additional condition 'when a *sārvadhātuka* follows' and so is *bahiraṅga.*

On Pāṇini 3.1.91

Dhātoḥ.

After a *dhatus* (acts a *pratyaya* to the end of the third *adhyāya*)

Vārttika Summary

Bhā. : Up to where is the *adhikāra* applicable ?

Vā. 1 : *Dhātu* governing rule applicable up to the substitutes of *la.*

Vā. 2 : When *ādeśas* follow because of (*vikaraṇas*) intervening it is not established.

Vā. a : In the first rule (after '*lasya*') *tiṅ* would not be applicable when *vikaraṇas* intervene.

Vā. b : The substitution of *e* he ordains in place of *ṭi* portion of those having an *it t* would not be applicable.

Vā. c : *Ādeśa eś* has to be formed having an *it ś.*

Vā. d : And what *ādeśas* he enjoins for *loṭ* would not be applicable.

Vā. e : And that stated previously when *laṅ* and *liṅ* follow would not be applicable. *Bhāśya* has a lengthy discussion.

Vā. 3 : One purpose is the prohibition of acting after a *prātipadika.*

Vā. 4 : Another purpose is in relation to *dhātus svap* etc.

Vā. 5 : (A purpose is forming) the technical name *aṅga.*

Vā. 6 : (A purpose is forming) the technical name *kṛt.*

Vā. 7 : (A purpose is forming) the technical name *upapada.*

Vā. 8 : Mention of *dhātu* is pointless because of the *dhātu* governing rule expressed in the *sūtra* ordaining *vaṅ.*

Vā. 9 : If there were no governing rule there would be absence of technical term *aṅga.*

Vā. 10 : However, mention of *hetumat* is a *jñāpaka* for expressing the absence of *ṇic* elsewhere.

Vā. 11 : And because of the rule expressing a special designation in relation to *kaṇḍū* etc. *yak* does not act after all *dhātus.*

Bhāṣya Summary

The disadvantage of regarding the *dhātu* governing *sūtra* as ending with the *ādeśas* of *la* is that the *tiṅ pratyayas* would not be applicable after *dhātus.*

"Should the *vikaraṇas* or the *ādeśas* be produced?", he asks after the first two *vārttikas*. *Ādeśas* have scope even where there are *luk* and *ślu vikaraṇas*, and when *liṅ* and *liṭ* (without *vikaraṇas*) follow.

Vā 2c is explained as referring to *1.1.55* to prevent the effect of *1.1.54*, namely two *e*'s. However, even if *1.1.52* applies instead, since there is no point in *e* acting in place of *e*. Even without *it ś* the whole of the original will be replaced.

Another consequence is the *ādeśas* for the imperative ordained by *3.4.85, 86, 86* and *88* would not be applicable. Moreover when *laṅ* or *liṅ* follows *3.4.99-103* would not be applicable.

Taking the example of *ādeśa a* (second person plural *parasmai* of the Perfect) in place of *tiṅ tha*, it is shown finally that since there is no purpose in enjoining *a* in place of *a* the *ādeśa* will be in place of the whole *sthānin* even without *it ś*. However, that *a* in place of an *a* does have the purpose of achieving 'the same number' of *ādeśas* and *sthānins*.

3.4.114 is shown not to be meaningful unless the *dhātu* governing rule follows on in context of *ādeśas* of *la*. Moreover, there is no problem of *vikaraṇas* intervening because *adeśas* which are *sārvadhātuka* apply first, as the condition for *vikaraṇas* acting. Even *sya* etc. require *dhātoḥ* as qualification of that ordained. It will also necessary to specify 'immediately adjoining after' in the case of reduplicated *dhātus* so *jus* doe not replace *jhi*.

In the case of *3.4.110*, after finally accepting *dhātu* as qualification of that immediately adjoining and *a* as qualification of *dhātu* and have avoided circularity when *lopa* applies before *jus* obtains, it is explained, first *anti* is enjoined, then *lopa* and derivation of the proper form.

The third *vārttika* is rejected because even where there is no *dhātu* governing rule *tavyat* etc. will not be applicable after a *prātipadika* because they are *sādhana* needing a *sādhya*.

On the fourth it is indicated one purpose is to prevent *samprasāraṇam* etc. in *svap* etc., while on the fifth the implied *sūtra* for *aṅga* is supplied, namely *1.4.13*.

The sixth and seventh are rejected since the technical names *kṛt* and *upapada* are established by their own governing *sūtras*.

On the eighth it is explained, *dhātu* follows on from *3.1.22*. However, if that were so *ṇic* would obtain after all *dhātus*, *Patañjali* explains on the ninth.

The tenth and eleventh are explained as showing that *3.1.26* and *3.1.27* do not allow *ṇic* or *yak* after all *dhātus*.

On Pāṇini 3.1.92

Tatropapadaṃ saptamīstham.

There (in the third *adhyāya* in the sphere of the *dhātu* governing rule), the word mentioned in the seventh case is called *upapada.*

Bhā. : '*Stha*' is used to indicate *upapada* is applicable to whatever is mentioned in the seventh case.

Vā. 1 : Mention of *tatra* is for restricting the sphere of application of the rule.

Vā. 2 : When there is the name *upapada* there is mention of *samartha* (having the same grammatical construction).

Vā. 3 : Mention of *upapada* as a condition.

Vā. 4 : When no mention of condition, a *pratyaya* would be applicable even when there is no *upapada.*

Vā. 5 : The special mention is for the purpose of making a technical name.

Vā. 6 : Mention of *tatra* (there) is for the purpose of simultaneous conjunction with the *upapada.*

Bhāṣya Summary

Mention is made of *stha* so that whether the seventh case is heard or not, or it is indicated by *saptamī* or another word, the term *upapada* is still applicable.

On the first *vārttika* it is explained, *tatra* refers to the sphere of the *dhātu* governing rule.

It is explained on the second that mention of *samartha* needs to be made for the sake of the *pratyaya* (*aṇ* etc.)

Upapada is explained as a term significant in itself, meaning 'a word uttered near to the main word'. Thus being a word/*pada* it is only applicable for words syntactically connected (*2.1.1*).

Aṇ is not applicable when a *cvi* ending word is *upapada,* because that which has expectancy cannot be *samartha.* He gives an exception.

The third is explained as stating the *upapada* is a condition for *pratyaya.*

When *pratyaya* is ordained in relation to an *upapada,* the *saṃjñā* is applicable, the fifth states.

On the sixth it is explained the other purpose of *tatra* is simultaneous conjunction with the *upapada.*

On Pāṇini 3.1.93

Kṛdatiṅ.

In the sphere of the *dhātu* governing rule any *pratyaya* other than *tiṅ* (verbal *pratyaya*) is called *kṛt.*

Bhāṣya Summary

The technical name *kṛt* is stated to be applicable for a *pratyaya* after a *dhātu* as far as the *ādeśas* of *la.*

The prohibition of the name *kṛt* is said to be for the *la* about to be replaced by *tiṅ*, since there would otherwise be the name *prātipadika* and *su* etc. wrongly arising. In fact *su* etc. will not apply in sense of singularity etc. since this meaning has already been expressed by *tiṅ*. However, *kṛt* will be applicable so *tap* etc. can express femininity.

From the master's usage it is known that *aṇ* etc. are not applicable after that ending in a *tiṅ* inasmuch as he makes mention of *tiṅ* in *taddhitas* (*5.3.55-56*).

Finally the *sūtra* serves to prevent application of *6.1.71* to *tiṅ* ending words.

On Pāṇini 3.1.94

Vā sarūpo'striyām.

In the sphere of the *dhātu* governing rule, a special/*apavāda pratyaya* which is to debar a general/*utsarga* one, not of the same form, optionally bars it, but not so in the case of feminine *pratyayas* (which always debar *utsarga pratyayas 3.3.94* etc.).

Bhā. : *Astriyām* means those not in context of the *adhikāra* '*striyām*'.

Vā. 1 : Optional statement of a *pratyaya* of dissimilar form is so that the general rule should not be barred (totally) in the context of a rule that cancels it.

Vā. 2 : There is occasion for optional arising of a *pratyaya* as in the case of a *taddhita pratyaya.*

Vā. 3 : It is established as valid by expression of option for the barring of a *pratyaya* of dissimilar form.

Vā. 4 : There is occasion for option in case of *pratyayas* with different indicatory letters.

Vā. 5 : (This is) established as valid because of the indicatory letters nature of not forming part of that to which it is attached.

Vā. 6 : (If) it is proper to state option for such *pratyayas* which are dissimilar in actual usage, there is prohibition in relation to the *ādeśas* of *la* (tense *pratyayas*).

Vā. 7 : When the prohibition is effected in the feminine, there is occasion for option in the presence of the *pratyayas kta, lyuṭ, tumum,* and those having the sense of *khal.*

Vā. 8 : If it is stated, 'As far as *striyām*' the expression of option in relation to *pratyaya ktvā* should be made.

Vā. 9 : When time and the rest are in composition, there is option in relation to the *pratyaya tumum.*

Vā. 10 : There is ordaining of the *pratyaya tṛc* in the sense of fitness (with regard to the agent).

Bhāṣya Summary

If '*astriyām*' means 'When feminine is being expressed' in *lav-ya* etc. *vāsarūpo* does not obtain.

If it means 'When feminine *pratyayas* follow', *vyavakrośī* etc. are not established.

Neither applies, as then it will be known prohibition is for those under the governing *sūtra 3.3.94.*

After showing *vāsarūpo* is not needed for *3.1.96* not to cease to be valid as *utsarga,* nor for *ṇuvl* and *tṛc* in relation to *ac,* but so that *3.1.135* should only optionally bar those three *utsargas.*

On the second *vārttika* it is explained that the comparison with *taddhitas* is not valid since all of those whether *utsarga* or *apavāda* either arise optionally or do not arise at all.

In the context of the third, it is explained that here there cannot be non-arising of a *pratyaya* since 'The *prakṛti* is not to be used alone, nor is the *pratyaya* to be used alone'. Capacity to express meaning exists in the case of *taddhitas* because another *pratyaya* expresses it.

Or else option is with regard to that having form. Thus the *apavāda* having form, arises and is preceded by another *utsarga* required to complete the sense, optionally bars it. Even *kvip* etc. have form in the *upadeśa.*

The fourth is illustrated by citing *3.2.1* (*a-ṇ*) and *3.2.3* (*k-a*).

On the fifth he quotes *Pari. 4* in support or else just ordains option only for dissimilar forms, in actual use.

In relation to the sixth, it is explained that either we may infer *vāsarūpo* is not applicable to *ādeśas* of *la* from *3.2.116* or simply because in the *upadeśa* all the *la-kāras* are in fact of the same form '*l*'.

The implied rule from *3.1.139* is that *pratyayas* having the same form without *it* letters are not different from them. Only dissimilarity of form is optionally barring when that dissimilarity exists in use and before use.

On the seventh, the appropriate examples are provided, as also for the eighth and ninth.

In relation to the tenth, it is explained that *kṛtyas* being enjoined in sense of *bhāva* and *karman* do not bar *utsarga tṛc* in sense of agent.

Liṅ (*3.3.168*) would bar *utsargas kṛtya* and *tṛc*, all in the sense of fitness.

On Pāṇini 3.1.95

Kṛtyāḥ.

From this *sūtra* as far as *ṇvul tṛcau 3.1.133* all the *pratyayas* will have the name *kṛtya.*

Vā. 1 : When the name *kṛtya* is stated, a statement that it is applicable as far as the *ṇvul* rule should be made.

Vā. 2 : The rule enjoining *kṛtya* and *tṛc* in the sense of fitness as a *jñāpaka* makes known the pointlessness of expressing 'as far as *ṇvul*'.

Bhāṣya Summary

The purpose of the first *vārttika* is so that *kṛtya* should not be the name of *ṇvul* etc.

The second is explained as referring to *3.3.169,* so that the first is unnecessary. However, since *jñapaka* only applies to the rule referred to, *kṛtya* would apply after *ṇvul* were it not for the first.

On Pāṇini 3.1.96

Tavyat-tavyānīyaraḥ.

The *pratyayas tavyat, tavya* and *anīyar* act after *dhātus.*

Vā. 1 : Additional enumeration of the *pratyaya kelimar.*

Vā. 2 : *Tavyat* acts after the *dhātu vas-ḷ* in the sense of agent and the *pratyaya ṇic.*

Vā. 3 : Or it should be regarded as the *taddhita* (form).

Bhāṣya Summary

The appropriate examples are provided, for the first *vārttika*. The two meanings of *vāstavya* derived by the second and the third are given.

Additional enumeration of the *pratyaya kelimar.* And by some this is desired in the sense of reflexive passive.

However, by the *bhāṣya-kāra* it is shown in the sense of object/*karman.*

On Pāṇini 3.1.97

Aco yat.

The *pratyaya yat* acts after a *dhātu* that ends in a vowel (in the sense of agent).

Bhā. : Why mention *ac*? So *yat* be applicable after *dhātus* which formerly ended in a vowel.

Vā. 1 : In the domain of *yat* additional enumeration of *jan* should be made.

Vā. 2 : Optionally after *han,* (*yat*) and *vadha* is *ādeśa* of *han.*

Vā. 3 : Or it should be regarded as a *taddhita* form.

Bhāṣya Summary

The purpose of mentioning *ac* is not to be bar acting after a consonant, but so that *yat* should be applicable after a *dhātu* which orginally ended in a vowel, namely *lav-yam* etc.

Addition is made to the first *vārttika* of the *dhātus śas-i, cat-i,* and *yat-i* with examples.

Having provided the examples for the second and the third, it is stated a *samāsa* is established not by the *taddhita* but by *yat* according to *vā 2* on *2.1.33,* otherwise there would be the wrong accent.

On Pāṇini 3.1.100

Gadamadacarayamaścānupasarge. car (to go, eat) and yam (to restrain)

The *pratyaya yat* acts after a *dhātu gad* (to speak), *mad* (to be mad), and *yam* (to restrain) when they do not take any *upasarga.*

Vā. 1 : *Yat* acts after *car* without an *upasarga* and when preceded by *upasarga āṅ* except when meaning teacher.

Bhāṣya Summary

The necessary example and counter example are provided.

On Pāṇini 3.1.103

Aryaḥ svāmivaiśyayoḥ.

The word *arya* is a *nipātana* when meaning lord and a *vaiśya.*

Vā. 1 : In the sense of Lord, (*arya*) has final *udātta* accent.

Bhā. : Provides the example.

On Pāṇini 3.1.105

A-jaryam saṅgatam.

Ajaryam is a *nipātana,* when qualifying the word *saṅgatam* (friendship) expressed or understood.

Vā. 1 : The word *ajaryam* occurs in the sense of agent.

Bhāṣya Summary

Having provided the counter examples, the first *vārttika* is introduced by asking why these have the sense of agent.

This need not be stated for *kta,* since it is ordained in the sense of agent and *karman* after *dhātus* of motion. But *jṝ* being intransitive obtains in the sense of *bhāva.*

Saṅgatam is a qualification of agent.

On Pāṇini 3.1.106

Vadaḥ supi kyap ca.

After the *dhātu vad* (to speak) governing a case inflected word as its *upapada* and not having an *upasarga* preceding, the *pratyaya kyap* also acts.

Vā. 1 : Secific mention of *kyap* after *vad* without an *upasarga* in the presence of a *sup pratyaya.*

Bhāṣya Summary

Having given the counter examples, it is explained that '*anupasarga*' follows on, in accord with the general principal that governing rules should follow on.

On Pāṇini 3.1.107

Bhuvo bhāve.

After the *dhātu bhū* in construction with a *sup* as *upapada* and when without an *upasarga, pratyaya kyap* acts to denote abstract action.

Bhāṣya Summary

Mention of *bhāve* is for the sake of subsequent *sūtras,* not to prevent the sense of *karman.*

On Pāṇini 3.1.108

Hanasta ca.

After *dhātu han* when in construction with a *sup* inflected word as its *upapada* and when without an *upasarga,* the *pratyaya kyap* acts in denoting abstract action/state and *t* is *ādeśa* of its final *n.*

Vā. 1 : In the *chandas* when forming a feminine noun (*kyap* with *it c* acts after *han* and *t* is the *ādeśa* of the final *n.*)

Bhāṣya Summary

The examples and counter examples are provided.

On Pāṇini 3.1.109

Etistuśāsvṛdṛjuṣaḥ kyap.

The *pratyaya kyap* acts after the *dhātus i, stu, śās, vṛ, dṛ,* and *juṣ.*

Bhā. : Why mention *pratyaya kyap* again ? So that whatever else obtains be not applicable.

Vā. 1 : In the context of the *kyap* rule there should be mention of the *dhātu vṛñ.*

Vā. 2 : And additional enumeration of *añj* when forming a name.

Bhāṣya Summary

The mention of *kyap* is so that *kyap* alone be applicable and *ṇyat* not be applicable.

The counter example is provided for the first *vārttika.*

On the second, having provided the example, it is explained because of *vṛddhi* there must be *ṇyat.* However, that would require *lopa* of the penultimate, therefore it is *kyap* with the *upasarga aṇ* preceeding *añj-i. Pada Pāṭha* conventions notwithstanding, rules of grammer prevail.

On Pāṇini 3.1.111

Ī ca khanaḥ.

The *pratyaya kyat* acts after the *dhātu khan* and long *ī* is *ādeśa* (for the final).

Bhā. : Long *ī* is not justified.

Bhāṣya Summary

After considering the purpose of long *ī* may be to prevent *tuk āgama* by *6.1.71*, it is acknowledged that the *guṇa* single *ādeśa* by 6.1.87, is not *asiddha* and therefore, short *i* should be stated in the *sūtra.*

85.6 ई च खनः।

Some say, when long *ī* is rejected by the *bhāṣyakāra* there is a second letter *i* (hidden) by reason of coalescence of vowels being indicated; on which view it is for the purpose of barring the long *ā* which is obtained by

ये विभाषा (6.4.43) (जनसनखनाम् आत्)

"There is optionally long *ā ādeśa* for the finals of *jan, san,* and *khan* before a *pratyaya* beginning with *ya* and marked with an indicatory *k* or *ṅ.*"

That is not right. (It is) by reason of the simultaneous conjunction with *kyap* due to the *antaraṅga* nature of the long *ī* being ordained.

However, when the letter *y* follows of a *pratyaya* actually arisen, due to the *bahiraṅga* nature of the long *ā* ordained for *aṅga* and due to the absence of conflict (of rules of equal force), there is absence of obtainment.

On Pāṇini 3.1.112

Bhṛño saṃjñāyām.

The *pratyaya kyap* acts after the *dhātu bhṛñ* when not used as a name.

Bhā. : Why not as a name? *Bhāryā* (female supported by another, wife).

Vā. 1 : When prohibition of *kyap* after *bhṛñ* to form a name, there is no prohibition in the feminine because of its being enjoined by another *sūtra.*

Vā. 2 : What is the purpose of the prohibition? For prohibiting a non-feminine name.

Vā. 3 : It is established as valid because of prohibition in the feminine in the sense of name.

Vā. a : Because of seeing *kyap* used in a masculine name your *bhāryā* is not established.

Vā. 1 : There is a governing rule *bhāve* in the feminine and by reason of that it is remembered that *bhāryā* is established as a valid form.

Vā. b : Otherwise it is remembered diveresely the *kṛtya pratyayas* are applicable in the sense of name.

Vā. 2 : As for example *yatyam, janyam,* and *bhitti.*

Vā. 4 : And diveresely *kyap* acts after *bhṛ* after *upasarga sam.*

Bhāṣya Summary

Having the counter example to 'When not used as a name', it is explained in relation to the first that *apratiṣedha* really means prohibition, since *kyap* is enjoined in the feminine by *3.3.99.* On the second it is stated that the purpose is prohibition of the non-feminine name of *kṣatriyas.*

The third is again referring to *3.3.99,* so that *kyap* does not come after *bhṛñ* in the feminine. There is no conflict because there *bhāve* follows on from *3.3.98,* and here the *pratyaya* is in sense of *karman.*

It is pointed out again in the first that *karman* is also there. Otherwise *ṇyat* is also applicable because of *bahulam 3.3.113.* The examples are provided for the fourth.

On Pāṇini 3.1.114

Rājasūyasūryasūryamṛṣodyarucya kupyakṛṣṭhapacyāvyathyāḥ.

The words *rājasūrya, sūrya, mṛṣodya, rucya, kupya, kṛṣṭha,* and *pacya* are *nipātanas* formed by the *pratyaya kyap.*

Vā. 1 : *Sūrya, rucya* and *avyathya* are laid down as irregular forms in the sense of agent.

Vā. 2 : *Kupya* occurs in the sense of name.

Vā. 3 : Final *udātta* for *kṛṣṭha* and *pacya* and *(kyap)* is in the sense of reflexive passive.

Bhāṣya Summary

It is explained on the first *vārttika* that these are *nipātanas.*

Derivations are given of *sūrya, rucya* and *avyathyaḥ.*

Having provided the counter example for the second, a Vedic example as well as etymology is provided for the third.

There is *k* in place of the initial of *gup* (to hide) for the form *kupya.*

Kupya is wealth, precious metal other than gold and silver.

On Pāṇini 3.1.118

Pratyapibhyām graheḥ.
After the *dhātu grah* preceded by the *upasargas prati* and *api*, *pratyaya kyap* acts.

Vā. 1 : *Kyap* acts after *grah* preceded by *prati* and *api* in the *chandas.*

Bhāṣya Summary

Suitable examples and counter examples are provided, on the *vārttika.*

Uddyota : Some say by the word *apigṛhya* is stated as (meaning) 'to be seized by the employment of force'.

On Pāṇini 3.1.122

Amāvasyad-anyatarasyām.
The word *amāvasya* is optionally *nipātana.*

Śloka Varttika : I put down irregularly absence of *vṛddhi* for *amāvasya* followed by *ṇyat* so that the one state of existence of the two (words) and the proper accent is established as valid for me.

Bhāṣya Summary

The *nipātana* is explained as absence of *vṛddhi* for *amāvasya* followed by *ṇyat* not *vun* (*4.3.30*) so both alternatives are established with final *svarita* not initial *udātta.*

On Pāṇini 3.1.123

Chandasi niṣṭarkya devahūya praṇīyonnī yocchiṣya marya staryā-dhvarya-khanyakhānya-devayajyā-pṛchya pratiṣīvya-brahmavādya-bhāvya-stāvya upacāyyapṛḍāni.
In the *chandas* the following words are laid down as *nipātana: niṣṭarkya, devahūya, praṇīya, unnīya, ucchiṣya, marya, staryā, dhvarya, khanya, khānya, devayajyā, pṛcchya, pratiṣīvya, brahmavādya, bhāvya, stāvya,* and *upacāyyapṛḍa.*

Śloka Varttika 1 : In *niṣṭarkya* there is inversion of *t* for *k*, cerebral *ṣ* in place of *s* of *nis* and *ṇyat* and *ay ādeśa* are put down irregularly in *upacāyya.*

Śloka Varttika 2 : *Ṇyat pratyaya* is enjoined after one *dhātu, kyap* after four, *ṇyat* again after one, and there is *ya*; two *kyaps* and four *ṇyats* finally are enjoined

Bhāṣya Summary

The irregular formation of *niṣṭarkya* from *kṛt* is explained, *Sikata* from *kās* and *sinha* from *hins.* The *śloka* adds that *ṇyat* and *āy* help from *upacāyya.*

An example of *niṣṭarkya* in context is given.

The second *śloka vārttika* is explained linking the *pratyayas* with the various *nipātanas.*

In the case of *upacāyyapṛḍam* there is also the *ādeśa ay.*

On Pāṇini 3.1.124

Ṛhalor ṇyat.

The *pratyaya ṇyat* acts after the *dhātus* that end in *ṛ* (short or long) or in a consonant.

Vā. 1 : When *pāṇi* is an *upapada, ṇyat* is ordained after *dhātu sṛj.*

Vā. 2 : *Ṇyat* acts after *sṛj* with *upasargas sam* and *ava* . . .

Vā. 3 : And *ṇyat* acts after *lap-i* and *dabh-i.*

Bhāṣya Summary

The necessary derived forms are provided for all three *vārttikas.*

Uddyota Vā. 1 *Ṇyat* is *apavāda* of *kyap* due to penultimate *ṛ* of *sṛj* when *pāni* is *(upapada).*

Vā. 3 : *Ṇyat* (instead of *yat*) after the *lap* and *dabh* having final and penultimate *a.*

On Pāṇini 3.1.125

Orāvaśyake.

The *pratyaya ṇyat* acts after a *dhātu* that ends in *u* short or long, when the sense is that of necessity.

Vā. 1 : If *āvaśyake* is (an *upapada*) there should be additional enumeration of it as the sense to be expressed by suggestion.

Vā. 2 : If it is the sense to be expressed by suggestion, the accent for compound is not applicable.

Vā. 3 : By reason of the prior rule being more powerful when in mutual conflict, *kyap* acts after *dhātu stu* (praise) in place of *ṇyat* in the sense of necessity.

Bhāṣya Summary

Having provided the examples for the first in the sense of necessity, the problem of wrong accent, if the sense is to be expressed by suggestion is overcome when such compounds are taken as part of '*mayūravyansaka*' *gaṇa* (*2.1.72*).

On the third it is explained there is scope for *ṇyat* after other *dhātus* ending in *u* by this very *sūtra*, but that in the case of *stu, kyap* by *3.1.109* is more powerful by *pūrva-vipratiṣedha.*

On Pāṇini 3.1.127

Ānnāyyo'nitye

The word *ānāyya* is a *nipātana* when meaning impermanent.

Śloka Varttika 1 : If *ānāyya* means impermanent it denotes the *dakṣināgni,* having one source (the *Garhapatya*) otherwise *āneyaḥ* would be the form.

On Pāṇini 3.1.129

Pāyya sānāyya nikāyya dhāyyā māna havirnivāsasāmidhenīṣu.

The word *pāyya, sānnāyya, nikāyya,* and *dhāyyā* are laid down as irregular forms meaning 'a measure', 'an oblation to fire', 'a dwelling', and 'a sacrificial prayer' respectively.

Vā. 1 : The irregular formation in the words *pāyya* and *nikāyya* is the initial *p* (for *m* of *mā*) and *k* (for *c* of *ci*)

Bhāṣya Summary

The regular forms of *meyam* and *niceyam* are provided.

Uddyota It should be known the *ādeśa āy* is also irregularly laid down.

On Pāṇini 3.1.130

Kratau kuṇḍapāyyasañcāyyau

The words *kuṇḍapāyya* and *sañcāyya* are laid down irregularly, meaning sacrifice.

Vā. 1 : The *pratyaya yat* is enjoined in forming the word *kuṇḍapāyya.*

Bhāṣya Summary

Reiterates the *sūtra* by saying *kuṇḍapāyya* is a sacrifice.

On Pāṇini 3.1.131

Agnau paricāyyopacāyyasamūhyāḥ.

The words *paricāyya, upacāyya* and *samūhya* are laid down as irregular forms when they are names of fire.

Vā. 1 : *Samūhya* is pointless because it has already been formed by the general *sūtra.*

Vā. 2 : If the irregular form is meant for *vah-i,* then it is established by *ūhi* because it has the same sense.

Vā. 3 : Because of the resolution of the compound *samūhya* into *sam* and *ūh-i* in the *Brāhmaṇas* it is established as valid.

Bhāṣya Summary

Samūhya can be derived by the general *sūtra 3.1.124.* Since *dhātus* have many meanings it is also possible for *ūhi* to occur in the sense of *vahi,* as found in the *Brāhmaṇas.*

On Pāṇini 3.1.132

Cityāgnicitye ca.

The words *citya* and *agnicitya* are *nipātanas.*

Bhāṣya Summary

Agnicitya is equivalent to *agnicayana.*

On Pāṇini 3.1.133

Ṇvultṛcau

The *pratyaya ṇvul* and *tṛc* act after all *dhātus* in expressing the agent.

Bhā. : '*C*' is for not hindering the general mention of *tṛ.*

Vā. 1 : When *ṇvul* follows there should be mention of action after intransitive *dhātus.*

Vā. 2 : Or else it should be applicable because *ṇvul* is seen to act after all *dhātus.*

Vā. 3 : In the case of *tṛc* etc. mention should be made of the present time for the sake of the forms *adhyāyaka* and *vedādhyāya.*

Vā. 4 : Or else it is not applicable, because of others being seen in the sense of all times.

Bhāṣya Summary

The purpose of the *it c* is not for accent, nor for distinguishing but for not hindering the general mention in *6.4.11.*

The necessary examples are provided for the first two *vārttikas* and on the third it is explained that the forms mentioned should not be used when one has already studied or one is going to study.

On Pāṇini 3.1.134

Nandigrahipacādibhyo lyuṇinyacaḥ

After the *dhātus nand* and the rest, *grahi* and the rest and *pac* and the rest, act the *pratyayas lyu* (*ana*), *ṇin* (*in*) and *ac* (*a*) respectively.

Vā. 1 : *Ac pratyaya* also acts after all *dhātus.*

Vā. 2 : There is a list of *pac* etc. for attaching indicatory letters and for barring an *apavāda pratyaya.*

Bhāṣya Summary

The first *vārttika* is stated so that *ac* be applicable for *bhāvaḥ* etc.

The list of *pac* etc. mentioned in the second is for the feminine forms *nadī* etc, *jarābharā* etc.

On Pāṇini 3.1.135

Igupadhajñāprīkiraḥ kaḥ.

After the *dhātus* ending in a consonant preceded by *i, u* or *ṛ* (long or short) or *ḷ* and after the *dhātus jña* (to know), *prī* (to please), *kṝ* (to scatter), acts the *pratyaya ka* (*a*).

Vā. 1 : *Pratyaya ka* is to be enjoined after *dhātus* with a penultimate *ik* vowel when an *upasarga* (precedes) for the sake of the words *meṣa* and the rest.

Vā. 2 : Or else *ka* is not enjoined because of seeing the words *budha* and the rest even not preceded by the *upasarga āṅ.*

Bhāṣya Summary

Deva and *seva* are also mentioned, as well as *meṣa* in *pac-ādi.*

Budha, bhida etc. are formed with *ka* even without *upasarga.*

On Pāṇini 3.1.137

Pāghrādhmādheṭ dṛśāḥ śaḥ.

Pratyaya śa acts after the *dhātus pā, ghrā, dhmā, dheṭ,* and *dṛś* when an *upasarga* precedes.

Vā. 1 : There is prohibition of *śa* after *jighra* when a name is expressed.

Bhāṣya Summary

The prohibition of *śa* not of *ādeśa jighra,* allows *lopa* of *a* and the form *vyāghraḥ.*

On Pāṇini 3.1.138

Anupasargāl-limpa-vinda dhāri-pāri-vedyudeji ceti-sāti-sāhibhyaśca.

The *pratyaya śa* acts after the following *dhātus* without an *upasarga: limp, vind,* (and the causatives) *dhār-i, pār-i, ved-i, udej-i, cet-i, sāt-i,* and *sāh-i.*

Vā. 1 : The *pratyaya śa* acts after the *dhātu limp* when preceded by the *upasarga ni.*

Vā. 2 : And *śa* acts after *dhātu vind-i* when *'go'* is *upapada* in expressing a name

Bhāṣya Summary

Having given the explanatory example for the first *vārttika* it is stated on the second that there are other words as *upapadas* like *aravindaḥ* etc.

On Pāṇini 3.1.140

Jvali-ti-kasantebhyoḥ ṇaḥ.

After the *dhātus* beginning with *jval* (to burn brightly) and ending with *kas* (to go) without an *upasarga* the *pratyaya ṇa* optionally acts.

Vā. 1 : Additional enumeration should be made of *na* as acting after the *dhātu tan* (to extend).

Bhāṣya Summary

The additional form of *avatānaḥ* is provided.

On Pāṇini 3.1.145

Śilpini ṣvun

The *pratyaya ṣvun* acts after a *dhātu* when the agent so expressed denotes an artificer.

Bhāṣya Summary

Only after *dhātus mṛt, khan,* and *rañj,* so not for *hvāyakaḥ* etc.

On Pāṇini 3.1.149

Prusṛ lvaḥ samabhihāre vun

After the *dhātus pru, sṛ,* and *lū* the *pratyaya vun* acts when repetition is meant.

Vā. 1 : There is enjoining of the *pratyaya* after the *dhātus pru, sṛ,* and *lū* in the sense of doing something well.

Bhāṣya Summary

The *vārttika* is so that *vun* should be applicable for one who does something well though only once, and not for one doing badly many times.

❖❖❖